Drug Therapy
in
Obstetrics and
Gynecology

Drug Therapy in Obstetrics and Gynecology

Editors

WILLIAM F. RAYBURN, M.D.
Assistant Professor
Director of Obstetrics
Department of Obstetrics and
  Gynecology
Women's Hospital
The University of Michigan
  Medical School
Ann Arbor, Michigan

FREDERICK P. ZUSPAN, M.D.
Professor and Chairman
Department of Obstetrics and
  Gynecology
The Ohio State University College
  of Medicine
Columbus, Ohio

Associate Editors

PHILIP J. SCHNEIDER, M.S., R.PH.
Associate Director,
Department of Pharmacy,
The Ohio State University
Hospitals; Clinical Instructor,
Department of Surgery, The
Ohio State University College
of Medicine; Clinical
Assistant Professor, College
of Pharmacy, The Ohio State
University, Columbus, Ohio

BRIAN D. ANDRESEN, PH.D.
Associate Professor
Department of Pharmacology
The Ohio State University
College of Medicine
Columbus, Ohio

CLIFTON J. LATIOLAIS, SC.D., R.PH.
Director, Department of
Pharmacy,
The Ohio State University
Hospitals; Professor, College
of Pharmacy, The Ohio State
University, Columbus, Ohio

APPLETON-CENTURY-CROFTS/Norwalk, Connecticut

84 85 86 / 10 9 8 7 6 5 4 3

Prentice-Hall International, Inc., London
Prentice-Hall of Australia, Pty. Ltd., Sydney
Prentice-Hall of India Private Limited, New Delhi
Prentice-Hall of Japan, Inc., Tokyo
Prentice-Hall of Southeast Asia (Pte.) Ltd., Singapore
Whitehall Books Ltd., Wellington, New Zealand

Library of Congress Cataloging in Publication Data

Main entry under title:

Drug therapy in obstetrics and gynecology.

   Includes bibliographies and index.
   1. Obstetrical pharmacology. 2. Gynecology—Formulae,
receipts, prescriptions. 3. Women—Drug use. I. Rayburn,
William F. II. Zuspan, Frederick P. [DNLM: 1. Pregnancy
complications—Drug therapy. 2. Genital diseases, Female
—Drug therapy. WQ 240 D7929]
RG131.D78   618   82–1829
ISBN 0–8385–1808–7   AACR2

Cover and text design: Gloria J. Moyer
Production Editor: Gerard G. East

PRINTED IN THE UNITED STATES OF AMERICA

Contributors

Craig W. Anderson, M.D., Assistant Professor, Division of Neonatology, Department of Pediatrics and Department of Obstetrics and Gynecology, The Ohio State University College of Medicine, Columbus, Ohio

Brian D. Andresen, Ph.D., Associate Professor, Department of Pharmacology, The Ohio State University College of Medicine, Columbus, Ohio

Larry L. Arwood, R.Ph., Clinical Pharmacist, Department of Pharmacy, The Ohio State University Hospitals, and Clinical Instructor, College of Pharmacy, The Ohio State University, Columbus, Ohio

John G. Boutselis, M.D., Professor, Director of Gynecologic Oncology, Department of Obstetrics and Gynecology, The Ohio State University College of Medicine, Columbus, Ohio

Gerald L. Cable, R.Ph., Clinical Pharmacist, Department of Pharmacy, The Ohio State University Hospitals, and Clinical Instructor, College of Pharmacy, The Ohio State University, Columbus, Ohio

William E. Copeland, Jr., M.D., Clinical Assistant Professor, Department of Obstetrics and Gynecology, The Ohio State University Hospitals, Columbus, Ohio

Leandro Cordero, Jr., M.D., Professor, Director of Newborn Services, Department of Pediatrics, The Ohio State University College of Medicine, Columbus, Ohio

James K. Crane, M.D., Clinical Assistant Professor, Department of Obstetrics and Gynecology, Peoria School of Medicine, The University of Illinois College of Medicine, Peoria, Illinois

Donald M. DeDonato, M.D., Clinical Instructor, Department of Obstetrics and Gynecology, The Ohio State University College of Medicine, Columbus, Ohio

Jeffrey M. Dicke, M.D., Clinical Instructor, Department of Obstetrics and Gynecology, The Ohio State University College of Medicine, Columbus, Ohio

Chad I. Friedman, M.D., Assistant Professor, Division of Reproductive Endocrinology and Infertility, Department of Obstetrics and Gynecology, The Ohio State University College of Medicine, Columbus, Ohio

Debra K. Gardner, R.Ph., Clinical Pharmacist, Department of Pharmacy, The Ohio State University Hospitals, and Clinical Instructor, College of Pharmacy, The Ohio State University, Columbus, Ohio

R. Michael Gendreau, M.D., Research Scientist, Battelle Laboratories, Columbus, Ohio

Paul E. Hafner, R.Ph., Pharmacist Coordinator, Clinic Pharmacy, Department of Pharmacy, The Ohio State University Hospitals, and Clinical Instructor, College of Pharmacy, The Ohio State University, Columbus, Ohio

Jay D. Iams, M.D., Assistant Professor, Department of Obstetrics and Gynecology, The Ohio State University College of Medicine and The Ohio State University Hospitals, Columbus, Ohio

George A. Johnston, M.D., Assistant Professor, Division of Gynecologic Oncology, Department of Obstetrics and Gynecology, The Ohio State University College of Medicine, Columbus, Ohio

Melanie S. Kennedy, M.D., F.A.C.P., Assistant Professor, Department of Pathology, The Ohio State University College of Medicine, and Associate Director, Transfusion Service, The Ohio State University Hospitals, Columbus, Ohio

Moon H. Kim, M.D., Professor, Director of Reproductive Endocrinology and Infertility, Department of Obstetrics and Gynecology, The Ohio State University College of Medicine, Columbus, Ohio

Joseph J. Kryc, M.D., Assistant Professor, Department of Anesthesiology, and Assistant Professor, Department of Obstetrics and Gynecology, The Ohio State University College of Medicine, Columbus, Ohio

Peg F. McKnight, R.Ph., Clinical Pharmacist, Department of Pharmacy, The Ohio State University Hospitals, and Clinical Instructor, College of Pharmacy, The Ohio State University, Columbus, Ohio

Robert M. McNulty, Pharm. D., Clinical Pharmacist, Department of Pharmacy, The Ohio State University Hospitals, and Clinical Instructor, College of Pharmacy, The Ohio State University, Columbus, Ohio

Timothy D. Moore, M.S., R.Ph., Associate Director, Department of Pharmacy, The Ohio State University Hospitals; Assistant Professor, Department of Family Medicine, The Ohio State University College of Medicine; and Clinical Assistant Professor, Division of Pharmacy Practice, College of Pharmacy, The Ohio State University, Columbus, Ohio

Richard W. O'Shaughnessy, M.D., Assistant Professor, Division of Maternal-Fetal Medicine, Department of Obstetrics and Gynecology, The Ohio State University College of Medicine, Columbus, Ohio

Stephen F. Pariser, M.D., Assistant Professor, Department of Psychiatry, The Ohio State University, and Clinical Instructor, Department of Obstetrics and Gynecology, The Ohio State University Hospitals, Columbus, Ohio

William K. Rand, III, M.D., Clinical Instructor, Department of Obstetrics and Gynecology, The Ohio State University College of Medicine, Columbus, Ohio

William F. Rayburn, M.D., Assistant Professor, Department of Obstetrics and Gynecology, Women's Hospital, The University of Michigan Medical School, Ann Arbor, Michigan

John S. Russ, M.D., Clinical Assistant Professor, Department of Obstetrics and Gynecology, The Ohio State University College of Medicine, Columbus, Ohio

Mervyn J. Samuel, M.D., M.R.C.O.G (ENG.), F.A.C.O.G., Clinical Assistant Professor, Department of Obstetrics and Gynecology, The Ohio State University College of Medicine, Columbus, Ohio

Randy F. Schad, M.S., R.Ph., Assistant Director, Pharmaceutical Services, William Beaumont Hospital, Royal Oak, Michigan

Laurence E. Stempel, M.D., Clinical Instructor, Department of Obstetrics and Gynecology, The Ohio State University College of Medicine, Columbus, Ohio

James A. Visconti, Ph.D., Associate Professor, College of Pharmacy, The Ohio State University, and Director, Drug Information Center, The Ohio State University Hospitals, Columbus, Ohio

Nichols Vorys, M.D., Clinical Associate Professor, Department of Obstetrics and Gynecology, The Ohio State University College of Medicine, Columbus, Ohio

Nicholas A. Votolato, R.Ph., Clinical Pharmacist, Department of Pharmacy, The Ohio State University Hospitals, and Clinical Instructor, College of Pharmacy, The Ohio State University, Columbus, Ohio

Carl P. Weiner, M.D., Fellow, Division of Maternal-Fetal Medicine, Department of Obstetrics and Gynecology, Prentice Women's Hospital, The Medical School, Northwestern University, Chicago, Illinois

Andrew L. Wilson, Pharm. D., Associate Director, Department of Pharmacy, The Ochsner Foundation Hospital, New Orleans, Louisiana

Frederick P. Zuspan, M.D., Professor and Chairman, Department of Obstetrics and Gynecology, The Ohio State University College of Medicine, Columbus, Ohio

Kathryn J. Zuspan, M.D., Senior Resident, Department of Obstetrics and Gynecology, University of North Carolina College of Medicine, Chapel Hill, North Carolina

Contents

Preface

Numerous drugs are prescribed to treat a variety of obstetric and gynecologic disorders in ambulatory and hospital settings. Furthermore, many drugs used in the treatment of other disorders may affect the course of a woman's pregnancy, the health of her fetus or neonate, or her reproductive function. Information about drug therapy is increasing as further clinical knowledge expands in the subspecialties of maternal-fetal medicine, reproductive endocrinology, and gynecologic oncology. With these considerations and despite heavy workloads, clinicians are asked to provide quality health care and be aware of implications from the use of currently prescribed drugs. Consequently, an effort to find in-depth information about drug therapy may be time-consuming and often frustrating.

Several texts are already available which discuss therapy of specific disorders in obstetrics and gynecology. Instead, this book provides information about specific drugs used in daily clinical practice. Current drug therapy is reviewed in a concise and comprehensive manner in each of the three major sections: obstetrics, gynecology, and drugs for general use. Each chapter introduces the nature of certain disorders or patient concerns and then describes the characteristics and indications for the use of each drug. The chapters were planned, written, and revised by the combined efforts of individuals within the following disciplines: obstetrics and gynecology, pharmacology, pharmacy, neonatology, anesthesiology, and psychiatry. Along with a review of the current literature, many useful tables and figures are included for quick reference. Over-the-counter drugs are discussed, and comparative cost considerations are also featured when appropriate.

We hope that this text is instructive to clinicians, house officers, and students for improving patient care through the safe, accurate, and rational use of drugs in the specialties of obstetrics and gynecology.

The editors wish to acknowledge the following persons for their assistance in the preparation of this text: Barbara Akers, Joseph Bianchine, Elaine Clark, Richard Early, Annette Haban, Marina Liscano, Ronald Lay, John McDonald, Grant Morrow, Pamela Rayburn, Kevin Scheckelhoff, and Mary Yates.

WILLAM F. RAYBURN, M.D.
Ann Arbor, Michigan
FREDERICK P. ZUSPAN, M.D.
Columbus, Ohio

xiii

PART ONE: OBSTETRICS

1. Principles of Perinatal Pharmacology

WILLIAM F. RAYBURN   BRIAN D. ANDRESEN

Pharmacology is the science which deals with the study of drugs and the complex interaction of pathways for the absorption, distribution, metabolism, and excretion of drugs (Fig. 1-1). The absorption of a drug across a membrane (gastrointestinal, placenta, or into breast milk) is related to the following factors: the chemical properties of the drug (molecular weight, spatial configurations, degree of protein binding, ionic dissociation or pKa, lipid solubility); tissue pH; drug concentration; and exposure time. Nonionized, low molecular weight, lipid-soluble compounds are usually well absorbed. The most common mechanism of drug transport across a membrane is passive or simple diffusion from a high to a low concentration. Facilitated diffusion which requires a carrier, and active transport, which requires energy transport across a concentration gradient, are less common transport mechanisms for drugs.

The distribution of absorbed drugs in the bloodstream and tissues is dependent on drug-binding to proteins, local blood perfusion, capillary permeability of the unbound or "free" drug, pH of the target tissue, and membrane permeability. A drug crosses cell membranes selectively by many transport mechanisms and binds to intracellular receptors. The duration of a drug effect is related to the route of administration, dissolution rate, dose, time required to reach equilibrium, half-life of the drug, and degree of drug-receptor binding.

The metabolism of a drug is a complex event occurring primarily in the liver, and is carried out by microsomal enzymes. Representative drug metabolism reactions include oxidation, reduction, dealkylation, and synthesis. These processes transform drugs into either active or inactive compounds. Most reactions form more polar, and therefore more water-soluble, compounds which can be eliminated by the kidney.

The excretion of metabolized drugs by the kidneys is related to the volume of distribution of the drug, glomerular filtration rate, renal tubular reabsorption, urine pH, and tubular secretion. Lipid-soluble, nonionized compounds are more likely to be reabsorbed than compounds which are significantly ionized at the pH of the urine. Excretion from the intestines (in bile), lungs, and sweat glands is less common but significant for certain drugs.

Drug-drug interactions are encountered frequently and can interfere with absorption, plasma and tissue protein-binding, access to cell receptors, and renal excretion. Certain drugs may also induce (phenobarbital) or inhibit (disulfiram) enzymes responsible for the metabolism of other drugs or endogenous substances.[1]

The identification and quantitation of drugs and their metabolites have been accomplished primarily by the newest techniques in radioimmunoassay (RIA), combined gas chromatography and mass spectrometer (GC-MS) computer systems, and high-pressure liquid chromatography (HPLC). Animal and human experiments utilizing these and other instru-

1

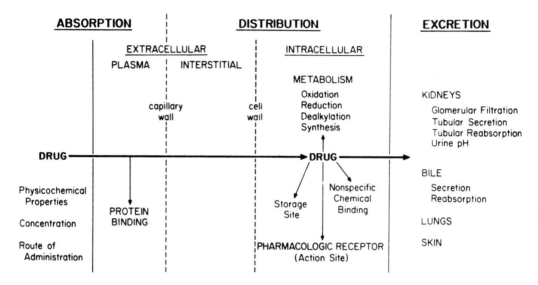

Figure 1-1. Pathways of drug metabolism.

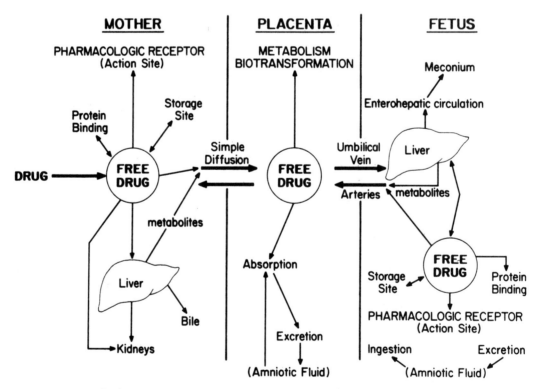

Figure 1-2. Drug pathways within the maternal, placental, and fetal units.

mental methods of analysis have revealed the potential deleterious effects and fate of drugs on the developing fetus. From these studies, new information has been gathered concerning the distribution and pharmacokinetic properties of drugs and metabolites in the maternal-fetal unit.

The study of perinatal pharmacology represents a complex interrelationship among maternal changes, placental factors, fetal development, and neonatal adaptation. These pathways are shown in Figure 1-2 and discussed in the sections that follow.

MATERNAL CHANGES

The absorption of drugs in the gastrointestinal tract during pregnancy has not been well studied but is thought to be similar to nonpregnant patients.[2] Decreased gastric tone and motility are related to progesterone effects. Hydrochloric acid secretion in the stomach is decreased during the first and second trimesters, but increased during the third trimester and postpartum periods. Whether this influences the preferential absorption of certain drugs is unclear. Pregnancy has little effect on gastrointestinal secretion, digestion, or absorption.

The distribution of a drug taken during pregnancy is influenced by many factors. Before or during conception the luminal secretions and drug concentrations in the semen, fallopian tubes, and uterus are influenced by certain drugs.[3] The extracellular volume (including intravascular volume), intracellular volume, and uterine blood flow increase gradually during pregnancy. Despite an increased production during pregnancy, serum albumin has a relatively lower concentration because of plasma volume expansion. The albumin-binding capacity to drugs is also decreased, and more unbound or "free" drug is therefore available for placental transfer.

The metabolism of drugs in the liver during pregnancy is influenced by increasing amounts of circulating steroid hormones. Enzyme induction or inhibition by the hepatic microsomes can arise by stimulation from certain drugs. Hepatic blood flow is not increased during pregnancy, and minimal centrilobular bile stasis occurs in the liver as pregnancy progresses.[4] The excretion of drugs by the kidneys can be more rapid because of increased renal perfusion and glomerular filtration. Renal blood flow increases by 25 to 50 percent during pregnancy (550 to 800 cc/minute) because of the increased cardiac output, while glomerular filtration is also increased by 50 percent.[4]

ROLE OF THE PLACENTA

The placental transfer of drugs and other substrates is complex and no method of study is ideal. Several models have been used to better understand placental transfer. Pregnant animals have been injected with drugs in varying concentrations and subsequently sacrificed at certain intervals to determine the concentration of drugs or metabolites in fetal tissues. Drug concentrations in umbilical cord or neonatal sera have also been measured and shown to correlate with maternal serum levels. Human placentas have been cultured and exposed to drugs to determine their metabolic capabilities. It has been determined that the transfer of drugs across the placenta is primarily by simple diffusion and is dependent on the chemical properties and concentration gradients of the free drug.[5] Most drugs have a molecular weight of 250 to 500. An unbound and unionized drug of molecular weight less than 1000 is usually lipid-soluble and will rapidly penetrate the trophoblast, connective, and endothelial tissues which separate the fetal and maternal circulations.[3] Drug transfer is greater during late gestation, and explanations[6] for this increased transfer are listed in Table 1-1. Any drug in sufficient concentration will eventually cross the placenta, especially when maternal therapeutic blood levels of a drug have been maintained for an extended period of time. Pathologic processes causing an inflammatory reaction, hypoxia, vascular degeneration, or partial separation of the placental

TABLE 1-1 REASONS FOR INCREASED PLACENTAL DRUG TRANSFER IN LATE PREGNANCY

1. Increased free drug available for transport
2. Increased utero-placental blood flow (500 ml/min)
3. Increased placental surface area.
4. Decreased thickness of the semipermeable lipid membranes (2 μm at term) between the placental capillaries
5. Greater physical disruption of placental membranes
6. More acidic fetal circulation to "trap" basic drugs

implantation can affect utero-placental blood flow and drug transfer. Uterine contractions, cord compression, and supine positioning of the mother can lead to transient utero-placental hypoperfusion.

Examples of drugs which readily cross the placenta within minutes after maternal administration include ampicillin, penicillin G, cephalothin, kanamycin, tetracycline, sulfonamides, streptomycin, diazepam, phenytoin, barbiturates, ethanol, meperidine, salicylate, lidocaine, mepivacaine, bupivacaine (with or without epinephrine), and propranolol.[3]

The placental metabolism of drugs is not well understood and is likely to be less active than metabolism within the fetal liver.[6] However, biochemical transformations may require enzymatic reactions at both sites. Certain substances may cross the placenta only after transformation by any of the four possible metabolic reactions (oxidation, reduction, dealkylation, and synthesis). The synthetic capabilities of the placenta (including conjugation or oxidative metabolism) has not been well demonstrated. Certain drugs can also induce or inhibit placental enzymes necessary for the metabolic conversion of endogenous substances or for energy-requiring transport mechanisms.[6] Furthermore, drugs may act on the fetus and placenta to reduce placental blood flow or interfere with the active trans-

port or other nutritive functions of the placenta.[7]

DRUG EFFECTS ON THE FETUS

Drugs that cross the placental barrier usually reach fetal levels which often correspond to 50 to 100 percent of maternal serum concentrations.[3] Exceptions are diazepam and the local anesthetics that reach drug levels in the fetus at equilibria which are greater than those in the mother. The total exposure of a drug in the fetus is more important than the rate of transplacental transport. Chronic drug exposure, rather than single-dose therapy, may influence fetal cell growth during the early (hyperplasia stages) or later (hypertrophy stages) periods of development.[7,8] Drugs may act as teratogenic agents in many ways: abortions, malformations, altered fetal growth, functional deficits, carcinogenesis, or mutagenesis (see Chap. 2).

Drugs transported in the umbilical vein travel to the fetal liver (portal vein) or are shunted through the liver to the right side of the heart (ductus venosus). Factors determining the flow direction through the ductus venosus or portal vein are not well understood. Cardiac output is proportionally greater in the fetus than in the adult, and blood is preferentially circulated to the essential organs (brain, heart, placenta) through less resistant pathways. Blood-brain permeability is greater in the fetus than in the adult. Mitochondria, the main intracellular sites for metabolism, increase in number in the fetal brain and heart and show increasing enzyme content with fetal age.[9] More than half of the cardiac output is directly returned to the placenta through the umbilical arteries. This is greater when fetal acidosis is present. The maternal-fetal concentration gradient is therefore decreased, and further transfer of drugs or metabolites is retarded.[10]

Despite preferential circulation to the heart and brain, drug distribution in the fetus eventually becomes diffuse. Total body water increases with fetal maturity but decreases proportionally with total body mass (95 percent at mid-gestation to 75 percent at term). The total concentration of plasma protein and the protein-binding properties are lower in the fetus than in the mother. More free drug is therefore available for tissue penetration or competitive protein-binding with other drugs or endogenous compounds. Conclusions about drug deposition within the fetus obtained from maternal or fetal serum levels alone may not accurately reflect fetal pharmacokinetics or drug distribution patterns.

Concentrations of drugs in the fetus vary but decrease when sampling from the umbilical vein, umbilical artery, and fetal tissue (fetal scalp), respectively. The rate of tissue permeability of a drug is unknown but probably increases with gestation.[11] Autonomic receptors (α and β) in the ileum, carotid artery, and aortic arch sinuses are present in fetal animal studies in the early second trimester and respond to catecholamine stimulation.[11,12] Response curves from drugs are considered similar throughout gestation, but the strength of receptor response increases remarkably with fetal development.[10,11] Some drugs may also have a higher affinity for specific target tissues. Examples of organs which are affected by specific drugs include the heart (digoxin, phenytoin); skeleton (tetracycline, warfarin); red blood cells (sulfonamides); central nervous system (diazepam, ethanol, narcotics); platelets (aspirin); adrenal gland (sex steroids, phenytoin); mullerian duct and vagina (diethylstilbestrol); and auditory nerve (gentamycin).[3]

Many fetal organs are capable of substantial metabolic activity, but drug metabolism occurs principally in the fetal liver. Human fetal liver microsomes have significant cytochrome P_{450} levels and NADPH–cytochrome c reductase which can be measured as early as the 14th week of gestation.[11] Oxidation and reduction reactions have been described as early as the 16th week.[13] The activity and concentration of certain hepatic microsomal enzymes and the rate of oxidative and conjugative reactions are probably less than in the adult.[13] Therefore, direct pharmacodynamic effects from drugs may be more pronounced and more prolonged in the fetus than in the mother. Certain drugs, such as phenobarbital or ethanol, which readily cross the placenta, may induce specific fetal liver enzymes.[3] Following chronic exposure, enzyme induction increases the smooth endoplasmic reticulum, and the hepatic drug metabolism capabilities of the fetus are activated. Prolonged phenobarbital, narcotic, or ethanol exposure has been shown to stimulate glucuronyl transferase to conjugate circulating bilirubin over several days and thereby diminish the amount of unconjugated hyperbilirubinemia in the neonate.[14] Furthermore, by stimulating hepatic enzymes, phenobarbital may enhance the metabolism and elimination of phenytoin.[15] An absence or excessive presence of one or more enzymes may go unrecognized if the embryo or fetus does not survive.

The excretion of most drugs is slower in the fetus than in the adult, since many systems are not fully developed. The primary routes of elimination involve the placenta and fetal urine. The placental transfer of drugs from the fetus to the mother is the primary route of drug elimination in early pregnancy and is dependent on simple diffusion, free drug chemical properties, and concentration gradients. Drug elimination in the latter half of pregnancy is determined by the immature fetal kidneys contributing to the amniotic fluid. In the absence of gastrointestinal atresia, great amounts of amniotic fluid can be swallowed by the fetus and can be recirculated into the enterohepatic circulation. The measurement of some drug and metabolite concentrations is possible by amniotic fluid sampling and by meconium analysis.

Drug therapy for various fetal complications is another area presently under investigation. Examples of prior treatment of fetal complications are listed in Table 1-2. Drug administration can occur by the passive, transplacental route or by direct intra-amniotic instillation or intramuscular injection. The direct route has clear invasive risks, but would quickly aid the fetus if drug-transplacental transfer is slow. These risks and benefits for

TABLE 1-2 DRUG THERAPY FOR VARIOUS FETAL CONDITIONS

Fetal Conditions	Therapeutic Agents
Heart failure, tachycardia	Digoxin
Hypothyroidism	Thyroxine
Syphilis exposure	Penicillin
Adrenal hyperplasia	Hydrocortisone
Respiratory distress syndrome	Glucocorticoids

fetal therapy remain uncertain and require further investigation.

NEONATAL PHARMACOLOGY

Drugs absorbed transplacentally from the mother before or during labor may remain in the neonate for a prolonged period. Drug effects on the fetus may be assessed immediately at birth by Apgar scores, drug concentration measurements of the umbilical blood, and a search for gross anomalies. Neurobehavioral examination of the neonate is also useful in the determination of more subtle and transient drug effects.[16] These include body tone, rooting reflex, Moro response, and response to pinprick stimulation.

Nearly all active or inactive drugs circulating within the mother can also be transferred into the breast milk or colostrum (see Chap. 15). Those drugs passing into the breastfed infant may be further metabolized in the gastrointestinal tract. Absorption processes in the untested gastrointestinal tract of the neonate are similar to the adult, and lipid-soluble drugs are well absorbed. The absorption of drugs administered intramuscularly or subcutaneously is dependent on an adequate local circulation.

Distribution of drugs in the newborn is similar to the adult. Circulatory alterations after the umbilical cord is clamped involve more blood flow to the lungs and extremities and less to the liver and brain. Total body water and extracellular volume are proportionally higher in the infant, while adipose tissue is less than in the adult. Total serum protein is less in the infant than in the adult, and competition between drugs and endogenous substrates (sulfonamides and bilirubin) for binding sites in albumin may displace more free drugs and bilirubin into the circulation.[17,18]

Metabolism in the premature and term infant occurs primarily within the liver. The four basic metabolic reactions (oxidation, reduction, dealkylation, and synthesis) for conversion or detoxification of foreign compounds are present but less active. Drugs such as salicylates, ethanol, and diazepam are therefore biotransformed much less rapidly than in the older child or adult and would contribute to any delays in neonatal adaptation.[16] Asphyxia, inadequate nutrition, hypoglycemia, insufficient body temperature control, inborn errors of metabolism, specific diseases, and toxic effects from drugs (local anesthetics, autonomic nervous system drugs, narcotic addiction, chronic barbiturate use) or endogenous and exogenous substrates can further retard metabolic processes.[3,18] Conversely, drugs may induce enzyme activity and accelerate the metabolism of certain drugs or other essential biochemicals. The measurement of serum bilirubin levels in the neonate can provide a better understanding of the metabolism of certain drugs (sulfonamides, diazepam, methyldopa, nitrofurantoins) since many metabolic processes are shared by other endogenous and exogenous compounds.[17]

Excretion of drugs is also delayed in the infant. Elimination processes are principally

TABLE 1-3 REASONS FOR MORE SERIOUS SIDE EFFECTS IN THE NEONATE

1. More free drug available
2. Greater cell membrane permeability
3. Reduced hepatic capacity
4. Delayed renal excretion

in the kidneys, while drug excretion by the lungs, bile, or sweat glands is less significant. Renal plasma flow, glomerular filtration, and tubular absorption and secretion are initially less than in the adult and become comparable only after several months of maturation. Individual drug properties, volume of drug distribution, and more basic urine pH also influence the rate of drug elimination.[18] Toxic or serious side effects of drugs are potentially more frequent in the neonate than in the older child or adult. The reasons for this phenomenon in the neonate include: greater concentration of free or unbound drug, greater membrane permeability, reduced hepatic capability, and delayed renal excretion capacity (Table 1-3). This observation is appreciated more in premature or growth-delayed infants.

DRUGS IN BREAST MILK

Principles of drug transfer across the placenta also apply to the transfer of drugs into the breast tissues. The dose, duration of exposure, and route of administration of drugs for the mother are important considerations. Local blood flow in breast tissue is increased during lactation, and therefore drug transfer into breast milk by passive or simple diffusion is facilitated. The chemical properties of each drug must be appreciated, but most drugs in high concentrations can be detected in breast milk. Because the breast is primarily adipose tissue, it is a potential storage site for drugs before and after delivery. A more detailed discussion of drugs in breast milk is found in Chapter 15.

DRUG USE DURING PREGNANCY

The average patient has been reported to consume four to five different prescribed drugs during pregnancy.[19] Excluding vitamin and iron preparations, drugs are prescribed to 82 percent of all pregnant women, and 65 percent of pregnant women take drugs *not* prescribed by a physician.[20] Certain compounds are taken from habit instead of physical need, and are not considered medicines by patients. The initial obstetrical examination should include questioning for any specific prescribed, over-the-counter, or "street" drugs. Additionally, questions concerning the mother's exposure to industrial chemicals in abnormal amounts should be included. A history of any drugs (including oral contraceptives and appetite suppressants) taken at conception or during the first trimester should be sought. A specific drug is to be continued during the first trimester only if the anticipated benefit is reasonable and considered to outweigh any known potential, suspected, or theoretical risk. Any indicated drug must be documented on the antepartum chart, and the pediatrician should be notified prior to the time of delivery.

The effects of a drug or its metabolites on the fetus are related to the dose, duration of administration, and developmental stage at exposure (see Chap. 2). Information from case reports, epidemiologic studies, and animal studies has definite limitations. Studies with many types of animal species frequently involve the administration of large doses of a specific agent administered during early gestation. Drugs taken in high dosages and near delivery may cause more immediate and sustained neonatal effects. The effects from indiscriminate use of many drugs are not usually overtly manifested in the neonate, and less pronounced effects may be undetected.

Relief of patient symptoms and the medical welfare of the pregnant patient must not be ignored. Drugs which improve maternal health often benefit the fetus. To minimize any fetal risks or adverse side effects to the mother, a prescribed medication should be closely monitored, using a therapeutic dose for the shortest duration. Individual variation in patient tolerance to a certain drug must be appreciated, since recommended dosages for nonpregnant women may be inadequate or may reach toxic levels.

REFERENCES

1. Conney AH: Pharmacological implications of microsomal enzyme induction, *Pharmacol Rev* 19:317, 1967

2. Winship DH: Gastrointestinal diseases, in Burrow G, Ferris T (eds): *Medical Complications of Pregnancy.* New York, Saunders, 1975, pp. 275–350

3. Mirkin BL, Singh S: Placental transfer of pharmacologically active molecules, in Mirkin BL (ed): *Perinatal Pharmacology and Therapeutics.* New York, Academic, 1976, pp. 1–70

4. Bynum TE: Hepatic and gastrointestinal disorders in pregnancy. *Med Clin North Am* 61:129, 1977

5. Ferris T: Renal disease, in Burrow G, Ferris T (eds): *Medical Complications of Pregnancy.* New York, Saunders, 1975, pp 1–70

6. Juchau MR, Dyer DC: Pharmacology of the placenta. *Pediatr Clin North Am* 19:65, 1972

7. Juchau MR: Drug biotransformation reactions in the placenta, in Mirkin BL (ed): *Perinatal Pharmacology and Therapeutics.* New York, Academic, 1976, p 71

8. Enesco M, Leblond CP: Increase in cell number as a factor in the growth of the organs and tissues of the young male rat. *J Embryol Exp Morphol* 10:530, 1962

9. Winick M, Noble A: Quantitative changes in D.N.A. and R.N.A. and protein during prenatal and postnatal growth in the rat. *Dev Biol* 12:451, 1965

10. Smith RJ: Mitochondria in fetal tissue. *J Embryol Exp Morphol* 11:424, 1964

11. Waddell WJ, Marlowe GC: Disposition of drugs in the fetus, in Mirkin M (ed): *Perinatal Pharmacology and Therapeutics.* New York, Academic, 1976, pp 119–269

12. Boreus LO: Pharmacology of the human fetus: Dose-effect relationship for acetylcholine during ontogenesis. *Biol Neonate* 11:328, 1967

13. McMurphy DM, Boreus LO: Pharmacology of the human fetus: Adrenergic receptor function in the small intestine. *Biol Neonate* 13:325, 1968

14. Mirkin BL: Biological maturation and drug disposition, in *Perinatal Pharmacology:* Mead Johnson Symposium on Perinatal and Developmental Medicine, no 5, 1974, p 31

15. Pippenger CE, Rasen TS: Phenobarbital plasma levels in neonates. *Clin Perinatol* 2:111, 1975

16. Seanion, JW, Alper MH: Perinatal pharmacology and evaluation of the newborn. *Int Anesthesiol Clin* 11:163, 1973

17. Vaisman SL, Gartner LM: Pharmacologic treatment of neonatal hyperbilirubinema. *Clin Perinatol* 2:37, 1975

18. Giacoia GP, Gorodisher R: Pharmacologic principles in neonatal drug therapy. *Clin Perinatol* 2:125, 1975

19. Bleyer, WA, Au WY: Studies on the detection of adverse drug reactions in the newborn: Fetal exposure to maternal medication. *JAMA* 213:2046, 1970

20. Fofar JO, Nelson MN: Epidemiology of drugs taken by pregnant women. *Clin Pharmacol Ther* 14:632, 1973

2. Drug Effects on the Fetus

JAY D. IAMS   WILLIAM F. RAYBURN

DRUGS IN EARLY PREGNANCY

Drug use among women of childbearing age is common, and does not decline during early pregnancy. Brocklebank et al. found that 15 percent of women surveyed took systemic medication in any given month during the 6 months prior to conception.[1] This figure rose to nearly 20 percent during the second and third months of pregnancy. Pregnant women may require drug therapy for an ongoing medical condition, may take drugs prior to confirmation of pregnancy, or may use over-the-counter drugs in the belief that nonprescription medications present no fetal hazard. The frequency of drug use in early pregnancy is a problem of some magnitude since there are few, if any, drugs known to be "safe" for the developing embryo. Although only a handful of drugs qualify as being definitely hazardous, most medications have unknown teratogenic potential.

Drugs as Teratogenic Agents: General Principles

The role of drugs in the etiology of fetal malformation is not entirely clear. Drugs are currently believed to account for 4 to 5 percent of malformations (Table 2-1). The impact of maternal medication on the incidence of miscarriage, fetal growth retardation, and other adverse sequelae is more difficult to estimate. Drugs taken by the mother may also contribute to the production of birth defects now classified as multifactorial or unknown in etiology.

The general principles of teratology, outlined by Wilson and Fraser and modified here, indicate the difficulty in establishing a simple cause-and-effect relationship between a given defect and teratogen.[2]

The effect of a teratogen is dependent upon:

1.   The dose reaching the developing embryo or fetus. This will be affected by the maternal dose, the volume of distribution in the mother, the metabolic clearance of the drug by the mother, and the molecular weight of the drug.

2.   The gestational age at the time of exposure. Teratogenic exposure in the first 2 to 3 weeks following conception may result in spontaneous abortion. The period of organogenesis from the 3rd to 10th postconceptional week represents the critical period for major organ malformation. Physiologic deficits and growth delay are the principal effects beyond the 10th postconceptual week.

3.   The duration of exposure. An agent given during the embryonic period of organogenesis and during the fetal period of growth may produce both morphologic and physiologic alterations.

4.   The genotypes of the mother and fetus. Species differences in teratogenic effect abound in the literature, and illustrate the difficulty in applying animal research to predict either the safety or adverse effects on human

TABLE 2-1 CAUSES OF HUMAN MALFORMATION (PERCENTAGE)

Known genetic transmission	20
Chromosome anomalies	5
Environmental factors	10
Irradiation—< 1%	
Infections—2–3%	
(rubella, cytomegalovirus, toxoplasmosis, syphilis)	
Maternal disorders—1–2%	
(diabetes, PKU, virilizing tumors)	
Drugs and chemicals—4–5%	
(see Tables 2 to 5)	
Multifactorial/unknown	65
(e.g, most congenital heart disease, neural tube	
defects, facial cleft)	

pregnancy. Individual differences in the maternal or fetal metabolism of a given drug may produce a marked increase or decrease in the dose reaching the fetus.

5. The effect of other agents to which the embryo or fetus is simultaneously exposed. For example, drug A may be teratogenic to a given species only in the presence or absence of drug B. The addition of drug C may yield an entirely different result.

The consequences of the principles cited above are several:

1. The effect of a teratogenic agent may include:
   a. No effect
   b. Abortion
   c. Malformation
   d. Altered fetal growth
   e. Functional deficit
   f. Carcinogenesis
   g. Mutagenesis

2. A given teratogenic effect may be induced by a variety of other teratogens, both pharmacologic and otherwise.

3. A single teratogen may have multiple effects, depending upon the dose, the time in gestation, as well as host and environmental factors.

4. Proof of the teratogenicity or safety of an individual drug is consequently difficult to establish. Teratogenicity may be more easily inferred if the defect produced is rare, for example, diethylstilbestrol (DES) and vaginal adenosis. Reports that a drug is associated with more common malformations such as cleft lip/palate or ventricular septal defects are much more difficult to evaluate. Conversely, the absence of reports of teratogenicity for a given drug does not imply safety. There is no drug proven to be safe for the developing fetus in human pregnancy. Data from animal studies may be either alarming or reassuring, but species differences preclude drawing conclusions about drug effects on the human fetus based on animal data. A drug which reliably produces defects in an animal species may not do so in humans. The converse is also true and was tragically demonstrated by the effects of thalidomide in infants, after animal studies revealed no teratogenic effects. Any drug must therefore be presumed to be a teratogen if given to a susceptible host in sufficient doses at a critical period of gestation.

The obvious conclusion is that all drugs, both prescription and over-the-counter, should be used with caution throughout pregnancy, given only for specific indication at the minimum effective dose, and for the shortest duration necessary. Pregnant women should be advised at the first prenatal care visit to consult with a physician before taking prescription or over-the-counter medications. This prospective counseling will avoid concern over the unknown effects of medication in pregnancy. Frequently, however, the physician is consulted retrospectively, after the drug has already been ingested. Before advising such a patient, the physician must first establish the exact medication, the dose and duration of the administration, and the gestational age of the pregnancy at the time of exposure. For all but the most commonly used drugs, the next step is a careful review of the recent literature. Shepard's *Catalog of Teratogenic Agents*[3] and *The Year Book of Obstetrics and Gynecology* are useful in this review. All too often these steps are ignored, and the patient is given either reassurance or alarm without ade-

quate data collection. Tabular listings of drug effects in pregnancy must be interpreted with caution in light of the principles of teratology outlined previously.

The birth of a child with a congenital defect should prompt a review of any maternal medication during pregnancy. The same meticulous documentation of dose, duration of therapy, gestational age at exposure, and literature review are required before any causal connection between maternal medication and malformation is even implied. Failure to follow this procedure may produce unwarranted maternal guilt and anxiety.

It is clinically useful to place drugs in one of three general categories: drugs with known adverse effects, drugs with suspected adverse effects, and drugs without known adverse effects at customary dosage levels. These are listed in Tables 2-2, 2-3, and 2-4 and are described in more detail below in the sections that follow.

TABLE 2-2   DRUGS WITH KNOWN TERATOGENIC EFFECT

Drug	Effect
Anticonvulsants Trimethadione, phenytoin	Facial dysmorphogenesis, mild mental retardation, growth retardation
Anticoagulants Coumadin and congeners	Nasal hypoplasia, epiphyseal stippling, optic atrophy
Alcohol	Fetal alcohol syndrome—growth retardation, mild mental retardation, increase in anomalies
Folic acid antagonists Methotrexate, aminopterin	Abortion, multiple malformations
Hormones Diethylstilbestrol and congeners	Vaginal adenosis, carcinogenesis, uterine anomalies, epididymal anomalies, microphallus, cryptorchidism, testicular hypoplasia
Androgens	Masculinization of female fetus
Methyl mercury	CNS damage, growth retardation
Thalidomide	Phocomelia

TABLE 2-3   DRUGS WITH SUSPECTED TERATOGENIC EFFECTS

Drug	Suspected Effect
Alkylating agents	↑ Abortion, anomalies
Hormones	
Oral contraceptives	↑ Limb and cardiac defects
Progestins	↑ Limb and cardiac defects
Lithium carbonate	Ebstein's anomaly
Nicotine	Growth retardation
Sulfonylureas	↑ Anomalies (?)
Tranquilizers	
Benzodiazepines	Facial clefts

Drugs with Known Adverse Effects

This category is small, and fortunately contains only one group of drugs—the anticonvulsants—where fetal risk does not conclusively exceed maternal benefit.

Anticonvulsants as teratogens are discussed extensively in Chapter 5. Trimethadione can conclusively be listed as a teratogen, producing growth retardation, microcephaly, facial dysmorphism, and other anomalies.[5] Principally used for petit mal seizures, it can frequently be avoided in pregnancy without

TABLE 2-4   DRUGS WITHOUT KNOWN TERATOGENIC EFFECT IN HUMANS AT CUSTOMARY DOSAGES*

Analgesics	Antiemetics
Acetaminophen	Bendectin
Narcotics	Promethazine
Salicylates	Corticosteroids
Antibiotics	Heparin
Penicillin	
Cephalosporin	
Sulfonamides	

* None of these drugs are *proven* safe. All have been associated in animal studies with malformations, but human studies have not confirmed suspected effects.

hazard to the mother. The status of phenytoin, on the other hand, is less clear. Although the literature is inconclusive about the teratogenic effect of phenytoin, there is sufficient data to suggest that it be avoided if possible.[6] This raises the question of the relative risks of maternal seizures versus the medications used to control them.

Coumadin may be avoided in situations where anticoagulation is necessary by the substitution of self-administered heparin (see Chap. 25).[7]

The use of cancer chemotherapeutic agents in pregnancy must be considered individually. While only the folate antagonists, methotrexate and aminopterin, are listed as demonstrated teratogens, it is logical to suspect that any drug designed to kill growing malignant cells may have the same effect upon the developing embryo. Surprisingly, few cases of malformation have been reported following maternal treatment with antineoplastic drugs. Wilson and Fraser speculate that this is due to their limited use in pregnancy because of demonstrated teratogenicity in laboratory animals, easy justification for elective abortion under the circumstances of use, and the high rate of treatment-induced abortions and intrauterine death.[8]

Excessive maternal use of alcohol has now been associated with a spectrum of teratogenic effects, including growth retardation, microcephaly, shortened palpebral tissues, and mild mental retardation.[9] The frequency of other anomalies, including cardiac defects, is also slightly increased. This appears to be a dose-dependent phenomenon. Although no cases of fetal alcohol syndrome have been reported with the consumption of less than 2 ounces of absolute ethanol daily, there is no known safe threshold dose. Pregnant women should be advised to omit alcohol, but need not become alarmed over occasional use.

The remaining drugs listed in Table 2-2 have no indication for use in pregnancy and do not ordinarily present therapeutic or counseling problems. Tetracycline is almost always a second line antibiotic; other, safer antimicrobials are available. Androgens, DES and related substances, and thalidomide are now proven teratogens.

Drugs with Suspected Adverse Effects

This category could conceivably include any drug which has been the subject of a case report suggesting possible teratogenicity. Such a compilation would be a book in itself, and so exhaustive as to be practically useless. Instead, a shortened list of drugs which are likely to achieve "proven" status is offered (Table 2-5). These medications may cause concern when inadvertent use during pregnancy is discovered. None is sufficiently studied to warrant pregnancy termination when exposure occurs.

Several of the agents in this category merit additional comment, because they illustrate some of the principles of teratogenicity. Lithium carbonate, used in the therapy of manic-depressive illness, has been associated with an increased frequency of Ebstein's anomaly, a rare congenital cardiac lesion with a reported incidence of 1 in 20,000 births. Nora et al. reported that 8 of 11 malformed infants born to mothers exposed to lithium in the first trimester had congenital heart disease.[10] Of the eight, four had the Ebstein anomaly, representing a 400-fold increase over the expected frequency. Though small, this series of patients is impressive because of the rarity of the reported defect, and the magnitude of the increase. Conversely, a large series of patients treated with progestins showed a doubling of the incidence of all forms of congenital heart disease.[11] Although the increase was statistically significant in a large population, this report must be interpreted with some care because of the relatively small increase in the incidence of a more common and less distinctive group of malformations.

Studies of the sulfonylureas in the treatment of maternal diabetes present problems similar to those of the anticonvulsants. Whether the malformations observed are secondary to the maternal disorder or to the medications is not clear. Diabetic women are known to have a two- to threefold increase

in the incidence of all malformations. Whether this is related to hyper- or hypoglycemia is unknown. This problem is now academic in the case of the sulfonylureas, since oral hypoglycemics have no place in the management of glucose intolerance in pregnancy.

Drugs Without Known Adverse Effects

Some commonly used medications have not been associated with anomalies in humans despite their widespread use. Analgesic compounds including narcotics, salicylates, and acetaminophen may be used in customary doses when indicated. Salicylates are perhaps the most commonly used medication in pregnancy, taken by 80 percent of gravidas in one study.[12] Despite demonstrated embryo-toxicity in animals,[13] and retrospective analysis associating aspirin use with malformation,[14] a prospective study by Slone et al.[15] failed to identify an increase in malformation among the offspring of 5128 mothers who ingested large quantities of aspirin, or among 9736 infants exposed to episodic maternal use of aspirin in early pregnancy. Turner and Collins also found no increase in anomalies in the offspring of 144 pregnant women who used salicylates regularly.[16] Acetaminophen is commonly believed to have fewer side effects than aspirin, and is often used in place of salicylates during pregnancy. The paucity of data about the teratogenic potential of acetaminophen does not permit the conclusion that it is more or less safe than aspirin in pregnancy. The recent increased use of acetominophen as an over-the-counter analgesic should prompt further investigation of its risks in pregnancy.

The summary of the known effects of medication in pregnancy in Table 2-5 provides data from human sources. Proven teratogens are identified by an asterisk.

DRUGS IN LATE PREGNANCY

Because of the possible adverse effects on fetal organ development during the first trimester,

TABLE 2-5   REPORTED EFFECTS FROM DRUG EXPOSURE ON THE FETUS

	Reported Effect on the Human Fetus	
Drugs	FIRST TRIMESTER EFFECTS	SECOND AND THIRD TRIMESTER EFFECTS
Analgesics		
Acetaminophen	None known	Nephrotoxicity
Narcotics	None known	Depression, withdrawal
Salicylates	Frequent reports—none proven (see text)	Prolonged pregnancy and labor, hemorrhage
Anesthetics		
General	Anomalies, abortion	Depression
Local	None known	Bradycardia, seizures
Anorexics		
Amphetamines	Possible cardiac defects	Irritable, poor feeding
Phenmetrazine	Possible skeletal anomalies	None known
Meclazine	Facial cleft (?)	None known
Anti-infection Agents		
Aminoglycosides	Possible nerve and renal anomalies	Nephrotoxic, ototoxic
Cephalosporins	None known	Positive neonatal cultures
Chloramphenicol	None known	"Gray baby" syndrome (?)
Clindamycin	None known	Unknown
Erythromycin	None known	None known
Ethambutol	None known	None known
Ethionamide	Anomalies	None known
Isonazid	None known	None known
Metronidazole	Mutagenesis (?)	None known
Penicillins	None known	↓Positive neonatal cultures
Rifampin	None known	None known
Sulfonamides	None known	Hemolytic anemia, thrombocytopenia, hyperbilirubinemia
Tetracyclines	Impaired bone growth	Bone growth, stained deciduous teeth (enamel hypoplasia)
Trimethaprim	None known (theoretic concern)	Hyperbilirubinemia
Anticoagulants		
Coumadin	Nasal hypoplasia, ophthalmic abnormalities, epiphyseal stippling	Hemorrhage, stillbirth
Heparin	None known	Hemorrhage, stillbirth
Anticonvulsants		
Barbiturates	None known	Bleeding, withdrawal
Carbamazepine	Unknown	Bleeding, withdrawal
Clonazepam	None known	Withdrawal, depression
Ethosuximide	None known	None known
Phenytoin*	IUGR, craniofacial, abnormalities, MR, hypoplasia of phalanges	Hemorrhage ⎫ Depletion of
Primidone	None known	Hemorrhage ⎬ vitamin K-
Trimethadione*	Mental retardation, facial dysmorphogenesis	Hemorrhage ⎭ dependent clotting factor

* Proven teratogen   (continued)

TABLE 2-5 Continued

	Reported Effect on the Human Fetus	
Drugs	FIRST TRIMESTER EFFECTS	SECOND AND THIRD TRIMESTER EFFECTS
Cancer Chemotherapy		
Alkylating agents	Abortion, anomalies	Hypoplastic gonads, growth delay
Antimetabolites		
Folic acid analogs (Methotrexate)*	Abortion, IUGR, cranial anomalies	Same as above
Pyrimidine analogs (arabinoside)	Same as above	" "
Purine analogs (cytosine, 5-FU)	" " "	" "
Antibiotics (actinomycin)	" " "	" "
Vinca alkyloids	" " "	" "
Cardiovascular Drugs		
Antihypertensives		
Methyldopa	None known	Hemolytic anemia, ileus
Guanethidine	None known	
Hydralazine	Skeletal defects (?)	Tachycardia
Propranolol	None known	Bradycardia, hypoglycemia, IUGR with chronic use
Reserpine	None known	Lethargy
β-Sympathomimetics	None known	Tachycardia
Digitalis	None known	Bradycardia
Cold and Cough Preparations		
Antihistamines	None known	None known
Cough suppressants	None known	None known
Decongestants	None known	None known
Expectorants	Fetal goiter	None known
Dextromethorphan	None known	None known
Diuretics		
Furosemide	None known	Death from sudden hypoperfusion
Thiazides	None known	Thrombocytopenia, hypokalemia, hyperbilirubinemia, hyponatremic
Fertility Drugs		
Clomiphene	Chromosomal anomalies (?)	Unknown
Hormones		
Androgens*	Masculinization of the female fetus	Adrenal suppression (?)
Corticosteroids	Cleft in animals, not in humans	Growth delay
Estrogens	Cardiovascular anomalies	None known
Progestins	Limb and CV anomalies, "VACTERL" syndrome	None known
Hypoglycemics		
Insulin	Does not cross placenta	None known
Sulfonylureas	Anomalies (?)	Suppressed insulin secretion
Laxatives		
Bisacodyl	None known	None known
Docusate	None known	None known
Mineral oil	Decreased maternal vitamin absorption	Decreased maternal vitamin absorption
Milk of magnesia	None known	None known

* Proven teratogen

TABLE 2-5 Continued

Drugs	Reported Effect on the Human Fetus	
	FIRST TRIMESTER EFFECTS	SECOND AND THIRD TRIMESTER EFFECTS
Psychoactive Drugs		
Antidepressants		
tricyclics	Limb defects (?)	None known
Benzodiazepines	Oral clefts (?)	Depression, floppy infant
Hydroxyzine	None known	None known
Meprobamate	Cardiac anomalies (?)	None known
Phenothiazines	None known	None known
Sedatives	None known	Depression
Thalidomide*	Phocomelia in 20 percent of cases	None known
Lithium	Facial clefts; Ebstein's anomaly	None known
Thyroid Drugs		
Antithyroid	Goiter	Goiter, airway obstruction
131I*	Abortion, anomalies	hypothyroid, mental retardation
Propylthiouracil	Goiter	Same
Methimazole	Aplasia cutis, goiter	Same, aplasia cutis
Thyroid USP	Does not cross	None known
Thyroxine	Does not cross	None known
Tocolytics		
Alcohol*	Fetal alcohol syndrome	Intoxication, hypotonia; lethal
Magnesium sulfate	None known	Hypermagnesemia, respiratory depression
β-Sympathomimetics	None known	Tachycardia, hypothermia, hypocalcemia, hypo- and hyperglycemia
Vaginal Preparations		
Antifungal agents	None known	None known
Podophyllin	Mutagenesis (?)	Laryngeal polyps (?) CNS effects (?)
Vitamins (high dose)		
A	Urogenital anomalies (?)	None known
B	None known	None known
C	None known	Scurvy after delivery
D	Mental retardation, facial cleft	None known
E	None known	None known
K	None known	Hemorrhage, if deficiency
Antiasthmatics		
Theophylline	None known	Decreased respiratory distress
Terbutaline	None known	Tachycardia, hypothermia, hypocalcemia, hypo- and hyperglycemia
"Street" Drugs		
LSD	None known	Withdrawal
Marijuana	None known	None known
Methaquaalone	None known	Withdrawal
Heroin	None known	Depression, withdrawal
Methadone	None known	Withdrawal
Pentazosine	None known	Withdrawal
Cocaine	None known	Withdrawal
Other		
Cimetidine	None known	None known
Caffeine	Anomalies (?) in high doses	Jitteriness
Azathiuprine	Skeletal defect(?)	None known

* Proven teratogen

drugs are frequently avoided or not used until later in pregnancy. The fetus is not entirely spared from possible toxic effects during the latter half of pregnancy, however, since histogenesis and functional maturation continue. Retarded growth of specific fetal organs may also occur, although malformation is unlikely after completion of organogenesis. Cells within the brain, gonads, liver, and special nervous system organs (eye, ear) continue to divide rapidly and are susceptible to drug effects. A toxic reaction within the fetus from a drug is often unpredictable and difficult to prove, since a drug may indirectly or directly act in any of the following pathways: induction or inhibition of certain enzymes, mutation of genes, changes in cell membrane integrity, competition for circulating protein-binding sites, or interactions with other drugs or teratogens.

Table 2-5 also lists specific drugs and reported effects on the fetus during the second and third trimesters of exposure. Antibiotics, antihistamines, antihypertensives, sedatives, and mild analgesics are the most commonly prescribed drugs in the latter half of pregnancy. Side effects seen in the mother may occur in the fetus with greater intensity and can interfere with normal physiologic or homeostatic processes. With the increase in utero-placental blood flow and placental size, and with a breakdown in the placental barrier as gestation progresses, serum levels of drugs or drug metabolites in the fetus may be increased and approach or exceed maternal serum concentrations. Furthermore, the untested and immature metabolic pathways in the fetus may not adequately detoxify or degrade certain drugs. Metabolic clearance may be hindered, especially if large doses are administered over prolonged periods. Principles of drug metabolism and elimination in the fetus are discussed in Chapter 1.

REFERENCES

1. Brocklebank JC, Ray WA, Federspiel CF, et al: Drug prescribing during pregnancy. *Am J Obstet Gynecol* 132:235, 1978
2. Wilson JG, Fraser FC (eds): *Handbook of Teratology*. New York, Plenum, 1979
3. Shepard TH: *Catalog of Teratogenic Agents*, ed 3. Baltimore, Johns Hopkins Univ Press, 1980
4. Pitkin RM, Zlatnik FJ (eds): *The Year Book of Obstetrics and Gynecology*. Chicago, Year Book Medical Publishers (whole series).
5. Feldman GL, Weaver DD, Lourien EW: The fetal trimethadione syndrome. *Am J Dis Child* 131:1389, Dec 1977
6. Hanson JW, Smith DW: The fetal hydantoin syndrome. *J Pediatr* 87:285, 1975
7. Stevenson RE, Burton OM, Ferlauto GJ, Taylor HA: Hazards of oral anticoagulants during pregnancy. *JAMA* 243:1549, 1980
8. Wilson JG, Fraser FC: *Handbook of Teratology*, Vol 1. p 323, New York, Plenum, 1977
9. Clarren SK, Smith DW: The fetal alcohol syndrome. *N Engl J Med* 298:1063, 1978
10. Nora JJ, et al: Lithium, Ebstein's anomaly, and other congenital heart defects. *Lancet* 2:594, 1974
11. Heinonen OP, Slone D, Monson RR, et al: Cardiovascular birth defects and exposure to female sex hormones. *N Engl J Med* 296:67, 1977
12. Bodendorfer TW, Briggs GG, Gunning JE: Obtaining drug exposure histories during pregnancy. *Am J Obstet Gynecol* 135:490, 1979
13. Warkany J, Takacs E: Experimental production of congenital malformations in rats by salicylate poisoning. *Am J Pathol* 35:315, 1959
14. Nelson MM, Forton JO: Associations between drugs administered during pregnancy and congenital abnormalities of the fetus. *Br Med J* 1:523, 1971
15. Slone D, Siskind V, Heinonen OP, et al: Aspirin and congenital malformations. *Lancet* 1:1373, 1976
16. Turner G, Collins E: Fetal effects of regular salicylate ingestion during pregnancy. *Lancet* 2:338, 1975

3. Iron Preparations, Vitamins, Antiemetics and OTC Drugs

RANDY F. SCHAD   WILLIAM F. RAYBURN

Despite growing patient awareness to avoid drugs during pregnancy, many medications are commonly used. Between 3.6 to 4.5 drugs are ingested during pregnancy which contain 8.7 different pharmacologic agents.[1,2] Drug ingestion is most common during the first and third trimesters, exposing the fetus during organogenesis and predelivery periods. Analgesics (especially aspirin), antihistamines, iron, antiemetics, antacids, and vitamin supplements are the most commonly used drugs. Many over-the-counter drugs are taken without physician knowledge and are not recognized by the pregnant patient as being potentially harmful. Furthermore, over-the-counter drugs have been reported to be taken four times more often than prescribed medications during pregnancy.[3] This chapter evaluates the drugs most commonly taken during pregnancy.

IRON

Requirements During Pregnancy

The natural course of pregnancy, due to increasing fetal and maternal needs, requires approximately twice the daily requirement of elemental iron as the nonpregnant state. A minimum of 750 mg of additional utilizable elemental iron is necessary during the course of pregnancy to meet the demands for increased maternal red blood cell volume (500 mg), fetal needs (200 mg), and placental and cord requirements (50 mg).[4] Additionally, the nursing mother loses 1 or 2 mg of iron per day via breast milk. Therefore, a total of 4 mg of absorbed elemental iron is required daily to meet the demands of normal adult losses and pregnancy or lactation needs.

The demands for iron during pregnancy are in excess of dietary sources (red meats, liver); hence, iron supplementation is recommended. Approximately 10 percent of iron contained in food and iron supplements is absorbed. Intestinal absorption of elemental iron increases further with gestational age and during iron deficiency (about 20 percent). Although no teratogenic effects have been reported in physiologic doses, iron is usually unnecessary until the second trimester, when the demand for iron increases. Iron may also be perceived by the patient as contributing to nausea of early pregnancy, which should subside by the second trimester.

Iron deficiency anemia is the most common form of anemia during pregnancy and occurs in 60 percent of gravid women if iron supplements are not given. Causes for this deficiency include inadequate dietary intake, occult hemorrhage, diminished gastrointestinal absorption, and fetal requirements. Additional iron therapy is necessary after iron deficiency anemia is confirmed. The prevention of iron deficiency anemia and the replenishment of iron stores during each pregnancy should prevent anemia in subsequent pregnancies.

Preparations

Many over-the-counter and prescription products are available which contain iron in varying dosages. Differences between oral products relate to the amount of elemental iron (10 to 33 percent) in the form of iron salt (Table 3-1). Iron-containing liquids should be taken if tablets cannot be tolerated or if intestinal absorption of iron from the tablets is questioned. Sustained release iron preparations are relatively expensive and are transported beyond the duodenum and proximal jejunum where iron is less likely to be absorbed, and have not proven to be more useful than other preparations. Other ingredients that are added to oral iron products include vitamin C and docusate sodium (Colace), a stool softener. Vitamin C promotes iron absorption, and docusate sodium counteracts the consti-

pating effect of iron. The added expense for these preparations must be considered and they must be proven to be beneficial.

Injectable iron contains elemental iron (iron dextran), and is available with a preservative (0.5 percent phenol) in multiple dose vials for intramuscular injection, or without a preservative in ampules for intravenous administration.

Modes of Administration and Dose

Oral iron therapy is the preferred and safest route of administration. Ferrous sulfate or gluconate, 325 mg daily, is sufficient to provide the iron requirements of pregnancy for those patients who are not iron-deficient. Patients with iron deficiency should receive 325 mg of ferrous sulfate two or three times daily. Six months of iron supplementation is necessary

TABLE 3-1   IRON PRODUCTS CURRENTLY AVAILABLE

Dosage Form	Trade Name	Generic Name	Strength (mg, unless otherwise indicated)	Elemental Iron (mg)	Cost*
Liquids	Fer-In-Sol	Ferrous sulfate	150 mg/5 ml	30	4
	Feosol Elixir	Ferrous sulfate	220 mg/5 ml	44	3
	Fergon Elixir	Ferrous gluconate	300 mg/5 ml	34	4
	Mol-Iron Liquid	Ferrous sulfate	244 mg/15 ml	49	3
Tablets/capsules	Feosol	Ferrous sulfate	325	65	2
	Fergon	Ferrous gluconate	320	37	2
	Fumasorb	Ferrous fumarate	200	66	2
	Ferancee-HP	Ferrous fumarate	330	110	6
		Ascorbic acid	600	—	
	Mol-Iron with	Ferrous sulfate	195	39	3
	Vitamin C	Ascorbic acid	75	—	
Sustained release oral preparations	Ferro Sequels	Ferrous fumarate	150	50	8
		Docusate sodium	100	—	
	Feosol Spansule	Ferrous sulfate	250	50	8
	Fergon Capsules	Ferrous gluconate	435	50	7
	Fero-Gradumet	Ferrous sulfate	525	105	7
	Fero-Grad-500	Ferrous sulfate	525	105	7
		Vitamin C	500	—	9
	Mol-Iron chronsule	Ferrous sulfate	390	78	5
Injection	Imferon	Iron dextran complex	50 mg/ml	50	3

* The number reflects the average wholesale cost of that dosage form rounded to the next whole dollar. It represents the cost of 100 tablets, capsules, or oral liquid doses of the indicated volume. For injections, it reflects the cost per ampule.

TABLE 3-2 REASONS FOR FAILURE OF ORAL IRON THERAPY

1. Inadequate patient compliance
2. Inability to tolerate or absorb the iron
3. Nonbioavailable iron preparation
4. Antacid therapy
5. Concurrent infection, inflammation, or malignancy
6. Undetected blood loss
7. Non–iron-deficient anemia

to replenish already depleted iron stores in the bone marrow. Parenteral administration of iron is necessary when the response to oral iron is inadequate or not tolerated (Table 3-2) by the patient. The total dose of parenteral iron needed to restore hemoglobin and to replenish iron stores in the bone marrow can be calculated by the following formula:

Milligrams total
iron to be injected*

$$= \frac{0.3 \times \text{body weight in pounds} \times (100 - \text{patient hemoglobin gram·percent} \times 100)}{14.8}$$

A test dose of 0.5 ml should be administered intramuscularly or intravenously initially if parenteral therapy is necessary. If no reaction occurs within several hours, a maintenance dose of 2 ml can be given. The patient can either receive an intramuscular dose daily or twice weekly until the desired total dose is administered. The Z-track technique for intramuscular injection should be performed using a 2- or 3-in, 19- or 20-gauge needle in the upper outer quadrant of the buttock only.† Needle size is important and should be judged upon the size of the patient.

Intravenous administration of iron dextran is approved by the Food and Drug Admin-

* To calculate the dose in milliliters of Imferon, divide the total milligrams by 50.
† The Z-track technique involves displacing the skin laterally prior to injection and not releasing the skin until the needle is withdrawn.

istration, but is reserved for those patients with poor muscle mass who would require multiple injections. Intravenous injection may involve a daily bolus of 100 mg (2 ml) over 2 minutes (Table 3-3). The rate of hemoglobin production is essentially the same whether iron is administered orally, intramuscularly, or intravenously.[5-7] Intramuscular and intravenous preparations are recommended only when oral iron fails.

Precautions

Ingested iron may irritate the gastrointestinal tract. Abdominal cramps, diarrhea, constipation, and nausea are frequent patient complaints. Taking the iron preparation with a meal may improve these side effects, but iron absorption may be reduced. Antacids also impair absorption and should not be taken simultaneously with iron. Black, tarry stools are caused by the accumulated unabsorbed iron.

Local effects from intramuscular injections include pain, sterile abscess formation, hematoma formation, and skin discoloration (lasting up to 3 years). Phlebitis may occur at the intravenous administration site. Systemic reactions from parenteral administration occur in less than 1 percent of all patients and are usually manifested within 10 minutes. Systemic signs and symptoms include headache, dyspnea, myalgia, arthralgia, flushing, dizziness, nausea and vomiting, fever, and death from severe anaphylaxis.

An overdose of iron therapy may occur, particularly in children who are attracted to the candy-like appearance of the tablets. The average lethal dose of ferrous sulfate is 200 to 250 mg/kg body weight.[8] Death has been reported in small children who have ingested 2 gm or less of ferrous sulfate. It results from metabolic derangements, liver necrosis, extensive gastrointestinal mucosal damage, and renal failure. The treatment of iron overdose requires the immediate induction of vomiting with syrup of ipecac (15 to 30 ml). The hospitalized patient should be treated with gastric lavage using sodium phosphate, administration of intravenous deferoxamine (an iron-binding compound), and supportive care.

TABLE 3-3 TOTAL VOLUME OF IRON DEXTRAN INJECTION NEEDED TO TREAT IRON DEFICIENCY ANEMIA*

Patient's weight (lb)	Observed Hemoglobin (gm/100 ml)				
	4.4%	5.9%	7.4%	8.9%	10.4%
100	42	36	30	24	18
110	46	39	33	26	20
120	51	43	36	29	22
130	55	47	39	31	23
140	59	50	42	34	25
150	63	54	45	36	27
160	68	57	48	38	29
170	72	61	51	41	31
180	76 ml	64 ml	54 ml	43 ml	32 ml

* From Huff BB (ed): *Physicians Desk Reference.* Oradell, NJ, Medical Economics Co, 1980, p 1213.

Anemia refractory to iron therapy may result from folic acid deficiency, hemoglobinopathies, chronic disease, or infection. A cause may not be found, and spontaneous remission may occur after delivery.

VITAMINS AND MINERALS

Requirements During Pregnancy

A balanced diet provides an adequate supply of vitamins and minerals for the pregnant patient and supplementation is usually unnecessary. The United States Recommended Daily Allowances (USRDA) for vitamins and minerals for pregnant and lactating patients have been established by the FDA and are listed in Table 3-4.[8]

Folic acid is an especially important vitamin for red blood cell production during the last trimester of pregnancy, for multiple gestations, and during lactation. A lack of folic acid affects nucleic acid metabolism. Folic acid deficiency with or without an adequate iron intake is the second leading cause of anemia during pregnancy. It is frequently seen in women of lower socioeconomic status, in adolescents with inadequate diets, and in high-risk pregnancies.

The daily adult requirement for folic acid is 0.4 mg, but increases to 0.8 mg during pregnancy.[9] Daily oral supplementation of 1 mg of folic acid should be prescribed for those patients who cannot maintain a well-balanced diet (including green vegetables) or those taking anticonvulsant medications with antifolate properties. Many of the prenatal vitamin preparations contain 1 mg of folic acid.

The routine prescribing of calcium salt tablets is unnecessary during pregnancy, as the dietary requirements for calcium during pregnancy and lactation are not thought to be increased. Because of fetal and nursing demands for calcium, the maternal parathyroid glands undergo hyperplasia, and parathormone (PT) levels are greater than in the nonpregnant state. Parathormone acts to increase the calcium available by increasing intestinal absorption, reabsorption at the distal renal tubules, and bone calcium mobilization. Calcium for fetal bone deposition represents only about 2.5 percent of the total maternal calcium. It crosses the placenta by active diffusion, so that adequate fetal levels are ensured. Even

**TABLE 3-4   UNITED STATES RECOMMENDED DAILY
ALLOWANCES (USRDA) OF VITAMINS AND IRON**

Vitamin	Nonpregnant	Pregnant or Lactating
A (IU)*	5000	8000
D (IU)	400	400
E (IU)	30	30
C (mg)	60	60
Folic acid (mg)	.4	.8
Niacin (mg)	20	20
B_1 (mg)	1.5	1.7
B_2 (mg)	1.7	2.0
B_6 (mg)	2.0	2.5
B_{12} (mg)	.006	.008
Iron (mg)	18	18
Calcium (mg)	800–1200	1200

* IU = International Units

though a patient may not tolerate the gastrointestinal effects from as little as 1 cup of milk each day (30 percent of daily requirements), calcium is supplied in other dairy products (cheese, cottage cheese, yogurt, ice cream) and in the standard prenatal vitamins (125 to 600 mg of elemental calcium, 15 to 50 percent of daily requirements). Natabec Rx has the greatest concentration of calcium (600 mg, 50 percent of daily requirements). Calcium supplementation should be considered only in treating hypoparathyroidism (see Chap. 7) or prolonged malabsorption conditions.

Preparations

Prenatal vitamin preparations are a source of folic acid, iron, and other vitamins. These products are not to be substituted for a minimum of three well-balanced meals each day. Table 3-5 lists many of the common prenatal vitamins. All contain varying amounts of folic acid, iron (usually the fumarate salt), and other vitamins. The amount of each ingredient either meets or exceeds the recommended daily allowances. The cost is approximately five times greater than ferrous sulfate tablets alone.

Over-the-counter vitamin preparations

are also listed in Table 5. Not all of these preparations contain folic acid and iron. Furthermore, absolute amounts of elemental iron and folic acid may be inadequate for pregnancy needs. The risks and benefits of taking separate vitamins (C, D, A, etc.) in differing amounts are poorly understood. Vitamins should not be taken without the physician's knowledge.

Precautions

A deficiency of folic acid or vitamin B_{12} from malabsorption can lead to megaloblastic anemia and neurologic damage (paresthesia, poor muscle coordination, confusion, mental slowness). Folic acid without vitamin B_{12} given to pregnant patients with pernicious anemia may correct the anemia, but will not affect neurologic sequelae from vitamin B_{12} deficiency. A monthly injection of 0.1 mg of vitamin B_{12} is therefore necessary in addition to the folic acid.

Folic acid is nontoxic in humans, but large doses of fat-soluble vitamins A and D have been associated with a broad spectrum of congenital abnormalities and toxic reactions.[10] Vitamin A toxicity occurs both in children and adults receiving more than 100,000 units per

TABLE 3-5 COMMON PRENATAL VITAMINS AND OVER-THE-COUNTER (OTC) VITAMINS

Trade Name	Elemental Iron Content† (mg)	Folic Acid Content‡ (mg)
Prenatal Vitamins		
Filibon*	18	0.4
Filibon F.A.	45	1
Filibon Forte	45	1
Materna 1–60	60	1
Natabec*	30	0.8
Natabec R$_x$*	30	1
Natabec-F.A.*	45	0.8
Natalins*	30	0.8
Natalins R$_x$	60	1
Pramilet-F.A.	40	1
Stuart Prenatal*	60	0.8
Stuart Prenatal with F.A.	65	0.3
Stuart Natal 1 + 1	65	1
OTC Vitamins		
Dayalets Plus Iron	18	0.4
One-A-Day	0	0.4
One-A-Day Plus Iron	18	0.4
Micebrin	15	0
Stresstabs 600 with Iron	27	0.4
Theragran-M	12	0
Theragran Hematinic	67	0.33

* OTC prenatal vitamins
† Minimum daily requirement of absorbed elemental iron during pregnancy and lactation is 4 mg. However, approximately 10% of elemental iron is absorbed.
‡ Minimum daily requirement of absorbed folic acid during pregnancy and lactation is 0.8 mg.

day over several months. The common signs and symptoms are fatigue, malaise, lethargy, abdominal upset, bone and joint pain, hair loss, brittle nails, and scaly skin. In addition to the above, infants have increased intracranial pressure, bulging fontanels, hypoprothrombinemia, decalcification of bone, and arrest or retardation of growth. Treatment consists of discontinuing the vitamin A.

Vitamin D toxicity is seen when doses exceed 50,000 units per day for prolonged periods (see Chap. 2). Toxic effects include anorexia, nausea, vomiting, weakness, weight loss, polyuria, constipation, soft tissue calcification, nephrocalcinosis, hypertension, hypercalcemia, acidosis, and renal failure. Treatment consists of a discontinuation of vitamin D, a low calcium diet, and an increased intake of fluid.

Mineral oil taken as a laxative may prevent the intestinal absorption of fat-soluble vitamins (A, D, E).

ANTIEMETICS

The "morning sickness" of early pregnancy is a frequent patient complaint. Although the etiology is unclear, increased levels of pregnancy-related hormones and certain psychologic factors have been implicated. Other conditions which may lead to persistent nausea and vomiting (urinary tract infections, influenza, appendicitis, cholecystitis, bowel obstruction, cerebral tumors) must also be considered.

Preparations

If psychologic reassurance and frequent small, dry meals of mostly carbohydrates offer no improvement, medications which contain a combination of an antihistamine and pyridoxine (Bendectin) or the phenothiazines (promethazine—Phenergan, prochlorperazine—Compazine) can be used with caution. The phenothiazines are thought to act by blocking the chemoreceptor trigger zone (CTZ) and the vomiting center in the brain, while the mechanism of action of Bendectin is unknown. These antiemetics are listed in Table 3-6.

Modes of Administration

If nausea is recurrent at predictable times, the medication may be taken before its onset. The antiemetic activity of Bendectin is delayed by a special coating which permits the nighttime dose to be effective in the morning hours. The two common phenothiazine preparations may be given rectally if oral administration is not tolerated. Parenteral administration is infrequent but necessary when oral or rectal therapy is inadequate. After initial treatment, the dosage of any medication should be adjusted to the smallest amount necessary to relieve symptoms.

Precautions

Studies in women receiving Bendectin during pregnancy have shown the incidence of birth defects to be no higher than women not taking the drug.[11-15] Bendectin contains an antihistamine (doxylamine, 10 mg) and pyridoxine (10 mg). The amount of pyridoxine is no more than what is found in many standard prenatal vitamins. Teratology studies in rabbits and reproduction studies in rats have been conducted and show Bendectin to have no adverse effect on pregnancy.[16] The Food and Drug Administration has revised the physician's prescribing information and now states that Bendectin should be prescribed only if significant nausea and vomiting is unresponsive to more conservative measures. No known anomalies are associated with phenothiazine usage (see Table 2-5). Phenothiazines are not approved for this use by the FDA; their liberal use as an antiemetic is therefore not encouraged.

Common side effects of antiemetics include drowsiness and relaxation. The concomitant use of analgesics, sedatives, and alcohol with antiemetics can further depress the central nervous system and should be avoided.

Table 3-6 Antiemetics Commonly Used During Pregnancy

Trade Name	Generic Name	Dose	Strength (mg, unless otherwise indicated)	Cost*
Bendectin	Doxylamine succinate pyridoxine HCL	2 tablets HS 1 to 2 tablets in AM 1 to 2 in mid-afternoon	10 10	13
Phenergan	Promethazine	25 mg repeated every 4 to 6 hr	25 25 mg suppository 25 mg/ml	10 5 /
Compazine	Prochlorperazine	5 to 10 mg every 4 to 6 hr	5 10 25 mg suppository 5 mg/ml injection	9 12 6 2

* The number reflects the average wholesale cost of that dosage form rounded to the next whole dollar. It represents the cost of 100 tablets, the cost per ampule, or the cost of 12 suppositories.

Patients should be cautioned against driving automobiles or performing any actions that require coordination. Occasional side effects of phenothiazines include hypotension, extrapyramidal effects, dyskinesias, dry mouth, skin reactions, jaundice, and blood dyscrasias.

Signs of Bendectin overdose include dilated pupils; dry, burning sensations of the mouth; thirst; difficulty swallowing; hyperthermia; generalized flushing; hot, dry skin; headache; nausea and vomiting; excitement; delirium; convulsions; rapid pulse; and respiratory and circulatory collapse. Treatment consists of inducing emesis, administering activated charcoal, and gastric lavage. Parenteral diazepam (Valium) is recommended to treat convulsions. A case has been reported of a 3-year-old child who died after ingesting 100 tablets of Bendectin.[17]

An overdose of the phenothiazines can cause central nervous system depression, coma, convulsions, fever, dry mouth, hypotension, ileus, extrapyramidal reactions, dystonic reactions, headache, vertigo, disorientation, and blurred vision. Treatment may require gastric lavage, along with symptomatic and supportive care. Emesis should be attempted cautiously, since a dystonic reaction of the head or neck may develop and lead to aspiration of vomitus. Persistent extrapyramidal signs are treated with trihexyphenidyl (Artane).

Excess prochlorperazine (Compazine) taken by children may cause dysphagia, convulsions or opisthotonus.[18]

OVER-THE-COUNTER DRUGS

The basic pharmacologic principles described in Chapter 1 also apply to over-the-counter drugs used during pregnancy. The initial obstetrical examination should include the questioning and documentation of any specific over-the-counter drugs taken at conception and during the first trimester. Effects from the indiscriminate use of over-the-counter drugs are not usually obvious in the neonate. Less pronounced effects can be unappreciated,

even though each preparation may contain several active ingredients and preservatives.

Certain over-the-counter preparations may be taken from habit, instead of physical need, and may not be considered as medicines by the patient. Relief of patient symptoms is important, and many over-the-counter preparations are permissible during the second and third trimesters in minimal dosages and for short durations. However, all drugs should be used cautiously during pregnancy. The cost of brand name preparations containing the same basic ingredients is similar and usually higher than generic preparations.

Mild Analgesics
Aspirin is effective and should not be absolutely discouraged. Certain aspirin preparations contain magnesium or aluminum buffers (Bufferin) or caffeine (Excedrin, Anacin, Doans Pills, Vanquish).[19] However, large doses or chronic use may inhibit prostaglandin synthetase activity and thereby prolong gestation or increase the duration of labor.[18] Excessive maternal hemorrhage can occur from aspirin effects by inhibiting platelet aggregation and inhibiting factor XII synthesis. Hemorrhage in the fetus and neonate and in utero closure of the fetus ductus arteriosus have also been reported.[20] Even in minimal doses, aspirin can cause decreased platelet aggregation in the fetus for several days. The clinical significance of this finding is uncertain. The effects of acetaminophen (Tylenol, Datril) in pregnancy are unknown. It does inhibit—in large doses only—prostaglandin activity (see Chap. 21) and may not necessarily be a better substitute for aspirin in late gestation. Acetaminophen does not alter platelet properties but can be toxic to the liver in large doses and may be less desirable.

Decongestants, Antihistamines, Antitussives
Decongestants, antihistamines, and antitussives are frequently requested and used during early pregnancy. All "cold" preparations combine a sympathomimetic, an antihistamine, and a mild analgesic (Dristan, Co-Tylenol,

Triaminicin).[19] Atropine and belladonna may also be present (Alka-Seltzer Plus, Contac). Cough syrups (Robitussin D. M., Vicks Cough Syrup, Nyquil, Romilar, Halls) contain an antitussive (dextromethorphan), an antihistamine, and alcohol. Decongestants (Neosynephrine, Sinex, Dristan, Sudafed) should be used in the lowest concentrations, because they contain a sympathomimetic which may influence uterine perfusion in large doses. They should not be used if utero-placental insufficiency is suspected. The teratogenic potential is unconfirmed, but withdrawal in infants born to chronic abusers of these agents can include tremulousness, agitation, irritability, and poor feeding.

Antacids

Antacids should be taken only after diet manipulation and conservative treatment for dyspepsia is unsuccessful. A buffered preparation of calcium carbonate (Tums, Camalox, Chooz), a mixture of magnesium and aluminum hydroxide (Gelusil, Maalox, Riopan, Digel, Kolantyl), or magnesium hydroxide alone (Phillip's Milk of Magnesia) is recommended. Excess sodium is related to fluid retention and possibly to the onset of toxemia. Sodium is present in certain preparations (Rolaids, Alka-Seltzer, Bromo-Seltzer).[19]

Laxatives and Stool Softeners

Laxatives and stool softeners are permitted for relief of constipation only after diet manipulation (additional fluids, fruits, bran foods) has been attempted unsuccessfully. Natural vegetable concentrates (Senokot, Metamucil, Serutan, Konsyl) are recommended bulk laxatives. Castor oil, epsom salts, or milk of magnesia may also be used occasionally. Laxatives usually contain phenophthalein (Ex-lax, Feen-A-Ment) or docusate sodium or calcium (Correctol, Regutol, Colace, Doxidan, Dialose).[19] Excess cathartic use may promote labor and should be taken with caution. In addition, enemas may contain high concentrations of sodium (Fleets enema). Antidiarrheals (Kaopectate, Donnagel) contain kaolin and pectin and may be used in moderation. Pepto-Bismol contains bismuth subsalicylate and significant amounts of salicylate are released with large doses. Preparation H contains no topical anesthetic and is perhaps the best hemorrhoidal preparation during pregnancy.

Sedatives

Sedatives (Nytol, Sominex, Quiet World, Sleep-Eze, Nervine, Compoz) contain the antihistamine, pyrilamine maleate. Excess use may cause a worrisome decrease in fetal activity. Withdrawal symptoms in the neonate can include irritability, tremulousness, a high-pitched cry, and poor feeding. Prescribed sedatives and hypnotics are described in more detail in Chapters 11 and 26.

Topical Preparations

Acne creams (Stridex, Clearasil, Phisoac, Fostex, Cuticura) and lotions contain benzoyl peroxide or sulfa, salicylate, and alcohol, and are safe in moderation.[19] Cis-retinoic acid in newer preparations is also probably safe to apply. First-aid ointments or lotions (Johnson & Johnson, Bacitracin, Neosporin, Betadine, Cruex, Calamine) and topical steroids (Cortaid, Lanacort) are likely safe with moderate use. Pain-relieving rubs (Mentholatum, Ben-Gay) contain methyl salicylate and menthol and should be used in moderation during pregnancy because they increase circulation to the skin, which may cause an increased absorption.

Aerosols and Chemicals

Aerosol and chemical-fume exposure from hair sprays, paint, pesticides, methane, spray adhesives, household cleaners, and laboratory chemicals are frequent patient concerns. The effect on fetal cerebral development is probably negligible, but patient exposure should be discouraged or minimized in a well-ventilated area. No fetal effects have been observed with hair dye application.

Caffeine

The structural similarity of caffeine to DNA base pairs adenine and guanine has prompted laboratory investigation to determine any teratogenic effect. Skeletal variations have been found in fetal rats exposed to high doses of caffeine.[21] It is not known whether caffeine or its principal metabolite, paraxanthine, is teratogenic in humans. In contrast to recent large epidemiologic studies, Weathersbee et al. found excess caffeine ingestion (at least 600 mg/day) to be associated with a high incidence of abortion, stillbirth, or premature birth.[22] Caffeine in coffee (125 mg), tea (65 mg), 6-oz service of cola soft drinks (50 mg), and mild analgesics (30 to 60 mg) is transferred to the fetus and breastfed infant. Stimulant tablets (NoDoz, Vivarin, Caffedrine) contain approximately 100 mg of caffeine and are to be discouraged. Drinking caffeinated beverages sparingly or in moderation with an adherence to a proper diet is strongly recommended.

Artificial Sweeteners

Artificial sweeteners (saccharin, sorbitol) in beverages or commercial preparations (Sucaryl, Sweeta) readily cross the placenta. However, no increase in abortion or teratogenic effects has been evident; however, such additives should be used in moderation during pregnancy.[23,24]

Diet Pills

Diet pills (Perathine, AYD's, Appedrine, Prolamine, Dexatrim, Thinz-span, Coffee-Off) contain phenyl propanolamine and caffeine, and their effect during early, unsuspected pregnancy is unknown. "Water" pills (Diurex, Dayspan, Aqua-Ban) contain caffeine and potassium or ammonium chloride and are to be discouraged.

Alcohol

The ingestion of alcoholic beverages (beer, wine, distilled spirits) at conception or during pregnancy is a frequent patient concern. Reports from human and animal studies have involved excessive or chronic exposure of alcohol to the fetus. A fetal alcohol syndrome has been delineated in the human and is described in Chapter 2. A 25 percent malformation rate, which includes cardiac anomalies and cleft palates, has been reported in children born

to alcoholic mothers. What effect in utero exposure to alcohol has on the child's subsequent neurobehavioral development is unclear. Other conditions such as inadequate nutrition (poor protein intake, pyridoxine or other vitamin B deficiencies), contaminants in the alcohol, and genetic factors may also play an important etiologic role. There is no safe threshold of alcohol consumption, but no cases of fetal alcohol syndrome have been reported with the mother ingesting less than 2 oz of absolute alcohol daily. Two ounces of absolute alcohol (100 percent) is equivalent to one-half glass of distilled spirits (50 percent), two glasses of wine (12 percent), or four glasses of beer (6 percent). The pregnant patient is discouraged from drinking alcoholic beverages during the first trimester and should avoid two or more drinks each day during the second and third trimesters.

Cigarette Smoking

The effects from fetal exposure to carbon monoxide and nicotine have been extensively studied in animals.[25] Both chemicals have been associated with delayed fetal growth. The incidence of neonatal mortality and congenital defects is not increased by smoking. Preterm rupture of the amniotic membranes may occur more frequently in heavy smokers. Whether or not cigarette smoking during pregnancy impairs the subsequent intellectual function of the exposed fetus is controversial. Davie et al. reported a 3 to 4 month delay in reading achievement, while Hardy and Mellitus could find no intellectual impairment in offspring of heavy smokers.[26,27] Other problems associated with smoking during pregnancy include spontaneous abortion, placental abruption, placenta previa, and decreased infant length. If the patient is unable to quit smoking during pregnancy, she is to be encouraged to smoke five or less cigarettes each day, using a low tar and nicotine brand.

REFERENCES

1. Peckham CH, King RW: A study of intercurrent conditions observed in pregnancy. *Am J Obstet Gynecol* 87:609, 1963

2. Bleyer WA, Au WY: Studies on the detection of adverse drug reactions in the newborn: Fetal exposure to maternal medication. *JAMA* 213:2046, 1970

3. Fofar JO, Nelson MM: Epidemiology of drugs taken by pregnant women: Drugs that may affect the fetus adversely. *Clin Pharmacol Ther* 14(pt 2):632, 1973

4. Hambidge KM, Mauer AM: Trace elements, in *Laboratory Indices of Nutritional Status in Pregnancy,* ed 1. National Academy of Sciences, 1978, pp 157–165

5. McCurdy PR: Oral and parenteral iron therapy. *JAMA* 191:859, 1965

6. Olsen KS, Weinfeld A: Availability of iron dextran for hemoglobin synthesis as studied with phlebotomy. *Acta Med Scand* 192:543, 1972

7. Pritchard, JA: Hemoglobin regeneration in severe iron deficiency anemia. *JAMA* 195:97, 1966

8. Arena JM: *Poisoning.* Springfield, Ill, Thomas, 1974, p 395

9. AMA Department of Drugs: *AMA Drug Evaluations.* Chicago, American Medical Association, 1980, pp 818–819

10. Gosselin RE, Hodge HC, Smith RP, et al: *Clinical Toxicology of Commercial Products.* Baltimore, Williams & Wilkins, 1976, p 173

11. Milkovich L, van den Berg BJ: An evaluation of the teratogenicity of certain antinauseant drugs. *Am J Obstet Gynecol* 125:244, 1976

12. Shapiro S, Heinonen OP, Siskind V, et al: Antenatal exposure to doxylamine succinate and dicyclomine hydrochloride (Bendectin) in relation to congenital malformations, perinatal mortality rate, birth weight, and intelligence quotient score. *Am J Obstet Gynecol* 128:480, 1977

13. Smithells RW, Sheppard S: Teratogenicity testing in humans: A method demonstrating safety of bendectin. *Teratology* 17:31, 1978

14. Bunde CA, Bowles DM: A technique for controlled survey of case records. *Curr Ther Res* 5:245, 1963

15. Rothman, KJ, Fyler DC, Goldblatt A, et al: Exogenous hormones and other drug exposures of children with congenital heart disease. *Am J Epidemiol* 109:433, 1979

16. Gibson JP, Staples RE, Larson EJ, et al: Teratology and reproduction studies with an antinauseant. *Toxic Appl Pharmacol* 13:439, 1968

17. *Bendectin* (revised) suppl 113. US Dept of Health, Education and Welfare, National Clearinghouse for Poison Control Centers, Jan 1977

18. Gosselin RE, Hodge HC, Smith RP, et al: *Clinical Toxicology of Commercial Products.* Baltimore, Williams & Wilkins, 1976, p 222

19. *Handbook of Nonprescription Drugs,* ed 6. Washington, D.C., American Pharmaceutical Association, 1980

20. Corby DG: Aspirin in pregnancy: Maternal and fetal effects. *Pediatrics* 62:930, 1978

21. Collins TF, Welsh JJ, Black TN, et al: A comprehensive study of the teratogenic potential of caffeine in rats when given by oral intubation, in *Report on Caffeine,* Food and Drug Administration, Sept 1980

22. Weathersbee PS, Olsen LK, Lodge JR: Caffeine and pregnancy. *Postgrad Med* 62:64, 1977

23. Kroes R, Peters P, Berkvens J, et al: Long term toxicity with cyclamate, saccharin, and cyclohexylamine. *Toxicology* 8:285, 1977

24. Kline J, Stern Z, Susser M et al: Spontaneous abortion and the use of sugar substitutes. *Am J Obstet Gynecol* 130:708, 1978

25. Landesman-Dwyer S, Emanuel I: Smoking during pregnancy. *Teratology* 19:119, 1979

26. Davie R, Butler N, Goldstein H: In *From birth to seven: A Report of the National Child Development Study.* London, Longman and the National Children's Bureau, 1972, pp 175–177

27. Hardy JB, Mellitus ED: Does maternal smoking have a long-term effect on the children? *Lancet* 2:1332, 1972

4. Drug Addiction in Pregnancy

FREDERICK P. ZUSPAN   KATHRYN J. ZUSPAN

The problems of drug addiction in pregnancy are frequently unrealized and may not become apparent until the problem of newborn withdrawal is identified. Most health care practitioners think of drug addiction as involving chronic heroin or methadone dependence. Other medications must also be considered, such as juveniles experimenting with different drugs and emotionally distraught individuals on psychotropic medications. Inadequate reporting is inherent to this problem, and the patients most likely to volunteer that they have a drug dependency are patients in a recognized methadone program. Most others will not admit to drug dependence and will go undetected unless a high degree of suspicion exists or a somatic problem emerges. Some of the questions that are necessary in the prenatal history concern drug dependence and usage of not just heroin or methadone but any of the psychotropic or off-street drugs, including marijuana.

Drug dependence during pregnancy involves all classes of society. The lack of awareness or inquisition about drug addiction is common in the United States. We tend to underestimate the existence of these problems because we find it socially unattractive. As a result, drug addiction creates a negative relationship between the patient and physician. Drug-dependence studies have classically involved heroin and methadone, but reports of neonatal withdrawal have also been seen in patients receiving drugs such as phenobarbi-

tal, alcohol, pentazocaine, propoxyphene, nicotine and caffeine.[1,2] Due to their low molecular weight, stimulants and depressants cross the placenta and are also excreted in breast milk. The drug reaction in the fetus is often the same as in the mother. A patient who is addicted to a narcotic such as heroin may be unable to sustain her habit or enter a recognized methadone maintenance program during her pregnancy. As a result, she and the fetus will have withdrawal symptoms with increased agitation, convulsions, and often intrauterine death.[3]

Street drug use is almost impossible to study except to recognize that it does exist. The most extensive experience in drug dependency in pregnancy comes from methadone maintenance programs, which have done an exemplary job of maintaining addicted women through their pregnancies. Each major city has a methadone maintenance program for pregnant and nonpregnant individuals.[4-6]

MENSTRUAL DYSFUNCTION AND FERTILITY

Menstrual abnormalities are common findings in drug-dependent women, especially those on heroin.[7] Table 4-1 identifies the different types of menstrual abnormalities seen in heroin abusers, polydrug abusers using heroin, and methadone-dependent women. Amenorrhea is the most frequently reported symptom[7,8]

31

TABLE 4-1 MENSTRUAL ABNORMALITIES

1. Heroin: Amenorrhea—frequent
2. Multiple drug abuse; including heroin: Menstrual irregularities with anovulation (60–90%)
3. Methadone: First 3–6 months—amenorrhea; after 6–12 months—normal menses (80–93%)

and it is not unusual to find a pregnant patient near term who has been amenorrheic for several years.

Fertility is difficult to assess among drug addicts. It is not uncommon to find sexually transmitted diseases with a high incidence of pelvic inflammatory disease, which may cause tubal occlusion. Coupled with the higher incidence of amenorrhea and anovulation, conception is often difficult in the drug-dependent patient. Women in methadone maintenance programs who abstain from other drugs, including alcohol, are more likely to resume normal menstrual functions.

DIAGNOSIS OF EARLY PREGNANCY

Early diagnosis of pregnancy is important so that any desire to terminate the pregnancy can be discussed openly. At the University of Chicago, we found less than 10 percent of drug-addicted patients desired an interruption of pregnancy, which was lower or about the same as in the conventional population. An abortion against the patient's will should not be urged, since the patient's psychological makeup is often quite fragile and may precipitate a worsening of the situation.[9] The pregnant drug addict is seldom seen early unless she is in a methadone maintenance program. The standard techniques for diagnosing pregnancy are more difficult in the pregnant drug addict. A history of amenorrhea *may* be present in the nonpregnant methadone patient, but is usually present in the nonpregnant heroin addict. The positive pregnancy test is not always valid in the drug

addict, since narcotics or narcotic metabolites may inhibit latex particle agglutination during the urine testing for pregnancy. Fatigue, headache, nausea and vomiting, and hot sweats or flushes can be signs and symptoms of either early pregnancy or withdrawal. Auscultation of fetal heart tones and sonographic visualization of a gestational sac are the only definitive techniques for the diagnosis of addict pregnancy.

ANTEPARTUM MANAGEMENT

The woman who is pregnant and drug-dependent deserves special attention and support throughout her pregnancy. A complete and comprehensive medical and drug history is of paramount importance. Table 4-2 identifies

TABLE 4-2 MEDICAL COMPLICATIONS ENCOUNTERED IN PREGNANT ADDICTS*

Anemia

Bacteremia

Endocarditis (valvular heart disease)

Cellulitis

Poor dental hygiene (peridontitis)

Edema and "woody" subcutaneous tissue

Hepatitis—acute and chronic

Pelvic inflammatory disease

Phlebitis and lack of available veins

Pneumonia (may be associated with granuloma lung), pulmonary edema

Septicemia

Tetanus

Tuberculosis

Urinary tract infections (cystitis, urethritis, pyelonephritis)

Venereal infection (condyloma accuminatum, gonorrhea, Hemophilis vaginalis, herpes, trichomonas, syphilis)

* Adapted from Finnegan et al., Ref. 10.

medical problems more commonly found among drug addicts who are pregnant. The most notable pertain to infection. These complications as reported by Finnegan[10] were similar to the University of Chicago study involving 106 patients,[9] where the incidence of specific prenatal complications included:

• Anemia	24.0%
• Syphilis	17.8%
• Urinary tract infections	15.3%
• Gonorrhea	5.1%
• Pulmonary pathology	4.2%
• Cellulitis or abscess	4.2%
• Severe edema	4.2%

A positive hepatitis history is common and was apparent in 23 percent of pregnant drug addicts in the University of Chicago study, and the use of contaminated needles may explain this high incidence. Over 12 percent of heroin addicts and former addicts have been reported to be chronic carriers of hepatitis B-antigen.[11]

Laboratory baseline studies should be performed in case a problem develops during the antenatal course (Table 4-3).

Nutrition

A diet of 100 gm of protein per day is beneficial in the drug-dependent patient, even though this is seldom accomplished despite nutrition counseling. Studies that we have done utilizing the urea nitrogen and creatinine ratio indicate poor protein nutrition in these women; hence, an extra effort must be made for nutrition counseling. The average protein intake proved to be less than 50 gm/day.

Prenatal vitamins are essential because of the inadequate diet in most pregnant drug addicts. Iron supplementation in the form of ferrous sulfate, 300 mg, or ferrous gluconate, 300 mg, twice daily is essential to correct the nutritional anemia seen in one-fourth of these patients.

Folic acid levels were routinely screened in 106 pregnant addicts, and 64 patients had abnormally low folic acid levels of less than 2.6 mg. All patients with low serum folic acid

TABLE 4-3 RECOMMENDED PRENATAL BASELINE LABORATORY TESTS

1. Complete blood count with indices
2. Blood smear
3. Urine culture (minimum of three during pregnancy)
4. Chest x-ray
5. TB skin test
6. Hemoglobin electrophoresis
7. Folic acid level
8. Total protein—A:G ratio
9. Liver function profile
10. Rubella titer
11. Serology VDRL and FTA
12. Gonorrhea culture (cervical and rectal) initial and repeat at 36 weeks
13. Hepatitis-associated antigens (HAA)
14. Pap smear
15. Blood type, Rh and indirect Coombs test
16. Ultrasound scan
17. Herpes culture (if positive history)

levels were treated with additional oral folic acid throughout pregnancy. In the absence of folic acid deficiency, drug-dependent women require the routine prenatal capsule with folic acid.

Fetal Assessment

It is important to understand that detoxification during pregnancy, if too rapid, will result in undesirable side effects to the fetus. Figure 4-1 identifies the sequence of events seen with rapid detoxification of fetal withdrawal, hyperactivity of the fetus, intrauterine convulsions, passage of meconium, and possible stillbirth. The methadone diminution of 2mg/week should obviate this problem. Figure 4-2 identifies marked stimulation of the fetal adrenal and the sympathetic nervous system in response to diminishing doses of methadone. Since increased fetal activity correlates with

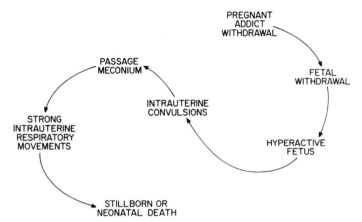

Figure 4-1. Sequence of events in fetal withdrawal.

the peak of epinephrine and norepinephrine in the amniotic fluid, a fetal kick count recorded during one or more convenient hours during the day is useful during the gradual methadone detoxification. A gradual reduction of methadone should occur in a controlled clinical atmosphere.

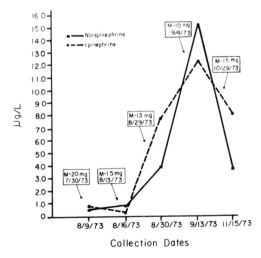

Figure 4-2. The response of the fetal adrenal and sympathetic nervous system in response to diminishing doses of methadone.

Any baseline laboratory tests that were abnormal earlier in the pregnancy should be repeated as pregnancy ensues, especially in the third trimester. At least two ultrasound examinations should be made to assess fetal growth. Of these patients, 10.2 percent had intrauterine growth retardation. When compared to a similar group of control patients, this is no higher than would be expected in that general population.[5] Ultrasound is also reliable to help redetermine the expected date of confinement and to provide an approximation of the weight of the fetus.

Nonstress tests and oxytocin challenge tests are usually not indicated, as there are few drug-related problems encountered during the antenatal period except for premature rupture of membranes found in 20 percent of patients. The addicted mother may have a less active fetus, and erroneous interpretations may be obtained with fetal testing.

It is undesirable to obtain estriol determinations, either serum or urine, as these often are misleading. Estriols were consistently more than 2 SD below what would be expected for the appropriate level of gestation in our study.[12]

Amniocentesis prior to the 37th week may reveal a delayed maturation of the L:S ratio for comparable weeks of gestation in the methadone-dependent patient. This does not apply after the 37th week of gestation.[13]

REHABILITATION AND DRUG WITHDRAWAL

The artificial sense of well-being in the patient who is a drug abuser inhibits the development of important psychologic and social skills. The emotional stresses of pregnancy are exacerbated in drug-dependent women, especially if they attempt to abstain from drugs. Drug abuse rehabilitation in the pregnant addict is often complicated by more intense fear, guilt, and shame than is seen in the nonpregnant patient.

The patient's reaction to rehabilitation may take two paths. She responds with either more profound drug use or attempts to achieve complete abstinence from drugs, which may affect the intrauterine environment and create profound physiologic changes in the fetus.[14] The patient is better managed with a maintenance dose of methadone followed by a gradual dose reduction of 2 mg/week until the dose is reduced to 20 mg/day or less, if tolerable.[5,15] The model proposed by Senay[16] and Davis[17] used methadone as a temporary support for the patients, while their basic human needs were met by psychotherapeutic and resocialization measures. During this period of approximately 6 to 8 months, the patient may gain psychological strength by working through some of the problems that are encountered during pregnancy. Instead of using high doses of methadone, the goal of therapy is to orient the patient to a low-dose regimen.[18-20] This is followed by an increased emphasis on the use of medical, legal, psychologic, vocational, and social services to help readapt the patient to her environment. The pregnant patient adopts an immature behavior, an inability to tolerate delayed gratification, and a poor control of her impulses. Requests for tranquilizing medication may further potentiate depressive traits in methadone patients.[21] Patients may turn to alcohol as the most easily accessible method to handle depression and anxiety, since alcohol consumption is estimated to range from 15 to 40 percent in patients in drug abuse programs. Alcohol and tranquilizers also act as major deterrents to mental health. Fetal wastage and perinatal loss have been shown to be 30 percent higher in a group of patients known to have been using central nervous system altering drugs.[17]

The following are recommendations for supportive care in the antepartum period: (1) avoid physical and emotional stresses that cause the pregnant addict to continue drug abuse, (2) emphasize prenatal classes and groups designed specifically to educate patients and help them work through issues related to drug use during pregnancy, (3) use intramural and extramural crisis intervention and counseling programs staffed by professionals and paraprofessionals (former drug addicts) to intervene in marital and family conflicts during pregnancy, and (4) collaborate frequently with the drug program staff and hospital staff to eliminate prejudicial attitudes.

Table 4-4 lists problems seen during drug withdrawal during pregnancy. The physician should be aware of how manipulative the pregnant drug addict can be and should prescribe sparingly any medicine other than methadone. Eliminating the use of alcohol is difficult, but the patient should understand that alcohol potentiates the problem and increases perinatal loss.

TABLE 4-4 PROBLEMS ASSOCIATED WITH DRUG WITHDRAWAL

1. The manipulative patient
2. Multiple drug regimens—not of value (use only methadone)
3. Diazepam—potentiates depressive traits
4. Alcohol—used by 15–40% of pregnant addicts
5. Multiple-abused drugs cause 30% increase in perinatal loss

The ideal drug-dependent patient is one who is only on methadone and no other medications. Table 4-5 identifies the different philosophies of therapy of the methadone programs. Three different programs (narcotic blockade, small-dose regimen, gradual detoxification) exist in this country, and each has cared for large numbers of pregnant addicts with impressive results.

We have been believers in utilizing the smallest dose possible to achieve control of the patient and using various supportive measures to help in this effort.[16,21] The maternal dose directly correlates with the percentage of patients having newborns exhibiting withdrawal symptoms. For example, if patients are on greater than 20 mg/day, the assumption can be made that at least 90 percent of newborns will have withdrawal symptoms of one form or another, and that half will need to have some form of therapy (methadone, diazepam, or phenobarbital) for at least 7 to 15 days.[22]

If a pregnant woman is taking street heroin, the most efficacious way to switch to a methadone program is to begin between 20 and 40 mg of methadone per day. An average dose of 30 mg is acceptable. Additional five-milligram increments every 3 to 5 days can then be given based on the individual needs of the patient to prevent withdrawal. If this is insufficient, then 10 mg every 3 to 5 days may need to be given. A weekly urinalysis should be obtained to check for any illicit drug

TABLE 4-5　PHILOSOPHY OF METHADONE THERAPY

1. Narcotic blockade:[11,12] Large doses of methadone 80–120 mg/day

2. Small dose regimen:[5,10] Controls the patient with less than 40 mg/day

3. Cold turkey or complete detoxification:[7] Has no place in therapy of the pregnant patient

4. Gradual detoxification:[5,8] Decreased dose (2 mg/week) only with caution, with an attempt to achieve 20 mg/day or less at delivery

use and to help manage the noncompliant patient. When the pregnant patient is converted and stable in the methadone maintenance program, a decision must then be made as to whether or not the patient feels that she would like to have a gradual detoxification program begun at 2 mg increments per week.

Narcotic Overdose

Whether narcotic overdose is intentional or unintentional, the route of administration determines how promptly action needs to take place. After oral dosages are taken, symptoms are most likely to appear 1 to 3 hours after ingestion, and gastric lavage is indicated. If awake, the patient may not need tracheal intubation. If comatose, tracheal intubation with inflation of the tube should be performed before gastric lavage. The usual supportive measures, including maintenance of the airway and an intravenous line for medications, should be performed.

It is imperative to know the drug taken in the overdose. For narcotics, the drug of choice to counteract the effect is naloxone (Narcan). Naloxone is a narcotic antagonist with almost no central nervous system depressant effects. It should be administered intravenously at doses of 0.01 mg/kg and readministered at short intervals every 5 to 10 minutes until the patient regains consciousness. Naloxone has a maximum duration of action of 2 hours, compared to most short-acting narcotics, which have a 6- to 8-hour duration of action, and methadone, which has a 12- to 48-hour duration of action. Great care must be given to the fetus during this period of time, and monitoring for movement and heart rate is essential. Naloxone will cause precipitous withdrawal symptoms in the fetus, and it may be necessary to administer intra-amniotic medications into the fetus to control abnormal fetal activity. Observation of fetal movement can be made by utilizing an external fetal heart rate and tocodynamometer or by real-time ultrasonography.

Neither peritoneal dialysis nor hemodialysis is indicated in pregnancy overdose, nor is hemodialysis, since narcotics are extensively bound to plasma proteins and are therefore not dialyzable.

LABOR AND DELIVERY

The incidence of delivery complications in drug-dependent women varies little from normal pregnant patients. There is no difference in the incidence of abruptio placenta or placenta previa. Less preeclampsia and hypertension are seen in this group as compared to conventional patients. Premature rupture of the membranes was noted in 21 percent of 119 pregnant drug addicts. This is 2½ times greater than in the normal population and underscores a need for careful attention to the microbiology of the vagina in the drug addict during pregnancy by repeated speculum examinations and appropriate culture in the early third trimester of pregnancy.

During labor, the adrenal glands in the mother excrete epinephrine which can be measured in maternal urine to monitor maternal adrenal gland activity. Measurable norepinephrine comes principally from the sympathetic nervous system and is a reflection of the neurohormonal milieu in the mother. Urine from pregnant addicts was assayed for epinephrine, norepinephrine, and creatinine, and these values were compared to similar urine collections from normal pregnant patients. Results revealed that the pregnant drug addict has a greater adrenal response than the nonaddict during pregnancy as evidenced by elevated urinary epinephrine levels (Fig. 4-3). There was no difference in sympathetic nervous system activity in the antepartum period.[23,24,26] The pregnant drug addict thus appears to have a hyperactive adrenal gland that further responds to labor, delivery, and the postpartum period by elevated epinephrine levels. The sympathetic nervous system, as indicated by urinary norepinephrine, is similar to normal except that it lacks the ability to react to labor and delivery (Fig. 4-4), but does respond in a late fashion in the postpartum period.

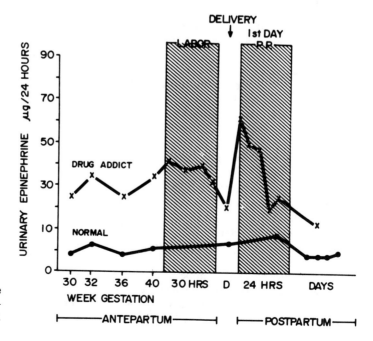

Figure 4-3. Urinary epinephrine levels in the normal pregnant patient and the pregnant drug addict.

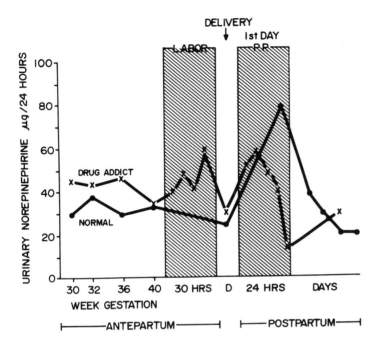

Figure 4-4. Comparison between urinary norepinephrine levels of the pregnant drug addict and the normal pregnant patient.

The heroin addict typically consumes a "bag of heroin" prior to admission and often enters the hospital in the acceleration phase of labor, delivering a short time after arrival. This is in contrast to the methadone-dependent pregnant patient who enters the hospital at variable periods, depending on when her labor begins or if she has premature rupture of membranes. It is important that she receive her daily dose of methadone and that supplemental pain medications be used in an appropriate manner for labor. The patient requires the methadone to avoid intrauterine fetal withdrawal if her labor is protracted. The analgesic agent of choice is meperidine (Demerol) if supplemental narcotic medication is necessary, and the dosage may be larger than customary because of the addict's tolerance of narcotics.

Satisfactory analgesia can be obtained by epidural analgesia, which can also be used for delivery. A pudendal block and supplemental nitrous oxide can also be used for delivery.

Barbiturates, if given to the methadone-dependent patient, may cause transient arterial hypotension and are not recommended. If the methadone maintenance dose was given that day, the pregnant addict usually does well in labor and delivery without major complications.

THE NEWBORN

The infant of the drug-dependent mother may be smaller than those of nondependent women. In a group of 117 infants born to drug addicts from our study, the mean birth weight was 2680 gm with 12.5 percent of the infants being considered small for gestational age. At birth, 88 percent had Apgar scores of 7 or above at 1 minute and 94 percent had scores of about 7 at 5 minutes. Of 117 infants, 8 had congenital malformations, of which three were minor and four major, two with talipes equinovarus and two with cardiac murmurs considered to be due to patient ductus arteriosis.[22] One infant with Potter's syndrome died; it is associated with renal agenesis.

Unless the nursery team is skilled in looking for special characteristics other than overt signs of withdrawal, these will be present before therapy can be instituted. Table 4-6 identifies newborn withdrawal signs and symptoms, not all of which need to be present before therapy is begun. Tremulousness is the first sign of withdrawal and can be evoked by startling the infant or by minimal tactile stimulation. In the severely affected infant undergoing withdrawal, tremulousness occurs without provocation. It is necessary to exclude hypocalcemia and hypoglycemia, as tremulousness is similar to both conditions. The offspring of the pregnant drug addict does not have an increased incidence of either hypocalcemia or hypoglycemia. An increase in flexor tone may accompany the tremulousness, and flexor rigidity is the most characteristic single sign of neonatal withdrawal. The attitude of flexion in the withdrawing infant increases to a point where there is marked resistance to extension and the infant becomes almost board-like, with the neck flexors sustaining the head in the same plane as the trunk for a prolonged period of time. Irritability is more pronounced than seen in normal patients, and the infant appears to be hyperalert and wakeful, with interferences being identified in the sleep cycle. The characteristic cry is shrill and high-pitched;

TABLE 4-7 NEWBORN WITHDRAWAL MEDICATIONS

Methadone	0.25 mg every 6 hr (maximum dose 0.5 MS)
Phenobarbital	5–8 mg/kg every 24 hr (given in divided doses every 8 hr)
Diazepam	0.5–2 mg every 8 hr

however, this is not frequently seen as the patient is usually treated prior to this degree of withdrawal. The infant often roots and sucks on its fist. Seizures should be uncommon since the infant should be treated before this occurs.

Madden studied 110 newborns in a randomized blind trial utilizing methadone, phenobarbital, and diazepam with the dosage schedules outlined in Table 4-7.[3,22] Withdrawal symptoms were noted in 94 percent of patients (103 out of 110) and 45 percent required therapy. The decision to treat the neonate was based on clinical assessment of severity and whether the condition worsened.

Treatment was started 2.7 days after delivery; the duration of treatment for methadone was 11.8 days; phenobarbital, 14.5 days; and diazepam, 10.2 days.

There was a direct correlation between maternal methadone maintenance dose and the presence or absence of newborn withdrawal. If the maternal dose was less than 20 mg/day, only 5 of 28 infants required therapy. When the dose was greater than 20 mg/day, 40 of 64 infants required therapy.

TABLE 4-6 NEWBORN WITHDRAWAL

1. Tremulousness (no hypoglycemia or hypocalcemia)
2. Flexor tone increase (characteristic sign)
3. Sweating, yawning, thermal instability
4. GI disturbances (i.e., vomiting and diarrhea)
5. Tachypnea (respiratory alkalosis)
6. Irritability (hyperalert, sleep disturbance)
7. Cry—shrill and high-pitched
8. Seizures (late findings)

OTHER ADDICTING DRUGS

A common misconception is that fetal addiction takes place only with narcotic-like drugs. Although the narcotic group of drugs has been studied more extensively, other abused drugs affect the mother and her fetus to alter newborn behavior during withdrawal.

The drugs in Table 4-8 are grouped according to their chemical and street names.

TABLE 4-8 DRUG ABUSE

Drug Groups	Signs and Symptoms of Overdose	Withdrawal Symptoms	Fetal Effects
Alcohol	Unusual behavior, mostly depressant with stupor, loss of memory, hypotension	Agitation, tremors	Microcephaly, mental retardation, altered facial expressions
Anticholinergics Atropine Belladonna Scopolamine	Pupils—dilated and fixed Heart rate—increased Temperature—increased; flushed skin Sensorium—clouded, amnesia	None	None
Cannabis Marijuana THC Hashish Hash oil	Pupils—normal but conjunctiva injected BP—decreased in standing Heart rate—increased Sensorium—clear, dreamy, fantasy state, time and space distorted	None	None known
CNS Sedatives Barbiturates Chlordiazepoxide Diazepam Flurazepam Glutethimide Meprobamate Methaqualone, etc.	Pupils—unchanged BP—decreased ± shock Respiration—depressed Tendon reflexes—decreased drowsiness, coma, lateral nystagmus, ataxia, slurred speech, deliriums, convulsions	Tremulousness, insomnia, chronic blink reflex, agitation, toxic psychosis	None
CNS Stimulants Antiobesity drugs Amphetamines Cocaine Methylphenidate Phenmetrazine	Pupils—dilated and reactive Respiration—shallow BP—increased Tendon reflexes—hyperactive Cardiac arrhythmias Dry mouth, tremors, hyperactivity, sensorium hyperacute	Muscle aches, abdominal pain, hunger, prolonged sleep, ± suicidal	Hyperactivity with increased kicks
Hallucinogens LSD Psilocybin Ketamine Mescaline 2.S-Dimethoxy-4-methylamphetamine Dimethyltryptamine Phencyclidine (PCP)	Pupils—dilated BP—elevated Heart rate—increased Tendon reflexes—increased Face flushed, euphoria, anxiety, inappropriate effect, illusions, hallucinations, realization Dysmorphic face Behavioral problems	No withdrawal symptoms	No known fetal effects
Narcotics Codeine Heroin Hydromorphone Meperidine Morphine Opium Pentazocine	Pupils—constricted Respiration—depressed BP—decreased Reflexes—hypoactive Sensorium—obtunded	Flu-like syndrome, agitation, dilated pupils, abdominal pain	Intrauterine withdrawal with increased fetal activity; newborn withdrawal

Signs and symptoms of an overdose, withdrawal symptoms, and any known fetal or neonatal effects are described. Frequently, abused drugs are mixed, which may cause different effects that may occur at lower threshold levels. Effects on the fetus are variable and may lead to an abortion or stillbirth, teratogenic effects, or developmental delays later in life.

REFERENCES

1. Zelson C: Infant of the addicted mother. *N Engl J Med* 288:1393, 1973
2. Tyson HK: Neonatal withdrawal symptoms associated with maternal use of proproxyphene (Darvon). *J Pediatr* 85:684, 1974
3. Madden JD, Chappel JN, Zuspan FP, Gumpel J, and Mejia A: Observation and treatment of neonatal narcotic withdrawal. *Am J Obstet Gynecol* 127:199, 1977
4. Harper RG, Solish GI, Purrow HM, et al: The effect of a methadone treatment program upon pregnant heroin addicts and their newborn infants. *Pediatrics* 54:300, 1974
5. Zuspan FP: Drug addiction in pregnancy: An invitational symposium. *J Reprod Med* 20:301, 1978
6. Blinick G, Jerez E, Wallach RC: Methadone maintenance, pregnancy, and progeny. *JAMA* 225:477, 1973
7. Gaulden EC, Littlefield DC, Putoff OE, Seivert AL: Menstrual abnormalities associated with heroin addiction. *Am J Obstet Gynecol* 90:155, 1964
8. Santen RJ, Sofsky J, Bilic N, Lippert R: Mechanism of action of narcotics in the production of menstrual dysfunction in women. *Fertil Steril* 26:538, 1975
9. Gumpel J, Mejia-Zelaya A: Prenatal management, labor and delivery care and postpartum follow-up of the drug addict. *J Reprod Med* 20:333, 1978
10. Finnegan L, Chappel JN, Kreek MJ, et al: Narcotic addiction in pregnancy, in Neibyl J(ed): *Drugs in Pregnancy*. Philadelphia, Lea and Febiger, 1981
11. Kreek MJ, Dodes L, Kane S, Knobler J: Long-term methadone maintenance therapy: Effects on liver function. *Ann Intern Med* 77:598, 1972
12. Zuspan, FP, Kim, M: Personal communication, 1981
13. Singh EJ, Mejia A, Zuspan FP: Studies of human amniotic fluid phospholipids in normal, diabetic, and drug-abuse pregnancy. *Am J Obstet Gynecol* 119:623, 1974
14. Blinick G, Wallach RC, Jerez E: Pregnancy in narcotic addicts treated by medical withdrawal. *Am J Obstet Gynecol* 105:997, 1969
15. Zuspan FP, Gumpel JA, Mejia-Zelaya A, Madden J, Davis R: Fetal stress from methadone withdrawal. *Am J Obstet Gynecol* 122:43, 1975
16. Senay EC, Wright M: The human need approach to the treatment of drug dependence, in *Proceedings of the International Council on Alcoholism and Addiction*. Amsterdam, 1972
17. Davis RC, Chappel JN, Mejia-Zelaya A, et al: Clinical observations on methadone maintained pregnancies. *Int J Addict Dis* 2:101, 1975
18. Dole VP, Nyswander M: Methadone maintenance and its implications for theories of narcotic addiction. *Res Publ Assoc Res Nerv Ment Dis* 46:359, 1968
19. Dole VP, Nyswander M: The use of methadone for narcotic blockade. *Br J Addict* 63:55, 1968
20. Davis RC, Chappel JN: Pregnancy in the context of addiction and methadone maintenance, in *Proceedings 5th National Conference on Methadone Treatment*, vol 2. New York, National Association for the Prevention of Addiction to Narcotics, 1973, p 1146
21. Davis RC, Psycho-social care of the pregnant narcotic addict. *J Reprod Med* 20:316, 1978
22. Madden JD: Problems pertaining to the care of newborn infants of drug-addicted women. *J Reprod Med* 20:303, 1978
23. Zuspan FP: Urinary excretion of epinephrine and norepinephrine during pregnancy. *J Clin Endocrinol Metab* 30:357, 1970
24. Zuspan FP: Urinary amine alterations in drug addiction pregnancy. *Am J Obstet Gynecol* 120:955, 1976
25. Golden, NL, Sokol, RJ, Rubin, IL: Angel dust: Possible effects on the fetus. *Pediatrics* 65:18, 1980

5. Anticonvulsant Therapy During Pregnancy

LAURENCE E. STEMPEL   TIMOTHY D. MOORE

Epilepsy is one of the most common disorders in the world with an incidence of 0.5 percent.[1,2] In most cases, the seizure disorder commences before the age of 20, making epilepsy a frequent accompaniment to the childbearing years.[2] In the past, marriage and reproduction by epileptics were limited by social stigma and public statutes. With improved social acceptance, advances in medical therapy, and decreased emphasis on the genetic transmission of epilepsy, many epileptics are now able to marry and lead nearly normal lives. Consequently, epilepsy is now a frequent medical complication of pregnancy, with an estimated incidence of 0.3 to 0.5 percent.[3-6] Without treatment, epilepsy is a socially, psychologically, and physically disabling condition, and hence it is almost always imperative that anticonvulsant medications be continued during pregnancy. The major concern of the obstetrician caring for the pregnant epileptic should be the prevention of seizures; however, it is also important that the adverse fetal effects of anticonvulsants be minimized as much as possible.

GENERAL CONSIDERATIONS

Definition and Classification

Epilepsy is not a disease, but rather a complex syndrome characterized by brief recurrent paroxysmal episodes of disturbed central nervous system (CNS) function, often with alteration in the state of consciousness. These episodes, known as seizures, may be accompanied by altered behavior, or by motor or sensory activity. The term "convulsion" is reserved for seizures which have a predominant motor component, such as the tonic-clonic movements of grand mal epilepsy. Seizures may vary in nature from a momentary absence spell, as in petit mal, to the repetitive convulsions of status epilepticus, which may last for hours or days. Patients who have a single isolated seizure should not be stigmatized as having epilepsy, as this term implies a recurrent disorder. Nevertheless, anyone who experiences even one seizure should be thoroughly evaluated and treated if the seizures recur.

There are many different forms of epilepsy, and the proper therapy depends on a correct diagnosis. There are a number of different classifications of epilepsy and a wide variety of atypical forms. However, most patients have either grand mal, focal motor, psychomotor, or petit mal epilepsy, or a combination of these forms.

Grand Mal Epilepsy. Over 70 percent of epileptics have grand mal epilepsy, either alone or in combination with petit mal or psychomotor epilepsy.[7] Grand mal seizures are characterized by total loss of consciousness, followed by a tonic phase during which the arms are flexed, the legs are extended, and the patient is apneic. This is soon followed by the clonic phase, with alternate contraction and relaxation of skeletal muscles. The convulsion often lasts only a few minutes and the patient usually experiences a postictal depression character-ized by drowsiness and confusion.

Focal Epilepsy. This form of epilepsy may be primarily motor or sensory. It is usually indica-tive of focal disease of the cerebral cortex, but it may also be seen with metabolic disorders such as hypoglycemia and hypocalcemia. Mo-tor seizures often begin peripherally with twitching of the thumb, big toe, or face, which are all disproportionally represented in the cerebral cortex. The seizure may remain con-fined to these twitchings, or may progress to a generalized tonic-clonic convulsion. It may be followed by Todd's paralysis, a transient paralysis of that part of the body correspond-ing to the epileptogenic focus.

Psychomotor Epilepsy. This bizarre form of epilepsy is caused by an epileptogenic focus in the temporal lobe. Seizures may include subjective experiences, such as altered mood, repetitive disturbing thoughts, a sensation of impending disaster, and visual distortions. The patient may also experience automatisms, such as lip smacking and chewing motions, and autonomic changes including salivation, perspiration, and pupillary dilatation. While often brief, these seizures may last from hours to days. Psychomotor seizures account for 15 percent of epilepsy.[7]

Petit Mal Epilepsy. Petit mal seizures are char-acterized by brief absence spells, often lasting less than 10 seconds. There is usually no major motor activity or loss of posture, although the patient may blink or roll her eyes. These sei-zures are not followed by postictal depression, and the patient can usually resume prior activi-ties. Although petit mal accounts for 10 per-cent of all epilepsy,[7] it rarely persists past ado-lescence, and therefore is infrequently seen during pregnancy.

Etiology

There are many causes of seizures, some of which are listed in Table 5-1. Unfortunately, in most cases, the etiology is unknown. Cor-rectable problems should always be diligently sought, since correction of underlying disor-ders is frequently as important as drug ther-apy.

There appears to be a familial component to epilepsy, although it is not nearly as strong as once believed. If one parent is epileptic, there is a 2.5 percent chance that the offspring will develop epilepsy;[8] this is five times the risk in the general population. The risk is even

TABLE 5-1 ETIOLOGY OF EPILEPSY

Infectious	Meningitis, encephalitis, brain abscess
Metabolic	Alkalosis, hypocalcemia, hypoglycemia, hyponatremia, porphyria
Toxic	Mercury, lead, carbon monoxide, amphetamines, phenothiazine, and tricyclic antidepressant toxicity
Traumatic	Cerebral injury (especially penetrating wounds)
Vascular	Cerebrovascular accident, A-V malformation
Drug withdrawal	Alcohol, barbiturate, anticonvulsant
Degenerative disease of the CNS	
Perinatal	Trauma, asphyxia, anomalies
Neoplastic	Primary or metastatic
Genetic	

higher if both parents are epileptic.[8] Forty-one percent of epileptics have a positive family history of epilepsy, while the corresponding figure for control patients is only 6.3 percent.[9] While this familial tendency is probably in part genetic, it may also represent environmental influences, such as maternal seizure-related hypoxia during pregnancy.

It is important to distinguish precipitating factors from etiologic factors. Edema, hyperventilation, stress, fatigue, and fever may provoke seizures in patients with a low seizure threshold, but do not in themselves cause seizures.[8] Nevertheless, they should be avoided by susceptible individuals.

Effects of Pregnancy on Epilepsy

Pregnancy has an unpredictable effect on the frequency and severity of seizures.[10,11] Almost half of gravid epileptics will experience an exacerbation of their seizure disorder during pregnancy, while another 45 to 50 percent will show no change. The remaining 5 to 10 percent will have fewer seizures during pregnancy.[10,12] The prognosis is unrelated to maternal age or age at onset of epilepsy.[10] Only 25 percent of patients with rare seizures, less than one every 9 months, will get worse during pregnancy, while virtually all patients who convulse at least once a month will deteriorate.[10] The course of epilepsy during previous pregnancies is not predictive either, since only half of epileptics show a similar response in subsequent pregnancies.[10] The effects of pregnancy on epilepsy are temporary, and most patients revert to their pregestational pattern after the puerperium.[10]

Many explanations have been offered for the rare improvement and frequent deterioration of epilepsy during pregnancy. Epilepsy shows natural fluctuations with time, and some of the changes may be totally unrelated to pregnancy. Improvement may also be related to better drug compliance.[12] There are numerous factors which may be responsible for the exacerbations that are so often seen during pregnancy. Many of the physiologic changes of pregnancy, such as hyperventilation, hyponatremia, hypocalcemia, and expansion of the extracellular fluid volume are well known to precipitate convulsions in susceptible individuals.[12,13] Indeed hyperventilation and hydration are frequently used in diagnostic testing to bring out electroencephalogram (EEG) abnormalities. Emotional stress and anxiety are frequent accompaniments of pregnancy, and are also known to precipitate seizures. However, the most important reason for the worsening of seizures in pregnancy may be the decrease in anticonvulsant serum levels which many patients experience.

Anticonvulsant serum levels are reduced during pregnancy for a variety of reasons. Patients may refuse to take their medications because of fears of teratogenesis, or they may fail to ingest or absorb their medication because of nausea and vomiting. Serum levels may also drop because of dilution by the expanded extracellular fluid volume, increased hepatic clearance, and possibly also because of fetoplacental drug metabolism.[14]

In a retrospective study, Mygind found increased plasma clearance of phenytoin during pregnancy, with half of the patients showing more than a 100 percent increase in clearance. He also found a correlation between loss of seizure control and decreased levels of phenytoin.[15] Mirkin found that gravid patients maintained on standard doses (300 to 400 mg/day) of phenytoin had a mean plasma level of 3.6 mcg/ml, far below the therapeutic range of 10 to 20 mcg/ml.[16] Lander et al. also found increased phenytoin requirements in 10 patients during pregnancy, with some patients needing as much as 50 percent more medication.[14] Serum levels of phenobarbital and primidone have also been shown to decrease during pregnancy, although there is considerable individual variation.[14] It is important that serum anticonvulsant levels be checked frequently during pregnancy, with appropriate adjustments made in dosage to maintain levels in the therapeutic range.

Effects of Epilepsy and Anticonvulsant Therapy on Pregnancy

Epilepsy and its therapy may have a variety of adverse effects on the pregnancy and the fetus. While some investigators have found no increase in spontaneous abortion, prematurity, toxemia, and multiple gestation,[10,17] others have found a significant increase in complications such as vaginal bleeding, toxemia, prematurity, and low birth weight.[18] Epileptics have a perinatal mortality twice that of the general population,[18,19] largely due to an increase in congenital malformations and neonatal hemorrhage.[19]

Because most epileptics are on chronic anticonvulsant therapy, it is often difficult to separate the effects of epilepsy from those of the therapy. Although it is sometimes helpful to compare treated and untreated epileptics, it is likely that untreated patients represent a heterogenous and quite different group, including those with mild disease, noncompliant patients, and patients resistant to prior treatment.[3] The problem is further complicated by the fact that most epileptics take multiple anticonvulsant drugs, all of which have overlapping side effects.

Several adverse effects of epilepsy and anticonvulsants that are of particular concern to the obstetrician include congenital malformations, altered maternal folate metabolism, vitamin D deficiency, and neonatal coagulopathy, depression, and drug withdrawal. While most of these problems are clearly due to anticonvulsants, others such as teratogenesis may be related to both anticonvulsants and epilepsy. These complications are discussed later with the individual anticonvulsant agents. However, because of the great concern that has been expressed about the teratogenicity of anticonvulsants, this subject is discussed in greater detail in the following sections.

Fetal Malformations. It has been demonstrated repeatedly that the offspring of epileptic women taking anticonvulsant medications have a two- to three-fold increase in congenital anomalies.[4,19-22] Nevertheless, the teratogenicity of most antiepileptic agents remains to be established, as there are several possible explanations for the increased incidence of malformations, including:

1. Epilepsy might in some way be linked to congenital anomalies. Dronamraju demonstrated a greater than expected number of epileptics among the first- and second-degree relatives of patients with orofacial clefts,[23] and Friis found three times the expected number of epileptics among the parents of children with facial clefts.[24] In a review from the Mayo Clinic, however, Annegers et al. were unable to confirm this relationship.[3] Further evidence that epilepsy and anomalies may be linked is the finding that the children of epileptic fathers may also have an increased incidence of malformations.[25] Finally, epileptics and their relatives have a higher than expected incidence of anomalies.[26]

2. Epileptic patients as a group have a number of characteristics associated with an increased risk of malformations, including older age, lower socioeconomic class, and a higher rate of past stillbirths.[20,22] However, Monson et al. found an increased incidence of anomalies in the children of mothers taking phenytoin during the first trimester, even after correcting for some of these confounding factors.[22]

3. Epileptic convulsions are often associated with hypoxia and acidosis, and these metabolic disturbances could be teratogenic during the first trimester.[1] However, Fedrick and others found no relationship between the frequency of seizures during pregnancy and congenital anomalies.[19,20]

Despite these considerations, most of the evidence supports the concept that some anticonvulsants are teratogenic, and that this teratogenicity accounts for most of the increase in anomalies in the offspring of epileptics.

Since Meadow's report in 1968 of six cases of orofacial clefts and other anomalies in fetuses exposed in utero to anticonvulsants,[27] there have been numerous epidemiologic surveys of the offspring of epileptic patients.[1,6,19-22] A variety of study designs have been used; some investigators have compared epileptics with the general population, while others have used matched controls. Some studies have differentiated between treated and untreated patients, while others have not. Furthermore, the definition of malformation, the patient follow-up, and the method of ascertainment of children with anomalies have varied widely. Although some investigators have found no increase in malformations among the offspring of treated epileptics,[17,28,29] the vast majority of studies have shown a two- to threefold relative increase in the incidence of anomalies in fetuses exposed to anticonvulsants.[6,19-22] In a review of over 2000 children of epileptics taking anticonvulsants, the most commonly reported defects were orofacial clefts (3.0 percent), skeletal anomalies (1.9 percent), heart defects (1.4 percent), CNS malformations (1.2 percent), gastrointestinal malformations (1.1 percent), facial anomalies (1.0 percent), mental retardation (0.7 percent), and genitourinary anomalies (0.6 percent).[30] A recent prospective study of infants exposed in utero to anticonvulsants has shown a 10 to 20 percent incidence of major anomalies and a similar incidence of decreased mental capacity.[31] While these figures are disturbing, most authorities agree that with the exception of trimethadione, anticonvulsant medications should not be discontinued during pregnancy.

ANTICONVULSANT THERAPY DURING PREGNANCY

General Guidelines

The primary objective of anticonvulsive therapy is to reduce the frequency and severity of seizures without causing excessive adverse effects. With appropriate therapy, seizures can be completely abolished in 65 percent of epileptics, while another 20 percent will show a reduction in the frequency and severity of seizures.[8] In designing an anticonvulsant regimen for the individual patient, the following principles should be kept in mind:

1. An appropriate primary drug should be chosen. This drug should have the best possible balance between efficacy and adverse effects. The patient should undergo thorough evaluation prior to the institution of therapy, as agents which are effective for some forms of epilepsy may exacerbate others.

2. The patient should be initially treated with a *single* anticonvulsant agent. It should be started at a moderate dosage, and increased gradually until either seizures are controlled or evidence of toxicity develops. The dose should not be increased any more frequently than once every three to four half-lives, to allow serum levels to reach a steady state.

3. If toxicity develops before seizures are controlled, the dosage should be reduced and a second drug should be added. These same principles apply to the second drug.

4. If complete seizure control is achieved with a second drug, the initial drug should be slowly tapered and even withdrawn, if possible.

5. Changes in the anticonvulsant regimen should be made slowly. Rapid changes may precipitate status epilepticus.

6. Serum levels of anticonvulsants should be maintained within the therapeutic range, which is the concentration of drug at which most patients show the best seizure control without evidence of toxicity. It is especially important to monitor serum levels after changing drugs or dosages, and in patients with renal or hepatic disease. Serum levels should also be checked if other medications are added or withdrawn, because of the potential for drug interactions. It is also helpful to measure the serum levels in patients with signs or symptoms of toxicity, or if seizures recur. It is sometimes necessary to monitor the levels of active metabolites, for example, phenobarbital in patients taking primidone. Low serum anticonvulsant levels may be caused by inadequate dosage, noncompliance, incomplete absorption, or abnormally rapid elimination. High serum levels may be caused by improper dosage, impaired elimination, or drug interactions.

7. In some cases, complete control of seizures may not be possible.

8. The most common reasons for the failure of anticonvulsants to control seizures are patient noncompliance and the use of the wrong drug or dosage.[8]

Treatment of Specific Disorders

Many drugs are available for the treatment of seizure disorders. The first- and second-line drugs for the various forms of epilepsy are shown in Table 5-2. Table 5-3 describes the mechanisms of action and biopharmaceutical properties of these agents. Dosage considerations and effective serum concentrations of these anticonvulsants are listed in Table 5-4. Finally, the adverse maternal and fetal effects of these agents are shown in Table 5-5.

Grand Mal and Focal Motor Epilepsy. Phenobarbital and phenytoin are the first-line drugs for the treatment of grand mal and focal motor epilepsy.[8] For women in the reproductive age group, phenobarbital is probably the drug of choice, as it appears to have less teratogenic potential than phenytoin.[4,5,20,32] However, phenytoin should be used when a second agent is required. Primidone is effective for both of these disorders, but should not be used in conjunction with phenobarbital, as this latter drug is one of the active metabolites of primidone. Other second-line drugs which are useful for grand mal and focal motor epilepsy are carbamazepine and occasionally, valproic acid.

Psychomotor Epilepsy. Primidone is the drug of choice for psychomotor epilepsy.[8,33] If a second agent is needed, then phenytoin may be added. Phenobarbital, carbamazepine, and valproic acid are other useful second-line drugs. This form of epilepsy may be especially difficult to control.[8]

Petit Mal Epilepsy. This disorder rarely persists past adolescence, and is therefore an uncommon complication of pregnancy. Ethosuximide is the drug of choice for petit mal, although occasionally acetazolamide or valproic acid may be necessary.[8] Trimethadione is highly teratogenic, and should never be used

TABLE 5-2 ANTICONVULSANT DRUGS OF CHOICE FOR TREATING SEIZURE DISORDERS DURING PREGNANCY

Seizure Disorder	Primary Drug	Secondary Drugs
Grand mal and focal motor	Phenobarbital	Phenytoin Primidone Carbamazepine Valproic acid
Psychomotor	Primidone	Phenytoin Phenobarbital Carbamazepine Valproic acid
Petit mal	Ethosuximide	Valproic acid Acetazolamide
Status epilepticus	Diazepam followed by phenytoin	Phenytoin Phenobarbital Paraldehyde Thiopental

TABLE 5-3   PROPOSED MECHANISM OF ACTION AND BIOPHARMACEUTICS OF ANTICONVULSANTS

Mechanism of Action	Biopharmaceutics
Phenytoin (Dilantin) (1) Alters intracellular-extracellular sodium transport, resulting in a change in ionic fluxes during depolarization, and (2) decreases calcium ion influx during depolarization[104]	Micronized forms are well absorbed.[105] Phenytoin is primarily metabolized by hepatic microsomal enzymes. It is chiefly parahydroxylated, which accounts for 60–70% of a single dose of the drug. Some patients have a genetic predisposition toward rapid or slow metabolism[104] and some may exhibit a biphasic elimination pattern. At lower doses first-order or linear pharmacokinetics are seen. Thus, the plasma half-life (24 hr with fourfold variations) increases proportionately to the size of the dose. In higher doses, zero-order elimination may occur. In this situation the elimination of the drug may become constant because of saturation of the hydroxylation capacity of the liver. Therefore, higher doses may lead to accumulation at a rate faster than predicted.[105] Phenytoin is 60–90% protein bound and the volume of distribution is approximately 65% of body weight. In pregnancy, serum levels may drop while the same dosage is continued because of an increase in the volume of distribution of the drug, which in turn may be the result of increased maternal plasma volume and fetal tissue volume. Other factors may include increased hepatic metabolism, malabsorption, and/or supplemental vitamin intake.[81] Maternal plasma levels of phenytoin increase over a number of weeks after birth until antepartum pharmacokinetics are seen. Plasma levels of the drug should be determined monthly during pregnancy and appropriate adjustments made to keep the serum levels between 10 and 20 mcg/ml. The total daily dose of phenytoin may be given in divided doses or at one time because of its long half-life. As of July 1, 1980 only those phenytoin products labeled "extended" may be given as a single daily dose. Other products labeled "prompt" must be given in divided doses. The extended dosage forms provide for gradual absorption of phenytoin into the circulation, whereas using the prompt form may result in rapid absorption of the drug. This can lead to transiently high levels of phenytoin and toxicity[106] with the single daily dosing regimen.
Phenobarbital Increases the convulsive threshold of the motor cortex[104]	Phenobarbital is well absorbed and is 40–60% protein bound.[104] Degradation occurs primarily in the liver (70%). Multiple metabolites have been identified. Plasma half-life is 2–6 days. Three to four weeks of continuous dosing may be needed to reach the steady state.[105] Thirty percent of phenobarbital may be eliminated unchanged by the kidney. Other inactive metabolites are eliminated in a similar fashion. Severe decreases in renal function can result in an accumulation of the drug.[104]
Primidone (Mysoline) (1) Resembles phenobarbital in its activity and (2) is more selective in its ability to modify electroshock seizure patterns in animal and humans[104]	Primidone is also well absorbed, but is not significantly protein bound. It is primarily metabolized by the liver. The serum half-life has been reported to be 21 hr. About 15% of the drug is oxidized to phenobarbital. The major metabolite is phenylethylmalonamide (PEMA), which is active ($t_{1/2} = 24$–48 hr). It should not be used with phenobarbital, since phenobarbital is an active metabolite.[104,105]

(continued)

TABLE 5-3 PROPOSED MECHANISM OF ACTION AND BIOPHARMACEUTICS OF ANTICONVULSANTS *(continued)*

Mechanism of Action	Biopharmaceutics
Carabamazepine (Tegretol) (1) It is related to actions of phenytoin, (2) blocks posttetanic reflexes, and (3) suppresses polysynaptic reflexes.[104]	Carabamazepine is absorbed rapidly. It is approximately 80% bound to plasma proteins. Its distribution is extensive. Metabolism occurs chiefly by the conversion of carbamazepine to 10, 11-epoxide, an active compound. The half-life after continuous dosing is 19–30 hr. The half-life of the 10, 11-epoxide metabolite has been reported to be 6–20 hr. There is subsequent metabolism of these compounds and less than 1% of the parent drug or epoxide is recovered in the urine.[105,107,108] Serum levels often drop during pregnancy in a similar fashion to phenytoin. Continual monitoring of serum levels and readjustment of dosage is necessary.[81,105,107] Observe the same cautions with carabamazepine as outlined under phenytoin for dosing.
Ethosuximide (Zarontin) (1) Decreases the activity of the motor cortex, (2) elevates the threshold of the central nervous system to convulsive stimuli, and (3) suppresses the paroxysmal spike and wave pattern commonly seen in petit mal activity.[104]	Ethosuximide's absorption has not been well studied. It is chiefly metabolized in the liver. Plasma half-life in adults is 60 hr. In children the plasma half-life is 30 hr. It is not significantly bound to plasma proteins. About 20% of the drug is excreted unchanged.[104,105]
Valproic acid (Depakene) Its mechanism of action is related to its ability to raise brain and cerebellar levels of γ-aminobutyric acid (GABA).[88]	Valproic acid is rapidly absorbed orally. Its peak concentrations are seen 1–4 hr after ingestion. The half-life is variable (8–15 hr). Plasma protein-binding is reported to be 80–95% and it displaces phenobarbital from plasma proteins. This may be significant when the ratio of sodium valproate to phenobarbital is high. The same displacement may be seen with phenytoin and primidone. This displacement may not be evident where serum phenytoin assays report only total phenytoin concentration. Therefore, clinical judgment must be used in adjusting dosage.[88,105] Distribution is restricted to the circulation and rapidly exchangeable extracellular water.[88,105] Elimination occurs chiefly (70%) via metabolites, mainly 2-propylglutaric acid.[88]
Trimethadione (Tridione) (1)Selectively suppresses the polysynaptic transmission of impulses resulting from a prolongation of synaptic recovery time, (2) suppresses the projection of seizure activity from cortical foci to the thalamus, and (3) elevates the cortical seizure threshold.[104]	Trimethadione is readily absorbed from the gastrointestinal tract. It is metabolized primarily by liver. The principal metabolite is 5, 5-dimethyl-2,4 oxazolidinedione (DMO), which is active against petit mal seizures. DMO's half-life is 5–10 days. Only about 3% of a single dose is eliminated in the urine.[104]

(continued)

TABLE 5-3 PROPOSED MECHANISM OF ACTION AND BIOPHARMACEUTICS OF ANTICONVULSANTS *(continued)*

Mechanism of Action	Biopharmaceutics
Diazepam (Valium) (1) Is mediated through the inhibitory neurotransmitter γ-aminobutyric acid, (2) augments presynaptic inhibition, and (3) reproduces profound CNS depression and muscle relaxation.[104]	Intramuscular injections during status epilepticus are not recommended because of diazepam's erratic absorption. Intravenous administration results in rapid action and seizure control. It is highly protein bound (90%) and well distributed through most body tissues. Diazepam is metabolized to the major metabolites, desmethyldiazepam, 3-hydroxy-diazepam, and oxazepam. Its duration of action intravenously is usually 15 min to 1 hr. Diazepam is chiefly eliminated as metabolites in the urine. Due to the long half-lives of some active metabolites (up to 200 hr), it may take days for the drug to be totally eliminated. Appears in the fetus in concentrations equal to or higher than that seen in maternal serum.[104]

in fertile women during the reproductive years.[34-36]

Status Epilepticus. Status epilepticus is the occurrence of repetitive grand mal seizures between which the patient does not regain consciousness. Without adequate therapy, the seizures may continue for hours or even days, frequently resulting in death or anoxic brain damage. Even with prompt treatment, mortality is still high, making status epilepticus a serious medical emergency. The patient's prognosis depends on the underlying cause of the seizures, the general condition of the patient, and the interval between the onset of seizures and the institution of therapy.[37] Although status epilepticus may be triggered by a variety of insults, the most common precipitating factor is the abrupt cessation of anticonvulsant medications.[38] While status epilepticus is no more common during pregnancy, it can be disastrous for both the mother and the fetus, though normal infants have been born after an episode of status epilepticus.[10]

Patients with status epilepticus should be hospitalized immediately, preferably in an intensive care unit. Supportive care includes an IV line, padded side rails, and maintenance of a patent airway. The underlying cause of the seizures should be diligently sought and promptly treated. The mainstay of treatment, however, is the use of large doses of intravenous anticonvulsant medications.

Because of its rapid effect on the CNS,

intravenous diazepam is the drug of choice for status epilepticus.[38] The benefits of prompt seizure control far outweigh the risks of hypotension and respiratory depression.[37] Diazepam is administered intravenously in a dose of 5 to 10 mg over a 2 to 4-minute period. It should not be given any faster than 5 mg/minute. If there is no response to the initial dose, then it may be repeated several times at 10-minute intervals; however, this may necessitate the use of artificial ventilation. The anticonvulsant action of intravenous diazepam lasts for only 15 to 20 minutes, and therefore treatment with long-acting agents such as phenytoin or phenobarbital must begin as soon as seizures have been stopped.[38]

Phenytoin is not often used as the primary therapy of status epilepticus, since it is effective in stopping seizures in only about half of the cases.[37] However, as soon as seizures are controlled with diazepam, the patient should receive an intravenous loading dose of phenytoin. This drug has a rapid onset of action, and unlike phenobarbital, it does not potentiate the depressant actions of diazepam. Even if the patient receives a modest overdose, the symptoms of nystagmus and ataxia are not dangerous.[39] Phenytoin should be given in a loading dose of 1000 to 1500 mg (18 mg/kg), at a rate not to exceed 50 mg/minute. When given any faster, phenytoin may cause hypotension, arrhythmias, and cardiac arrest.[37-39] The blood pressure and electrocardiogram (ECG) should be carefully monitored while the

TABLE 5-4 DOSAGE CONSIDERATIONS OF ANTICONVULSANTS

Drug	Available Strength	Dosage Range[109]	Route of Administration	Effective Serum[105] Concentration (mcg/ml)
Phenytoin (Dilantin)	30- and 100-mg capsules 50-mg chewable tablet 30 mg/5 ml suspension 125 mg/5 ml suspension	300–500 mg daily,* single dose or divided doses+	Oral or IV	10–20
Phenobarbital	10-, 15-, 20-, 25-, 30-, 40-, 60-, 75-, and 100-mg tablets	100–200 mg/day in divided doses	Oral	15–30
Primidone (Mysoline)	50- and 250-mg tablets	250 mg at bedtime, increased by 250 mg weekly until adequate response or serum levels are obtained. Not to exceed 2 gm* daily in divided doses.	Oral	5–15
Carbamazepine (Tegretol)	100- and 200-mg tablets	200 mg twice daily initially, increased by 200 mg daily until serum levels are obtained or adequate response is seen. Should not normally exceed 1.2 gm daily* in divided doses.	Oral	4–10
Ethosuximide (Zarontin)	250-mg capsule	500 mg/day in divided doses. May increase daily dose every 4–7 days until serum levels are achieved or response is seen up to 1.5 gm* daily in divided doses.	Oral	40–100
Valproic Acid (Depakene)	250-mg capsule	600 mg/day, increased by 200 mg every third day until serum levels are achieved or adequate response is seen, up to 2.6 gm* daily in divided doses.	Oral	50–100
Trimethadione (Tridione)	150-mg chewable tablet, 300-mg capsule	300 mg three times daily increased by 300 mg/week. Maintenance range 900-mg to 2.4-gm daily doses.	Oral	Above 700 mcg/ml of dimethadione, the active metabolite
Diazepam (Valium)	5 mg/ml injection	For status epilepticus: 5–10 mg IV (not to exceed 5 mg/min administration rate). Repeat as needed up to 20–30 mg. May repeat dose in 2–4 hr.†	IV	

* The dosage range may have to be exceeded during pregnancy in order to maintain appropriate serum levels.
† Loading doses required in status epilepticus of 500–1000 mg (18 mg/kg).

TABLE 5-5 ADVERSE MATERNAL AND FETAL EFFECTS FROM ANTICONVULSANT USE

Anticonvulsant	Maternal[110]	Fetal/Neonatal
Phenytoin	Cardiovascular collapse after rapid IV injection, ataxia, nystagmus, GI upset, increased incidence of seizures, gingival hyperplasia, behavioral changes, osteomalacia, megaloblastic anemia, hirsutism, lymphadenopathy, skin rashes, Stevens-Johnson syndrome, lupus syndrome, and hepatic necrosis.	Probable teratogenicity, possible carcinogenicity, neonatal coagulopathy, and neonatal hypocalcemia and tetany
Phenobarbital	Drowsiness (transient), ataxia, respiratory depression, sleep abnormalities, hypotension, allergic reaction, megaloblastic anemia, agranulocytosis, thrombocytopenia.	Possible low-level teratogenicity, neonatal coagulopathy, neonatal depression, neonatal withdrawal
Primidone	Ataxia, vertigo, headache, nausea, morbilliform rash, edema, nystagmus, impotence, leukopenia, and megaloblastic anemia.	Possible teratogenicity, neonatal coagulopathy, neonatal depression
Carbamazepine	Diplopia, drowsiness, leukopenia, transient blurred vision, rash, disturbance of equilibrium, transient paresthesias, proteinuria, neutropenia, systemic lupus erythematosus, left ventricular failure, hypertension, hypotension, syncope and collapse, edema.	None known
Ethosuximide	Hematopoietic complications, including aplastic anemia, pancytopenia, agranulocytosis, and eosinophilia. Morphologic and functional changes in the liver, GI upset, nausea, vomiting, diarrhea. Hyperactivity, hypoactivity, behavioral changes, paranoid and suicidal ideations. Stevens-Johnson syndrome, systemic lupus erythematosus, and pruritic erythematous rash.	Possible low-level teratogenicity
Valproic acid	GI upset, sedation, ataxia and incoordination, hepatotoxicity, and thrombocytopenia.	Hyperglycemia, teratogenic in animals
Trimethadione	Sedation, blurred vision in bright light, nonspecific GI and neurologic effects, skin rashes, lupus syndrome.	Definite teratogenicity
Diazepam	Depressed respiration, bradycardia, hypotension, cardiovascular collapse, and paradoxical hyperexcitability. Caution should be exercised not to use small veins or the dorsum of the hand or wrist to administer diazepam. Extreme care should also be taken to avoid intra-arterial administration or extravasation because of the irritating properties of the drug.	Decreased fetal heart rate variability, possible low-level teratogenicity, neonatal depression, neonatal hypotension, neonatal withdrawal, impaired neonatal thermoregulation

loading dose is being given. After the patient has received her loading dose, daily maintenance therapy should be started.

Intravenous phenobarbital has been used to treat status epilepticus, but its slow onset of action (15 to 30 minutes) makes it less useful than diazepam.[38] When administered in conjunction with diazepam, the hypotensive and respiratory depressant actions of the two drugs are additive.[38] Phenobarbital may be used to treat status epilepticus caused by barbiturate withdrawal. In these cases, it should be given intravenously in a dose of 250 mg administered over 3 to 5 minutes. This dose may be repeated once after 30 minutes. It should be noted that it may be necessary to artificially support respiration when large doses of intravenous phenobarbital are given.

Paraldehyde and general anesthesia have been used on occasion to treat status epilepticus, but are only rarely needed.

Special Considerations in Pregnancy

Phenytoin. Phenytoin requirements generally increase during pregnancy, although there is considerable individual variation,[14-16] and dosage changes should be dictated by serum levels. Phenytoin crosses the human placenta rapidly, so that with chronic usage, maternal and fetal serum levels are identical.[40] This drug is eliminated quite slowly by the neonate, with a half-life of approximately 60 hours, compared to only 24 hours in the adult.[16] Although phenytoin may have a number of adverse effects on the fetus and neonate, including teratogenesis, coagulopathy, and vitamin deficiency, it differs from some of the other anticonvulsants in that it is not associated with neonatal depression or withdrawal.[16]

TERATOGENICITY. Phenytoin is known to be teratogenic in some laboratory animals.[2,41,42] In mice, the severity of malformations is related to both the dosage and the stage of gestation at which it is administered.[42] The numerous difficulties involved in defining the teratogenic potential of an anticonvulsant drug in humans have already been discussed. Nevertheless, there is considerable evidence that phenytoin is teratogenic in humans. In

a retrospective study, Monson et al. found that infants exposed to phenytoin on a daily basis early in pregnancy had a 6.1 percent incidence of selected malformations, including orofacial clefts, neural tube defects, congenital heart lesions, and limb defects. Even after correcting for confounding variables such as age, race, and socioeconomic status, this incidence of malformations was 2.4 times higher than that of nonepileptics, and also considerably higher than the rate among fetuses exposed to phenytoin sporadically or later in pregnancy. There was no evidence that the risk of anomalies was dose-related.[22] Fedrick also found that phenytoin was much more likely to produce defects than phenobarbital, although the combination was additive. Infants exposed in utero to phenytoin had a 15.2 percent incidence of malformations, compared with 4.9 percent with phenobarbital alone and 22.0 percent when both agents were used. Of the control patients, 5.6 percent gave birth to anomalous infants. Fedrick also was unable to find a relationship between phenytoin dosage and the risk of malformations.[20]

Hanson has described a fetal hydantoin syndrome (FHS) consisting of pre- and postnatal growth deficiency, microcephaly, mental retardation, developmental delay, and a wide variety of dysmorphic features (Table 5-6). These infants may manifest a variety of limb abnormalities, including distal phalangeal and nail hypoplasia and finger-like thumbs.[43,44] Other frequently reported lesions include congenital heart defects and diaphragmatic hernias. In a retrospective review of data from the Collaborative Perinatal Study, Hanson and co-workers found that 11 of 104 infants exposed in utero to phenytoin had FHS.[43] In a companion prospective study of 35 infants exposed to phenytoin during pregnancy, he found that 11 percent manifested FHS, while an additional 31 percent showed some of the features of the syndrome. None of the infants exposed only to phenobarbital had features of FHS.[43] The permanent impairment of neurologic function in some of these infants has caused greater concern than the structural defects, most of which are readily

TABLE 5-6 FEATURES OF THE FETAL HYDANTOIN SYNDROME

Intrauterine growth retardation

Postnatal growth retardation

Microcephaly

Mental or motor deficiency

Ridging of metopic suture

Facial dysmorphisms
  Low-set or abnormal ears
  Broad, depressed nasal bridge
  Short nose
  Anteverted nostrils
  Wide mouth
  Prominent upper lip
  Inner epicanthal folds
  Ptosis
  Strabismus
  Cleft lip and/or palate
  Hypertelorism

Limb anomalies
  Hypoplastic nails
  Hypoplastic distal phalanges
  Finger-like thumbs

Congenital heart defects

Hernias
  Diaphragmatic
  Inguinal

Genitourinary anomalies

Abnormal genitalia

correctable.[30] It should be noted, however, that some investigators have questioned Hanson's figures.[4,25,26,45]

The current feeling is that infants exposed to phenytoin in utero have a somewhat increased risk of mental retardation, and a two- to threefold increased incidence of congenital malformations. These risks appear to be unrelated to dosage, although this has never been studied prospectively. Phenytoin is probably more teratogenic than phenobarbital, and several authorities have recommended that when possible, women in the reproductive age group should be treated with phenobarbital alone.[4,5,32] However, when needed to control seizures, the benefits of phenytoin far outweigh the risks.

CARCINOGENICITY. There have been four reported cases of neuroblastoma in children with FHS. Because of the rarity of these two conditions it has been calculated that it should take approximately 60 years to produce three cases of FHS with neuroblastoma if the two conditions are not related.[46] The fact that these four cases were reported over only a 3-year period suggests that phenytoin may be carcinogenic.

NEONATAL COAGULOPATHY. Another serious complication of anticonvulsant use during pregnancy is neonatal hemorrhage, which contributes significantly to the high perinatal mortality in the offspring of epileptics. First reported in 1957, it was a number of years before the nature of this problem became clear. It is now known that almost half of all infants exposed in utero to anticonvulsants will exhibit a severe coagulopathy, and half of these children will experience significant bleeding if they are not given vitamin K at birth.[47] These infants tend to bleed soon after birth, often during the first 24 hours of life.[48,49] This is in contrast to hemorrhagic disease of the newborn (HDN), in which the infants usuallly bleed during the second to fifth day. This syndrome also differs from HDN in that these infants may bleed in unusual places, such as into the pleural, pericardial, or peritoneal cavities, or into the retroperitoneal space. Intracranial bleeding may also occur.[9,19,48,49] This bleeding appears to be unrelated to prematurity, hypoxia, or birth trauma.

Anticonvulsant-associated coagulopathy is characterized by a deficiency of the vitamin K-dependent coagulation factors, that is, numbers II, VII, IX, and X.[47,49] It can usually be prevented by treating the infant at birth with 1 mg of intramuscular vitamin K.[47-50] As this vitamin is used prophylactically in many hospitals in the United States, most of the reports of neonatal bleeding have come from Europe. Because infants may occasionally bleed despite treatment with vitamin K at birth,[9] it has been recommended that epileptics be treated with vitamin K prophylactically during the final months of pregnancy.[47-49] Clotting studies should be obtained on the cord blood from all newborns exposed in utero to anticonvulsant agents; if these studies are severely abnormal, the infant should be treated with additional doses of vitamin K and with fresh frozen plasma, as some infants will die if treatment is delayed until there is clinical evidence of bleeding.[47,48]

Anticonvulsant-associated coagulopathy is usually seen only after treatment with barbiturates or primidone,[47,48] but it may occasionally be seen with phenytoin alone.[48] In fact, phenytoin has been shown to depress vitamin K-dependent clotting factors in animals in a dose-dependent fashion, and this drop can be prevented by the administration of vitamin K.[49] Other anticonvulsants besides phenytoin, phenobarbital, and primidone have not been reported to cause this syndrome.

FOLATE DEFICIENCY. Folate deficiency is a frequent complication of several anticonvulsant agents, including phenytoin, phenobarbital, and primidone.[50,51] Because of the increased metabolic demands of pregnancy, this problem can be especially severe in the pregnant epileptic. Between 33 and 91 percent of patients taking anticonvulsants are folate-deficient, depending on the population being studied, the definition of normal, and the particular test which is used.[52] Only a small fraction of these patients demonstrate macrocytosis, and fewer yet have megaloblastic anemia.[51-53] All of these changes respond readily to folic acid supplementation.[51]

Anticonvulsants may cause folate deficiency through several mechanisms. By inducing hepatic microsomal enzymes, these drugs increase the demand for folates, which act as cofactors in the hepatic reactions responsible for drug hydroxylation.[54] In addition, phenytoin has been shown to interfere with intestinal absorption of folates.[55,56]

The only complication of pregnancy that has been definitely linked to folate deficiency is megaloblastic anemia.[57] However, folate antagonists, such as aminopterin, are well known to be potent teratogens,[58] and folate deficiency has been shown to induce malformations in some animals.[52] Although several retrospective studies have suggested a relationship between folate deficiency and malformations in humans,[59,60] other studies have failed to confirm this.[61,62] Furthermore, a prospective study of approximately 3000 patients showed no relationship between serum folate levels during early pregnancy and fetal anomalies.[63] At the present time, the relationship between folate and congenital malformations remains controversial.[52]

Some authorities have recommended that all pregnant epileptics be given prophylactic folic acid. However, correction of folate deficiency may increase hepatic drug hydroxylation, with a resultant decrease in serum phenytoin levels.[54,64] This drop is usually small, and rarely results in the loss of seizure control.[52,53] Nevertheless, patients receiving supplemental folic acid should have their anticonvulsant levels monitored carefully.

ALTERED CALCIUM METABOLISM. Another complication of chronic phenytoin therapy is abnormal calcium metabolism. Phenytoin is thought to induce the enzymes which increase the metabolism of cholecalciferol to inactive compounds.[65] Phenytoin may also interfere with intestinal absorption of calcium.[66] These changes may cause hypocalcemia, rickets, or osteomalacia. In addition, cases have been described of severe, prolonged neonatal hypocalcemia and tetany refractory to calcium therapy in infants exposed to phenytoin and phenobarbital during pregnancy.[67] This has led some investigators to suggest that pregnant epileptics be given supplemental vitamin D.[50,67]

BREASTFEEDING. Phenytoin crosses poorly into the breast milk, attaining levels which are only one-fourth to one-third of those in the maternal serum.[16] These low levels have not been shown to be harmful, despite slow elimination by the neonate.[16] Hence, breastfeeding is not contraindicated in patients taking phenytoin.

Phenobarbital. Phenobarbital levels frequently decrease during pregnancy, often necessitating increases in the daily dosage.[14] Barbiturates cross the placenta without difficulty, rapidly reaching an equilibrium between mother and fetus.[68] At birth, levels in the cord blood are approximately 95 percent of those in the maternal serum.[69] After delivery, the neonate excretes phenobarbital slowly, clearing only 1 to 20 percent every 24 hours.[69] Although phenobarbital is probably less teratogenic than phenytoin, it has some of the same adverse effects. For example, phenobarbital often contributes to folate deficiency in the mother, and coagulation defects in the neonate. In addition, phenobarbital has several adverse effects that are not seen with phenytoin, such as neonatal depression and withdrawal. Nonetheless, it remains the drug of choice for the young epileptic woman with grand mal or focal motor epilepsy.[5,32]

TERATOGENICITY. Phenobarbital appears to have much less teratogenic potential than phenytoin.[4,5,20,32] However, several retrospective studies have shown a significant association between maternal phenobarbital ingestion and congenital anomalies, even among nonepileptic patients.[70-72] There is also recent evidence that a fetal barbiturate syndrome may exist.[73] These findings have been contradicted by other studies. Shapiro found no evidence of fetal damage in approximately 8000 nonepileptic patients who took phenobarbital during pregnancy.[25] Thus, the question of phenobarbital's teratogenicity remains controversial. Most authorities are convinced, however, that even if phenobarbital is teratogenic, it is probably much less so than phenytoin.

NEONATAL COAGULOPATHY. Phenobarbital and primidone, which is partially metabolized to phenobarbital, are the anticonvulsants most commonly associated with neonatal coagulopathy. The diagnosis, prevention, and therapy of this disorder are discussed in the section on phenytoin.

FOLATE DEFICIENCY. Like phenytoin, phenobarbital and primidone may cause maternal folate deficiency, and occasionally megaloblastic anemia. This problem is discussed in a previous section.

NEONATAL DEPRESSION. Maternal ingestion of barbiturates during the last few days of pregnancy may cause neonatal depression, manifested by decreased alertness, respiratory depression, and hypotonia.[74] In addition, barbiturates may cause a 48-hour lag in the neonate's ability to adapt to breastfeeding.[75]

NEONATAL WITHDRAWAL. Barbiturates are well known to possess addictive potential in adults, and recently a neonatal withdrawal syndrome has been described.[74] Between 10 and 20 percent of neonates exposed to as little as 60 mg/day of phenobarbital during the third trimester will exhibit symptoms of withdrawal.[74] These symptoms frequently commence after the infant has left the hospital, usually between the fourth and seventh days of life. The neonatal phenobarbital withdrawal syndrome is characterized by generalized neuromuscular excitability, with hyperactivity, tremulousness, hyperreflexia, excessive crying, sleep disturbances, vomiting, diarrhea, hyperphagia, and occasionally seizures. Some of these symptoms may persist for 2 to 6 months. This syndrome differs from neonatal heroin withdrawal in that the onset is much later and the infant is usually appropriately grown. Phenobarbital withdrawal is treated by minimizing stimulation of the newborn and, when necessary, sedation with phenobarbital, phenothiazines, or paregoric.

BREASTFEEDING. As noted above, barbiturates may cause a 2-day lag in the newborn's ability to nurse.[75] Barbiturates enter the breast milk, attaining levels of 10 to 30 percent of those in the maternal serum.[76] This level, combined with the slow rate of elimination of the drug by the neonate, may lead to continued depression in a small percentage of newborns.[69,77] Breastfeeding is not contraindicated in mothers taking phenobarbital unless the neonate manifests signs or symptoms of generalized depression.

Primidone. Primidone crosses the placenta to a variable degree. Nine out of 10 patients given a single 250-mg tablet during labor had detectable primidone in the cord blood.[78] Because phenobarbital is one of its major active metabolites, patients taking primidone during pregnancy can expect all of the same problems that are seen with phenobarbital, including folate deficiency, and neonatal coagulopathy, depression, and withdrawal. There is one report which suggests the possibility of a primidone embryopathy, consisting of craniofacial and cardiac malformations.[79] In addition, Shapiro found an 8 percent (2 of 26) malformation rate in the fetuses of epileptics taking primidone alone.[25] Primidone crosses poorly into breast milk,[80] and nursing should be avoided only in those infants showing signs of generalized depression.

Carbamazepine. Although some investigators have found that serum levels of carbamazepine decrease during pregnancy,[80,81] others have not found this to be true.[14] Carbamazepine readily crosses the placenta in humans, with drug levels in the cord blood approximating those in the maternal circulation.[80] Carbamazepine is eliminated by the neonate at approximately the same rate as adults, with a half-life of 8 to 28 hours.[82] The teratogenicity of carbamazepine in humans has not been fully investigated, as relatively few pregnant epileptics have received this agent and of those who have, most have been taking other anticonvulsants as well. Of the 94 reported cases of infants exposed to carbamazepine, only five took this agent alone. Four of these 94 patients delivered anomalous infants.[80] Although this incidence is no greater than expected in the general population, there is not yet enough data to recommend switching pregnant patients from other potentially more harmful drugs to carbamazepine. Conversely, carbamazepine should not be discontinued when the epileptic patient becomes pregnant.

Carbamazepine crosses poorly into breast milk, with levels less than 40 percent of those in the maternal serum.[80] Since chronically exposed neonates are able to metabolize this drug as efficiently as adults, nursing is not contraindicated in epileptic patients taking this drug.

Ethosuximide. Like most other anticonvulsants, ethosuximide crosses the placenta.[83] It appears to be far less teratogenic in humans than trimethadione, the other first-line drug used for petit mal epilepsy.[84] Because petit mal is rare after adolescence, there is little data on the effects of ethosuximide on the fetus; however, one estimate puts the risk of malformations at approximately 6 percent, somewhat higher than the general population.[84]

Ethosuximide is eliminated slowly by the neonate, with a half-life of 41 hours.[83] Levels in the breast milk are only slightly lower than those in the maternal serum.[83] However, toxicity has not been observed in nursing infants, and there is therefore no contraindication to breastfeeding in mothers who must take this drug.

Valproic Acid. Valproic acid readily crosses the placenta, with fetal and maternal serum levels being about equal or slightly higher in the fetus.[85-87] This drug produces a transient neonatal hyperglycinemia; while serum levels of glycine are not high enough to impair neuronal development, they may cause a false-positive screen for aminoacidemia.[86] Valproic acid has been shown to have a dose-related teratogenic effect in mice, rats, and rabbits,[88] but there is currently too little data to evaluate its teratogenicity in humans. In one series of 26 patients who received this drug during pregnancy, only one delivered an anomalous infant. This infant had a cleft lip and palate. However, it is highly unlikely that these defects were caused by valproic acid, as the patient was on three other anticonvulsants during the entire pregnancy, and took valproic acid for only 1 week during her seventh month.[88,89] Dalens and co-workers recently reported a severely malformed infant which was born to a woman who took valproic acid throughout her pregnancy.[90] At the present time, there is not enough evidence to warrant changing anticonvulsant therapy to valproic acid during pregnancy, nor should this agent be discontinued if it is necessary to maintain adequate seizure control.

Valproic acid crosses poorly into the breast milk, with levels less than 2 percent of those in the maternal serum.[87] Therefore, there is no contraindication to nursing in mothers taking this drug.

Trimethadione. Trimethadione is the most potent teratogen among the anticonvulsants. The fetal trimethadione syndrome, described in Table 5-7, includes a variety of congenital defects, many of which are also seen with FHS.[34,36] When used during pregnancy, trimethadione is associated with an 83 percent incidence of major fetal malformations among live-born infants, and a high rate of spontaneous abortion. In one review of exposed patients, 87 percent of pregnancies were complicated by either fetal anomalies or first trimester loss.[34] Several families have been reported in which numerous consecutive pregnancies resulted in spontaneous abortion or fetal malformations while the mother was taking the drug, followed by several consecutive normal children after the drug was discontinued.[34,35] Trimethadione is useful only

TABLE 5-7 FEATURES OF THE FETAL TRIMETHADIONE SYNDROME

Intrauterine growth retardation

Postnatal growth deficiency

Microcephaly

Mild to moderate mental retardation

Developmental delay

Speech difficulties

Facial dysmorphisms
  V-shaped eyebrows
  Hypertelorism
  Strabismus
  Inner epicanthal folds
  Visual impairment
  Low-set ears with anterior folded helix
  Hearing loss
  Broad, depressed nasal bridge
  High, arched palate
  Orofacial clefts
  Irregular teeth

Congenital heart defects

Tracheo-esophageal anomalies

Hypospadias

Inguinal hernias

Assorted gastrointestinal and genitourinary defects

for the treatment of petit mal epilepsy, a relatively benign disorder which is rarely seen after adolescence. This drug should be avoided by women during the reproductive years.

Diazepam. Diazepam crosses the human placenta within seconds, with fetal levels of the parent drug and its active metabolites exceeding maternal levels for the first 4 to 6 hours.[91-94] The neonate metabolizes diazepam very slowly, and it frequently takes more than a week for drug elimination.[95]

Diazepam is used only for the control of status epilepticus. This disorder is so life-threatening for both the mother and the fetus that almost any adverse fetal effect is acceptable. Diazepam administered during labor may cause numerous neonatal problems, including low Apgar scores, apneic spells, hypotonia, poor suckling, reluctance to feed, impaired metabolic response to cold stress, and hypothermia. These effects are most pronounced when the mother has received more than 30 mg of the drug during the 15 hours preceding delivery.[95,96] When used during labor, diazepam depresses short-term, beat-to-beat variability of the fetal heart rate.[94] A syndrome resembling narcotic withdrawal has been observed in neonates after prolonged intrauterine exposure to diazepam,[97] but this is rarely a problem in the epileptic patient.

Diazepam crosses the placenta as early as the first trimester.[98] In rats, benzodiazepines are not teratogenic, even in high doses.[99] In a study in humans, there was no increase in the incidence of malformations when diazepam was used in cases of threatened abortion.[32] One group found that a related compound, chlordiazepoxide, was associated with a fourfold increase in congenital malformations when used in early pregnancy,[100] but this was not confirmed in a larger study.[101] However, four retrospective case control studies in three countries have shown an association between oral clefts and first trimester exposure to diazepam.[102] The risk was increased by three to four times, but the absolute risk for any fetus was quite small. Therefore, diazepam should not be withheld in cases of status epilepticus during pregnancy because of fears of teratogenesis.

Diazepam crosses into the breast milk and may cause lethargy and impaired suckling.[103] Because neonates eliminate diazepam slowly, it is best avoided in nursing mothers. This is rarely a problem, as it is unlikely that a woman who has recently been treated for status epilepticus will be in any condition to breastfeed.

GUIDELINES FOR MANAGEMENT OF EPILEPSY IN PREGNANCY

1. Epileptic women should not be discouraged from becoming pregnant unless seizures are difficult to control, making the patient incapable of responsible parenthood.

2. If the mother has idiopathic epilepsy, she should be advised that the risk of her child developing epilepsy is approximately 2 to 3 percent, or five times higher than the general population.

3. If the patient is not pregnant when first seen, has been seizure-free for several years, and has a normal EEG, an attempt should be made to withdraw anticonvulsants over a period of several months prior to the patient attempting pregnancy.

4. If the patient is not pregnant, and is taking a combination of anticonvulsants, an attempt should be made to see if she can be controlled with only one agent, preferably phenobarbital. However, the patient should be maintained on as many medications as are necessary to control her seizures, since seizure control is of more concern than teratogenesis. The only exception to this rule is that trimethadione should never be used in young women during the reproductive years.

5. If the patient is first seen during pregnancy and is well controlled on her current regimen, anticonvulsant agents should not be withdrawn, as this may put the patient into status epilepticus.

6. Status epilepticus should be treated vigorously, without regard for the pregnancy.

7. Patients should be advised that the risk of fetal anomalies is increased two- to threefold in patients taking anticonvulsants, and that there is a somewhat increased risk of mental retardation with certain agents.

8. Pregnant epileptics should be warned that excessive weight gain and sudden fluid retention may increase the risk of seizures.

9. Patients should be advised that there is a 50 percent risk that epilepsy will worsen during pregnancy, and that this risk is even higher if she has frequent seizures.

10. Anticonvulsant serum levels should be measured monthly during pregnancy and the puerperium, with adjustments in dosage to keep levels in the therapeutic range.

11. Pregnant epileptics receiving phenytoin, phenobarbital, or primidone should be given prophylactic folic acid, with careful monitoring of serum anticonvulsant levels.

12. Pregnant epileptics taking phenytoin, phenobarbital, or primidone should be given vitamin K, 5 to 10 mg daily by mouth during the last 1 or 2 months of pregnancy to prevent neonatal coagulopathy. Coagulation studies should be obtained on the cord blood, and the infants should be given 1 mg of vitamin K IM at birth.

13. During labor, anticonvulsants should be administered parenterally whenever possible in order to prevent intrapartum or postpartum seizures.

14. The infants of mothers receiving phenobarbital or primidone should be carefully observed for evidence of generalized depression or neonatal withdrawal symptoms.

15. There is no contraindication to breastfeeding in mothers taking anticonvulsants, as long as the infant shows no signs of generalized depression.

REFERENCES

1. Speidel BD, Meadow SR: Epilepsy, anticonvulsants and congenital malformations. *Drugs* 8:354, 1974
2. Mercier-Parot L, Tuchmann-Duplessis H: The dysmorphogenic potential of phenytoin: Experimental observations. *Drugs* 8:340, 1974
3. Annegers JF, Elveback, LR, Hauser WA, et al: Do anticonvulsants have a teratogenic effect? *Arch Neurol* 31:364, 1974
4. Committee on Drugs, American Academy of Pediatrics: Anticonvulsants and pregnancy. *Pediatrics* 63:331, 1979
5. Golbus MS: Teratology for the obstetrician: Current status. *Obstet Gynecol* 55:269, 1980
6. Janz D: The teratogenic risk of antiepileptic drugs. *Epilepsia* 16:159, 1975
7. Bowman WC, Rand MJ: *Textbook of Pharmacology*, ed 2. Oxford, Blackwell, 1980
8. Parker WA: Epilepsy, in Herfindal ET, Hirschman JL (eds): *Clinical Pharmacy and Therapeutics*, ed 2. Baltimore, Williams & Wilkins, 1979, pp 569–580
9. Hill RM, Verniaud WM, Horning MG: Infants exposed in utero to antiepileptic drugs. *Am J Dis Child* 127:645, 1974
10. Knight AH, Rhind EG: Epilepsy and pregnancy: A study of 153 pregnancies in 59 patients. *Epilepsia* 16:99, 1975
11. Sabin M, Oxorn H: Epilepsy and pregnancy. *Obstet Gynecol* 7:175, 1956
12. Suter C, Klingman WO: Seizure states and pregnancy. *Neurology* 7:105, 1957
13. Dimsdale H: The epileptic in relation to pregnancy. *Br Med J* 2:1147, 1959
14. Lander CM, Edwards VE, Eadie MJ, et al: Plasma anticonvulsant concentrations during pregnancy. *Neurology* 27:128, 1977
15. Mygind KI, Dam M, Christiansen J: Phenytoin and phenobarbitone plasma clearance during pregnancy. *Acta Neurol Scand* 54:160, 1976
16. Mirkin BL: Diphenylhydantoin: Placental transport, fetal localization, neonatal metabolism, and possible teratogenic effects. *J Pediatr* 78:329, 1971
17. Janz D, Fuchs U: Are anti-epileptics harmful in pregnancy? *Dtsch Med Wochensch* 89:24, 1964
18. Bjerkedal T, Bahna SL: The course and outcome of pregnancy in women with epilepsy. *Acta Obstet Gynecol Scand* 52:245, 1973
19. Speidel BD, Meadow SR: Maternal epilepsy and abnormalities of the fetus and newborn. *Lancet* 2:839, 1972
20. Fedrick J: Epilepsy and pregnancy: A report from the Oxford record linkage study. *Br Med J* 2:442, 1973
21. Lowe CR: Congenital malformations among infants born to epileptic women. *Lancet* 1:9, 1973
22. Monson RR, Rosenberg L, Hartz SC, et al: Diphenylhydantoin and selected congenital malformations. *N Engl J Med* 289:1049, 1973
23. Dronamraju KR: Epilepsy and cleft lip and palate. *Lancet* 2:876, 1970
24. Friis ML: Epilepsy among parents of children with facial clefts. *Epilepsia* 20:69, 1979
25. Shapiro S, Hartz SC, Siskind V, et al: Anticonvulsants and parental epilepsy in the development of birth defects. *Lancet* 1:272, 1976
26. Stumpf DA, Frost M: Seizures, anticonvulsants, and pregnancy. *Am J Dis Child* 132:746, 1978
27. Meadow SR: Anticonvulsant drugs and congenital abnormalities. *Lancet* 2:1296, 1968
28. Bird AV: Anticonvulsant drugs and congenital anomalies. *Lancet* 1:311, 1969
29. Livingston S, Berman W, Pauli LL: Maternal epilepsy and abnormalities of the fetus and newborn. *Lancet* 2:1265, 1973
30. Hill RM: Teratogenesis and antiepileptic drugs. *N Engl J Med* 289:1089, 1973
31. Hill RM: Anticonvulsant medication. *Am J Dis Child* 133:449, 1979
32. Tuchmann-Duplessis H: *Drug Effects on the Fetus*. Sydney, ADIS, 1975, pp 142–194
33. Millichap JG: Drug treatment of convulsive disorders. *N Engl J Med* 286:464, 1972
34. Feldman GL, Weaver DD, Lovrien EW: The fetal trimethadione syndrome. *Am J Dis Child* 131:1389, 1977
35. German J, Ehlers KH, Kowal A, et al: Possible teratogenicity of trimethadione and paramethadione. *Lancet* 2:261, 1970
36. Zackai EH, Mellman WJ, Neiderer B, et al: The fetal trimethadione syndrome. *J Pediatr* 87:280, 1975
37. Sodha NB: Neurologic emergencies, in Costrini NV, Thomson WM (eds): *Manual of Medical Therapeutics*, ed 22. Boston, Little Brown, 1977, pp 363–378
38. Cloyd JC, Gumnit RJ, McLain W: Status epi-

lepticus: The role of intravenous phenytoin. *JAMA* 244:1479, 1980

39. Easton JD: Diphenylhydantoin and epilepsy management. *Ann Int Med* 77:421, 1972

40. Mirkin BL: Placental transfer and neonatal elimination of diphenylhydantoin. *Am J Obstet Gynecol* 109:930, 1971

41. Gibson JE, Becker BA: Teratogenic effects of diphenylhydantoin in Swiss-Webster and A/J mice. *Proc Soc Exp Biol Med* 128:905, 1968

42. Harbison RD, Becker BA: Relation of dosage and time of administration of diphenylhydantoin to its teratogenic effect in mice. *Teratology* 2:305, 1969

43. Hanson JW, Myrianthopoulos NC, Sedgwick MA, et al: Risks to the offspring of women treated with hydantoin anticonvulsants, with emphasis on the fetal hydantoin syndrome. *J Pediatr* 89:662, 1976

44. Hanson JW, Smith DW: The fetal hydantoin syndrome. *J Pediatr* 87:285, 1975

45. Shapiro S, Slone D, Hartz SC, et al: Are hydantoins (phenytoins) human teratogens? *J Pediatr* 90:673, 1977

46. Allen RW, Ogden B, Bentley FL, et al: Fetal hydantoin syndrome, neuroblastoma, and hemorrhagic disease in a neonate. *JAMA* 244:1464, 1980

47. Mountain KR, Hirsh J, Gallus AS: Neonatal coagulation defect due to anticonvulsant drug treatment in pregnancy. *Lancet* 1:265, 1970

48. Bleyer WA, Skinner A: Fatal neonatal hemorrhage after maternal anticonvulsant therapy. *JAMA* 235:626, 1976

49. Solomon GE, Hilgartner MW, Kutt H: Coagulation defects caused by diphenylhydantoin. *Neurology* 22:1165, 1972

50. Seip M: Effects of antiepileptic drugs in pregnancy on the fetus and newborn infants. *Ann Clin Res* 5:205, 1973

51. Reynolds EH: Anticonvulsants, folic acid, and epilepsy. *Lancet* 1:1376, 1973

52. Norris JW, Pratt RF: Folic acid deficiency and epilepsy. *Drugs* 8:366, 1974

53. Grant RHE, Stores OPR: Folic acid in folate-deficient patients with epilepsy. *Br Med J* 4:644, 1970

54. Maxwell JD, Hunter J, Stewart DA, et al: Folate deficiency after anticonvulsant drugs: An effect of hepatic enzyme induction. *Br Med J* 1:297, 1972

55. Gerson CD, Hepner GW, Brown N, et al: Inhibition by diphenylhydantoin of folic acid absorption in man. *Gastroenterology* 63:246, 1972

56. Dahlke MB, Mertens-Roesler E: Malabsorption of folic acid due to diphenylhydantoin. *Blood* 30:341, 1967

57. Strauss RG, Ramsay RE, Willmore LJ, et al: Hematologic effects of phenytoin therapy during pregnancy. *Obstet Gynecol* 51:682, 1978

58. Milunsky A, Graef JW, Gaynor MF: Methotrexate-induced congenital malformations. *J Pediatr* 72:790, 1968

59. Fraser JL, Watt HJ: Megaloblastic anemia in pregnancy and the puerperium. *Am J Obstet Gynecol* 89:532, 1964

60. Hibbard ED, Smithells RW: Folic acid metabolism and human embryopathy. *Lancet* 1:1254, 1965

61. Pritchard JA, Scott DE, Whalley PJ, et al: Infants of mothers with megaloblastic anemia due to folate deficiency. *JAMA* 211:1982, 1970

62. Scott DE, Whalley PJ, Pritchard JA: Maternal folate deficiency and pregnancy wastage. *Obstet Gynecol* 36:26, 1970

63. Hall MH: Folic acid deficiency and congenital malformation. *J Obstet Gynaecol Br Commonw* 79:159, 1972

64. Baylis EM, Crowley JM, Preece JM, et al: Influence of folic acid on blood-phenytoin levels. *Lancet* 1:62, 1971

65. Stamp TCB, Round JM, Rowe DJF, et al: Plasma levels and therapeutic effect of 25-hydroxycholecalciferol in epileptic patients taking anticonvulsant drugs. *Br Med J* 4:9, 1972

66. Goldberg MA: Anticonvulsant drugs, in Bevan JA (ed): *Essentials of Pharmacology*, ed 2. Hagerstown, Harper & Row, 1976, pp 239–247

67. Friis B, Sardemann H: Neonatal hypocalcaemia after intrauterine exposure to anticonvulsant drugs. *Arch Dis Child* 52:239, 1977

68. Flowers CE: The placental transmission of barbiturates and thiobarbiturates and their pharmacological action on the mother and the infant. *Am J Obstet Gynecol* 78:730, 1959

69. Melchior JC, Svensmark O, Trolle D: Placental transfer of phenobarbitone in epileptic women, and elimination in newborns. *Lancet* 2:860, 1967

70. Crombie DL, Pinsent RJFH, Slater BC, et al: Teratogenic drugs—R.C.G.P. survey. *Br Med J* 4:178, 1970

71. Greenberg G, Inman WHW, Weatherall JAC, et al: Maternal drug histories and congenital abnormalities. *Br Med J* 2:853, 1977

72. Nelson AM, Forfar JO: Associations between drugs administered during pregnancy and congenital abnormalities of the fetus. *Br Med J* 1:523, 1971
73. Smith DW: Teratogenicity of anticonvulsive medications. *Am J Dis Child* 131:1337, 1977
74. Desmond MM, Schwanecke RP, Wilson GS, et al: Maternal barbiturate utilization and neonatal withdrawal symptomatology. *J Pediatr* 80:190, 1972
75. Brazelton TB: Psychophysiologic reactions in the neonate. *J Pediatr* 58:513, 1961
76. Donaldson JO: *Neurology of Pregnancy*. Philadelphia, Saunders, 1978, pp 190–210
77. Tyson RM, Shrader EA, Perlman HH: Drugs transmitted through breast milk. *J Pediatr* 13:86, 1938
78. Martinez G, Snyder R: Transplacental passage of primidone. *Neurology* 23:381, 1973
79. Rudd NL, Freedom RM: A possible primidone embryopathy. *J Pediatr* 94:835, 1979
80. Niebyl JR, Blake DA, Freeman JM, et al: Carbamazepine levels in pregnancy and lactation. *Obstet Gynecol* 53:139, 1979
81. Montouris GD, Fenichel GM, McLain WL: The pregnant epileptic: A review and recommendations. *Arch Neurol* 36:601, 1979
82. Rane A, Bertilsson L, Palmer L: Disposition of placentally transferred carbamazepine in the newborn. *Eur J Clin Pharmacol* 8:283, 1975
83. Koup JR, Rose JQ, Cohen ME: Ethosuximide pharmacokinetics in a pregnant patient and her newborn. *Epilepsia* 19:535, 1978
84. Fabro S, Brown NA: Teratogenic potential of anticonvulsants. *N Engl J Med* 300:1280, 1979
85. Gugler R, von Unruh GE: Clinical pharmacokinetics of valproic acid. *Clin Pharmacokinet* 5:67, 1980
86. Simila S, von Wendt L, Hartikainen-Sorri A-L: Sodium valproate, pregnancy, and neonatal hyperglycinemia. *Arch Dis Child* 54:985, 1979
87. Dickinson RG, Harland RC, Lynn RK, et al: Transmission of valproic acid (Depakene) across the placenta: Half-life of the drug in mother and baby. *J Pediatr* 94:832, 1979
88. Pinder RM, Brogden RN, Speight TM, et al: Sodium valproate: A review of its pharmacological properties and therapeutic efficacy in epilepsy. *Drugs* 13:81, 1977
89. Hiilesmaa VK, Bardy AH, Granstrom M-L, et al: Valproic acid during pregnancy. *Lancet* 1:883, 1980
90. Dalens B, Raynaud EJ, Gaulme J: Teratogenicity of valproic acid. *J Pediatr* 97:332, 1980
91. Gamble JAS, Moore J, Lamki H, et al: A study of plasma diazepam levels in mother and infant. *Br J Obstet Gynaecol* 84:588, 1977
92. Idanpaan-Heikkila JE, Jouppila PI, Puolakka JO, et al: Placental transfer and fetal metabolism of diazepam in early human pregnancy. *Am J Obstet Gynecol* 109:1011, 1971
93. McAllister CB: Placental transfer and neonatal effects of diazepam when administered to women just before delivery. *Br J Anaesth* 52:423, 1980
94. Scher J, Hailey DM, Beard RW: The effects of diazepam on the fetus. *J Obstet Gynecol Br Commonw* 79:635, 1972
95. Cree JE, Meyer J, Hailey DM: Diazepam in labour: Its metabolism and effect on the clinical condition and thermogenesis of the newborn. *Br Med J* 4:251, 1973
96. Gillberg C: "Floppy infant syndrome" and maternal diazepam. *Lancet* 2:244, 1977
97. Rementeria JL, Bhatt K: Withdrawal symptoms in neonates from intrauterine exposure to diazepam. *J Pediatr* 90:123, 1977
98. Erkkola R, Kanto J, Sellman R: Diazepam in early human pregnancy. *Acta Obstet Gynecol Scand* 53:135, 1974
99. Beall JR: Study of the teratogenic potential of diazepam and SCH 12041. *CMA Journal* 106:1061, 1972
100. Milkovich L, Van den Berg BJ: Effects of prenatal meprobamate and chlordiazepoxide hydrochloride on human embryonic and fetal development. *N Engl J Med* 291:1268, 1974
101. Hartz SC, Heinonen OP, Shapiro S, et al: Antenatal exposure to meprobamate and chlordiazepoxide in relation to malformations, mental development, and childhood mortality. *N Engl J Med* 292:726, 1975
102. Safra MJ, Oakley, GP: Valium: An oral cleft teratogen? *Cleft Palate J* 13:198, 1976
103. Patrick MJ, Tilstone WJ, Reavey P: Diazepam and breast-feeding. *Lancet* 1:542, 1972
104. Rall TW, Schleifer LS: Drugs effective in the therapy of the epilepsies, in Gilman AG, Goodman LS, Gilman A (eds): *The Pharmacologic Basis of Therapeutics*, ed 6. New York, Macmillan, 1980, pp 448–474
105. van der Kleijn E, Schobben E, Vree TB: Clinical pharmacokinetics of antiepileptic drugs. *Drug Intell Clin Pharm* 14:674, 1980
106. Dilantin vs generic phenytoin. *Med Lett* 22(12):49, June 13, 1980

107. Bertilsson L: Clinical pharmacokinetics of carbamazepine. *Clin Pharmacokinet* 3:128, 1978

108. Browne TR: Drug therapy reviews: Clinical pharmacology of antiepileptic Drugs. *Am J Hosp Pharm* 35:1048, 1978

109. Moore TD: Guidelines for anticonvulsant therapy, in Housten M (ed): *Modern Medicine Practice Guide,* ed 5. New York, Harcourt Brace Jovanovich, 1981, pp 39–47

110. Dukes MNG: Anticonvulsants, in Dukes MNG (ed): *Meylers Side Effects of Drugs,* ed 9. Amsterdam, Excerpta Medica, 1980, pp 90–101

6. Acute and Chronic Hypertension During Pregnancy

FREDERICK P. ZUSPAN KATHRYN J. ZUSPAN
ANDREW L. WILSON

HYPERTENSION DURING PREGNANCY

Hypertension of pregnancy is best understood if divided into four different types of pregnancy-related elevations of blood pressure. Such a classification follows: (1) acute hypertension in pregnancy, preeclampsia-eclampsia, and pregnancy-induced hypertension (PIH); (2) chronic hypertension during pregnancy; (3) chronic hypertension during pregnancy with superimposed acute hypertension (preeclampsia); and (4) transient hypertension in pregnancy which occurs during labor or immediately postpartum, then subsides.

The first two categories, acute and chronic hypertension, are well described and treated with specific drugs and regimens. These are discussed in ensuing sections. Chronic hypertension with a superimposed acute component is managed using the drug regimens for chronic hypertension, with that of acute hypertension added when superimposed by preeclampsia. Finally, transient hypertension in the absence of signs of preeclampsia is treated with intravenous hydralazine as needed, just as in the regimens which follow.

Acute Hypertension of Pregnancy

Acute hypertension during pregnancy is a condition that is synonymous with the terms toxemia of pregnancy, preeclampsia-eclampsia, and pregnancy-induced hypertension. The latter is the most current and commonly used term. Conditions related to this form of hypertension are listed in Figure 6-1.

The description of the patient with mild preeclampsia is an individual who, after the 24th week of gestation, develops, in sequential fashion: overt edema of the face or hands; hypertension, that is, blood pressure greater than 140/90, or an incremental increase in the diastolic of greater than 15, or in the systolic greater than 30; and the development of proteinuria noted in clean-catch specimen on two successive days. Usually there are no other clinical signs. It is important to understand that in more than 90 percent of patients, this will be a sequential development of edema, hypertension, and proteinuria. If other signs or symptoms are seen, then a suspicion should be entered that perhaps other conditions also exist.

The mild forms of PIH are treatable but not preventable. With proper identification and management of the severe forms, their complications are completely preventable and should not occur. These severe forms have a maternal mortality of 10 percent and a perinatal mortality exceeding 30 percent. The treatment protocol for PIH outlined as follows has been shown to decrease eclampsia-related maternal mortality to zero, and perinatal loss to less than 10 percent, and represents the best

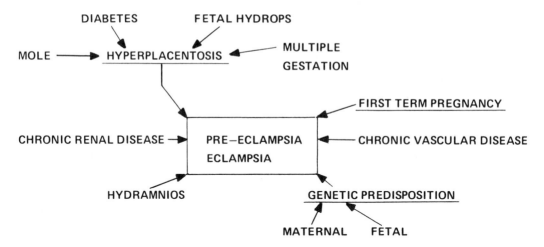

Figure 6-1 The cause of preeclampsia-eclampsia is multifaceted. Many different maternal and fetal conditions can act as catalytic agents in its development. When these conditions are present, meticulous prenatal care and diagnosis are essential for prevention.

maternal/fetal salvage rate in the literature. The common denominator of therapy is a pharmacologic amount of magnesium sulfate and the relative absence of other medications, except for antihypertensive medications to prevent stroke.

The key to treatment is prevention. Patients who are prone to develop PIH must be identified early and seen at weekly intervals. The development of PIH consists of mild preeclampsia progressing on to severe preeclampsia and then to eclampsia. The rapidity in which one stage passes to another is variable and dependent upon many factors, including the individual variations of patients. It would be most unusual for a patient to present first with eclampsia without progressing through the milder forms of the disease.

Once the diagnosis of mild preeclampsia is made, the patient must be hospitalized on complete bedrest (laying on her side) with a nutritious diet. The only medication given is a sedative, that is, phenobarbital 30 mg three times daily to improve comfort during bedrest. Diuresis is expected in 36 to 48 hours, with symptoms abating in 3 to 5 days. If the patient is at or near term, oxytocin induction of labor should be considered.

The diagnosis of the severe form of preeclampsia is based on one or more of the following criteria:

1. Systolic pressure of 160 or diastolic pressure of 100 taken two times, recorded 6 hours apart, with the patient at bed rest

2. Proteinuria of greater than 5 gm in 24 hours or a 3 to 4+ protein on dipstick

3. Oliguria, defined as urinary output of less than 400 ml in 24 hours

4. Cerebral or visual disturbances, including eye-ground changes

5. Pulmonary edema or cyanosis

The patient with severe preeclampsia is seriously ill and must be hospitalized on bedrest, with frequent blood pressure recordings and evaluation of deep tendon reflexes. The major therapy is administration of magnesium sulfate either intravenously or intramuscularly. The IV route is both more appropriate for the disturbed pathophysiology and less painful. Magnesium sulfate is given via a controlled administration system such as an infusion pump, with 4 to 6 gm magnesium sulfate being given slowly IV over 20 minutes as a loading dose, then 1 gm/hour thereafter. The patient is monitored by examination of (1) deep tendon reflexes which should be hypoactive but present, (2) urine output which should be greater than 25 ml/hour, and (3) respirations that are in excess of 10 per minute. Loss of reflexes, decrease in urine output, and depressed respirations are signs of magnesium overdose. Magnesium toxicity is managed by decreasing the rate of magnesium infusion or, in severe toxicity, by intravenous administration of 1 gm of intravenous calcium chloride.

If the diastolic blood pressure is greater than 100 mm Hg, hydralazine is given to prevent a cerebrovascular accident. A 5-mg IV bolus is infused and followed by administration using an infusion pump, with the hydralazine placed in an intravenous solution container. The diastolic blood pressure should range from 90 to 100 mm Hg.

Most patients with severe preeclampsia should be delivered. Labor is easily induced with small doses of oxytocin given by infusion pump (see Chap. 10). Electronic fetal heart rate surveillance is essential during this process. Table 6-1 provides a listing of the relative risk of fetal mortality with an increase of maternal blood pressure.

Following a generalized clonic convulsion, the patient may be obtunded, and the possibility always exists of aspiration during the seizure. An aggressive action-oriented program that is the same as the one outlined for severe preeclampsia should be instituted. Once the patient is under good control (a process requiring no more than 2 hours), a decision must be made concerning delivery. Convulsions are controlled with 4 to 6 gm of magnesium sulfate IV, and not with other drugs. Diuretics are not used, and antihypertensive therapy should be instituted only to prevent stroke, as described previously using hydralazine (Figs. 6-2 and 6-3).

Chronic Hypertension of Pregnancy

Chronic hypertension during pregnancy is defined as hypertension usually antedating pregnancy or seen prior to the 24th week of gestation. Pregnancy tends to provoke the unmasking of chronic hypertension, which is seen more commonly in the multigravida. Fetal wastage in patients with mild hypertension is 16 percent, whereas in those with severe hypertension (blood pressure greater than 160/100), fetal wastage is as high as 40 percent.

Chronic hypertension is subdivided into primary and secondary. Primary hypertension is that which is not related to any specific disease and comprises 95 percent of chronic hypertensive patients. Secondary hypertension

TABLE 6-1 RELATIVE RISK OF FETAL MORTALITY WITH INCREASED MATERNAL BLOOD PRESSURE

Diastolic Pressure Maximum (mm Hg)	Proteinuria	Relative Fetal Risk*
94	≥1+	20×
94	None	4×
85	≥2+	10×
85	≥1+	7×
75–84	≥1+	4×

* Compared with a diastolic pressure maximum of 75 to 84 mm Hg with no proteinuria.

PRINCIPAL RX – MgSO$_4$ $\Big\langle$ IV 4-6 GM THEN 1 GM/HR.
IM 10 GM THEN 5 GM/4 H

SECONDARY RX – HYDRALAZINE 5 MG BOLUS THEN IV INFUSION

DEFINITIVE RX – DELIVERY, AVOID MAJOR CONDUCTION
ANESTHESIA

Figure 6-2. The major therapy for preeclampsia/eclampsia in the United States is the use of parenteral magnesium sulfate. An antihypertensive (hydralazine) is used to prevent a stroke in the mother. *(Note:* The IV route is preferred to avoid pain and assure accurate drug delivery.)

is hypertension related to a known disease process. A specific diagnosis is mandatory, since some forms are treatable, such as some neurohumoral disorders, endocrine factors, renal pressor mechanisms, and cardiovascular factors.

Initial management involves electrocardiogram (ECG) chest x-ray, and laboratory studies. The patient is maintained on the antihypertensive and diuretic medications used prior to pregnancy, with the diuretics being discontinued after 20 weeks' gestation. For a mild to moderate increase in blood pressure, the patient is placed on self-blood pressure determinations twice a day and frequent prenatal visits (every 1 or 2 weeks).

A second trimester decline in blood pressure is expected, and when absent is an ominous sign. Hospitalization with controlled bedrest may be necessary to see a response. Phenobarbital, 30 mg three times daily may improve patient compliance during bedrest. When the blood pressure no longer responds to bedrest, antihypertensive medications are used starting with α-methyldopa (Aldomet) 250 mg four times daily and increased to 500 mg four times daily if necessary. If salt and fluid retention are necessary, the periodic use of a diuretic such as hydrochlorothiazide or diazide may be employed. If the patient's blood pressure shows minimal or no response to this therapy, the amount of bedrest is fur-

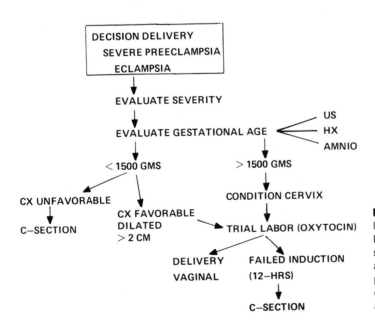

Figure 6-3. The decision for delivery is outlined in this flowchart. It must be stressed that the decision should be made early in the affected patient. Delivery mode depends upon the condition of the cervix, fetal size, and gestational age.

ther increased and 10 mg propranolol is added four times daily and gradually increased to 40 mg four times daily. If an acute hypertensive episode intervenes, the patient is admitted to the intensive care unit and treated with intravenous hydralazine. A bolus injection of 5 mg IV gives an indication of response. The hydralazine is then added to the IV bag and infused via infusion pump at a rate adequate to control the diastolic blood pressure between 80 and 100 mm Hg. If preeclampsia superimposes on the chronic hypertension, the preeclampsia is treated with intravenous magnesium sulfate (4 mg loading dose and then 1 gm/hour maintenance dose).

In cases of the latter severity, the option of pregnancy termination should be considered. Evaluation of fetal pulmonary maturity is carried out by amniocentesis. If less than 34 weeks' gestation, intravenous hydrocortisone 1 gm every 8 hours for a total of 4 gm in 1 day is given to maturate fetal lungs, if the lecithin-sphingomyelin ratio is less than 1:1. We have found no increase in blood pressure using this drug. Delivery is then induced, using oxytocin or, in cases of an unfavorable cervix, abdominal delivery is indicated.

In summary, the drugs used in the treatment regimen described for acute hypertension include magnesium sulfate to prevent or control convulsions, hydralazine as an antihypertensive agent, phenobarbital for sedation, calcium chloride as an antidote for magnesium toxicity, and oxytocin for induction of labor. The drugs used in chronic hypertension therapy as outlined include α-methyldopa as an antihypertensive, with propranolol and intravenous hydralazine added if needed; a diuretic such as hydrochlorthiazide or diazide used periodically; phenobarbital for sedation; hydrocortisone to maturate fetal lungs; and oxytocin for induction.

The challenge for the obstetrician in chronic hypertension is to choose the appropriate drug with maximum safety for the fetus and therapeutic response in the mother. Over the past several years many drugs have been used, but until recently randomized clinical trials had not been undertaken. The objectives

of therapy include delivery of a viable baby with no morbidity, and prevention of maternal cardiac decompensation, stroke, and morbidity.

A number of drugs are employed in different treatment regimens. Blood pressure control is sought using sympatholytics such as reserpine and α-methyldopa; β-adrenergic agents such as propranolol and metoprolol; vasodilators such as prazosin, hydralazine, minoxidil, diazoxide, and sodium nitroprusside; and diuretics such as thiazide, furosemide, ethacrynic acid, chlorthalidone, and spironolactone. Each of these agents is discussed in this chapter and is listed in Table 6-2.

DIURETICS

The use of diuretics, particularly the thiazides, in the treatment of hypertension is well established.[1] Although recommended as the primary drugs in the stepped-care approach to the treatment of hypertension, they are probably not indicated during pregnancy.[2-8] Diuretics do not alter the incidence of preeclampsia and eclampsia, and do not influence perinatal mortality or birth weight.[5,8] The use of diuretics may induce maternal hypovolemia and a decrease in placental and uterine perfusion.[9-12]

The thiazides are the most commonly used diuretics in treating hypertension. Maternal side effects include those seen in nonpregnant patients: hypokalemia, hypovolemia, pancreatitis, decreased carbohydrate tolerance, and hyperuricemia.[13] In addition, there have been case reports of hypokalemia and metabolic alkalosis,[14] hemorrhagic pancreatitis,[15] and maternal death[16] when thiazide diuretics are administered to the pregnant patient.

Reported perinatal side effects include hyponatremia,[2,17] thrombocytopenia[18,19] jaundice,[7] and the possibility of hypertension at maturity.[20] Chlorothiazide appears to freely cross the placenta, with essentially equal maternal and neonatal levels being found at birth.[21] Fetal heart rate abnormalities have been reported in a pregnant patient with hypo-

TABLE 6-2 ADVERSE EFFECTS ON THE MOTHER AND FETUS OF DRUGS USED TO TREAT HYPERTENSION DURING PREGNANCY

Drug	Placental Transfer	Maternal Adverse Effects	Fetal Adverse Effects	Sources
Diuretics				
Thiazides	Yes, chlorothiazide—fetal levels equal to maternal[30]	Hypokalemia, hyperglycemia, hyperurecemia, hypercalcemia, skin rashes, pancreatitis, hypovolemia	Hyponatremia, thrombocytopenia, jaundice, increased risk of hypertension at maturity	87–94
Furosemide	Unknown	Hypokalemia, hyperuricemia, hyperglycemia, gastro-intestinal upset, hypovolemia	None reported	87, 95
Ethacrynic acid	Unknown	Same effects as furosemide plus hearing loss	Deafness	96, 97
Spironolactone	Unknown	Hyperkalemia, gynecomastia, amenorrhea	Unknown	
Triamterene	Unknown	Leg cramps, dizziness, hyperkalemia	No available data	
Chlorthalidone	Unknown	Same effects as furosemide	Unknown	98,99
Sympatholytics				
Reserpine	Yes—not quantified	Depression, sedation, bizarre dreams, nasal congestion, calactorrhea, increased gastric acid secretion, abdominal cramps, diarrhea, breast cancer (?)	Bradycardia, lethargy, nasal congestion, altered thermoequilibrium, stillbirth and congenital anomalies, anorexia, death	
α-Methyldopa	Unknown	Sedation, decreased mental acuity, fatigue, sodium retention, hepatitis, drug fever, positive Coombs test, hemolytic anemia, galactorrhea, postural hypotension	None reported	100–106

	Crosses Placenta	Maternal Side Effects	Fetal Effects	References
β-Adrenergic Agents Propranolol	Yes—fetal levels, similar to maternal	Sodium retention, aggravation of heart failure, bradycardia, depression, aggravation of broncho-constrictive disease, vivid dreams, interference of diabetic control, CNS disturbances	Intrauterine growth retardation, hypoglycemia, respiratory depression, bradycardia	87, 107–109
Metoprolol, Abdolol, Timolol	Unknown	Similar to propranolol	No available data	
Vasodilator Clonidine	Unknown	Sedation, dry mouth, sodium retention, orthostatic hypotension, constipation, CNS disturbances, rebound hypertension when stopped	Embryotoxic in animals; none reported in humans	100, 107
Guanethidine	Unknown	Postural hypotension, diarrhea, depression, sodium retention, aggravation of heart failure	No available data	87
Hydralazine	Unknown	Tachycardia, palpitations, flushing, headache, sodium retention, aggravation of angina, Lupus syndrome, neuropathy, dizziness	None reported in long-term use; fetal heart rate changes when given acutely at term	87, 110, 111
Prazosin	Unknown	Sodium retention, sudden hypotension, palpitations, tachycardia	No available data	112
Minoxidil	Unknown	Tachycardia, hypotension, palpitations, hypertrichosis	No available data	
Magnesium Sulfate	Yes—fetal levels similar to maternal	Overdose—decreased respirations, absent reflexes Increased urine calcium loss, increased parathyroid hormone secretion	Excess level excreted in 4 to 24 hr; rare bladder atony and myotonia	

kalemia secondary to diuretics.[22] Lethargy and poor Apgar scores secondary to hyponatremia were found in two infants whose mothers received thiazide diuretics antepartum.[17] However, the rarity of these complications in practice is pointed out by several large studies which reported no adverse fetal or neonatal effects.[8,23,24]

Furosemide has been used throughout pregnancy with no adverse effects on the fetus.[2,25] Although fetal hyponatremia has not been reported, the electrolyte effects in nonpregnant hypertensives make this a possibility, as with thiazide diuretics. It has been suggested by several authors[2,26,27] that the use of furosemide should be limited to patients with pulmonary edema or heart failure, and those receiving diazoxide for preeclampsia or toxemia. Furosemide has been reported to freely cross the placenta, leading to equal maternal and fetal blood levels.[25]

Ethacrynic acid is similar in mechanism of action and clinical effects to furosemide. The use of ethacrynic acid during pregnancy should be avoided because of the potential for ototoxicity and nephrotoxicity.[3,26]

The use of chlorthalidone[28,29] and spironolactone[4] in pregnant patients has been reported, but their routine use cannot be recommended because of a paucity of data.

SYMPATHOLYTICS

Reserpine exerts its hypotensive effect via depletion of catecholamines from peripheral nerve endings. Adverse effects reported in adults include depression, nasal congestion, and galactorrhea. Fetal and neonatal adverse effects reported are: bradycardia, lethargy, alteration of thermal equilibrium, congenital anomalies, and mucous membrane engorgement.[30-32] Because of these problems, the use of reserpine during pregnancy should be avoided.

α-Methyldopa is currently one of the most widely used hypotensive agents in pregnancy. Side effects in nonpregnant adults include drowsiness, fatigue, and rarely, Coomb's positive hemolytic anemia and hepatic disorders. Methyldopa is the most extensively studied hypotensive drug used in pregnancy. Fetal and neonatal adverse effects have not been reported up to the present time.[33-38] Leather et al.[36] and Redmon et al.[34,35] showed increases in fetal survival rates, decreases in maternal blood pressure, and an increase in the length of gestation of approximately 2 weeks when compared with an untreated control group. The major difference that made these studies statistically significant was the decrease in midtrimester fetal loss. Doses of methyldopa in both trials ranged from 0.5 to 2 gm daily, and allowed the addition of hydralazine or a diuretic if indicated by less than optimal response. Other authors have noted similar results,[33,37,39] but the work of Leather and Redmon are the only randomized trials yet published in the literature.

The transfer of methyldopa across the "placental barrier" has been noted.[37,39] Samples of amniotic fluid contained higher total levels of drug, but with a greater percentage of conjugated drug than in the maternal or fetal circulation. Free or unconjugated drug appears to cross the placenta where it is conjugated and excreted by the fetus. The specific effect of methyldopa on fetal amines has yet to be studied.[40]

To summarize, methyldopa's effectiveness and apparent safety make it an agent of choice for the treatment of chronic hypertension in pregnancy.

β-ADRENERGIC BLOCKING AGENTS

β-Adrenergic blocking agents form a large part of antihypertensive therapy today. They have been found to be useful alone[41] or in combination with a diuretic[42] in the treatment of hypertension in the nonpregnant patient. Potential maternal adverse effects are the same as those found in nonpregnant patients: interference with diabetic control, bradycardia, drowsiness, aggravation or precipitation of heart failure, or bronchoconstrictive disease.[43]

Propranolol constitutes the greatest portion of β-adrenergic blocking agents used in the United States. Propranolol appears to cross the placenta freely, leading to essentially equal maternal and fetal concentrations.[44] Reported fetal complications include neonatal hypoglycemia, intrauterine growth retardation, and neonatal respiratory depression and bradycardia.[44-56] Caution must be used in interpreting the incidence of these side effects, as all of these reports are anecdotal. No teratogenic effects have been reported for propranolol, and there is a paucity of data for other, newer agents. Some side effects of β-blockers may be dose-related,[48] and can possibly be prevented by using lower doses or by discontinuing the drug 1 to 2 weeks prior to the expected delivery date. The inability to accurately predict the date of delivery and the increase in maternal pressure which follows drug discontinuation probably preclude the use of propranolol during pregnancy. In the only random double-blind study of the effects of propranolol on the fetus, a 5- to 6-minute delay occurred in the onset of spontaneous respiration, possibly requiring intubation in babies born to mothers receiving 1 mg of propranolol IV prior to cesarean section.[55]

Propranolol is not routinely indicated for antihypertensive use during pregnancy, since there are insufficient clinical data to evaluate their role in the management of maternal hypertension.[56] The effects on the fetus and neonate have been discussed in Chapter 2. We have followed many pregnant patients with cardiac disease (notably mitral valve prolapse) and symptomatic hyperthyroidism who were on propranolol, and all delivered without event to either mother or baby. The lowest necessary dose of propranolol should be taken for the shortest time.

VASODILATORS

Prazosin, hydralazine, minoxidil, diazoxide, and sodium nitroprusside reduce blood pressure through direct effects on arterioles. They are useful when added to previously ineffective therapy with maximal doses of other antihypertensive agents or, for the latter three, when used acutely to treat hypertensive exacerbations. Treatment with these agents is limited by a reflex increase in sympathetic activity and heart rate, an increase in plasma renin activity, and the corresponding retention of sodium, fluid, and circulation plasma volume. Combination therapy with a diuretic and β-blocker or sympatholytic obviates these problems in chronic use.

Hydralazine, when used parenterally, is the drug of choice in pregnancy, and is an effective agent when used acutely to control exacerbations of maternal blood pressure.[57] Adverse effects in pregnant and nonpregnant patients include tachycardia and palpitations, flushing, and headaches. The use of hydralazine in combination with methyldopa in two large studies found no adverse effects in the fetus and neonate.[58-60] There are conflicting reports of the effects of hydralazine on uteroplacental blood flow, though the possibility of decreased flow must be considered. Fetal heart rate changes occur when hydralazine is administered acutely[61] and the blood pressure drops precipitously. Although fetal adverse effects have rarely been reported, the possibility of neonatal thermoregulatory problems and hypothermia exist.[62] Due to the amount of experience with hydralazine, and inexperience with other agents, hydralazine can therefore be recommended for use in pregnancy as the drug of choice. The use of oral hydralazine is only minimally effective and is not used routinely.

Diazoxide is a thiazide congener available for intravenous use only. Major problems with its use include sodium and fluid retention and reflex sympathetic stimulation. Diazoxide is usually successful in lowering blood pressure, even after failures with other indirectly acting agents. Its use in pregnancy is, however, not without controversy. Diazoxide has a powerful relaxant effect on uterine smooth muscle and may stop labor (see Chap. 8), necessitating the use of oxytocins to reestablish it.[63,64] Diazoxide crosses the placenta[64] and can cause neonatal hyperglycemia, as well as hyperbilirubinemia by displacement from protein-binding sites. Maternal side effects include hyperglycemia through a direct effect on pancreatic β cells and hyperuricemia. Both of these effects are mild and rarely present problems with short-term use. Headache, flushing, tachycardia, and palpitations may be seen acutely as with other vasodilators.[65] The most distressing problem associated with the use of diazoxide is the unpredictability of the initial response. Reports of systolic and diastolic pressures decreasing to below 60 mm Hg are distressing and cause acute fetal distress and hypoxia. The implications for utero-placental perfusion of this drop in pressure are grave. Fetal heart rate decelerations immediately following the use of diazoxide have been reported. This, along with hyperbilirubinemia and problems with fetal and maternal carbohydrate metabolism, make diazoxide a poor choice in pregnancy, and it should only be used if the blood pressure can not be controlled with hydralazine. However, diazoxide is a good agent for use in the immediate postpartum state to control acute exacerbations of high blood pressure.

Sodium nitroprusside has not been widely used or studied because of potential fetal cyanide poisoning. Because of this problem, it cannot currently be recommended. Its only use may be to control an acute blood pressure rise during anesthesia for cesarean section, when the fetus is to be extracted in a short time.

MAGNESIUM SULFATE

The most important agent used in the United States in the treatment of severe preeclampsia and eclampsia is parenteral magnesium sulfate. Of a group of academic obstetricians and gynecologists recently surveyed, 100 percent utilize this drug for severe preeclampsia and eclampsia. Similarly, 98 percent of clinical obstetricians and gynecologists in the United States use magnesium sulfate, as contrasted to 2 percent of practicing obstetricians and gynecologists in the United Kingdom.[66] This discrepancy between the two countries is felt to be due to the American promotion of the drug by academic obstetricians and gynecologists, especially by the teachings and writings of Pritchard[67] and Zuspan.[68] The use and role of magnesium sulfate in acute hypertension in pregnancy follows.

Magnesium Metabolism

Magnesium is the fourth most common cation in the body and the second most plentiful intracellular cation. The human body contains approximately 2000 mEq of magnesium. The majority, at least 50 percent, is found in bone, and the remainder is equally distributed in muscle and nonmuscular tissue.[69-71] Magnesium is absorbed mainly in the small intestine, and disorders or alterations of the intestine such as a jejunoileal bypass can result in magnesium deficiency. The excretion of magnesium, when it is administered intravenously, is principally in the urine, as only 1 to 2 percent is recovered in the feces.[72]

Magnesium is an activator of a host of enzyme systems which are critical to cellular metabolism. In addition, it is a required cofactor for oxidative metabolism in vitro. Since it is the most abundant divalent intracellular cation, it is used in many metabolic pathways.

Magnesium and calcium have a complex interdependent influence on the excitability of the components of the neuromuscular junction. There are no known studies showing that magnesium deficiency is the cause of toxemia of pregnancy nor that its use in toxemia provides a correction of such a deficiency. Magnesium and calcium depletion do not lead to increased neurohormonal excitability nor do they enhance neuromuscular transmission. Some of the effects of calcium and magnesium, however, are antagonistic to neurohormonal transmission. Magnesium in pharmacologic doses has a curariform action on the neuromuscular junction, presumably interfering with the release of acetylcholine from motor-nerve terminals. Another hypothesis is that there is a change in membrane potential by replacement of calcium with magnesium, thus altering neuromuscular transmission and excitability of the motor-nerve terminal which prevents eclamptic convulsions.

Magnesium Excess

The studies on magnesium excess in the human have resulted from clinical pharmacologic studies, most notably those in toxemia of pregnancy. It is known that infusions to animals and humans lead to an impairment of neuromuscular transmission. The sequential clinical development suggestive of magnesium excess can be noted first when deep tendon reflexes become hypoactive at serum magnesium concentrations between 8 and 10 mEq/liter, followed by respiratory paralysis developing when concentrations exceed 13 to 15 mEq/liter. Finally, cardiac conduction is affected with serum concentrations greater than 15 mEq/liter. Cardiac arrest does not occur until extremely high concentrations take place, usually in excess of 25 mEq/liter, with cardiac arrest occurring in diastole.

Use of Magnesium in Preeclampsia and Eclampsia

Since 1906 magnesium sulfate has been used for the treatment of preeclampsia and eclampsia.[73] Administration has been parenteral, with a very few clinicians in the world using intrathecal magnesium to control eclamptic convulsions. Lazard, in 1925, was the first to use intravenous magnesium sulfate to treat eclampsia. He gave hourly doses of 20 ml of 10 percent solution of magnesium sulfate until the convulsions ceased. The following year, Dorsett used intramuscular magnesium sulfate to treat toxemia of pregnancy. Eastman is credited with establishing the current acceptable intramuscular regimen for magnesium sulfate by giving an initial dose of 10 gm (20 ml of 50 percent solution), followed by 5 gm at 6-hour intervals.[74] He regarded magnesium therapy as the single most valuable agent in the treatment of severe preeclampsia, and this has not changed to this day in the United States. Pritchard popularized a regimen similar to Eastman's, except that the initial dose is 4 gm of magnesium sulfate IV and thereafter, intramuscular injec-

tions.[67,75] Zuspan popularized the use of intravenous magnesium sulfate using 4 to 6 gm initially, then 1 to 2 gm/hour thereafter, depending on the clinical condition of the patient.[76,77] The reports of Pritchard and Zuspan in the literature identify the use of parenteral magnesium sulfate as the most efficacious means of reducing eclampsia-related perinatal mortality to 10 percent and maternal mortality to zero. Their reports, published more than 15 years ago, represent the best fetal salvage rates for this severe disease reported in the literature (Fig. 6-4).

Magnesium Sulfate Regimens

All doses of magnesium sulfate refer to the hydrated form $MgSO_4 \cdot 7 H_2O$. The anhydrous salt contains twice as much magnesium as the hydrated salt. Various methods are available to monitor the therapeutic administration of magnesium. Flowers proposed monitoring the urine magnesium as well as the plasma levels at periodic intervals using formula calculations, thus allowing appropriate adjustment of magnesium dosage.[78] Periodic monitoring of plasma magnesium is advisable, and the ideal level is 6 to 8 mEq/liter. The difficulty stems from the protracted amount of time required to obtain the magnesium level, thus rendering this method of little value except to monitor a trend of therapy.

Most clinicians monitor the patient using reflexes, respiration, and urine output as parameters. Reflexes should be present, respirations adequate, and urine output should be more than 100 ml every 4 hours. To assure this: (1) deep tendon reflexes should be checked on an hourly basis and, if absent, the dosage should be lowered (reflexes should be hypoactive and present); (2) respirations should be counted at hourly intervals and should remain above 12 per minute; and (3) urine output should exceed 100 ml every 4 hours since magnesium is only excreted in the urine. In the event of oliguria, a plasma magnesium level should be obtained and the amount of magnesium gradually diminished; an antidote to combat a hypermagnesium state is calcium gluconate or calcium chloride in a

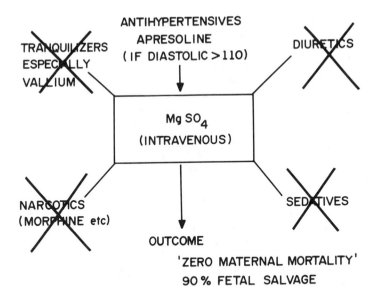

Figure 6-4. The major therapy used in preeclampsia-eclampsia is intravenous magnesium sulfate in pharmacologic doses.

10 percent solution; 10 ml or 1 gm is injected IV for magnesium overdose.

Pritchard demonstrated in toxemia therapy involving parenteral MgSO₄ that plasma levels average 6 mEq/liter and often approach 8 to 10 mEq/liter. The concentration of magnesium in the cerebral spinal fluid is only slightly increased and is considered essentially normal. Cerebral spinal fluid magnesium thus does not correlate with plasma magnesium.

Several investigators in the past used intrathecal magnesium to control convulsions and, despite previous information, this was an effective method, although it is not generally accepted at the present time.[79]

A major misconception concerning magnesium sulfate centers around its hypotensive qualities. Magnesium is not a hypotensive agent, even though it decreases intrinsic resistance in the uterine vessels. Occasionally a transient decline in blood pressure occurs within the first hour of administration of intravenous magnesium; however, it returns to baseline levels following this brief period. If blood pressure needs to be controlled, an antihypertensive drug should be used. Therapeutic levels of magnesium seem to blunt the vasospastic fluctuations of the blood pressure

often seen in the severe preeclamptic patient with an elevated blood pressure. It is hypothesized that magnesium may also protect the fetus by increasing uterine blood flow, a finding in experimental animals not yet documented in humans.[80] Magnesium has no direct general anesthetic property, and changes at serum concentrations above 12 mEq/liter do not indicate suppressed EEG activity.[81]

Adverse Effects on the Neonate and Uterine Activity

There is divided opinion concerning the effect of magnesium sulfate on uterine activity. Zuspan was not able to show a lengthening of eclamptic labor or inductions in spite of doses of magnesium as high as 3 gm/hour.[82] This is in contrast to Hall et al., who were able to demonstrate in muscle tissue excised from the gravid human uterus at the time of cesarean section that increasing concentrations of magnesium in the muscle-bath solution caused a diminution in spontaneous uterine activity.[83] Their conclusions were that magnesium inhibits the contractility of isolated muscle tissue excised from the gravid human uterus and that additionally, the magnesium ion may have a depressant action on uterine motility in vivo.

These workers substantiate their latter statements by looking at the length of labor of 300 patients who, in toxemia of pregnancy, received either no magnesium, low magnesium, or high magnesium. The high magnesium patients had labor of approximately 18 hours, versus 14-hour labor in the low magnesium patients and 9-hour labor in patients without magnesium.

Pritchard also was not able to document a causal relationship of magnesium and alterations in uterine contractions by direct transabdominal percutaneous recordings of uterine pressure. There were no changes in frequency, duration, or intensity of uterine contractions following the parenteral injection of magnesium.[75]

The effect of magnesium on the fetus is such that amniotic fluid levels are roughly 25 to 30 percent of plasma levels. Cruikshank and Pitkin sampled in a sequential manner the maternal and cord levels of magnesium with a follow-up of newborn blood levels revealing that it takes 24 to 48 hours for magnesium levels to return to normal after therapeutic doses are present in the mother.[84] Over a 14-year period, Stone and Pritchard studied some 7000 infants whose mothers had received parenteral magnesium and found no problem in its use with relation to newborns.[85] They found that the serum level of magnesium in the fetus rapidly approached that of the mother but could not be correlated with any ill effects on the newborn. Lipsitz has noted that when magnesium sulfate is given intramuscularly to the mother, the newborn is usually not compromised by excess magnesium but may be affected. However, when continuous infusion of magnesium sulfate is used and given for more than 24 hours, anticipation of the newborn manifesting signs of hypermagnesemia may be present.[86] This is in contrast to the experience of Zuspan, who has utilized therapeutic doses of magnesium sulfate since 1960. Excessive magnesium levels present in the newborn are cleared by renal excretion if the newborn did not suffer hypoxia during labor or the birth process. Only two exceptions are notable in 20 years, and both involved urinary retention

most likely due to magnesium effects on the detrussor muscle of the newborn. The point at issue is that magnesium remains the best drug for the toxemic patient, and although it may affect the fetus, it has the lowest number of side effects.

REFERENCES

1. Moser M, et al: Report of the Joint National Committee on Detection, Evaluation, and Treatment of High Blood Pressure. *JAMA* 237:255–262, 1979
2. Kelly JV: Drugs used in the management of toxemia of pregnancy. *Clin Obstet Gynecol* 20:395–420, 1977
3. Welt SI, Crenshaw MC: Concurrent hypertension and pregnancy. *Clin Obstet Gynecol* 21:619–648, 1978
4. Campbell DM, MacGillivary I: The effect of a low caloric diet or a thiazide diuretic on the incidence of preeclampsia and on birthweight. *Br J Obstet Gynecol* 82:572–578, 1975
5. Kraus GW, Marchese HR, Yen SSC: Prophylactic use of hydrochlorothiazide in pregnancy. *JAMA* 198:1150–1154, 1966
6. Gray J: Use and abuse of thiazides in pregnancy. *Clin Obstet Gynecol* 11:568–578, 1968
7. Limited usefulness of diuretics in pregnancy. *FDA Drug Bull.* Sept 1977
8. Lindheimer MD, Katz AI: Sodium and diuretics in pregnancy. *JAMA* 198:1150–1154, 1966
9. Gant NF, Madden JD, Siiteri PK, MacDonald PK: The metabolic clearance rate of dehydroisoandrosterone sulfate: III. The effect of thiazide diuretics in normal and preeclamptic pregnancies. *Am J Obstet Gynecol* 123:159–163, 1975
10. Gant NF, Madden JD, Siiteri PK, MacDonald PK: The metabolic clearance rate of dehydroisoandrosterone sulfate: IV. Acute effects of induced hypotension and natriuresis in normal and hypertensive pregnancies. *Am J Obstet Gynecol* 124:143–148, 1976
11. Arias F: Expansion of intramuscular volume and fetal outcome in patients with chronic hypertension and pregnancy. *Am J Obstet Gynecol* 123:610–616, 1975
12. Soffronoff EC, Kaufman RM, Connaughton JF: Intravascular volume determination and fetal outcome in hypertensive diseases of pregnancy. *Am J Obstet Gynecol* 127:4–9, 1977
13. Riddiough MA: Preventing, detecting, and

managing adverse reactions of antihypertensive agents in the ambulant patient with hypertension. *Am J Hosp Pharm* 34:465–479, 1977

14. Pritchard JA, Walley PJ: Severe hypolkalemia due to prolonged administration of chlorothiazide during pregnancy. *Am J Obstet Gynecol* 81:1241, 1961

15. Minkowitz S, Soloway HB, Hall JE, Yermakov V: Fatal hemorrhagic pancreatitis following chlorothiazide administration in pregnancy. *Obstet Gynecol* 24:337, 1964

16. Schifrin BS, Spellacy WN, Little WA: Maternal death associated with excessive ingestion of a chlorothiazide diuretic. *Obstet Gynecol* 34:215, 1969

17. Alstatt LB: Transplacental hyponatremia in the newborn infant. *J Pediatr* 66:785–788, 1965

18. Merenstein GB, O'Laughlin EP, Plunkett DC: Effects of maternal thiazides on platelet counts of newborn infants. *J Pediatr* 76:766–767, 1970

19. Rodriguez SU, Leikin SL, Hiller MC: Neonatal thrombocytopenia associated with antepartum administration of thiazide drugs. *N Engl J Med* 270:881–884, 1964

20. Grollman A, Grollman EF: The teratogenic induction of hypertension. *J Clin Invest* 41:710–714, 1962

21. Garnet JD: Placental transfer of chlorothiazide. *Obstet Gynecol* 21:123–125, 1963

22. Anderson GG, Hanson TM: Chronic fetal bradycardia. *Obstet Gynecol* 44:896, 1974

23. Jerner K, Kutti J, Victorin LA: Platelet counts in mothers and their newborn infants with respect to antepartum administration of oral diuretics. *Acta Med Scand* 194:473–475, 1973

24. Andersen JB: The effect of diuretics in late pregnancy on the newborn infant. *Acta Paediatr Scand* 59:659–663, 1970

25. Riva E, Farina P, Togoni G, et al: Pharmacokinetics of furosemide in gestosis of pregnancy. *Eur J Clin Pharmacol* 14:361–366, 1978

26. Finnerty FA: Hypertension in pregnancy. *Clin Obstet Gynecol* 18:145–154, 1975

27. Berkowitz RL: Antihypertensive drugs in the pregnant patient. *Obstet Gynecol Surv* 35:191–204, 1980

28. Sanders JG, Gillis OS III, Marketo DL Jr, Gready TG Jr: Chlorthalidone in edema of pregnancy. *NY State J Med* 65:762–764, 1965

29. Tenvila L, Vartainen E: The effects and side effects of diuretics in the prophylaxis of toxemia of pregnancy. *Acta Obstet Gynecol Scand* 50:351–356, 1971

30. Stirrat GM: Prescribing problems in the second half of pregnancy and during lactation. *Obstet Gynecol Surv* 31:1–6, 1976

31. Desmond MM, Rogers SE, Lindley JE, et al: Management of toxemia of pregnancy with reserpine: II. The newborn infant. *Obstet Gynecol* 10:140, 1957

32. Budnich IS, Leikth S, Hoek LE: Effect in the newborn infant of reserpine administered antepartum. *Am J Dis Child* 90:286–289, 1955

33. Kincaid-Smith P, Bullen M, Mills J: Prolonged use of methyldopa in severe hypertension of pregnancy. *Br Med J* 1:275, 1966

34. Redmon CWG, Beitin LJ, Bonnar J, Ounsted MK: Fetal outcome in trial of antihypertensive treatment in pregnancy. *Lancet* 1:753–756, 1976

35. Redmon CWG, Beitin LJ, Bonnar J: Treatment of hypertension in pregnancy with methyldopa: Blood pressure control and side effects. *Br J Obstet Gynecol* 84:419–426, 1977

36. Leather HM, Humphreys DM, Baker P, Chadd MA: A controlled trial of hypotensive agents in hypertension in pregnancy. *Lancet* 2:488–490, 1968

37. Jones HMR, Cummings AJ: A study of the transfer of alpha-methyldopa to the human fetus and newborn infant. *Br J Clin Pharmacol* 6:432–434, 1964

38. Hans SF, Kopelman H: Methyldopa in the treatment of severe hypertension of pregnancy. *Br Med J* 1:736–739, 1964

39. Jones HMR, Cummings AJ, Sebchell KDR, Lawson AM: A study of the disposition of alpha-methyldopa in newborn infants following its administration to the mother for the treatment of hypertension during pregnancy. *Br J Clin Pharmacol* 8:833–840, 1979

40. Zuspan FP, O'Shaughnessy R: Chronic hypertension in pregnancy. In Pitkin RM, Zlatnik FL (eds): *Yearbook of Obstetrics-Gynecology.* Chicago, Yearbook Medical Publishers, 1979, pp 11–36

41. Zacharias FJ, Kowen KJ, Presst J, Vickers J, Wall BG: Propranolol in hypertension: A study of long-term therapy. *Am Heart J* 83:755–761, 1972

42. Joint National Committee on Detection, Evaluation, and Treatment of High Blood Pressure: Report. *JAMA* 237:255–262, 1977

43. Riddiough MA: Preventing, detecting, and managing adverse reactions of antihypertensive agents in the ambulant patient with hypertension. *Am J Hosp Pharm* 34:465–479, 1977

44. Sabom MB, Curry C, Wise DE: Propranolol therapy during pregnancy in a patient with idiopathic hypertrophic subaortic stenosis: Is it safe? *South Med J* 71:328–329, 1978

45. Levitan AA, Manion JC: Propranolol therapy during pregnancy and lactation. *Am J Cardiol* 32:247, 1973

46. Fiddler GI: Propranolol and pregnancy. *Lancet* 2:722–723, 1974

47. Read RL, Cheney CB, Fearon RE, et al: Propranolol throughout pregnancy: A case report. *Anesth Analg* 53:224–228, 1974

48. Cottrill CM, McAllister RG, Genes L, et al: Propranolol therapy during pregnancy, labor and delivery: Evidence for transplacental drug transfer and impaired neonatal drug disposition. *J Pediatr* 91:872–874, 1977

49. Tcherdekoff PH, Colliard M, Berrard E, et al: Propranolol in hypertension during pregnancy. *Br Med J* 2:670, 1978

50. Eliahou HE, Silverberg DE, Reisin E, et al: Propranolol for the treatment of hypertension during pregnancy. *Br J Obstet Gynecol* 85:431–436, 1978

51. Lieberman BA, Stirrat GM, Cohen SL, et al: The possible adverse effects of propranolol on the fetus in pregnancies complicated by severe hypertension. *Br J Obstet Gynecol* 85:678–683, 1978

52. Habib A, McCarthy JS: Effects on the neonate of propranolol administered during pregnancy. *J Pediatr* 91:808–811, 1977

53. Gladstone GE, Hordof A, Gersony WM: Propranolol administration during pregnancy: Effects on the fetus. *J Pediatr* 86:962–964, 1975

54. Barnes AB: Chronic propranolol during pregnancy. *J Reprod Med* 5:179–180, 1970

55. Tunstall ME: The effect of propranolol on the onset of breathing at birth. *Br J Anaesth* 51:792–793, 1969

56. Pruyn SC, Phelan JP, Buchanan GC: Long-term propranolol therapy in pregnancy: Maternal and fetal outcome. *Am J Obstet Gynecol* 135:485–489, 1979

57. Kelly JV: Drugs used in the management of toxemia of pregnancy. *Clin Obstet Gynecol* 20:395–420, 1977

58. Redmon CWG, Beilin LJ, Bonnar J, Ounsted MK: Fetal outcome in trial of antihypertensive treatment in pregnancy. *Lancet* 1:753–756, 1976

59. Redmon CWG, Beilin LJ, Bonner J: Treatment of hypertension in pregnancy with methyldopa: Blood pressure control and side effects. *Br J Obstet Gynecol* 84:419–426, 1977

60. Leather HM, Humphreys DM, Baker P, Chadd MA: A controlled trial of hypotensive agents in hypertension in pregnancy. *Lancet* 2:488–490, 1968

61. Vink GJ, Moodley J, Philpott RH: Effect of dihydralazine on the fetus in the treatment of maternal hypertension. *Obstet Gynecol* 55:519–522, 1980

62. Gordon II: Toxemia of pregnancy, in Hawkins DF (ed): *Obstetric Therapeutics.* Baltimore, Williams & Wilkins, 1974, pp. 274–276

63. Koch-Weser J: Diazoxide. *N Engl J Med* 294:1271–1274, 1976

64. Boulos BM, Davis LE, Almond CH, et al: Placental transfer of diazoxide and its hazardous effect on the newborn. *J Clin Pharmacol* 11:206–210, 1971

65. Morris JA, Arce JJ, Hamilton CJ, et al: The management of severe preeclampsia and eclampsia with intravenous diazoxide. *Obstet Gynecol* 49:675, 1977

66. Lewis PJ, Bulpitt CJ, Zuspan FP: A comparison of current British and American practice in the management of hypertension in pregnancy. *J Obstet Gynaecol Br Commonw* 1:78–82, 1980

67. Pritchard JA, Stone SR: Clinical and laboratory observations on eclampsia. *Am J Obstet Gynecol* 99:754, 1967

68. Zuspan FP, Ward MC: Improved fetal salvage in eclampsia. *Obstet Gynecol* 26:893, 1965

69. Widdowson EM, McCance RA, Spray CM: Chemical composition of human body. *Clin Sci* 10:113, 1951

70. Wacker WEC, Parisi AF: Magnesium metabolism. *N Engl J Med* 278:658, 1968

71. Wacker WEC, Parisi AF: Magnesium metabolism. *N Engl J Med* 278:712, 1968

72. Silver L, Robertson JS, Dahl LK: Magnesium turnover in human studied with Mg[28]. *J Clin Invest* 39:420, 1960

73. Chesley LE, Tepper I: Plasma levels of magnesium attained in magnesium sulfate therapy for preeclampsia and eclampsia. *Surg Clin North Am* April: 353–367, 1957

74. Eastman NJ: *Williams Obstetrics*. New York, Appleton-Century-Crofts, 1950

75. Pritchard JA: The use of the magnesium ion in the management of eclamptogenic toxemias. *Surg Gynecol Obstet* 100:131, 1955

76. Zusman FP, Ward MC: Improved fetal salvage in eclampsia. *Obstet Gynecol* 26:893, 1965

77. Zuspan FP: Problems encountered in the treatment of pregnancy induced hypertension. *Am J Obstet Gynecol* 131:591, 1978

78. Flowers CE Jr: Magnesium sulfate in obstetrics: A study of magnesium in plasma, urine and muscle. *Am J Obstet Gynecol* 91:763, 1965

79. Watehorn E, McCance RA: Inorganic constituents of cerebralspinal fluid. *Biochem J Lond* 26:54, 1932

80. Harbert G: Personal communication, 1980

81. Aldrete JA, Barnes DR, Aikawa JK: Does magnesium produce anesthesia? Anesthesia and analgesia *Curr Res* 47:428, 1968

82. Zuspan FP, Talledo OE, Rhodes K: Factors affecting delivery in eclampsia: The condition of the cervix and uterine activity. *Am J Obstet Gynecol* 100:672, 1968

83. Hall DG, McGaughey HS Jr, Corey EL, Thornton WN: The effects of magnesium therapy on the duration of labor. *Am J Obstet Gynecol* 78:27, 1959

84. Cruikshank D, Pitkin R: Personal communication, 1981

85. Stone SR, Pritchard JA: Effect of maternally administered magnesium sulfate on the neonate. *Obstet Gynecol* 35:574, 1970

86. Lipsitz PJ: The clinical and biochemical effects of excess magnesium in the newborn. *Pediatrics* 47:501, 1971

87. Kelly JV: Drugs used in the management of toxemia of pregnancy. *Clin Obstet Gynecol* 20:395–420, 1977

88. Limited usefulness of diuretics in pregnancy. *FDA Drug Bull*, Sept 1977

89. Gant NF, Madden JD, Siiteri PK, MacDonald PK: The metabolic clearance rate of dehydro-isoandrosterone sulfate: III. The effect of thiazide diuretics in normal and pre-eclamptic pregnancies. *Am J Obstet Gynecol* 123:159–163, 1975

90. Gant NF, Madden JD, Siiteri PK, MacDonald PK: The metabolic clearance rate of dehydro-isoandrosterone sulfate: IV. Acute effects of induced hypotension and natriuresis in normal and hypertensive pregnancies. *Am J Obstet Gynecol* 124:143–148, 1976

91. Alstatt LB: Transplacental hypoatremia in the newborn infant. *J Pediatr* 66:785–788, 1965

92. Rodriquez SU, Leikin SL, Hiller MC: Neonatal thrombocytopenia associated with antepartum administration of thiazide drugs. *N Engl J Med* 270:881–884, 1967

93. Grollman A, Grollman EF: The teratogenic induction of hypertension. *J Clin Invest* 41:710–714, 1962

94. Garnet JD: Placental transfer of chlorothiazide. *Obstet Gynecol* 21:123–125, 1963

95. Riva E, Farina P, Togoni G, et al: Pharmacokinetics of furosemide in gestosis of pregnancy. *Eur J Clin Pharmacol* 14:361–366, 1978

96. Welt SI, Crenshaw MC: Concurrent hypertension and pregnancy. *Clin Obstet Gynecol* 21:619–648, 1978

97. Finnerty FA: Hypertension in pregnancy. *Clin Obstet Gynecol* 18:145–154, 1975

98. Sanders JG, Gillis OS III, Marketto DL Jr, Gready TG Jr: Chlorthalidone in edema of pregnancy. *NY State J Med* 65:762–764, 1965

99. Tervila L, Vartainen E: The effects and side effects of diuretics in the prophylaxis of toxaemia of pregnancy. *Acta Obstet Gynecol Scand* 50:351–356, 1971

100. Stirrat GM: Prescribing problems in the second half of pregnancy and during lactation. *Obstet Gynecol Surv* 31:1–6, 1976

101. Budnick IS, Leikin S, Hoek LE: Effect in the newborn infant of reserpine administered antepartum. *Amer J Dis Child* 90:286–289, 1955

102. Kincaid-Smith P, Bullen M, Mills J: Prolonged use of methyldopa in severe hypertension of pregnancy. *Br Med J* 1:275, 1966

103. Redmon CWG, Beilin LJ, Bonnar J, Ounsted MK: Fetal outcome in trial of antihypertensive treatment in pregnancy. *Lancet* 1:753–756, 1976

104. Redmon CWG, Beilin LJ, Bonnar J: Treatment of hypertension in pregnancy with methyldopa: Blood pressure control and side effects. *Br J Obstet Gynecol* 84:419–426, 1977

105. Leather HM, Humphreys DM, Baker P, Chadd MA: A controlled trial of hypertensive agents in hypertension in pregnancy. *Lancet* 1:488–490, 1968

106. Jones HMR, Cummings AJ: A study of the transfer of alpha-methyldopa to the human fetus and newborn infant. *Br J Clin Pharmacol* 6:432–434, 1978

107. Sabom MB, Curry C, Wise DE: Propranolol

therapy during pregnancy in a patient with idiopathic hypertrophic subaortic stenosis: Is it safe? *South Med J* 71:328–329, 1978

108. Gladstone GR, Hordof A, Gersony WM: Propranolol administration during pregnancy: Effects on the fetus. *J Pediatr* 86:962–964, 1975

109. Pruyn SC, Phelan JP, Buchanan GC: Long-term propranolol therapy in pregnancy: Maternal and fetal outcome. *Am J Obstet Gynecol* 135:485–489, 1979

110. Soffronoff BC, Kaufman RM, Connaughton JF: Intravascular volume determination and fetal outcome in hypertensive diseases of pregnancy. *Am J Obstet Gynecol* 127:4–9, 1977

111. Vink GJ, Moodley J, Philpott RH: Effect of dihydralazine on the fetus in the treatment of maternal hypertension. *Obstet Gynecol* 55:519–522, 1980

112. Brogden RN, Heel RC, Speight TM, et al: Prazosin: A review of its pharmacological properties and therapeutic efficacy in hypertension. *Drugs* 14:163–197, 1977

7. Endocrine Disorders During Pregnancy

Robert M. McNulty   William F. Rayburn
Richard W. O'Shaughnessy

With improved medical, obstetrical, and neo-natal care, remarkable progress has been made in treating pregnancies complicated by endocrine disorders. Today, many more patients with endocrinopathies are able to conceive and successfully maintain their pregnancies as compared to several decades ago. Diabetes mellitus and thyroid diseases are the most common endocrine disorders seen during pregnancy, and these conditions, along with all endocrinopathies, require careful monitoring during the antepartum, intrapartum, and postpartum periods. Derangements in parathyroid, adrenal, or pituitary glands are quite uncommon but may be amenable to drug therapy. This chapter provides detailed information on the use of insulin, thyroid, and antithyroid medications during pregnancy. In addition, drugs proposed for treating other endocrine conditions are listed and briefly discussed.

DIABETES MELLITUS

The reported incidence of diabetes mellitus during pregnancy is approximately 2 to 3 percent.[1] Diabetes is due to faulty pancreatic activity with the subsequent disturbance of normal insulin release and carbohydrate metabolism, resulting in hyperglycemia, glycosuria and polyuria, and symptoms of thirst, hunger, and weakness.

An increased number of patients with diabetes are now becoming pregnant and seeking early prenatal care. A diabetic pregnancy is considered high risk, since maternal morbidity and unfavorable perinatal outcomes are significantly increased when compared to nondiabetic pregnancies. Maternal complications may arise from metabolic, vascular, and infectious derangements. Fetal complications include premature delivery, congenital anomalies, metabolic alterations, and respiratory distress. Specific fetal metabolic derangements include hypoglycemia, hypocalcemia, hypomagnesemia, hyperkalemia, and hyperbilirubinemia. Not all complications can be avoided completely during pregnancy, but maternal and fetal complications may be minimized with early screening and careful medical management.[1-6]

Pregnancy is associated with many physiologic alterations in metabolism which are hormonally influenced. Glucose intolerance may not become apparent until the onset of pregnancy. In order to adequately diagnose and treat diabetes during pregnancy, it is necessary to understand the metabolic changes of pregnancy and appreciate the pathophysiologic principles of diabetes.

Carbohydrate Metabolism During Pregnancy

During pregnancy, many energy-producing metabolic pathways are modified through hormonal influence. These modifications are necessary to provide essential nutrients to the fetus, while maintaining normal circulating glucose levels in the mother. As the primary regulator of carbohydrate metabolism, insulin at increased levels results in increased glycogen synthesis, protein synthesis, and the conversion of carbohydrates to fat with an increased uptake of free fatty acids. Basal levels of insulin are lower or unchanged in early pregnancy, but higher levels are secreted in the second half of pregnancy from the hyperplastic β cells in the islets of Langerhans.[7,8] Insulin secretion is noted to increase rapidly after eating during pregnancy and reaches levels which are approximately twice those that would be expected in a nonpregnant patient (Fig. 7-1).

Despite this hyperinsulinemic state during the second half of pregnancy, glucose tolerance is impaired. Compared to nonpregnant values, basal glucose values after an overnight fast are lower in the first trimester and decrease progressively during gestation. This tendency toward fasting hypoglycemia, termed as "accelerated starvation" by Freinkel, is related to the following conditions: (1) increasing insulin levels, (2) increasing placental and fetal uptake of glucose, (3) subnormal hepatic production of glucose, and (4) less renal reabsorption of glucose at all levels of the filtered load.[9] After an oral glucose challenge, peak values of glucose are higher and occur later when compared to values in the early or non-

TABLE 7-1 GTT VALUES DURING PREGNANCY*

	Whole Blood (mg/100 ml)	Serum (mg/100 ml)
Fasting (hr)	≤ 90	≤105
1	165	190
2	145	165
3	125	145

* 100-gm glucose challenge.

pregnant state (Fig. 7-1). As pregnancy continues, serum glucose levels show decreasing fasting levels, increasing 1-hour levels, and essentially unchanged 2-hour levels after a glucose challenge. Glucose tolerance test (GTT) standards must be adjusted upward to correct for this physiologic response. The standards of O'Sullivan and Mahan for the 3-hour, 100-gm oral test have been accepted widely and are listed in Table 7-1.[10]

Postprandial glucose intolerance is a diabetogenic phenomenon explained by the insulin-antagonistic effects of cortisol, progesterone, and placental lactogen (hPL). Insulin-sensitive tissues are exposed to increasing levels of prolactin, which has been suggested as

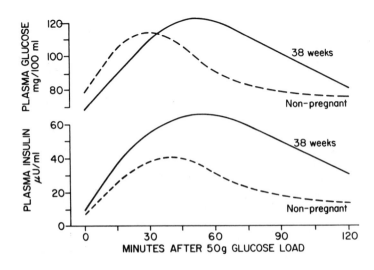

Figure 7-1. Relationship between circulating glucose and insulin levels during late pregnancy and the nonpregnant state. *(From Lind T: Changes in carbohydrate metabolism during pregnancy. Clin Obstet Gynecol 2:401, 1975, with permission.)*

a possible insulin antagonist at target cell receptor sites, as well as increasing concentrations of free cortisol during pregnancy. The role of catecholamines in the metabolic changes of pregnancy is uncertain. Although the secretion of glucagon from the pancreas increases during pregnancy, its counterinsulin effects are offset by the relatively increased secretion of insulin.[11] In addition, the placenta is capable of synthesizing and secreting increasing levels of progesterone and hPL which are antagonists to insulin at the cellular level.

The elimination of endogenous and exogenous insulin is unchanged during pregnancy. Although influenced by the increased extracellular volume, placental metabolism, and lowered renal clearance, the half-life of insulin is considered to be the same in pregnancy as in nonpregnant controls or in women in the late puerperium.[12,13]

The fetus and placenta constantly drain nutrients such as glucose and amino acids from the mother. Although the placenta is impermeable to maternal or fetal insulin, glucose is known to cross the placenta by facilitated diffusion. There is a direct relationship between glucose intolerance in the mother and glucose utilization by the fetus and neonate.[14] The worse the maternal tolerance, the more rapidly glucose is assimilated by the fetus. Although fetal insulin and glucagon concentrations within the pancreas are greater than in

the adult as early as the first trimester, secretory mechanisms are immature.[15] Carbohydrate metabolism is apparently independent of these hormones until the third trimester, when insulin takes over the dominant role (Fig. 7-2). An elevated maternal blood glucose level causes fetal hyperglycemia, and whether the fetus is protected from severe hyperglycemia is presently unclear.[16] Fetal hyperinsulinemia with hyperplasia of the islets of Langerhans may occur in response to high fetal glucose concentrations secondary to persistent maternal hyperglycemia. With prolonged hyperglycemia and resultant hyperinsulinemia, macrosomia and delayed lung maturation are possible. Fetal macrosomia results from the insulin-induced deposition of fat and glycogen. Delayed fetal lung maturity can occur from the antagonism of insulin to the maturing effects of cortisol, or from a decrease in the precursors for phospholipid synthesis.

Guidelines for Therapy

Most pregnant patients tolerate well increased demands on carbohydrate metabolism. However, when metabolic requirements at the cellular level are not met by an adequate secretion of insulin, maternal hyperglycemia may persist. A positive relationship has been shown between maternal hyperglycemia with fluctuating maternal glucose levels and subsequent perinatal morbidity and mortality. The

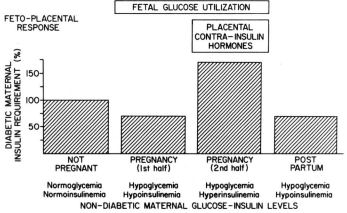

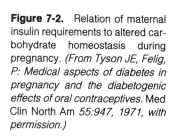

Figure 7-2. Relation of maternal insulin requirements to altered carbohydrate homeostasis during pregnancy. *(From Tyson JE, Felig, P: Medical aspects of diabetes in pregnancy and the diabetogenic effects of oral contraceptives.* Med Clin North Am *55:947, 1971, with permission.)*

goal of diabetic management during pregnancy is to control serum glucose values (100 to 140 mg/dl) while treating any medical complications and carefully planning the delivery. [17–19] Strict control of blood glucose levels requires the periodic sampling of urine and blood for glucose determination, a proper diet, and the administration of insulin if necessary.

An adequate diet may be sufficient to control glucose intolerance. Most approved diabetic diets involve a daily intake of 30 to 35 kcal/kg of ideal body weight. The calories are to be distributed more in favor of the carbohydrates (45 percent carbohydrate, 30 to 35 percent fat, 20 to 25 percent protein) and to be taken evenly throughout the day (20 percent at breakfast, 30 percent at lunch, 35 percent at dinner, and 15 percent as a late snack). Adjustments in this schedule are dependent on individual patient desires and corresponding glucose values. Prolonged periods of fasting are to be avoided.

Oral hypoglycemic agents (chlorpropamide, talozamide, tolbutamide, acetohexamide) are contraindicated during pregnancy. Although maternal glucose levels may be decreased with these agents, they can cross the placenta to stimulate the fetal pancreas. No teratogenic effect on the major organs has been reported in human studies using oral hypoglycemic agents, but pancreatic hyperplasia and fetal hyperinsulinemia can result from persistent sulfonylurea-agent stimulation. Neonatal macrosomia and profound hypoglycemia may be apparent.[20] These drugs are to be discontinued when pregnancy is being planned or immediately after pregnancy is confirmed.

Insulin should be continued in all insulin-dependent diabetics during pregnancy. In addition, many patients who have abnormally high glucose values on screening tests will require insulin, despite an initial attempt at diet control. It is usually recommended that the patient be admitted to the hospital for instruction on the management of her condition, to obtain the appropriate baseline tests and consultations, and either to begin or adjust insulin therapy according to serum glucose levels.

Insulin

Insulin is a protein composed of two chains of amino acids linked by two disulfide bridges. It acts to lower serum glucose levels by inhibiting glucose production and by promoting the peripheral utilization of glucose in the liver and peripheral tissues. At low concentrations, the hypoglycemic effect from insulin is primarily from a decrease in either glycogenolysis and/or gluconeogenesis within the liver. At higher physiologic concentrations, (100 mU/liter or more), insulin also contributes to the peripheral utilization of glucose to decrease circulating glucose concentrations. In normal subjects, endogenous insulin probably acts primarily in the liver to block glucose production, while peripheral concentrations of insulin remain low. In insulin-dependent diabetics, however, portal vein concentrations of insulin are equal to or lower than peripheral concentrations of insulin. Because of this relative increase in peripheral insulin concentration, glucose utilization contributes more to the lowering of serum glucose.

The actions of insulin are many. Insulin is thought to bind to specific receptors on membranes of skeletal muscle and adipose cells to facilitate the transmembranous passage of glucose. Glucose metabolism for the production of energy in skeletal muscle and for triglyceride synthesis in adipose tissue is also stimulated by insulin. Insulin favors protein synthesis, nucleic acid (DNA, RNA) synthesis, glycolysis, and glycogenesis, and it inhibits glycogenolysis, gluconeogenesis, lipolysis, and proteolysis.

Following injection, insulin is rapidly degraded in the peripheral tissues by the cleavage of the disulfide bridges by the enzyme insulinase, which is found in all tissues, especially the liver and kidney. Protease enzymes further degrade the two insulin chains into individual amino acids. Placental insulinase can also degrade insulin to prevent maternal insulin from reaching the fetal circulation.[21] Its effect on insulin resistance during pregnancy is probably minimal.

Preparations and Routes of Administration. Insulin is digested after oral intake, so subcutaneous or intravenous administration is necessary. The properties of the various insulin preparations (onset of action, duration of action) serve only as a guide, and insulin regimens must be adjusted according to individual responses after an adequate period of surveillance. Since circulating insulin is degraded rapidly, the duration of action is dependent on absorption from the injection site. The available preparations are grouped as being either fast acting, intermediate acting, or long acting (Table 7-2). Only fast acting (regular, Semilente insulin) and intermediate acting (NPH, Lente) preparations are used during pregnancy. Long acting preparations are not used during pregnancy because of their variable onsets of action and prolonged duration.

Recent progress in purification of insulin products has resulted from gel-filtration chro-matography and ion-exchange chromatography techniques. As a result, concentrations of contaminants such as proinsulin, glucagon, somatostatin, and pancreatic polypeptides are decreased. Enhanced purification has led to a decreased risk of lipodystrophy, antibody formation, and local or systemic allergic reactions. In addition, dosage requirements of insulin may decrease when changing to a more purified insulin product. In the future, all commercially available insulin will be in the form of purified preparations.

The various insulin products may be safely stored for long periods. Cost differences between the various fast-acting and intermediate-acting preparations are minimal.

Dosing. A rigid control of serum glucose levels (< 115 mg/dl) and the avoidance of keto-acidosis are desired throughout pregnancy,[5,6,22-25] although this may be difficult to obtain.[26] The dosing of insulin is dependent on periodic glucose determinations using serum glucose determinations by venipuncture

TABLE 7-2   PROPERTIES OF VARIOUS INSULIN PREPARATIONS

Type	Preparation	Route	Onset (hr)	Peak (hr)	Duration (hr)	Compatible Mixed with:
Fast acting	Regular	SQ	½–1	2–6	5–8	All preparations
		IM	¼–½	1–3	2–4	
		IV	$\frac{1}{12}$	$\frac{1}{12}$	¼	
	Prompt zinc (semilente)	SQ	½–1	3–9	12–16	Lente
Intermediate acting	Isophane (NPH)	SQ	1–2	7–12	24–30	Regular insulin
	Insulin zinc suspension (lente)	SQ	1–4	7–12	24–30	Regular, semilente
	Globin insulin	SQ	1–4	6–16	16–24	—
Long acting	Protamine zinc	SQ	1–8	12–24	30–36	Regular
	Extended insulin zinc, suspension (ultralente)	SQ	4–8	10–30	34–46	Regular, semilente
Mixtures	Regular 30 percent Isophane 70 percent	SQ	See individual components			—

or capillary glucose determinations by finger stick using an optical reflectometer (Dextrostix-Eyetone) or enzymatic method (Chemstip bG).[27] The latter method offers the advantage of patient participation in a relatively inexpensive manner at home. Urine glucose determinations are less reliable and predictable, since the renal threshold for glucose is decreased during pregnancy.

Exogenous insulin requirements may either decrease or remain unchanged during the first half of pregnancy, while requirements should increase during the latter half when insulin-antagonistic effects become more apparent. Caloric intake and distribution and the mother's activity must be considered when insulin dosing regimens are changed.

After gestational-onset diabetes is confirmed by an abnormal GTT, insulin is started when diet alone has failed to properly regulate glucose levels. A brief course of "sliding scale" regular insulin may be necessary to correct any high glucose levels, that is, for 150 to 200 mg/100 ml, give 2 to 5 units; for 200 to 250 mg/100 ml, give 5 to 10 units; for 250 to 300 mg/100 ml, give 10 to 15 units. Intermediate-acting insulin (NPH, Lente) is then begun in low doses (5 to 10 units) each morning. Although some patients may be well controlled with a single early morning dose of NPH or Lente, most are better controlled with both early morning (two-thirds total daily dose) and early evening doses (one-third total daily doses) before meals. This "split-dose" regimen may result in improved glucose control throughout a 24-hour period without an increased risk of hypoglycemia. When converting a patient from one injection to two injections per day, less total daily insulin may be required, resulting in a decreased risk of significant hypoglycemia, particularly in the late afternoon. An additional advantage to the split-dose regimen is that the time of the evening meal can be varied without risk of hypoglycemia. The success of any insulin regimen is dependent upon adherence to a prescribed diet.

A pregestational, insulin-dependent diabetic will require insulin during pregnancy. Split-dose insulin regimens and the mixing of regular with NPH insulin are usually necessary. The addition of regular insulin with the NPH insulin is often used to control the rapid increase in glucose levels after a meal. The mixing of regular with NPH insulin in a syringe does not appreciably alter their respective onsets and durations of action. Recently, pumps have been used to continuously administer regular insulin by SC and IV routes, but their effectiveness during the antepartum period has not been well studied.[28,29,30]

Diabetic keto-acidosis is fortunately uncommon in closely regulated patients but may result from profound hyperglycemia and ketosis. Dehydration, acidosis, and potassium depletion are particular concerns. Along with the appropriate replacement of fluids and electrolytes and the infusion of bicarbonate, insulin administration is necessary. An initial 50 unit IV bolus of regular insulin is immediately followed by a 10 to 50 unit subcutaneous dose. The desired goal is a serum glucose level of less than 300 mg/100ml with no urinary ketone bodies. Should there be little or no decline in serum glucose values, a double dose of IV regular insulin (up to 200 units or more) may be necessary within the next two hours. Once satisfactory control is achieved, only subcutaneous regular insulin is required using a sliding scale dose regimen.

The management of the diabetic during the intrapartum period is similar to the diabetic about to undergo surgery. Frequent monitoring of the blood glucose level by finger stick or venipuncture is essential, since strict glucose control (80 to 140 mg/dl) is necessary to avoid ketoacidosis from marked hyperglycemia or marked hypoglycemia.[31]

Glucose control during labor and delivery is achieved by balancing the intravenous infusion of dextrose solutions with intermittent or continuous insulin therapy. Regular insulin may be given intermittently by subcutaneous administration every 4 hours, depending on the capillary or venous glucose values. One advantage of this method is the variability and delay in absorption of insulin. Continuous intravenous infusion of regular insulin (50 units regular insulin/500 ml of normal saline or 5 percent dextrose in water) is an alternate method, wherein the onset of action is more rapid and the duration of action is shorter.[30] Hypoglycemia, detected from blood determinations or maternal complaints of nausea, weakness, or lightheadedness, can be reversed quickly by stopping the insulin infusion and maintaining a dextrose infusion. Since insulin infusion must be carefully titrated, a constant infusion pump should be used, beginning at 0.5 to 1 unit "rations" of regular insulin per hour.

Following delivery of the placenta, insulin requirements drop dramatically for 24 to 72 hours, then rise to approximately two-thirds of the normal pre-pregnancy dose. Insulin requirements should be expected to return to pre-pregnancy requirements during the next 6 weeks. Breastfeeding usually decreases insulin requirements despite the increase in necessary caloric intake. Regular insulin is usually administered on a sliding scale every 6 hours, with the dose being dependent on the glucose concentration.

Precautions. Insulin administered in excess can cause iatrogenic hypoglycemia with a resultant stimulation in endogenous catecholamines, cortisol, glucagon, and growth hormone secretion to raise circulating glucose levels. This rebound hyperglycemic effect (Somogyi phenomenon) usually develops in the morning and may lead to the erroneous administration of more insulin to compound the problem. It is diagnosed by the demonstration of wide fluctuations in serum glucose levels which are unrelated to food intake.

Antibodies to insulin are rarely responsible for glucose intolerance. Insulin resistance is apparent when exogenous insulin demand exceeds 200 units per day and anti-insulin antibodies of IgG type exceed 30 mU/ml.[31] Therapy for this condition usually requires a change in insulin to a monospecies (pork) preparation and may require glucocorticoids in large doses (prednisone 80 mg/day) or a change to Lente, which does not contain protamine.

When insulin is infused intravenously, it may adhere to the walls of glass or plastic containers and tubing to reduce the actual amount of insulin administered to the patient. Reports of 10 to 80 percent of insulin adhering to the delivery system make it difficult to predict the actual dose being infused, and it is recommended that the tubing and container be primed with an insulin solution.[32]

Local allergic reactions usually occur within 1 month after initiation of insulin treatment and involve edema, induration, and pruritis. Treatment is usually unnecessary, since insulin is destroyed rapidly in the tissues; however, a change in preparation may be necessary and could require a pure pork preparation. Signs of systemic reactions are rare but include anaphylaxis and generalized urticaria. Therapy requires supportive care.

Lipoatrophy with a loss of subcutaneous fat may be minimized by using the purified pork preparation and rotating the sites of injection. Lipohypertrophy will disappear gradually by avoiding the same injection site.

Many factors should be considered when insulin requirements are increased or decreased during pregnancy. Increased insulin requirements may result from increasing pregnancy demands, acute infection, drugs (thyroid supplementation, glucocorticoids, diuretics), and certain endocrine disorders (hyperthyroidism, hyperadrenocorticism, hyperparathyroidism). Decreased insulin requirements may result from a degenerating placenta or utero-placental insufficiency, inactivity, renal disease, inadequate caloric intake, or certain endocrine disorders (hypothyroidism, hypoadrenocorticism). Wide fluctuations in glucose levels may result from errors in management (diet, exercise, insulin administration, glucose determinations) or emotional disturbances.

HYPERTHYROIDISM

Changes in thyroid metabolism during pregnancy relate to increased circulating levels of steroid hormones. The synthesis and release of carrier proteins by the liver are increased during pregnancy from estrogen stimulation. In particular, the serum concentration of thyroid-binding globulin (TBG) increases gradually to twice the nonpregnant value and provides an increased number of sites for thyroid hormone-binding. Although concentrations of total thyroxine (T_4) and tri-iodothyronine (T_3) are increased as early as the second trimester, circulating levels of free T_3 and T_4 are not increased throughout pregnancy because of their 99 percent protein-binding property. The measurement of resin T_3 uptake (RT_3U) is inversely proportional to the number of binding sites on TBG and is therefore found to be decreased during pregnancy. The pituitary glycoprotein required for thyroid stimulation, TSH, is unchanged during pregnancy. Placental transfer is negligible for T_4 and TSH and is poor for T_3.

Fetal thyroid function has been described as early as the end of the first trimester, with circulating levels of T_4 and TBG increasing gradually during the second half of pregnancy.[33] Production of T_3 is primarily by peripheral conversion from T_4 and increases gradually after 30 weeks of fetal life. With the development of neuroendocrine control during the latter half of pregnancy, the negative feedback by thyroid hormones on the fetal pituitary gland is found to eventually mature.

Hyperthyroidism is the second most common endocrine disorder during pregnancy. Graves' disease is the most common form and is characterized by a diffuse goiter. Toxic nodular goiter and thyroid hyperfunction from excess pituitary TSH secretion are very uncommon. A search for trophoblastic disease (hydatidiform mole, choriocarcinoma) is necessary when biochemical signs of hyperthyroidism are apparent during pregnancy. The signs and symptoms of thyroid hyperfunction include tachycardia, weakness, increased appetite, and shortness of breath and may be difficult to distinguish from the usual patient complaints during pregnancy.

Therapy is necessary to avoid serious maternal and fetal complications. Many patients may become more symptomatic and may de-velop thyrotoxicosis, which is a medical emergency, especially during labor and delivery. Fetal goiter and hyperthyroidism may occur when stimulated by LATS, a long-acting thyroid stimulator of IgG type which crosses the placenta from the maternal circulation. If maternal hyperthyroidism is untreated, stillbirth rates have been reported to increase to 8 to 15 percent, and premature delivery is considered to be increased to 11 to 25 percent.[34,35]

Guidelines for Therapy

Treatment of hyperthyroidism in the nonpregnant state includes radioactive iodine, medical therapy, and surgical correction. Radioiodine (^{131}I) in therapeutic doses is contraindicated during pregnancy because of its damaging effect in the fetal thyroid after placental transfer. Hypothyroidism in the fetus is also possible, even with a brief course of radioactive iodide.

Subtotal thyroidectomy is reserved for patients who fail on medical management because of poor compliance, severe disease, or need for excessive antithyroid medication. Postoperative complications may include hypothyroidism, hypoparathyroidism, airway obstruction, recurrent laryngeal nerve paralysis, and infection.

Medical therapy of hyperthyroidism is the primary form of treatment during pregnancy. Prescribed medications are intended to decrease the amount of circulating thyroid hormones (antithyroid drugs) and to relieve severely bothersome maternal symptoms (β-adrenergic blocking agents).

Antithyroid Drugs

Two principal antithyroid preparations have been used to inhibit excess hormone production within the thyroid gland. Propylthiouracil (PTU) and methimazole (Tapazole) are thiourea derivatives which prevent the iodination of tyrosine by inhibiting the oxidation of iodide to iodine (Figure 7-3). Within the first 24 to 48 hours of therapy, propylthiouracil may also produce a 25 to 40 percent reduction in the peripheral conversion of T_4 to T_3 (which is three to four times more metabolically active than T_4).[36]

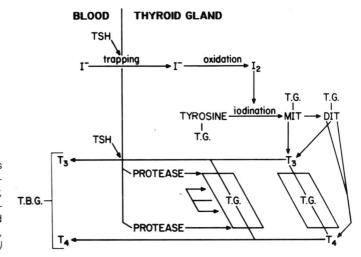

BLOOD | **THYROID GLAND**

Figure 7-3. Synthetic pathways for hormone production in the thyroid. *(From Gibson M, Tulchinsky, D: The maternal thyroid in Tulchinsky D, Ryan K (eds):* Maternal and Fetal Endocrinology, *Philadelphia, Saunders, 1980, with permission.)*

Oral absorption is rapid, and the duration of action is moderately short (2 to 3 hours for PTU). The drugs and their metabolites are eliminated primarily via the kidneys. The placenta is permeable to each drug, but PTU is preferred over methimazole during pregnancy because transfer is less rapid.

Propylthiouracil. Propylthiouracil is available as 50-mg tablets which are usually prescribed in 100- to 400-mg daily doses (100 mg each day or every 6 hours). Because of the relatively short duration of action, frequent use each day may be necessary. The response of hyperthyroidism to therapy is governed by the long time needed to deplete thyroid stores which may persist until 3 to 6 weeks after the beginning of therapy. The adjustment in daily dosage is begun after this initial period and is dependent on relief of patient symptoms and circulating levels of free T_4. To avoid hypothyroidism and to minimize the effective dose necessary, serum-free T_4 levels should be maintained within an upper normal or slightly elevated range during pregnancy. Tapering the dose and even discontinuing the drug are possible during pregnancy. Daily doses exceeding 300 mg should be avoided because of potential fetal effects.

Side effects in the mother from PTU are uncommon and are usually well tolerated. Agranulocytosis is reported to occur in 1 in 500 cases, so a leukocyte count should be determined periodically.[37] Allergic reactions or a mild, sometimes purpuric rash may resolve spontaneously without discontinuing the drug. Arthralgias, especially of the hands and wrist, are very uncommon.

Because of placental transfer, antithyroid substances may impair fetal thyroid function and cause an increase in fetal TSH levels. Goiter formation has been reported in up to 10 percent of all infants and is dependent on the dose and duration of in utero exposure. Neonatal hypothyroidism is short-lived, lasting only a few days.[38] The minimum effective dose to the mother is therefore recommended. However, the risks to the fetus do not appear to be reduced with low-dose thyroid supplementation to the mother.[39]

No other anomaly has been consistently found with antithyroid use, and the perinatal outcome is usually favorable in 70 to 95 percent of the pregnancies.[34,40] In a study involving 28 children with in utero exposure to antithyroid drugs, Burrow found that long-term intellectual development was not impaired when compared to their siblings.[41] If ablative doses of radioactive iodine are inadvertently given during early pregnancy, PTU and saturated solutions of potassium iodine have been given to blunt the fetal uptake of the radioactive isotope.

Breastfeeding while ingesting PTU is not recommended, even though concentrations are less in breast milk than maternal serum.

Methimazole. Methimazole offers no advantage over PTU during pregnancy and may have more adverse effects to the fetus. In comparable doses, methimazole lacks the ability to inhibit peripheral monodeiodination of T_4 to T_3. It is metabolized more slowly and transferred more rapidly across the placenta than PTU. A maldevelopment of the fetal scalp, aplasia cutis, has also been described with methimazole use.[43]

β-Adrenergic Blocking Agents

Tachycardia, tremors, hyperreflexia, and palpitations are frequent findings in hyperthyroidism which relate to enhanced sympathomimetic activity and increased responsiveness to β-adrenergic stimulation (see Chap. 8). β-Adrenergic blocking agents are used when these findings are severe. Clinical experience with β-blocking agents has been greatest with propranolol hydrochloride (Inderal). Propranolol may also inhibit the peripheral conversion of T_4 to T_3, thus decreasing the elevated circulating levels of the more metabolically active thyroid hormones.

Propranolol is a naphthyloxy propanolamine derivative which is absorbed well after any route of administration. Following absorption from the gastrointestinal tract, propranolol is metabolized in the liver. Only a fraction of the original drug remains in the circulation and at least eight metabolites have been detected in the urine. Oral doses of 10 to 30 mg three or four times daily are usually adequate for symptomatic relief. An IV dose of 1 to 3 mg may be given slowly, either during thyrotoxicosis or to avoid thyrotoxicosis before or during an operation. Prolonged use of propranolol is to be avoided, and the dose should be titrated to maintain a maternal pulse of 80 beats/minute and to control tremors and nervousness.

Maternal side effects from propranolol use in otherwise healthy women are uncommon, and are dose-dependent. Toxic effects may be seen in a variety of tissues but most commonly in the heart. Bradycardia, hypotension, and congestive failure may result from the decreased inotropic, chronotropic, and metabolic effects. These adverse effects are more apparent if a preexisting heart disorder is present. In select cases, propranolol has been used as an antihypertensive agent (see Chap. 6), but hypotension is an undesired effect in treating symptoms of hyperthyroidism. Since bronchial spasm is possible, propranolol should be given with caution in any patient with a history of asthma. Propranolol may compete with β_2-adrenergic agents used to inhibit premature labor (see Chap. 8) and may increase uterine muscle tone.

Propranolol does cross the placenta, but no congenital anomalies have been linked with its use. The increased incidence of growth-retarded fetuses may be attributable to the underlying medical condition. A mild bradycardia of the fetal heart rate may be observed during the antepartum and intrapartum periods.[44] Propanolol concentrations in the neonate are reported to be 20 percent of the maternal concentrations. Although neonatal glucose, calcium, and electrolyte balance are usually not impaired, hypoglycemia should be suspected. Furthermore, transient neonatal respiratory depression has been associated with intravenous propranolol use prior to anesthesia for cesarean section.[45]

HYPOTHYROIDISM

Thyroid hypofunction is much less common than hyperthyroidism in reproductive-age women. It is most apparent following subtotal thyroidectomy; hypothyroidism from iodine deficiency is very unusual. Symptoms of hypothyroidism (myxedema) include increased fatigability, cold intolerance, hyporeflexia, and lethargy. Many patient complaints during pregnancy may overlap with these classical symptoms. Documented hypothyroidism by low free-T_4 levels has been reported to be associated with an increased risk of infertility and an unfavorable perinatal outcome.[46] Whether an impaired intellectual development of the offspring or an increased incidence of spontaneous abortion is more common in hypothyroid pregnant patients remains controversial.[46,47] It is recommended that thyroid supplementation be continued during pregnancy only if laboratory evidence exists and patient symptoms persist.

Thyroid Supplements

Thyroid preparations are used to supplement low serum concentrations of free thyroid hormones. The metabolic rate is increased by several mechanisms to enhance energy-requiring oxidation processes in tissues and to stimulate protein synthesis. Table 7-3 lists thyroid supplements currently available. All products are taken orally and are inexpensive. The two most commonly used preparations, thyroid extract and synthetic levothyroxine sodium, contain thyroxine (T_4). In addition, thyroid extract contains levotriiodothyronine (T_3) in variable concentrations.

Levothyroxine is the preferred drug during pregnancy, as patients seem to tolerate this therapy better than thyroid extract. There are many advantages of ingesting a thyroid supplement with T_4 alone, instead of a combination T_3:T_4 preparation. Thyroxine mimics normal thyroid physiology more closely, and 80 percent of T_3 produced is by peripheral monodeiodination from T_4.[48,49] Serum T_3 levels with combination preparations may fluctuate more, and nonphysiologic concentrations of T_3 are more common.

Fifty to eighty percent of an oral dose of levothyroxine is absorbed. Absorption is decreased by meals, intestinal flora, plasma protein in the gut, and other substances to which thyroxine may bind. Levothyroxine is 99 percent bound to plasma proteins (thyroid-binding globulin, thyroid-binding prealbumin, albumin). Each day, approximately 85 percent of T_4 is peripherally converted to T_3 at many sites, including the liver and kidney. Thyrox-

TABLE 7-3 THYROID SUPPLEMENTATION PREPARATIONS

Preparation	Trade Name	Equivalent Dose	T_3 Content	T_4 Content	Comments
Thyroid extract	Various	60 mg	Variable	Variable	Reputable company standardizes thyroid content. Cheapest, but all products inexpensive. Inactive iodinated protein contamination. Variable potency.
Thyroglobulin extract	Proloid	60 mg	Variable	Variable	Inactive iodinated protein removed. Variable potency.
Liotrix	Thyrolar Euthyroid	# 1 tablet # 1 tablet	12.5 mcg 15 mcg	50 mcg 60 mcg	No advantage. Nonphysiologic replacement.
Levothyroxine	Synthroid Letter Levoid	0.05–0.1 mg	0	100 mcg	Converted to thyronine peripherally. Most physiologic replacement. Long half-life duration.
Liothyronine	Cytomel	25 mcg	25 mcg	0	Absorption and onset rapid. Hormone content standardized. Physiologic fluctations with thyrotoxic levels. Expensive. Drug of choice in emergency, such as myxedema coma.

ine may also be monodeiodinated to form reverse thyronine (RT$_3$) under such conditions as surgical stress, renal failure, acute or chronic starvation, cirrhosis, or chronic illness. Reverse T$_3$ is biologically inactive, and patients may remain clinically euthyroid despite low T$_3$ levels. Thyroxine may also be conjugated in the liver and undergo recirculation in the enterohepatic pathways.

Thyroid supplements do not pass the placental barrier in any appreciable amounts and should have no effect on the autonomous fetal thyroid-pituitary function. Direct administration of levothryroxine into the fetal buttock by the transabdominal route has led to the successful treatment of one fetus thought to be hypothyroid.[50] The only major complication with thyroxine therapy is overdosage, and signs of hyperthyroidism may range from subclinical to overt. Cardiovascular disease is less

likely to be exacerbated by thyroxine than by thyroid hormone combinations. The response to thyroid supplementation should therefore be determined by the standard thyroid tests.

The dosage of levothyroxine should be such that the serum thyroxine and free thyroxine index are in the upper limits of normal, and TSH is less than 10 mUnits/ml. The pregnant hypothyroid patient may require a higher dose of thyroxine, up to 0.4 mg/day.

OTHER ENDOCRINE DISORDERS

Pregnancies complicated by disorders of the parathyroid, pituitary, or adrenal gland are rare. Medical treatment should be continued during pregnancy, using either the same or lesser doses unless the condition worsens. Disorders involving hormone deficiency or hy-

TABLE 7-4   DRUGS USED IN THE MANAGEMENT OF ENDOCRINE DISORDERS DURING PREGNANCY

Gland	Disorder	Drug	Sources
Pancreas	Insulinoma	Corticosteroids	51
	Diabetes mellitus	Insulin, glucagon	
Parathyroid	Hypoparathyroidism	Calcium salts	52–54
		Vitamin D	
		Calcitriol	
		Phosphate-binding antacids	
	Hyperparathyroidism	Oral phosphates	55, 56
Thyroid	Hyperthyroid	Propylthiouracil	
	Hypothyroid	Levothyroxine	
Pituitary	Hypophysectomy	Vasopressin	58
	and	Levothyroxine	57, 58
	Sheehan's syndrome	Corticosteroids	57
		Mineralocorticoids	
		Estrogen-progestin	
		Human menopausal gonadotropin	
		Human chorionic gonadotropin	
	Diabetes insipidus	Vasopressin	59
		Diuretics (i.e., ethacrynic acid)	
	Pituitary tumors	Bromocriptine	60–65
		Corticosteroids	
Adrenal	Addison's disease	Corticosteroids	66–68
		Mineralocorticoids	
	Cushing's syndrome	None	69–71

pofunctional states (hypoparathyroid, hypophysectomy, diabetes insipidus, Addison's disease) require appropriate hormone replacement. Surgery is often the treatment of choice when glandular hyperfunction (Cushing's syndrome, hyperparathyroid, pituitary tumor, insulinoma) exists. Hormonal replacement therapy may be necessary postoperatively. Because of the sparsity of reported cases and the possible adverse fetal effects from drug use, controlled clinical trials comparing different drug regimens are lacking. Literature on the medical management of these rare conditions is therefore limited. Medications used to treat specific endocrinopathies and appropriate references for further reading are listed in Table 7-4.

REFERENCES

1. Beard RW, Oakley NW: The fetus of the diabetic, in Beard RW, Nathanietz PW (eds): *Fetal Physiology and Medicine.* London, Saunders, 1976, p 137
2. White P: Diabetes in pregnancy, in Loslen EP (ed): *The Treatment of Diabetes Mellitus,* Philadelphia, Lea and Febiger, 1928, p 861
3. Hagbard L: Pregnancy and diabetes mellitus. *Acta Obstet Gynecol Scand* 35(suppl 1): Chap 4, 1956
4. Cornblath M, Schwartz R: Infant of the diabetic mother, in Cornblath M, Schwartz R (eds): *Disorders of Carbohydrate Metabolism in Infancy,* Philadelphia, Saunders, 1976, p 115
5. Pedersen J, Pedersen L, Andersen B: Assessors of fetal perinatal mortality in diabetic pregnancy. *Diabetes* 23:302, 1974
6. Raversi GD, Garguilo M, Nicolini U, et al: A new approach to the treatment of diabetic pregnant women: Report of 479 cases seen from 1963 to 1975. *Am J Obstet Gynecol* 135:567, 1979
7. Aerts L, Assche, FA: Ultrastructural changes of the endocrine pancreas in pregnant rats. *Diabetologia* 11:284, 1975
8. Van Assche FA, Hoeb JJ, Jack PM: The endocrine pancreas of the pregnant mother, fetus, and newborn, in Beard RW, Nathanietz PW (eds): *Fetal Physiology and Medicine.* Philadelphia, Saunders, 1976, pp 121–136
9. Freinkel N, Metzger BE, Nitzan M, et al: "Accelerated starvation" and mechanisms for the conservation of maternal nitrogen during pregnancy. *Isr J Med Sci* 8:426, 1972
10. O'Sullivan JB, Mahan CM: Criteria for the oral glucose tolerance test in pregnancy. *Diabetes* 13:278, 1964
11. Kitzmiller JL: The endocrine pancreas and maternal metabolism, in Tulchinsky D, Ryan KJ (eds): *Maternal-Fetal Endocrinology.* Philadelphia, Saunders, 1980, p 58
12. Burt RL, Davidson IW: Insulin half-life and utilization in normal pregnancy. *Obstet Gynecol* 43:161, 1974
13. Bellmann O, Hartman E: Influence of pregnancy on the kinetics of insulin. *Am J Obstet Gynecol* 122:829, 1975
14. Wood GP, Sherline DM: Amniotic fluid glucose: A maternal, fetal, and neonatal correlation. *Am J Obstet Gynecol* 122:151, 1975
15. Schaeffer LD, Wilder ML, Williams RH: Secretion and contents of insulin and glucagon in human fetal pancreas slices in vitro. *Proc Soc Exp Biol Med* 143:314, 1973
16. Danforth DN (ed): *Obstetrics and Gynecology,* ed 3. Hagerstown, Harper & Row, 1977, p 450
17. Gabbe Steven G: Diabetes mellitus in pregnancy, in Quilligan EJ, Kritchmer, N (eds): *Fetal and Maternal Medicine.* New York, Wiley, 1980, p 587
18. Gugliucci CL, O'Sullivan MJ, Apperman W, et al: Intensive care of the pregnant diabetic. *Am J Obstet Gynecol* 125:435, 1976
19. Gyves MT, Rodman HM, Little AB, et al: A modern approach to management of pregnant diabetics: A two-year analysis of perinatal outcomes. *Am J Obstet Gynecol* 128:606, 1977
20. Adam PA, Schwartz R: Diagnosis and treatment: Should oral hypoglycemic agents be used in pediatric and pregnant patients? *Pediatrics* 42:819, 1968
21. Posner BI: Insulin receptors in human and animal placental tissue. *Diabetes* 23:209, 1974
22. Churchill JA, Berendes HW: Intelligence of children whose mothers had ketonusic during pregnancy, in *Perinatal Factors Affecting Human Development* (scientific publication no 185). New York, Pan American Health Organization, 1969, p 30
23. Karlsson K, Kjellmer I: The outcome of diabetic pregnancies in relation to the mother's blood sugar level. *Am J Obstet Gynecol* 112:213, 1972
24. Tyson JE, Hock RA: Gestational and pregestational diabetes: An approach to therapy. *Am J Obstet Gynecol* 125:1009, 1976

25. Coutan DR, Berkowitz RL, Hobbins JC: Tight metabolic control of overt diabetes in pregnancy. *Am J Med* 68:845, 1980

26. Leveno J, Hauth JC, Gilstrap LC, et al: Appraisal of "rigid" blood glucose control during pregnancy in the overtly diabetic woman. *Am J Obstet Gynecol* 135:853, 1979

27. Sonksen PH, Judd SL, Lowy C: Home monitoring of blood-glucose. *Lancet* 1:729, 1978

28. Tamborlane WV, Sherwin RS, Genel M, et al: Reduction to normal of plasma glucose in juvenile diabetes by subcutaneous administration of insulin with a portable infusion pump. *N Engl J Med* 300:573, 1979

29. Rudolf, M, Coustan, D, Sherwin, R, et al: Efficacy of the insulin pump in the home treatment of pregnant diabetics. *Diabetes* 30:891, 1981

30. Yeast JD, Porreco RP, Ginsberg HN: The use of continuous insulin infusion for the peripartum management of pregnant diabetic women. *Am J Obstet Gynecol* 131:861, 1978

31. Freitag JJ, Miller LW (eds): *Manual of Medicine Therapeutics*, ed 23. Boston, Little Brown, 1980, pp 358–359

32. Whalen FJ, LeCain WK, Latiolais CJ: Availability of insulin from continuous low-dose infusion of insulin. *Am J Hosp Pharm* 36:330, 1979

33. Fesher DA, Dussault JH, Sack J, et al: Ontogenesis of hypothalamic-pituitary-thyroid function and metabolism in man, sheep, and rat. *Recent Progr Horm Res* 33:59, 1977

34. Talbert LM, Thomas CG, Holt WA, et al: Hyperthyroidism during pregnancy. *Obstet Gynecol* 36:779, 1970

35. Worley RJ, Crosby WM: Hyperthyroidism during pregnancy. *Am J Obstet Gynecol* 119:150, 1974

36. Saberi M, Sterling FH, Utiger RD: Reduction in extrathyroidal triiodothyronine production by propylthiouracil in man. *J Clin Invest* 55:218, 1975

37. Gilman AG, Goodman LS, Gilman A (eds): *The Pharmacological Basis of Therapeutics*, ed 6. New York, MacMillan, 1980, p 1410

38. Refetoff S, Ochi Y, Selenkow HA, et al: Neonatal hyperthyroidism and goiter in one infant of each of two sets of twins due to maternal therapy with antithyroid drugs. *J Pediatr* 85:240, 1974

39. Gibson M, Tulchinsky D: The maternal thyroid, in Tulchinsky D, Ryan KA (eds): *Maternal-Fetal Endocrinology*. Philadelphia, Saunders, 1980, p 115

40. Mujtaba Q, Burrow GN: Treatment of hyperthyroidism in pregnancy with propyl thiouracil and methimazole. *Obstet Gynecol* 46:282, 1975

41. Burrow GN: Hyperthyroidism during pregnancy. *N Engl J Med* 298:150, 1978

42. Burrow GN: Thyroid diseases, in Burrow GN, Ferris TF (eds): *Medical Complications During Pregnancy*. Philadelphia, Saunders, 1975, pp 196–241

43. Milharn S, Elledge W: Maternal methimazole and congenital defects in children. *Teratology* 5:125, 1972

44. Gladstone GR, Harelof A, Gersony WM: Propranolol administration during pregnancy: Effects on the fetus. *J Pediatr* 86:962, 1975

45. Turnstall ME: The effect of propranolol on the onset of breathing at birth. *Br J Anaesth* 41:792, 1969

46. Lachelin GC: Myxedema and pregnancy. *J Obstet Gynaecol Br Commonw* 77:77, 1970

47. Greenman GW, Gabrielson MO, Howard-Flanders J, et al: Thyroid dysfuretion in pregnancy: Fetal loss and follow-up evaluation of surviving infants. *N Engl J Med* 267:426, 1962

48. Brennan MD: Thyroid hormones. *Mayo Clin Proc* 55:33, 1980

49. Dong Betty J: Diseases of the thyroid, in Koda-Kimble Mary Anne, Katcher BS, Yound LY (eds): *Applied Therapeutics for Clinical Pharmacists*, ed 2. San Francisco, Applied Therapeutics, Inc., 1978, pp 494–529

50. Van Herle AJ, Young RT, Fisher DA, et al: Intra-uterine treatment of a hypothyroid fetus. *J Clin Endocrinol Metab* 40:474, 1975

51. Rubens R, Carlier A, Thiery M, et al: Pregnancy complicated by insulinoma. *Br J Obstet Gynecol* 84:543, 1977

52. Goodenday LS, Gordon GS: No risk from vitamin D in pregnancy. *Ann Intern Med* 75:807, 1971

53. O'Leary JA, Klainer LM, Newwirth RS: The management of hypoparathyroidism in pregnancy. *Am J Obstet Gynecol* 94:1103, 1966

54. Bolen JW; Hypoparathyroidism in pregnancy. *Am J Obstet Gynecol* 117:178, 1973

55. Salem R, Taylor S: Hyperparathyroidism in pregnancy. *Br J Surg* 66:648, 1979

56. Dorey LG, Gell JW: Primary hyperparathyroidism during the third trimester of pregnancy. *Obstet Gynecol* 45:469, 1975

57. Grimes HG, Brooks MH: Pregnancy in Sheehan's syndrome: Report of a case and review. *Obstet Gynecol Surv* 35:481, 1980

58. Corral J, Calderon J, Goldzieher JW: Induction of ovulation and term pregnancy in a hypophysectomized woman. *Obstet Gynecol* 39:397, 1972

59. Pico I, Greenblatt RB: Endocrinopathies and infertility: IV. Diabetes insipidus and pregnancy. *Fertil Steril* 20: 384, 1969

60. Husami N, Jewelewicz R, Vande Wiele RL: Pregnancy in patients with pituitary tumors. *Fertil Steril* 28:920, 1977

61. Bigazzi M, Ronga R, Lancranjan I, et al: A pregnancy in an acromegalic woman during bromocriptine treatment: Effects on growth hormone and prolactin in the maternal fetal and amniotic compartments. *J Clin Endocrinol Metab* 48:9, 1979

62. Magyar DM, Marshall JR: Pituitary tumors and pregnancy. *Am J Obstet Gynecol* 132:739, 1978

63. Kinch RA: The use of bromocriptine in obstetrics and gynecology. *Fertil Steril* 33:463, 1980

64. Bergh T, Nillius SJ, Wide L: Clinical course and outcome of pregnancies in amenorrhocic women with hyperprolactinaemia and pituitary tumors. *Br Med J* 1:875, 1978

65. Griffith RW, Turkalj I, Braun P: Pituitary tumours during pregnancy in mothers with bromocriptine. *Br J Clin Pharmacol* 7:393, 1979

66. Khunda S: Pregnancy and Addison's disease. *Obstet Gynecol* 39:431, 1972

67. Barber HRK, Graber EA, O'Rourke JJ: Pregnancy and delivery after previous bilateral total adrenolectomy. *Obstet Gynecol* 27:414, 1966

68. Poorai A, Jelercic F, Pop-Lazic B: Pregnancy with diabetes mellitus, Addison's disease and hypothyroidism. *Obstet Gynecol* 49(suppl. 86S):865, 1977

69. Grimes EM, Gayez JA, Miller GL: Cushing's syndrome and pregnancy. *Obstet Gynecol* 42:550, 1973

70. Reschini E, Giustina G, Crosignani PG, et al: Spontaneous remission of Cushing syndrome after termination of pregnancy. *Obstet Gynecol* 51:598, 1978

71. Check J H, Caro JF, Kendall B, et al: Cushing's syndrome in pregnancy: Effect of associated diabetes on fetal and neonatal complications. *Am J Obstet Gynecol* 133:846, 1979

8. Glucocorticoids to Enhance Fetal Pulmonary Maturity

FREDERICK P. ZUSPAN   LARRY L. ARWOOD
LEANDRO CORDERO, JR.

The major cause of death in the premature newborn is from respiratory distress complications which occur in the first 3 to 4 days of life. The role of antepartum administration of corticosteroids in the prevention of the respiratory distress syndrome (RDS) deserves careful scrutiny. It is known that: (1) RDS is the major cause of death in infants weighing less than 1500 gm; (2) RDS is primarily the result of an inadequate production of pulmonary surfactant, which subsequently lowers the surface tension in the alveoli, allowing expansion; (3) glucocorticoids administered to both animals and humans increase surfactant production by the type II pneumocytes in the lung; (4) the neonatologist's success in managing the low-birth-weight infant is dependent on the respiratory condition of the infant when delivered; and (5) intensive care by the neonatologist has increased the survival and long-term prognosis for the very low-birth-weight infant.[1-7]

Until 34 weeks' gestation, the major survival problem for the very low-birth-weight baby is the development and maturation of the pulmonary tree, including the invasion of capillaries into the alveoli and the thinning of the alveoli to facilitate the transfer of oxygen. The development of type II pneumocytes in the terminal pulmonary tree is also important, since these specialized cells are responsible for pulmonary surfactant synthesis.

The finding that glucocorticoids have an effect on fetal lung maturation through increased pulmonary surfactant production was discovered serendipitously. While studying the effects of corticosteroids to induce premature labor in sheep, Liggins observed in 1968 that dexamethasone injected directly into fetal lambs in utero resulted in a longer than expected survival after premature delivery.[8] Microscopic examination of the treated fetal lambs revealed partial aeration of the lung. Liggins postulated that dexamethasone might have enhanced the production of pulmonary surfactant prior to its normal biologic appearance. This finding was supported by De Lemos et al., who in 1970 reported that the in utero infusion of cortisol into one of twin lambs produced an advanced maturation of the pulmonary tree in the treated but not in the untreated twin.[9]

Having discovered the beneficial effects of prenatal steroid administration, other important observations which were made include: (1) the postnatal administration of steroids does not appear to influence the course of RDS,[10] (2) the prenatal administration of corticosteroids enhances the production of fetal pulmonary surfactant,[1] and (3) the biochemical effect of these steroids in animals does not necessarily correlate with the conditions observed in the human.[11-13]

MECHANISM OF ACTION OF GLUCOCORTICOIDS

The exact mechanism by which glucocorticoids induce pulmonary maturation is not fully understood, but is probably related to an in-

99

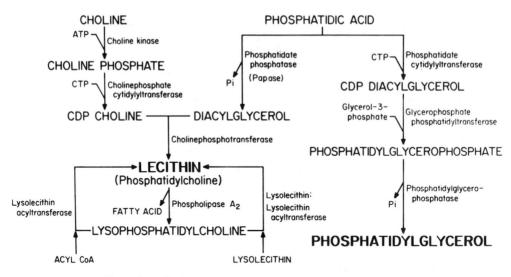

Figure 8-1. Pathways for lecithin and phosphatidylglycerol synthesis.

creased enzyme activity for the biosynthesis of surface active phospholipids in the type II pneumocytes. Choline phosphotransferase and phosphatidic acid phospatase (papase) are the primary enzymes responsible for the synthesis of the two principal surface-active phospholipids, phosphatidyl-choline and phosphatidyeglycerol (Fig. 8-1).[14,15] The choline pathway is thought to be the more important pathway for fetal lung development. Phosphatidic acid phosphatase catalyzes the hydrolysis of phosphatidic acid into diacylglycerol, which is a major substrate used in the biochemical pathway leading to the production of phosphatidylcholine. Phosphatidylcholine, phosphatidylglycerol, other lipids, and specific proteins are the primary constituents of lecithin, the major component of pulmonary surfactant.

The type II pneumocyte in the alveolar space is considered to be the principal site of glucocorticoid action (Fig. 8-2). After crossing the cell membrane, the glucocorticoid binds to specific intracytoplasmic receptors for transfer to the nucleus.[16] It is within the nucleus that RNA is synthesized for the eventual enzyme production and surfactant synthesis.[10] Intracytoplasmic lamellar bodies store the surfactant until its release into the alveolar space.

Although the lamellar bodies may be found as early as at 20 weeks' gestation, sufficient concentrations of surfactant to sustain lung stability are usually absent until about 33 weeks' gestation. Due to the prerequisite development of the pneumocytes, the ability of

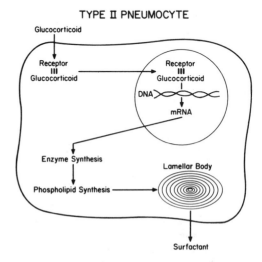

Figure 8-2. Model for glucocorticoid action in type II cells involving receptors and *de novo* synthesis of proteins.

the fetal lung to respond to glucocorticoid administration is also dependent upon gestational age.

Exogenous glucocorticoids administered to the mother have been shown to cause diverse effects on the fetal lung within 24 to 72 hours. These changes include morphologic, biochemical, and physiologic alterations. Whatever the exact biochemical mechanism, the significant increases in the L:S ratio after therapy have been reported by several authors, including our own studies.[1,17] However, when administered to the mother, betamethasone apparently does not cause an increased L:S ratio, despite lowering the incidence of respiratory distress.

PROBLEMS IN STUDIES ON PULMONARY MATURATION

There are so many variables involved in studies on pulmonary maturation in both animals and humans that it is almost impossible to draw precise scientific conclusions. The problem is further clouded by the fact that the very-low-birth-weight baby has a notoriously poor survival rate, and emotion often enters into therapy judgment. Some investigators state that the use of glucocorticoids to maturate fetal lungs may indeed be salutary, but its long-term safety has not been proven. Still another group of investigators questions the efficacy of corticosteroids to mature the fetal lung.

The diagnosis of neonatal respiratory distress, even though standardized for the neonatologist, has some degree of uncertainty, and incidence figures depend upon the severity of the disease. Few studies in the literature are double-blind trials, and even in double-blind trials patient selection is not as precise as one would hope. Furthermore, the information is often not standardized or detailed enough to allow regular statistical comparison. Despite these limitations, the combined data from published double-blind trials reveal the incidence of respiratory distress to be three times lower for infants whose mothers were prenatally treated with glucocorticoids when compared to untreated, "control" groups. The data in Table 8-1 was assembled from the literature.

An example of trials which illustrate such problems would include the classic study of Liggins and Howie, published in 1972.[16] A group of 282 mothers were randomly selected to receive 12 mg of betamethasone IM. The rationale for the choice of cortisone acetate as a placebo which has one-fiftieth the relative corticosteroid potency of betamethasone is not discussed and would not make it a true control group. The study later included 884 patients through 1974, using a dosage of betamethasone that was doubled. There was no rationale for doubling this dosage; the results were essentially the same.

The criteria of patient selection is another important consideration, and a subset of patients with hypertension, edema, and proteinuria were included in the initial Liggins and Howie study. At least 24 hours intervened after the administration of the second dose of betamethasone before the delivery of a

TABLE 8-1 COMPARISON BETWEEN THE INCIDENCE OF RESPIRATORY DISTRESS AND NEONATAL MORTALITY FROM RESPIRATORY DISTRESS IN PREGNANCIES DELIVERING PREMATURELY WITH OR WITHOUT PRENATAL GLUCOCORTICOID TREATMENT

Condition	Total Incidence	Untreated	Treated
Respiratory distress*	142/703 (20.2%)	101/353 (28.8%)	41/350 (11.7%)
Neonatal mortality†	226/1431 (15.8%)	181/824 (21.9%)	45/607 (7.4%)

* Data based on five double-blind studies.
† Data based on 10 double-blind studies treated with betamethasone (8) or hydrocortisone (2).

hypertensive or normotensive patient. The hypertensive group was found to have an increased incidence of antepartum and intrapartum fetal death, 12 of 47 in the hypertensive group as compared to 3 of 47 in the control group. Liggins and Howie concluded that patients with preeclampsia and other forms of hypertension should not be given betamethasone because of the increased fetal loss. When the report is analyzed more critically, it is apparent that the fetal loss is not directly related to the betamethasone administration as much as it is to the antepartum testing methods to determine the ideal time for delivery.

As scientists, we would all like to offer our patients the maximum protection learned from animal studies before any trials in humans are begun. Animal studies have used proportionally larger doses of glucocorticoids than in humans, and are therefore not comparable on that basis alone. Even if dosages were proportional, the extrapolation of data from the animal to the human is clearly not possible, since final proof always rests in the human.

EFFECTS OF CORTICOSTEROIDS ON FETAL DEVELOPMENT

The classical assumption that toxic effects of medications are related to dosage and duration of therapy may lead to a false sense of security regarding corticosteroid therapy. Many animal studies involving corticosteroids involve therapies of relatively short duration with large doses. Glucocorticoids injected directly into the fetus for as short a time period as 3 days have resulted in somatic and lung growth retardation.

Particular concern has been expressed over data indicating that dendritic and synaptogenic growth has been altered in rats. Our research group studied brains of rat fetuses treated with hydrocortisone. Using a dosage scheme similar to human therapy, hydrocortisone was given intraperitoneally on days 12 and 15 of gestation in pregnant rats. The offspring were studied at days 20 to 21 of gestation and days 12 to 13 in the neonatal period.

The amine systems of the hydrocortisone and saline groups showed equal cerebral maturation, and both groups demonstrated nerve cell bodies in areas A-1 to A-13 and axon terminals in all examined regions. The distribution in the fluorescent intensity in the brains did not show any differences in either group, and the cerebral concentrations of dopamine, epinephrine, and norepinephrine were also similar. These results indicate that hydrocortisone given during pregnancy does not influence the proliferation of amine cell bodies or the arrival of axon terminals in regions where formed in the fetus.[13]

Unlike that of the rat, the human cortex has developed more fully by the time glucocorticoid therapy would be given to promote pulmonary maturation. Neuronal multiplication in the human in the developing brain is followed by a migration to the outer cortical zones which occurs up to 24 weeks' gestation. It is unlikely that many neurons will enter the cerebral cortex beyond 24 weeks of gestation, but dendritic growth continues to 35 or 36 weeks and synaptogenesis probably continues through term. Glial development and myelinization are probably not completed until the second year of postnatal life. It is therefore possible that the different temporal patterns of brain development in the human may prevent some of the detrimental effects of glucocorticoid treatment observed in the rat. Prenatal glucocorticoid therapy treatment commits the physician team and the institution to careful and long-term follow-up, which is often unavailable outside tertiary-care-level facilities.

INDICATIONS FOR GLUCOCORTICOID THERAPY

The initiation of glucocorticoid therapy is based upon analysis of amniotic fluid. Unfortunately, not enough data are available to indicate the gestational age group that is most likely to respond favorably to corticosteroid therapy, but the fetus from 28 to 34 weeks probably has an optimum chance of response.

The beneficial effects for infants less than 28 weeks of gestation cannot be determined at the present time, and the fetus beyond 34 weeks of gestation has a low incidence of respiratory distress.

A time lapse must exist between maternal treatment and fetal response of at least 24 hours after the last dose of steroid therapy.[1,18-24] If the underlying antepartum complication does not permit this period of nonintervention, glucocorticoid therapy should not be given, and delivery should take place. On the other hand, if the pregnancy continues for more than 10 days after therapy, an amniocentesis should be repeated, and the amniotic fluid should be reanalyzed prior to another course of therapy.

The cornerstone of therapy rests upon the prompt and accurate diagnosis of fetal pulmonary activity by amniotic fluid analysis. The four commonly used tests to analyze amniotic fluid for pulmonary surfactant production include the lecithin: spinogomyelin (L:S) ratio, phosphatidyl glycerol determination, the "shake" test, and optical density OD_{650} determination. Although the L:S ratio and phosphatidyl glycerol determination are performed at regional perinatal centers, the shake test and OD_{650} determination can be easily performed at any hospital and at awkward times such as at night, on weekends, and during holidays when specialized technicians are less accessible. Glucosteroid therapy is to be administered only after there is laboratory evidence of fetal pulmonary immaturity (L:S less than

2:1, OD_{650} less than 0.15, negative phosphatidyl glycerol, or negative or suspicious shake test). If conditions remain favorable to delay delivery, an immature result using either the OD_{650} or shake test should be later confirmed with an L:S ratio determination. When using the OD_{650} to assess pulmonary maturity, we have not experienced a false positive determination, that is, if the OD_{450} is greater than 0.15 at 650 mm, RDS has not been found, which confirms the observation by Sbarra who initially published the test.[25,26]

CONTRAINDICATIONS TO GLUCOCORTICOID THERAPY

The absolute and relative maternal and fetal contraindications for glucocorticoid therapy are straightforward (Table 8-2). Absolute contraindications are fortunately uncommon, but relative contraindications require individualization.

Premature Rupture of Membranes

Most authors conclude that there is no association between fetal/maternal infection and prenatal steroid treatment, since the dosage levels are quite small. Tauesch et al.,[27,28] however, reported maternal infections in 5 of 10 women treated as compared to 1 of 17 placebo patients. All patients studied had premature rupture of membranes greater than 48 hours, and

TABLE 8-2 CONTRAINDICATIONS TO PRENATAL GLUCOCORTICOID THERAPY

	Absolute	Relative
Maternal	Tuberculosis Viral keratitis Active herpes, type II Febrile illness or infection	Hypertensive disorder Diabetes mellitus Hyperthyroidism Uterine bleeding Peptic ulcer
Fetal	Amnionitis Imminent delivery Mature amniotic fluid test result Inability to monitor the fetus	Premature rupture of membranes (PROM) Placental insufficiency

none had signs of infection prior to cortico-steroid or placebo therapy. No author has been able to document an increase in infant infections in corticosteroid-treated infants, but this may be explained by the liberal use of prophylactic antibiotics in the newborn period. Although any decreased resistance to infection during corticosteroid therapy remains controversial, it is recommended that corticosteroid therapy be withheld in patients with amnionitis or other infections. Glucocorticoids are known to increase the white blood count, so cultures and clinical criteria remain the best methods to monitor for any infection. The Gram stain and a search for white cells in amniotic fluid may also be helpful.

A review of the data at The Ohio State University has not confirmed the fact that premature rupture of membranes promotes an acceleration of pulmonary surfactant, but controversy continues.[29-35] It is our practice that if the patient has premature rupture of membranes, amniotic fluid is obtained from either the vaginal pool or from ultrasound-guided amniocentesis for pulmonary maturity testing. A culture of the material and microscopic examination with Gram stain are also done. Any advantage to the use of glucocorbicoids in the conservative management of this complication remains unclear.

Hypertensive Disorders

There has been speculation but no data that glucocorticoids may compromise placental function in hypertensive patients. This speculation is based on urinary and serum estriol values diminishing precipitously after glucocorticoid therapy. This decreased value is instead a reflection of maternal adrenal suppression. The analysis of Liggins' original data indicates that the increased perinatal death rate in preeclamptic patients is closely related to the degree of proteinuria and the severity of the disease. As an example, patients excreting more than 3 gm of protein had a perinatal mortality rate of 43 percent, while those with less proteinuria had a perinatal mortality rate of only 14 percent.[36] It probably was not the

glucocorticoid, but the severity of the disease that resulted in these stillbirths.

At least four different investigators have treated hypertensive patients with glucocorticoids, with all reporting similar results of hypertension not exacerbated and fetal mortality not increased.

The group at The Ohio State University recently evaluated 32 hypertensive gravidas who were treated in the third trimester of pregnancy with intravenous hydrocortisone to enhance fetal lung maturity. Blood pressure was determined throughout the 24 hours of steroid therapy, and no significant increase in maternal blood pressure was found.[18] The two antepartum fetal deaths in our study group were similar to those in the Liggins and Howie control group. In addition, 15 different studies utilizing various drugs such as betamethasone, hydrocortisone, and dexamethasone have treated 1,214 patients with only 22 stillbirths following prenatal glucocorticoid therapy, or a 2 percent fetal mortality for these high-risk patients. The fear of steroid-induced exacerbation of maternal hypertension has therefore not been supported as a valid reason to withhold steroid therapy in hypertensive patients if indications are present for its use and the maternal condition is stable.

Diabetes Mellitus

Glucocorticoids increase insulin requirements by inhibiting glucose utilization, by mobilizing amino acids for their conversion to glucose and glycogen, and by the induction of liver enzymes involved in gluconeogenesis. This increase in insulin requirement occurs within minutes after initiation of therapy. β-Adrenergic tocolytic agents (terbutaline, isoxsuprine, ritodrine) are often used concurrently with glucocorticoids and may also increase circulating glucose levels. Thus, the concurrent administration of β-sympathomimetics and corticosteroids may compound the management problem of the diabetic mother and requires a diligent monitoring of maternal blood glucose levels. Since it is extraordinarily difficult to control the severe diabetic, glucocorticoid therapy is not recommended.

Peptic Ulcer

The exact relationship between peptic ulcer and the use of glucocorticoids is unclear and may not actually exist. A history of ulcer disease, along with additional stress, and the concomitant use of other gastrointestinal irritants will predispose patients to the ulcerogenic effects of corticosteroids. These patients should therefore receive parenteral glucocorticoid therapy with caution.

Bleeding

Glucocorticoid therapy may decrease the platelet number and function. A negative history of excessive bleeding and a normal platelet count are desirable before therapy. Severe vaginal bleeding necessitates prompt delivery, but a pregnancy complicated by placenta previa may be a candidate for glucocorticoid therapy if conservative treatment is successful.

DRUG CHOICE AND DOSAGE SCHEDULE

The specific drug of choice and the dosage of drug are presently unknown. No agent has been shown to offer any advantages in promoting pulmonary maturity, but there are certain differences in their pharmacology which deserve consideration.

The durations of anti-inflammatory effects based on approximately equivalent one-time doses may be used as a guideline and are shown in Table 8-3. Since anti-inflammatory effects may reflect immunosuppressant capability, hydrocortisone may offer some ad-

vantage to decrease the risk of infections for both mother and child. A potential disadvantage of hydrocortisone is the significant mineralocorticoid activity with associated fluid retention which is not present with dexamethasone and betamethasone therapy.

The most expedient route of administration is intravenous, and the slower intramuscular absorption of betamethasone and dexamethasone would appear to be less desirable.

The transport of glucocorticoids across the placenta and to the fetal pulmonary target tissue is worthy of consideration. All agents rapidly cross the placenta, and any difference in metabolic conversion by the 11-dehydrogenase enzyme system is thought not to be significant. In addition, any 11-keto compound metabolite formed during placental transfer may also be effective in promoting type II pneumocyte stimulation. Steroid-binding to carrier proteins in the fetus is less with dexamethasone and betamethasone (to albumin only) as compared to hydrocortisone (to albumin and cortisol-binding globulin). If urinary estriol excretion is identified as an index of suppression of the fetal adrenal activity, hydrocortisone shows the most rapid effect, that is, maximum depression of urinary estrogen is seen in less than 12 hours, whereas with betamethasone 24 hours is required.

A therapy regimen utilizing the minimal effective dose for the shortest duration is not established for any of the glucocorticoids. Table 8-4 identifies dosage regimens that have been used at many institutions. An advantage of hydrocortisone is that the L:S ratio has been shown to increase in 80 percent of treated

TABLE 8-3 COMPARISONS BETWEEN ANTI-INFLAMMATORY EFFECTS WITH HYDROCORTISONE, DEXAMETHASONE, AND BETAMETHASONE

Drug	Dose (mg)	Duration of Anti-Inflammatory Effect (days)
Hydrocortisone	250	1.25–1.5
Dexamethasone	5	2.75
Betamethasone	6	3.25

TABLE 8-4 GLUCOCORTICOID DOSAGE REGIMENS USED TO PROMOTE FETAL LUNG MATURATION

Drug	Dosage Schedule	Total Dose (mg)
Betamethasone (6 mg acetate/6 mg phosphate—Celestone)	12 mg IM every 24 hr for two doses	24
Dexamethasone (Decadron, Deronil)	4 mg IM every 8 hr for six doses	24
Hydrocortisone (Cortisol, Cortef, Cortril, etc.)	500 mg IV every 8 hr for four doses	2000

cases, while no change has been reported with betamethasone.

A time lapse of at least 24 hours after the last dose until delivery is necessary. If more than 7 days have elapsed after completion of therapy, amniotic fluid testing should be repeated before administering another course of therapy. The effectiveness of the second weekly dose has not been proved to be effective.

In conclusion, the short-term benefits from the use of prenatal glucocorticoid therapy to promote fetal lung maturity has been established from animal and human investigations. The appropriate agent and dosage regimen, and the proper selection of prospective candidates remain unclear. Absolute safety to the mother and fetus requires that there be further short- and long-term investigation. Glucocorticoid therapy should be initiated only after informed patient consent has been obtained and after amniotic fluid testing suggests fetal pulmonary immaturity.

ADDENDUM

The response of the fetal lung to antenatally-administered glucocorticoids seems to be greater in females than in males. Cord blood betamethasone and the degree and duration of the adreno-cortical axis suppression seem to be similar in treated infants disregarding sex,* hence the reason for the different responsiveness still remains obscure.

Preliminary results from the antenatal glucorticoid collaborative study† recently documented the overall effectiveness of the treatment, the absence of maternal and neonatal complications, and the lack of neurological abnormalities in treated infants when tested at 40 weeks of gestation.

REFERENCES

1. Zuspan FP, Cordero L, Semchyshyn S: Effects of hydrocortisone on lecithin-sphingomyelin ratio. *Am J Obstet Gynecol* 128:571, 1977
2. Farrell PM, Zachman RD: Induction of choline phosphotransferase and lecithin synthesis in the fetal lung by corticosteroids. *Science* 179: 297, 1973
3. Grub L: Administration of cortical steroids to induce maturation of fetal lung. *Am J Dis Child* 130:976, 1976
4. Ballard RA, Ballard PL: Use of prenatal glucocorticoid therapy to prevent respiratory distress syndrome. *Am J Dis Child* 130:982, 1976
5. Ballard PL, Ballard RA: Corticosteroid and respiratory distress syndrome: Status 1979. *Pediatrics* 63:163, 1979

* *Ballard P et al: Fetal sex and prenatal betamethasone therapy. J Pediatr 97:451, 1980.*
† *Collaborative group on antenatal steroid therapy. Am J Obstet Gynecol 141:276, 1981.*

6. Hallman M, Grub L: Development of the fetal lung. *J Perinat Med* 5:3, 1977

7. Taeusch HW, Heitner M, Avery ME: Acceleration of lung maturation and increased survival in premature rabbits treated with hydrocortisone. *Am Rev Resp Dis* 105:971, 1972

8. Liggins GC: Premature delivery of foetal lambs infused with glucocorticoids. *J Endocrinol* 45: 515, 1969

9. De Lemos R, Shermeta D, Knelson J, et al: Acceleration of appearance of pulmonary surfactant in the fetal lamb by administration of corticosteroids. *Am Rev Resp Dis* 102:459, 1970

10. Buckingham S, McNary WF, Sommers SC, et al: Is lung an analog of Moog's intestine? Phosphatase and pulmonary alveolar differentiation in fetal rabbits (abstract). *Fed Proc* 27:328, 1968

11. Schapiro S, Salas M, Vukovich K: Hormonal effects on the ontogeny of swimming ability in the rat: Assessment of CNS development. *Science* 168:147, 1970

12. De Lemos RA: Glucocorticoid effect: Organ development in monkeys, in *Proceedings of the 70th Ross Conference on Pediatric Research.* Columbus, Ohio, Ross Laboratories, 1975, pp 77–80

13. Van Geijn H, Copeland K, Vorys A, et al: *The Effects of Hydrocortisone on the Development of the Amine Systems in the Fetal Brain* (abstract). Society for Gynecologic Investigation, 1979

14. Ballard P, Benson B, Brehier A: Glucocorticoid effects in the fetal lung. *Am Rev Resp Dis* 115 (suppl):29, 1977

15. Weischel M: Glucocorticoid effect upon thymidine kinase in the developing cerebellum. *Pediatr Res* 8:361, 1974

16. Liggins GC, Howie RN: A controlled trial of antepartum glucocorticoid treatment for prevention of the respiratory distress syndrome in premature infants. *Pediatrics* 50:515, 1972

17. Morrison JC, Whybrew WE, Bucovaz ET, et al: Injection of corticosteroids into mother to prevent neonatal respiratory distress syndrome. *Am J Obstet Gynecol* 131:358, 1978

18. Iams JD, Semchyshyn S, O'Shaughnessy R, Moynihan V, Zuspan FP: Blood pressure response in hypertensive pregnancies treated with cortisol. *Clin Exp Hypertension* 2:923, 1980

19. Kennedy JL: Antepartum betamethasone in the prevention of RDS (abstract). *Pediatr Res* 8:447, 1974

20. Kennedy JL: Prenatal glucocorticoid treatment: Prevention of respiratory distress syndrome, in *Proceedings of the 70th Ross Conference on Pediatric Research.* Columbus, Ohio, Ross Laboratories, 1975, pp 105–110

21. Taeusch HW: Catecholamines, insulin, glucocorticoids and respiratory distress syndrome: Tribulations of controlled trials, in *Proceedings of the 70th Ross Conference on Pediatric Research.* Columbus, Ohio, Ross Laboratories, 1975, pp 92–97

22. Caspi E, Schreyer P, Weinraub Z, et al: Prevention of the respiratory distress syndrome in premature infants by antepartum glucocorticoid therapy. *Br J Obstet Gynecol* 83:187, 1976

23. Ballard RA, Ballard PL, Granberg JP, et al: Prenatal administration of betamethasone for prevention of respiratory distress syndrome. *J Pediatr* 94:97, 1979

24. Thornfeldt RE, Franklin RW, Pickering NA, et al: The effect of glucocorticoids on the maturation of premature lung membranes. *Am J Obstet Gynecol* 131:143, 1978

25. Copeland W Jr, Stempel L, Lott J, Copeland W Sr, Zuspan FP: Assessment of a rapid test on amniotic fluid for estimating fetal lung maturity. *Am J Obstet Gynecol* 130:225, 1978

26. Sbarra A: Personal communication, 1980

27. Taeusch HW, Frigoletto F, Kitzmiller J, et al: Risk of respiratory distress syndrome after prenatal dexamethasone treatment. *Pediatrics* 63:64, 1979

28. Taeusch HW, Wang NS, Baden M, et al: A controlled trial of hydrocortisone therapy in infants with RDS: 11. Pathology. *Pediatrics* 52:850, 1973

29. Jones MD, Burd LL, Bowes WA, et al: Failure of association of premature rupture of membranes with respiratory distress syndrome. *N Engl J Med* 292:1253, 1975

30. Berkowitz RL, Bontz BW, Warshaw JE: The relationship between premature rupture of the membranes and the respiratory distress syndrome. *Am J Obstet Gynecol* 124:712, 1976

31. Thibeault DW, Emmanouilides GC: Prolonged rupture of fetal membranes and decreased frequency of respiratory distress syndrome and patent ductus arteriosus in preterm infants. *Am J Obstet Gynecol* 129:43, 1977

32. Christensen KK, Christensen P, Ingermarsson I, et al: A study of complications in preterm deliveries after prolonged premature rupture of the membranes. *Obstet Gynecol* 48:670, 1976

33. Zachman RD: Premature rupture of the membranes and the incidence of respiratory distress syndrome. *Perinat Press* 1:4, 1976

34. Sell EJ, Harris TR: Association of premature

rupture of membranes with idiopathic respiratory distress syndrome. *Obstet Gynecol* 49:167, 1977

35. Mead PD: Does prolonged rupture of the membranes protect against respiratory distress? *Perinat Press* I:4, 1977

36. Liggins GC: Prenatal glucocorticoid treatment: Prevention of respiratory distress syndrome, in *Proceedings of the 70th Ross Conference on Pediatric Research.* Columbus, Ohio, Ross Laboratories, 1975, pp 97–105

9. Drugs to Inhibit Premature Labor

DONALD M. DEDONATO
WILLIAM K. RAND, III WILLIAM F. RAYBURN

Despite the remarkable success achieved in neonatal intensive care units, the majority of perinatal morbidity and mortality occurs in premature infants. Although less than 10 percent of all infants are delivered before term, 75 percent of perinatal deaths are directly related to premature birth.[1] Significant neonatal morbidity, such as permanent intellectual and physical handicaps, also occurs more commonly in premature infants. The prevention of premature delivery is therefore one of the primary objectives of prenatal care. When premature labor occurs, the use of pharmacologic agents to suppress labor is an alternative to delivering the premature infant. Delaying delivery for even 1 or 2 weeks may offer psychologic, financial, and physical advantages, and may avoid death or significant central nervous system handicaps for some infants.

Premature labor is usually defined as the onset of labor before the 38th week of amenorrhea. The incidence of premature delivery varies with the population studied. In American women the incidence of premature birth is estimated to be 8 to 10 percent.[2] Only 3.3 percent of infants in East Germany are born prematurely, in contrast to nearly one-fourth being premature in impoverished areas of India.[3]

The events leading to the onset of labor are poorly understood. The etiology is most likely multifactoral; conditions associated with an increased incidence of premature labor are listed in Table 9-1. The difference between true and false labor is often subtle, and may

be so unclear that it is too late for therapy to be successful. The most widely accepted criteria for the clinical diagnosis of premature labor requires palpable contractions occurring every 10 minutes for at least 30 minutes and lasting 30 seconds or more.[4] When using these criteria, 40 to 70 percent of patients who are managed with sedation and bedrest alone will not deliver prematurely. Unless contraindicated, a drug to inhibit uterine contractions (tocolytic drug) should be administered early, even though some patients may be treated for false labor.

The earliest gestational age at which premature labor is to be arrested is controversial. Attempts at precise determination of gestational age must be obtained from pertinent clinical information and ultrasonographic findings. The frequency of anomalies occurring in pregnancies with spontaneous labor before 20 weeks may preclude tocolysis. Arresting labor after the 37th week is not beneficial, since perinatal morbidity and mortality have not been shown to decrease. Amniocentesis to assess fetal pulmonary maturity is helpful, especially when fetal age is uncertain, so that the risks of neonatal respiratory distress can be predicted before tocolytic therapy is begun.

The arrest of premature labor may not benefit all fetuses. Certain underlying fetal or maternal conditions may predispose to premature labor or may be deleterious if intrauterine existence is continued. The criteria for selecting patients for tocolytic therapy are listed in

109

TABLE 9-1   CONDITIONS ASSOCIATED WITH THE ONSET OF PREMATURE LABOR

Maternal
Acute severe systemic illness
Chronic severe systemic illness
Pyelonephritis
Chronic hypertension
Hyperthyroidism
Hyperparathyroidism
Hyperadrenocorticism
Previous history of premature labor
Fever
Inadequate nutrition
Age (under 16, over 40 years)
Excess smoking

Uterine
Polyhydramnios
Multiple gestation
Foreign body (IUD)
Trauma
Cervical incompetence or trauma
Uterine anomalies
Amniocentesis
Surgery
Chorioamnionitis

Fetoplacental
Fetal death
Placenta previa
Abruptio placenta
Fetal anomalies
Multifetal gestation
Preterm ruptured amniotic membranes (PROM)

TABLE 9-2   CRITERIA FOR SELECTING PATIENTS FOR TOCOLYTIC THERAPY

Clinical Diagnosis
   Gestational age between 20 and 36 weeks
   Estimated fetal weight less than 2500 gm
   Uterine contractions every 10 min, lasting 30 sec
      or more, for 30 min or more
   Cervical dilation of 4 cm or less

No Remarkable Antepartum Complication
   Maternal
      Cardiac disease
      Hypertension
      Symptomatic hypotension
      Diabetes mellitus
      Thyrotoxicosis
      Fever or disseminated infection

   Fetoplacental
      Intrauterine infection
      Placenta previa or placental abruption
      Suspected severe fetal growth retardation
      Fetal anomaly
      Polyhydramnios
      Fetal demise

No Evidence of Fetal Pulmonary Maturity

Table 9-2. Most patients in premature labor have no other discernible antepartum complication and therefore qualify for inhibition of uterine contractions. Vaginal cultures for gonorrhea and group B β-streptococci are performed when determining whether the amniotic membranes are ruptured. Bedrest is necessary with the patient lying on her side in a Trendelenburg position.

Tocolytic drugs may be identified by their presumed mechanisms of action. Premature labor may be arrested by using agents that prevent the synthesis or release of a uterine stimulant (ethanol, antiprostaglandin) or by suppressing the contractile response at the tar-

get organ, the myometrial cells (magnesium sulfate, β-adrenergic agents). More specific mechanisms of actions of each drug group remain uncertain but are shown in Figure 9-1. Dose regimens, side effects, and contraindications for use are described in Tables 9-3 and 9-4. More detailed comments and the relative effectiveness of each drug group are described further.

TOCOLYTIC AGENTS

Ethanol

Ethanol has been the most widely used tocolytic agent in the past for inhibiting premature labor. Despite its widespread use, the effectiveness of ethanol in improving perinatal outcome is debatable. The intravenous administration of ethanol became popular after a clinical trial by Fuchs and associates was published in 1967.[5] Ethanol was thought to act

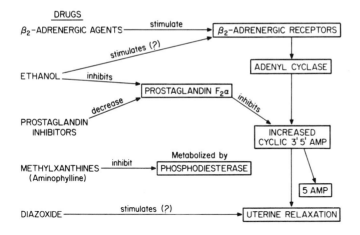

Figure 9-1. Proposed sites for pharmacologic action of drugs to inhibit preterm uterine contractions.

on the central nervous system by blocking the release of oxytocin, and on the myometrium by a direct suppressant action. Intravenous ethanol was reported to prolong pregnancy in 67 percent of the cases for greater than 72 hours, when the membranes were intact and the cervix was dilated less than 4 cm. A randomized study in 1972 by Zlatnick and Fuchs reported a delay in delivery for at least 72 hours in 81 percent of women treated with ethanol as compared to 31 percent of those treated with placebo.[6] Subsequent nonran-

TABLE 9-3 DOSAGE REGIMENS FOR TOCOLYTIC DRUGS

Drug	Preparation	Loading Dose	Maintenance Dose	
			SHORT TERM	LONG TERM
Ethanol	10% solution in dextrose 5% solution in dextrose	7.5 ml/kg/hr IV for 2 hr	1.5 ml/kg/hr IV for 6–12 hr	(?) Oral administration advised
Magnesium sulfate	40 gm in 1000 ml in 5% dextrose in water and 0.45 normal saline (40 gm/liter)	4 gm in 100 cc over 20 min	1–4 gm IV/hr for 8–12 hr (25–100 cc/hr)	No oral administration
Isoxsuprine (Vasodilan)	0.02% solution in 5% dextrose and 0.45 normal saline (200 mg/liter)	0.2–1.0 mg IV over 10 min	0.1–0.3 mg/min IV for 12 hr (30–90 ml/hr)	10–20 mg PO every 4–6 hr
Terbutaline (Brethine, Bricanyl)	0.001% solution in 5% dextrose and 0.45 normal saline (10 mg/liter)	0.25 mg IV over 1–2 min	0.01–0.025 mg/min IV for 12 hr (60–150 ml/hr)	0.25 mg SC every 4 hr 2.5–5.0 mg PO every 4–6 hr
Ritodrine (Yutopar)	0.03% solution in 5% dextrose and 0.45 normal saline (150 mg/500 ml)	None	0.1–0.35 mg/min IV for 12 hr (20–70 ml/hr)	10 mg PO every 2 hr or 10–20 mg PO every 4–6 hr

TABLE 9-4   SIDE EFFECTS AND CONTRAINDICATIONS FOR TOCOLYTIC AGENTS

| Drug | Side Effects | | Contraindications |
	MATERNAL	FETAL	
Ethanol	Intoxication Nausea and vomiting Aspiration Restless Hypoglycemia Lactic acidemia Diuresis with dehydration Headache Tachycardia	Intoxication Depression	Liver disease (A)* Alcoholism (A) Diabetes mellitus (R)†
Magnesium sulfate	Cutaneous flushing Nausea and vomiting Respiratory depression Depressed reflexes Intracardiac conduction delays (cardiac arrest)	Depression (rare)	Heart block (A) Myocardial damage (A) Impaired renal function (R)
Antiprostaglandins (Indomethacin, Naproxen)	GI bleeding and ulceration Nausea and vomiting Allergic rashes Bone marrow depression	Premature closure of the ductus arteriosus‡ Pulmonary hypertension Coagulopathy Hyperbilirubinemia	Active or recurrent GI lesion (A) Epilepsy (R) Psychiatric disturbances (R)
β-adrenergics	Tachycardia Hypotension Hyperglycemia Restlessness Headache Nausea and vomiting Palpitations Tremor, anxiety Hypokalemia Angina (occult cardiac disease) Pulmonary edema	Tachycardia Transient hypoglycemia Hypotension	Heart disease (A) Hyperthyroidism (R) Hypertension (R) Diabetes mellitus (R)

* A = Absolute contraindication
† R = Relative contraindication
‡ Limited Data

domized studies with control populations and with comparisons to other tocolytic agents have reported widely different success rates, ranging from no better than placebo to 81 percent success.[7,8] Some of these differences in success are explained by differing criteria for diagnosis and success and differing ethanol dosages and durations of therapy. Two recent, randomized, controlled studies have shown ethanol to be less effective than magnesium sulfate or ritodrine in delaying premature delivery.[9,10] Furthermore, seldom has ethanol been shown to stop labor for more than 48 hours in patients with ruptured membranes, and it is likely to be no more effective than conservative management with bedrest.

Intravenous ethanol may cause side effects in the mother. Inebriation should be expected when ethanol is infused at dosages described in Table 9-4, since the usual serum level of alcohol is above the legal definition of intoxication (100 mg%). Serum ethanol concentrations at the standard infusion rates range from 100 to 210 mg%.[11] Serum concentrations of 250 mg% may be anesthetic, and concentrations above 300 mg% may cause coma or death.[12] Because of a depressed consciousness and an impaired gag reflex, the risk of aspiration pneumonitis (Mendelson's syndrome) is increased. The monitoring of the patient's mental status and the administration of antiemetics and antacids may minimize this hazard. Metabolic alterations resulting from ethanol exposure include hypoglycemia and lactic acidemia with an inhibition of gluconeogenesis.

Despite its rapid transfer across the placenta, the adverse effects of ethanol on the premature fetus have been more theoretical than real. Some newborns exhibit transient signs of lethargy, hypotonia, and intoxication at birth, but significant depression and respiratory difficulties are surprisingly rare. The fetal alcohol syndrome (see Chap. 2) is not associated with acute alcohol exposure in late pregnancy.

Magnesium Sulfate

Along with its anticonvulsant properties in managing toxemia, parenteral magnesium sulfate has also been found to inhibit uterine contractions.[13] Ionic magnesium is thought to antagonize calcium flow and to exert its effects on myometrial cells in three possible ways: (1) decrease the frequency of muscle-cell action potentials, (2) uncouple the excitation and contraction of smooth muscles, and (3) relax the contractile elements. Clinical studies in patients with premature labor are scarce. Observations have been primarily by Harbert et al. and by Steir and Petrie.[9,14] The data from Steir and Petrie suggest that magnesium sulfate is superior to ethanol for the management of premature labor. The inhibition of uterine contractions is dose-related and a serum concentration of 4 to 8 mg/dl of magnesium should effectively reduce uterine contractions.

For effective tocolysis, magnesium sulfate is to be infused at maintenance doses of 2 gm or more per hour after a 4 gm loading dose. This use is not FDA-approved, and lower doses (1 gm/hour) for seizure prophylaxis are likely to be ineffective in inhibiting uterine contractions.

Clinical signs of hypermagnesemia in the patient are not infrequent. The mother's knee reflexes, urine output, and respiratory rate must be closely monitored.[4] The knee-jerk reflex disappears at serum concentrations of 10 to 12 mg/dl. Respiration is depressed when the serum magnesium level reaches 12 to 15 mg/dl. Abnormalities in electrocardiograph tracings (increased P-R interval, prolonged QRS interval, increased T wave) have been related to serum concentrations as low as 6 mg/dl. Cardiac arrest does not occur until the serum magnesium concentration is 30 mg/dl or greater.[15] Serum magnesium levels are usually drawn only when worrisome clinical signs are evident (see Chap. 6).

The maternal administration of magnesium sulfate usually does not compromise the neonate.[16] Magnesium does cross the placenta promptly by active diffusion and can produce fetal serum concentrations which are comparable to the mother's.[17,18] However, only isolated reports of neonatal depression have appeared, and Apgar scores do not relate to serum concentrations of magnesium in the cord blood. Respiratory depression from hypermagnesemia can be reversed in the mother (calcium gluconate 10 ml of 10 percent solution IV) but not in the neonate.

Prostaglandin Synthetase Inhibitors

Prostaglandins have been implicated in the onset of uterine contractions. Their synthesis in the uterus is dependent on prostaglandin synthetase, an enzyme complex necessary for the conversion of arachidonic acid to prostaglandins (see Chap. 10 and 21). Antiprostaglandin agents are thought to inhibit spontaneous uterine contractions in pregnant rats and subhuman primates by reducing the amount of prostaglandins synthesized and released by the myometrial cells.[19,21] Human investigations by Lewis and Schulman[22] and by Zuckerman and co-workers[23] have involved pregnancies undergoing therapeutic abortion. Large doses of aspirin or indomethacin were found to either inhibit or prolong labor. Evidence from animal studies have revealed that aspirin, indomethacin, and naproxen are effective in prolonging gestation and labor.[24] Their use in clinical obstetrics has largely been as prophylaxis to avoid the onset of recurrent premature labor. Niebyl et al. found indomethacin to be effective in inhibiting premature labor in a prospective, randomized, double-blind study involving 30 patients.[25] The lowest effective dose for each drug has not yet been determined.

Prostaglandin synthetase inhibitors are not approved by the Food and Drug Administration for inhibiting uterine contractions. Potential side effects in the mother and fetus may result from acute or chronic exposure. Adverse effects in the mother include peptic ulceration, bleeding, bone marrow depression, and gastrointestinal perforation, and are usually related to the dose and duration of the specific drug. Reported effects on the fetus include in utero closure of the ductus arteriosus and decreased platelet aggregation.[26,27] Adaptive adjustments from fetal to neonatal life may be impaired.[28] Double-blind, controlled, prospective studies are necessary to establish the effectiveness of prostaglandin synthetase inhibitors in inhibiting the onset or duration of premature uterine contractions.

Progesterone

Progesterone, which is synthesized in the placenta, has been proposed by Csapo to block uterine activity.[29] The onset of labor in several animal species may not be delayed by decreasing the placental production of progesterone. In contrast, increasing levels of estrogen during pregnancy may promote uterine contractions, perhaps by increasing the release of or sensitivity to oxytocin. The direct injection of progesterone into the uterine wall or the intravenous infusion of the progesterone precursor, pregnenolone, may inhibit oxytocin effects. In contrast, several studies by Fuchs and Stakemann[30] and by Brenner and Hendricks[31] have failed to demonstrate any labor-inhibit-

ing effect of progesterone in women with premature labor. The prescribed dosages of progesterone may be inadequate to supplement the placental production for inhibiting the onset of labor. Progesterone is probably ineffective after the onset of labor.

The most promising work has been by Johnson et al. in a prospective, double-blind study involving the prophylactic weekly injections of 250 mg of 17-α-hydroxy progesterone caproate (Delalutin) begun *after* the 14th week of gestation.[32] Premature delivery did not occur in the 18 patients receiving the progestational agent, whereas 9 of the 22 patients receiving placebo had premature delivery. The safety and effectiveness of these prophylactic injections are being studied at other institutions, but further investigation is necessary before FDA approval can be obtained for this indication.

β-Adrenergic Drugs

β-Adrenergic drugs have gained the attention of many investigators during recent years because of their efficacy in inhibiting spontaneous or induced uterine contractions. These agents are structurally similar to epinephrine and act by binding to adrenergic receptors on uterine smooth muscle cells. Rucker, in 1925, was the first investigator to report the inhibiting effect of infused epinephrine on the gravid uterus;[33] however, the transient nature and unwanted cardiovascular side effects limited its clinical use. Being structurally similar to catecholamines and capable of stimulating adrenergic receptors, isoxsurprine was later found to diminish uterine contractile activity with fewer cardiovascular side effects. Other adrenergic drugs such as terbutaline and ritodrine were soon studied, and adrenergic receptor function became better understood.

Pharmacology. Adrenergic receptors in many tissues were initially categorized by Ahlquist in 1944 according to their vasoactive properties.[34] α-receptor stimulation caused vasoconstriction, while β-receptor stimulation provoked vasodilation and tachycardia. In 1967 Lands et al. further subdivided β-receptor

TABLE 9-5 EFFECTS FROM ADRENERGIC RECEPTOR STIMULATION

Adrenergic Receptor	Tissue	Observed Effect
α	Uterus	Uterine contractions
	Blood vessels	Hypertension
β_1	Heart	Tachycardia
	Adipose	Lipolysis
	Small intestine	Gastrointestinal relaxation
β_2	Uterus	Uterine relaxation
	Bronchioles	Bronchial relaxation
	Blood vessels	Hypotension
	Muscles	Glycogenolysis
	Liver	

function into β_1 and β_2 groups.[35] Specific effects from stimulation of these three types of adrenergic receptors (α, β_1, β_2) are listed in Table 9-5. A betamimetic drug with primarily β_2 adrenergic activity is most desirable in premature labor. A subset of β_2 receptor stimulants acting on uterine smooth-muscle receptors rather than on blood vessel or bronchial receptors would be ideal.

β_2-Adrenergic drugs bind to specific receptors on the outer smooth-muscle cell membrane to activate the enzyme, adenyl cyclase.[36] Adenosine 5'-triphosphate (ATP) is then rapidly converted to cyclic adenosine 5'-monophosphate (cAMP) which causes protein kinases to phosphorylate cell membrane proteins. The phosphorylated proteins sequester intracellular calcium to prevent the activation of muscle cell contractile elements for uterine smooth-muscle contraction.

All β-adrenergic drugs are metabolized in the liver and eliminated primarily by the kidneys in either unchanged or inactive, conjugated forms.

Preparations and Dosages. All preparations that have been used clinically are structurally similar to epinephrine (Fig. 9-2). Observed effects relate to differences in substitutions on the aromatic ring, the α- and β-carbons, and the terminal amine group.

Isoxsuprine (Vasodilan), terbutaline (Brethine, Bricanyl), and ritodrine (Yutopar) have been used in the United States. Only ritodrine has been approved by the FDA for inhibiting preterm labor, and it has been studied for more than 10 years at various medical centers in the United States and Europe. The wholesale cost of ritodrine is considerably higher than the cost of an equivalent dose of terbutaline.

The preparations and dose regimens for initial and maintenance therapy are listed in Table 9-3. Unlike many other tocolytic agents,

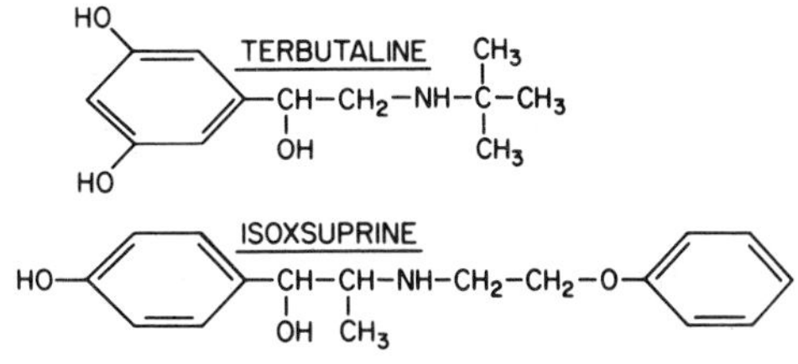

Figure 9-2. Structures of the β-adrenergic agents.

the β-adrenergic drugs can be administered by intravenous, subcutaneous, or oral routes. The parenteral dose is titrated according to contraction frequency and side effects. Intravenous treatment should be continued for approximately 12 hours after contractions cease. Oral therapy may then be started during SC injections or IV therapy. Therapy can be reinstituted if labor returns after successful tocolysis, but the persistence of labor despite the maximal recommended IV dose warrants discontinuation of the drug. Because side effects outweigh the benefits, β-adrenergic therapy is discontinued after the 37th gestational week, or if fetal pulmonary maturity has been established.

ISOXSUPRINE.   Reports from controlled studies by Das[37] and by Csapo and Herczeg[38] have supported the use of isoxsuprine in arresting premature labor. This gained further acceptance from studies by Bishop and Woutersz[39] and by Hendricks.[40] Success rates judged by delay of delivery 3 days or more were 80 percent. Frequent severe side effects including maternal tachycardia and hypotension from α- and β-receptor stimulation have limited the routine use of isoxsuprine. The average maternal blood pressure decreased by 8 mm Hg and average maternal heart rate increased by 10.9 beats/minute in the isoxsuprine-treated group. There was a slight average increase in fetal heart rate (FHR) of 6 beats/minute,[41] in addition to some patients developing transient dizziness, weakness, nausea, sweating and headaches.

Glycogenolysis from β_2-receptor stimulation in the liver and muscles can cause hyperglycemia, lactic acidemia, and elevated levels of free fatty acids. Transient increases in insulin secretion and a moderate decrease in serum potassium levels may occur. As a result of fetal hyperinsulinemia in response to the hyperglycemia, transient hypoglycemia may be seen in the neonate. No increase in neonatal morbidity has been reported in a 2-year follow-up after ritodrine use.

TERBUTALINE.   Terbutaline is a selective β_2-agonist which has wide clinical use in the treatment of bronchial asthma. Most of the initial studies on terbutaline's effectiveness in the therapy of premature labor were done by Anderson and Ingemarsson in Sweden.[42,43] In 1975 Anderson demonstrated that terbutaline in concentrations of 0.2 to 1.0 μg/ml inhibited spontaneous contractile activity of isolated strips of myometrium in vitro from seven patients undergoing cesarean section at term. The effects of terbutaline were inhibited by propranolol (β_1- and β_2-blocker); however, a selective β_1-blocker had no effect on the actions of terbutaline in vitro. A small number of patients in labor received a terbutaline infusion of 10 to 15 μg/minute for 20 to 40 minutes, which inhibited both spontaneous as well as oxytocin-induced labor. The intensity and the frequency of the contractions were diminished in all patients.

The safety of terbutaline has been supported by animal studies by Caritis et al.[44] Terbutaline successfully suppressed spontaneous and oxytocin augmented uterine activity in the pregnant baboon when administered intravenously. Mean maternal arterial pressure was not significantly changed although a mild maternal tachycardia occurred and was dose-related. Significant alterations in maternal or fetal acid base status did not occur despite the presence of hyperglycemia. In infusion rates in excess of labor-inhibiting doses in pregnant ewes, terbutaline did not cause adverse changes in uterine blood flow.[45] Akerlund and Andersson determined that intravenous terbutaline caused an inhibition of myometrial activity and an increase in local endometrial blood flow in the human uterus at all phases of the menstrual cycle.[42]

In 1974, Andersson et al. administered intravenous terbutaline at a rate of 10 to 20 μg/min to 14 patients in normal term labor.[46] In all patients studied, uterine contractions were inhibited with a decrease in amplitude and frequency of contractions. Inhibition was not affected by the use of oxytocin and no rebound was noted after discontinuation of the drug. Most patients had an increase in systolic pressure but a decrease in diastolic pressure, thereby increasing pulse pressure. The most significant change was an increase in maternal heart rate while on terbutaline. The fetal heart rate also increased up to a maximum rate of 160 beats/minute.

This study was followed by the first double-blind, placebo-controlled study with terbutaline by Ingemarsson.[47] Thirty patients in premature labor with intact membranes were randomized and matched. Cervical dilation in all patients was less than 4 cm. In the terbutaline-treated group, 12 of 15 (80 percent) of the patients delivered at week 37 or beyond, while only 3 patients (20 percent) in the placebo group reached term. No serious side effects occurred with terbutaline. Maternal tachycardia occurred in all patients treated with terbutaline with an average increase of 30 percent, and fetal tachycardia was also observed.

Wallace et al.[48] performed an uncontrolled study of 50 women in premature labor. An initial IV bolus of 250 μg of terbutaline was followed by a maintenance infusion of 10 to 80 μg/minute. Success, as defined by a prolongation of gestation for 72 hours or more, involved 78 percent of the study group. There was an average prolongation of gestation of 3.7 weeks, with 48 percent of patients reaching 36 weeks or more.

Most side effects encountered with terbutaline are mild and careful attention must be placed on monitoring blood pressure and pulse. The patient must be well hydrated prior to administration of the drug. There have been some isolated reports of pulmonary edema occurring in patients simultaneously treated with terbutaline and steroids to enhance lung maturity.[49,50]

RITODRINE.   Ritodrine hydrochloride is a β-adrenergic agonist with a preferential affinity for β_2-receptors that was developed specifically for inhibiting uterine contractions in premature labor. It is only a weak β_1-agonist and has no α-sympatholytic effects; therefore, it has minimal direct cardiovascular effects. It is presently the only drug approved by the FDA for use in premature labor. Its safety and patient acceptance of the drug have been proven in extensive worldwide clinical trials. Evidence for its efficacy in improving neonatal

outcome is attested to by some but not all individual studies of the agent. It is the most well studied of the β-adrenergic agonists for the treatment of premature labor.

Trials of ritodrine in the United States were judged as providing sufficient evidence of efficacy and safety for the FDA in 1980 to approve the drug for clinical use. The study was a collaborative attempt to assemble data from 11 investigators in a prospective, randomized or double-blind manner by comparing ritodrine to either ethanol or placebo.[51] Unfortunately, only a partially standardized protocol was used. Over a 5-year period (1975–1979), 313 pregnancies with premature labor were evaluated. A statistically significant difference was noted between the ritodrine versus controls in a variety of parameters. Neonatal deaths and respiratory distress syndrome were noted to be significantly less in the treated versus the control groups. The average number of days gained prior to delivery was 32.6 in the ritodrine group and 21.3 days in the control group. Significantly, more infants in the treated group obtained birth weights of greater than 2500 gm or gestation ages of 36 weeks or more. In all categories the most benefit was gained by the neonates whose estimated gestational age at the onset of treatment was less than 33 weeks.

The pharmacokinetics of ritodrine have been extensively studied in animals and humans.[52] Animal studies show that between 50 and 80 percent of the drug is excreted in the urine. Ninety percent of the drug is excreted in 24 hours, the majority in the form of inactive metabolites. Almost twice as much of the drug is excreted unchanged when given intravenously. In sheep, the drug crosses the placenta and reaches 20 percent of the maternal concentration of the drug. The lethal dose was ascertained in many animal studies, and in the two most sensitive species the LD_{50} was 80 times the effective therapeutic level in humans. No ill effects were noted in the animals on short or protracted courses of therapy, and the only fetal effect noted in some species was an increase in fetal weight. Uterine blood flow studies have not shown consistent results, but indicate some decrease in blood flow may occur that is not associated with acid-base changes in the fetus.

Human studies reveal that 32 percent of the drug is bound to albumin, and 71 to 93 percent of the drug is excreted in the urine with a maximum rate of excretion 1 hour after oral administration. As in animals, approximately 20 percent of the drug crosses the placenta.

Several maternal cardiovascular effects have been noted in patients treated with intravenous ritodrine; these include a dose-related rise in maternal heart rate of 19 to 40 beats/minute, a widening of the pulse pressure by 3 to 18 mm Hg, and a slight increase in cardiac output. The mean fetal heart rate increases consistently. All cardiovascular effects can be blocked with β-blockers. Serious side effects are rare, but two maternal deaths have been reported.[52] One patient had unsuspected idiopathic pulmonary hypertension, the other was on multiple medications including corticosteroids. Pulmonary edema has been reported in patients who were also receiving corticosteroids, usually when excessive fluids were administered intravenously. Metabolic changes include transient increases in glucose, free fatty acids, and insulin, with a moderate decrease in potassium.[53] Unpleasant but probably physiologically insignificant side effects include tremor (10 to 15 percent), palpitations (33 percent), and nervousness or restlessness in 20 percent. There have been no reports of an increase in postterm pregnancies, abnormal labor, or uterine atony. No increase in neonatal morbidity has been noted in the 2-year follow-up of the infants delivered during these trials.[54] In addition, transient hypoglycemia was common in neonates delivered by mothers receiving ritodrine.

The dosage of ritodrine for treating premature labor is begun at 100 μg/minute IV and is usually increased in increments of 50 μg/minute up to 350 μg/minute as needed to inhibit contractions. Accurate fluid balance is necessary, and isotonic saline solutions should be avoided. The manufacturer recommends continuing intravenous treatment for 12 hours after contractions cease. Oral maintenance therapy is started 30 minutes prior to the discontinuation of the intravenous regimen at 10 mg every 2 hours or 20 mg every 4 hours. The maximal dose should not exceed 120 mg/day. If labor recurs and there are no contraindications to tocolysis, the infusion may be restarted. Once fetal lung maturity is evident, the drug may be discontinued without the need for tapering.

OTHER DRUGS WITH UTERINE INHIBITORY ACTIVITY

Diazoxide (Hyperstat)
Diazoxide is a potent vasodilating agent which is a nondiuretic thiazide. It has been noted to markedly inhibit uterine activity when used to treat hypertensive crisis in pregnancy.[55] The mechanism for tocolysis is uncertain but may be a direct effect on uterine smooth muscle or through the release of catecholamines.[56] The cardiovascular effects (tachycardia, hypotension) and metabolic effect (hypoglycemia) of diazoxide are similar to those of the β_2-adrenergic agents, but they are not reversed by β-blocking agents (propranolol) and are more pronounced. In studies using sheep, uterine blood flow was not reduced with a slow infusion.[57] Studies in humans with doses that inhibited contractions resulted in only mild tachycardia and a small reduction in blood pressure. Controlled, convincing studies of the effectiveness of diazoxide are lacking and are unlikely to be undertaken, since β_2-adrenergic agonists have been shown to be effective and probably less hazardous.

Aminophylline
Aminophylline is a xanthine derivative used to treat asthma during pregnancy. It has been postulated that aminophylline may indirectly inhibit uterine motility by its phosphodiesterase inhibitory action.[58] The inhibition of phosphodiesterase may cause an accumulation of cAMP, which is an important regulator in myosin light-chain phosphorylation for smooth muscle contractility. A study by Coutinho and

Lopes supported this theory by infusing aminophylline to 60 women at various phases of their menstrual cycles.[59] Uterine activity was decreased in all patients. Aminophylline is not approved by the FDA for premature labor therapy, and a paucity of data supports its effectiveness. Recent evidence in rabbit and rat fetal exposure and supported by human investigation has suggested that phosphodiesterase inhibitors may increase alveolar surfactant concentration and synthesis.[60,61] The principal result is thought to be an increase in phosphatidylcholine levels.

GUIDELINES FOR SELECTING TOCOLYTIC AGENTS

The proper choice of an appropriate tocolytic agent frequently is not easy. Many agents described in this chapter (ethanol, magnesium sulfate, isoxsuprine, diazoxide, aminophylline) were found to have tocolytic potential only as a result of incidental use. The mechanism of uterine contraction has become better understood in recent years, and β_2-adrenergic drugs have been found to be most useful clinically because of their more specific interaction with myometrial receptors. They are effective and can be used repetitively and chronically as oral agents. Ritodrine is the only drug that is currently FDA-approved for tocolysis and is the drug of choice in the majority of pregnancies treated for premature labor.

No group of drugs described in this chapter has been proven to be ideal for inhibiting uterine contractions. Adverse effects to the mother and fetus must be considered as cases are selected for tocolysis. Patient education and informed consent are essential. Close monitoring is a prerequisite, and package inserts describing each drug must be read and understood.

The choice of tocolytic agent must be tailored to the individual clinical situation. Anticipated side effects from each drug may require a change in drugs or a discontinuation of therapy. This is especially true if heart disease, hypertension, thyroid disease, liver disease,

impaired renal function, diabetes mellitus, or vaginal bleeding is present. A well-supervised delivery near an intensive care nursery may be preferred to inhibiting uterine contractions when fetal lung maturity is evident. Very little information is available about the combined use of tocolytic agents. Uterine contractions may be more effectively inhibited, while unwanted side effects may not be increased or may be reduced, if smaller dosages can be administered.

Further clinical investigation is necessary to better understand the etiology of premature labor, the endocrinology of parturition, and the effectiveness of the various tocolytic drug regimens. Double-blind, prospective studies involving control groups must be continued at regional perinatal centers. Along with determining what percentage of pregnancies remain undelivered within a few days or several weeks after initiating therapy, the long-term effects on the fetus and infant must be assessed. The practicality of tocolytic therapy also requires further investigation of conditions in which preterm ruptures of amniotic membranes are present or for selected pregnancies in which prophylactic therapy may decrease the risk of subsequent premature labor.

REFERENCES

1. *Monthly Vital Statistics Report* 22(7) suppl 7. US Dept of Health, Education and Welfare, Health Resources Administration, Oct 1973
2. Zuspan FP: Premature labor: Its management and therapy. *J Reprod Med* 9:93, 1972
3. Wynn M, Wynn A: *The Prevention of Preterm Birth.* London, Foundation for Education and Research in Child-Bearing, 1977
4. Caritis SN, Edelstone DI, Mueller-Heubach E: Pharmacologic inhibition of preterm labor. *Am J Obstet Gynecol* 133:557, 1979
5. Fuchs F, Fuchs AR, Poblete VF Jr, Risk A: Effect of alcohol on threatened premature labor. *Am J Obstet Gynecol* 99:627, 1967
6. Zlatnick FJ, Fuchs F: A controlled study of ethanol in threatened premature labor. *Am J Obstet Gynecol* 112:610, 1972
7. Watring WG, Benson WL, Wiebe RA, Vaughn DL: Intravenous alcohol—a single blind study

in the prevention of premature delivery: A preliminary report. *J Reprod Med* 16:35, 1976

8. Castren O, Gummerus M, Saarikoski S: Treatment of imminent premature labour. *Acta Obstet Gynecol Scand* 54:95, 1975

9. Steir CM, Petrie RH: A comparison of magnesium sulfate and alcohol for the prevention of premature labor. *Am J Obstet Gynecol* 129:1, 1977

10. Lauersen NH, Merkatz IR, Tejani N, Wilson KH, Roberson A, Mann LI, Fuchs F: Inhibition of premature labor: A multicenter comparison of ritodrine and ethanol. *Am J Obstet Gynecol* 127:837, 1977

11. Fuchs F: Prevention of prematurity. *Am J Obstet Gynecol* 126:809, 1976

12. Ritchie JM: The aliphatic alcohols. In Goodman LS, Gilman A (eds): *The Pharmacologic Basis of Therapeutics*, ed. 5. New York, Macmillan, 1975, pp 137–151

13. Kumar D, Zourlas PA, Barnes AC: In vitro and in vivo effects of magnesium sulfate on human uterine contractiligy. *Am J Obstet Gynecol* 86:1036, 1963

14. Harbert GM, Cornell GW, Thornton WN Jr: Effect of toxemia therapy on uterine dynamics. *Am J Obstet Gynecol* 105:94, 1969

15. Wacker WEC, Parisi AF: Magnesium metabolism. *N Engl J Med* 278:658, 1968

16. Stone SR, Pritchard JA: Effect of maternally administered magnesium sulfate on the neonate. *Obstet Gynecol* 35:574, 1970

17. Lipsitz PJ: The clinical and biochemical effects of excess magnesium in the newborn. *Pediatrics* 47:501, 1971

18. Pritchard JA: The use of magnesium sulfate in pre-eclampsia-eclampsia. *J Reprod Med* 23:107, 1979

19. Aiken JW: Aspirin and indomethacin prolong parturition in rats: Evidence that prostaglandins contribute to expulsion of foetus. *Nature* 240:21, 1972

20. Csapo AI, Csapo EF, Fay E, Henzl MR, Salau G: The delay of spontaneous labor by naproxen in the rat model. *Prostaglandins* 3:827, 1973

21. Novy MJ, Cook MJ, Manaugh L: Indomethacin block of normal onset of parturition in primates. *Am J Obstet Gynecol* 118:412, 1974

22. Lewis RB, Schulman JD: Influence of acetylsalicyclic acid, an inhibitor of prostaglandin synthesis, on the duration of human gestation and labour. *Lancet* 2:1159, 1973

23. Zuckerman H, Reiss U, Rubinstein I: Inhibition of human premature labor by indomethacin. *Obstet Gynecol* 44:787, 1974.

24. Johnson WL, Harbert GM, Martin CG: Pharmacologic control of uterine contractility. *Am J Obstet Gynecol* 123:364, 1975

25. Niebyl JR, Blake DA, White RD, et al: The inhibition of premature labor with indomethacin. *Am J Obstet Gynecol* 136:1014, 1980

26. Starling MB, Elliott RB: The effects of prostaglandins, prostaglandin inhibitors, and oxygen on the closure of the ductus arteriosus, pulmonary arteries and umbilical vessels in vitro. *Prostaglandins* 8:187, 1974

27. Haslam RR, Ekert H, Gilliam GR: Hemorrhage in a neonate possibly due to maternal ingestion of salicylate. *J Pediatr* 84:556, 1974

28. Bleyer WA, Breckenridge RT: Studies on the detection of adverse drug reactions in the newborn: II. The effects of prenatal aspirin on newborn hemostasis. *JAMA* 213:2049, 1970

29. Csapo AI: The regulatory interplay of progesterone and prostaglandin F₂ in the control of the pregnant uterus, in Josimovich JB (ed): *Uterine Contraction*, New York, Wiley 1973, pp 223–255

30. Fuchs F, Stakemann G: Treatment of threatened premature labor with large doses of progesterone. *Am J Obstet Gynecol* 79:172, 1960

31. Brenner WE, Hendricks CH: Effect of medroxyprogesterone acetate upon the duration and characteristics of human gestation and labor. *Am J Obstet Gynecol* 83:1094, 1962

32. Johnson JWC, Austin KL, Jones GS, Davis GH, King TM: Efficacy of 17-hydroxyprogesterone caproate in the prevention of premature labor. *N Engl J Med* 293:675, 1975

33. Rucker MP: The action of adrenalin on the pregnant human uterus. *South Med J* 18:412, 1925

34. Ahlquist RP: A study of the adrenotropic receptors. *Am J Physiol* 153:586, 1948

35. Lands AM, Luduena FP, Buzzo HJ: Differentiation of receptors responsive to isoproterenol. *Life Sci* 6:2241, 1967

36. Steer ML, Atlas D, Levitzki A: Inter-relations between α-adrenergic receptors, adenylate cyclase and calcium. *N Engl J Med* 292:409, 1975

37. Das RK: Isoxsuprine in premature labour. *J Obstet Gynaecol India* 19:1076, 1965

38. Csapo AI, Herczeg J: Arrest of premature labor by isoxsuprine. *Am J Obstet Gynecol* 129:482, 1977

39. Bishop EH, Woutersz TB: Arrest of premature labor. *JAMA* 178:116, 1961

40. Hendricks CH: The use of isoxsuprine for the arrest of premature labor. *Clin Obstet Gynecol* 7:687, 1964

41. Stander RW, Barden TP, Thompson JF, Pugh WR, Werts CE: Fetal cardiac effects of maternal isoxsuprine infusion. *Am J Obstet Gynecol* 89:792, 1964

42. Akerlund M, Andersson K-E: Effects of terbutaline on human myometrial activity and endometrial blood flow. *Obstet Gynecol* 47:529, 1976

43. Andersson K-E, Bengtsson L Ph, Gustafson I, Ingemarsson I: The relaxing effect of terbutaline on the human uterus during term labor. *Am J Obstet Gynecol* 121:602, 1975

44. Caritis SN, Morishima HO, Stark RI, Daniel SS, James LS: Effects of terbutaline on the pregnant baboon and fetus. *Obstet Gynecol* 50:56, 1977

45. Caritis SN, Mueller-Heubach E, Morishima HO, Edelstone DI: Effect of terbutaline on cardiovascular state and uterine blood flow in pregnant ewes. *Obstet Gynecol* 50:603, 1977

46. Andersson K-E, Ingemarsson I, Persson CGA: Effects of terbutaline on human uterine motility at term. *Acta Obstet Gynecol Scand* 54:165, 1975

47. Ingemarsson I: Effect of terbutaline on premature labor. *Am J Obstet Gynecol* 125:520, 1976.

48. Wallace RL, Caldwell DL, Ansbacher R, Otterson WN: Inhibition of premature labor by terbutaline. *Obstet Gynecol* 51:387, 1978

49. Stubblefield PG: Pulmonary edema occurring after therapy with dexamethasone and terbutaline: For premature labor. *Am J Obstet Gynecol* 132:341, 1978

50. Jacobs MM, Knight AB, Areas F: Maternal pulmonary edema resulting from betamimesic and glycocorticoid therapy. *Obstet Gynecol* 56:56, 1980

51. Merkatz IR, Peter JB, Barden TP: Ritodrine hydrochloride: A betamimetic agent for use in preterm labor. *Obstet Gynecol* 56:7, 1980

52. Barden TP, Peter JB, Merkatz IR: Ritodrine hydrochloride: A betamimetic agent for use in preterm labor. *Obstet Gynecol* 56:1, 1980

53. Spellacy WN, Cruz AC, Buhi WC, et al: The acute effects of ritodrine infusion on maternal metabolism: Measurement of levels of glucose, insulin, glucagon, triglycerides, cholesterol, placental lactogen and chorionic gonadotropin. *Am J Obstet Gynecol* 131:673, 1978

54. Freysz H, Willard D, Lehr A, et al: A long-term evaluation of infants who received a betamimetic drug while in utero. *J Perinat Med* 5:94, 1977

55. Pennington JC, Picker RH: Diazoxide and the treatment of the acute hypertensive emergency in obstetrics. *Med J Aust* 2:1051, 1972

56. Wohl AJ, Hausler LM, Roth FE: Studies on the mechanism of antihypertensive action of diazoxide: In vitro vascular pharmacodynamics. *J Pharmacol Exp Ther* 158:531, 1967

57. Caritis SN, Morishima HO, Stark RI, James LS: The effect of diazoxide on uterine blood flow in pregnant sheep. *Obstet Gynecol* 48:464, 1976

58. Polson JB, Krzanowski JJ, Fitzpatrick DF, et al: Studies on the inhibition of phosphodiesterase-catalyzed cycle AMP and cycle GMP breakdown and relaxation of canine tracheal smooth muscle. *Biochem Pharmacol* 27:254, 1978

59. Coutinho EM, Vieira Lopes AC: Inhibition of uterine motility by aminophylline. *Am J Obstet Gynecol* 110:726, 1971

60. Brinkman CR, Nuwayhid B, Assali NS: Renal hypertension and pregnancy in sheep. I. Behavior of uteroplacental vasomotor tone during mild hypertension. *Am J Obstet Gynecol* 121:931, 1975

61. Karotkin EH, Kido M, Cashore WJ, et al: Acceleration of fetal lung maturation by aminophylline in pregnant rabbits. *Pediatr Res* 10:722, 1976

10. Uterine Stimulants

John S. Russ William F. Rayburn
Mervyn J. Samuel

Many theories concerning uterine stimulation during pregnancy exist, and explanations have paralleled knowledge about uterine physiology. Despite our inability to completely explain the mechanisms involved in uterine contractility, nature continually illustrates the process. At some critical time, which almost always seems appropriate and purposeful, the uterus is stimulated for the evacuation of its contents. Almost unerringly the process begins and ceases, being timed perfectly for mother and child.

The initiation and maintenance of uterine activity involves a complex interaction between maternal, uterine, and fetal factors. Progress in understanding the mechanisms for initiation of parturition have led to advances in uterine stimulation by pharmacologic agents. With continued clinical application these uterine stimulators have been modified and improved for use during the intrapartum and postpartum periods.

The three major groups of drugs to induce uterine stimulation include oxytocin, ergot alkaloids, and prostaglandins. An appreciation of their properties, indications, and effects on the target tissues should increase the clinician's competence in managing the induction of labor and in diminishing uterine blood loss in the postpartum period.

OXYTOCIN

In 1906 Dale was the first person to describe the chemical properties and elucidate the pharmacology of oxytocin from pituitary extracts.[1] It was not until the early 1950s, however, that duVigneaud and co-workers did the pioneering and Nobel prize-winning work on the structure of oxytocin.[2] Once commercially prepared quantities became available, knowledge about oxytocin paralleled advances in the comprehension of mechanisms of labor and the effects of labor on the uterus and on the fetus. Oxytocin is now the most widely used uterine stimulant and the most potentially harmful agent, if used improperly.

Pharmacology

Oxytocin is an octapeptide which is synthesized in the supraoptic and paraventricular nuclei of the hypothalamus. It is transported by carrier proteins from the hypothalamus to the posterior pituitary, where it is eventually released. Oxytocin has a half-life of 3 to 4 minutes and is rapidly metabolized and degraded by oxytocinase.[3] The component amino acids are either redistributed or eliminated via the kidneys.

The mechanism wherein oxytocin facilitates smooth muscle contraction is not fully understood. Oxytocin is thought to bind to receptors on myometrial cell membranes, where cyclic adenosine 5'-monophosphate (cAMP) is eventually formed for a dose-dependent increase in amplitude and frequency of uterine contractions.[4] Bound intracellular calcium near the cell membrane is eventually mobilized from the sarcoplasmic reticulum to activate the contractile proteins. Oxytocin is also thought to act with prostaglandins. The uterine response to oxytocin stimulation depends on the uterine threshold of excitation, with the sensitivity of the uterus to oxytocin increasing gradually during gestation and sharply increasing before parturition.[5] Oxytocin is secreted in increasing amounts as labor progresses.

Clinical Use

Oxytocin is used to induce uterine contractions in term and preterm pregnancies requiring uterine evacuation (Fig. 10-1). Pregnancy complications requiring uterine evacuation with oxytocin and uterine curettage would include incomplete or inevitable abortion, missed abortion, trophoblastic disease, and elective abortion. The uterine sensitivity to oxytocin infusion increases with gestational age and stage of labor.

Oxytocin may also be used during the intrapartum period to augment uterine contractions which are mild or infrequent (hypotonic contractions).[6] Postpartum hemorrhage is reduced when oxytocin is given with uterine massage. In our experience, an emptied uterus which does not contract well at cesarean section may respond to a direct 10-unit intramyometrial injection. Except for small hematomas, no immediate adverse effects have been observed.

Oxytocin is either contraindicated or should be used with extreme caution when certain obstetrical complications exist (Table 10-1). The risks and benefits must be carefully considered on an individual basis. Careful uterine and fetal monitoring is essential with close labor and delivery personnel supervision. Oxytocin should not be used to force cervical dilation.

Preparations and Doses

When taken orally, oxytocin is rapidly degraded in the gastrointestinal tract. Ampules of 10 units/ml of oxytocin (Pitocin, Syntocinon) are currently available for parenteral use. Tablets for application to the buccal cavity are no longer available, since the variable absorption caused unpredictable uterine understimulation and overstimulation.

The administration of oxytocin by IM injection, IV bolus, or nasal drip is to be discouraged during labor. Compared to these routes of administration, the slow, continuous intravenous infusion has more predictable absorption, distribution, and response patterns.

Solutions for intravenous use usually contain 10 units of oxytocin (10 mU/ml). More concentrated solutions are possible when appropriate monitoring of the dose can be arranged. Infusion pumps are recommended for the accurate control of the rate of infusion.

The goal of induction is the presence of uterine contractions occurring every 2 to 3 minutes and lasting approximately 45–60 seconds.[7] When an intrauterine pressure catheter is used, a 50 mm H_2O recording is considered to be reasonable evidence of an adequate contraction. The infusion is begun at 2 mU/minute and increased at 2-mU/minute increments every 15 to 20 minutes until adequate contractions are palpated and observed. The maximal rate of infusion for delivery purposes should generally not exceed 20 mU/minute, and the uterine response generally will not improve if a rate of 30 mU/minute or more is administered.[8] Table 10-2 lists the intravenous infusion schedules of oxytocin using a 10 units/liter solution mixture.

Side Effects

Side effects from oxytocin use are usually easily predicted. Adequate supervision with monitoring of the uterine contractions, the fetus, and the infusion is necessary. Hyperstimulation with strong (hypertonic) or prolonged (tetanic) contractions, or a resting tone of 15 to 20 mm H_2O or more between contractions can lead to uterine rupture, utero-placental hypoperfusion, and fetal distress from hypoxia. Under these circumstances the infusion should be stopped immediately.

Cardiovascular side effects including premature ventricular contractions may occur when an IV bolus of one or more units is given.[9] Hypotension from direct peripheral vasodilation may also occur, especially when oxytocin is used in combination with a general anesthetic such as cyclopropane.

SENSITIVITY OF THE HUMAN UTERUS TO OXYTOCIN
DURING PREGNANCY

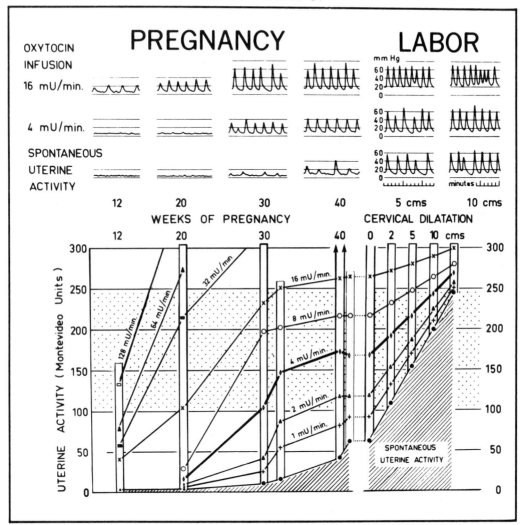

Figure 10-1. Sensitivity of the human uterus to oxytocin during pregnancy. Uterine activity tracings in the upper section illustrate the increasing sensitivity of the human uterus to oxytocin. The mean values of the uterine response to increasing doses are plotted against the duration of pregnancy and cervical dilation. (From Caldeyro-Barcia R, Heller, eds: *Oxytocin.* Oxford, Pergaman, 1961, with permission.)

Natural and synthetic oxytocin is structurally similar to antidiuretic hormone (ADH), and fluid reabsorption from the glomerular filtrate may cause fluid retention (Fig. 10-2). To avoid this, large quantities of intravenous crystalloid solutions are not to be infused with high concentrations of oxytocin. The infusion of 20 mU/minute may lead to a decrease in urine output, while 40 mU/minute or more of oxytocin with excessive fluid infusion has led to fluid overload and convulsions or coma.[10] Hypoglycemia and decreased circulat-

TABLE 10-1 CONDITIONS IN WHICH OXYTOCIN IS EITHER USED WITH CAUTION OR IS CONTRAINDICATED

Used with Caution
  Cephalopelvic dysproportion
  Multiple fetuses
  Polyhydramnios
  Suspected fetal distress
  Grand multiparity
  Delivery of second twin
  Severe hypertension
  Breech
  Repeat cesarean section (low transverse uterine incision)

Contraindicated
  Repeat cesarean section (vertical uterine incision)
  Unfavorable fetal position (transverse lie)
  Placenta previa

ing triglyceride levels have also been associated with prolonged oxytocin use, although the mechanism is unclear.[11]

Oxytocin does not cross the placenta, so no direct effects on the fetus have been observed. However, uterine hypertonicity from overzealous oxytocin use may lead to variable decelerations of the fetal heart rate and fetal hypoxia. A greater incidence of hyperbilirubinemia has been reported in infants delivered after oxytocin was used during labor.[12] This was found when large amounts of oxytocin had been given and may have resulted from fetal hemorrhage during the birthing process.

ERGOT ALKALOIDS

The earliest report of ergot alkaloid use for uterine stimulation was in the 1582 *Kreuterbuch* by Adam Lonicer. In the 1700s, the grain source of this stimulant was identified, and by the early 1800s, John Stearns introduced ergot into obstetrical practice. It was not until the beginning of the 1950s that the contractile properties of the ergots became well understood. Work on the purification of these compounds and advancements in receptor pharmacology have resulted in the practical use of the ergots for uterine stimulation.

TABLE 10-2 INTRAVENOUS INFUSION SCHEDULE OF OXYTOCIN (USING A 10 μM/LITER SOLUTION MIXTURE)*

Infused Oxytocin (mU/min)†	Eyeball (drops/min)	IVAC (drops/min)	IMED (ml/hr)
2	2	2	12
4	4	4	24
6	6	6	36
8	8	8	48
10	10	10	60
12	12	12	72
14	14	14	84
16	16	16	96
18	18	18	108
20	20	20	120

* In the prescribed mixture, 1 drop contains 1 mU of pitocin and 1 ml of solution contains 10 drops or 10 mU of pitocin.
† Oxytocin infusion is routinely begun at 2 mU/min and increased at 2 mU/min increments every 15 to 20 min as necessary. Hyperstimulation and water intoxication are to be avoided, and infusion at 16 mU/min or more is discouraged.

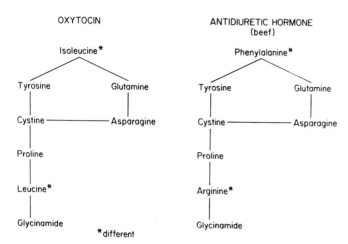

OXYTOCIN

Isoleucine*

Tyrosine   Glutamine

Cystine —————— Asparagine

Proline

Leucine*

Glycinamide
*different

ANTIDIURETIC HORMONE
(beef)

Phenylalanine*

Tyrosine   Glutamine

Cystine —————— Asparagine

Proline

Arginine*

Glycinamide

Figure 10-2. Chemical structures of oxytocin and antidiuretic hormone.

Pharmacology

The natural ergot alkaloids are derived from a fungus *(Claviceps purpurea)* which is grown commercially. The semisynthetic derivatives contain a chemical modification which causes more specific actions with fewer side effects. The ergots affect many organ systems, particularly the cardiac, nervous, and uterine organs. The mechanism of action is by direct smooth-muscle cell receptor stimulation. The uterus is very sensitive to ergot stimulation, and powerful contractions may persist for hours. Vasoconstriction from direct smooth muscle stimulation is usually observed. The ergot alkaloids are detoxified in the liver and eliminated in the urine.

Most currently used drugs are semisynthetic derivatives of the ergot alkaloids. Each consists of a lysergic acid amide moiety combined with a condensed polypeptide. The amine alkaloids are of particular interest because of their direct stimulation of the uterine smooth muscle.

The uterine response to ergot alkaloid stimulation increases steadily during pregnancy. The characteristic uterine activity pattern in the preterm period consists of frequent, weak contractions with hypertonus, while hypercontractility is more evident at term.[13] During labor, this uncoordinated pattern of uterine activity during ergot administration is more similar to that observed with sparteine sulfate rather than with oxytocin use.[14]

Clinical Uses

Because of the potential for sustained uterine contractions and fetal compromise, which are not pharmacologically reversible, ergot products should not be used during labor.[13] Fetal and maternal injuries and deaths have been reported from such violent uterine contractions.[15] Therefore, ergot preparations are used in obstetrics only to promote uterine involution in the postabortion or postpartum periods.

Preparations and Doses

The two amine alkaloids used for uterine stimulation include ergonovine maleate (Ergotrate) and methylergonovine maleate (Methergine). Both drugs are prepared in tablet or solution forms and, unlike most ergot derivatives, they have the advantage of being well absorbed in the gastrointestinal tract. The 0.2-mg tablets are used three or four times each day for 3 days to 1 week to diminish bleeding after uterine evacuation. Immediate effects are seen when a 0.1-mg intravenous infusion or a 0.2 mg-intramuscular injection is given. The onset of action is usually 40 seconds with intravenous infusion and 7 minutes with intramuscular injection.[3]

Side Effects

Ergonovine and methylergonovine have relatively poor vasoconstrictive properties. Hypertension and signs of cardiac ischemia occur rarely in the postpartum period, but transient elevations in blood pressure may be severe and are most prominent after intravenous infusion.

Central nervous system effects are variable, but the dramatic results in preventing or treating migraine headaches with certain ergot alkaloids are not seen with ergonovine and methylergonovine. Nausea and vomiting may occur.

Along with serious injuries to the fetus and mother, ergot alkaloids are not to be used for labor induction, since eclampsia and cardiovascular collapse have been reported.[16,17] Pregnancies complicated by hypertension should therefore not receive ergot preparations. In addition, the placenta may become trapped if the ergot is given too early after delivery.

PROSTAGLANDINS

Prostaglandins are the most recent addition to the uterine stimulants. More than 3000 original publications and 10 years of clinical experience have led obstetricians to realize the enormous potential of these compounds on human parturition.

Prostaglandins were first discovered in 1935, when von Euler found substances in seminal fluid which promoted smooth muscle stimulation and relaxation, especially on the uterus.[18] With the recent development of synthetic processes to make prostaglandins, our understanding of their pharmacology and uses has increased greatly. Within the last decade, the Food and Drug Administration has approved the use of prostaglandins for abortion and for experimental use during labor.

Pharmacology

Prostaglandins are 20-carbon compounds formed by the action of the enzyme prostaglandin synthetase on the precursor, arachidonic acid (see Chap. 21). Enzymes for prostaglandin synthesis are present in most cells, and prostaglandins are formed rapidly in response to physiologic changes. All prostaglandins are structurally similar, and individual variations in chemical structure would explain differing binding characteristics to cell receptors and different effects. Prostaglandins released from decidual and myometrial cells are thought to act on specific cell receptors to alter or inhibit the action of adenyl cyclase, subsequently inhibiting formation of cAMP, the mediator of most hormone action.[19] It is also postulated that calcium release is influenced by these compounds.[4] The observed effects result primarily from changes in smooth muscle tone and modulation of hormonal activity. While their action is influenced by estrogen and progesterone, prostaglandins can effect uterine contractions at any stage of pregnancy.[3] The effect on uterine smooth muscle is not completely specific, and systemic use of these compounds can also overstimulate the gastrointestinal, circulatory, and respiratory tracts. The subsequent degradation of prostaglandins is usually rapid, since many tissues are capable of utilizing and converting these compounds. The metabolites are considered to be biologically inactive.

Preparations

Although many prostaglandins exist, the major types important in reproduction are prostaglandin E_2 (PGE_2) and F_2 (PGF_2). They differ from the parent compound, prostanoic acid, by the substitution at C-9 and C-11 of the cyclopentane ring and the addition of a double bond (Fig. 10-3).

PGF_2 (Prostin) is commercially available in 5 mg/ml concentrations in 20- and 40-mg ampules. It is administered by intra-amniotic instillation, rather than by IV or IM routes, since systemic effects are less pronounced. The IM injection of PGF_2 does not offer any advantages over the direct intra-amniotic route.

PGE_2 is prepared in a 20-mg vaginal suppository. Advantages to the suppository preparation are the ability to efface the cervix and

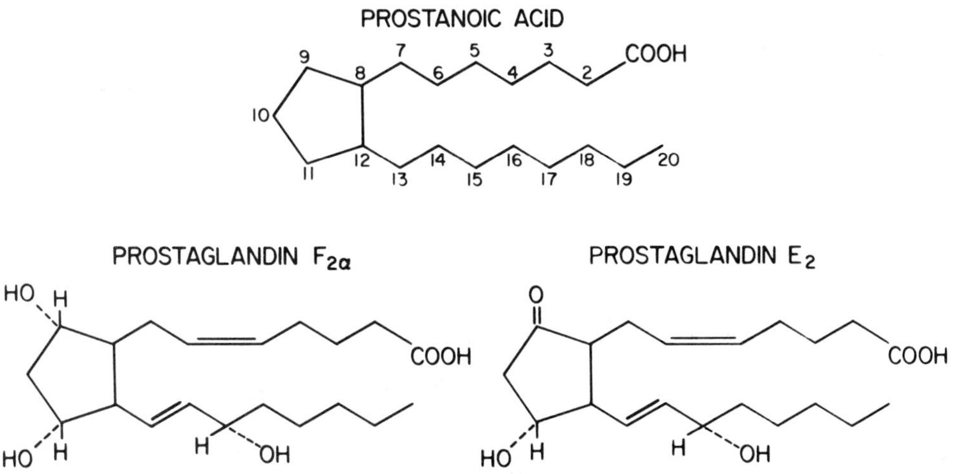

PROSTANOIC ACID

Figure 10-3. Chemical structure of the parent prostaglandin compound (prostanoic acid), prostaglandin $F_{2\alpha}$, and prostaglandin E_2.

the rapid reversal of undesired effects by removal of the suppository. A gel containing prostaglandins, which is not yet commercially available, is considered effective in effacing the cervix when applied topically.[20]

The relative cost difference between PGF_2 and PGE_2 for the desired effect is negligible.

Clinical Uses

Both PGE_2 and PGF_2 are used only for the stimulation of uterine contractions for pregnancy termination. PGF_2 is FDA-approved for intra-amniotic instillation in terminating pregnancies from 13 to 20 weeks' gestation. PGE_2 is also marketed for the termination of pregnancies complicated by intrauterine fetal demise, missed abortion (up to 28 weeks), nonmetastatic gestational trophoblastic disease, and therapeutic abortion between the 12th and 27th weeks.[21] The use of prostaglandins for the induction of labor in uncomplicated pregnancies is not recommended until investigations on uterine and fetal effects are better understood and the drugs are proven safe. Furthermore, the use of PGE_2 suppositories to decrease postpartum bleeding has been reported, but is not recommended for routine use.[22]

Dose and Effectiveness

Before the instillation of intra-amniotic PGF_2, laminaria tents may be used to dilate the cervix. After starting a precautionary IV line, a 5-mg (1 ml) intra-amniotic test dose should be instilled using a 20-gauge spinal needle under local anesthesia to search for any systemic reactions such as dyspnea, tachycardia, nausea, or vomiting. These undesired effects would indicate intravascular injection and are reversed only by discontinuation of the medication and expectant management. In the absence of these effects after 5 minutes, the remaining 35-mg (7-ml) dose is slowly instilled (Table 10-3). If amniocentesis is unsuccessful, the PGF_2 may be administered by an extraovulatory, transcervical route, using an infant feeding tube or pediatric Foley catheter.[23] Strong uterine contractions may become readily apparent. A second dose may be necessary if abortion has not occurred and the membranes remain intact after 24 hours. Oxytocin may also be infused at approximately 40 mU/minute for 2 hours after each injection.

If PGE_2 suppositories are to be used, laminaria tents may also be inserted in the cervical canal; premedication using an antinauseant (prochlorperazine 10 mg IM) and an antidiar-

TABLE 10-3   AGENTS USED FOR SECOND TRIMESTER PREGNANCY TERMINATION (13–24 weeks)

Agent	Preparation	Dose Regimen	Initiation-to-Abortion Time
Prostaglandin $F_{2\alpha}$	20- and 40-mg ampules (5 mg/ml)	40 mg (8 ml) intra-amniotically every 24 hours	12–19 hr (mean: 17 hr)
Prostaglandin E_2	20-mg vaginal suppository	One suppository every 3–5 hr	10–22 hr (mean: 14 hr)
Hypertonic saline	20% saline solution	200 ml intra-amniotically every 24 hr	16–43 hr (mean: 29 hr)
Urea	40–80-gm solution	40 gm intra-amniotically every 24 hr	>48 hr

Note: Laminaria tents are useful in dilating the cervix to avoid extensive lacerations, and oxytocin may be used to augment uterine contractions and decrease the dose required for each agent.

rheal agent (Lomotil 5 mg orally) is recommended 1 hour before the suppository insertion. A narcotic (Meperidine 50 mg IM) and an antipyretic (acetaminophen 325 mg rectal suppository) are often necessary to relieve pain from the uterine contractions and to control elevated temperatures (38 C or more). Hypertonic saline or urea has also been instilled to decrease the likelihood of delivering a viable fetus. In addition, urea (40 mg) instilled with PGF_2 should decrease the necessary effective dose of PGF_2.

The initiation-to-abortion time using PGF_2 or PGE_2 is approximately the same and ranges between 12 and 23 hours (mean: 16 hours) (Table 10-3). The use of laminaria and an increased gestational age are associated with a shorter initiation-to-abortion time.[24-26] Failures are uncommon with either preparation but have been reported to occur in 2 to 8 percent of all cases.[24-26] The risk of failed abortion is greatest among nulliparous patients before 16 weeks' gestation. A dilatation and evacuation procedure or a hysterotomy may then be necessary.

Side Effects

The major complications associated with prostaglandin use involve gastrointestinal com-

plaints which occur in less than half of the patients. Elevated temperatures requiring medication may occur in 29 percent of those patients being treated with PGE_2 suppositories. Perhaps the greatest concern with prostaglandin use is the delivery of a viable fetus, which has been reported to occur in 3 to 4 percent of the PGE_2 group and less than 1 percent of the PGF_2 group.[23,25]

Absolute contraindications to prostaglandin use include hypersensitivity to the compound and acute pelvic inflammatory disease (Table 10-4). Although not absolutely contraindicated, prostaglandins should be used with caution in patients with a history of asthma, hypertension, cardiovascular disease, renal disease, peptic ulcer disease, anemia, jaundice, diabetes, or epilepsy. It is necessary that these medical conditions be sufficiently treated before attempting to evacuate the uterus.

Signs of uterine rupture or extensive cervical tears should be sought when prostaglandins are used on patients who have had uterine surgery or overdistension. The patient should also be advised before treatment that uterine emptying is sometimes incomplete and may require curetting.

Systemic effects vary according to the type

TABLE 10-4 CONDITIONS WHERE PROSTAGLANDINS SHOULD BE USED WITH CAUTION OR ARE CONTRAINDICATED

Used with Caution
  Asthma
  Hypertension
  Cardiovascular disease
  Renal disease
  Peptic ulcer disease
  Anemia
  Jaundice
  Diabetes mellitus
  Seizure disorder
  Prior uterine surgery
Contraindications
  Hypersensitivity
  Pelvic inflammatory disease
  Unfavorable fetal position (transverse lie)
  Placenta previa

of prostaglandin and the route of administration. Although nausea, vomiting, diarrhea, and headaches are particularly common, organic causes must be considered.

The use of each prostaglandin has its own special precautions. When using intra-amniotic prostaglandins, care should be taken to avoid intramyometrial (myonecrosis) or IV (systemic reactions) injection. The risk of subsequent endometritis and parametritis is greater with the intra-amniotic instillation of any abortifacient.[26] Uterine exploration after evacuation is routine. The patient should be given a prescription for a 3 to 7-day course of a broad-spectrum antibiotic (doxycycline, tetracycline, ampicillin) following a pharmacologically induced abortion.

The use of PGE_2 suppositories requires careful monitoring of uterine contractions. Placement of an intrauterine pressure catheter may be necessary if intense and sustained contractions are suspected by external monitoring methods. To minimize any risk of a uterine rupture, removal of the suppository and infusion of a β-adrenergic tocolytic drug (see Chapter 9) may be necessary.

OTHER UTERINE STIMULANTS

Other uterine stimulants such as urea and hypertonic saline have been used for pregnancy termination. Despite their extensive use in the past, these agents will probably have limited application in the future with the advent of more specific stimulators (prostaglandins).

Hypertonic Saline
This hypertonic solution is assumed to act as an irritant to promote uterine contractions by drawing fluid from the extravascular space. The procedure is performed for therapeutic abortion, usually between 16 and 22 weeks, or as soon as the uterus is large enough for safe injection. After removing approximately 100 ml of amniotic fluid using a 20-gauge spinal needle under local anesthesia, 200 ml of a 20 percent solution of sodium chloride is instilled over a 10-minute period. If abortion has not occurred and the membranes remain intact at 24 hours, reinstillation is necessary using the same dose.

Advantages of hypertonic saline over other agents would include the greater likelihood of stillbirth, the higher percentage of complete uterine evacuation, and less uterine bleeding.[27,28] The time of the abortion process is not shortened with saline injection, and potential cardiovascular effects may result from the sodium load. A coagulopathy from thromboplastin release into the maternal circulation may occur in less than 1 percent of the cases.[28] When compared to the prostaglandins with or without oxytocin or laminaria tents, intra-amniotic saline was not found to be more effective.

Urea
Urea was originally used as a single agent for intra-amniotic instillation to terminate second trimester pregnancies. Because of its long instillation-to-abortion time (2 to 5 days), urea is instead instilled with PGF_2, so that less PGF_2 is necessary and the abortion and fetal-death processes are accelerated.[29] The usual dose of urea is 40 to 80 gm in 35 ml of 5 percent

dextrose in water. Like hypertonic saline, a disadvantage of urea instillation is myonecrosis if injection is in the uterine muscle. Other side effects include nausea and vomiting and a transient increase in blood urea nitrogen (BUN) levels.

Dextrose

Large volumes of high-dextrose concentrations (50 percent dextrose in water) have been used as an intra-amniotic agent for pregnancy termination. A long instillation-to-abortion time combined with an increased risk of infection or metabolic problems have curtailed its use.[30]

REFERENCES

1. Dale HH: Some physiologic actions of ergots. *J Physiol* 34:163, 1906
2. duVigneaud V, Ressler C, Tripett S: The sequence of amino acids in oxytocin, with a proposal for the structure of oxytocin. *J Biol Chem* 205:949, 1953
3. Rall T, Schleifer L: Oxytocin, prostaglandins, ergot alkaloids, and other agents. In Gilman AF, Goodman LS, Gilman A (eds): *The Pharmacological Basis of Therapeutics*, ed 6. New York, Macmillan, 1980, pp 935–950
4. Huszar G: *Cellular Aspects of Labor.* In Premature Labor: Mead Johnson Symposium on Perinatal and Developmental Medicine, no 15, 1980, pp 16–25
5. Tepperman HM, Beydoun SN, Abdul-Karim FW: Drugs affecting myometrial contractility in pregnancy. *Clin Obstet Gynecol* 20:423, 1977
6. Hendricks CH, Eskes TK, Saameli K: Uterine contractility at delivery and in the puerperium. *Am J Obstet Gynecol* 83:890, 1962
7. Friedman EA: *Labor: Clinical Evaluation and Management*, ed 2. New York, Appleton-Century-Crofts, 1978, p 336
8. Pritchard JA, MacDonald PC (eds): *Williams Obstetrics*, ed. 16. New York, Appleton-Century-Crofts, 1980, p 790
9. Hendricks CH, Brenner WE: Cardiovascular effects of oxytocic drugs used postpartum. *Am J Obstet Gynecol* 108:5, 1970
10. Abdul-Karim R, Assali NS: Renal function in human pregnancy: V. Effects of oxytocin on renal hemodynamics and water and electrolyte excretion. *J Lab Clin Med* 57:522, 1961
11. Burt RL, Leake NH, Dannenburg WN: Effect of synthetic oxytocin on plasma nonesterified fatty acids, triglycerides, and blood glucose. *Obstet Gynecol* 21:708, 1963
12. D'Souza SW, Black P, MacFarlane T, Richards B: The effect of oxytocin in induced labour on neonatal jaundice. *Br J Obstet Gynecol* 86:133, 1979
13. Cibils LA, Hendricks CH: Effect of ergot derivatives and sparteine sulfate upon the human uterus. *J Reprod Med* 3:147, 1969
14. Hendrick CH, Reed DW, Praagh IV, et al: Effect of sparine sulfate upon uterine activity in human pregnancy. *Am J Obstet Gynecol* 91:1, 1965
15. Browning DJ: Serious side effects of ergometrine and its use in routine obstetric practice. *Med J Aust* 19:741, 1957
16. Berde B: Pharmacology of ergot alkaloids in clinical use. *Med J Aust* (special suppl) 11/78:3, 1978
17. Valentine BH, Martin MA, Phillips NV: Collapse during operation following I.V. ergometrine. *Br J Anaesth* 49:81, 1977
18. Csaky TZ: *Cutting's Handbook of Pharmacology: The Actions and Uses of Drugs*, ed. 6. New York, Appleton-Century-Crofts, 1979, p 338
19. Challis JR: Endocrinology of parturition. In Huszar G. *Cellular Aspects of Labor:* Mead Johnson symposium on Perinatal and Developmental Medicine, no 15, 1980, pp 8–15
20. Ulmsten U: Aspects on ripening of the cervix and induction of labor by intracervical application of PGE_2 in viscous gel. *Acta Obstet Gynecol Scand* 84 (suppl):5, 1979
21. Prostin E2 Vaginal Suppository. The Upjohn Company, October 1977.
22. Hertz R, Sokol R, Dierker L: Treatment of postpartum uterine atony with prostaglandin E vaginal suppositories. *Obstet Gynecol* 56:129, 1980
23. Brenner WE: The place of prostaglandins in modern obstetrics, in Aladjem S (ed): *Risks in the Practice of Modern Obstetrics*. St Louis, Mosby, 1975, pp 210–244
24. Grimes DA, Cates W: The comparative efficacy and safety of intraamniotic prostaglandin F_{2a} and hypertonic saline for second-trimester abortion. *J Reprod Med* 22:248, 1979
25. Robins J, Surrogo E: Alternatives in midtrimester abortion induction. *Obstet Gynecol* 56:716, 1980
26. *Methods of Midtrimester Abortion:* ACOG Technical Bulletin no 56, Dec 1979

27. Grimes DA, Cates W Jr: The brief for hypertonic saline. *Contemp Obstet Gynecol* 15:29, 1980

28. Kerenyi TD, Mandelman N, Sherman DH: Five thousand consecutive saline inductions. *Am J Obstet Gynecol* 116:593, 1973

29. Burnett L, King T, Atienza M, et al: Intra-amniotic urea as a midtrimester abortifacient: Clinical results and serum and urinary changes. *Am J Obstet Gynecol* 121:7, 1975

30. Pritchard J, Whalley P: Abortion complicated by *Clostridium perfringens* infection. *Am J Obstet Gynecol* 111:484, 1971

11. Management of Pain During Labor

Joseph J. Kryc   William F. Rayburn

Relief of pain during labor and delivery has been a topic of interest since the banishment of Adam and Eve from the Garden of Eden. Pain during childbirth was Eve's punishment for her role in the fall of mankind and was to be suffered by all her descendents. In the Middle Ages, any attempts to relieve the pain and suffering associated with childbirth was considered blasphemous by the Church. Despite these prevailing religious attitudes, many psychological and physical techniques were devised to comfort the patient in labor.

The discovery of nitrous oxide by Joseph Priestley in 1772 marked the introduction of modern analgesia and anesthesia. However, the utilization of these techniques in obstetrics did not occur for approximately 70 years. Ether was first administered in 1847 to a patient in labor by James Y. Simpson, a professor of midwifery at the University of Edinburgh. Because of strong religious teachings, acceptance was delayed until 1853, when Queen Victoria received chloroform analgesia for the birth of her eighth child. Obstetrical analgesia and anesthesia have since evolved into a complex science utilizing many pharmacologic agents and anesthetic techniques. The relief of pain during labor may be accomplished by one or more of the following analgesic methods: psychologic, systemic, regional, and inhalation (Table 11-1).

Since fear and anxiety can contribute to the pain experienced during labor, recent emphasis has been placed on educating and preparing women for childbirth. Psychological techniques such as hypnosis, Lamaze, LeBoyer, and acupuncture may result in excellent analgesia in selected patients. In those patients where successful analgesia is obtained, there is no obtundation of maternal laryngeal reflexes, hypotension, or drug depression to the mother or fetus. These techni-

TABLE 11-1   ANALGESIC/ANESTHETIC TECHNIQUES USED FOR PAIN RELIEF DURING LABOR

Psychologic
  Hypnosis
  Lamaze—psychoprophylaxis
  Acupuncture

Systemic Analgesics and Sedatives
  Narcotics
  Barbiturates
  Benzodiazepines
  Phenothiazines
  Amnesic agents

Regional Anesthesia
  Minor conduction
    Local infiltration
    Paracervical block
    Pudendal block
  Major conduction
    Spinal (subarachnoid) block
    Lumbar/caudal epidural block

Inhalation Anesthesia
  Nitrous oxide
  Halogenated agents

ques rely on positive conditioning responses to produce analgesia. Although psychoprophylaxis reduces the amount of pharmacologic agents required, between one-third and two-thirds of patients still require supplemental analgesia.[1]

SYSTEMIC ANALGESICS AND SEDATIVES

Systemically administered medications are used frequently to relieve pain and anxiety during labor. Narcotics, sedatives, and tranquilizers are the pharmacologic agents most commonly used. Dissociative and amnesic drugs are used less often. There is no ideal drug, and maternal and fetal depression are related to the route of administration, the dose, and the timing of administration during labor of the specific agent as well as any underlying obstetrical complication.

Sedatives, hypnotics, and tranquilizers are used during labor to decrease fear and anxiety and to induce sleep. Their differentiation is based on the degree of action, which is also dose-dependent. Tranquilizers produce a decrease in anxiety without a sedative effect. Sedatives relieve tension and anxiety by producing a calmness that allows the patient to fall asleep. Hypnotics are central nervous system (CNS) depressants that enable patients to fall asleep. These agents are all capable of depressing the vasomotor and respiratory centers; however, they have no analgesic activity.

Narcotics

Narcotics are the most widely used systemic medications used to reduce pain during the first and second stages of labor. Many narcotic agents are currently available (Table 11-2), but their pharmacologic properties and observed effects are similar. The exact mechanism by which narcotics exert their effects is unknown. They interact with neurotransmitters to decrease the release of acetylcholine from some central and peripheral cholinergic nerves and are also able to influence catecholamine release.[2] Highly specific opiate receptors have

Table 11-2 CLASSIFICATION OF NARCOTIC DRUGS

Natural Alkaloids
  Morphine
  Codeine

Semisynthetic Compounds
  Diacetyl morphine (Heroin)
  Dihydromorphinone (Dilaudid)
  Oxymorphone (Numorphan)

Synthetic Compounds
  Meperidine derivatives
    Meperidine (Demerol)
    Alphaprodine (Nisentil)
  Methadone and Derivatives
  Fentanyl
  Pentazocine (Talwin)

been identified within the CNS of vertebrates. Located in the thalamus, hypothalamus, and substantia gelatinosa of the spinal cord, these receptors may be bound by narcotics, producing profound analgesia. Endogenous polypeptides, called endorphins, have recently been identified as having potent analgesic action.[3] These compounds are capable of modifying pain impulses traveling to the central nervous system and are considered to bind to opiate receptors.

Maternal Effects. Effects from narcotic use are seen in a variety of organ systems.[2] In small to moderate doses, narcotics produce drowsiness, changes in mood, mental clouding, and analgesia without loss of consciousness. They also raise the pain threshold and dampen pain perception. Large doses cause a greater depression of the central nervous and respiratory systems and may lead to apnea. CNS effects may be potentiated by other depressants and can result in a decrease in all respiratory parameters (respiratory rate, minute volume, tidal volume).

Cardiovascular parameters such as blood pressure, central venous pressure, and cardiac output remain essentially unchanged with usual doses. A slight bradycardia may occur from vagal stimulation. Peripheral vasodilation following large-dose administration results from histamine release and can result in orthostatic hypotension.

Narcotics decrease gastric motility and emptying, and may induce nausea and vomiting by stimulating the chemoreceptor trigger zone of the medulla.

The effects of narcotics on uterine contractility during labor are variable and depend on the severity of pain and apprehension, the dose, the route of administration, and the stage of labor. In studies where narcotics have been reported to shorten labor, the major mechanism is related to a decrease in anxiety and pain, rather than to a direct uterine effect.[4,5] Narcotics may actually prolong labor and impair the mother's ability to voluntarily assist in the delivery.

Fetal and Neonatal Effects. All narcotics are capable of easily crossing the placenta. CNS depression of the fetus is a major concern, since respiratory efforts and neurobehavioral adjustments may be delayed.[6,7] These effects have been studied most extensively using meperidine. Decreased beat-to-beat variability of the fetal heart rate, decreased respiratory motion, and altered electroencephalograms in the fetus have been reported. It is postulated that IV injection during a uterine contraction will slow narcotic transfer to the fetus. Theoretically, blood flow through the placental bed is slowed, thereby allowing the bolus of medication to bypass this area.

Neonatal respiratory depression is uncommon and usually mild and transient. Its presence and severity are related to the dose, the time from administration to delivery, and the use of other depressant agents (e.g., barbiturates).[6] The risk of neonatal depression after intramuscular meperidine is not great if delivery occurs within 1 hour of administration. If delivery occurs 2 to 3 hours after administration, the incidence of neonatal depression is increased. The reason for this delay is uncertain, but may be due to an active metabolite unique to meperidine.[8] The metabolites show a slow rise in serum levels with gradual elimination that may be as long as 3 to 6 days. Meperidine metabolites include normeperidine, meperidinic acid, and normeperidinic acid. Normeperidine is an active metabolite and has been implicated as the agent causing neurobehavioral or respiratory depression in the neonate for up to 48 to 72 hours after delivery. Naloxone (Narcan) may be given to the infant to reverse any depression from narcotic use (see Chap. 13).

Selecting the Proper Narcotic. The selection of an appropriate narcotic is dependent upon the effects desired. The various narcotics differ with respect to the dosage range, onset of action, duration of action, and side effects (Table 11-3). Meperidine (Demerol) is the most widely accepted narcotic for pain relief during labor and delivery. Other narcotics seem to offer no distinct advantage, and neonatal depression may be greater.[9]

Morphine is the most important alkaloid extracted from opium and represents the parent compound of the narcotic analgesics. Like meperidine, it is absorbed rapidly after intravenous or intramuscular administration. Biotransformation in the liver is by oxidation and conjugation with glucuronic acid. The conjugated compound is then excreted into the urine. Morphine provides no better analgesic effect than equipotent doses of meperidine and may have more of a respiratory depressant effect on the fetus.[10]

Pentazocine (Talwin) is a weak synthetic analgesic agent that has not been used extensively in labor. It does not seem to have any advantages when compared to meperidine, except for a slight decrease in the incidence of nausea and vomiting. When given in large doses (60 mg or more), pentazocine has been associated with hallucinations and nightmares.[11] Narcotic antagonist properties make this agent dangerous in the narcotic-dependent mother. α-Prodine (Nisentil) is a synthetic narcotic with a rapid onset and short duration of action, which makes this a popular drug. It may also be given subcutaneously. In equianalgesic doses, there seems to be no advantage of α-prodine over meperidine. Sinusoidal fetal heart rate patterns have been associated with α-prodine use.[12]

TABLE 11-3　COMPARATIVE EFFECTIVENESS OF NARCOTIC ANALGESICS

	70–90% Relief of Pain with Sedation and Euphoria				
Efficacy	MORPHINE	MEPERIDINE (DEMEROL)	ALPHAPRODINE (NISENTIL)	PENTAZOCINE (TALWIN)	FENTANYL (SUBLIMAZE)
Obstetrical					
Dosage IM (mg)	5–10	50–100	30–40	20–30	50–100 µg
IV (mg)	2–5	25–50	10–20	10–20	25–50 µg
Onset of Action					
IM (min)	10–20	10–20	10–20	5–20	7–8
IV (min)	3–5	3–5	3–5	2–3	Immediate
Duration of Action					
IM (hr)	2–4	2–3	1½–2	3–4	1–2
IV (hr)	1–2	1½–2	1½–2	2–3	½–1
Side Effects Maternal	—Large doses–Orthostatic, hypotension, respiratory depression, nausea and vomiting, delayed gastric emptying, histamine release with morphine			—Minimal cardiovascular effects —Minimal nausea and vomiting —Psychotropic effects with pentazocine	
Fetal	Mild to marked depression dependent upon dosage. Neurobehavioral effects of up to 72 hr				
Placental Transfer	Rapid for all narcotic agents				
Active Metabolites	No	Yes (normeperidine)	No	No	No

Fentanyl (Sublimaze) is a relatively new synthetic narcotic agent that is extremely potent, with a rapid onset and a short duration of action. Respiratory depression has been reported to outlast its analgesic properties, so its use during labor has been very limited.[13]

Barbiturates

Barbiturates are sedative-hypnotics; these are no longer popularly used during labor. Their primary indication is for sedation during the early stages of labor. The four major groups of barbiturates have the same pyrimidine derivation, and an intimate relation exists between their structures and activities.

Pharmacology. In sedative and hypnotic doses, barbiturates are thought to act by interfering with the transmission of impulses to the cortex at the thalamus and ascending reticular formation. Barbiturates are well absorbed or-

ally and most compounds are biotransformed within the liver and eliminated in the kidneys. With repeated usage, they are capable of inducing liver enzymes.

With standard oral doses, there are minimal cardiovascular effects including a slight decrease in blood pressure and heart rate. The medullary vasomotor center is depressed, but reflexes remain intact. When used as an induction agent for anesthesia, thiopental causes direct myocardial depression in proportion to the concentration and dose used. It is also associated with histamine release and vasodilation, a decrease in cardiac output and cerebral blood flow, and either an increase or no change in heart rate.

Barbiturates may affect the respiratory system by influencing neurogenic, chemical, and hypoxic mechanisms for maintaining breathing.[14] The neurogenic center for breathing is located in the reticular activating system and is important in the normal awake state. Its function is extremely sensitive to the hypnotic effects of barbiturates. The breathing control center is influenced by cerebral spinal fluid, pH, and $Paco_2$, and is located in the medulla. The chemical drive for respiration is depressed at about three to four times the usual barbiturate dose. The hypoxic driving mechanism is the least sensitive to barbiturate exposure. Although extreme respiratory depression can occur, barbiturates do not obtund protective reflexes such as laryngeal reflexes.

Preparations. Barbiturates are characterized by their duration of action including ultrashort, short, intermediate, and long acting. The various preparations are described in Table 11-4.

Thiopental sodium (Pentothal) is an ultrashort-acting barbiturate used intravenously for the induction of anesthesia. The rapid recovery from the original dose is explained by its lipid solubility and redistribution properties. Following a bolus injection of a thiobarbiturate, blood concentrations in richly perfused organs, including the brain, are high. After a few circulations, it is then redistributed to other areas of the body, such as muscle and adipose tissue, resulting in lower levels in vital organs and a subsequent loss of activity. Although very little drug has been metabolized or excreted during this brief time interval, its clinical action has been terminated because of the lowered plasma concentration.

Secobarbital (Seconal) and pentobarbital

(Nembutal) are short-acting agents which provide brief hypnosis and mild sedation. Amobarbital (Amytal) and phenobarbital have longer onsets of action and durations and are therefore not used after the onset of uterine contractions.

Maternal Effects. In the usual prescribed oral doses, barbiturates should have no adverse effects on the mother. They exhibit no known inhibitory effects on uterine tone or contractility. The central nervous system, however, is exquisitely sensitive to these drugs, and depression varies from mild sedation to coma.[14] Effects are dependent on the type of barbiturate, the dose, and the route of administration.[15] Orally administered barbiturates cause drowsiness for a few hours, followed by subtle alterations in mood, impairment of judgment, and diminished fine motor skills for up to 24 hours. Unlike gaseous and volatile anesthetic agents, barbiturates do not obtund pain sensation. With small doses, they increase the reaction to painful stimuli, possibly by depressing some inhibitory pathways in the brain. In larger anesthetic doses, all barbiturates exhibit anticonvulsant activity. Phenobarbital is especially popular in this regard because of its selective anticonvulsant activity without producing anesthesia (see Chap. 5). Although overdose during labor is rare, severe respiratory depression may require ventilatory assistance.

Fetal and Neonatal Effects. Barbiturates rapidly cross the placenta. Fetal serum levels of

TABLE 11-4 ONSET AND DURATION OF ACTION OF BARBITURATES AFTER IM INJECTION

	Ultrashort	Short	Intermediate	Long
Onset of Action	Seconds	Minutes	1 hr	1+ hr
Duration	Minutes	4–8 hr	6–8 hr	10–12 hr
Preparations	Thiopental (Pentathal)	Secobarbital (Seconal) Pentobarbital (Nembutal)	Amobarbital (Amytal)	Phenobarbital (Luminal)

the highly lipid-soluble, short-acting barbiturates approach maternal levels in only a few minutes.[16,17] With excessive use or in high doses, prolonged CNS depression can occur and lead to respiratory depression and neurobehavioral abnormalities during the first 48 hours of life. The flaccid infant may also have initial feeding problems. The neonate's attention span may be shortened, even with small doses. All these undesired effects may be further accentuated with combined narcotic use during labor.[6] Induction of fetal hepatic microsomal enzymes with these agents has already been discussed in Chapter 1.

Benzodiazepines

The benzodiazepines are tranquilizers which include diazepam (Valium), chlordiazepoxide (Librium), and flurazepam (Dalmane). Their use for relief of maternal anxiety during labor has become less popular and is not considered to be any more effective than barbiturates. Any direct muscle relaxant action is not appreciable during labor. Diazepam has been most widely used and is most effective during the antepartum and intrapartum periods to control seizures from grand mal epilepsy or eclampsia (see Chap. 5).

The mechanism of action of benzodiazepines is unknown. Serotonin and catecholamines are not released, and monoamine oxidase inhibitors (MAO) are unaffected (see Chap. 26). Accumulation may occur, since excretion is usually delayed. Toxic reactions are uncommon but include ataxia, vertigo, syncope, and drowsiness. Hypotension may occur with rapid intravenous infusion. Respiratory depression is also possible.

Although the margin of safety is great in the mother, intravenous diazepam can easily cross the placenta and may reach fetal serum levels equal to or greater than the mother's (see Chap. 1). Desmethydiazepam, an active metabolite of diazepam with a biologic half-life of greater than 90 hours, may accumulate and cause CNS toxicity.[18] Acid-base derangements are uncommon with diazepam, but a loss of variability of the fetal heart rate may be seen in IV doses as little as 5 to 10 mg.

In larger doses (30 mg or more), lethargy, poor feeding, and poor temperature control may persist for several days.[19] Diazepam has also been associated with hyperbilirubinemia of the newborn. Sodium benzoate, a buffer of the injectable form, has been implicated as a bilirubin albumin uncoupler, which may cause increased levels of free bilirubin.[20] All of these undesired effects may be compounded further with the administration of a systemic analgesic.

Phenothiazines and Hydroxyzine

The phenothiazines represent a large group of tranquilizers used primarily in treating psychiatric disorders. Their common use during labor has been to control nausea and vomiting, to sedate, and to prolong the effects from narcotics. Phenothiazines are three ringed amino compounds with a basic configuration, shown in Figure 11-1. Substitutions at positions R_1 and R_2 independently alter the pharmacologic activity of these agents. Substitutions at the R_2-position tend to depress motor activity and increase antipsychotic and antiemetic properties. Substitutions at position R_1 result in three major groups: (1) the dimethylamino group, which includes promethazine (Phenergan) and propiomazine (Largon); (2) the piperidine group, which includes thioridazine (Mellaril); and (3) the piperazine group, which includes perphenazine (Trilafon).

The primary mechanism of action of phenothiazines is to inhibit uptake of norepinephrine and 5-OH-tryptophan on the CNS (see Chap. 26). As a group, they are very similar pharmacologically and therapeutically. Promethazine (Phenergan) 25 mg or propiomazine (Largon) 10 mg are commonly given parenterally with meperidine. They are absorbed well and distributed widely. Biotransformation is within the liver, and excretion in the kidneys or feces is partly as sulfoxide.

Toxic effects using recommended dosages in the mother are quite uncommon. Therapeutic doses usually result in sedation and indifference to surroundings with a concomitant loss of anxiety. For this reason, reduced narcotic doses are usually necessary to relieve

DIMETHYLAMINO GROUP

CHLORPROMAZINE (Thorazine)

PROMAZINE (Sparine)

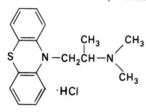

PROMETHAZINE (Phenergan)

PROPIOMAZINE

PIPERIDINE GROUP

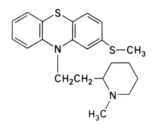

THIORIDAZINE (Mellaril)

PIPERAZINE GROUP

PROCHLORPERAZINE (Compazine)

Figure 11-1. Chemical structure of the phenothiazine drugs. (From Csáky TZ: Cutting's Handbook of Pharmacology: The Actions and Uses of Drugs, ed. 6, New York, Appleton-Century-Crofts, 1979, pp 325, 596–598, with permission.)

pain. Phenothiazines also lower the seizure threshold and should be used with extreme caution in patients with a history of a seizure disorder. Extrapyramidal effects such as Parkinsonian movements are prominent and thought to result from a blockage of dopamine receptors in the brain. The phenothiazines in general and chloropromazine (Thorazine) in particular are potent antiemetics and directly inhibit the chemoreceptor trigger zone. The cardiovascular effects of these agents are complex. Direct depression of myocardial contrac-

tility and hypotension from α-adrenergic blockade of the blood vessels are possible.

Placental transfer varies between the different groups of phenothiazines but is usually rapid. In recommended doses, promethazine and propiomazine are not responsible for any detrimental effects on the fetus or neonate, even though a loss of fetal heart rate beat-to-beat variability may occur.[21]

The antihistamine hydroxyzine (Atarax, Vistaril) is another rapidly acting, mild sedative. Unlike the barbiturates, its effects are not dose-dependent. Along with its antihistamine properties, the use of hydroxyzine during labor is similar to the phenothiazines. Hydroxyzine may relieve anxiety and reduce the dose of narcotics needed without increasing the risk of neonatal depression.[22] This drug is very irritating to tissues and should be given by deep IM injection in the buttocks. Intravenous, subcutaneous, or prolonged intravenous injections are not recommended.

Amnesia Drugs

Amnesic or dissociative drugs include ketamine and scopolamine and are no longer popular or recommended for sedation during labor. In low IV doses, these drugs can cause a dream-like state, which is no longer desired by most patients. The analgesic effect of ketamine is not observed with scopolamine, and narcotic supplementation is required. Transient hallucinations and delirium may occur with high or excessive dosages of either agent.

Ketamine (Ketalar, Ketaject). Ketamine is an intravenously administered anesthetic which is a cyclohexanone compound similar in structure to phencyclidine (PCP). Its anesthetic and sedative properties are similar to the ultrashort-acting barbiturates (thiobarbiturates) when IV doses of 1 mg/kg are given. The mechanism of action is unknown. The onset of action and clearance are usually rapid. Systemic vasopressor effects with ketamine do not apparently reduce uterine blood flow. In the usual low doses (0.25 to 0.5 mg/kg), uterine contractions are unaffected; however, with doses greater than 0.5 mg/kg, there is an increase in the frequency of contractions.[22] Ketamine may be administered every 2 to 5 minutes, but a total dose of 100 mg over 30 minutes is to be avoided. Placental transfer is rapid, but neonatal depression is seen only after high doses (> 1 mg/kg body weight or > 100 mg total dose). The frequency of low Apgar scores is not significantly greater with low-dose ketamine than with regional, local, or general anesthesia.[23]

Scopolamine (Hyoscine). Like atropine, scopolamine is a belladonna alkaloid. It acts centrally by inhibiting the uptake of acetylcholine at binding sites on postganglionic receptors. The distribution is wide and may be prolonged, but dangerous toxicity to the mother is very uncommon. After the intravenous administration of 0.3 to 0.6 mg, maternal amnesia occurs and may be intense. Pain suppression and further sedation require the addition of a narcotic to produce "twilight sleep." Physostigmine has been used to reverse sedative and delirium effects from scopolamine. Scopolamine has no apparent effect on uterine contractility and can cross the placenta rapidly. Fetal tachycardia and a loss of beat-to-beat variability may be readily apparent and may last for 60 to 90 minutes.[24] Respiratory depression in the newborn is not more common after scopolamine alone.

LOCAL ANESTHETICS

Regional anesthesia provides a temporary interruption of painful impulses from any portion of the body without a loss of consciousness. Local infiltration and major regional blocks using local anesthetics are used frequently for pain relief during labor and delivery. Local anesthetics are capable of reversibly inhibiting the transmission of impulses in neural tissue. These agents exhibit marked selectivity, since they can inhibit neural transmissions from one part of the body without significantly affecting other areas. This selectivity and the reversibility of action make their use in obstetrics ideal.

Cocaine was the first identified, naturally occurring local anesthetic. It was isolated from the coca shrub in 1860 by Albert Niemann but was not utilized as an anesthetic agent for 25 years. Because of extreme toxicity, its clinical usefulness was limited. A search for a less toxic material led to the discovery of procaine in 1904 by Einhorn. This drug remained the cornerstone of local anesthetics for almost 50 years, until Löfgren, a Swedish chemist, discovered the amide local anesthetic, lidocaine, in 1948. This discovery led to the development of other amide agents that are more potent, longer acting, and less toxic.

Physiology of Neural Transmission

Neural tissue has the unique capability of transferring messages in the form of electrical potentials from one area of the body to another. These electrical potentials are initiated by mechanical, electrical, or thermal stimuli. Each nerve cell or neuron consists of a cell body, axon, and multiple dendrite extensions. The axon or nerve fiber is a cylinder of axoplasm which is encased in a semipermeable membrane. (A diagram of the nerve fiber membrane is shown later in Figure 11-3.) The membrane consists of a double-thickness layer of phospholipid molecules. This structure is thinly covered by inner and outer layers of protein. A larger portion of the protein molecule is distributed in the bimolecular phospholipid layer, giving rise to a mosaic-type pattern on the surface. The nerve membrane also contains small channels which connect the extracellular and intracellular spaces. These channels vary in size and are selective for either sodium or potassium. Located on the internal portion of the channel are voltage-dependent "gates" which open and close to either block or allow ionic migration (Fig. 11-2A). The ionic separation created by the semipermeability of the membrane gives rise to an electrochemical gradient known as the resting membrane potential. At rest, the sodium channel is relatively impermeable to the passage of sodium ions. The potassium channel is considerably more permeable, allowing the easy passage of potassium between the extracellular and intracellular spaces. During the resting state, a small amount of ionic leakage occurs which allows sodium to enter and potassium to exit from the cell. Since potassium is more permeable, it flows out of the cell leaving larger, negatively charged ions behind. These negative ions impart a net negative charge to the interior of the cell and eventually halt the outward flow of potassium. In an effort to maintain this electrochemical gradient, sodium is also transported out of the cell by an energy-dependent system known as the sodium-potassium pump.

When a stimulus is applied to the nerve, the generated electrical field causes the gates in the sodium and potassium channels to open. This results in an inward surge of sodium ions with a change in electrical potential (Fig. 11-2B). If the stimulus is weak, only a few gates will open, and the sodium will be quickly pumped out of the cell. With a larger stimulus, many gates are opened, and a threshold is reached eventually where sodium influx matches sodium efflux (firing threshold). When this is reached, depolarization and sodium influx occur at an extremely rapid rate (Fig. 11-3). For a short period, the interior of the cell is more positive than the exterior of the cell, until potassium efflux begins. This process of depolarization gives rise to an impulse or action potential and is rapidly followed by repolarization of the nerve membrane. During repolarization, the sodium channels close, and sodium is actively pumped out of the cell to reestablish the original resting membrane potential. If the process of depolarization is interrupted along the axon, an impulse cannot be transmitted and the nerve becomes blocked.

Many nerve fibers are surrounded by myelin, a fatty material. The myelin sheath is interrupted at regular intervals by gaps, known as nodes of Ranvier, at which a small portion of the nerve membrane is exposed to the surrounding medium. The myelin sheath acts as an electrical insulator which enables the nerve to conduct an impulse at a faster rate than an unmyelinated nerve of comparable width.

Mechanism of Action

Local anesthetics are thought to obstruct the inward surge of sodium ions associated with depolarization.[25] When a local anesthetic is applied to a nerve, impulse conduction ceases. Failure of impulse conduction occurs gradually to progressively lower the height of the action potential, reduce its rate of rise, elevate

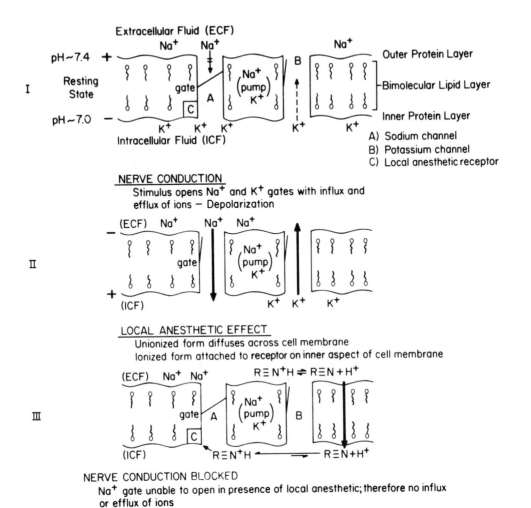

NERVE CONDUCTION
    Stimulus opens Na+ and K+ gates with influx and
    efflux of ions – Depolarization

LOCAL ANESTHETIC EFFECT
    Unionized form diffuses across cell membrane
    Ionized form attached to receptor on inner aspect of cell membrane

NERVE CONDUCTION BLOCKED
Na+ gate unable to open in presence of local anesthetic; therefore no influx
or efflux of ions

Figure 11-2. Local anesthetic effect on nerve fiber membrane function.

the threshold level, and eventually block conduction.

    There is no change in the resting potential. Local anesthetics therefore prevent depolarization. The site of action of local anesthetic agents is the internal surface of the cell membrane at a receptor site located on the opening of the sodium channel (Fig. 11-2C). Some binding also occurs at the potassium channel, but the receptor-binding affinity is much less.

    Although it is generally agreed that local anesthetics bind to receptor sites, the mechanism for impulse blockade remains controversial.[26] One potential mechanism of action involves a change in the surface charge of the sodium channel which prevents the sodium ion from entering the channel. A second mechanism may involve membrane expansion to decrease the size of the sodium channel.

    Sensitivity to local anesthetics is also influenced by fiber width and myelin thickness. The wider and more myelinated the nerve, the more excitable and rapidly it conducts an impulse. Small, thin, unmyelinated nerves which

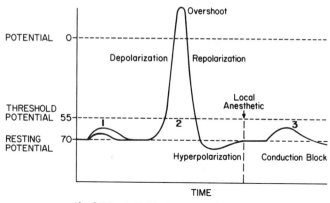

POTENTIAL 0

Depolarization | Repolarization

Overshoot

THRESHOLD
POTENTIAL 55

Local
Anesthetic

RESTING
POTENTIAL 70

Hyperpolarization | Conduction Block

TIME

1) Subthreshold Stimulus – no action potential generated
2) Threshold Stimulus – action potential generated
3) Effect of Local Anesthetic – no action potential generated

Figure 11-3. Electrochemical events in nerve cell stimulation: (1) subthreshold stimulus—no action potential generated, (2) threshold stimulus—action potential generated, (3) effect of local anesthetic—no action potential generated.

transmit pain, temperature, and autonomic effects are slowly conducting and not easily excitable.

The minimum anesthetic concentration (C_M) is the lowest concentration of an anesthetic agent necessary to cause an impulse blockade within a specified time.[26] A nerve will not be solidly blocked until this concentration is reached. Each local anesthetic agent has its own C_M. Nerve fibers also have different C_M's, based on their size and amount of myelin present. Thin, unmyelinated nerves which transmit pain are adequately blocked, while thicker, myelinated fibers transmitting motor or touch remain unblocked. This selectivity or differential nerve block is clinically important, since motor function, touch, and pressure sensation may remain intact during regional anesthesia even though pain has been completely abolished.

Preparations

Local anesthetics have pharmacologic properties that are influenced by their structure, pKa, lipid solubility, and protein-binding. Although many agents are commercially available, as a group they are quite similar.

Local anesthetics contain three structural portions: (1) a hydrophilic amino portion, which is almost always a tertiary amine; (2) an intermediate chain, which is either an ester or an amide; and (3) a lipophilic aromatic residue (Fig. 11-4). Based on the type of linkage between the aromatic residue and the intermediate chain, the local anesthetics can be classified as either esters or amides. Changes in any portion of the molecule result in a change in anesthetic properties.

Amides and esters are biotransformed differently.[26] The ester agents are metabolized by plasma pseudocholinesterase, while the amide agents are metabolized in the liver. The amide agents therefore have a longer half-life than the esters.

Although local anesthetics can be classified as either esters or amides, each possesses a substituted amine group and therefore is considered to be a weak base. In the free-base form these local anesthetics are unstable and only slightly soluble in water. Therefore, to confer stability to the parent compounds and to generate water-soluble drugs suitable for injection, the local anesthetics such as amine hydrochloride salts are generally used. When salts are formed, an uncharged tertiary amine is converted to a quaternary ammonium salt:

(1) Local anesthetic — N + HCl →
(weak base)   (acid)

local anesthetic — NH$^+$Cl$^\ominus$
(salt)

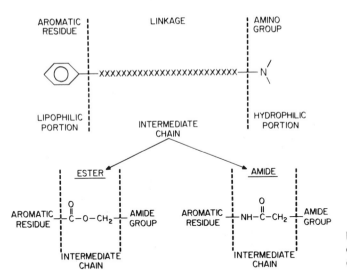

Figure 11-4. Chemical structure of the ester and amide local anesthetics.

When placed in an aqueous solution, the salt dissociates into a cation and anion:

$$(2)\ \text{Local anesthetic} - \overset{|}{\underset{|}{N}}\text{H}^+\text{Cl}^- \rightleftharpoons$$
(salt)

$$\text{local anesthetic} - \overset{|}{\underset{|}{N}}\text{H}^+ + \text{Cl}^\ominus$$
(cation)   (anion)

and establishes an equilibrium with the union-ized base:

$$(3)\ \text{Local anesthetic} - \overset{|}{\underset{|}{N}}\text{H}^+ \overset{pKa}{\rightleftharpoons}$$
(cation)

$$\text{local anesthetic} - \overset{\oplus}{N} + \text{H}^+$$
(base)

The amount of dissociation is dependent upon the dissociation constant (pK_a) of the cation and on the pH of the solution. When the pK_a of the anesthetic is equal to the pH, there is an equal concentration of ionized and nonionized molecules. As the pH is increased (less H^+ available), Eq. (3) is forced to the right, and a higher concentration of the non-ionized drug is apparent. Conversely, as the pH is lowered (more H^+ available), Eq. (3) is forced to the left, producing a higher concentration of the ionized form.

The site of action of local anesthetics is on the interior of the nerve cell membrane.[25] At this location, the positively charged molecule (cation) is the active form. This ionized molecule is not lipid soluble and as such cannot traverse the cell membrane. It has been demonstrated that a local anesthetic at a nerve exists in both a charged and uncharged form, as described by Eq. (3). The uncharged form is extremely lipid soluble and diffuses easily through the cell membrane. Since the interior of the cell is slightly more acidic than the exterior, more hydrogen ions are available to interact with this uncharged molecule. This causes the molecule to become charged and "trapped" to bind with a receptor at the opening of the sodium channel.

Following injection of a local anesthetic, its subsequent uptake and distribution is dependent on the site of injection, dosage, agent, and addition of any vasoconstrictor. Table 11-5 lists the local anesthetics in common use in obstetrics. Agents that are highly lipid soluble and not strongly protein bound will be absorbed by the target tissues and removed slowly into the blood stream. This results in

TABLE 11-5 THERAPEUTIC PROPERTIES OF LOCAL ANESTHETICS

Agent	Concentrations (%)	Class	pK$_a$	Relative Potency	Maximum Dose (mg)	Duration (min)
I. Low Potency, Short Duration						
Procaine (Novacaine)	1.0–2.0	Ester	8.9	1	1000	45–90
Chloroprocaine (Nesacaine)	2.0–3.0	Ester	8.9	1	1000	45–69
II. Intermediate Potency, Intermediate Duration						
Mepivacaine (Carbocaine)	1.0–2.0	Amide	7.6	2	500	120–140
Lidocaine (Xylocaine)	1.0–2.0	Amide	7.9	2	500	90–200
III. High Potency, Long Duration						
Tetracaine (Pontocaine)	0.15–0.25	Ester	8.5	8	200	180–600
Bupivacaine (Marcaine)	0.25–0.75	Amide	8.1	8	300	180–600
Etidocaine (Duranest)	0.5–1.5	Amide	7.7	6	300	180–600

lower blood levels. Vasoconstrictors are also very useful in slowing vascular absorption and prolonging the duration of action. The use of epinephrine may, however, interfere with uterine activity when used with epidural analgesia.[26] Because of the marked amount of vasoconstriction produced by this agent, its use with paracervical block is contraindicated.

The distribution of local anesthetics occurs in two phases. The first or α-phase is very rapid (less than 1 hour) and relates to the rapid redistribution of the anesthetic agent throughout the body. The second or β-phase is much slower (several hours) and relates to metabolism and excretion of the drug.

Bupivacaine is the preferred local anesthetic of choice for obstetrical anesthesia. Its onset of action is reasonably rapid, and the duration of action is long (3 to 10 hours). Because of its high pK$_a$ (8.1) and its 95 percent protein-binding property, bupivacaine is less likely to cross the placental barrier and affect the fetus (Table 11-5). Both xylocaine and carbocaine have rapid onsets of action, but each is only 50 to 70 percent protein bound and has a lower pK$_a$. Therefore, fetal effects are more apparent than with bupivacaine and may last up to 24 to 48 hours after delivery.[27]

Chloroprocaine (Nesacaine) has until recently been widely popular in obstetrical units. It represents the "ideal" agent for use in obstetrical conditions because of its rapid onset and short duration. Since it is an ester compound which is metabolized by plasma pseudocholinesterase, the effective half-life in the fetus is 45 seconds. Recently, choloroprocaine has been associated with prolonged neural blockade and adhesive arachnoiditis with inadvertent subarachnoid injections of large volumes. It has therefore been suggested that if the agent is used, small amounts should be given.

Etidocaine is a new amide agent very similar to bupivacaine. It is much more lipid soluble and approximately equal in protein-binding to bupivacaine. However, etidocaine use for regional anesthesia is associated with more pronounced and prolonged muscle relaxation than analgesia.[28] This may interfere with the patient's ability to bear down and the dynamics of the second stage of labor.

Maternal Effects

Since local anesthetics block conduction of nerve impulses, they may interfere with any organ where impulse transmission occurs. Effects on the central nervous and cardiovascular systems are particularly noteworthy. When local anesthetics are absorbed systemically, they can easily cross the blood-brain barrier. Toxic levels produce central nervous stimulation followed by marked depression or coma. Circulatory support and assisted ventilation may be necessary. Other signs of local anesthetic toxicity include tinnitus, drowsiness, slurred speech, tremors, and convulsions. Respiratory arrest can also occur with large doses. The apparent stimulation and subsequent CNS depression observed is related to the extreme sensitivity of inhibitory cortical neurons to local anesthetics. With inhibitory pathways blocked, excitatory neuronal pathways are unopposed, and excitation and convulsions may occur. As the local anesthetic concentration increases, the excitatory pathways also become blocked.

CNS toxicity usually follows inadvertent intravascular injection and is dependent on the potency of the agent being used (Table 11-5). The susceptibility of the brain can be altered by the prophylactic administration of benzodiazepines or barbiturates. Neither sedative is routinely used in obstetrical practice, so meticulous technique should be used to prevent an intravascular injection of a local anesthetic.

Local anesthetics may affect the cardiovascular system by acting directly on the heart and peripheral vasculature and indirectly on sympathetic blockade. When applied directly to the myocardium, local anesthetics decrease the electrical excitability, the rate of conduction, and the force of contractility. Vasodilation is seen when an anesthetic is injected into peripheral vessels, including the pudendal artery. However, when injected into the uterine artery, intense vasospasm which is dose dependent occurs.[29]

Allergic reactions to local anesthetics are uncommon. Localized edema, urticaria, and pruritis are related to breakdown products of metabolized esters and should be treated with antihistamines. Anaphylactic reactions are rare and require epinephrine injection and supportive care. Allergic reactions do not occur with amide use.

Fetal Effects

Direct fetal effects may occur following the injection of a local anesthetic in a highly vascular space (epidural, pudendal, paracervical) and may result in significant maternal serum concentrations. Despite metabolism in the liver and elimination in the kidneys, local anesthetics may reach the intervillous space. Their ability to cross the lipid placental membrane is related to the drug's chemical properties (see Chap. 1). Since fetal blood is more acidic than maternal blood, local anesthetics become ionized and therefore "trapped" in the fetal circulation. This "trapping" phenomenon is more pronounced in the presence of fetal acidosis. The binding of these drugs to fetal protein is not well understood, but fetal tissue affinity for local anesthetics is high. The fetus is capable of detoxifying local anesthetics by hepatic microsomes, but not to the extent of the maternal counterpart.

Indirect fetal effects of these agents are produced by alterations of maternal homeostasis that secondarily involve the fetus. This includes alterations in uterine blood flow, caused by their direct action on the uterine arteries and myometrium, and maternal hypotension secondary to autonomic blockade.[30]

Despite the possibility of adversely affecting the maternal-fetal unit, the local anesthetics have been used extensively and safely in obstetrics. The route of administration and the specific agent used is extremely important. Paracervical blocks pose a greater threat to the fetus than do either epidural or subarachnoid blocks.

The incidence of significant fetal bradycardia with paracervical blocks approaches 25 percent. Lidocaine and mepivacaine tend to produce fetal bradycardia more frequently than bupivacaine, but bupivacaine can produce fetal bradycardias of extremely long duration (90 minutes to 2 hours).[31] These effects are not dependent on the concentration of the anesthetic used.

No fetal deaths have been reported when epidural anesthesia has been used. However, certain agents may cause neonatal depression, which principally involves transient motor retardation that is not reversed with any drug.[32] Lidocaine and mepivacaine are more likely to cause these transient effects because of their described chemical properties. Bupivacaine has chemical properties which prevent large amounts from entering the fetal compartment and causing significant fetal effects.

INHALATION AGENTS

Inhalation agents are occasionally used for pain relief during labor, even though their popularity has declined in recent years. With close supervision, analgesia may be obtained in subanesthetic doses, so that the patient will remain conscious and cooperative. In higher concentrations, delirium and a progressive loss of vital function may become apparent. Inhalation agents may also be used when uterine relaxation is necessary. Conditions requiring uterine relaxation would include delivery of a second twin (intrauterine manipulation), manual removal of an adherent placenta, or replacement of an inverted uterus.

All inhalation agents are inspired and absorbed as gases, metabolized to some degree and eliminated in the lungs and kidneys. Their mechanisms of action remain unclear.

The risks of inhalation agents used during labor and delivery are several. In anesthetic doses, respiratory depression to the mother

may cause inadequate oxygenation, loss of laryngeal reflexes, and aspiration of gastric contents. A 30 ml dose of an antacid is usually given one half hour prior to administration of any general anesthetic to neutralize gastric acid (pH_2). Halogenated agents produce uterine relaxation, which is dose-dependent, and may increase uterine bleeding. All agents rapidly cross the placental barrier, and a transient depression on the fetal central nervous, cardiovascular, and respiratory systems is possible. This depression is directly proportional to the duration and depth of maternal anesthesia, since fetal concentrations rapidly approach the mother's as the anesthetic is continued. The properties of each agent are discussed in the sections which follow. A comparison of their effects is given in Table 11-6. Techniques used for administration of these agents must be performed by qualified personnel and are described in several standard anesthesiology texts.[33]

Nitrous Oxide

Nitrous oxide is the most commonly used inhalation agent for analgesia because of its relative safety, rapid onset, and short duration of activity. It is an inert, colorless gas which is nonflammable and stored in a tank as a liquid. It is relatively nonirritating, nontoxic, and rapidly reversible. Concentrations may vary up to 70 percent, but inhalation of 50 percent nitrous oxide with 50 percent oxygen is standard. At this concentration, maternal or fetal depression is unlikely.[34] Analgesic effects are obtained with intermittent use prior to the onset of each contraction or with continuous use during labor. Continuous analgesia is often more reliable, since the onset of uterine contractions may be unpredictable. The self-administration of 50 percent nitrous oxide with 50 percent oxygen (Nitronox) has been used successfully during the late first stage and the second stage of labor.

Methoxyflurane (Penthrane)

Methoxyflurane is a potent inhalation agent which is an effective analgesic in subanesthetic doses. It is a halogenated (F and Cl) methyl-

TABLE 11-6 COMPARATIVE EFFECTS OF INHALATION AGENTS

Agent	Analgesia (Subanesthetic Dose)	Uterine Relaxation	Neonatal Depression	Toxicity
Nitrous oxide	+++*	—	±†	Cardiac (if heart disorder), nausea, leukocyte suppression
Methoxyflurane	+++	±	±	Cardiodepression, hypotension, hepatotoxicity, nephrotoxicity
Halothane	—	+++	++‡	Cardiodepression, hypotension, hepatotoxicity
Enflurane	—	+++	++	Cardiodepression, hypotension, hepatotoxicity
Isoflurane	—	+++	++	Cardiodepression, hypotension, hepatotoxicity

* +++ = pronounced effect
† ± = negligible effect
‡ ++ = moderate effect

ethyl ether and is nonexplosive. A concentration of 0.35 percent administered intermittently is ideal. The analgesic effect is comparable to nitrous oxide, and the two agents have been used in combinations of lesser concentrations to produce a greater analgesic effect.[35]

Renal effects from methoxyflurane may be a concern. Its metabolic products, inorganic fluoride and oxalic acid, may be associated with subclinical renal toxicity with an increase in blood urea nitrogen (BUN), creatinine, and uric acid values during 48 hours after delivery.[36] Serum inorganic fluoride levels have also been increased in the neonate. What effect this may have on the renal and central nervous systems is presently unknown. Methoxyflurane should be avoided if preexisting renal disease or nephrotoxic drugs are being used.

Halothane (Fluothane)
Halothane is a potent, halogenated anesthetic agent with depressant effects on the respiratory and cardiovascular system. Induction of anesthesia is rapid when inhaled concentra-

tions of 3 to 4 percent are used. Relaxation of the uterus at these concentrations is extremely rapid, but analgesia is obtained only in anesthetic doses.[37] Because of its associated hepatic toxicity, halothane is not recommended in patients with hepatic dysfunction.

Other Agents
Enflurane is another halogenated inhalational agent. Its use for pain relief during labor is very limited, since its properties are similar to halothane (myometrial depression, hypotension, myocardial depression, analgesia in anesthetic doses).

Cyclopropane was once popular for obstetrical anesthesia. However, it is highly explosive and may cause profound maternal hypotension and diminished uterine blood flow.

Ether was also popular because of its rapid action and uterine relaxation effects. It is also highly flammable and explosive in air (1.8 to 36 percent),[2] and the unpleasant odor may cause nausea and vomiting.

Isoflurane is a new halogenated agent similar to halothane and enflurane. Although uterine relaxant effects are good, analgesia occurs only when anesthetic concentrations are used.[37]

REFERENCES

1. Shnider SM, Levinson G: Psychological anesthesia for obstetrics. In Shnider SM, Levinson G (eds): *Anesthesia for Obstetrics*. Baltimore, Williams & Wilkins, 1979, p 67

2. Goodman LS, Gelman, H.: Morphine and other alkaloids. In Gilman AF, Goodman LS, Gilman A (eds): *The Pharmacologic Basis of Therapeutics*, ed. 5. New York, Macmillan, 1979, p 250

3. Stoelting RK: Opiate receptors and endorphins: Their role in anesthesiology. Anesth Analg 59:874, 1980

4. DeVoe SJ, DeVoe K Jr, Rigsby WC, et al: Effect of meperidine on uterine contractility. *Am J Obstet Gynecol* 105:1004, 1969

5. Filler WW Jr, Hall WC, Filler NW: Analgesia in obstetrics. *Am J Obstet Gynecol* 96:832, 1967

6. Shnider SM, Moya F: Effects of meperidine on the newborn infant. *Am J Obstet Gynecol* 89:1009, 1964

7. Brackbill Y, Kane J, Manniello RL: Obstetric meperidine usage and assessment of neonatal status. *Anesthesiology* 40:116, 1974

8. Morrison JC, Whybrew WD, Rosser SI, et al: Metabolites of meperidine in the fetal and maternal serum. *Am J Obstet Gynecol* 126:997, 1976

9. Flowers CE: *Obstetrical Analgesia and Anesthesia*. New York, Harper & Row, 1967, p 76

10. Way WL, Costley EC, Way EL: Respiratory sensitivity of the newborn infant to meperidine and morphine. *Clin Pharmacol Ther* 6:454, 1965

11. Paddock R, Beer EG, Bellville JW, et al: Analgesic and side effects of pentazocine and morphine in a large population of postoperative patients. *Clin Pharmacol Ther* 10:355, 1969

12. Gray JH, Cudmore DW, Luther ER, et al: Sinusoidal fetal heart rate patterns associated with alphaprodine administration. *Obstet Gynecol* 52:678, 1978

13. Kaulman RD, Aqleh KQ, Bellville TW: Relative potencies and durations of action with respect to respiratory depression of intravenous meperidine, fentanyl, and alphaprodine in man. *J Pharmacol Exp Ther* 208:73, 1979

14. Frost E: Update on therapeutic barbiturate coma. *Curr Rev Clin Anesthesiol* 1:1–8, 1980

15. Myers R, Meyers S: Use of sedative, analgesic and anesthetic drugs during labor and delivery: Bane or boon. *Am J Obstet Gynecol* 133:83, 1979

16. Root B, Eichner E, Sunshine I: Blood secobarbital levels and their clinical co-relation in mothers and newborn infants. *Am J Obstet Gynecol* 81:948, 1961

17. Kosaka Y, Takahashi T, Mark LC: Intravenous thiobarbiturate anesthesia for cesarean section. *Anesthesiology* 31:849, 1969

18. Cree IE, Meyer J, Hailey DM: Diazepam in labour: Its metabolism and effect on the clinical condition and thermogenesis of the newborn. *Br Med J* 4:251, 1973

19. Yeh SY, Paul RH, Cordero L, et al: A study of diazepam during labor. *Obstet Gynecol* 43:363, 1974

20. Schiff D, Chan G, Stern L: Fixed drug combinations and the displacement of bilirubin from albumin. *Pediatrics* 48:139, 1971

21. Powe CE, Kiem IM, Fromhagen C, et al: Propiomazine hydrochloride in obstetrical analgesia. *JAMA* 181:290, 1962

22. Zsigmond EK, Patterson RL: Double blind evaluation of hydroxyzine hydrochloride in obstetric anesthesia. *Anesth Analg* 46:275, 1967

23. Downing JW, Mahomedy MC, Jeal DE, et al: Anaesthesia for caesarean section with ketamine. *Anaesthesia* 31:883, 1976

24. Boehm FH, Smith BE, Egilmez A: Physostigmine's effect on diminished fetal heart rate variability caused by scopolamine. In *Abstracts of Scientific Papers:* Annual Meeting, Society for Obstetric Anesthesia and Perinatalogy, Philadelphia, 1975, p 18

25. DeJong R: *The Neural Target in Local Anesthetics*, ed. 2. Springfield, Ill, Thomas, 1977, p 10

26. Covino BG: Pharmacology of local anesthetic agents. *Surg Rounds*, pp 32–51, July 1978

27. Brown WU, Bell GC, Jurie AO, et al: Newborn blood levels of lidocaine and mepivacaine in the first postnatal day following maternal epidural anesthesia. *Anesthesiology* 42:698, 1975

28. Phillips G: A double-blind trial of bupivacaine (Marcaine) and etidocaine (Duranest) in extradural block for surgical induction of labour. *Br J Anaesth* 47:1305, 1975

29. Ralston DH, Shnider SM: The fetal and neonatal effects of regional anesthesia in obstetrics. *Anesthesiology* 48:34, 1978

30. Usubiaga JE: Neurologic complications following epidural analgesia. *Int Anesthesiol Clin* 13:1–157, 1975

31. Salts L, Orr M, Walson PD: Local anesthetic agents—pharmacologic basis for use in obstetrics: A review. *Anesth Analg* 55:829–838, 1976

32. Tronick E, Wise S, Als H, et al: Regional obstetrical anesthesia and newborn behavior: Ef-

fect over the first ten days of life. *Pediatrics* 58:94, 1976

33. Shnider SM, Levinson G: *Anesthesia for Obstetrics.* Baltimore, Williams & Wilkins, 1979

34. Marx GF, Joshi CW, Orkin LR: Placental transmission of nitrous oxide. *Anesthesiology* 32:429, 1970

35. Jones PL, Rosen M, Mushin WW, et al: Methoxyflurane and nitrous oxide as obstetric analgesics: II. A comparison by self-administered intermittent inhalation. *Br Med J* 3:259, 1969

36. Creasser CW, Stoelting RK, Krishna G, et al: Methoxyflurane metabolism and renal function after methoxyflurane analgesia during labor and delivery. *Anesthesiology* 41:62, 1974

37. Munson ES, Embro WJ: Enflurane, isoflurane, and halothane and isolated human uterine muscle. *Anesthesiology* 46:11, 1977

12. Drug Therapy for Immediate Care of the Newborn

CRAIG W. ANDERSON

Almost from the time of conception the fetus is frequently exposed to drugs and drug metabolites which cross the placenta from the mother. At birth, nearly 95 percent of all babies make the transition from intrauterine to extrauterine life without difficulty; however, a small percentage may require resuscitation and need certain pharmacologic agents within the first few minutes of life. Regardless of the newborn's condition, routine eye and bleeding prophylaxis should be performed. Thus, from conception to after delivery, the developing fetus and newborn are repeatedly exposed to various pharmacologic agents in the perinatal period. The discussion in this chapter includes those drugs used for both routine care of the newborn as well as pharmacologic agents utilized in emergency situations during immediate postnatal life.

EYE PROPHYLAXIS

Prophylaxis against gonococcal ophthalmia neonatorum in the first hour of life remains mandatory. This action is supported by the known increase in asymptomatic genital gonococcal infection and the estimated 28 percent occurrence of gonococcal ophthalmia in untreated infants born to infected mothers.[1] Silver nitrate ophthalmic drops, tetracycline and erythromycin ointments, and penicillin G intramuscularly have all been given for gonococcal eye prophylaxis.

Silver Nitrate

Silver nitrate is a water-soluble, colorless crystal and is known to be directly germicidal against *Neisseria* gonorrhea.[2] The 1 percent ophthalmic solution in single-dose ampules is instilled into the conjunctiva immediately after birth. Irrigation of the eyes with water is unnecessary and does not apparently reduce the incidence of chemical conjunctivitis commonly seen in the first week of life.[3] Since the silver ions precipitate with the chloride ions, flushing with saline will produce a temporary black staining of surrounding tissues. Although silver nitrate may theoretically postpone eye-to-eye maternal-infant bonding, its value in preventing eye damage from gonococcal infection is well substantiated and would appear to outweigh the temporary inconvenience.[2] Silver nitrate has been the major therapeutic drug for gonococcal prevention; however, other treatments have been recently recommended.

Tetracycline and Erythromycin Ointments

Tetracycline ointment (1 percent) and erythromycin ointment (0.5 percent) are topical antibiotics which have been recently approved and recommended for eye prophylaxis by the Center for Disease Control and the American Academy of Pediatrics.[3] They are supplied in single-use tubes and are effective against *Neisseria* gonorrhea. In addition, both antibiotics have been shown to be effective in vitro against *Chlamydia trachomatis,* an important organism contributing to neonatal conjunctivitis and subsequent respiratory illnesses. Clinical trials have revealed an appreciable decrease in chlamydial conjunctivitis with erythromycin ointment but not with tetracycline ointment.[4] Allergic reactions to these topical antibiotics have been reported but are rare.[5] Presently, the significant cost of the topical ointments favors the continued use of the effaciously proven silver nitrate drops.

Penicillin G

The intramuscular use of 50,000 units of aqueous penicillin G given intramuscularly within the first 30 minutes of life for prophylaxis against gonococcal conjunctivitis is another alternative. This mode of therapy cannot be recommended, however, until the incidence of disease from evolving penicillin-resistant organisms, including *Neisseria* gonorrhea, is more clearly delineated.[4] Furthermore, penicillin sensitization within the first year has been reported, and a greater incidence of penicilloyl-sensitive IgM antibodies has been shown in those treated with single-dose penicillin at birth as compared to those receiving local eye prophylaxis. These differences in penicillin sensitivity were no longer present by 5 years of age.[6]

BLEEDING PROPHYLAXIS (VITAMIN K)

The newborn, and especially the premature infant, has only 20 to 40 percent of the normal adult level of the vitamin K-dependent clotting factors II (prothrombin), VII (proconvertin), IX (Christmas or plasma thromboplastin component) and X (Stuart-Prower). The administration of exogenous vitamin K is therefore necessary to arrest the further physiologic decline of these vitamin K-dependent factors which occurs during the first few days of life.[7] Following the establishment of the normal enteric flora, bacterial synthesis and oral intake provide an adequate supply of vitamin K.[8]

A failure to administer this vitamin soon after birth may result in hemorrhagic disease of the newborn, which occurs within the first 48 hours of life. This condition presents as bleeding from the gastrointestinal tract, umbilical cord, circumcision site, nose or intracranial structures.[8] Newborns who are breastfed are also susceptible to this deficiency if untreated, since human milk contains 15 μg/liter of vitamin K in comparison to 60 μg/liter found in cow's milk. The calculated daily requirement of vitamin K is 15 μg/day for the first 3 years of life.[9]

Vitamin K consists of a group of lipid-soluble structures that are cofactors for the activation of clotting factor precursors. Biochemically, the glutamic acid peptide residue is converted to γ-carboxyglutamic acid in the microsomal enzyme system. This alteration then allows calcium ion-binding and phospholipid surface-binding which are important steps for the activation of the clotting factor cascade.[2]

The three forms of vitamin K are shown in Figure 12-1. Vitamin K_1 or phytonadione (2-methyl-3-phytyl-1,4-naphthoquinone) is present in plants and is the only natural vitamin used therapeutically. Vitamin K_2 or menaquinone is synthesized by bacteria and

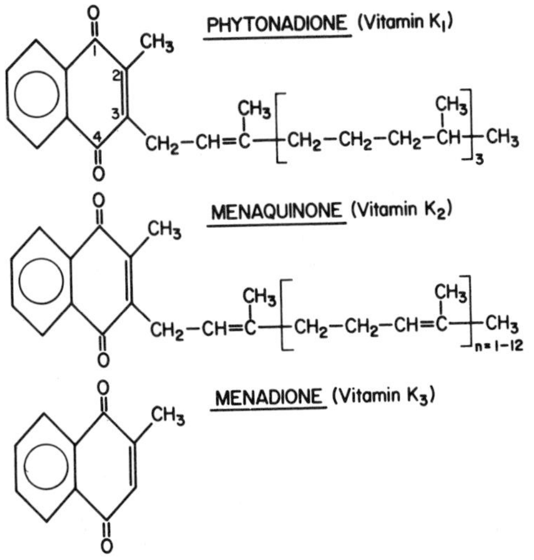

Figure 12-1. Chemical structure of three vitamin K compounds.

represents a group of compounds where a side chain of prenyl units is substituted for the phytyl side chain. Vitamin K_3 or menadione (2-methyl-1,4 naphthoquinone) is the most biologically active of the synthetic derivatives.[1]

Hemorrhagic disease of the newborn from vitamin K deficiency is easily prevented by the intramuscular administration of 1 mg of a phytonadione (vitamin K_1) preparation. Aquamephyton (neonatal) is a yellow, viscous liquid containing phytonadione (1 mg/0.5 ml) dispersed in polyoxyethylated fatty acid derivatives, dextrose, sterile water, and benzyl peroxide (0.9 percent). Konakion uses polysorbate and propylene glycol to disperse phytonadione.[2]

Certain synthetic analogues of menadione or vitamin K_3 (Hykione and Synkonite) should not be administered during the neonatal period because of potentially serious sequelae. Hemolytic anemia, hyperbilirubinemia, kernicterus, and an increase in mortality may occur with excessive doses, which may be partly related to competition between vitamin K_3 and bilirubin for the albumin binding sites.[8]

PHARMACOLOGY OF RESUSCITATION

Several informative and helpful articles on resuscitation of the newborn are available.[10,11] The prevention of birth asphyxia and the knowledge of proper resuscitative techniques can often preclude the use of a pharmacologic agent in the first minutes of life. The appropriate use of drugs in the newborn will depend on the experience of medical personnel and the condition of the neonate at 1 and 5 minutes after birth, as evaluated by the Apgar scoring system[12] (see Tables 12-1 and 12-2). If the newborn's status reflects significant asphyxia (Apgar score 0 to 4), thermal neutrality must be maintained (drying and placing the infant under a radiant warmer), the head and neck must be correctly extended, the airway should be gently cleared of secretions and ventilated by mouth-to-mouth resuscitation, and

bag breathing and/or endotracheal intubation must be performed. Pharmacologic intervention after these crucial basic steps may then be instituted.

Oxygen

Since its discovery in the late 1700s by Priestley, oxygen therapy has become a major pharmacologic agent. This colorless, odorless, therapeutic gas is required in all delivery rooms where potential resuscitation of a newborn may be necessary. Although most newborns do well without the use of oxygen (including those with peripheral cyanosis or acrocyanosis), asphyxiated infants with hypoxia and acidosis greatly benefit from its administration. In those emergency situations where oxygen is needed, a 5- to 7-liter flow of warmed, humidified oxygen is placed in front of the infant's face. The prerequisite of warmed oxygen eliminates the potential for cold stimulation of the trigeminal nerve which may cause reflex apnea and bradycardia. Excessive flow of the gas may cause marked turbulence and jeopardize optimal oxygenation of the patient. Oxygen is supplied through both pressurized wall outlets or from pressurized cylinders, which must be well supported for safety precautions. Regulators, flow meters, humidifers, and heating units should be understood by responsible persons. The importance of minimizing and reversing hypoxia by oxygen administration in the acute situation at birth clearly outweighs any potential toxicity seen in the newborn intensive care unit. (Retrolental fibroplasia and bronchopulmonary dysplasia are usually associated with chronic exposure to oxygen.) The normal physiologic adjustments involving fetal transitional structures are facilitated by oxygenation at birth. The ductus arteriosus, although influenced by various vasoactive substances, responds principally to an increasing arterial blood oxygen tension (> 80 mm Hg). Additional effects of oxygen on the central nervous system, pulmonary system, and peripheral receptors in the neonate continue to be an area of intense investigation.[13]

TABLE 12-1 EVALUATION OF THE NEWBORN USING THE 1- AND 5-MINUTE APGAR SCORING SYSTEM: POINTS ASSIGNED

	Score		
Sign	0	1	2
Heart rate	Absent	≤100	>100
Respiratory effort	Absent	Weak, irregular	Good, crying
Muscle tone	Flaccid	Some flexion of extremities	Well flexed
Reflex irritability (catheter in nose)	No response	Grimace	Cough and sneeze
Color	Blue, pale	Body pink, extremities blue	Pink

Intravenous Fluids

Parenteral fluid administration is paramount in certain neonatal conditions such as prematurity, diabetic progeny, small-for-gestational age, septic shock, and severe birth asphyxia. Both water and glucose supplementation support important critical functions.

From 32 weeks' gestational age until term, water constitutes roughly 80 percent of the total body weight in the newborn. In the sick infant, for whom oral feedings are unwise and potentially dangerous, IV solutions are needed to replace fluid losses (insensible,

urine, and stool) and to support intravascular volume.

Glucose is known to be the major substrate utilized for metabolic processes in the neonate. It is necessary for continued function and preservation of the cardiovascular and central nervous systems and to prevent hypoglycemia and its serious sequelae. A reduction in tissue catabolism[14] and an improvement in survival rate in prematures[15] have been documented following early intravenous administration of water and glucose. Ten percent dextrose (10 gm of dextrose/100 ml water)

TABLE 12-2 DEGREE OF ASPHYXIA AND CLINICAL APPEARANCE OF THE NEWBORN USING THE APGAR SCORING SYSTEM

Degree of Asphyxia	1-minute Apgar Score	Ph	Clinical Presentation
None	7–10	≥7.25	Heart rate > 100, good respirations, well flexed, reflex irritability present, acrocyanosis/pink color
Moderate	4–6	7.10– 7.25	Heart rate > 100, gasping respirations, some flexion, some reflex irritability, pale blue color
Severe	0–3	≤7.10	Heart rate < 100, apneic, flaccid, poor to no reflex irritability, pale color

without electrolytes is used for all term newborns and low-birth-weight infants (1000 to 2500 gm) who require IV fluids within the first 24 hours of life. In very low-birth-weight (VLBW) infants (< 1000 gm), 7.5 percent dextrose in water (7.5 gm dextrose/100 ml water) or 5 percent dextrose in water (5 gm dextrose/100 ml water) should be used to avoid hyperglycemia and the subsequent rise in serum osmolarity. An appropriate fluid load is 60 to 80 ml/kg/day, although VLBW infants may require more to counteract their increased insensible water loss. Fluid therapy is regulated by frequent evaluations of body weight, urine output, urine specific gravities, and degree of insensible water losses, quite variable depending on gestational age. All affected infants should have serum sodium, potassium, and chloride levels measured within 24 hours after birth and prior to adding electrolytes to the IV fluids.

Sodium Bicarbonate

Cardiovascular support in asphyxiated, high-risk infants requires a patent airway, supplemental oxygen, and IV fluids (water and glucose). Occasionally, a buffering agent is necessary to combat lactic acidosis. Sodium bicarbonate ($NaHCO_3$) is a sterile, hypertonic solution used intravenously as a systemic alkalizer. The 4.2 percent solution (infant dosage) contains 0.5 mEq/ml of sodium, 0.5 mEq/ml of bicarbonate, with an osmolality of 1000 mOsm and a pH of 8.0. This agent is used in the newborn to increase the buffering capacity of the blood which is diminished following such situations as anemia, hypoxemia, and ischemia. An appropriate dosage of $NaHCO_3$ is 2 mEq/kg, diluted in equal volumes with sterile water to reduce the osmolality. Infusion should occur over a minimum of 10 to 15 minutes through a peripheral IV or central umbilical catheter line. An upper limit of 6 to 8 mEq/kg over a 24-hour period is recommended.[3] The bicarbonate buffering system is based on the following equation:

$$H^+ + HCO_3^- \rightleftharpoons H_2CO_3 \rightleftharpoons H_2O + CO_2\uparrow.$$

Elimination of carbon dioxide (CO_2) is required in order for bicarbonate to work effectively and is symbolized on the right side of the above equation. Obviously, proper ventilation of the newborn is a prerequisite to bicarbonate administration.

The complications associated with the use of this drug in the newborn include hypernatremia, increased osmolality, fluid overload, hypocalcemia, respiratory acidosis, and intracranial hemorrhage in the premature infant. Administration concomitantly with calcium mixtures should be avoided because of the precipitation of calcium-bicarbonate admixtures.[16]

Naloxone Hydrochloride (Narcan)

Narcotic-induced depression of the newborn is uncommon, but to ensure sufficient oxygenation and to prevent hypercarbia and acidosis, early recognition and prompt resuscitation are required. Proper technique in resuscitation and adequate supportive care diminish significantly the need for a narcotic-antagonist.

Naloxone (Narcan) is an almost pure antagonist of opioid-like compounds with virtually no agonistic effects. It is this characteristic which makes naloxone the drug of choice for narcotic-induced depression when compared to other antagonists that have combined actions (nalorphine hydrochloride and levallorphan tartrate). The neonatal preparation of naloxone (0.02 mg/ml) is recommended at a dose of 0.01 mg/kg IV. Less predictable absorption occurs with subcutaneous, intramuscular, and intralingual administration. Due to its short-lasting action, naloxone may be readministered within 5 minutes if the initial positive response of rhythmic respirations is not sustained.[17]

Naloxone and other narcotic-antagonists act centrally by direct competition for the opiate receptor sites. These receptors seem to be intimately involved with the enkephalin neurotransmitters distributed with the spinal cord, brain stem, pituitary, thalmus, and amygdala.[18] Further studies of these peptide structures and receptor sites may lead to the development of synthetic nonaddicting analgesics.

Naloxone should be used very discriminately in the newborn. Although short-term side effects seem to be negligible, the long-term safety of naloxone is still being investigated. Acknowledgment of the role of endogenous polypeptides (endorphins and enkephalins) in the central nervous system has raised serious questions about the routine use of a narcotic-antagonist. Alterations in release of prolactin, growth hormone, luteinizing hormone and follicle-stimulating hormone have been documented in animals following naloxone administration.[17] It should not be given to infants of narcotic-dependent mothers wherein withdrawal may be abrupt.

Additional Drugs

Critically ill newborns who continue to have difficulty adjusting to extrauterine life despite oxygenation, ventilation, intravenous glucose, volume expansion, and bicarbonate may need additional pharmacologic agents to support their heart rate, blood pressure, and cardiac output. These drugs are summarized in Table 12-3 and described below.

Epinephrine. Effects from epinephrine, a mediator of the adrenergic nervous system, are directly related to the stimulation of α- and β-adrenergic receptor sites.[19] During resuscitation, this drug raises blood pressure through vasoconstriction of the precapillary vascular beds and increases cardiac output by its direct

TABLE 12-3 DRUGS FOR RESUSCITATION OF THE NEONATE

Drug	Dose	Route	Indication	Complications
Sodium bicarbonate (4.2% solution)	2 mEq/kg* (dilute 1:1 with sterile water)	IV slowly†	Severe asphyxia, metabolic acidosis	Hypernatremia, hyperosmolarity, volume overload, intraventricular hemorrhage, respiratory acidosis
Epinephrine	1 ml 1:10,000 dilution	IV or IC	Bradycardia (HR < 80) despite ventilation	Ventricular fibrillation
Volume expander (saline, blood, plasma)	10 ml/kg	IV slowly	Hypotension, volume depletion	Volume overload, intraventricular hemorrhage
Narcan (neonatal)	0.01 mg/kg	IV or IM	Depression, with maternal narcotic history	Minimal; antagonism with enkephalins
Atropine	0.01 mg/kg	IM, SC	Continued bradycardia	Marked tachycardia
Isuprel	1 Amp (0.2 mg) per 50 ml D5W Dose: 0.1–0.4 ug/min	IV	Low cardiac output, bradycardia	Arrhythmias, reduced cardiac output if heart rate > 200
Dopamine	5–10 ug/kg/min	IV	Low cardiac output	Arrhythmias; gangrene, increased pulmonary artery pressure

* Calculated dose mEq NAHCO$_3$ = .3 × weight (kg) × base deficit
† IV = intravenous, IC = intracardiac, IM = intramuscular, SC = subcutaneous

stimulation of the myocardium. An increase in the strength of ventricular contraction (positive inotropic effect) and an increase in heart rate (positive chronotropic effect) further contributes to the improvement in arterial blood pressure. Epinephrine (1 ml) in a 1:10,000 dilution (0.1 mg/ml) should be administered intravenously to the asphyxiated newborn when bradycardia (heart rate < 80 beats/minute) continues despite proper resuscitation. If this is unsuccessful in improving the heart rate, intracardiac administration using a subxiphoid approach should be attempted.

Catecholamines appear to work less effectively in an acid medium; therefore buffering with sodium bicarbonate may increase their effectiveness. Epinephrine and bicarbonate should not be given simultaneously in the identical IV line however, since their interaction may cause precipitation, and thus inactivate the catecholamines.[20]

Atropine. By inhibition of vagal effects on the sino-atrial node, atropine may increase heart rate during newborn resuscitation. Known as an antimuscarinic agent, atropine competes directly with the neurotransmitter acetylcholine at the postganglionic receptor sites. Subcutaneous administration of 0.01 mg/kg will inhibit parasympathetic effects and allow sympathomimetic pharmacologic agents to elevate the contraction frequency of the heart.

Dopamine. Dopamine, an endogenous catecholamine, stimulates β_1-adrenergic receptors and, at higher doses, α-adrenergic receptors. Its unique characteristics have made it the drug of choice in critically ill infants needing continued cardiovascular support. Dopamine selectively dilates renal, coronary, splanchnic, and cerebral vessels by causing a decrease in their vascular resistance.[21] Its positive inotropic and chronotropic effects increase cardiac output, support arterial blood pressure, and allow perfusion of vital organs.[22] Potential complications include increased pulmonary arterial pressure and peripheral ischemia.

Isoproterenol. Isoproterenol, a β_1- and β_2-adrenergic agonist, causes significant inotropic

and chronotropic cardiac stimulation. However, its powerful chronotropic effect often prevents improvement in cardiac output. Additionally, its strong β-stimulation of the periphery leads to vasodilation and subsequent hypotension. Unlike dopamine, isoproterenol fails to selectively increase flow to vital organ systems.[22] Further investigation into the pharmacologic actions of dopamine, isoproterenol, and dobutamine is necessary.

REFERENCES

1. Davidson HH, Hill J, Eastman JJ: Penicillin in the prophylaxis of ophthalmic neonatorum. *JAMA* 145:1052, 1951
2. Harvey S: Antiseptics and disinfectants; fungicides; ectoparasiticides, in Gilman AG, Goodman LS, Gilman A (eds): *The Pharmacological Basis of Therapeutics*, ed. 6 New York, Macmillan, 1980, pp 976–977
3. Segal S, Brann A, Mortimer E, et al: Prophylaxis and treatment of neonatal gonococcal infections. *Pediatrics* 65:1047, 1980
4. Siegel JD, McCracken GH, Threlkeld N, et al: Single-dose penicillin prophylaxis against neonatal group B streptococcal infections. *N Engl J Med* 303:769, 1980
5. Hammerschlag, M, Chandler, J, Alexander, E, et al: Erythromycin ointment for ocular prophylaxis of neonatal chlamydial infection. *JAMA* 244:2291, 1980
6. Fellner MJ, Klaus MV, Baer RL, et al: Antibody production in normal children receiving penicillin at birth. *J Immunol* 107:1440, 1971
7. Owen GM, Nelson EC, Baker GL, et al: Use of vitamin K_1 in pregnancy. *Am J Obstet Gynecol* 99:368, 1967
8. Oski FA: Hematologic problems. In Avery 6B (ed): *Neonatology: Pathophysiology and Management of the Newborn*, ed 2. Philadelphia, Lippincott, 1981, p 569–571
9. Anderson TA, Foman SJ: Vitamins. In Foman SJ (ed): *Infant Nutrition*, ed 2. Philadelphia, Saunders, 1974, pp 222–223
10. Anderson CW, Iams J: Resuscitation of the newborn infant. In Zuspan FP, Quilligan EJ (eds): *Practical Manual of Obstetrical Care*, ed 1 St Louis, Mosby, 1981, in press
11. Fisher DE, Paton JB: Resuscitation of the newborn infant. In Klaus MH, Fanaroff AA (eds): *Care of the High-Risk Neonate*, ed 2. Philadelphia, Saunders, 1979, pp 23–44
12. Apgar V: A proposal for a new method of eval-

uation of the newborn infant. *Anesth Analg (Paris)* 32:260, 1953

13. Nelson NM: Respiration and circulation after birth, in Smith CA, Nelson NM (eds): *The Physiology of the Newborn Infant,* ed 4. Springfield, Ill, Thomas, 1976, pp 143–152

14. Auld PA, Bhangananden P, Mehta S: The influence of an early caloric intake with IV glucose on catabolism of premature infants. *Pediatrics* 37:592, 1966

15. Cornblath M, Forbes AE, Pildes RS, et al: A controlled study of early fluid administration on survival of low birth weight infants. *Pediatrics* 38:547, 1966

16. Bowen FW, Lewis WJ: The use and abuse of bicarbonate in neonatal acid-base derangements. *Resp Care* 23:5, 1978

17. Segal S, Anyan WR, Hill RM, et al: Naloxone use in newborns. *Pediatrics* 65:667, 1980

18. Snyder S: Opiate receptors in the brain. *N Engl J Med* 296:5:266–271, 1977

19. Weiner N: Norepinephrine, epinephrine and the sympathomimetic amines, in Gilman AG, Goodman LS, Gilman A (eds): *The Pharmacological Basis of Therapeutics,* ed 6. New York, Macmillan, 1980, pp 144–151

20. Holbrook PR, Mickell J, Pollack MM, et al: Cardiovascular resuscitation drugs for children. *Crit Care Med* 8:588, 1980

21. Goldberg L: Dopamine—clinical uses of an endogenous catecholamine. *N Engl J Med* 291:707, 1974

22. Driscoll DJ, Gillette PC, Lewis RM, et al: Comparative hemodynamic effects of isoproterenol, dopamine and dobutamine in the newborn dog. *Pediatr Res* 13:1006, 1979

13. Rho(D) Immune Globulin

MELANIE S. KENNEDY

Isoimmune hemolytic disease of the newborn is the destruction of the red blood cells of the fetus and neonate by antibodies produced by the mother. The mother can be stimulated to form the antibodies in any of a number of ways (Table 13-1). In about 95 percent of the cases of hemolytic disease of the newborn, the antibodies in the mother are directed against the red blood cell antigens called Rho or D.[1] The incidence of the disease due to Rho(D) has decreased in the United States from 40.5 cases per 10,000 total births in 1970 to 14.3 per 10,000 in 1979.[2] This decreased incidence can be attributed to the development and release in 1968 of the hyperimmune γ-globulin called Rho(D) immune globulin [Gamulin Rh (Parke-Davis), MICRhoGAM (Ortho), HypRho-D (Cutter), RhoGAM (Ortho)].

TABLE 13-1 CAUSES OF MATERNAL IMMUNIZATION TO RHO(D)

1. Previous pregnancy of Rho(D)-positive fetus
   a. No Rho(D) immune globulin
   b. Insufficient Rho(D) immune globulin
2. Previous transfusion of Rho(D)-positive blood
3. Current pregnancy of Rho(D)-positive fetus
   a. Spontaneous fetal maternal hemorrhage
   b. Amniocentesis
   c. Spontaneous or induced abortion
   d. Ectopic pregnancy
4. Rho(D)-positive mother (grandmother theory)

MECHANISM OF ACTION

The prevention of active immunization by the simultaneous administration of red cell antigen and antibody was first observed in 1900.[3] However, it was not until the 1960s that the application of this principle was investigated for the prevention of Rho(D) immunization by the use of anti-D(Rho). During pregnancy and at delivery, the mixing of fetal and maternal blood occurs. If the mother is Rho(D)-negative and the infant is Rho(D)-positive, the mother has about an 8 percent chance of being stimulated to form anti-D(Rho).[4-6] As little as 1 ml of fetal red blood cells can elicit a response.[7] Antenatally, the risk of sensitization is about 1.8 percent,[3] indicating that a significant amount of fetal red blood cells can enter the maternal circulation during pregnancy. However, the greatest risk is at delivery.

The passively administered Rho(D) immune globulin attaches to the fetal Rho(D)-positive red blood cells in the maternal circulation. This coating antibody prevents the recognition of the Rho(D) antigen by the mother's immune system, and, therefore, prevents the active formation of anti-D(Rho).

DRUG PREPARATION

The only source of Rho(D) immune globulin is plasma from Rho(D)-negative women immunized by pregnancy and Rho(D)-negative men deliberately immunized by repeated

Rho(D)-positive red blood cell injections.[8] In the United States, the immune globulin is prepared by the Cohn cold ethanol fractionation method from pooled raw plasma from at least 20 different human donors. All immune globulins prepared by this method cannot be injected intravenously. In Europe, products are prepared by column separation and can be injected intravenously.[3] This method is being developed for application in the United States. Although immune globulins, regardless of the method of preparation, cannot be pasteurized, they do not transmit hepatitis for unknown reasons.

Each regular single-dose vial contains about 300 μg of anti-D(Rho) and the microdose vial contains about 50 μg. A multiple dose vial is also available (RhoGAM, Ortho). The products also contain 0.3 M glycine as a stabilizer and 0.01 percent thimerosal as a preservative. Rho(D) immune globulin should be stored between 2 and 8 C and must not be frozen.

INDICATIONS

At Delivery

Since the highest risk for Rho(D) immunization occurs at the time of delivery, the unsensitized mother should receive Rho(D) immune globulin soon after. The original studies of the efficacy of the product in prisoners were carried out using 72 hours between the injection of the Rho(D)-positive red blood cells and the injection of the Rho(D) immune globulin. The 72-hour time interval was selected because of weekends and the usual postpartum stay.[4] Complete protection from immunization was shown for the 72-hour time period, although administration beyond 72 hours probably is protective as well, and is certainly not a contraindication.[4]

The mother should be Rho(D)-negative as well as D^u-negative (Fig. 13-1) since Rho(D) immune globulin is incompatible with Rho(D)-positive red blood cells, and will cause shortened survival of Rho(D)- or D^u-positive red

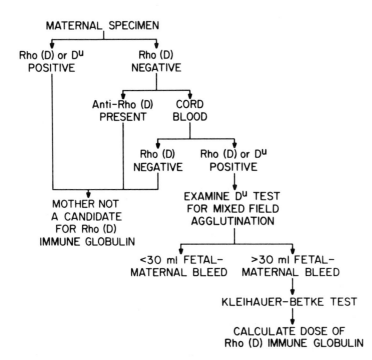

Figure 13-1. Decision tree for the indications and dose of Rho(D) immune globulin as determined by laboratory test results. The maternal blood specimen, collected after delivery, is essential. If the cord or neonatal blood specimen is unavailable, assume that the fetus is Rho(D)- or D^u-positive.

blood cells. The infant should be Rho(D)- or D^u-positive. Rho(D) immune globulin should also be administered if the Rh type of the infant is unknown (e.g., stillborn or abortus).[4]

Routine Antenatal Prophylaxis

Since there is some risk of immunization during pregnancy, some practitioners advocate the use of Rho(D) immune globulin antenatally.[3,6,9] In Winnipeg, Canada, the investigation of the prenatal injection of Rho(D) immune globulin, which was begun in 1968,[3,6] has shown that single injections at 28 weeks' gestation and again at delivery are effective in preventing nearly all cases (> 98 percent) of Rho(D) immunization.

Routine antenatal use is controversial,[5,8,10] however, since those mothers who develop anti-D do not necessarily have severely affected infants.[5,10] A recent survey in Great Britian[10] showed that only 1.82 percent of infants of sensitized mothers died and only 17.4 percent of the infants required transfusion. Considering the low incidence of immunization, 8 percent per pregnancy, and the fact that a single dose after delivery will prevent more than 50 percent of these cases, the cost-effectiveness of an additional dose during pregnancy is very low. In 1980 Tovey[10] estimated that the annual cost of additional routine antenatal prophylaxis in Great Britain to be about £1.8 million or about $3.5 million, for a population of about 50 million. Nusbacher and Bove[8] pointed out that approximately 40 percent of Rho(D)-negative women will be carrying a Rho(D)-negative fetus, so that the amount of antenatal Rho(D) immune globulin would be almost twice that required at delivery. In addition, since humans are the only source of the product, the risks to the donors—hepatitis, immunization to leukocyte and platelet antigens, immunization to non-Rho(D) antigens, and death due to mixup in the red cells returned—become substantial when the benefits are small.[8] Tovey[10] estimated that antenatal prophylaxis would prevent at the most 0.1 deaths/million population annually, or about 6 in Great Britain and 20

in the United States. Some authors[5,10] have also noted that infants are less likely to be severely affected by hemolytic disease of the newborn if Rho(D) immune globulin has been administered after a previous pregnancy.

Amniocentesis

Several authors[3,6,9] have recommended the administration of Rho(D) immune globulin after amniocentesis in the nonimmunized Rho(D)-negative woman, since the risk of fetal maternal hemorrhage is increased. It would seem that the administration of Rho(D) immune globulin would pose a risk to an Rho(D)-positive fetus, since maternal IgG is actively transported across the placenta during pregnancy.[11] This would presumably include Rho(D) immune globulin. However, 300 μg of Rho(D) immune globulin causes an albumin titer to be 1:1 or 1:2 in the mother,[3] which does not cause hemolytic disease of the newborn, although the newborn may have a positive direct antiglobulin (Coomb's) test.

The half-life of IgG is about 25 days, so that 300 μg administered at 28 weeks' gestation would be expected to be about 30 μg at 40 weeks. This is not sufficient to protect against the possible sensitization of delivery. An additional regular dose would be required at delivery. It is very important that the laboratory be informed of any woman receiving Rho(D) immune globulin during gestation, since the remaining anti-D(Rho) in the maternal circulation after delivery may be detected by the routine blood bank type and screen. This could be interpreted as active rather than passive immunization and further administration of Rho(D) immune globulin would appear to be contraindicated. The omission of an additional dose may lead to active Rho(D) sensitization.

Abortion and Ectopic Pregnancy

About 2 to 3 percent of Rho(D) negative women who abort spontaneously or therapeutically will become sensitized, with a higher risk at 10 to 12 weeks than at 6 to 8 weeks.[3] The risk of immunization is about twice that of antenatal sensitization during a normal pregnancy, so that the indication for administration is clear. Fetal red blood cells are formed at about the sixth week of gestation.[12] Abortions and ectopic pregnancy before 12 weeks' gestation can receive the microdose of 50 μg, which is sufficient to protect against 2.5 ml of packed red blood cells. The regular dose of 300 μg should be given for terminations after 12 weeks' gestation.

Accidental Transfusion

Rho(D)-positive red blood cells accidentally transfused to a Rho(D)-negative woman of childbearing age can cause Rho(D) immunization in those 70 percent who are "good responders."[7] An appropriate dose of Rho(D) immune globulin can prevent immunization.

DOSE AND ADMINISTRATION

The regular vial in the United States contains 300 μg of anti-D(Rho), which is sufficient to protect against 15 ml of packed red blood cells, or 30 ml of whole blood (Table 13-2). The regular vial in the United Kingdom contains 100 μg, whereas in most other countries each vial contains between 200 and 300 μg.[7] A small proportion (less than 1 percent) of women delivering after 20 weeks' gestation will have fetal maternal hemorrhages of more

than 30 ml of whole blood. These massive hemorrhages can lead to sensitization if adequate Rho(D) immune globulin is not administered. The existence of a possible massive fetal maternal hemorrhage may be detected by the routine use of the indirect antihuman globulin (Coomb's reagent) test, reading the result microscopically. This test is the same as the D^u test (Fig. 13-1), and can detect 10 ml of Rho(D)-positive fetal red blood cells in the maternal circulation. Quantitation of the actual amount of hemorrhage must be done by the Kleihauer-Betke test. In this test, a thin smear of the maternal blood is subjected to acid and then stained. The fetal cells contain hemoglobin that is resistant to acid and will remain dark. The maternal hemoglobin is eluted by the acid, and therefore maternal cells will appear as ghosts. After several hundred cells are counted, the percentage of fetal cells is determined, and the volume of fetal hemorrhage is calculated using the formula:

$$\frac{\text{No. of fetal cells} \times \text{maternal blood volume}}{\text{Number of maternal cells}} =$$

Volume of fetal maternal hemorrhage

The calculated volume of fetal maternal hemorrhage is then divided by 30 to determine the number of required vials of Rho(D) immune globulin.

TABLE 13-2 INDICATIONS AND DOSE

Indications	Dose

Gestational age < 12 weeks:
    Abortion, spontaneous or induced
    Ectopic rupture
    Amniocentesis
	50 μg (microdose)

Gestational age > 12 weeks:
    Abortion, spontaneous or induced
    Ectopic rupture
    Amniocentesis
    Delivery: spontaneous, induced,
    section, or stillbirth
	300 μg (minimum)

Massive fetal-maternal hemorrhage > 30 ml whole blood	Calculate by Kleihauer-Betke test
Sterilization postpartum	

The microdose of 50 μg is sufficient for abortions up to 12 weeks' gestation, since the total fetal blood volume is estimated at less than 5 ml at 12 weeks. The use of the microdose vial will save the patient from 45 to 55 percent of the cost of the regular vial.

The number of vials for transfusion accidents is calculated by dividing the volume of Rho(D)-positive packed red blood cells transfused by 15 ml, the amount of red blood cells covered by one vial of 300 μg. The amount of Rho(D) immune globulin required can be large, so that the entire dose is often divided and administered in several injections at separate sites.

Rho(D) immune globulin, prepared by the Cohn fractionation technique, as available in the United States, must be injected intramuscularly only. IV injection can cause severe reactions due to the anticomplementary activity of the product. The entire calculated dose should be administered within 72 hours of delivery or accidental transfusion, since nearly all clinical studies use this time span. It is unknown how much delay would still allow complete protection, but if the administration of the Rho(D) immune globulin is inadvertently delayed beyond 72 hours, the dose should still be given.

PRECAUTIONS

Contraindications

Rho(D) immune globulin is of no benefit once a person has been actively immunized and has formed anti-D(Rho). Therefore, before administering Rho(D) immune globulin, the potential recipient should be tested for immune antibodies against red cell antigens. If anti-D(Rho) is identified, administration of Rho(D) immune globulin is not indicated, unless it can be shown that the presence of anti-D(Rho) is due to the previous administration of Rho(D) immune globulin.

Rho(D) immune globulin is not indicated for mothers who are Rho(D)- or D^u-positive, since the product is incompatible with their red blood cells and would cause their rapid destruction. It is also not to be given to the newborn infant. In determining the Rh type of the mother, it is important that fetal red blood cells in the maternal circulation not be interpreted as maternal, since the mother would then be assumed to be D^u-positive. In this case, the correct interpretation should be that a massive fetal maternal hemorrhage has occurred. The difference can be distinguished by examining the D^u test microscopically, since the presence of D(Rho)-positive fetal cells in the D(Rho)-negative maternal blood would have the typical "mixed field" appearance. Confirmation should then be made with the Kleihauer-Betke test.

Rho(D) immune globulin is not indicated for the mother if the infant is found to be Rho(D)- and D^u-negative. This is usually not possible to determine for abortions, stillbirths, and ectopic pregnancies; therefore, Rho(D) immune globulin should be administered in these circumstances.

Adverse Effects

Local reactions to the injections are frequent, and fever occurs occasionally. Rarely, severe reactions may occur from anaphylaxis. Individuals receiving Rho(D) immune globulin may be stimulated to form antiglobulin antibodies which may be due to aggregated IgG in the Cohn fractionation process.[10] It is not known if these antibodies have any clinical significance, or if their passage across the placenta would cause any long-term effect in a future fetus.[10]

Failures

Since about 2 percent of unsensitized Rho(D)-negative women may become immunized during gestation, these cases should not be considered failures. However, the level of antibody at the time of delivery may be too small to detect except by very sensitive techniques. Thus the mother would be considered unsensitized, given Rho(D) immune globulin, and then termed a "failure" at the next pregnancy. As discussed previously, these women generally have less severely affected infants at the next pregnancy.[5,10]

TABLE 13-3   CAUSES OF APPARENT FAILURES OF RHO(D) IMMUNE GLOBULIN

1. Antenatal immunization
2. Inadequate dose
3. Misinterpretation of maternal Rh type
4. Previous Rho(D)-positive transfusion
5. Failure of administration when indicated
6. Immunization to cross-reacting antigen (G or C + D)
7. Delay in administration

The cause of the largest group of "failures" is the failure to give the Rho(D) immune globulin when indicated. About half of the women sensitized in the series by Tovey,[10] and nearly all reported by Mitchell et al.,[5] were due to failures of administration. Table 13-3 lists these and additional causes of apparent failures.

FUTURE DIRECTIONS

The development and marketing of Rho(D) immune globulin prepared by column separation would permit IV injection, and allow a reduction in the cost of the product, since this method results in a higher yield and a lower required dose. Use during gestation for all unimmunized women requires a careful study of cost-effectiveness, and the risks for the human donors of the plasma (incompatibility problems, hepatitis, and even death), the mothers, and their infants. Educational efforts and increased surveillance should decrease any failures of administration, and thus further reduce the incidence of hemolytic disease of the newborn without a need for routine antenatal administration.

REFERENCES

1. Rh hemolytic disease, United States, 1968–1977. *Morbid Mortal Wkly Rep* 27:487–489, 1978
2. Rh hemolytic disease—Connecticut, United States, 1970–1979. *Morbid Mortal Wkly Rep* 30:13–15, 1981
3. Bowman JM: Prevention of Rh-isoimmunization: Remaining problems. In Sherwood WC, Cohn A (eds): *Transfusion Therapy: The Fetus, Infant, and Child.* New York, Masson, 1980, pp 23–36
4. Freda VJ, Gorman JG, Pollack W, et al: Prevention of Rh hemolytic disease—ten years' clinical experience with Rh immune globulin. *N Engl J Med* 292:1014–1016, 1975
5. Mitchell R, O'Donnell R, Blair RG, et al: Antenatal anti-D prophylaxis (letter). *Lancet* ii:798, 1980
6. Bowman JM, Chown B, Lewis M, et al: Rh isoimmunization during pregnancy: Antenatal prophylaxis. *Can Med J* 118:623–627, 1978
7. Mollison PL: *Blood Transfusion in Clinical Medicine,* ed 6. Oxford, Blackwell, 1979, pp 292–352
8. Nusbacher J, Bove JR: Rh immunoprophylaxis: Is antepartum therapy desirable? *N Engl J Med* 303:935–937, 1980
9. Zipursky A: The conquest of Rh disease. *Can Med J* 118:609–610, 1978
10. Tovey GH: Should anti-D immunoglobulin be given antenatally? *Lancet* ii:466–468, 1980
11. Mollison PL: Haemolytic syndromes due to alloantibodies. In Gell PGH, Coombs RRA, Lachman PJ (eds): *Clinical Aspects of Immunology,* ed 3. Oxford, Blackwell, 1975, pp 1043–1060
12. Oski FA, Schwartz E: Hematology of the newborn. In Williams WJ, Beutler E, Erslev AJ, Rundles RW (eds): *Hematology.* New York, McGraw-Hill, 1972, p 52

14. Puerperal Lactation Suppressants

WILLIAM E. COPELAND, Jr.

Despite the resurgence of interest in breast-feeding, there is a significant number of women who choose not to nurse or are unable to do so due to various maternal or neonatal factors. Pharmacologic methods for lactation suppression offer an option to traditional, symptomatic measures of breast-binding, ice packs, fluid restriction, and analgesics. The concepts involved in the complex mechanism of lactation have only recently been understood. This information has significantly influenced the development of specific therapeutic modalities for lactation suppression.

PHYSIOLOGY OF LACTATION

Anatomically, the mature mammary gland is comprised of 15 to 25 lobes, arranged in a radial fashion and separated by fat. Each lobe is made up of several lobules, which are composed of large numbers of alveoli. Each alveolus is lined by a layer of milk-secreting epithelial cells and covered by a layer of contractile myoepithelial fibers. The alveolus secretes milk into the lumen, which subsequently drains into connecting intralobular ducts and finally, into the major lactiferous ducts for each lobule. The growth of this ductal system is estrogen-dependent, while alveolar growth and development are stimulated by progesterone. Although ovarian hormones are primarily involved in breast development, complete differentiation requires an integrated effect from insulin, cortisol, thyroxine, prolactin, and growth hormone, along with human placental lactogen in pregnancy.

During pregnancy, there are progressive increases in the levels of circulating prolactin, estrogen, and progesterone. Prior to parturition and during the early puerperium, only nonmilk colostrum is produced. Colostrum contains desquamated epithelial cells and a transudate, which contains higher levels of fat, protein, and immunoglobulins and less lactose than normal breast milk. Despite the high levels of prolactin, milk production is absent. This is thought to be the result of an inhibitory effect of placental estrogen and progesterone, which exert local effects on the breast.[1-4] Following parturition, circulating levels of estrogen and progesterone fall precipitously. Prolactin levels initially remain elevated and fall more slowly to normal levels. This process is prolonged in the nursing mother. Breast engorgement and milk secretion usually begin on the third or fourth postpartum day. These events probably reflect the loss of inhibitory effects from estrogen and progesterone on the breast. Engorgement is a self-limited phenomenon in the puerperium, lasting 48 to 72 hours, and manifested by swollen, firm, tender breasts.

Lactation is a complex process involving multiple neuroendocrine functions (Fig. 14-1). Suckling or breast stimulation signals tactile sensors in the areola, to activate hypothalamic centers via a neural arc. These centers may also be activated by the mother thinking of the newborn, seeing the baby, or hearing a

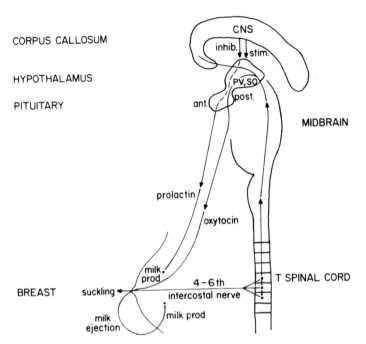

Figure 14-1. Neuroendocrine reflexes involved in lactation. (From Tulchinsky D: The postpartum period, in Tulchinsky D, Ryan K, eds: *Maternal-Fetal Endocrinology,* Philadelphia, Saunders, 1980, with permission.)

cry. The hypothalamic centers synthesize and transport oxytocin to the posterior pituitary gland. Oxytocin is then released to stimulate the alveolar myoepithelial fibers to contract; this results in the emptying of the alveoli and lactiferous ducts and the ejection of milk from the nipple and is known as milk "let-down."

Suckling also activates a similar feedback mechanism resulting in the inhibition of prolactin inhibitory factor (PIF) secretion from the hypothalamus, which leads to an increased production of prolactin from the anterior pituitary gland. Prolactin stimulates the breast to produce milk composed of proteins, casein, fatty acids, and lactose. Prolactin secretion also controls the volume of milk produced through a supply-and-demand system triggered by suckling. The absence of suckling results in cessation of let-down and restoration of normal levels of PIF production in non-nursing mothers. Breast engorgement diminishes, and milk secretion ceases within a few days. Suckling stimulates let-down and milk production long after serum prolactin levels have returned to normal in nursing women (Fig. 14-2). This may result from transient elevations in prolac-

tin associated with suckling in the early puerperium. Later, milk secretion will continue despite normal serum levels of prolactin when suckling is continued. It is hypothesized that this event involves increased sensitivity of the breast to lower levels of prolactin.

TREATMENT FOR LACTATION SUPPRESSION

A significant percentage of patients will experience symptomatic breast engorement, lactation, and breast pain during the first few days postpartum. Studies on the incidence of symptoms vary widely but reveal a range of subjective and objective symptomatology of 25 to 80 percent in placebo-controlled populations.[5-9] Marked symptoms in these individuals ranged from 15 to 49 percent for engorgement, 15 to 33 percent for breast pain, and 15 to 20 percent for excessive lactation.[5-8] While these numbers are significant, many patients are asymptomatic, or require modest symptomatic treatment, and have an uncomplicated resolution of symptoms. Pharmacologic

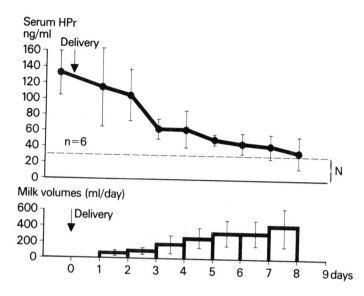

Figure 14-2. Suckling stimulates let-down and milk production long after serum prolactin levels have returned to normal in nursing women. (From Brun del Re R, del Pozo E, deGrandi P, et al: Prolactin inhibition and suppression of puerperal lactation by a Br-ergocryptine (CB-154). *Obstet Gynecol* 41:885, 1973, with permission.)

agents demonstrated to be effective for lactation suppression during the puerperium include chlorotrianisene, the combination of estradiol valerate and testosterone enanthate, and bromocriptine mesylate.

Chlorotrianisene (TACE)

Chlorotrianisene is a synthetic, orally effective, nonsteroidal substance. This compound (tri-*p*-anisylchloroethylene) is classified as a proestrogen, as it is presumably altered in the body prior to exerting its effect. The prolonged estrogenic effect results from storage in adipose tissue and gradual release into the systemic circulation. The recommended dosage is 1 tablet (72 mg) orally twice daily for 2 days, beginning within 8 hours of delivery. Alternative dosages include 12 mg orally four times daily for 7 days or 24 mg orally four times daily for a total of six doses. The mechanism of lactation suppression by estrogenic substances is felt to result from local effects on breast tissue. Animal studies have shown that estrogen implants in rat breast tissue decreased milk secretion, while similar implants in the pituitary gland and median eminence stimulated a release of prolactin.[1] Subsequent human clinical trials failed to show reductions in serum prolactin levels during therapy with exogenous estrogens despite demonstrable lactation suppression.[2,3] These data suggest a localized inhibitory effect at the breast.

Chlorotrianisene has been demonstrated to be significantly better than a placebo in the prevention of breast engorgement, pain, and lactation.[5-7] These findings were present in 10 to 35 percent of women receiving chlorotrianisene, but symptoms were severe in less than 10 percent of treated individuals. A rebound phenomenon of engorgement and lactation following completion of therapy was found in early studies,[6] but these findings were not substantiated by other investigators.[7] Lochial flow, uterine involution, and return of menstrual function were not significantly altered when compared to a placebo group.[5,7]

Testosterone Enanthate and Estradiol Valerate (Deladumone OB, Ditate-DS)

This compound contains the long-acting steroid esters testosterone enanthate (360 mg) and estradiol valerate (16 mg). The recommended dose is a single 2-ml IM injection administered at the beginning of the second stage of labor or within the first hour following parturition. The mechanism of action is considered to be due to local inhibitory effects of estrogen on breast tissue rather than a central effect. Previous experience suggested a reduction in estrogenic side effects when these substances were combined with androgenic compounds.[8] Androgens alone suppress lactogenesis, but are unsatisfactory therapy due to their side effects. Other double-blind studies have demonstrated more effective lactation suppression with combined androgen-estrogen preparations when compared to estrogens alone.[6,7]

In previous controlled studies, testosterone enanthate and estradiol valerate were found to be significantly more effective than a placebo in the prevention of breast engorgement, pain, and lactation.[6-10] These symptoms were present in 1 to 20 percent of patients in pooled series, but most studies demonstrated an incidence of severe symptoms which was less than 5 percent. Initial concerns regarding maternal effects from the androgenic component were unfounded, since virilization has not occurred when the androgen is administered with estrogen. No statistical difference was found in the occurrence of rebound lactation, amount of lochial flow, progress of uterine involution, or return of menstrual function when this compound was compared to a placebo.[7-9] Local discomfort and the risks associated with IM injection must be taken into account prior to administration.

Bromocriptine Mesylate (Parlodel)

Bromocriptine is a nonestrogenic, nonhormonal agent, whose action is systemic rather than local. Bromocriptine is a dopamine receptor agonist with a direct effect on the anterior pituitary gland resulting in an inhibition of prolactin secretion.[11] Some experimental evidence also suggests a hypothalamic effect that increases PIF.[12]

The recommended dosage is one tablet (2.5 mg) orally twice daily for 14 days, with an additional 7 days of treatment should rebound effects occur. Bromocriptine has been found to be significantly better than a placebo in the prevention of breast engorgement, pain, and lactation in clinical trials.[12,13] The specific effect of bromocryptine is demonstrated by a prompt decrease in prolactin suppression during treatment (Fig. 14-3).[3] The transient rise in prolactin levels in response to suckling is also abolished by bromocriptine therapy (Fig. 14-4).[3] Bromocriptine has even been demonstrated to suppress previously initiated lactation in a high percentage of patients.[11,13] This condition is unresponsive to hormonal therapy.

The absence of symptoms with bromocriptine use for postpartum women has been reported in 98 to 99 percent for engorgement, 77 to 85 percent for lactation, and 94 to 95 percent for rebound mammary congestion

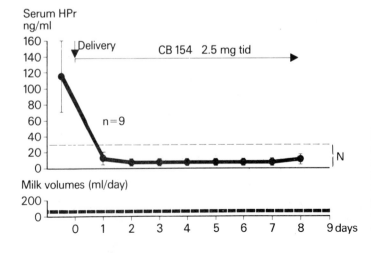

Figure 14-3. Prompt suppression of prolactin secretion with bromocriptine. (From Brun del Re R, del Pozo E, deGrandi P, et al: Prolactin inhibition and suppression of puerperal lactation by a Br-ergocryptine (CB-154). *Obstet Gynecol* 41:887, 1973, with permission.)

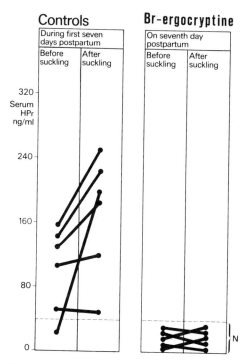

Figure 14-4. The transient rise in prolactin levels in response to suckling is also abolished by bromocriptine therapy. (From Brun del Rey R, del Pozo E, deGrandi P, et al: Prolactin inhibition and suppression of puerperal lactation by a Br-ergocryptine (CB-154). *Obstet Gynecol* 41:886, 1973, with permission.)

with pain when compared to placebo controls.[3,11-13] Side effects from the medication are infrequent but include headache, nausea, and dizziness. A potentially significant side effect was the occurrence of hypotension in over 25 percent of cases in earlier studies, though syncopal episodes were noted in less than 1 percent of cases (product insert). A recommendation has subsequently been adopted to delay administration of the drug until vital signs are stable and a minimum of 4 hours has elapsed since delivery. Mild to moderate rebound breast symptoms have been reported in 18 to 40 percent of cases, but these effects are controlled by continuation of treatment for an additional 7 days.

Gynecologic uses for bromocriptine in-

clude the treatment of various amenorrhea-galactorrhea syndromes, induction of ovulation, and symptomatic relief of the premenstrual syndrome (see Chap. 18).[14,15]

Special Considerations

Thromboembolism with Lactation Suppressants. Significant concern has arisen over the use of estrogens in the puerperium and the possible potentiation of thromboembolic events. An epidemiologic review indicates that the risk of thromboembolism during pregnancy and postpartum is greater than five times that for nonpregnant control subjects.[16] The pathophysiology of puerperal thromboembolism is a complex entity involving numerous contributing factors, particularly advanced maternal age and an operative vaginal or abdominal delivery. The additive effect of estrogens utilized for lactation suppression seemed to contribute toward an increased risk of thromboembolic disease in British studies.[16-18] The incidence of deep vein thrombophlebitis (DVT) was not statistically different in women under the age of 25 having pharmacologic lactation suppression following normal spontaneous vaginal deliveries when compared to a similar, untreated group. Women over the age of 25 and those patients undergoing operative delivery were found to have a higher incidence of thromboembolic disease. The incidence of DVT and embolism ranged from 2- to 10-fold higher in the group treated with estrogen when compared to an untreated control group. The studies indicate an increase from a baseline of 1 to 2 cases of thromboembolism per 1000 deliveries of lactating mothers to 6 to 10 thromboembolic events per 1000 deliveries treated with estrogens for lactation suppression. Women over the age of 35 undergoing cesarean section were at highest risk. It should be emphasized that the estrogens studied were ethinyl estradiol and diethylstilbestrol, but that similar concerns must be applied to all estrogens used for lactation suppression. The decision for use of estrogenic compounds in the puerperium must have the potential bene-

TABLE 14-1   DOSAGES, ROUTES OF ADMINISTRATION, AND COST CONSIDERATIONS AMONG LACTATION SUPPRESSANTS

Drug	Route of Administration	Dose	Cost
Chlorotrianisene (TACE)	Oral	72 mg twice daily for 2 days	equal
Testosterone enanthate/ estradiol valerate (Deladumone OB, Ditate-DS)	IM	2 ml IM	equal
Bromocriptine mesylate (Parlodel)	Oral	2.5 mg twice daily for 14 days	3–4X other substances

fit of lactation suppression weighed against the possible risk of thromboembolic disease.

Bromocriptine is nonestrogenic and is not associated with an increased risk for thromboembolic disease or in any demonstrable alteration in coagulation factors studied to date.[11,13]

Cost Comparison. Presently, chlorotrianisene and the testosterone-estradiol compounds are comparably priced. Bromocriptine is three to four times this cost, depending on length of treatment (Table 14-1).

REFERENCES

1. Bruce JO, Ramirez VD: Site of action of the inhibitory effect of estrogen upon lactation. *Neuroendocrinology* 6:19,1970
2. L'Hermite M, Stavric V, Robyn C: Human pituitary prolactin during pregnancy and postpartum as measured in serum by a radioimmunoassay. *Acta Endocrinol* (KBH) 159(Suppl):37, 1972
3. Brun del Re R, del Pozo E, de Grandi P, et al: Prolactin inhibition and suppression of puerperal lactation by a Br-ergocryptive (CB-154). *Obstet Gynecol* 41:884, 1973
4. Turkington RW, Hill RL: Lactose synthetase: Progesterone inhibition of the induction of α-lactalbumin. *Science* 153:1458, 1969
5. Tyson JEA: A high-dosage estrogen for lactation suppression. *Obstet Gynecol* 27:729, 1966
6. Schwartz DJ, Evans PC, Garcia C-R, et al: A clinical study of lactation suppression. *Obstet Gynecol* 42:599, 1973
7. Morris JA, Creasy RK, Hohe PT: Inhibition of puerperal lactation. *Obstet Gynecol* 36:107, 1970
8. Womack WS, Smith SW, Allen GM, et al: A comparison of hormone therapies for suppression of lactation. *South Med J* 55:816, 1962
9. Iliya FA, Safon L, O'Leary JA: Testosterone emanthate (180 mg.) and estradiol valerate (8 mg.) for suppression of lactation: A double-blind evaluation. *Obstet Gynecol* 27:643, 1966
10. Markin KE, Wolst MD: A comparative controlled study of hormones used in the prevention of postpartum breast engorgement and lactation. *Am J Obstet Gynecol* 80:128, 1960
11. Cooke I, Foley M, Lenton E, et al: The treatment of puerperal lactation with bromocriptine. *Postgrad Med J* 52:75, 1976
12. Rolland R, Schellekens, L: A new approach to the inhibition of puerperal lactation. *J Obstet Gynaecol Br Commonw* 80:945, 1973
13. Nilsen PA, Meling A-B, Abildgaard U: Study of the suppression of lactation and the influence on blood clotting with bromocriptine (CB-154) (Parlodel): A double blind compari-

son with diethylstilboestrol. *Acta Obstet Gynecol Scand* 55:39, 1976

14. Parkes D: Drug therapy—bromocriptine. *N Engl J Med* 301:873, 1979

15. Elsner CW, Buster JE, Schindler RA, et al: Bromocriptine in the treatment of premenstrual tension syndrome. *Obstet Gynecol* 56:723, 1980

16. Jeffcoate TNA, Miller J, Roos RF, Tindall VR: Puerperal thromboembolism in relation to the

inhibition of lactation of oestrogen therapy. *Br Med J* 4:19, 1968

17. Turnbull AC: Puerperal thromboembolism and suppression of lactation. *J Obstet Gynaecol Br Commonw* 75:1321, 1968

18. Tindall VR: Factors influencing puerperal thromboembolism. *J Obstet Gynaecol Br Commonw* 75:1324, 1968

15. Drugs in Breast Milk

DEBRA K. GARDNER   WILLIAM F. RAYBURN

The prevalence of breastfeeding has increased dramatically during the past decade. A recent survey of 10,000 mothers by Ross National Mothers Survey indicates that the number of mothers who breastfeed at the time of hospital discharge has increased from 33 percent in 1975 to 43 percent in 1977.[1] The emergence of this trend coincides with the general condemnation of artificial products and processes and the preservation of nature's way. Psychologists have demonstrated the importance of the maternal-infant bond during the early days of life, and the advantages of breastfeeding are well documented.[2] Members of all health care professions are involved in educating parents on breastfeeding, and organizations have been formed to encourage nursing mothers.

As a result of the increased interest in breastfeeding, knowledge about drug therapy and exposure to environmental pollutants during lactation are becoming more important. The long-term consequences to infants being fed breast milk containing drugs and other chemicals remain unknown. Weaning as a precaution during drug therapy can only be altered after accurate information is gathered about the drug's level in breast milk and its effect on the infant.

Thorough pharmacokinetic studies on drugs and chemicals consumed during lactation are unfortunately lacking, with most human data including only a small number of patients or a single case report. Single determinations of a drug in breast milk are of limited value. Animal studies may be misleading due to species variations in pH, milk composition, and metabolic differences. Certain drug assay procedures in the past lacked sensitivity and specificity, and extraction from either the aqueous or lipid phase was often not quantitative. Manufacturer's unpublished data and the use of phrases such as "may" or "might" when referring to the possible effect of the drug on the nursing infant are often understood to mean the drug is contraindicated in nursing mothers. An understanding of the pharmacokinetic properties of the drug and serial measurements of drug levels in maternal plasma, breast milk, and infant plasma are necessary. Drug therapy which is beneficial for the mother and not detrimental to the infant is the ultimate goal.

SYNTHESIS AND COMPOSITION OF MILK

Mammary glands are morphogenetically similar to sweat glands. They are composed of alveolar cells, which produce and secrete milk into a lumen, and myoepithelial cells, which have contractile properties that permit expulsion of milk from the alveoli into the duct system. A biologic membrane comprised of a basement membrane and low columnar glandular cells separates the luminal contents from the extracellular space.

The synthesizing machinery of the alveolar cell is provided energy by plasma glucose, and its product is an isotonic mixture of proteins, carbohydrates, fats, ions, and vitamins. Casein, the primary milk protein, is assembled in the ribosomes of the rough endoplasmic reticulum. Other proteins in milk include serum albumin, α-lactalbumin, β-lactoglobulins, immunoglobulins, and other glycoproteins. The predominant carbohydrate nutrient in milk is lactose, which is synthesized from maternal glucose and galactose in the Golgi apparatus by the enzyme, lactose synthetase. Lactose creates an osmotic gradient drawing water into the alveoli, forming the aqueous phase of milk and therefore regulating milk volume. Protein is combined with its carbohydrate complement within the Golgi apparatus prior to its secretion into the alveolar lumen. Lipid droplets in milk are primarily composed of cholesterol and its esters, phospholipids, triglycerides, and free fatty acids. These droplets are engulfed in the apical membrane and are eventually discharged into the lumen. Ions are either free in solution or bound to milk proteins, and are usually transported into alveolar cells by passive diffusion. A low sodium concentration is maintained in milk by active extrusion of sodium ions by the basal portion of the secretory cell back into plasma.[3] Calcium, magnesium, and amino acids appear to be actively transported into the alveolus.[4]

Variations in milk composition and yield become important when dealing with drug excretion, as the distribution will depend on their degree of solubility in either the aqueous or lipid fraction of milk and their degree of binding to milk proteins. As colostrum progresses to mature milk, the profile of protein and lipid content changes. Total lipid content increases and protein decreases. The milk the infant receives initially during a feeding (foremilk) differs in composition from that received during the latter part of a feeding (hind-milk). The rate of fat production and fat concentration, along with protein concentration, increases during the last half of feeding.[3] Fat excretion has diurnal variations, with its minimum content being the first morning feeding and its highest concentration being the mid-morning feeding with a progressive decline throughout the day.[5]

PRINCIPLES OF DRUG TRANSFER INTO MILK

Principles of drug transfer into milk and the effect on the infant encompass absorption, distribution, metabolism, and elimination of a drug in both the mother and the infant. This concept is illustrated in Figure 15-1, and is described in detail in the sections which follow.

Drug transfer and concentration in breast milk is influenced by the drug's physical and chemical properties (molecular weight, degree of ionization, solubility characteristics, and protein-binding). Most clinically useful drugs have molecular weights between 250 and 500, and their passage into breast milk depends on their lipid solubility and degree of ionization, since usually the unionized lipid-soluble form passes through the cell membrane. The degree of ionization of weak acids and bases is related to the pH of the medium and to the drug dissociation constant (pKa). The breast milk pH ranges from 6.8 to 7.3 which is lower than plasma and interstitial fluid.[6] Weak bases are more unionized in the higher pH of the plasma and pass readily into the more acidic milk where they become ionized and "trapped," creating a higher concentration in milk than in plasma. Weak acids such as barbiturates, organic acids, sulfonamides, diuretics, and benzyl penicillin have an equal or lower concentration in milk than in plasma.

Drugs and pollutants present in maternal blood must cross the capillary endothelium, extracellular spaces, and the hydrophobic barrier created by the alveolar cell membrane before entering the milk. Most drug transfer occurs by passive diffusion, in which the concentration gradient governs solute movement. As maternal plasma levels decrease, the drug concentration in the milk decreases by back diffusion.[5] Some ionized particles and small hydrophilic drugs with molecular weights less than 200 penetrate the membrane through aqueous channels or pores.[7] Facilitated diffusion, an uncommon method of drug transfer, explains the passage of water-soluble substances too large to pass through mem-

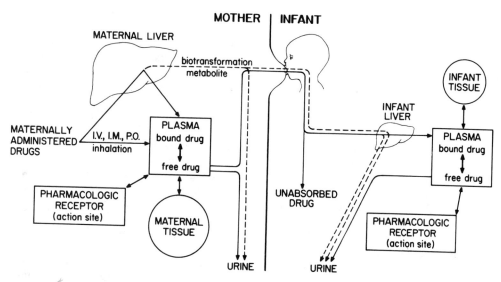

Figure 15-1. Drug disposition in the maternal infant unit. (From Giacoia GP, Catz CS: Drugs and pollutants in breast milk. *Clin Perinatol* 6:182, 1979, with permission.)

brane pores.[8] Active transport mechanisms requiring energy provide a process whereby substances are carried from a lower concentration to a higher concentration. Substances which are actively transported include glucose, amino acids, calcium, and magnesium, but very few drugs have been found to use this mechanism of transfer.[3] Pinocytosis and reverse pinocytosis are involved in the transport of very large molecules and proteins.

Since only the unbound fraction of a drug exerts the pharmacologic action and can be metabolized and excreted, the extent and affinity of drug-binding to both plasma and milk proteins affect drug concentration in milk. The displacement of a particular drug from albumin can occur by competitive binding with endogenous or exogenous substances and creates a higher concentration of free drug.

Pharmacokinetic parameters of a drug affect its excretion rate and concentration in breast milk. The amount of drug present in the milk and consumed by the infant depends on the dose, frequency and duration of exposure, route of administration, and the relationship between the time of drug administration to the time of feeding. The blood flow to the breast is another important factor that determines the rate of a drug's presentation to the milk.

ABSORPTION AND ELIMINATION OF DRUGS BY THE NURSING INFANT

The nursing infant is constantly maturing and the manner in which it absorbs, tolerates, and metabolizes drugs can vary within a short period of time. The bioavailability of compounds ingested by the infant depends on the functional readiness of the gastrointestinal tract. The gastric emptying time, gastrointestinal motility, gastric pH, interaction of drugs with components of the gastrointestinal tract, dissolution rate of salts and particles, dietary factors, and effective surface area must be considered. The gastric emptying time is generally prolonged, and the gastric pH is higher in the newborn.[8] A slower transit time in the upper small intestine may enhance absorption of certain drugs. Synthesis and pool size of bile salts are relatively small compared to those of an adult. The increased permeability of the gastrointestinal mucosa to macromolecules may be responsible for sensitization to certain substances found in milk.[8] Some drugs (tetracyclines) form complexes with components in the milk, which limits their absorption.

Drug distribution in the neonate differs from that of an adult in that the neonate has a smaller extracellular fluid volume and a greater deposition of fat.[8] Premature infants have lower albumin levels, which limits available protein-binding sites. Jaundice may occur when drugs (sulfonamides) displace bilirubin from plasma protein-binding sites.

During the first few months of life, drug-metabolizing pathways and kidney function are not fully developed. The half-lives of certain drugs are prolonged and make the infant susceptible to toxicity from drug accumulation (see Chap. 1). Hepatic glucuronyl transferase is deficient in the neonate which accounts for cases of hyperbilirubinemia when certain drugs (estrogens, progestins) are ingested by the nursing infant.[9] The rate of drug metabolism and excretion is like that of the adult only after two months of age.[8]

ASSAY TECHNIQUES

The presence and concentration of drugs and chemicals in breast milk are determined by standard analytical procedures using gas-liquid chromatography and gas chromatography-mass spectometry. Breast milk differs from other commonly analyzed body fluids because high concentrations of fatty acids and lipids reduce extraction efficiency and interfere with certain analyses. Analysis of compounds with a high lipid solubility therefore requires multiple solvent extractions. The removal of lipids by washing with a low polarity solvent may also lower recovery of the drug. Other techniques include protein precipitation prior to extraction and lyophilization.

DRUGS THAT AFFECT
THE PRODUCTION OF MILK

Mammary blood flow determines the rate of drug presentation to the breast. Factors regulating mammary blood flow include the metabolic activity in the mammary gland, the release of lactogenic hormones in response to suckling, a decrease in intramammary pressure due to the removal of accumulated secretions in the alveoli as sucking occurs, and the use of certain drugs. Mammary blood vessels are extremely sensitive to vasoconstrictors. Drugs with sympathomimetic activity (stimulants, decongestants) can decrease blood flow and milk yield. Large amounts of nicotine in mothers who smoke heavily (1 to 2 packs/day) can decrease milk supply.[7] Vasodilating drugs can increase the rate of excretion of substances that are rapidly excreted by the alveolar epithelium, since their transport is flow dependent.

Prolactin secretion is susceptible to drug modification. Levodopa, ergocriptine, bromocriptine, pyridoxine, and monoamine oxidase inhibitors cause stimulation of dopamine receptors either directly or indirectly in the hypothalamus, which increases the release of prolactin inhibitory factor (see Chap. 14). Conversely, drugs acting on the hypothalamus to suppress prolactin inhibitory factor secretion include phenothiazines, cimetidine, metoclopramide, methysergide, and certain antihypertensive agents (reserpine, clonidine, and methyldopa).[10] Metoclopramide, a potent stimulator of prolactin release, has been used to restore milk flow in women whose volume has decreased.[11]

COMMONLY ENCOUNTERED
DRUGS DURING LACTATION

Physicians often encounter the following classes of drugs when treating nursing mothers or answering their questions. Specific information concerning individual drugs are found in the Appendix and discussed in further detail as follows.

Alcohol, Caffeine, and Nicotine

Most babies are periodically or chronically exposed to alcohol through breastfeeding. Ethanol in plasma rapidly equilibrates in breast milk, and the milk to plasma concentration ratio (M:P) is 0.9.[3] Almost every source of information dealing with the presence of alcohol in breast milk recounts a case report published in 1936 involving a mother who ingested 750 ml of port wine during a 24-hour period. The affected infant displayed unarousable sleep with snoring, deep respiration, and no reaction to pain.[12] If a moderate social drinker (2 to 3 cocktails, 2 to 3 glasses of wine, or two to three 340-ml bottles of beer) had a blood alcohol concentration of 50 mg/dl, the nursing infant would receive about 82 mg of alcohol, which would produce insignificant blood concentrations.[3] Mild sedation can occur in the infant whose mother's blood alcohol concentration is 300 mg/dl. This is probably the highest alcohol concentration at which a mother would still be capable of nursing her infant. Furthermore, there is no evidence that occasional moderate ingestion of alcohol by the mother is harmful to the infant. For obvious reasons, intoxicated mothers should not breastfeed their babies, and chronic alcoholic mothers who will not stop drinking should be discouraged from breastfeeding.

Although the concentration of caffeine in breast milk is 1 percent of the mother's plasma level, caffeine can accumulate in the infant.[13] If a breastfeeding mother drinks six to eight cups of caffeine-containing beverages including coffee, tea, and colas, her infant is likely to show signs of caffeine stimulation such as hyperactivity and wakefulness.[13] It is therefore recommended that nursing mothers limit their intake of caffeine-containing beverages to 1 to 2 cups/day.

Nicotine can enter the milk and reach relatively low levels (0.01 to 0.05 mg/dl) if 20 cigarettes are smoked per day.[7] Since nicotine is not readily absorbed by the infant's intestinal tract and is rather quickly metabolized, signs of nicotine intoxication are unlikely. If maternal smoking exceeds 20 to 30 cigarettes/day, milk yield may significantly decrease and may explain any symptoms of nausea, vomiting, abdominal cramping, and diarrhea in the infant.

Analgesics

Narcotic analgesics (morphine, codeine, meperidine, and methadone) appear in human milk in low levels, and the amount absorbed by the infant is insignificant. Mothers maintained on 50 to 80 mg of methadone/day may still breastfeed.[14]

Salicylates may be found in breast milk but usually in low concentrations, as transport from plasma into milk is not favored since acids exist primarily in the ionized form. A risk of interference with the infant's platelet function and blood-clotting mechanisms is possible if the mother is ingesting antiarthritic doses of salicylates.[15]

A breastfeeding infant weighing 5.4 to 7.3 kg could theoretically receive up to 1 mg of propoxyphene/day if the mother were to continually consume the maximum dose.[14] This may be difficult for the infant to metabolize due to immature liver enzymes. One infant was reported to have unusually poor muscle tone when the mother was taking propoxyphene every 4 hours.[13]

Antibiotics

Most antibiotics appear in breast milk, and their concentration in milk depends mainly upon the pKa of the drug, its lipid solubility, and protein-binding capabilities.

Sulfonamides appear in milk in varying concentrations according to their pKa values. Sulfapyridine readily passes into milk because it is a very weak acid (pKa 8.4) and is therefore unionized. Only rarely has an adverse reaction been reported from the presence of sulfas in milk. Hyperbilirubinemia and jaundice can occur in the early weeks of life due to displacement of protein-bound bilirubin.[16] One case of hemolytic anemia has been reported in a glucose-6-phosphate dehydrogenase-deficient infant.[7]

Penicillins and cephalosporins are excreted in milk in relatively low concentrations with M:P ratios ranging from 0 to 0.2.[3] The risk of sensitization is possible, and an allergic reaction has been reported in an infant whose mother was being treated for syphilis with penicillin.[5] Cephalothin and cefazolin are not well absorbed into the systemic circulation when ingested orally through breast milk.

Tetracyclines appear in milk in concentrations ranging between 60 and 80 percent of the maternal plasma concentration, but are usually undetected in the infant's plasma.[3] The relative gastric achlorhydria of newborns may decrease solubility and absorption of tetracyclines.[3] Calcium and proteins bind tightly to tetracyclines, which limits the absorption of this group of drugs. The theoretical risks of teeth staining and delayed bone growth have not been reported during breastfeeding. Some authors still do not negate this possibility and recommend alternate therapy if possible.[17]

The aminoglycoside antibiotics are generally considered safe to use during lactation because of poor gastrointestinal absorption in the infant. If gastrointestinal inflammation or diarrhea exists in the infant, there may be increased absorption of aminoglycosides, and ototoxicity and nephrotoxicity become a greater risk. Infant plasma concentration should be monitored in such circumstances.

Chloramphenicol concentrations in milk are half that of the mother's plasma. Its use is contraindicated in the very early postpartum period because even small absorbed amounts can accumulate in the very young infant and cause bone marrow depression.[18]

Some antibiotics concentrate in the milk and their observed M : P ratios are greater than 1. These include erythromycin, metronidazole, isoniazid, and trimethoprim.[3] If a mother has active tuberculosis, breastfeeding is contraindicated. If treatment with isoniazid is necessary, the infant should be monitored closely for signs of toxicity (vomiting, respiratory distress, and central nervous system depression).

Anticoagulants

The major anticoagulants are safe during breastfeeding. Heparin has a molecular weight of 17,000 and is too large to pass into breast milk. Warfarin is highly bound to plasma proteins, weakly acidic, and usually ionized, and therefore goes undetected in breast milk, even

with very sensitive assays.[19,20] Dicumarol also appears to be safe for nursing mothers.[21] Bleeding problems and increases in the infant's prothrombin time have been associated with phenindione and ethylbiscoumacetate.

Laxatives

It is believed that anthraquinone cathartics (senna, cascara sagrada, danthron, and casanthrol) may appear in breast milk. The exact form of the drug absorbed and the extent of absorption into the maternal circulation is unknown. Infant gastrointestinal effects such as diarrhea and colic when lactating mothers were given anthraquinone derivatives have been reported.[22] Another laxative, phenolphthalein, is seldom found in breast milk, and is therefore not often associated with diarrhea in the infant. Bisacodyl is not excreted in breast milk.[7] Anionic surfactants (dioctyl sodium sulfosuccinate) and bulk formers including bran, methylcellulose, and psyllium hydrophyllic mucilloid are the laxatives of choice for lactating mothers because they are not absorbed into the maternal circulation.

Oral Contraceptives

Progestins and estrogens contained in oral contraceptives may reach the milk in concentrations up to 1 percent of the oral dose.[7] Effects from oral contraceptive use during lactation include the potential decrease in milk production and possible side effects in the nursing infant. Diminished lactation is more likely if oral contraceptive use is instituted before the fourth postpartum week. If contraceptive therapy is instituted after an adequate milk supply is established, it will not influence lactation, but may affect the composition of milk. Some studies reveal a change in protein, fat, and mineral content in mother's milk, but changes observed were still within the normal ranges, and the clinical significance is unclear.[23] Proliferation of vaginal epithelium in female nurslings has been ascribed to maternal contraceptive use,[24] while ingestion of the comparatively high sex steroid doses contained in earlier contraceptive preparations was reported to cause gynecomastia in one male infant.[25] If large amounts of estrogens and progestins are absorbed from the ingested milk into the baby's circulation, hyperbilirubinemia may result since the steroids compete for binding of glucuronic acid in the liver and displace bilirubin from plasma protein-binding sites.[9] Oral contraceptive preparations containing 2.5 mg or less of a progestin (19-nortestosterone derivatives) and 50 mcg or less of ethinyl estradiol, or 100 mcg or less of mestranol present no hazard to the mother's milk yield to the infant.[7] No adverse effects on the infant during the ensuing years in bone maturation, genital development, or impaired fertility have been substantiated.

REFERENCES

1. Lawrence RA: Breast-Feeding: *A Guide for the Medical Profession.* St. Louis, Mosby, 1980, pp 5–6

2. Jelliffee DB, Jelliffee EFP: "Breast is best": Modern meanings. *N. Engl J Med* 297:912, 1977

3. Wilson JT, Brown RD, Cherek DR, et al: Drug excretion in human breast milk, principles, pharmacokinetics, and projected consequences. *Clin Pharmacokinet* 5:1, 1980

4. Gaginella TS: Drugs and the nursing mother infant. *US Pharmacist* 3:39, 1978

5. Catz CS, Giacoia GP: Drugs in breast milk (Symposium on pediatric pharmacology). *Pediatr Clin North Am* 19:151, 1972

6. Lien EJ, Kuwahara J, Koda RT: Diffusion of drugs into prostatic fluid and milk. *Drug Intell Clin Pharm* 8:470, 1974

7. Vorherr H: Drug excretion in breast milk. *Postgrad Med* 56:97, 1974

8. Giacoia GP, Catz CS: Drugs and pollutants in breast milk (Symposium on pharmacology). *Clin Perinatol* 6:181, 1979

9. Wong YK, Wood BS: Breast-milk jaundice and oral contraceptives. *Br Med J* 4:403, 1971

10. Dickey RP: Drugs affecting lactation. *Semin Perinatol* 3:279, 1979

11. Sousa PLR, et al: Reestablishment of lactation with metoclopramide. *J Trop Pediatr* 21:214, 1975

12. Bisdom CJW: Alcohol and nicotine poisoning in nurslings. *Maandschr Kindergeneeskd* 6:332, 1936

13. Lawrence RA: Drugs in breast milk, in *Breast-Feeding: A Guide for the Medical Profession.* St. Louis, Mosby, 1980, pp 157–170

14. Ananth J: Side effects in the neonate from psychotropic agents excreted through breast-feeding. *Am J Psychiatry* 135:801, 1978

15. Bleyer W, Brenkenridge RT: Studies on the detection of adverse drug reactions in the newborn: II. The effects of prenatal aspirin on newborn hemoatasis. *JAMA* 214:2049, 1970

16. Forrest JM: Drugs in pregnancy and lactation. *Med J Aust* 2:138, 1976

17. Hervada AR, Feit E, Sagraves R: Drugs in breast milk. *Perinat Care* 2:19, 1978

18. Abramowicz M (ed): Update: Drugs in breast milk. *Med Lett Drug Ther* 21:21, 1979

19. Orme ML 'E, Lewis PJ, Sweit M, et al: May mothers given warfarin breast-feed their infants? *Br Med J* 1:1564, 1977

20. DeSwiet M, Lewis PJ: Excretion of anticoagulants in human milk. *N Engl J Med* 297:1471, 1977

21. Bambel CE, Hunter RE: Effect of dicoumarol on the nursing infant. *Am J Obstet* 59:1153, 1950

22. Knowles JA: Breast milk: A source of more than nutrition for the neonate. *Clin Toxicol* 7:69, 1974

23. Lonnerdal B, Forsum E, Hambraeus L: Effect of oral contraceptives on composition and volume of breast milk. *Am J Clin Nutr* 33:816, 1980

24. Lauritzen C: On endocrine effects of oral contraceptives. *Acta Endocrinol* 124(supp):87, 1967

25. Curtis EM: Oral-contraceptive feminization of a normal male infant. *Obstet Gynecol* 23:295, 1964

26. Anderson PO: Drugs and breast-feeding—a review. *Drug Intell Clin Pharm* 11:208, 1977

27. O'Brien TE: Excretion of drugs in human milk. *Am J Hosp Pharm* 31:844, 1974

28. Bauer JH, Pape B, Zajecek J, et al: Propranolol in human plasma and breast milk. *Am J Cardiol* 43:860, 1979

29. Sovner R, Orsulak PJ: Excretion of imipramine and desipramine in human breast milk. *Am J Psychiatry* 136:4A, 1979

30. Yoshioka H, Cho K, Takimoto M, et al: Transfer of cefazolin into human milk. *J Pediatr* 94:151, 1979

31. Niebyl JR, Blake DA, Freeman JM, et al: Carbamazepine levels in pregnancy and lactation. *Obstet Gynecol* 53:139, 1979

32. Allgen LG, Holmberg G, Person B, et al: Biological fate of methenamine in man. *Acta Obstet Gynecol Scand* 58:287, 1979

33. Tegler L, Lindstron B: Antithyroid drugs in milk. *Lancet* 2:591, 1980

34. Rey E, Giraux P, D'Athis Ph, et al: Pharmacoki-

netics of the placental transfer and distribution of clorazepate and its metabolite nordiazepam in the feto-placental unit and in the neonate. *Eur J Clin Pharmacol* 15:181, 1979

35. Santo GH, Huch A: Passage of Cefoxitin into breast milk. *Infection* 7(suppl):90, 1979
36. Knowles JA: Excretion of drugs in milk—a review. *J Pediatr* 66:1068, 1965
37. Yurchak AM, Jusko WJ: Theophylline secretion into breast milk. *Pediatrics* 57:518, 1976
38. Kaneko S, Sata T, Suzuki K: The levels of anti-convulsants in breast milk. *Br J Clin Pharmacol* 7:624, 1979
39. Levy M, Granit LB, Laufer N: Excretion of drugs in human milk. *N Engl J Med* 297:789, 1977
40. Somogyi A, Gugler R: Cimetidine excretion into breast milk. *Br J Clin Pharmacol* 7:627, 1979
41. Cruikshank DP, Varner MW, and Pitkin RM: St Louis, Society for Gynecologic Investigation, March, 1981

APPENDIX DRUG OR CHEMICAL, QUANTITY EXCRETED IN BREAST MILK, AND NEONATAL EFFECTS (AT MATERNAL THERAPEUTIC DOSES)

Drug (Brand)	Quantity Excreted in Milk	Neonatal Effect at Maternal Therapeutic Doses	Source(s)
Analgesics and Anti-inflammatory Drugs			
Acetaminophen	Excreted	Detoxified in liver. Avoid during immediate postpartum period. Otherwise NS.*	13
Aspirin	M:P < 1, milk level 1–3 mg/dl when plasma level is 1–5 mg/dl†	Transfer to milk not favored. At maternal dose of 12–16 tablets per day, no ill effects on infant. When mother requires high antiarthritic doses, monitor infant for bruiseability. May interfere with infant's platelet function.	26
Codeine	Trace amount	NS	26
Heroin	Variable amounts	Can cause addiction. Levels in milk not high enough to prevent withdrawal in addicted infants.	13, 26, 27
Indomethacin (Indocin)	Excreted	Case report of convulsions in breastfed infant. Used to close patent ductus arteriosus. Insufficient data on the effect on other vessels. May be nephrotoxic.	13
Mefenamic acid (Ponstel)	Negligible amounts	NS	26, 27
Methadone	Trace amounts	Breastfeeding permissible during methadone maintenance. Up to 80 mg/day, no ill effects on infant.	14
Meperidine (Demerol)	Trace amounts	NS	26
Morphine	Trace amounts	Amount excreted probably insignificant in clinical use, but may be excreted in higher amounts in addicts. Potential for accumulation. May be addicting to neonate.	13, 26, 27
Pentazocine (Talwin)	Not excreted	None	4, 13, 36
Phenylbutazone (Butazolidin)	6.3 µg/ml 1.5 hr after 750-mg IM dose; M:P = 0.13	Infant serum levels 3–20 µg/ml after 750-mg IM dose. Risk to infant not well defined. May accumulate in infant. Caution due to possible idiosyncratic blood dyscrasias.	13, 26
Propoxyphene (Darvon, Darvocet)	0.4% of material dose (manufacturer states M:P = 0.5)	Only symptoms detectable would be failure to feed and drowsiness. If mother ingests maximum recommended dosage in a 24-hr period, the infant could receive 1 mg/day, a significant dose in a neonate.	13, 14
Oxyphenbutazone (Tandearil)	Not detectable in 53 of 55 subjects; 10–80% of material plasma level.	No known effect. Oxyphenbutazone is a metabolite of phenylbutazone; caution is advised.	27

(Appendix continues on pages 184–196.)

Drug (Brand)	Quantity Excreted in Milk	Neonatal Effect at Maternal Therapeutic Doses	Source(s)
Antibiotics			
Amantadine (Symmetrel)	Excreted, not quantified	May cause vomiting, urinary retention, skin rash.	26, 27
Ampicillin	0.07 μg/ml; M:P = 0.06–0.3	NS, possibility of allergic sensitization exists, can produce candidiasis and diarrhea in infant.	3, 26, 27
Carbenicillin (Geopen)	0.265 μg/ml 1 hr after 1-gm dose	NS	27
Cefazolin (Ancef, Kefzol)	Peak level 1.51 μg/ml 3 hr after 2-gm IV dose; M:P = 0.023	NS, not absorbed well orally.	30
Cefoxitin (Mefoxin)	0.8–1.0 μg/ml at maternal dose of 3 gm/day	Infant could receive 0.7 mg/day, NS.	35
Cephalexin (Keflex)	Peak levels: 5μg/ml	Infant could receive up to 0.1 mg/ oz of milk. This amount should have no deleterious effect.	3
Cephalothin (Keflin)	Has not yet been found in milk.	NS	13
Chloramphenicol (Chloromycetin)	15–25 μg/ml; M:P = 0.5; 50% of drug in milk is inactive metabolite.	Contraindicated due to possibility of bone marrow depression. Infant does not excrete drug well, may accumulate.	3, 7, 18, 26
Chloroquine (Aralen)	< 2 μg/ml	Reports to date have failed to consider chloroquin's 5-day half-life. Probably NS.	27
Clindamycin (Cleocin)	2.1–3.8μg/ml peak 2–4 hr after therapeutic dose.	NS	26
Colistin (Coly Mycin)	0.05–0.09 mg/100 ml	Not well absorbed orally. NS.	7
Cycloserine (Seromycin)	M:P = 0.3–1.18 (aver. 0.72); 6–19 μg/ml after 250 mg PO four times daily.	No adverse effects reported in infants.	26
Demeclocycline (Declomycin)	Not detected at dose of 300 mg/day. 60 ng to 1.4 μg/ml at doses > 600 mg/day. Aver. M:P = .7. Detectable for up to 3 days after last dose.	Same precautions as tetracycline.	26
Doxycycline (Vibramycin)	Aver. 770 ng/ml 3 hr after second dose (200 mg × 1, 100 mg every 24 hr). 380 ng/ml 24 hr after second dose. M:P = 0.3–0.4.	Same precautions as tetracycline.	26
Erythromycin (Ilosone, E-mycin)	3–5 μg/ml; M:P = 0.5–3.0. Milk concentration can be up to six times plasma.	Use not recommended due to its ability to concentrate in milk. Principally excreted in the liver. Infant's liver function is not fully developed. Risk of jaundice.	3, 26, 27

* NS = Not significant in therapeutic dose to affect infant.
† M:P = Ratio of breast milk concentration to maternal plasma concentration.

Drug (Brand)	Quantity Excreted in Milk	Neonatal Effect at Maternal Therapeutic Doses	Source(s)
Gentamicin (Garamycin)	Unknown	Not well absorbed from GI tract. May change gut flora. If GI inflammation or diarrhea exists, monitor infant's serum levels to avoid otoxicity and nephrotoxicity.	13
Isoniazid	0.6–1.2 mg/100 ml after 10-mg/kg dose; M:P > 1	If mother has active tuberculosis, breastfeeding is contraindicated. Monitor infant for signs of isoniazid toxicity.	7, 24, 36
Kanamycin (Kantrex)	18.4 μg/ml after 1-gm IM dose. 0.05% of administered drug appears in the milk per day. M:P = 0.4–1.0.	Probably NS. (Same precautions as Gentamicin.)	3, 27
Lincomycin (Lincocin)	0.5–2.4 μg/ml; M:P = 0.15–2.25	NS	3, 26, 27
Mandelic acid (Methenamine mandelate—Mandelamine is 50% mandelic acid)	300 mg every 24 hr after dose of 12 gm/day.	NS	13, 27
Methacycline (Rondomycin)	50–260 μg/100 ml; M:P = 0.5 after therapeutic dose	Same precautions as tetracycline.	7, 27
Methenamine hippurate (Hiprex)	71.4 μmol/liter after 1-gm dose; M:P = 1.08	Infant would receive 0.05–0.1 mg/kg. No untoward effects.	32
Metronidazole (Flagyl)	6–12 μg/ml; M:P = 0.45–1.8 after therapeutic dose	Contraindicated due to possibly carcinogenic effect (in animal studies) and high milk concentrations.	26
Minocycline (Minocin)	0.8 μg/ml after 200-mg dose	Same precautions as tetracycline.	3, 26
Nalidixic acid (NegGram)	4 μg/ml at dose of 1 gm four times daily	NS. One case of hemolytic anemia in G6PD-deficient infant.	5, 26
Nitrofurantoin (Macrodantin)	Trace amount	NS, except in G6PD-deficient infants.	26
Nystatin (Mycostatin)	Not found, not absorbed orally	None	13
Oxacillin (Prostaphlin)	Not found	None	27
Oxytetracycline (Terramycin)	2–3 μg/ml	Same precautions as tetracycline.	3, 27
Para-aminosalicylic acid	Not found	None	13
Penicillin, benzathine	10–12 units/100 ml	NS; possibility of allergic sensitization.	3, 7, 26, 27
Penicillin G	0.06–0.96 units/ml; M:P = 0.03–0.2	NS; possibility of allergic sensitization.	3, 7, 26, 27
Penicillin VK	0.05–0.3 units/ml	NS; possibility of allergic sensitization.	27

Drug (Brand)	Quantity Excreted in Milk	Neonatal Effect at Maternal Therapeutic Doses	Source(s)
Pyrimethamine (Daraprim)	3.1–3.3 µg/ml, peak at 6 hr after 50–75-mg dose, detectable up to 48 hr after single dose.	Quantity excreted not sufficient to treat malaria in infants less than 6 months old, although there have been cases where this has been accomplished via drug in milk.	26
Quinine sulfate	0.4–1.6 µg/ml, peak 1.5–6 hr after 600–1300-mg dose.	Probably NS	26
Streptomycin	M:P = 0.4–1.0	NS. (Same precautions as Gentamicin.)	3, 4, 27
Sulfacetamide	M:P = 0.08	Probably NS. Neonatal jaundice due to displacement of bilirubin from protein-binding sites. Hemolytic anemia in G6PD-deficient infants. Rash.	4
Sulfadiazine	M:P = 0.21	Probably NS. (Same precautions as sulfacetamide.)	4
Sulfamethazine	M:P = 0.51	Same as sulfacetamide.	4
Sulfamethoxazole (Gantanol)	Excreted, not quantified	Caution during first 2 weeks of life. Same precautions as sulfacetamide.	27
Sulfanilamide	M:P = 1.0, 90 µg/ml after dose of 2–4 gm/day	Greater risk of hyperbilirubinemia encephalopathy because of high concentration in milk.	3, 4
Sulfapyridine	M:P = 0.85, 30–130 µg/ml after dose of 3 gm/day	Same as sulfanilamide.	4
Sulfathiazole	M:P = 0.43, 5 µg/ml after dose of 3 gm/day.	Probably NS. (Same precautions as sulfacetamide.)	4
Sulfisoxazole (Gantrisin)	Milk concentrations similar to plasma level.	Same precautions as sulfacetamide.	27
Tetracycline (Somycin)	0.5–2.6 µg/ml after dose of 500 mg four times daily, M:P = 0.2–1.4 (aver. 0.7)	Infant serum levels less than lower limit of assay. Use not recommended due to possibility of mottling of teeth and delayed bone growth.	3, 17, 26
Trimethoprim (Trimpex; also in combination with sulfamethoxazole in Bactrim and Septra)	1.2–5.5 µg/ml; M:P ≥ 1	Newborns absorb approximately 0.75–1.0 mg/day. May accumulate due to immature renal function. Toxicity includes vomiting, bone marrow depression, and thrombocytopenia.	26
Anticoagulants			
Bishydroxycoumarin (Dicumarol)	0.2 mg/100 ml; M:P = 0.01–0.02	Usually NS. Monitor infant. Vitamin K may be given to infant if PT warrants or if infant to undergo surgery.	3, 7, 21
Ethyl Biscoumacetate (Tromexan)	0–0.17 mg/100 ml. No correlation with dosage, unidentified active metabolite found in milk.	Avoid use due to reported episodes of hemorrhage of umbilical stump and cephalohematoma.	3, 7, 26
Heparin	Does not pass into milk.	None.	3, 20, 26

Drug (Brand)	Quantity Excreted in Milk	Neonatal Effect at Maternal Therapeutic Doses	Source(s)
Phenindione (Hedulin)	Secretion erratic. Levels less than 1 μg/ml; M:P = 0.012–0.06	Case report of increased PT and PTT in infant, and incisional and scrotal hemorrhage after inguinal herniotomy.	3, 5, 7, 26
Warfarin (Coumadin)	< 25 ng/ml (lower limit of assay)	NS. May safely breastfeed. Monitor PT.	19, 26
Anticonvulsants			
Carbamazepine (Tegretol)	M:P = 0.4–0.7, 1.9 ± 1.6 μg/ml; at maternal doses of 1000 mg/day skim milk fraction = 2.3 μg/ml, lipid fraction = 1.4 μg/ml, maternal plasma = 5.8 μg/ml.	A 4-kg infant would receive approximately 0.5 mg/kg, which is pharmacologically insignificant.	31, 38
Ethosuximide (Zarontin)	21.3 ± 2.8 μg/ml, M:P = .788 ± .328 at therapeutic dose.	No specific data.	38
Phenobarbital	Marked individual variation 10.4 ± 10.8 μg/ml; M:P = 0.459 ± 0.249 at therapeutic dose.	Maternal doses of 60–200 mg/day usually safe for infant. May induce hepatic microsomal enzymes; drowsiness in some cases.	3, 14, 38
Magnesium sulfate	Excreted	Levels in colostrum increase modestly over the first or second day and return to normal by day 3. Calcium levels are unaffected.	41
Phenytoin (Dilantin)	0.8 ± 0.3 μg/ml, M:P = 0.181 ± 0.059.[38] When maternal plasma level = 4.5 ± 1.4 μg/ml, M:P = 0.45.[3,7] One report of 6 μg/ml in breast milk when maternal plasma level was 28 μg/ml.	Usually no effect at maternal doses of 300–600 mg/day. Possibility of enzyme induction. One case report of methemaglobinemia and cyanosis in infant whose mother was taking phenytoin and phenobarbital.	3, 7, 38
Primidone (Mysoline)	2.3 ± 2.2 μg/ml, M:P = 0.81 ± 0.176 at therapeutic doses.	Drowsiness and decreased feeding. May cause bleeding due to hypoprothrombinemia. Avoid use during lactation.	4, 27, 38
Antihistamines and Decongestants			
Dexbrompheniramine Maleate, 6 mg with d-isophedrine 120 mg (sustained release tablets) (Drixoral)	Excreted	One case report of irritability, excessive crying, and disturbed sleeping patterns of 5 days' duration. Avoid long-acting preparations.	3
Diphenhydramine (Benadryl)	Excreted	NS. May cause sedation, decreased feeding, or may produce stimulation and tachycardia.	3, 27
Trimeprazine (Temaril)	Excreted	NS. (Same precautions as diphenhydramine.)	3, 27
Tripelennamine (Pyribenzamine)	Excreted	NS. (Same precautions as diphenhydramine.)	3, 27

Drug (Brand)	Quantity Excreted in Milk	Neonatal Effect at Maternal Therapeutic Doses	Source(s)
Autonomic Drugs			
Atropine	0.1 mg/100 ml	Hyperthermia, atropine toxicity (infants especially sensitive). Inhibits lactation.	27, 13
Carisoprodol (Soma, Rela)	May be present at concentrations two to four times that of maternal plasma.	CNS depression, GI effects.	27
Ergotamine (Cafergol)	Excreted, not quantified.	Most infants will have signs of ergotism. Vomiting, diarrhea, weak pulse, and unstable blood pressure.	13
Mepenzolate bromide (Cantil)	Not excreted	None	4, 27
Methocarbamol (Robaxin)	Trace amounts	NS	27
Neostigmine	Not excreted	None	13
Propantheline bromide (Probanthine)	Uncontrolled data indicate no measurable amounts.	Drug is rapidly metabolized in maternal system to inactive metabolite. Avoid long-acting preparations.	13, 27
Scopolamine (Hyoscine)	Trace amounts	NS	26
Cardiovascular Drugs			
Digoxin (Lanoxin)	0.5–1.0 ng/ml; M:P = 0.45–1.0	Due to large volume of distribution, the total daily excretion of digoxin in mothers with therapeutic serum concentrations would not exceed 1–2 μg. This amount is not sufficient to affect the child.	39
Dextrothyroxine (Choloxin)	Excreted, not quantified	NS	27
Guanethidine (Ismelin)	Excreted, not quantified	NS	13, 27
Hydralazine (Apresoline)	Excreted, not quantified	Jaundice, thrombocytopenia, electrolyte disturbances possible.	13
Methyldopa (Aldomet)	Excreted, not quantified	No specific reports.	27
Propranolol (Inderal)	M:P = 0.4–0.67	NS at dosages up to 160 mg/day	28, 13
Quinidine	Excreted, not quantified	Arrhythmias may occur.	13
Reserpine	Excreted, not quantified	May cause nasal stuffiness, lethargy, diarrhea, increased tracheobronchial secretions with difficulty breathing. Also reported to produce galactorrhea.	3, 4, 26, 27

* NS = Not significant in therapeutic dose to affect infant.
† M:P = Ratio of breast milk concentration to maternal plasma concentration.

Drug (Brand)	Quantity Excreted in Milk	Neonatal Effect at Maternal Therapeutic Doses	Source(s)
Chemotherapeutic Agents			
Cyclophosphamide (Cytoxan)	Excreted, not quantified	Contraindicated.	13, 26
Methotrexate	Minor route of excretion, M:P = 0.08–1.0; 2.6 ng/ml at 10 hr after 22.5-mg dose.	Infant could receive 0.26 µg/100 ml, which researchers consider nontoxic for infant.	13
Diuretics			
Bendroflumethazide (Rauzide, Naturetin)	Excreted, not measured	Lactation suppressed.	26
Chlorthalidone (Hygroton)	M:P = 0.03	One author suggests interruption of breastfeeding due to its long half-life (60 hr) in adults and lack of pharmacokinetic data in the neonate.	3
Chlorthiazide (Diuril)	Trace amount	Risk of dehydration and electrolyte imbalance. Monitor weight and wet diapers and occasional urine specific gravity and serum sodium to assure status of infant. Risk, however, is extremely low. May suppress lactation due to dehydration of mother.	13
Furosemide (Lasix)	Not found to be excreted	None	27, 13
Hydrochlorthiazide (Hydrodiuril)	Trace amount	Same precautions as chlorthiazide.	13, 26, 27
Spironalactone (Aldoctone)	Principal active metabolite, canrenone, present.	Unknown	
Environmental Agents			
Aldrin	Varies by location	Not a reason to wean. No need to test milk unless inordinate exposure.	13
Dieldrin	Varies by location	Not a reason to wean. Also, found in permanently mothproofed garments. Avoid.	13
DDT	Varies by location, highest in blacks in Mississippi and Arkansas. Aver. American 0.05–0.1 ppm.	No need to test milk unless inordinate exposure.	13
Halothane	2 µg/ml found in breast milk of anesthesiologists.	Possibility of hepatic and renal damage. No reports of effects on infants.	8
Heptachlor epoxide	Varies by location	Not a reason to wean. No need to test milk unless inordinate exposure.	13

* NS = Not significant in therapeutic dose to affect infant.
† M:P = Ratio of breast milk concentration to maternal plasma concentration.

Drug (Brand)	Quantity Excreted in Milk	Neonatal Effect at Maternal Therapeutic Doses	Source(s)
Hexachlorobenzene	Less than 8 ppb	Severe porphyria and some deaths occurred in nursing infants whose mothers had eaten wheat seed contaminated with hexachlorobenzene in Turkey in 1956.	8
Kepone	Varies by location, concentrates in milk	70 documented cases of poisoning of persons working with kepone. No need to test milk unless inordinate exposure.	8
Mercury	Excreted, varies by location	Several outbreaks of mercury poisoning have occurred in Japan, Iraq, Pakistan, and Guatemala. Poisoning of nursing infants has been documented.	8
Polybrominated biphenyl (PBB)	Concentrated in milk	PBB entered animal food chain when cattle feed was contaminated in Michigan; effects unknown.	8
Polychlorinated biphenyl (PCB)	Concentrated in milk	If mother at high risk from environment or diet (usually contaminated fish), measure milk level. Breastfed infants of Japanese women who ingested PCBs in contaminated rice oil appeared enervated, expressionless, apathetic, hypotonic, and lacked endurance. Three presented with abnormalities 5 years later. Induction of microsomal liver enzymes.	8
Texachlorethylene	Excreted	Obstructive jaundice.	8
Gastrointestinal Drugs			
Aloe (found in over-the-counter laxative combinations)	Detectable, not quantified	Possible diarrhea.	26
Bisacodyl (Dulcolax)	Not excreted	NS	3, 7
Cimetidine (Tagamet)	4.88–6.0 μg/ml after 1000 mg/day $\times$ 4 days. M:P = 4.6–11.76	The maximum amount of cimetidine an infant could ingest assuming 1 liter/day and fed at times of peak levels, would be 6 mg (1.5 mg/kg for a 4-kg infant). Therefore, caution may be warranted. (Study included only one subject.)	40
Casanthrol (in combination with stool softener in Dialose Plus and PeriColace)	Excreted, not quantified	Possible diarrhea and colic. Usually NS.	3

* NS = Not significant in therapeutic dose to affect infant.
† M:P = Ratio of breast milk concentration to maternal plasma concentration.

Drug (Brand)	Quantity Excreted in Milk	Neonatal Effect at Maternal Therapeutic Doses	Source(s)
Cascara sagrada	Excreted, amount not quantified	Possible diarrhea and colic.	3
Castor oil	Believed not to be excreted	NS	3
Dioctyl sodium sulfosuocinate (Colace)	Not excreted	None	3
Danthron (Modane, Doxidan)	Excreted, amount not quantified	Possible diarrhea and colic. Usually NS.	3
Magnesium citrate	Magnesium appearance in milk unknown	NS	3
Milk of magnesia	Magnesium appearance in milk unknown	NS	3, 26
Mineral oil	Not excreted	None	3, 26
Phenolphthalein (Correctol, Ex-Lax, Feen-A-Mint)	< 300 mg/ml	NS	3, 26
Psyllium hydrophillic mucilloid (Metamucil)	Not excreted	None	3
Senna (Senokot)	Less than lower limit of assay (340 mg/ml)	Possible diarrhea and colic, Senokot appears to have no effect on infant.	3, 26

Heavy Metals

Drug (Brand)	Quantity Excreted in Milk	Neonatal Effect at Maternal Therapeutic Doses	Source(s)
Arsenic	Excreted	Can accumulate in infant's blood. Check level if there is reason to suspect exposure.	13
Copper	Excreted	Unknown	13
Fluorine	Excreted	Monitor infant for excessive dose (excessive salivation and GI disturbances)	13
Gold thiomalate	0.022 μg/ml when mother given 50 mg/week	No proteinuria or aminoaciduria observed. Hematologic aberrations, rashes, nephritis, and hepatitis theoretically may occur. No harmful effects have been reported.	8, 13
Iron	Excreted	Intake of iron is beneficial to mother and infant.	13
Lead	Unknown	Nursing contraindicated if maternal serum 40 mcg/ml. Conflicting reports: breast milk not always cause of lead poisoning in nurslings.	13
Mercury	Excreted	Hazardous to infant.	13

* NS = Not significant in therapeutic dose to affect infant.
† M:P = Ratio of breast milk concentration to maternal plasma concentration.

Drug (Brand)	Quantity Excreted in Milk	Neonatal Effect at Maternal Therapeutic Doses	Source(s)
Hormones and Synthetic Substances			
Contraceptives	Less than 1% of dose	Reports of proliferation of vaginal epithelium in female nurslings and gynecomastia in male infants if daily dosage is greater than that recommended below. Diminished lactation if OC use instituted before fourth postpartum week.	7
Ethinyl estradiol	Trace amount	Not significant if daily dose is 50 μg or less.	7
Mestranol	Trace amount	Not significant if daily dose is 100 μg or less.	7
Progestins (19-nor-testosterone derivatives) Norethindrone Norgestrel Noresthindrone acetate Norethynodrel	Trace amount	Not significant if maternal daily dose is 2.5 mg or less.	7
Corticotropin	Excreted, not quantified	Destroyed in infant's GI tract.	5, 26, 27
Cortisone	Excreted, not quantified	Corticosteroids have not been studied sufficiently to assess their potential for harm to the infant. One study in rats found deaths and retarded development after 20 mg/day of cortisone (a high dose in a rat) was given to mothers. Most sources advise against breast-feeding in women taking corticosteroids.	5, 26, 27
Dihydrotachysterol (Hytakerol)	Excreted	May cause hypercalcemia. Need to monitor infant serum and urine calcium.	5
Epinephrine	Excreted	Destroyed in infant's GI tract.	5
Fluoxymesterone (Halotesin)	Excreted	Suppressed lactation. Masculinization.	26
Insulin	Unknown	Destroyed in infant's GI tract.	5
Prednisolone	Aver. 0.07–0.23% of dose/liter of milk over 48 hr.	Thought to be insignificant, but only a single-dose study.	26
Prednisone	2.67 μg/dl prednisone and 0.61 μg/dl Prednisolone after a single 10-mg PO dose.	Long-term effects unknown. Minimum amount in breast milk not likely to cause effect on infant in short course.	3, 8, 13
Psychoactive Substances			
Antidepressants			
Amitriptyline (Elavil, Endep)	Less than lower limit of assay (100 ng/ml) 4 and 12 hr after a single 25–50-mg dose.	Probably NS, but long half-life not taken into consideration. Watch for depression or failure to feed.	14, 26, 29

Drug (Brand)	Quantity Excreted in Milk	Neonatal Effect at Maternal Therapeutic Doses	Source(s)
Desipramine (Norpramin, Pertofrane)	Milk levels similar to plasma levels 17–35 ng/ml after 200 mg/day for 16 days of imipramine.	NS at this level. Unknown at maternal therapeutic levels.	14, 29
Doxepin	M:P = 0.33 in one patient receiving 75 mg/day for 3 months.	None known.	3
Imipramine (Tofranil)	Milk levels similar to plasma levels 12–29 ng/ml after 200 mg/day.	NS at this level. Unknown at maternal therapeutic blood levels.	26, 29
Nortriptyline (Aventyl, Pamelor)	Not detectable after a 25-mg dose.	Unknown at therapeutic levels.	26, 29
Tranylcypromine (Parnate)	Trace amounts	NS. May inhibit lactation.	14
Alcohol	M:P = 0.9–1.0	Not significant in moderation. Lethargy and prolonged sleeping when mother consumes excessive amounts.	14
Barbiturates	Low levels	Usually NS. May induce liver microsomal enzymes.	14
Barbital	< 40 μg/ml after 325–650-mg dose	NS. One case of sedation.	4, 26
Butabarbital (Butisol)	0.37 μg/ml 1.5 hr after seventh dose of 8 mg every 12 hr	NS	3
Pentobarbital (Nembutal)	0.17 μg/ml 19 hr after third dose of 100 mg/day	NS	3
Phenobarbital (see Anticonvulsants)	0.45–3.8 μg/ml	2 of 11 infants became difficult to awaken and slept excessively after mother received hypnotic doses (90 mg) for 5 days. NS in maternal antiepileptic doses (60–200 mg/day). May induce liver microsomal enzymes.	3, 26
Secobarbital (Seconal)	Detectable 14 hr after unspecified dose	NS	3, 26
Thiopental (Pentothal)	20 μg/ml after IV dose of 1.125 gm	NS	3, 26
Benzodiazepines			
Chlordiazepoxide (Librium)	Excreted	Amount secreted usually insufficient to affect infant, although CNS depression has been reported.	14
Diazepam (Valium)	78 ng/ml after 10 mg three times daily for 6 days. Total benzodiazepines excreted at 50% of serum level.	Reports of lethargy and weight loss. Infant most susceptible during first 4 days of life. Hyperbilirubinemia. Most sources do not advise its use during breastfeeding. Drug accumulation may occur.	14

Drug (Brand)	Quantity Excreted in Milk	Neonatal Effect at Maternal Therapeutic Doses	Source(s)
Chlorazepate (Tranxene)	M:P = 0.13–0.3 of chlorazepate and its metabolite nor diazepam.	Drowsiness. Infant younger than 2 months may have prolonged drug half-life due to immaturity of drug-metabolizing enzymes. Possibility of accumulation on chronic administration. Caution because of long half-life.	34
N-Demethyldiazepam	Active metabolite of diazepam, excreted	Caution, due to long half life.	14
Oxazepam (Serax)	Excreted, metabolite of diazepam	Monitor infant for drug intoxication.	14, 27
Bromides	67 μg/ml maximum after 1 gm NaBr five times a day for 3 days.	Drowsiness and rash. Possibility of allergic reactions.	4, 26
Caffeine	8.2 μg/ml after 1 cup coffee (100 mg)	Accumulates when intake moderate and continual. Causes jitteriness, wakefulness, and irritability.	3, 13
Chloral hydrate (Noctec)	Chloral hydrate and its metabolite trichlorethanol reach 50–100% of blood levels.	Sedation, usually not significant.	26
Chloroform	Excreted	Deep sleep.	3, 5
Dextroamphetamine (Dexedrine)	Excreted, not quantified	No effects on infants when given to 103 postpartum women for depression. Avoid long-acting preparations.	3, 14
Ether	Milk levels about equal to plasma levels for 8–10 hr after dose.	Sedation	26
Flurazepam (Dalmane)	Excreted	Some sedation, but usually not significant.	14
Glutethimide (Doriden)	Aver. peak of 270 ng/ml at 8–12 hr after 500-mg dose.	Some sedation, usually not significant.	26
Haloperidol (Haldol)	Milk concentration similar to plasma level.	Unknown. Rabbit studies showed behavioral changes.	3, 14
Lithium	Aver. 0.6 mEq/liter when maternal plasma level 1.5 mEq/liter. M:P = 0.25–0.77 (aver. 0.5)	Measurable lithium in infant's serum. Infant kidney can clear lithium. Reports of cyanosis, hypothermia, poor muscle tone, and ECG changes in nursing infants.	3, 4, 13
Marijuana	Excreted	Conflicting reports; use not recommended. No beneficial effect.	3, 13
Meprobamate	M:P = 2–4	Monitor infant for drug intoxication since drug accumulates in milk.	14, 27
Phenothiazines			
Chlorpromazine (Thorazine)	M:P = 0.3, not detectable at dose of 600 mg twice daily	NS at doses up to 1200 mg/day.	3, 14
Mesoridazine (Serentil)	Excreted, not quantified	None known.	14, 27

Drug (Brand)	Quantity Excreted in Milk	Neonatal Effect at Maternal Therapeutic Doses	Source(s)
Perphenazine (Trilafon)	M:P = 1	None known.	3, 14
Piperacetazine (Quide)	Excreted, not quantified	None known.	14
Prochlorperazine (Compazine)	Excreted, not quantified	None known.	27, 14
Thioridazine (Mellaril)	Excreted, not quantified	None known.	27, 14
Trifluoperazine (Stelazine)	0.4–1.5 mg/100 ml in dogs after daily dose of 200 mg	None known.	27, 14

Radiopharmaceuticals and Diagnostic Materials

Drug (Brand)	Quantity Excreted in Milk	Neonatal Effect at Maternal Therapeutic Doses	Source(s)
Barium	Not excreted	None	13
[131]I	1.3–2.0 nCi/ml 24 hr after 100-mCi dose. Peak of 39 nCi/ml at 6 hr. Appears to concentrate in milk.	Breastfeeding contraindicated after large therapeutic dose, and should be withheld for 24 hr minimum after smaller diagnostic doses. Check milk prior to resuming feeding.	26
[131I]labeled macroaggregated Albumin	4.2–28.0 nCi/ml after 200-mCi dose.	Discontinue breastfeeding for 10–12 days. Extreme avidity for iodine by the thyroid of young infants. 1/10 of the International Commission on Radiological Protection (ICRP) for drinking water reached 10 days after IV dose of 200 MCi.	26, 8
Iopanoic acid (Telepaque)	Peak iodide level at 5–19 hr; 3–11 mg iodide/feeding at this time.	No adverse effects. Iodine excretion can cause rash. Probably no problem with just one dose.	13, 26, 27
Gallium citrate	70 nCi/ml 96 and 120 hr. after 3-mCi dose	Discontinue nursing until 2 weeks. ^{69}Ga has cleared, usually	8
^{90}Sr	M:P = 1.0	NS. Less than in cow's milk.	13
^{99}TcO$_4^-$	3.0–5.2 times plasma level at 17 and 20 hr, respectively	Breastfeeding contraindicated for 32–72 hr after 10-mCi dose. Breastfeeding can be resumed 24 hr after 2-mCi dose for lung scanning.	26, 27
Tuberculin test	Not excreted	Tuberculin-sensitive mothers can passively immunize their infants through breast milk. Immunity may last several years.	13

Thyroid Drugs

Drug (Brand)	Quantity Excreted in Milk	Neonatal Effect at Maternal Therapeutic Doses	Source(s)
Liothyronine (Cytomel)	Not excreted	None	27
Methimazole (Tapazole)	Average M:P = 1.16 ± 0.12	Infant could receive 7–16% of maternal dose. Could interfere with thyroid function. Inhibits synthesis of thyroid hormone.	33

Drug (Brand)	Quantity Excreted in Milk	Neonatal Effect at Maternal Therapeutic Doses	Source(s)
Potassium iodide	3 mg/100 ml	May alter thyroid function in infant. May cause goiter.	13, 27
Propylthiouracil	M:P = 0.13–0.47	Infant could receive 0.5 mg/day at maternal dose of 600 mg/day. Thought to be harmless. Infant could ingest 0.07% of mother's daily dose.	33
Thyroid	Excreted	NS	13
Levo-Thyroxine (Synthroid)	Excreted in significant amounts	May delay clinical symptoms of congenital hypothyroidism in nurslings. Improves milk supply in hypothyroid mothers. Not contraindicated.	8, 13
Miscellaneous			
DPT Vaccine	Excreted in minimal amounts	Does not interfere with immunization schedule.	13
Ergonovine (Ergotrate)	Excreted, not quantified	Causes lowered prolactin levels in postpartum patients. Multiple doses may suppress lactation.	26
Isoproterenol (Isoprel)	Not excreted	NS	3
Poliovirus vaccine	Not excreted	Live virus taken orally. Not necessary to withhold nursing 30 minutes before and after dose. Provide booster after infant no longer nursing.	13
Rh antibodies	Excreted	Destroyed in GI tract.	13
Rubella virus vaccine	Minimal amounts	Will not confer passive immunity.	13
Smallpox vaccine	Not excreted	Exposure is by direct contact. Live virus. Contraindicated when mother has infant under 1 year.	13
Theobromine	M:P = 0.82	No adverse effects observed in infants. 4 oz chocolate contains 240 mg theobromine.	3, 13
Theophylline	Aver. M:P = 0.7 with rapid equilibration; peak levels 1–3 hr after dose.	Usually not significant. Some reports of irritability and insomnia in infant. Premature infants 3–15 days old have average half-lives of 30.2 hr. Caution with sustained release theophylline products. Maximum amount of theophylline that an infant could ingest is 8 mg/liter milk per day. Avoid nursing at time of peak serum level.	3, 26, 37
Tolbutamide	Milk level is 9–40% of serum level, 3–18 mcg/ml 4 hr after 500-mg dose.	Unknown.	26

PART TWO: GYNECOLOGY

16. Oral Contraceptives

NICHOLS VORYS   WILLIAM F. RAYBURN

Since the Food and Drug Administration approved the marketing of the oral contraceptive in 1960, it has become the most popular reversible contraceptive method. An estimated 50 million women in developed and developing countries are taking "the Pill." The United States, Canada, the Netherlands, New Zealand, West Germany, and Australia report that 25 percent of women in the reproduction era take oral contraceptives, while 5 to 10 percent of the women in third world countries are using the pill.[1] Oral contraceptive use is more popular among women married less than five years (65 percent) than among women married longer.[2] Women intending to have future births have found the pill to be an effective, temporary method of contraception. The oral contraceptive remains one of the most widely prescribed medications for the reproductive-age woman. This chapter is intended to review current information on the pharmacology, metabolic effects, and effectiveness of the various preparations, and to offer guidelines for oral contraceptive use.

PHARMACOLOGY

Each oral contraceptive combines a synthetic estrogen with a progestin component. These synthetic progestins and estrogens are discussed separately, as they differ from natural steroids in the normal menstrual cycle.

Synthetic Progestins

The synthetic progestins in combination oral contraceptives are formed by the removal of the 19-C atom from testosterone. They are called 19-nor compounds, and are shown in Figure 16-1. The effect of removing the 19-C atom is to remove nearly all the adrogenic and anabolic activity of testosterone. The progestational activity is enhanced by the addition of methyl (CH_3), ethinyl ($C\equiv CH$), or acetate ($OCOCH_3$) groups at the 3-, 17-, or 18-β-positions. The 19-nor compounds (norethindrone,

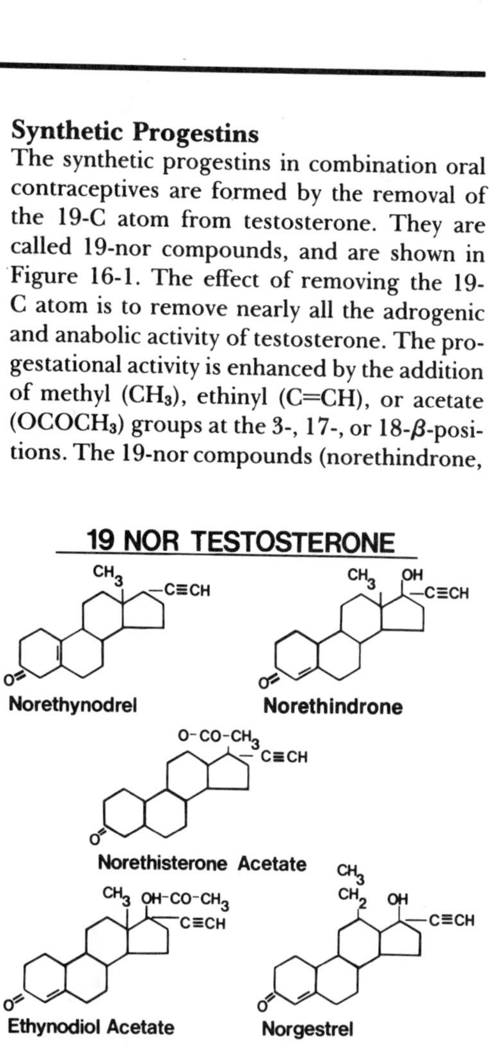

Figure 16-1. Synthetic progestins in oral contraceptives.

197

norethindrone acetate, and ethynodiol diacetate) differ only by the number of additional acetate groups at the 3- and 17-positions.

Molecular structural differences make some of these synthetic progestins act not only biologically as progesterone, but they also have inherent estrogen and androgen activity (Fig. 16-2). Two such compounds with estrogenic activity include norethynodrel and ethynodiol diacetate. Another oral progestin, norgestrel, has greater androgen activity and marked antiestrogen effect.

All oral contraceptives act on specific intracellular estrogen and progesterone receptors. Briggs has studied the protein receptor binding of synthetic progestins.[3] Norethynodrel, norethindrone acetate, norethindrone, and ethynodiol diacetate are metabolized to norethindrone in the liver before they are capable of receptor-binding. Norgestrel, the most potent available synthetic progestin, binds strongly to the progesterone receptor, which accounts for its potent biologic activity.[4,5]

Synthetic Estrogens

Oral contraceptives contain one of the two synthetic estrogens, ethinyl estradiol and mestranol (Fig. 16-3).[6] Ethinyl estradiol is formed by adding an ethinyl group to estradiol, while a methyl ether group is added to estradiol to synthesize mestranol. Mestranol is converted in the body to ethinyl estradiol, and without this conversion, mestranol is inactive. Factors which influence potency include the rate of conversion and the rates of metabolism into inactive derivatives.[7] Ethinyl estradiol is the synthetic estrogen of choice, and has been esti-

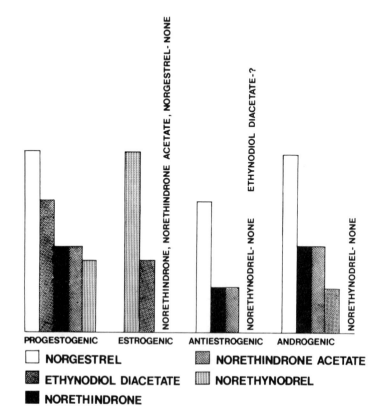

Figure 16-2. Inherent biologic effects of the synthetic progestins.

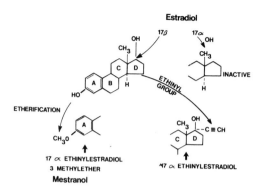

Figure 16-3. Mestranol and ethinyl estradiol, the two synthetic estrogens derived from estradiol and found in oral contraceptives.

mated to be slightly more potent than the equivalent weight of mestranol.[8,9]

The structural difference, route of administration, dosage schedule, and metabolism between natural and synthetic estrogens are important factors when considering the intracellular biologic action of estrogen. The 17-ethinyl group in synthetic estrogens allows for oral administration and biologic potency. The metabolism of synthetic estrogens differs from estradiol 17-β in the amount of ethinyl estradiol that is metabolized, and there is a failure of ethinyl estradiol to have significant alternate pathways leading to such biologically weak metabolites as 2- and 16-hydroxy compounds as is seen with natural estradiol metabolism. The differences in biologic half-lives between the natural and synthetic estrogens relate to the different metabolic and conjugation processes and to the enterohepatic circulation.

The pharmacologic properties of the estrogen molecule determine the cellular response at the target organ. The sensitivity of the end organ is determined by the presence of cytosol receptor proteins within the cell.[10] The transport of natural or synthetic estrogen through the cell membrane has a mitigating effect on the concentration of estrogen within the cell. The intracellular concentration of the hormone and the occupation of receptor sites are a function not only of estrogen dose and duration, but the presence of synthetic progestins.[11]

Dujovne measured cytosol receptor uptake of radiolabeled estrone and mestranol in monolayer tissue culture and found it altered by dose, duration of incubation, and the presence of the progestin, norethynodrel.[11] His experiments revealed that both estrone and mestranol have dose-related biologic effects on the liver cell. However, in the presence of norethynodrel, the uptake of mestranol was doubled. It was presumed that synthetic progestins such as norethynodrel and northindrone affect cell membrane permeability to estrogen. Therefore, the intracellular biologic activity of estrogen also depends on the progestin molecule with which it is administered, and the combination affects the intracellular pharmacodynamics at the end organ.

Oral Contraceptive Cycle Versus Natural Menstrual Cycle

For sex steroids to be biologically effective, one must consider the route of administration and the significance of the structure of the molecule. Oral contraceptives are absorbed into the intestinal wall, and pass through the portal circulation and liver prior to entering the general circulation. Ninety percent of oral contraceptives reach the liver in the active form, but only 20 percent of the administered dose is active at the target organs.[12] Conversely, estrogens produced in the ovary enter the vena cava and pass into the general circulation without having to first pass through the portal circulation. For orally administered sex steroids to achieve serum and tissue levels comparable to those of naturally secreted sex steroids, the liver must receive levels of steroids approximately five times as great as when the same steroid is derived from ovarian production.

Another important difference between oral contraceptive pill cycles and the normal menstrual cycle is that the synthetic estrogens and progestins are delivered concomitantly, and in a constant-dosage form. In the normal menstrual cycle, natural estrogen is secreted unopposed from day 7 to day 14 only, and with a mid-cycle peak. Natural progesterone is secreted only during the last 14 days of the menstrual cycle, and invariably in the presence of natural estrogen. The ratio of estrogen to progestin is constant in oral contraceptives, but varies according to the day of the normal menstrual cycle for sex steroids produced by the ovary. The ratio of synthetic estrogen in progestin ranges from 1:10 to 1:50 throughout the cycle in the various oral contraceptives, with the most frequently used range being 1:20. The ratio of estradiol and estrone to progesterone secreted by the ovary varies from 1:10 in the early proliferative phase, 1:1.2 in the late proliferative phase, and 1:60 in the luteal phase.

Thus, the differences between the oral contraceptive and the natural menstrual cycle are: (1) route of administration, which influences the pharmacologic impact on the liver; (2) difference in ratio of estrogen and progestin from the normal menstrual cycle; and (3) the administration of synthetic estrogen and progestin, which are administered concomitantly throughout the entire treatment cycle. These factors, and the metabolism of synthetic estrogen and progestins, undoubtedly account for some of the annoying clinical side effects (nausea, cyclic swelling, weight gain, breakthrough bleeding, etc.) and the metabolic adverse consequences, particularly as they involve the excretory function and protein synthesis by the liver.[13]

EFFECT ON REPRODUCTIVE ORGANS

The administration of a combined estrogen and progestin preparation interferes with fertility in many ways. The primary mechanism of action for contraception involves an inhibition of the hypothalamus and pituitary. This effect, along with the effects on other target tissues such as the cervix and endometrium, are dependent on the dose, progestin/estrogen ratio, and duration of therapy. Most changes are similar to changes during preg-

nancy, and are usually reversed by discontinuation of the preparation.

Hypothalamus and Pituitary

Estrogen administered on a cyclic basis suppresses follicle-stimulating hormone (FSH) secretion. When mestranol is administered, this effect diminishes as the dose is decreased from 100 to 80 to 40.[14] The effect of estrogen on luteinizing hormone (LH) secretion is less consistent, but repeated cyclic administration of mestranol suppresses both FSH and LH excretion. Ethinyl estradiol, in daily doses of 50 given from day 5 through 24 of the cycle, can cause an abolition of the mid-cycle surge of serum FSH and LH.[5] Sporadic surges of LH may be seen even after 12 cycles of treatment, and low doses of mestranol (10) may add a stimulatory rather than a suppressive action on the excretion of both FSH and LH in the urine.[15]

Progestins act by suppressing the mid-cycle LH peak. Different progestin molecules have varying effects—norgestrel and ethyndiol diacetate being the more potent.[16] Those women receiving even microdoses of progestins exhibit suppression of the mid-cycle peak of LH.[17] Progestins alone do not lower the baseline level of either FSH or LH.[14]

Goldzieher demonstrated that combination oral contraceptives suppress baseline plasma FSH to about 70 percent of control values, and LH to about 20 to 30 percent of control values, while eliminating the mid-cycle surge.[14] The differences between the follicular and luteal phase levels of FSH and LH were preserved. In addition, the combination oral contraceptives may have an effect on the pituitary gland by increasing prolactin release.[18] This was particularly obvious when thyroid-releasing hormone (TRH) and luteinizing hormone releasing factor (LHRF) were administered to combination oral contraceptive patients.[19]

The post-pill effect on reproduction has been studied at great length. After 3 months of discontinuation of combination oral contraceptives, plasma gonadotropin values should be in the range of normal cycles. Eighty-five percent of people discontinuing oral contraceptives are capable of becoming pregnant within 6 to 12 months.[20] There is, however, the possibility of post-pill amenorrhea continuing after 6 months, with the occurrence of this condition estimated to be between 2 and 2.6 percent.[21-23] If this figure were true in practice, 200,000 to 250,000 women currently using oral contraceptive pills would eventually require diagnosis and treatment for post-pill amenorrhea.

Post-pill amenorrhea is not a homogeneous entity. When such patients are compared with spontaneous amenorrhea patients, a number of subgroups become apparent. They have been identified by Jacobs as (1) primary ovarian failure, (2) hyperprolactinemia, (3) clomiphene-responsive amenorrhea, (4) anorexia nervosa, and (5) amenorrhea associated with psychiatric disease and/or environmental stress.[22] Dickey identified three endocrine groups of post-pill amenorrhea patients related to serum, prolactin, LH, and estradiol levels.[21] Group 1 cases had high prolactin with low or normal LH values. In these, post-pill amenorrhea was due to increased prolactin, and such patients responded to bromergocriptine with ovulation. Group 2 cases had normal prolactin, low LH, and low estradiol values. These amenorrhea patients were thought to have a suppressed or immature hypothalamus, and required estrogen priming and clomiphene or human menopausal gonadotropin (HMG), followed by human chorionic gonadotropin (HCG). Group 3 cases had a normal prolactin level, with elevated LH and normal or elevated estradiol values. Such patients were thought to have persistent, uninterrupted estrogen stimulation, but responded to progesterone withdrawal, and invariably to clomiphene with ovulation.

Most normally ovulating and menstruating patients will respond with ovulatory cycles after oral contraceptive discontinuation. Those patients that have hypothalamic-pituitary-ovarian dysfunction prior to the initiation of oral contraceptives almost invariably revert to their pre-oral contraceptive treatment pattern after cessation of oral contraceptive therapy.[13] The incidence of secondary anovulation and/or amenorrhea, with or without galactorrhea, is higher in the latter type of patient than is found in the normal ovulating patient.

Ovary

Steroidal contraceptives affect both ovarian morphology and function. The ovaries appear grossly small and inactive, and show no evidence of corpus lutea formation.[24] Histologically, these ovaries have a thick collagenous capsule with no maturing follicles. Ryan estimated that the number of primordial follicles remained in the normal range in women treated for periods up to 2 years with norethynodrel.[25] Inactive cystic and atretic follicles are often present after oral contraceptive use, and there appears to be a focal condensation of stroma.

Along with these morphologic changes, ovarian steroidogenesis is profoundly affected by combination therapy. Estradiol 17-β and estrone synthesis is decreased markedly. Testosterone production is generally decreased by one-half or more, and androstenedione production is decreased by one-third. Less change in dehydroeprandosterone sulfate (DHEAS) is seen during oral contraceptive consumption.

Functional ovarian cyst formation is reduced with oral contraceptive use. However, the risk of developing other benign ovarian tumors or ovarian carcinoma is unrelated to oral contraceptive exposure.

Oviducts

Ovarian hormones regulate segmental contraction of the oviduct and ciliogenesis of the endosalpinx, and control oviductal secretion and flow. These findings indicate that ovum transport and muscular activity of the oviduct are regulated by estrogen and progesterone, and a delicate balance is a prerequisite to normal function.[26] Motility of the human oviduct is known to be influenced by combination oral contraceptives, which inhibit the spontaneous motility of the isolated human oviduct.[27] With a scanning electron microscope, Brenner did not show any alteration of ciliary pattern of endosalpingeal epithelium in women receiving combination oral contraceptives.[28]

Various protein substances, enzymes, and trace elements in the oviductal fluid also play a major role in fertilization and in early stages of differentiation and development of the embryo.[26] The alteration and their concentration as a result of hormonal changes may lead to the inhibition of fertilization and the cleavage process.

Uterus

Steroidal contraceptives affect the myometrium. The uterus becomes soft, cyanotic, and enlarged; and this effect is more pronounced when higher-dose oral contraceptives are used. Prolonged use produces either no change, or a slight decrease in the size of the uterus. Histologically, the myometrium shows some cellular hypertrophy, dilated sinusoids, and edema.

Hendricks, in 1977, recorded spontaneous uterine activity during oral contraceptive use.[29] The transport of spermatozoa through the uterus and oviduct depends, to a large extent, on myometrial and oviductal muscular activity. It was noted that estrogen administration was followed by uterine contractions, and sperm were found in the uterine cavity shortly after coitus. With the administration of an estrogen/progestin combination, alterations in myometrial motility patterns, sperm transport, and egg implantation have also been noted.

Ovarian hormones bring about well-recognized morphologic changes in the endometrium during the menstrual cycle. The effect of oral contraceptives on the endometrium depends on the preparation, the dosage, the duration of administration, and the ratio of estrogen to progestin. These effects consist of a rapid progression from proliferation to early secretory changes within a few days following the start of the compound. By 7 days, a mixed hormonal effect is observed. Thereafter the endometrium shows regressive changes, characterized by a compact stroma dotted with sparse atrophic glands, which are lined with cuboidal or flattened epithelium. Glandular

secretory activity and tortuosity are either completely absent, or minimal.[27] Marked decidualization of the stroma is observed with most combination preparations. With prolonged use, the endometrium usually becomes progressively thin and inactive, but minimal cyclic changes occur even after long-term administration.[30] Withdrawal bleeding is often scanty, and shows no daily variation compared to normal menses. The lack of withdrawal bleeding is not to be taken lightly, and is an indication for cessation of therapy or a change in preparation.

Reports indicate that adenomatous hyperplasia has never been observed during combination contraceptive therapy, but that sequential oral contraception therapy is suspect.[31,32] The development of endometrial carcinoma in users of sequential oral contraceptives has been reported, but no absolute cause-and-effect relationship between the sequential formulations and endometrial cancer has been demonstrated.[33] Some experimental and clinical data suggest that cyclic-combination oral contraceptive pills contain an adequate amount of progestin to prevent hyperplasia, and those with a low estrogen dosage may provide a certain degree of protection against endometrial cancer.[33]

Cervix

Like the myometrium, the cervix is extremely sensitive to estrogen and progestins. Changes in the composition and properties of cervical secretion have been used for many years as an in vivo biologic assay for sex steroids. The response of the cervix to oral contraceptives depends largely on the type of compound, dosage used, the potency, and specific activity of the progestin. The cervix often becomes moderately soft and bluish, and assumes an appearance similar to that during pregnancy. There is an increased incidence of cervical erosion, because of the advancement of the squamocolumnar junction, which is believed to be hormonally dependent.

The secretion of cervical mucus is regulated by ovarian hormones. Estrogen stimulates the production of large amounts of thin, watery, elastic, acellular cervical mucus with intense ferning, spinnbarkheit, and sperm receptivity. Progesterone and all synthetic oral progestins, alone or in combination with estrogen, inhibit the secretory activity of cervical epithelium, and produce a scanty, viscous, and cellular mucus with low spinnbarkheit and an absence of ferning. Spermatozoa are usually unable to penetrate this luteal-phase type of cervical mucus. The chemical constituents of cervical mucus show definite cyclic variations during the menstrual cycle, or with administration of estrogen/progestins. The extent of the physical and chemical alteration of the cervical mucus results from the administration of progestational agents, and depends on the preparation and dosage. Higher dosages of progestins add a more profound sustained effect than lower doses; but even microdose progestins have been shown to inhibit, or greatly reduce, sperm migration through the cervical mucus.

Cervical erosion and eversion are commonly observed in oral contraceptive users. A variety of expressions of mild atypia may be seen in the areas of epidermalization. These changes include nuclear disarray and hyperchromatism, cellular crowding, and variability in glandular cell size. An atypical endocervical hyperplastic pattern, which is reversible and benign, can be mistaken for adenocarcinoma in many women taking oral contraceptives.

Frederick has reported ultrastructural changes in the cervix following treatment with combination oral contraceptives.[34] The configuration of the cells and the distribution of their organelles were generally comparable to those of the normal menstrual cycle, and differences appeared to be only quantitative.

Pincus reported a decreased incidence of abnormal pap smears in users of oral contraceptives compared to controls.[35] Since these pioneer studies, many publications have confirmed no difference in the prevalence or incidence rate of abnormal cytology between oral contraceptive users and controls.[36,37] Cervical dysplasia is usually considered a precancerous lesion. Richard and Barron estimated that cervical dysplasia lesions progress to in situ cancer in about 12 to 86 months, depending on

their severity.[38] Women diagnosed as having cervical dysplasia or carcinoma in situ, who received combination estrogen/progestin medication, showed no progressive changes of lesions. The prevalence of carcinoma in situ and cervical dysplasia in their study was higher, 2.64 percent in oral contraceptive users as compared to 1.5 percent in control users. Factors that seem of more relevance to the development of carcinoma of the cervix than the use of oral contraceptives are early age of sexual activity, multiple partners, and lower socioeconomic population, and have led some investigators to search for a transmissible disease as the etiologic cause.

Vagina

The cytologic response in the vagina to oral contraceptives depends on the type of estrogen/progestin, the relative and absolute amounts of estrogen/progestin, and the sensitivity of the vaginal mucosa to these steroids. Although one may occasionally encounter an appreciable number of superficial cells in the vaginal smears during oral contraceptive use, the usual pattern resembles more closely the late luteal phase, with intermediate cells predominating. Inflammatory cell patterns are occasionally observed. On rare occasions, parabasal cells, usually found in atrophic smears, are seen.

In contrast to the normal menstrual cycle, the vaginal cytology and karypknotic index in women treated with combination oral contraceptives do not exhibit a biphasic pattern in the relative number of superficial to intermediate or basal cells throughout the treatment cycle. Vaginal secretions of women receiving oral progestogens are scanty, multicellular, and contain large numbers of leukocytes and bacteria, and may account for inadequate lubrication during coitus.

Because of the heavy deposit of galactogen in vaginal mucosa and marked reduction of *Döderlein* bacilli produced by progestins, vaginal infections (particularly *Candida albicans*) are more likely to occur in women taking oral contraceptives.[39] Furthermore, it appears that there is progressive increase in this infection as the duration of oral contraceptive medication is increased. Whether oral contraceptives will increase the incidence of vulvo/vaginitis for each patient depends on her personal hygiene, life style, and other factors, including the estrogen/progestin in the combination oral contraceptive.

Breast

Breast development is directed by genetic potential and sex steroid stimulation. Estrogen causes breast duct growth, and progesterone stimulates the development of the peripheral breast glands (lobule alveolus). Oral contraceptives may cause an increase in breast size (the same phenomena as seen in normal pregnancy), and some degree of breast tenderness has been associated with oral contraceptive use. The latter symptom is dose-related, and decreases with a lower-dose estrogen component.

Lactation is also, in part, controlled by sex steroids. Oral contraceptives have been shown to decrease the volume of milk, to shorten the duration of lactation, and sometimes to alter the constituents of milk. Primiparous women are affected more than multiparous women.[40] It is universally agreed that the estrogen component of the oral contraceptive is at fault, and the larger the dose, the greater the adverse effect on successful nursing.

Benign mammary disease (fibrocystic disease) is a relatively common disorder, and is associated with a higher risk of breast cancer development. These benign neoplasms appear less frequently in oral contraceptive users than in the general population,[41] and the risk of fibrocystic disease of the breast in oral contraceptive users has been estimated to be 25 to 80 percent of that found in nonusers. In addition, long-term users of oral contraceptives seem to have less risk of benign breast dysplasia (fibrocystic disease) than short-term users. The progestin component of oral contraceptives is considered to be primarily responsible for this protection, especially if the progestin is less estrogenic (norgestrel in Ovral versus norethynodrel in Enovid). Oral contraceptive users in England were found to have signifi-

cantly fewer benign breast tumors than patients using diaphragms and intrauterine devices (IUDs). There is no substantial information that would identify oral contraceptives as a causative factor in benign breast neoplasms.[42] However, oral contraceptives should not be administered to any patient with a single or multiple breast lump until carcinoma has been ruled out.

In monkeys, both estrogens and oral contraceptives have failed to elicit an observable increase in incidence in mammary tumors.[43] There appears to be neither a positive nor negative association with mammary cancer in short-term use (up to 4 years) of steroid contraceptives in human subjects.[44] Despite these findings, any patient on oral contraceptives with a history of benign breast disease or a strong family history of breast cancer requires frequent examination.

Teratogenicity

The inadvertent use of oral contraceptives during early pregnancy has prompted much investigation to determine any teratogenic effects. Spontaneous abortion may represent a severe manifestation of a teratogen. The relationship of chromosome abnormalities in spontaneous abortion in women conceiving shortly after discontinuing or while on oral contraceptives is controversial. Carr reported on the types of chromosome abnormalities in spontaneously aborted conceptuses in which conception occurred after oral contraceptive use.[45] He found the percentage of chromosome anomalies in a control series to be 22 percent, while that in the post-oral contraceptive series was 48 percent. The striking difference between the control and study groups was in the incidence of polyploidy. Triploid abortuses were 4.5 times more common in the post-oral contraceptive group than in the control group. However, others have not confirmed this observation.

There are no good data to substantiate the increase of chromosome abnormalities in intrauterine pregnancies going to term in patients who have received oral contraception. In a well-done newborn study population, the observed control abnormality was 5.4/1000, and did not differ significantly from a rate of 6.9/1000 for post-oral contraceptive newborn patients.[46]

Janerich published a report that linked oral contraceptives with congenital limb reduction defects.[47] These authors found that 15 of the 108 women with babies who have malformations were exposed to exogenous sex steroids at one time or another, as compared to 4 of 108 controls. There may also be some evidence to implicate exogenous estrogen/ progestin exposure during pregnancy with congenital heart defects. These claims have not been established beyond reasonable doubt, or confirmed in depth by others.[48] A combination of anomalies involving the vertebrae, anal, cardiac, trachea, esophagus, and limbs was termed the "VACTERL" syndrome by Nora and Nora in 1973.[49] Although rare, this syndrome has been linked to sex steroid exposure in early pregnancy, but not substantiated.

EFFECTS ON OTHER ORGAN SYSTEMS AND METABOLISM

Effects on other organ systems and alterations in metabolism during oral contraceptive use were not fully realized at the time of initial marketing. After 20 years of use, many changes are now well appreciated. Although serious complications associated with oral contraceptive use are relatively rare, changes in laboratory test results may be caused by physiologic alterations. (These are listed in Table 16-1.) These test results usually remain within the normal range, and seldom reflect true pathologic changes. Most alterations result primarily from estrogen rather than progestin stimulation, and preparations containing less estrogen are less likely to influence laboratory tests.

Liver
Treatment of normal human subjects with large doses of estradiol does not produce any histologic or electronic microscopic alteration in the hepatic cell. However, treatment with regular-dose oral contraceptives is associated with canaliculi dilation, loss of canilicular microvilli, and a pericanalicular deposit of acid phosphatase.[50] Lactic dehydrogenase and transaminase values are not altered remarkably, but alkaline phosphatase may be increased.[51] Infusion of bromsulphalein (BSP) dye is invariably associated with BSP retention.[52,53] The observed decreased albumen/globulin ratio and serum cholinesterase are an early indication of derangement in hepatic protein synthesis of serum proteins and enzymes.[54]

Enterohepatic Circulation
The parenchymal cells of the liver have the capacity to take up and excrete into biliary channels organic anions of both endogenous and exogenous origin, at concentrations exceeding their plasma levels. The excretion of bilirubin and bile salts is a major hepatic function. The liver efficiently extracts bile acids from the portal blood, so that under normal circumstances the bile salt pool is confined largely to the enterohepatic cycle (liver-bile-intestine-portal blood-liver). In hepatobiliary disease, the liver often loses this high extraction efficiency, and increased amounts of circulating bile salts appear in peripheral plasma.

The capacity of the liver to excrete organic anions (bile salts or organic dyes) is consistently decreased by steroid hormones and pregnancy. Gross clinical tests, such as serum bilirubin concentration and the standard BSP test, do not detect these pregnancy-induced alterations in hepatic excretory function, but such studies are readily identified by kinetic studies. Like pregnancy, combination oral contraceptives appear to impair the final transport of bilirubin or BSP from the liver cell to the bile canaliliculi.

Mueller and Kappas described abnormal BSP metabolism in patients treated with the natural estrogens, estradiol and estriol.[53] Other natural steroids (progesterone, testosterone, and cortisol) do not alter BSP disposal by the liver,[55,56] but synthetic progestins and estrogens, given continuously, may be associ-

TABLE 16-1 EFFECTS OF ORAL CONTRACEPTIVES ON LABORATORY TESTS

Laboratory Test	Effects	Probable Mechanism
Serum, Plasma, Blood		
Albumin	Slightly decreased	Decreased hepatic synthesis
Aldosterone	Increased	Activates renin-angiotensin system
Amylase	Slightly increased (common)	Not established
	Markedly increased (rare)	Pancreatitis
Antinuclear antibodies	Become detectable	Not established
Bilirubin	Increased (rare)	Reduced secretion into bile
Ceruloplasmin	Increased	Increased hepatic synthesis
Cholinesterase	Decreased	Decreased hepatic synthesis
Coagulation factors	Increased II, VII, IX, X	Increased synthesis
Cortisol	Increased	Increased cortisol-binding globulin
Fibrinogen	Increased	Increased hepatic synthesis
Folate	Decreased or no change	Decreased folate absorption
Glucose tolerance tests	Small decrease in tolerance	Several mechanisms proposed
γ-Glutamyl transpeptidase	Increased	Altered secretion in bile
Haptoglobin	Decreased	Decreased hepatic synthesis
HDL cholesterol	Increased with estrogens and decreased with progestins	Not established
Iron-binding capacity	Increased	Increased transferrin levels
Magnesium	Decreased or no change	Decreased bone resorption
Phosphatase, alkaline	Increased (rare)	Altered secretion in bile
Plasminogen	Increased	Increased hepatic synthesis
Platelets	Slightly increased	Not established
Prolactin	Increased	Not established
Renin activity	Increased	Increased synthesis of renin substrate
Thyroxine (total)	Increased	Increased thyroxine-binding globulin
Transaminases	Slightly increased	Not established
Transferrin	Increased	Increased hepatic synthesis
Triglycerides	Increased	Increased synthesis
Triiodothyronine resin uptake	Decreased	Increased thyroxine-binding globulin
Vitamin A	Increased	Increased retinol-binding protein
Vitamin B_{12}	Decreased	Not established
Zinc	Decreased	Shift of zinc into erythrocyte
Urine		
Δ-Aminolevulinic acid	Increased	Increased hepatic synthesis
Ascorbic acid	Decreased or no change	Not established
Bacteria	Increased incidence of bacteriuria	Not established
Calcium	Decreased	Decreased bone resorption
Cortisol (free)	Unchanged	
Porphyrins	Increased (may precipitate porphyria in susceptible patients)	Increased Δ-aminolevulinic acid synthetase
17-OHCS	Slightly decreased or no change	Increased binding proteins
17-KS	Slightly decreased or no change	Increased binding proteins

ated with jaundice, pruritus, and laboratory evidence of intrahepatic cholestasis, that is, elevated serum alkaline phosphatase, elevated bile salt levels, and liver biopsies revealing dilated bile canaliculi with bile plugs.[51,55,56] Patients demonstrating this sensitivity are also prone to jaundice of pregnancy.

Estrogen and 17-alkylated progestins exert a general inhibitory effect on hepatic conjugation of bilirubin with glucuronic acid. The steroids that produce cholestasis inhibit the hepatic formation of the bile salt taurocholate, which provides the major osmotic force for bile flow.[57] 17-Aklylated progestins also produce a striking decrease in the 16-hydroxylation of estradiol, and thereby slow the metabolism of administered estradiol and its oxidative product, estrone. In addition, estrogens may cause a leak in the plasma membranes of the liver cell, causing a back diffusion from the bile canaliculi of conjugated bilirubin. Hence, the action of certain sex steroids on the liver are multiple, and may result in the development of intrahepatic cholestasis and, rarely, hyperbilirubinemia.

The enterohepatic circulation plays an important role in the metabolism of estrogen.[58] This circulation forms a second anatomic pool, from which estrogens are being continuously transported back and forth. Partial or complete interruption of the enterohepatic circulation of estrogens occurs in recurrent intrahepatic cholestatic jaundice of pregnancy and, to a degree, in patients on oral contraceptives. Accordingly, there may be a retention of estrogens in the liver following conjugation; these steroids are transported back to the blood instead of being secreted into the bile. Since the synthetic estrogens are excreted via the bile, they exert a greater effect in the liver when cholestasis and partial failure of excretory function occur. In frank or occult liver disease, the hepatic uptake of estrogen is increased and protein synthesis activities of the liver are altered.

Gallstone Formation

Bile excretion may also be impeded from progestin effects on ductal mobility. The composition of bile may also contain a higher concentration of cholesterol because of a reduced cholesterol clearance, initiated by exogenous estrogen and progestins. The incidence of cholelithiasis has been reported to double in patients taking oral contraceptives,[59] but the actual number of patients is less than 0.1 percent per year among oral contraceptive users. Progestins not only contribute to bile stasis and cholelithiasis, but have also been implicated in the hepatic metabolism of certain drugs. Progestins have been shown to have an effect on the smooth endoplasmic reticulum, whose microsomal fraction plays an important role in enzyme induction for drug metabolism (see Table 16-2).[55,56]

Hepatic Tumors

Another serious oral contraceptive related disorder is the development of benign tumors of the liver (estimates are 5 per 1 million users). This hepatoma tends to involve the right lobe, but may also appear in the left lobe. It is usually superficial and solitary, but may be multiple. Intrahepatic or intraperitoneal hemorrhage is the presenting clinical complaint one-half the time. The suspicion from palpation of a liver mass requires radiographic confirmation or liver biopsy. It is virtually impossible to predict which users of synthetic sex steroids will develop these tumors. Baum et al. first suggested the association in 1973.[60] Mays and co-workers,[61] at the University of Louisville, and Nissen and Kent,[62] at the University of California, Irvine, have established tumor registries. Fechner recently reported a critical analysis of the Anglo-American literature in benign hepatic tumors between 1940 and 1976.[63] Prior to 1960, the incidence of liver tumor had no association with oral contraceptives, and such cases served as a control group. Approximately 300 instances of benign liver tumors have been reported since 1973 in oral contraceptive users, but the actual incidence remains unknown.[64]

In the late 1950s, Edmonson clearly defined and separated the two most common forms, focal nodular hyperplasia and liver cell adenomas, by gross and microscopic pathology.[65] This has practical application, since the risk of potential hemorrhage is much

TABLE 16-2   DEVIATION OF THE PLASMA PROTEIN CONCENTRATION FROM THE NORMAL MEAN DURING LATE PREGNANCY COMPARED WITH THAT DURING USE OF MEGESTROL-MESTRANOL

Serum Proteins	Mean Change in Concentration	
	DURING USE OF CONTRACEPTIVE STEROIDS (%)	DURING LATE PREGNANCY (%)
Haptoglobin	− 25	0
Albumin	− 12	− 10
Immunoglobulins	(0)	(0)
α_2-Macroglobulin	+ 7	+ 40
Lipoproteins	+ 15	+ 45
Transferrin	+ 26	+ 40
Plasminogen	+ 47	+ 50
α_1-Antitrypsin	+ 51	+100
Thyroxine-binding globulin	+ 65	+ 65
Ceruloplasmin	+188	+200

greater with liver cell adenomas. Focal nodular hyperplasia (FNH) is characterized by one or more visible nodules in an otherwise normal liver, with bile ductules concentrated at the edge of the nodules. In contrast to FNH, liver cell adenoma was an extremely rare lesion prior to 1960.[64] Young women are the most likely group to develop this liver tumor. Adenomas may be single or multiple, and tend to be sharply circumscribed with a thin capsule and no nodularity. Small adenomas often have no capsule, and are confluent with normal cells. The possibility of malignant transformation must be viewed with extreme caution. Hepatocellular carcinoma is reported in both young and old, but its association with oral contraceptives appears highly unlikely.

The most reliable information on the clinical occurrence of liver tumors and oral contraceptive use emanates from the hepatic registries. The University of Louisville registry was established in 1973, and its clinical data were recently published.[61] Forty-four tumors were classified as focal nodular hyperplasia, 40 as hepatocellular adenoma, and 13 as hepatocel-lular carcinomas. Of the 101 tumors, 81 occurred in oral contraceptive users (the majority had taken large-dose oral contraceptives for a long period of time), three were long-term users of estrogen, one had a thecoma, and six were either pregnant or immediately postpartum. The average age of onset was 29, but most of the benign liver tumors, either pill-associated or spontaneous, were found during the reproductive years. Nissen and Kent found 85 percent of liver tumors from their registry were in patients under 35 years of age.[62] Eighty-five percent of those patients in which the association of pill and tumor was present had been on oral contraceptives over 4 years. The actual risk of long-term estrogen exposure in the presence of synthetic 17-alkylated progestins for increased mitosis and cell replication (which progresses to hepatic cell adenoma) is unknown.

Protein Synthesis
Many plasma proteins are synthesized by the hepatocyte.[66] Estrogen can influence the synthesis, distribution, degradation, and function

of RNA, which has a central role in the control of protein synthesis.[67] Estrogen may activate genes and allow transcription of new species of mRNA, which then code the synthesis of specific plasma proteins by the hepatocyte.[68,69]

A change in the serum concentrations of a broad variety of proteins synthesized within the liver is seen during oral contraceptive use.[66,69,70] Table 16-2 lists these changes, and shows how such alterations are similar to those seen during late pregnancy. Ramcharan, Honger and co-workers have demonstrated a decrease in serum albumin levels, as well as a number of other specific serum proteins.[66,71] There is a known relationship between the hepatic production of albumin and serum cholinesterase, both of which are significantly decreased during oral contraceptive use. The α_1-, α_2-, and β-protein globulins are increased, and the albumin/globulin ratio is further decreased. Oral contraceptives play a role in the increased synthesis of many carrier proteins (thyroxine-binding globulin, corticosteroid-binding globulin, pre-β and β-lipoprotein, testosterone-estrogen-binding globulin, transferrin, casuloplasmin) and vitamin K-dependent coagulation factors (II, VII, IX, X, and plasminogen). Of all the serum proteins, cortisol-binding globulin (CBG) shows the best correlation of estrogen dose to hepatocyte protein synthesis, since estrogen is the only factor known to increase CBG.[72]

Haptoglobin, cholinesterase, orosomucoid, antithrombin III, and γ-globulin show a decrease. Subgroups of the immunoglobulins IgG, IgA, IgM have been studied, and changes resulting during oral contraceptive use have been small and are not considered statistically significant or clinically pertinent.

Thyroid Function

Despite the increased hepatic synthesis of thyroid-binding globulin (TBG), oral contraceptives do not adversely affect thyroid function.[54] The evaluation of thyroid status by determination of free thyroxine and radioiodine tests suggest normal thyroid function. Total thyroxine (T_4) is elevated, and indirect tests of thyroid function, like resin uptake of [^{131}I], triodothyronine (T_3), are decreased. The latter test

reflects an alteration secondary to the increase in TBG.

Carbohydrate Metabolism

The data in glucocorticoid metabolism and its endocrine effect in patients who are chronically administered oral contraceptives are more complex than for the thyroid gland. Plasma 17-hydroxycorticosteroids (17-OHCS) are higher, and urinary 17-OHCS are unchanged or slightly decreased.[73] Cortical secretions are not increased, but the metabolic clearance rate (MCR) is decreased because the biologic half-life is prolonged from increased binding to increased CBG levels. The tissue concentrations of cortisol are not increased in patients treated with long-term and high doses of estrogen, and these patients do not appear cushinoid.

A blunting of the adrenocorticotropic hormone (ACTH) response to the metapyrone challenge test has been observed. This may be caused by the increased reservoir of bound cortisol or by the decreased pituitary reserves of ACTH. The latter seems unlikely, since the pituitary-adrenal response to stress is normal. In patients treated with oral contraceptives, the two constant features are an elevated CBG, which is dose-dependent with estrogen, and an elevated total serum cortisol, which are both reversed when the oral contraceptives are discontinued.

Although signs of hyperadrenocorticism are not clinically evident with oral contraceptive use, there are certain metabolic findings in pill users that are similar to glucocorticoid-like activity. Wynn has suggested that the persistently decreased tolerance to a glucose challenge and the resultant transient hyperinsulinemia during oral contraceptive use are similar to glucocorticoid-induced diabetes.[74] More specifically, he considered the metabolic picture to be similar to that found after the prolonged daily administration of 5 mg of prednisone. This may produce an excess in glucocorticoid metabolic activity without showing obvious symptoms of Cushing's syndrome. Others have found glycosuria in female patients challenged with low-dose oral glucocorticoids coupled with oral contraceptives.[75,76] Glucocorticoids promote liver gluconeogenesis and glycogenolysis, in contrast to hyperinsulinemia, which stimulates both the conversion of glucose to glycogen and its metabolism by glycolysis. Estrogens are thought to elevate glucose levels, while progestins may cause a hyperinsulinemia state. The estrogen/progestin ratio is, therefore, important to consider. The changes in glucose tolerance tests are likely minimal and reversible, and as a measure of carbohydrate metabolism, the oral glucose tolerance test is preferred over the intravenous test.[75,76]

A chronic stress to pancreatic β-cell production is strongly implied in long-term oral contraceptive users. This appears to be dose-dependent, that is, less in low-dose combination. Clinically, those patients who may have relative islet cell insufficiency (gestational diabetes, women with large babies, stillborns, obesity, and family history of diabetes) do not appear to be good candidates for high-or intermediate-dose combination oral contraceptives.

Lipid Metabolism

Whereas carbohydrate metabolic changes seem to be related to exogenous estrogen and progestin, alterations of lipid metabolism are influenced by estrogen. Wynn, in 1968, observed an increase in low-density lipoprotein levels with combination oral contraceptives, particularly those whose progestin had inherent estrogen activity.[74] Others have demonstrated elevated β-lipoproteins and pre-β-lipoproteins, both synthesized in the liver and increased by exogenous estrogen. It is now generally agreed that very low-density lipoproteins (VLDL) and their binding with triglyceride (TG) are greater. High-density lipoproteins (HDLP) levels increase from estrogen stimulation. There seems to be a worrisome increase in triglycerides, a commensurate rise in phospholipids, and a questionable elevation of cholesterol.[77]

The coincidental appearance of Fredrickson class II or IV hyperlipemia has been associated with combination oral contraceptives. Class IV patients with elevated pre-β-lipopro-teinemia and trigylcerides are a clinical concern, because of the association with eruptive xanthoma and early or accelerated atherosclerosis (with or without a propensity for coronary artery disease).

Hypertension

Weir et al., in a carefully monitored study, found systolic and diastolic blood pressure to increase 13.5 mm and 6.2 mm, respectively, in all combination oral contraceptive users.[78] Laragh et al. suggest that angiotensinogen synthesis is augmented by estrogen to variably increase levels of angiotensin II.[79] This potent vasopressor and stimulator of aldosterone may eventually cause sodium retention, an increased blood volume, and hypertension.

The exact changes in renin-substrate, plasma renin, and angiotensin II concentration are not universally agreed upon. Combination oral contraceptives consistently raise circulating levels of renin-substrate. Plasma renin activity is also usually increased, even though plasma renin concentration is not increased, and may fall. An impaired feedback mechanism has been suggested to explain the normal or reduced plasma renin concentration and augmented renin activity.

To summarize, a combination pill with a low dose of estrogen (0.05 mg or less) is recommended. Discontinuation of an oral contraceptive should reverse any blood pressure elevation within the first 3 months. Periodic blood pressure determinations are necessary in oral contraceptive users, particularly whenever there has been a history of pregnancy-induced hypertension.

Vitamin and Mineral Metabolism

The literature on oral contraceptives and their effect on vitamins and minerals is moderate.[80] When a tryptophane load is administered, vitamin B_6-(pyridoxine) deficient subjects have an increased excretion of xanthurenic acid (XA). This phenomenon may be seen in pregnancy or in oral contraceptive users, and is reversed by giving 30 mg of pyridoxine hydrochloride each day.[81] The need for riboflavin may be greater when increased amounts of pyridoxine are required for tryptophane metabolism. Folic acid deficiency in oral contraceptive users has been documented by decreased serum folate and red blood cell folate levels.[82,83] It is generally accepted that there is a reduced gastrointestinal absorption of folate from foods during oral contraceptive use. Serum vitamin B_{12} levels decrease, and the binding capacity increases during pregnancy and with oral contraceptive use.[84] The increased ceruloplasmin levels catalyze the oxidation of ascorbic acid (vitamin C), and vitamin C levels fall during pregnancy and oral contraceptive use. Therefore, there is a general consensus that selective vitamin replacement during oral contraceptive therapy is theoretically justifiable.

Along with vitamin metabolism, minerals undergo rather profound changes with oral contraceptive use. Marked elevation of serum copper has occurred, because of the increased copper absorption and the increase in serum ceruloplasmin. Serum iodine and iron are also elevated, because of increased TBG and transferrin levels. Persistent findings of iron metabolism in patients on oral contraceptives reveal an increased serum iron, total iron-binding capacity, and red blood cell volume.[83] Since albumen levels are decreased, less calcium, magnesium, and phosphorous are bound, and levels are decreased with oral contraceptive use.[85]

Coagulation Changes and Thromboembolism

Most of the serious complications reported in association with oral contraception involve problems of the vascular system, the vast majority occurring as a result of inappropriate coagulation.[59,86-90] Blood platelets may be slightly increased, and certain vitamin K-dependent coagulation factors (II, V, VII, IX, X) that are manufactured in the liver are increased. There is endothelial proliferation and thickening of the interna in medium-sized arteries of women receiving oral contraceptives. Fibrinogen, which is important to blood clot formation, increases 50 percent in oral contraceptive users. Blood-clotting factor V is elevated in 25 percent of users, factors II and

IX are elevated in 75 percent, and factor XII is increased in almost all users. Other investigators have found that blood clot lysis was found to decrease significantly. Such changes are reversible after oral contraception therapy is terminated.

These changes in the clotting mechanisms are associated with an increased incidence of thrombosis in the pelvis and lower extremity, as well as pulmonary embolism in the lung. In April 1979, two companion articles published in the *British Medical Journal* reported that women taking oral contraception have a higher incidence of thrombophlebitis and pulmonary embolus.[87,88] Other factors found to influence the incidence rates of thrombophlebitis were obesity, genetics (three times as common in mothers and sisters), major surgery, blood group (lower incidence in group O patients, higher in blood group A), chronic disease, and immobility. In a prospective study, The Royal College of General Practice found deep-vein thrombosis to be 5.6 times greater in oral contraceptive users.[90] The risk of deep-vein thrombosis was dose-dependent—the greater the estrogen dose, the greater the risk of thrombosis:[87,89] Use of a low-dose (35 μg ethinyl estradiol or 0.4 mg norethindrone) pill is not associated with an increased procoagulant risk and do not significantly enhance coagulation.

- 50 mcg estrogen pill: 81 cases of blood clots per 100,000 users
- 100 mcg estrogen pill   111 cases of blood clots per 100,000 users

Whenever thrombosis is evident, the oral contraceptive should be immediately discontinued and not restarted after successful therapy. An alternate method of birth control is also recommended in the presence of appreciable varicose veins or superficial thrombophlebitis.

Cardiovascular Disease

British data reveal a fourfold increase in the relative chance of developing a cerebrovascular accident in women taking oral contraceptives.[91] This risk is related to the dosage of the estrogen component. The pill is contraindicated if there is a strong family history of stroke, or is to be discontinued if persistent migraine-like headaches or hemiparesis occurs.

The risk of myocardial infarction is significantly altered in women taking oral contraceptives and who have hypertension, hypercholesterolemia, are smokers; this risk increases with age. The relative risk of a cardiovascular accident among oral contraceptive users who smoke is shown below:

Oral contraceptive + smoker + age 27 to 39 =
1 cardiovascular accident
per 8400 patients annually

Oral contraceptive + smoker + age 40 to 45 =
1 cardiovascular accident
per 250 patients annually

Goldzieher emphasized the inexactness of "anecdotal" reports and retrospective case/control studies in his investigation, and concluded:[48]

1. Women aged 40 to 44 are at no greater risk from pill use than younger women.

2. Smoking, and particularly heavy smoking, is a much more important risk factor (as is obesity) than pill use.

3. There appears to be an additive effect between smoking and pill use, especially in heavy smokers over the age of 35.

Conversely, Jick (1978) concluded that it is advisable not to prescribe oral contracep-

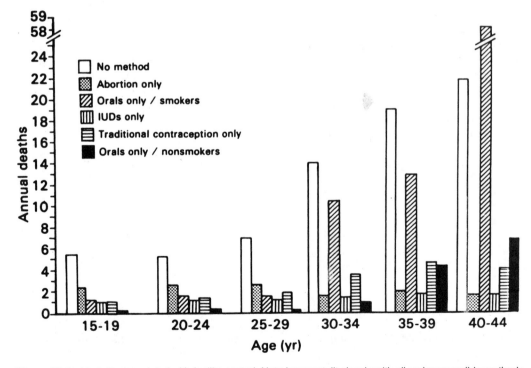

Figure 16-4 Mortality associated with fertility control. Note low mortality levels with all major reversible methods including oral contraceptives, compared to risk of death from pregnancy and childbirth when no fertility control is used, except for women who use oral contraceptives and also smoke. (Modified from Tietze C: *Family Planning Perspectives* 9:74, 1977, with permission.)

tives to women older than 37 years with conditions predisposing to heart attacks, such as hypertension, diabetes, hyperlipoproteinemia (type II hyperlipoproteinemia), obesity, and smoking.[92] Oral contraceptives are not recommended in the obese patient over 35 years of age. Certainly, smokers should be advised that they are subject to greater risk, and oral contraceptives should not be prescribed for smokers over the age of 40 (Fig. 16-4). Finally, oral contraception should be discontinued 4 weeks prior to elective major surgery.

PREPARATIONS

Combination Oral Contraceptives

In 1981, 27 oral contraceptive products are being marketed by a number of pharmaceutical firms, and prescribed to an estimated 10 million domestic users. These preparations contain 20 to 150 mcg of ethinyl estradiol or mestranol, and usually 1 mg or less of a progestin, in varying ratios. Table 16-3 lists those preparations which are currently available.

Each active tablet contains a specific concentration of each steroid, and is to be taken daily for 21 days each month. The tablets are packaged in calendar-like containers which aid the user in counting the days. The containers holding 28 tablets have an additional 7 inactive tablets, which permit the patient to take 1 pill daily throughout the menstrual cycle.

The effectiveness of these combined estrogen and progestin preparations is nearly 100 percent when taken properly, and is better than any other nonpermanent method of contraception. Even preparations containing 20 mcg of ethinyl estradiol are associated with a pregnancy rate of less than 0.2 percent per 100 women. The differences in effectiveness between the various preparations is, therefore, too small to recommend a higher-containing estrogen formulation.

An alternate regimen to high- and intermediate-dose combination estrogen/progestin was made possible by the synthesis of the potent progestin, norgestrel. This progestin molecule permitted the formulation of a low-dose combination estrogen/progestin. In this

TABLE 16-3 COMPOSITION AND DOSES OF SOME ORAL CONTRACEPTIVES

µg-Estrogen	Mg-Progestin		Trade Name
Less than 50 µg:			
20 Ethinyl estradiol	0.3	Norgestrel	Lo/Ovral
20 Ethinyl estradiol	1	Norethindrone	Loestrin 1/20; Zorane 1/20
30 Ethinyl estradiol	1.5	Norethindrone	Loestrin 1.5/30; Zorane 1.5/3
35 Ethinyl estradiol	0.4	Norethindrone	Ovcon-35
35 Ethinyl estradiol	0.5	Norethindrone	Brevicon; Modicon
35 Ethinyl estradiol	1.0	Norethindrone	Norinyl 1 + 35
50 µg:			
50 Mestranol	1	Norethindrone	Norinyl 1 + 50; Ortho-Novum 1:5
50 Ethinyl estradiol	0.5	Norgestrel	Ovral
50 Ethinyl estradiol	1	Ethynodiol diacetate	Demulen
50 Ethinyl estradiol	1	Norethindrone	Ovcon-50; Zoranel 1/50
50 Ethinyl estradiol	1	Norethindrone acetate	Norlestrin, 1
50 Ethinyl estradiol	2.5	Norethindrone acetate	Norlestrin, 2.5
More than 50:			
60 Mestranol	10	Norethindrone	Ortho-Novum, 10 mg
75 Mestranol	5	Norethynodrel	Enovid 5 mg
80 Mestranol	1	Norethindrone	Norinyl 1 + 80; Ortho-Novum 1/80
100 Mestranol	1	Ethynodiol diacetate	Ovulen
100 Mestranol	2	Norethindrone	Norinyl, 2 mg; Ortho-Novum, 2 mg
100 Mestranol	2.5	Norethyndrel	Enovid-E
150 Mestranol	9.85	Norethynodrel	Enovid 10 mg

instance, the synthetic estrogen was reduced to 20 mcg. Similarly, the progestin was reduced when estrogen was given in combination with norgestrel, and it became possible to use 0.3 mg of progestin (Lo Ovral). Other weaker progestins, such as norethindrone and norethindrone acetate, have been used with low-dose estrogen in a combination pill (Table 16-3). The reported incidence of breakthrough bleeding using Loestrin (1.5/30) is 20 percent, while using Norinyl 1 + 35 is 12 percent. Most reproduction endocrinologists prefer these low-dose estrogen/progestin preparations to their higher-dose counterparts for oral contraception.[28,93-95]

Sequential Oral Contraceptives

In 1967 an alternative formulation to combination oral contraception was proposed and marketed. Estrogen-progestin sequential preparations provided for 15 days of unopposed estrogen, and 6 days of estrogen/progestin. This formulation was adopted and marketed by several pharmaceutical companies. It was accompanied by clinical and metabolic side effects from large doses of exogenous, unopposed estrogen, which included leukorrhea, fluid retention, weight gain, escape ovulation, and unexpected pregnancies. The sequential preparation was also associated with an abnormal histologic appearance to the endometrium, suggesting a premalignant lesion, or carcinoma of the endometrium.[11] Such formulations were removed from the market for these reasons.

GUIDELINES FOR ORAL CONTRACEPTIVE USE

Patient Selection

Oral contraception selection requires an interested patient and an informed physician or physician's assistant. Pertinent clinical information is necessary before an oral contraceptive may be prescribed. A knowledge of the patient's menstrual history, growth and secondary sex characteristics, and general medical and social background is necessary. The menstrual history should include the patient's age at menarche, the presence or absence of regular menstrual cycles during adolescence, any current history of irregular or infrequent periods, and the presence or absence of dysmenorrhea. The presence or history of certain medical complications (breast disease, phlebitis, liver disease, hypertension, diabetes, epilepsy, estrogen-sensitive tumor) must be sought. Questions dealing with coital exposure, pregnancy plans, and any desire for sterilization are also informative. The general physical examination should assess the patient's growth and secondary sexual development. Along with height and weight determinations, signs of hyperandrogenism (acne, inappropriate hair growth) and a thorough breast and pelvic examination are recommended.

After the pertinent clinical information is gathered, it must be decided whether the patient is a suitable candidate for oral contraceptive use. Table 16-4 lists those conditions in which oral contraceptives are either relatively or absolutely contraindicated. Another temporary method of contraception (IUD, diaphragm) or permanent method (vasectomy, tubal ligation) method of contraception may be preferred.

Oral Contraceptive Selection

It is important to remember that women using oral contraception are not receiving this medication because they are ill, but for family planning purposes. Therefore, the medication should fulfill the following criteria: (1) not initiate any medical problems, (2) not aggravate any preexisting medical problems, (3) successfully eliminate unwanted pregnancies, and (4) not be associated with any danger to an inadvertent pregnancy or interfere with future pregnancies. Oral contraceptives fulfill criteria 3 and 4, but selection must be carefully individualized for criteria 1 and 2.

Table 16-5 provides guidelines to combination oral contraceptive selection. It is preferable to begin with a low-dose preparation (less than 50 mcg of estrogen, 1 mg or less of progestin). A change to an intermediate

TABLE 16-4 ABSOLUTE (A) AND RELATIVE (R) CONTRAINDICATIONS TO ORAL CONTRACEPTIVE USE

Vascular

A.	1.	Phlebitis—leg vein, pelvic blood clots (i.e., thrombosis)
A	2.	Pulmonary embolus—blood clots in lung
A	3.	Cerebral vascular accident—stroke
A	4.	Coronary occlusion—heart attack
A	5.	Blood dyscrasias—leukemia, sickle cell anemia, polycythemia are associated with intravascular blood clotting

Liver

A	1.	Jaundice—chronic or recurrent
A	2.	Hepatitis—with decreased liver function
A	3.	Recurrent pruritis of pregnancy
A	4.	Cirrhosis with decreased liver function
A	5.	Hepatic porphyria
A	6.	Hepatic tumor

Metabolic

R	1.	Predisposition to diabetes mellitus
		a. Family history
		b. Family history and obesity
		c. History of large babies (9 lb +)
A	2.	Hypertension
		a. Blood pressure 140/90
		b. Previous history of high blood pressure
		c. Black, with family history of high blood pressure
A	3.	Lipids
		a. Increased triglycerides
		b. Age 38 and over

Obstetrics and Gynecology (OB-GYN) Reproduction

A	1.	Pregnancy
R	2.	Lactation—i.e., nursing
A	3.	1° amenorrhea—i.e., no previous menstrual period
A	4.	2° amenorrhea—i.e., history of repeated cessation of menstrual periods for 3 or more months *or* chronic infrequent periods
R	5.	2° amenorrhea and/or lactation while on OCs—i.e., cessation of menstrual periods and or breast discharge
R	6.	Chronic breakthrough bleeding on OCs—i.e., unpredictable bleeding while on OCs
A	7.	Chronic cystic mastitis in smoker and/or a heavy caffeine user

Miscellaneous Concurrent Diseases

A	1.	Epilepsy
R	2.	Migraine headache
A	3.	Porphyria
R	4.	Fibroid tumors of uterus
R	5.	Benign breast tumors
R	6.	Varicose veins—severe
R	7.	Gallstones or chronic biliary symptoms
A	9.	Hyperthyroidism
R	10.	Diabetes Mellitus

Associated Side Effects and Symptoms

R	1.	Chronic weight gain
R	2.	Chronic fluid retention
R	3.	Chronic gastrointestinal symptoms—nausea, vomiting, dyspepsia
R	4.	Chronic premenstrual symptoms—nervous, irritable, depressed, headache, fatigue, lassitude
R	5.	Chronic unmanageable leg cramps
R	6.	Recurrent vaginal monilla (fungus) infection

dose or, eventually, a high dose is necessary if undesired side effects persist. The adolescent desiring oral contraceptives or the patient who is in between pregnancies requires special attention (see Tables 16-6 and 16-7). The prior menstrual history and signs of secondary sex characteristics and hyperandrogenism are important to consider when choosing the appropriate preparation.

Oral contraceptives are routinely started on the fifth day of menses. The effectiveness of the agent should be apparent within the first 2 to 3 days. Women with irregular menses may begin the pill anytime, but a barrier

TABLE 16-5   GUIDELINE TO "COMBINATION PILL" SELECTION

Estrogenic Combination		Intermediate	Androgenic Combination
Low Dose—First Choice None available	A	Brevicon, modicon, Norinyl 1 + 35 Loestrin 1/20	B Lo-Ovral
Intermediate Dose—Alternate Choice C Demulen	D	Orthonovum 1/50 mcg Norinyl 1 + 50 mcg	E Ovral.
High Dose—Final Choice F Ovulen	G	Orthonovum 2 mg, Norinyl 2 mg Norlestrin 2.5 mg	H Ovral 1/80
	I	Provera 10 mg (day 15–25) with barrier contraception	
	J	Follicular estrogen (Premarin 1.25 day 1–15) with luteal, estrogen/progestin (Premarin 1.25 plus Provera 10 mg day 15–25 day) with barrier contraception	

method (condoms, diaphragm) is recommended during the first few weeks.

Following pregnancy, it is encouraged that oral contraceptives be avoided during the initial postpartum period to minimize any risk of thromboembolic formation. Instead, the Pill may be safely started at the initial postpartum visit, unless a medical complication (hypertension, poorly controlled diabetes, liver disease) remains present. Persons past spontaneous or induced abortion may safely begin taking oral contraceptives within the first week.

Side Effects

Side effects during oral contraceptive use in otherwise healthy patients are many and variable in nature. Table 16-8 lists undesired effects expressed by the patient, and describes the likely etiology and recommended management. It is known that the majority of side effects occur in the first 3 months, and that 66 percent of users discontinue the Pill in 1 year. All oral contraceptive users should be seen 3 months after beginning oral contraceptive therapy, and have a yearly office visit for

TABLE 16-6   GUIDELINE TO "COMBINATION PILL" SELECTION: PUBERTY AND ADOLESCENCE (AGE 11 TO 18)

A, B	1. Contraception—mature 2° sex characteristics
A, B	2. Contraception—regular menstrual periods
C, F	3. (±) Hyperandrogenism—acne, hirsutism
C, D, E, F	4. (±) Dysmenorrhea—cramps with menstrual periods
J	5. Amenorrhea
I	6. Infrequent menstrual periods (2–8 per year)
C, F	7. Infrequent menstrual periods (2–8 per year), with evidence of transient or early hyperandrogenism, premenstrual acne, acne, or hirsutism*
C, D, E, F, G*	8. Irregular menstrual periods†

* An option is C or F day 15–25 of treatment cycle.
† An option is C, D, E, F, G day 15–25 of treatment cycle.

**TABLE 16-7 GUIDELINE TO "COMBINATION PILL"
SELECTION: REPRODUCTION YEARS (AGE
15 TO 35); AND PREGNANCY SPACING**

A, B	1.	Contraception—regular menstrual periods
C, F	2.	Contraception—(±) hyperandrogenism (acne, hirsutism)*
C, D, E, F	3.	Contraception—(±) dysmenorrhea (cramps with menstrual period)†
C, D, E, F	4.	Contraception— with or without irregular menstrual periods
C, D, F	5.	Contraception—with or without infrequent menstrual periods (3–6 years)‡
C, I, J	6.	Contraception—with cessation of menstrual periods
E, F, G	7.	Alternate choice for breakthrough bleeding (BTB)
A	8.	Alternate choice for weight gain, nausea, headache, fatigue, lassitude
A, B	9.	Alternate choice for recurrent vaginitis
B	10.	After 38 years, only as a final option

* An option is day 15–25 of treatment cycle, with barrier contraception.
† With antiprostaglandins: (1) Motrin, (2) Ponstel.
‡ Administer day 5–25, or day 15–25, the latter with barrier contraception.

TABLE 16-8 PATIENT CONCERNS

Problem	Etiology	Recommendations
Hyperandrogenism Acne Hirsutism Weight gain	1. Ovral steroid decreases hormone-binding globulin and serum albumin 2. Norgestrel in Ovral is anabolic and androgenic 3. Norethindrone and Norethindrone acetate are anabolic at 1 mg+ dose 4. Estrogen promotes fluid retention	1. For acne and hirsutism, cycle with Ovulen, Norinyl 2 mg or Demulin, which increases steroid hormone-binding globulin 2. For weight gain, minimize estrogen/progestin (i.e., Ovcon −35, Norinyl 1 + 35)
Breast Mastodynia Cystitis-mastitis Enlarged breasts	1. Estrogens increase ductal proliferation 2. Progestins increase alveolar proliferation	1. Use lower dose estrogen/progestin (progestin should be androgenic, i.e., LoOvral or Ovral)
Amenorrhea	1. Inadequate priming of endometrium 2. Excess progestin/estrogen ratio	1. Rule out pregnancy 2. Discontinue OCs for 3 months 3. Recycle with higher-dose estrogen component

(Table 16-8 continues on page 218.)

TABLE 16-8   PATIENT CONCERNS *(Cont.)*

Problem	Etiology	Recommendations
Post-Pill Amenorrhea	1. Hypothalamic-pituitary dysfunction 2. Hypoestrogenism 3. Elevated prolactin	1. Hormone profile 2. Cycle with natural estrogen (Premarin 1.25 mcg) day 1–25, and Provera 10 mg day 15–25 3. Ovulation stimulation after hormone profile if pregnancy desired
Amenorrhea-Galactorrhea	1. Hypothalamic-pituitary dysfunction	1. Serum prolactin 2. Rule out tumor 3. Pap smear of any unilateral breast discharge 4. Discontinue OCs if annoying

Premenstrual Tension-like Symptoms
  Fluid retention
  Nervous
  Irritable
  Headache
	1. Estrogen associated with fluid retention
	2. Estrogen/progestins have an unknown effect on the renin-angiotensin-aldosterone system
	3. Estrogen/progestin associated with pelvic congestion and cerebral edema, and lowered albumin/globulin ratio affecting osmolarity
		1. Use minimal-dose estrogen/progestin
		2. Sodium restricted diet
		3. Minimize use of diuretics

Breakthrough Bleeding (BTB)	1. Inadequate estrogen priming 2. Inadequate progestin 3. Insufficient estrogen/progestin ratio	1. Higher dose estrogen/progestin preparation 2. If BTB continues, discontinue OCs
Chloasma	1. Estrogen stimulates melanocyte-stimulating hormone secretion (?)	1. Use minimal-dose estrogen/progestin 2. Avoid exposure to sunlight

CNS Symptoms
  Fatigue
  Lassitude
  Decreased libido
  Mild depression
	1. Similar to third trimester of pregnancy changes
	2. Vitamin B_{12}, alteration
	3. Relative pyridoxine deficiency
		1. Use low-dose estrogen/progestin
		2. Multiple vitamin replacement
		3. Pyridoxine 30 mg QID

GI Disturbances
  Nausea
  Vomiting
  Epigastric distress
  Bloating
  Pruritis
	1. Pregnancy-like GI symptoms
	2. Oral synthetic estrogen induces cholestasis
	3. Progestin relaxes smooth muscle and GI motility
	4. Cholelithiasis and pancreatitis
		1. Low-dose estrogen/progestin
		2. Pruritis associated with BSP retention and occasional peripheral bile salts; therapy with oral cholestyramine and discontinue OC.

Monilial Vaginitis	1. More glycogen in vagina 2. Alter vaginal pH, flora	1. Monilial treatment (Chap. 20)

blood pressure, breast exam, pelvic, Pap smear, and follow-up clinical history.

Many physiologic changes may be managed by reassurance alone (especially during the initial three cycles) or by changing the preparation to a different estrogen and/or progestin component. An increase in the estrogen component to more than 50 mcg is rarely necessary. The activity of these synthetic steroids at receptor tissues may be either greater or less than the activity of the patient's own natural ovarian steroids. Effects similar to those seen premenstrually (nausea, nervousness, irritability, edema, headaches) are likely from estrogen excess, while symptoms similar to those occurring during pregnancy

TABLE 16-9   DRUGS THAT INTERACT WITH ORAL CONTRACEPTIVES

Class of Compound	Drug	Supposed Method of Action	Suggested Management
Drugs that May Reduce the Efficacy of Oral Contraceptives			
Anticonvulsant drugs	Barbiturates: phenobarbital, primidone, phenytoin, ethosuximide	Induction of microsomal liver enzymes. Fluid retention caused by OCs may precipitate seizures.	20–35 mcg combination OCs or progestin-only pills or another method.
Cholesterol-lowering agents	Clofibrate	Reduce elevated serum triglycerides and cholesterol; this reduces OC efficacy.	Use another method.
Phenylbutazone and allied drugs	Phenylbutazone, indomethacin, ibuprofen	Hepatic microsomal enzyme induction.	Use alternate method.
Antibiotics	Rifampicin, penicillin V	Enzyme induction: rapid breakdown of estrogen in liver; intestinal motility increased with penicillins.	Higher-dose OCs during short course of antibiotics or additional contraceptives. For long course, use another method.
Sedatives and hypnotics	Benzodiazepines, barbiturates, chloral hydrate	Enzyme induction, increased estrogen metabolism.	Alternative method.
Modification of Other Drug Activity by Oral Contraceptives			
Anticoagulants	All	Efficacy impaired, as OCs increase clotting factors.	Do not use OCs with anticoagulant therapy.
Antidiabetic agents	Insulin and oral hypoglycemic agents	High-dose estrogen pills cause impaired glucose tolerance.	Use 20–35 mcg OCs or progestin only. Consider other methods.
Antihypertensive agents	Guanethidine and occasionally methyldopa	Estrogen component involved with Na^{++} retention and increased angiotensenogen.	Use progestin-only pill or another method.
Phenothiazine	All phenothiazides: Reserpine, tricyclic antidepressants	Serum prolactin alters, while combination OCs are associated with increased response of serum prolactin to TRH.	Use alternative method.

(fatigue, lassitude, depression, increased appetite, weight gain) are primarily from progestin excess. An organic etiology must always be considered, especially when symptoms are severe or persist after the appropriate change or discontinuation of the preparation.

Interaction with Other Drugs

Oral contraceptives may interact with other drugs to alter absorption or affect metabolic pathways. Microsomal enzymes within the liver may be inhibited or induced and thereby affect drug metabolism and clearance. Because of this interaction, the desired effect of each drug may be antagonized or potentiated, and undesired side effects from oral contraceptive use may occur. Another form of contraception may therefore be necessary when interaction from chronic exposure is thought to either reduce the efficacy of the contraceptive or modify the activity of the other drug(s). Table 16-9 lists those known drugs with which oral contraceptives may interact and describes the presumed mechanism of action and recommended management.

THE FUTURE

The exploding world population frequently brings the medical profession face to face with the contemporary geopolitical and sociologic problems of our times. (Figure 16-5 displays those contraceptive methods used among married women.) The year 2,000 will see 8 billion people on this earth, with grave doubts about the ability to sustain ourselves. The oral contraceptive, IUD, and other temporary forms

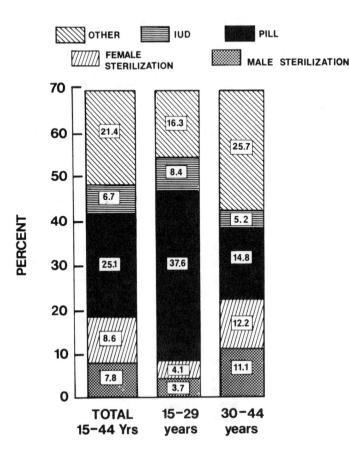

Figure 16-5. Contraception methods used by currently married women in the United States, 1973. (From Ford K: Contraception utilization among currently married women 15–44 years of age: United States, 1973. *Monthly Vital Statistics Report* 25 (no 7 suppl), Oct 1976, with permission.)

of contraception have made little progress in thwarting this specter. Immunologic contraception to β-subfractions of HCG and to specific sperm or ovum antigens hold much promise for the future.

The future of sex steroid treatment in preventing contraception is uncertain. The oral synthetic estrogen/progestin preparation is pharmacologically inappropriate, especially when adverse pathophysiology to the liver and coagulation system is considered. Investigations involving a more physiologic follicular phase and luteal phase replacement by another route of delivery (transvaginal, transdermal) must be continued if the problems caused by overpopulation are to be avoided.

REFERENCES

1. Arrata WSM: Oral contraceptives: General considerations. In Hafez ESE, et al (eds): *Human Reproduction: Conception and Contraception,* ed. 2. New York, Harper & Row, 1980, pp 509–520
2. Rock J, Garcia CR, Pinkus G: Oral contraception. *Recent Progr Horm Res* 13:323, 1957
3. Briggs M: Biochemical effects of oral contraceptives. *Adv Steroid Biochem Pharmacol* 5:65, 1976
4. Dickey RP, Stone SC: Progestational potency of oral contraceptives. *Obstet Gynecol* 47:106, 1976
5. Edgren RA: Relative potency of oral contraceptives. In Moghissi KS (ed): *Controversies in Contraception.* Baltimore, Williams & Wilkins, 1979, p 1
6. Chihal HJW, Peppler RD, Dickey RP: Estrogen potency of oral contraceptive pills. *Am J Obstet Gynecol* 212:75, 1975
7. Reed MJ, Fotherby K, Steel SJ, Addison J: *In vivo* and *in vitro* metabolism of ethynlestradiol. *Proc Soc Endocrinol* 53:28, 1972
8. Goldzieher JW, DeLaPena A, Chenault CB, et al: Comparative studies of the ethinyl estrogens used in oral contraception: II. antiovulatory potency. *Am J Obstet Gynecol* 122:619, 1975
9. Goldzieher JW, DeLaPena A, Chenault CB et al: Comparative studies of the ethinyl estrogens used in oral contraception: III. Effect on plasma gonadotropins. *Am J Obstet Gynecol* 122:625, 1975
10. Chen L, O'Malley BW: Mechanism of action of the sex steroid hormones. *N. Engl J Med* 294:1322, 1976
11. Dujovne CA: Cytotoxic interactions between estrogens and progestins on liver cell cultures. Unpublished data, 1976
12. Vorys N: The effect of sex steroids on the liver, in Givens JR (ed): *Clinical Use of Sex Steroids.* Chicago, Year Book Medical Publishers, 1980, pp 184–206
13. Editorial: Metabolic effects of oral contraceptives. *Lancet* 2:783, 1969
14. Goldzieher JW, Maqueo M, Ricand L, et al: Effect of combination oral contraceptives on pituitary gonadotropins. *Am J Obstet Gynecol* 96:1078, 1966
15. Vorys N, Stevens V: The effect of varying progestogen-estrogen ratios on pituitary gonadotropins (Proceedings of a symposium). *Clin Trails J (Lond),* Jan 1966, pp 73–75
16. Diczfalusy E: Mode of action of contraceptive drugs. *Am J Obstet Gynecol* 100:136, 1968
17. Krog W, Aktories K, Jurgensen O, et al: Contrasting effects of combined and sequential oral contraceptives on LH-RH stimulated release of LH and FSH as compared to minipills. *Acta Endocrinol (KBH)* 32(suppl):21, 1975
18. Dickey RP: The pill: Physiology, pharmacology, and clinical use. In Typer LB, Isenman AW (eds): *American College of Obstetrics and Gynecology Seminar in Family Planning.* Chicago, Knox, 1974, pp 24–37
19. Israel R, March CM, Kletzkz O: Post-pill amenorrhea: investigative and therapeutic response, in Crosignami PG, Mishell DR Jr (eds): *Ovulation in the Human.* London, Academic, 1976, p 181
20. Mishell DR Jr: The effects of contraceptive steroids on hypothalamic-pituitary function. *Am J Obstet Gynecol* 128:60, 1977
21. Dickey RP, Stone SC: Effect of bromergocriptine on serum in PRL, HLH, FSH, and estradiol 17B in women with glactorrhea-amenorrhea. *Obstet Gynecol* 48:84, 1976
22. Jacobs HS, Franks SM, Murray MAF, et al: Clinical and endocrine features of hyperprolactinemic amenorrhea. *Clin Endocrinol* 5:439, 1976
23. Tyson JE: Neuroendocrine dysfunction in galactorrhea-amenorrhea after oral contraceptive use. *Obstet Gynecol* 46:1, 1975
24. Maques J, Rice-Wray E, Calderon JJ, et al: Ovarian morphology after prolonged use of steroid contraceptives. *Contraception* 5:177, 1972

25. Ryan KJ: Estrogens and atherosclerosis. *Clin Obstet Gynecol* 19:805, 1976

26. Mastioianni L, Urzua M, Avalos M, et al: Some observations in fallopian tube fluid in the monkey. *Am J Obstet Gynecol* 103:703, 1969

27. Moghissi KS: Effects of steroidal contraceptives on the reproductive system. In Hafez ESE (ed): *Human Reproduction.* Hagerstown, Harper & Row, pp 529–567

28. Brenner RM: Ciliogenesis in the primate oviduct. In Sherman AI (ed): *Pathways to Contraception.* Springfield, Ill, Thomas, 1971, pp 50–54

29. Hendricks CH: Inherent motility patterns and response characteristics of the nonpregnant human uterus. *Am J Obstet Gynecol* 96:824, 1966

30. Maques M, Becerra C, Mungria H, et al: Endometrial changes in women using hormonal contraceptives for periods up to 10 years. *Conception* 1:115, 1970

31. Kaufman RH, Reeves KO, Daugherty CM: Severe atypical endometrial changes and sequential contraceptive use. *JAMA* 236:923, 1976

32. Kreutner A, Johnson D, Williamson HO: Histology of endometrium in long-term use of a sequential oral contraceptive. *Fertil Steril* 27:906, 1976

33. Grusberg SB: The histogenesis of endometrial cancer. *Obstet Gynecol* 30:287, 1967

34. Frederick ER: The effect of oral contraceptives on the cytology of the secretory cells of the cervix. In Blandau R, Moghissi KS (eds): *Biology of the Cervix.* Chicago, Univ Chicago Press, 1977, p 102

35. Pincus G: *The Control of Fertility.* New York, Academic, 1977 pp 240–255

36. Weid GL, Davis E, Frank R et al: Statistical evaluation of the effect of hormonal contraceptives on the cytologic smear pattern. *Obstet Gynecol* 27:327, 1966

37. Bibbo M, Bartils DH, Weid GI: Abnormal cytologic and cervical neoplasia in users of oral contraceptives and IUD's. In Moghissi KS (ed): *Controversies in Contraception.* Baltimore, Williams & Wilkins, 1979, p 151

38. Richard RM, Barron BA: A followup study of patients with cervical dysplasia. *Am J Obstet Gynecol* 105:386, 1969

39. Spellacy WN, Azias N, Buhi WC, et al: Vaginal yeast growth and contraceptive practice. *Obstet Gynecol* 38:342, 1971

40. Barsivala VM, Vikar RD: The effect of oral contraceptives on concentrations of various components of human milk. *Contraception* 7:307, 1973

41. Drill VA: Oral contraception: Relation to mammary cancer, benign breast lesions, and cervical cancer. *Ann Rev Pharmacol Toxicol* 15:367, 1975

42. Goldrath MH: Contraception and endometrial, cervical, and breast cancers. In Hafez ESE (ed): *Human Reproduction.* New York, Harper & Row, 1980, pp 312–331

43. Drill, VA: Experimental and clinical studies in relationship of estrogen and oral contraceptives to breast cancer. In Duncan WAM (ed): *Experimental Model Systems in Toxicology and Their Significance in Man:* Proceedings of the European Society of Drug Toxicology, vol 15, 1977, p 113

44. Donnelly PK, Baker KW, Camez JA, et al: Benign breast lesions and subsequent breast carcinoma in Rochester, Minnesota. *Mayo Clin Proc* 50:650, 1975

45. Carr DH: Chromosomes after oral contraception. *Lancet* 2:830, 1967

46. Klinger HP, Glasser M, Glebatis DM: Contraceptives and the conceptus: I. Chromosome abnormalities of the fetus and neonate related to maternal contraceptive history. *Obstet Gynecol* 48:40, 1976

47. Janeruh RF, Piper JM, Glebatis DM: Oral contraceptives and congenital limb reduction defects. *N Engl J Med* 291:597, 1974

48. Goldzieher JW. In defense of the pill. *J Contin Educ Obstet Gynecol,* Oct 1978, p 15

49. Nora AH, Nora JJ: A syndrome of multiple congenital anomalies associated with teratogenic exposure. *Arch Environ Health* 30:17, 1975

50. Schaffner F, Popper H: Electron microscopic study of cholestasis. *Proc Soc Exp Biol Med* 101:777, 1959

51. Hecker RW: The liver toxicity of oral contraceptives: A critical review of the literature. *Med J Aust* 2:682, 1968

52. Combes B, Shibata H, Adams R, et al: Alteration in BSP removal mechanism from blood during normal pregnancy. *J Clin Invest* 42:1431, 1963

53. Muller MN, Kappas A: Estrogen pharmacology: The influences of estradiol and estriol on hepatic disposal of sulfa bromophthalein. *J Clin Invest* 43:1903, 1964

54. Mishell DR Jr, Colodyn SZ, Swanson LA: The effect of an oral contraceptive on tests of thyroid function. *Fertil Steril* 20:339, 1969

55. Jones AL, Emans JB: The effects of progesterone on hepatic endoplasmic reticulum: An electron microscopic and biochemical study.

In Salhanick HA, Kipnis DM, Vande Wiele RL (eds): *Metabolic Effects of Gonadal Hormones and Contraceptive Steroids*. New York, Plenum, 1969, pp 68–85

56. Bianchetti JA, Prestine PE: Effect of contraceptive agents on drug metabolism. *Eur J Pharmacol* 7:196, 1969

57. Forker EL: The effect of estrogen on bile formation in the rat. *J Clin Invest* 48:654, 1969

58. Addlercreutz H, Luukkainen T: Biochemical and clinical aspects of the enterohepatic circulation of estrogens. *Acta Endocrinol* 124(suppl):101, 1967

59. Boston Collaborative Drug Surveillance Program: Oral contraceptives and venous thromboembolic disease, surgically confirmed gallbladder disease, and breast tumors. *Lancet* 1:1399, 1973

60. Baum JK, Holtz F, Bookstein JJ, et al: Possible association between benign hepatomas and oral contraceptives. *Lancet* 2:926, 1973

61. Mays ET, Christopherson WM, Barrows GH: Focal nodular hyperplasia of the liver: Possible relationship of oral contraception. *Am J Clin Pathol* 61:735, 1974

62. Nissen ED, Kent DR: Liver tumors and oral contraceptives. *Obstet Gynecol* 46:460, 1975

63. Fechner RE: Pathologic aspects of tumors and tumor-like lesions in women taking oral contraceptives, in Silverberg SG, Mayor FJ (eds): *Estrogen and Cancer*. New York, Wiley, 1978, pp 111–123

64. Sturtevant FM: Oral contraceptives and liver tumors. In Moghissi SK (ed): *Controversies in Contraception*. Baltimore, Williams & Wilkins, 1979, p 93

65. Edmondson HA, Henderson BB: Liver cell adenomas associated with the use of oral contraceptives. *N Engl J Med* 294:470, 1976

66. Ramcharan S, Sponzelli E, Wingerd MA: Serum protein fractions. *Obstet Gynecol* 48:211, 1976

67. Jensen E, Brecher PE, Mobla S, et al: Receptor transformation in estrogenic action—molecular events in hormone action. *Acta Endocrinol* 191(suppl):159, 1974

68. Doe RP, Mellinger GT, Swain WR, Seal US: Estrogen dosage effects on serum proteins: A longitudinal study. *J Clin Endocrinol* 27:1081, 1967

69. Musa BU, Doe RP, Seal US: Serum protein alterations produced in women by synthetic estrogens. *J Clin Endocrinol Metab* 27:1463, 1967

70. Laurell CB, Kullander S, Thorell J: Effect of administration of a combined estrogen-progestin contraceptive on the level of individual plasma proteins. *Scand J Clin Lab Invest.* 21:337, 1967

71. Honger PE, Rossing N: Albumin metabolism and oral contraception. *Clin Sci* 36:41, 1969

72. Robertson ME, Stiefel M, Landlaw, JC: The influence of estrogens on the secretory disposition and biologic activity of cortisol. *J Clin Endocrinol Metab* 19:1381, 1959

73. Pulkkinen MO: The levels of 17-hydroxycorticosteroids in the plasma of users of oral contraception. *Acta Endocrinol (KBH)* 119(suppl):156, 1967

74. Wynn V: Some metabolic effects of oral contraceptives. Proceedings of a symposium. *Clin Trails J (Lond)* Jan 1966, pp 171–180

75. Spellacy WN: A review of carbohydrate metabolism and the oral contraceptives. *Am J Obstet Gynecol* 104:448, 1969

76. Gershberg G, Javier A, Hulse M: Glucose tolerance in women receiving an ovulatory suppressant. *Diabetes* 13:378, 1964

77. Sachs BA, Wolfman L, Herzig N: Plasma lipid and lipoprotein alterations during oral contraceptive administration. *Obstet Gynecol* 34:530, 1969

78. Weir RJ, Briggs E, Mack A, Naismith L, Taylor L, Wilson E: Blood pressure in women taking oral contraceptives. *Br Med J* 1:535, 1974

79. Laragh JH, Sealey JE, Ledingham JG, Newton MA: Oral contraception: Renin aldosterone and high blood pressure. *JAMA* 201:918, 1967

80. Theuer RC: Effect of oral contraceptive agents on vitamin and mineral needs: A review. *J Reprod Med* 8:1, 1972

81. Wachstein M, Gudaitis A: The disturbance of vitamin B_6 metabolism in pregnancy. *J Lab Clin Med* 42:99, 1953

82. McLean R, Heine MW, Held B, Streiff B: Relationship between the oral contraceptive and folic acid metabolism. *Am J Obstet Gynecol* 104:745, 1969

83. Mandell J, Symmons C, Zilva JF: Comparison of the effects of oral contraceptives and pregnancy on iron metabolism. *J Clin Endocrinol* 29:1489, 1969

84. Bianchine JR, Bonnlander B, Placido VJ, et al: Serum vitamin B_{12} binding capacity and oral contraceptive hormones. *J Clin Endocrinol Metab* 29:1425, 1969

85. Young MM, Jasani C, Smith DA, et al: Some effects of ethinyl estradiol on calcium and

phosphorous metabolism in osteoporosis. *Clin Sci* 34:411, 1968

86. Walters WAW, Linn YL: Haemodynamic changes in women taking oral contraception. *J Obstet Gynecol Br Commonw* 77:1007, 1970

87. Inman WH, Vessey MP, Westerholm B, Engelund A: Thromboembolic disease and steroidal content of oral contraceptives: A report to the Committee for Safety of Drugs. *Br Med J* 2:203, 1970

88. Vessey MP, Doll R: Investigation of relation between use of oral contraceptives and thromboembolic disease: A further report. *Br Med J* 2:251, 1969

89. Sartwell PE, Masi AT, Arthes FG, et al: Thromboembolism and oral contraceptives: An epidemiology case-control study. *Am J Epidemiol* 90:365, 1969

90. The Royal College of General Practitioners: *Oral Contraceptives and Health.* New York, Pitman; 1974

91. Inman WH, Mann JI: Oral contraceptives and death from myocardial infarction. Br Med J 2:245, 1975

92. Jick H, Duran B, Rothman KJ: Oral contraception and nonfatal myocardial infarction. *JAMA* 239:1403, 1978

93. Dickey RP, Door CH: Oral contraceptives: Selection of the proper pill. *Obstet Gynecol* 33:273, 1969

94. Speroff L: Which birth control pill should be prescribed. *Fertil Steril* 27:997, 1976

95. Preston SN: A report of a collaborative dose-response clinical study using decreasing doses of combination oral contraceptives. *Contraception* 6:17, 1972

17. Therapeutic Uses of Estrogens and Progestins

CHAD I. FRIEDMAN   PEG F. MCKNIGHT
MOON H. KIM

The intent of this chapter is to review the uses of estrogens and progestins in clinical practice excluding their use as contraceptives. The magnitude of this task is reflected by the fact that almost every American female has utilized an estrogen or progestational compound during some period in her life. Use of estrogens and progestins has been a matter of controversy producing a massive collection of conflicting recommendations and warnings. A complete review of the literature surrounding their use is beyond the scope of this text, which attempts only to acquaint the reader with the present status of therapy with estrogens and progestins.

ESTROGENS

Chemistry and Metabolism

Based on their chemical structure, estrogens may be divided into two groups, steroid and nonsteroid compounds. While their biologic properties are similar, the metabolic fate of the steroid estrogens is quite different from the nonsteroid compounds.

Steroid Estrogens

NATURAL ESTROGEN. The naturally occurring estrogens include estradiol, estrone, estriol, equelin, and equilenin. The steroid structure consists of 18 carbons. All contain an unsaturated A-ring, a methyl group at C-13, a phenolic hydroxyl group at C-3, and a ketone or hydroxy group at C-17, as shown in Figure 17-1. Natural estrogens circulating in the blood are bound to albumin and testosterone-estradiol-binding globulin (sex hormone-binding globulin) with only a small fraction being free steroid. They are distributed throughout most body tissues with high concentrations occurring in fat deposits.

Estradiol 17-β is the major estrogen secreted from the maturing follicle and corpus luteum in ovulatory women. Among the naturally occurring estrogens it has the greatest biologic potency and the highest affinity for the estrogen receptor in target tissues.

Estrone is formed extensively in extraglandular tissue sites by the aromatization of androstenedione, which is produced primarily in the adrenal cortex and in the ovary. After menopause, depletion of the follicles occurs and peripheral conversion of androstenedione becomes the primary source of estrogen. Extraglandular aromatization occurs in liver, brain, kidney, and adipose tissue. Production is noncyclic though not necessarily static. Ovarian disease states may result in increased production of androstenedione. Also, metabolic processes associated with an increased capacity for aromatization may result in increased estrone production. This has been observed to occur with obesity, hepatic disease, hyperthyroidism, compensated congestive heart failure, and starvation.

Estriol is formed by 16-α-hydroxylation and reduction of the ketone at C-17. It is a major metabolite of estradiol and estrone and is readily excreted in the urine.

NATURAL ESTROGENS

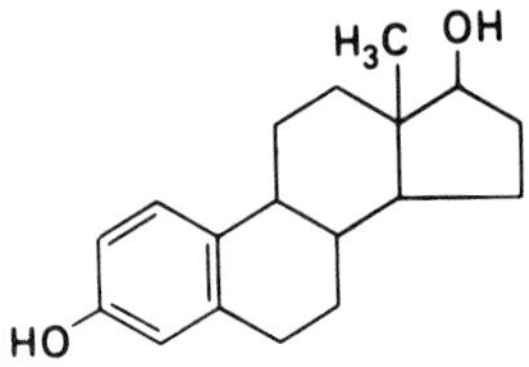

ESTRADIOL 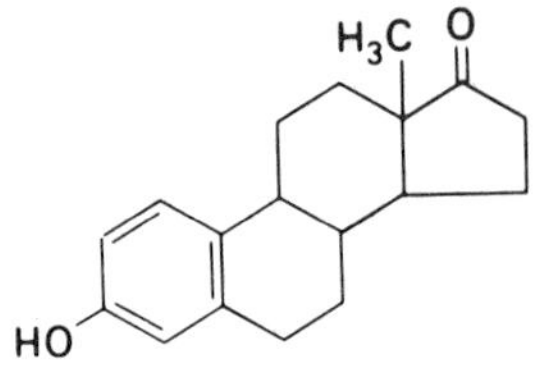   ESTRONE 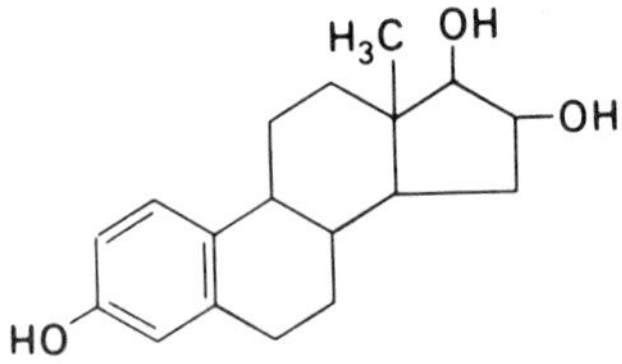   ESTRIOL

SYNTHETIC STEROIDAL ESTROGENS

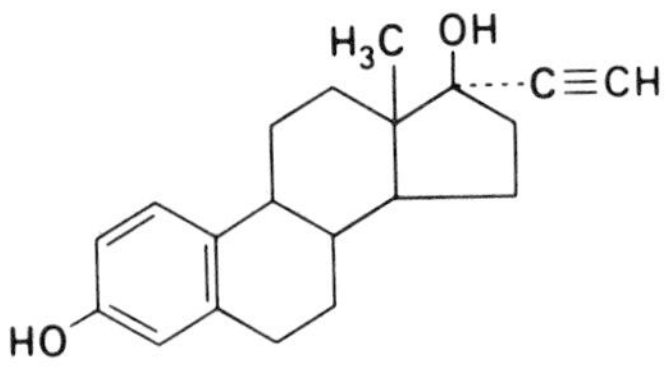

ETHINYL ESTRADIOL 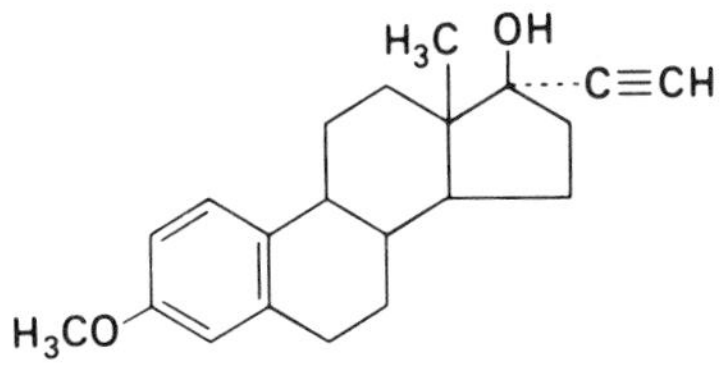   MESTRANOL

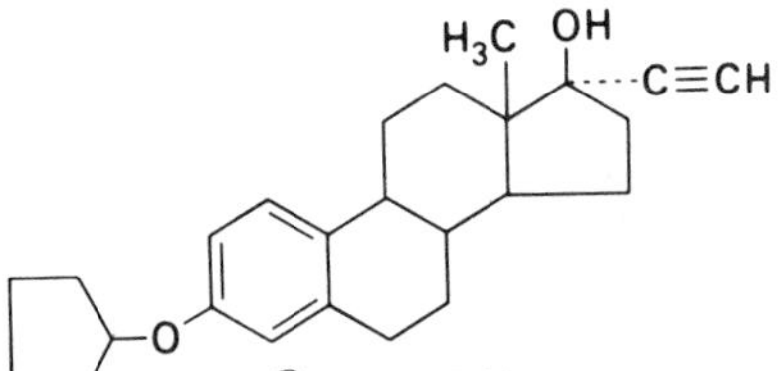

QUINESTROL

NONSTEROIDAL ESTROGENS

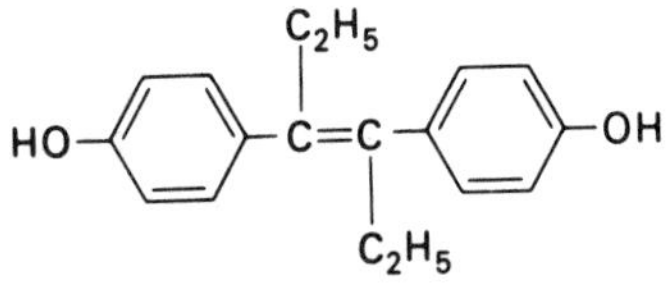

DIETHYLSTILBESTROL (Stilbestrol) 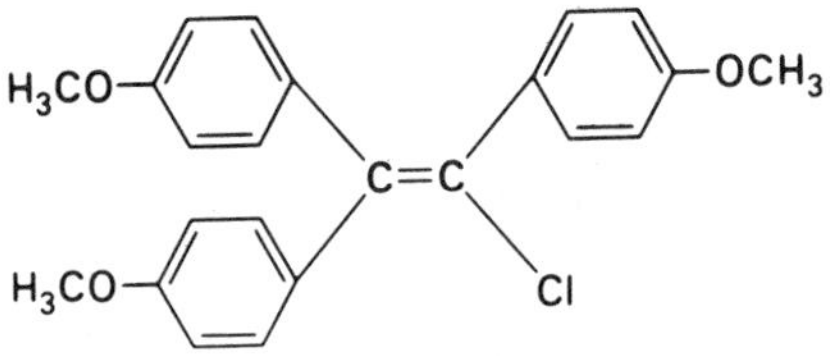   CHLOROTRIANISENE (Tace)

Figure 17-1. Chemical structure of natural estrogens, synthetic steroidal estrogens, and nonsteroidal estrogens. (From Csáky, TZ: *Cutting's Handbook of Pharmacology: The Actions and Uses of Drugs*, ed. 6, New York, Appleton-Century-Crofts, 1979, pp 373–375, with permission.)

Equelin and equilenin are found in the urine of pregnant mares and cannot be produced by humans.

The metabolic pathways of estrogen have not been fully elucidated. 17-β-hydroxysteroid dehydrogenase is considered a key enzyme in estrogen metabolism allowing for the conversion of estradiol to estrone. It is present in most tissues, including the gut and target tissues.

Estrone serves as a substrate for the hydroxylating enzymes (estrogen-2-hydroxylase and estrogen-16-α-hydroxylase), and is oxidized to form the 2-hydroxy (catechol) estrogens and other hydroxylated metabolites (i.e., estriol). Polyhydroxylated estrogens are very polar and water soluble, and may be excreted in the urine. Other, more lipid-soluble forms must be conjugated with glucuronic or sulfuric acid as a prerequisite for their excretion via urine or bile. Conjugation may occur in kidney tissue and intestinal mucosa as well as in the liver. The conjugated estrogens excreted in bile may be hydrolyzed by bacteria present in the gut, permitting reabsorption via the enterohepatic pathway. One conjugate, estrone-3-sulfate, may represent a storage form of estradiol. Its plasma levels exceed those of estradiol and it may be reconverted in the liver and other organs, including the uterus, to estrone and estradiol.[1]

SYNTHETIC STEROID ESTROGENS. Naturally occurring estrogens given orally are metabolized in a "first-pass effect" through the liver and are thus relatively ineffective. When natural estrogens are given intramuscularly, metabolism is rapid. Synthetic forms have been developed to improve absorption and slow inactivation. Changes in the steroid structure, which do not cause loss of estrogenic activity, include interconversion of the hydroxy and ketone groups and the addition of various side chains at C-3 and C-17.

The addition of an ethinyl group to the C-17 position of estradiol produces ethinyl estradiol, the most biologically active of the synthetic steroid estrogens. Its prolonged activity is due to slower elimination from the circulation, as compared to estradiol. From a quantitative viewpoint, the major metabolic pathway for ethinyl estradiol is aromatic hydroxylation, as it is for the natural estrogens.[1] Due to the substitution at C-17, the production of estriol analogue is reduced, accounting for the slower inactivation. However, some deethinylation does occur. Controversy exists in the literature regarding the quantitative extent of this reaction. Ethinyl estradiol-sulfate is the principal circulating form of ethinyl estradiol. This may represent a storage form with functions comparable to those of estrone sulfate. Unlike estradiol, substantial amounts of ethinyl estradiol are excreted in the feces with the ratio of excretion being 4:6 for feces and urine.[1]

Mestranol differs from ethinyl estradiol by the addition of a methoxy group at C-3. About 54 percent of this compound is demethylated in the liver to ethinyl estradiol. Because demethylation is not complete, more mestranol must be administered at low doses to achieve an equal therapeutic effect to ethinyl estradiol. The 3-methoxy group of mestranol causes it to be more lipophilic than ethinyl estradiol.

Quinestrol is another synthetic estrogen having a high affinity for adipose tissue, where it is stored in a chemically unaltered form and slowly released over a period of days. The unstored portion is rapidly metabolized, mainly to ethinyl estradiol. Excretion occurs mostly in urine and bile. Slow release results in an extended biologic half-life which has been reported to be 120 ±7 hours.[2]

Longer-acting parenteral forms of synthetic estrogens have also been developed. Esterfication or polymerization of the natural estrogens slows absorption from the injection site and prolongs the action so that a single dose may be effective for several days up to several weeks.

Nonsteroid Estrogens. Nonsteroid compounds have also been developed to overcome the problems encountered with natural estrogens. These are synthetic substances with estrogenic activity which are closely related structurally to stilbene. Metabolic pathways are not fully determined.

Like steroid estrogens, diethylstilbesterol (DES) and its metabolites undergo enterohepatic circulation. Metabolic pathways include: (1) aromatic ring hydroxylation and methylation of the catechol, (2) hydroxylation at one of the ethyl side chains, and (3) oxidation at the stilbene double bond. This latter pathway leads to the formation of dienestrol.[1]

Chlorotrianisene (Tace) is derived from DES. It has weak estrogenic properties but is metabolized to a more active compound. It is stored in fat tissues with a slow release resulting in prolonged action.

Mechanism of Action

Intracellular actions of estrogen have been well studied, although their specific interactions with DNA remain speculative. In contrast to protein hormones, which interact with cell membrane receptors, estrogens enter the target cells by passive diffusion. Estrogen concentrates within the cell by binding to a high-capacity, low-affinity protein conceptually similar to the steroid-binding globulin in serum. The estrogen receptor is a protein with very high affinity for estrogen compounds and is essential for transport of estrogen into the nucleus. Saturation of the estrogen receptors is readily achieved due to the limited number of receptors and the ability to bind only a single estrogen molecule per receptor. Some alterations in structure occur during this process, accounting for a change in sedimentation rate. Once inside the nucleus the steroid receptor complex interacts with DNA, resulting in RNA and protein synthesis. Transport of estrogen into the nucleus results in both short- and long-acting effects.[3] Short-acting effects have a rapid on-and-off mechanism and involve the majority of nuclear receptors. Biologic effect appears to correlate well with the number of receptors occupied. Fluid imbibition in the uterus is perhaps the best-studied short-acting effect of estrogen. Teleologically, the short-acting effects could be involved in feedback mechanisms, although this has not been shown.

Long-acting effects of estrogen are involved with cellular growth and division. They have been better studied due to their significance to neoplastic changes. Long-acting effects involve a limited number of nuclear receptors which are readily saturated. Biologic effect requires nuclear retention of the steroid receptor complex for a prolonged period of time. Given similar steroid receptor complex concentrations, the "biologically weaker" estrogens (i.e., estriol) can be shown to disappear from the nucleus at a more rapid rate than biologically more potent estrogens (i.e.,

estradiol).[4] Differences in dissociation between the estrogens and the nuclear receptors may be compensated for by persistent reassociation of the substrate with the limited number of nuclear receptors. The differences in biologic potency demonstrated by bolus injection studies become inapparent when the substrate is provided in a steady state at the low concentrations required for saturation.[5]

Replenishment of the cytosol receptor, as well as continued substrate receptor transport into the nucleus, appears necessary for continued cellular stimulation. Some estrogens are unable to stimulate receptor replenishment despite prolonged nuclear retention. This appears to be one of the major mechanisms for the antiestrogens used in clinical practice.[3]

Estrogens may also have actions not mediated by cytosol receptors (i.e., inhibition of bone resorption and vascular permeability). The means by which estrogens work in these situations are not well understood.

Pharmacologic Actions

Some of the major pharmacologic actions of estrogens are shown on Table 17-1. Many other drug interactions[6] and alterations in laboratory values[7] are known.

Clinical Use. It is appropriate for estrogens to be used in the lowest effective dose. Some individuals require higher doses than others to achieve a therapeutic response. Most patients are given estrogens on a cyclic basis: 21 days on, 7 days off, or for the first 25 days of each month. There are few data to support this regimen for the prevention of endometrial carcinoma, although it appears to be more physiologic and may be used to establish the need for estrogens in patients being treated for relief of vasomotor symptoms. Prior to starting estrogen in postmenopausal patients, a thorough breast exam and pelvic examination are performed. A Pap smear is obtained and an endometrial biopsy may be taken.

Progestational compounds should be used for at least 7 days each month in all patients with a uterus receiving estrogen replacement. In patients without a uterus, progestins

TABLE 17-1 PHARMACOLOGIC ACTIONS OF ESTROGENS

Genital Tract:
  Stimulation of endometrial glandular and stromal compartment
  Stimulation of myometrium
  Proliferation of vaginal and urethral epithelium
  Increase in vascular flow to genital tract
  Increase in cervical gland secretions
  Stimulation of production of receptors for progesterone and luteinizing hormone
Breast:
  Stimulation of ductular growth
Skin:
  Increase in content of hyaluronic acid and water
  Reduction in breakdown of collagen
  Decrease in sebum production
  Decrease in epithelial proliferation
Bone:
  Decrease in bone resorption
  Increase in parathyroid hormone concentrations
Liver:
  Stimulation of production of multiple binding globulins (i.e., steroid-binding globulin, cortisol-binding globulin, thyroid-binding globulin)
  Increase in concentration of bile salts
Pituitary-Hypothalamus:
  Suppression of vasomotor symptoms
  Suppression and stimulation of gonadotropin secretion
  Increase in prolactin secretion
Coagulation:
  Stimulation of factor VII, VIII, IX, X, and prothrombin
  Depression of antithrombin III
  Increase in platelet adhesiveness
Lipids:
  Changes in ratios of lipoprotein have had variable results depending on dose and estrogen used

concentrations of the administered estrogens are of little value in assessing dose equivalents. Estrogen production rates vary widely between patients and the hormones are subject to rapid interconversion and metabolism. Attempts to determine the estrogenic activity of various proportions have not been uniformly in agreement. Some comparative dosages of different estrogens are given in Table 17-2. As may be appreciated from the discussion, there is considerable controversy on the issue of the equivalency of different preparations.

Clinical Use After the Reproductive Years. Despite continuing controversy, the most common indications for estrogens are noted after menopause.

VASOMOTOR SYMPTOMS. The "hot flush" is the best known symptom of the menopausal syndrome. Following a physiologic menopause it is noted in up to 70 percent of women. Only 20 percent of these women seek medical treatment for the symptoms, although 50 percent of reproductive-age females undergoing castration may request treatment. Clinically, there is no reasonable means to follow the response to treatment other than subjective symptomatic improvement. Using double-blind crossover studies, estrogens have been shown to be effective in reducing the frequency of vasomotor symptoms. Such studies are necessary not only to eliminate a considerable placebo effect but to correct for the spontaneous abatement of symptoms which occurs with time. Doses for replacement therapy should be individualized to obtain the lowest dosage required to achieve a reasonable clinical response and should be reevaluated every 6 months. Short-

are seldom used, although consideration should be given for their use if data become available suggesting beneficial effects on the incidence of breast carcinoma.

Throughout this chapter, doses of estrogens given are expressed predominantly as the equivalent of conjugated estrogens, since this is the most commonly used preparation. The most frequently used conjugated estrogen preparation, Premarin, is a mixture of at least nine different estrogens. Serum and urinary

TABLE 17-2 COMPARATIVE DOSAGES OF VARIOUS ESTROGENS (MILLIGRAMS)

Ethinyl estradiol	0.015
Mestranol	0.02
Conjugated estrogens	0.625
Diethylstilbestrol	0.25

acting estrogen compounds given for 21 to 25 days per month will allow for assessment of the spontaneous reduction in vasomotor symptoms. Reduced symptomatology during the drug-free period is frequently found within 2 years of the menopause. An example of the proposed treatment regimen is shown in Figure 17-2. Alternate medications suggested for the relief of vasomotor symptoms include medroxyprogesterone[8] and clonidine.[9]

VAGINAL ATROPHY. Dyspareunia is the most common complaint associated with vaginal atrophy. Clinical inspection and vaginal cytology showing estrogen deficiency are adequate parameters for the physician to consider the use of estrogen therapy. While estrogens do not increase vaginal depth or caliber, the resulting increase in vascularity and epithelial proliferation allow greater lubrication and reduced vaginal trauma with coitus. Dosages of

estrogen equivalent to 1.25 mg of conjugated estrogens are given initially to produce a rapid response. Once this is achieved, the dose may be decreased or given at less frequent intervals and intermittent progesterone therapy implemented. Local treatment has not been shown to be more effective than systemic administration, and estrogens administered via the vaginal route are well absorbed for systemic distribution.[10] Treatment should continue until the patient is no longer sexually active. Lubricants have been used as alternatives to estrogens, but their inability to stimulate the vaginal mucosa has limited their utility.

DYSURIA. Dysuria is classically a symptom of a urinary tract infection, although estrogen depletion may be a cause of it. The distal vagina and urethra are derived from similar embryologic structure and are both sensitive to estrogen stimulation and depletion.

Baseline evaluation: No historical contraindications for estrogen use. Pelvic exam, cytology, breast exam and endometrial biopsy benign.

Begin estrogen therapy at lowest available dose from days 1–25 of each month. An oral progestin, medroxyprogesterone, 10 mg/day, or norethindrone acetate, 5 mg/day, is given from day 16–25.

↓ 4 weeks

If vasomotor symptoms are intolerable, increase to a higher estrogen dosage, continue progestin therapy day 16–25.

↓ 4 weeks

If symptoms are tolerable, continue present regimen.

↓ 6 months

If symptoms are tolerable with fewer flushes noted while off medication, reduce daily estrogen dosage.

↓ 6 months

If symptoms are tolerable but still bothersome during the drug-free period, continue present regimen and perform annual endometrial sampling.

↓ 6 months

If symptoms are tolerable with minimal symptoms during the drug-free period, attempt to terminate estrogen treatment.

Figure 17-2. Treatment of vasomotor symptoms. The lowest effective dose of estrogen is determined based on the patient's symptomatic response. Patients with an intact uterus are given progestin for 10 days during each cycle. The drug-free period is used to assess the natural course of the climacteric.

Prior to attempts at treatment with estrogen, an infectious etiology must be ruled out. Estrogen therapy similar to that for vaginal atrophy is appropriate. Maintenance dosages should again be as low as necessary to achieve the desired clinical response.

The increased vascularity resulting from estrogen therapy is associated with increased blood flow through the periurethral venous plexus. This may result in small increases in periurethral pressures, occasionally sufficient to correct urinary stress incontinence in some postmenopausal subjects.

OSTEOPOROSIS. The prophylactic treatment of osteoporosis remains a disputed indication for the use of estrogens. Multiple studies have demonstrated that estrogens are effective in decreasing the rate of bone resorption.[11,12] In contrast to treatment of vasomotor symptoms, estrogen therapy for a minimum of 6 years appears necessary to maintain the beneficial effects.[13] Accelerated bone loss is found after discontinuation of estrogen replacement. While the classic patient who develops osteoporosis is slender and an inactive Caucasian, the present clinical use of estrogen for prophylaxis has not been selective enough to demonstrate value when evaluated by cost-benefit analysis.[14] Special consideration for treatment should be given to patients who develop ovarian failure prior to the age of 40.

The majority of studies evaluating the ability of estrogen to prevent accelerated bone loss have dealt with high dosages of estrogens (i.e., 1.25 to 2.5 mg of conjugated estrogens). Mestranol in a dose of 20 mcg/day has been shown effective in preventing bone loss and capable of increasing bone density in subjects 3 to 6 years following castration.[15] Conjugated estrogens at a dose of 0.625 mg/day appear effective in reducing the incidence of subsequent fractures during a prolonged study period.[13] It has been suggested that the use of supplemental calcium prior to discontinuing estrogen replacement may prevent accelerated bone loss after estrogen withdrawal.[12] Further long-term studies to determine the lowest effective dose of estrogen and the value

of calcium supplementation are necessary before prophylactic treatment of osteoporosis becomes a generally accepted indication for estrogen therapy.

Estrogen is used in the treatment of established osteoporosis. While few studies have shown that estrogens started beyond 3 years after menopause can increase bone mass, estrogens alone or in conjunction with other agents (vitamin D and calcium) can decrease the incidence of new fractures.[16,17] Equivalents of conjugated estrogens in excess of 0.625 mg/day were used in most reports. Other agents proposed for the treatment of osteoporosis include sodium fluoride, calcitonin, and vitamin D metabolites.[12]

PSYCHOLOGICAL ASPECT. Estrogens may be of benefit in improving the sense of well-being in normal menopausal subjects at a daily dose of 0.625 mg of conjugated estrogens.[18] One mechanism of accomplishing this is to reduce the incidence of vasomotor symptoms. Others have suggested that estrogen can increase the duration of time spent in REM sleep and reduce the sleep-latency period, thereby causing an elevation in mood.[19] The data, however, are not consistent and appear dependent on population as well as testing modalities.[19] It is of interest that while estrogens are effective in reducing vaginal atrophy they have not been shown to improve libido. Estrogens, however, are not approved nor are they reliable as psychotherapeutic agents.

Clinical Uses During the Reproductive Years

DYSFUNCTIONAL UTERINE BLEEDING. Abnormal, heavy uterine bleeding in a reproductive-age female is most commonly caused by anovulation. Due to the absence of progesterone, the endometrium overgrows its blood supply and rests tenuously on an unstable matrix. Bleeding follows breakdown and sloughing of the endometrium without the normal hemostatic controls induced by progesterone. If treated early, progesterone alone is usually effective in stabilizing the endometrium and controlling the bleeding. If extensive endometrial sloughing has occurred, as is seen following a prolonged course of bleeding, exogenous estrogens (i.e., conjugated estrogen 5 mg/day for 14 days) may be required to induce proliferation and stabilization of the now denuded endometrium. Concurrently, the exogenous estrogens will stimulate production of progesterone receptors, making the endometrium more responsive to the effects of exogenous progestins, such as medroxyprogesterone 10 mg/day for the last 7 days of treatment. Treatment regimens have included intravenous administration of estrogens (25 mg of conjugated estrogen) every 4 hours until the bleeding stabilizes, or a maximum of six doses.[20] This form of treatment is reserved for patients requiring a rapid response. In these cases, once the patient is stabilized, oral contraceptives with intermediate-strength progestin may be administered for 21 days, and a synchronized planned withdrawal bleed will then result. Failure to stabilize with intravenous estrogens should in most cases necessitate a diagnostic curettage. Bleeding resulting from the prolonged use of progestin or progestin-dominant oral contraceptives may be treated by the addition of 1.25 to 2.5 mg/day of conjugated estrogens for 2 weeks.

While estrogens are extremely useful and effective in cases of dysfunctional uterine bleeding, an examination must rule out the presence of a pregnancy, cervical lesion, traumatic vaginal lesion, or a coagulopathy.

In cases of bleeding secondary to anovulation, a progestin administered each month or every 2 months following the last menstrual period will prevent such a recurrence. Attempts should be made to determine the cause of the anovulation. Consideration should be given for an endometrial biopsy before treatment to safeguard against a neoplastic lesion or the presence of a premalignant lesion (i.e., adenomatous hyperplasia).

DYSMUCORRHEA. In infertility patients with scanty or poor-quality cervical mucus at the presumed time of ovulation, exogenous estrogens have been used to improve the quality of the cervical mucus. Estrogen administration to hypogonadal females causes changes in the water content, pH, electrolytes, and protein concentrations of cervical mucus. These are clinically demonstrated by increased volume, transparency, ferning, spinnbarkeit, and sperm penetration. A dose of 0.3 to 0.625 mg of conjugated estrogens can be given daily during the mid- to late-follicular phase, days 8 through 14. The mechanism whereby estrogens are effective in patients with dysmucorrhea is not known. Patients with dysmucorrhea have not been shown to be hypoestrogenic. Estriol has been promoted as an estrogen with preferential actions on cervical mucus and vaginal epithelium, although recent clinical studies have failed to support this suggestion.[21] Higher dosages of estrogens have been used effectively to counteract the antiestrogen effects of clomiphene citrate on cervical mucus. It is important to discontinue the use of exogenous estrogens following ovulation to reduce the chance of any teratogenic effect. The use of estrogens in excess of 0.625 mg of conjugated estrogens may delay ovulation.

INTERCEPTION. High doses of estrogens have been used to prevent pregnancy following unprotected intercourse. Diethylstilbesterol 25 mg twice a day or conjugated estrogens 30 mg/day for 5 days may be used within 72 hours of coitus to prevent pregnancy. A failure rate of 0.5 percent has been reported.[22] Treatment should be limited to unpredictable and potentially conceptual exposures (e.g., rape, mechanical contraceptive defects). Treatment is associated with significant nausea, possible vomiting, and an increased incidence of ectopic pregnancy in failed treatments.[22] The patient must be fully counseled concerning potential teratogenic effects of high-dose estrogens if a pregnancy is already established or treatment is ineffective.

Uses During Adolescence

HYPOGONADAL STATES. Exogenous estrogens may be utilized to stimulate sexual development in hypogonadal female individuals. A thorough investigation should precede any such treatment. Failure to diagnose a brain tumor, sex chromosomal anomaly with a Y chromosome, other endocrinologic disorders, or systemic disorders associated with certain hypogonadal states (e.g., cardiac and renal abnormalities) could be extremely detrimental to the patient.

Cyclic administration of a daily dose of estrogen equivalent to 1.25 to 2.5 mg of conjugated estrogens for 3 weeks out of 4 is sufficient to maximally stimulate development of secondary sex characteristics. After a plateau in breast development is achieved, the dose may be readjusted. A progestational compound should be added for the last 7 to 10 days of estrogen therapy each month. Menstruation, a desired response in young individuals, should occur with these dosages. Long-acting oral estrogens may also be used for maintenance therapy. The cyclic administration of a progestin will still be required each month. Oral contraceptives are not appropriate substitutes for replacement therapy as the dosage of estrogen in oral contraceptives necessary to induce secondary sex characteristics and maintain menstrual function exceeds that required in substitutional therapy.

TREATMENT OF TALL STATURE. Administration of estrogens prior to attainment of peak growth velocity is capable of prematurely closing epiphyses and thereby reducing a subject's potential height. While the indication remains controversial, considerable experience has been gained.[23] Dose equivalents of 2.5 to 20 mg/day of conjugated estrogens have been used with success. Predicted heights are calculated from available charts after obtaining films to assess the present bone age. Treatment should be started at a bone age around 11 years to assure a reliable response. Following initiation of treatment a relative increase in growth velocity is noted, as well as accelerated maturation of the bone age. After achieving a bone age of 15 to 16 years, treatment is discontinued. Minimal further growth may be expected beyond this point. The long-term effects of such treatment are not known. It is essential that the patient, her parents, and the physician feel such treatment is justified prior to commencing therapy. The addition

of a progestational agent for 7 to 10 days each month is advised.

Adverse Effects of Estrogen Therapy

ENDOMETRIAL CARCINOMA. The incidence of low-grade endometrial carcinoma is increased by the use of unopposed estrogen therapy. Estimated increases in relative risk vary between 1.7- and 15-fold.[24,25] Dose and duration of therapy positively correlate with the occurrence of endometrial carcinoma. Cyclic therapy has not been shown to reduce the occurrence of endometrial carcinoma. Because of these findings, the indications and duration of therapy have been reassessed. The addition of a progestational compound is now strongly encouraged during estrogen replacement when the uterus is present. Some studies have suggested that 10 days of a progestational compound each month reduce the incidence of endometrial carcinoma to or below that found in an untreated population.[26,27] A further discussion of the use of progestins in replacement therapy is presented later in this chapter.

BREAST CARCINOMA. A recent study has suggested an increased incidence of breast cancer associated with estrogen replacement.[28] Statistical significance is noted only if oophorectomized patients are eliminated from the study population. The majority of studies have been unable to confirm an increased risk in postmenopausal women taking estrogen therapy.[29-31] Progestational therapy has not been shown to be effective in reducing the incidence of breast carcinoma.

THROMBOPHLEBITIS. In contrast to the findings with oral contraceptives, menopausal estrogen therapy has not been associated with an increased incidence of idiopathic thrombophlebitis.[31] The lower dosages of estrogens used in replacement therapy may in part explain the failure of association. In addition, mestranol, a common estrogen in oral contraceptives, may cause a greater stimulation of fibrinogen and a greater depression of antithrombin III than is seen with comparable doses of conjugated estrogens. The use of estrogens in patients with a previous history of thrombophlebitis or in situations predisposing to thrombophlebitis (i.e., surgery) is contraindicated.

CORONARY VASCULAR DISEASE. While the use of oral contraceptives in older-age females is associated with an increased risk of coronary vascular disease, few data are available to support this association with menopausal estrogen replacement. Several studies have found no increased risk.[32,33] One study reported a reduced incidence of expected myocardial infarctions in hysterectomized patients started on estrogens and followed for 5 to 28 years.[34]

CEREBRAL VASCULAR DISEASE AND HYPERTENSION. In contrast to oral contraceptives, replacement therapy has not been found to increase the likelihood of a stroke nor is there a strong association with hypertension.[33]

GALLBLADDER DISEASE. The Boston Collaborative study reported a 2.5-fold increase in gallbladder disease during estrogen replacement therapy.[31] This finding is supported by reports of higher concentrations of cholesterol found in bile after estrogen treatment. Oral administration of estrogens, causing the liver to be exposed to high concentrations of estrogens, may in part explain these findings despite the relatively low doses used. Parenteral or vaginal administration of estrogens potentially may reduce this complication.

GLUCOSE INTOLERANCE. The detrimental effect of estrogens on glucose tolerance is a dose-related phenomenon. Menopausal replacement dosages exert little influence on fasting glucose concentrations. The alteration in glucose tolerance must be considered in the treatment of borderline diabetics and patients receiving hypoglycemic agents.

LEIOMYOMATA. Stimulation of leiomyomata may be found following estrogen therapy. The growth, however, is probably dose-related. Using estrogen therapy equivalent to 0.625 mg of conjugated estrogen or less, this complication is unlikely.

POSTMENOPAUSAL BLEEDING. Using a dose of estrogen capable of suppressing vasomotor symptoms and a progestational com-

pound, most postmenopausal subjects with intact uteri will be expected to bleed during the withdrawal phase. The use of estrogens without progestins increases the occurrence of unexpected postmenopausal bleeding. Bleeding at times other than the drug-free interval is an indication for endometrial sampling.

TERATOGENIC EFFECTS. The effects of large doses of estrogen administered during early pregnancy have been extensively studied in DES progeny. The inadvertent use of replacement doses of estrogens has not been proven to be teratogenic. In potentially fertile subjects estrogen therapy should be limited to the preconception period.

Estrogen Dose Forms

For most patients, short-acting oral estrogens are the preferred agents allowing for cyclic therapy and ease in dose adjustments. Whether natural or synthetic estrogens are more clinically beneficial has not been established. Well-designed studies documenting therapeutic superiority of either form are lacking. The proven carcinogenic effect of DES, along with the availability of equally effective steroid estrogens, suggests that DES and its cogeners should be used cautiously.

Oral Preparations. See Table 17-3.

Oral Combination Preparations. Oral dosage forms are available from various manufacturers; these combine estrogen with antianxiety agents (Melprin, Menrium). Use of these products is not rational for most patients. As with any fixed-combination preparation, doses of individual drugs cannot be adjusted without altering the dose of other components. The recommended dose schedule is 1 tablet three times daily for 21 days followed by a 1-week, drug-free period. This schedule is irrational both for the estrogen and the antianxiety components, and is not recommended.

Parenteral Preparations. Many estrogen preparations are available for parenteral use. Due to the inconvenience and cost, short-acting forms are seldom utilized. Longer-acting es-

TABLE 17-3 ESTROGEN PREPARATIONS AND TABLET STRENGTHS

Preparation	Tablet Strength
Steroidal	
Conjugated estrogens (Premarin, Menotab, Ovest, and others): 50–60% sodium estrone sulfate and 20–35% sodium equilin sulfate	0.3, 0.625, 1.25, and 2.5 mg
Esterfied estrogens (Menest, Femogen, Estratabs and others): 75–85% sodium estrone sulfate and 6–15% sodium equilin sulfate	0.3, 0.625, 1.25, and 2.5 mg
Evex (esterified estrogens)	0.625 and 1.25 mg
Piperazine estrone sulfate (Ogen): Crystalline estrone solubilized as the sulfate and stabilized with piperazine	0.625, 1.25, 2.5, and 5 mg
Combined estrogen (Hormonin) Hormonin #1: 0.135 mg estriol, 0.7 mg estrone, and 0.3 mg estradiol Hormonin #2: 0.27 mg estriol, 1.4 mg estrone, and 0.6 mg estradiol	
Ethinyl estradiol (Estinyl, Feminone, and others)	0.02, 0.05, and 0.5 mg
Estradiol-17β (Estrace)	1 and 2 mg
Quinestrol (Estrovis)	100 μg
Nonsteroidal	
Diethylstilbestrol (various): Also available as enteric-coated tablets	0.1, 0.25, 0.5, 1 and 5 mg

trogens and subcutaneous implants offer the advantage of infrequent administration and are not presented to the liver as a large bolus, as is found with oral preparations. Variability in absorption, difficulties in individualizing the dosage, and the increased cost limit their utility. (Table 17-4)

Vaginal Preparations. For postmenopausal patients, when vulvovaginitis or urethritis are the only symptoms, use of vaginally applied estrogens may be indicated. Both estradiol and estrone are rapidly absorbed by the vaginal epithelium with plasma levels peaking in 3 to 4 hours after application.[10] Recommended doses have been shown to produce high blood levels of estrogen. Plasma levels may exceed those normally found in reproductive-age women. Since vaginal absorption may give levels similar to those achieved by oral dosing

regimens, dosing schedules currently recommended by manufacturers of vaginal creams and suppositories may be higher than needed. The recommended daily dose of 2 to 4 gm of conjugated estrogen creams contains 1.25 to 2.5 mg of estrogens. A more conservative dose of 1.25 mg daily of conjugated estrogens (or estrogen equivalent) used intravaginally for 1 week should be tried. After initial stimulation of the vaginal mucosa, administration of 1 gm once or twice weekly may control symptoms.

Vaginal Products
  Creams
    Conjugated estrogens 0.625 mg/gm (Premarin)
    Piperazine estrone sulfate 1.5 mg/gm (Ogen)
    Dienestrol 0.01 percent (DV, Estraguard, others)

TABLE 17-4 ESTROGENS FOR PARENTERAL USE

Available Parenteral Estrogens	Manufacturer's Recommended Dosage (mg)	Approximate Frequency of Administration
Estrone aqueous or oil suspensions	0.5–2	Once a week
Estradiol aqueous or oil suspension	0.2–1.5	Once a week
Estradiol cypronate	1–5	Once every 3–4 weeks
Estradiol valerate	10–20	Once every 4 weeks
Estradiol subcutaneous pellets	25	Once every 3 months

Suppositories
   Diethylstilbestrol 0.1 mg, 0.5 mg, 0.7 mg
   (various)
   Estrone 0.2 mg (ATV, Prinn-VS)
   Estradiol 0.5 mg, and testosterone 5 mg
   (test-Estrin)

PROGESTERONE AND PROGESTINS

The terms progestins and gestagens are used to describe the compounds with progesterone-like activity. One bioassay of progestin activity involves the ability of a compound to convert an estrogen-primed endometrium into a histologically luteal phase endometrium (Clauberg test in rabbits, Kaufman test in humans). Another assay tests the ability to support a pregnancy in an ovariectomized pregnant rat. The Greenblatt test evaluates the capacity of the drug to prolong the luteal phase after spontaneous ovulation. The Kaufman test comes closest to evaluating the physiologic phenomena as required in clinical practice. The test relies on descriptive characteristics, but the dosage of estrogen required for priming has not been standardized.

Chemistry and Metabolism

Progesterone, as shown in Figure 17-3, is secreted primarily by the corpus luteum but also by the placenta and adrenal glands. It is synthesized from cholesterol, which is converted to pregnenolone. This immediate precursor is converted to progesterone by a combined dehydrogenase and isomerase reaction.

Exogenous progesterone from any route is rapidly absorbed. Because progesterone is almost completely metabolized in one passage through the intestinal mucosa and liver, low doses administered orally are ineffective. In the blood stream progesterone shows a high affinity for cortisol-binding globulin and albumin and is 88.9 percent protein bound. A small amount is stored in body fat. The half-life of intravenously administered progesterone has been reported to range from 3 to 90 minutes.[35] Once-daily dosing regimens are usually effective, indicating a more prolonged action upon body tissues. Progesterone is metabolized in the liver, the endometrium, and the myometrium. Liver metabolism, which accounts for about two-thirds of all metabolic pathways, converts progesterone to pregnanediol. This and other metabolites are conjugated in the liver with glucuronic acid. Following injection of labeled progesterone, 50 to 60 percent of the metabolites are excreted via the kidney and 10 percent in the bile and feces, with the remainder unaccounted for.

Progesterone is most effective by parenteral administration. In equal doses, oral administration is about one-twelfth as effective, buccal about one-eighth effective, and intravaginal one-fifth as effective.[35] Buccal and intravaginal routes give variable absorption. Progesterone in oil (25 mg) given intramuscularly will achieve plasma levels equivalent to

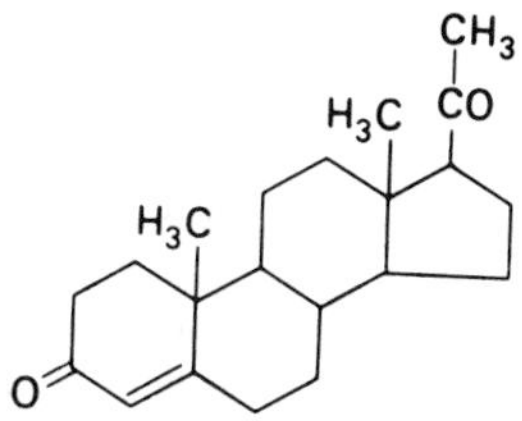

PROGESTERONE

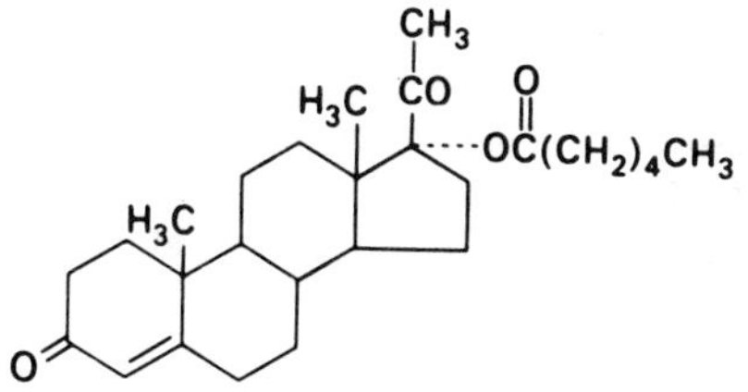

HYDROXYPROGESTERONE CAPROATE (Delalutin)

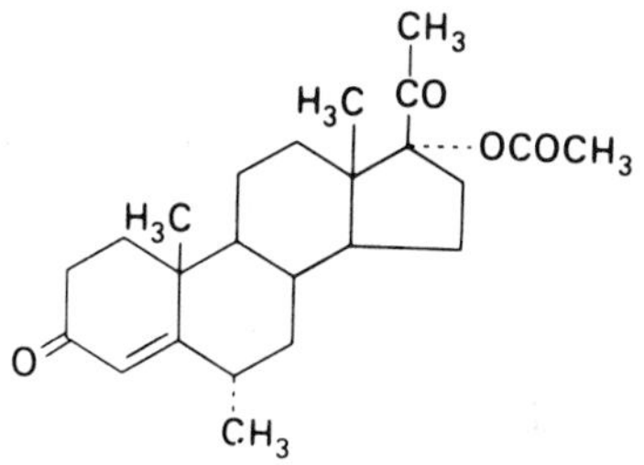

MEDROXYPROGESTERONE ACETATE (Provera)

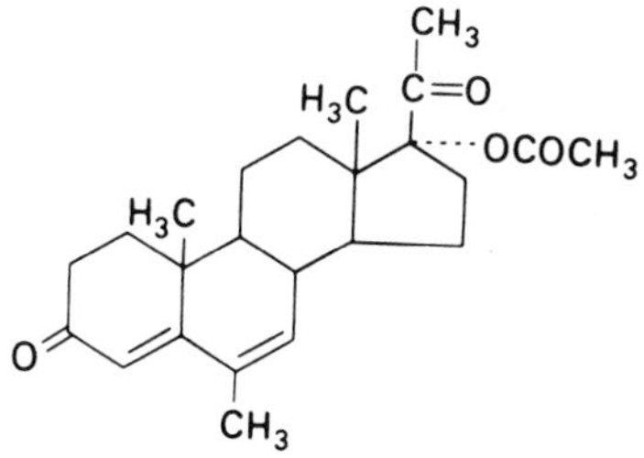

MEGESTROL ACETATE (Megase)

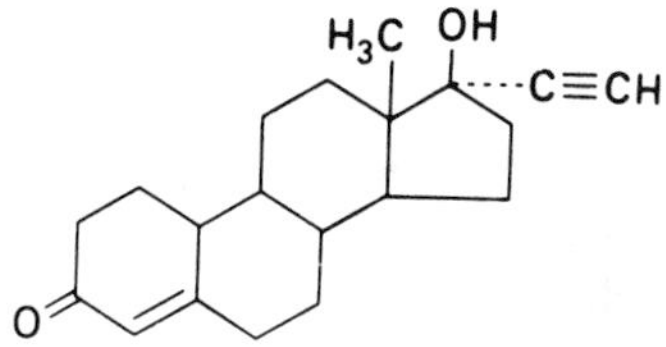

NORETHINDRONE

Figure 17-3. Chemical structure of progestins and natural progesterone. (From Csáky, TZ: *Cutting's Handbook of Pharmacology: The Actions and Uses of Drugs*, ed. 6, New York, Appleton-Century-Crofts, 1979, pp 377, 380, 381, 383, with permission.)

the concentrations seen during the midluteal phase.[36]

Synthetic progestins have been developed to overcome limitations of the naturally occurring hormone. Products are available that are orally effective, longer acting, and cause less irritation at injection sites.

C-19 and 19-Nor Progestins. These compounds are derived from testosterone. Addition of an ethinyl group at C-17 on the steroid ring reduces the androgenicity of the parent compound, increases its oral activity, and elicits progestational characteristics. Removal of the methyl group (C-19) attached at C-10 (thus, 19-nor testosterone) further enhances progestational activity and reduces the androgenic activity of the parent compound. These two modifications of testosterone are responsible for the potent oral progestin, norethindrone (17-α ethinyl-19-nortestosterone). In attempting to prolong the half-life of norethindrone, an acetate group may be added at C-17, forming norethindrone acetate. In humans, the acetate on norethindrone acetate is readily cleaved, accounting for the relatively equal potency of norethindrone and norethindrone acetate.

Norethindrone has a half-life approaching 8 hours. Excretion is predominantly via the urinary system as conjugated metabolites. The C-19 progestins are metabolized similarly to progesterone, undergoing reduction of the 4-ene-3-one group in ring A. The C-17 ethinyl group is not cleaved during in vivo metabolism and is believed to be responsible for preventing conversion of the C-19 progestins to ethinyl estradiol.

Progesterone-like Synthetic Progestins (C-21). Adding a hydroxyl group at C-17 of progesterone in the α-position dramatically reduces progestational activity. Esterification with a relatively long alkyl group at this position produces modestly potent but long-acting progestins. This is the case for 17-α hydroxyprogesterone caproate, shown in Figure 17-3, an effective, parenteral progestational agent. Methylation at C-6 of 17-α hydroxyprogesterone acetate produces medroxyprogesterone acetate with increased progestational activity permitting oral as well as parenteral administration. The addition of a double bond between C-6 and C-7 of medroxyprogesterone acetate still further increases the progestational activity (Megesterol).

Changing the methyl group on C-19 of progesterone from the β-position to the α-position (dydrogesterone) increases the progestational activity on the endometrium following oral administration. This change in spatial configuration appears to result in loss of hypothalamic activity (i.e., thermogenic changes and suppression of ovulation).

The metabolism of these progestins is similar to the parent compound. Metabolism occurs predominantly in the liver involving hydroxylation and conjugation. The majority of metabolites are excreted in the urine.

Mechanism of Action

Progesterone appears to function intracellularly in a manner similar to estrogen. Entry into the cell is by passive diffusion. The high-affinity, low-capacity binding protein differs from the estrogen receptor; it consists of two subunits and binds two molecules of progesterone per complex. Bound to the receptor, progesterone enters the nucleus and interacts in some fashion with DNA. In contrast to the estrogen receptor, progesterone, rather than stimulating an overall replenishment of cytosol receptors, actually decreases the number of progesterone receptors. Progesterone not only decreases its own receptors but also those of estrogen. This is one mechanism to explain inhibition of estrogen activity by progesterone. Progesterone is capable of inducing estradiol-17β dehydrogenase, an enzyme responsible for conversion of estradiol to estrone. Reducing the tissue concentration of estradiol, progesterone further antagonizes the action of estrogens. The antagonism of estrogen by progesterone is a consistent finding in the myometrium and the epithelial component of the endometrium. Several studies have suggested that when estrogen and progesterone are administered, the stromal compartment fails to recognize the suppressive action of progesterone.[37,38] Progesterone may not be uniformly suppressive on the effects of estrogen; it does not decrease the efficacy of estrogen in reducing bone reabsorption.

Progesterone also functions as an antagonist for aldosterone. It is presumed to act as a competitive inhibitor, although further investigation is needed to clarify its mechanism of action.

Pharmacologic Actions

The majority of actions of progesterone require the concurrent or prior administration of estrogen. A list of progesterone actions is given in Table 17-5.

Clinical Uses during the Menopausal Years. In the first portion of this chapter the use of a progestin during estrogen replacement was advised in patients with an intact uterus. However, the value of progestins in reducing the occurrence of endometrial carcinoma has not been uniformly accepted. Recommendations

TABLE 17-5   PHYSIOLOGIC EFFECTS OF PROGESTERONE

Genital Tract
  Endometrial glandular epithelium
    Reduces mitotic activity
    Increases glandular secretions
    Suppresses estrogen stimulation
  Endometrial stroma
    Increases mitotic activity in response to estrogen
    Causes vascular tortuosity
  Myometrium
    Reduces myometrial activity
  Cervix
    Reduces glandular secretions
    Inhibits ferning of cervical mucus
    Decreases elasticity of mucus
Breast
  Stimulates alveolar growth
Skin
  Reduces hair follicle responsiveness to androgens (inhibits 5-α-reductase)
Bone
  Decreases bone resorption
Kidney
  Inhibits aldosterone activity
Coagulation
  No effect
Lipids
  Decreases serum concentrations of high-density lipoprotein

to prolong progestational treatment to 10 days each month is in part a reaction to questions raised concerning the efficacy of progesterone when used for 7 days or less. A study by Jick[39] is the most commonly quoted epidemiologic study failing to show beneficial effects of progesterone. The retrospective study was biased by the use of a high proportion of orthopedic patients as controls. Gambrell et al.[40] have previously shown that 10 mg of medroxyprogesterone or 5 mg norethindrone acetate for 7 to 10 days each month is effective in treating various degrees of endometrial hyperplasia. In a prospective study from Wilford Hall[27] the protective influence of progestins in preventing endometrial carcinoma was demonstrated. A prospective study from Great Britain[26] and

a retrospective study by Hammond and co-workers[41] further emphasized the protective influence of progestins in preventing endometrial carcinoma. All three studies have suggested that the greatest benefit may be seen if progestins are used for 10 or more days each month.

Progestins may be effective in relieving vasomotor symptoms. Intramuscular medroxyprogesterone acetate in doses of 150 mg monthly relieves vasomotor symptoms in up to 89 percent of treated patients.[8] Less frequent injections and oral administration also appear to be of benefit. Temporary depression has been associated with the use of progestins as well as worsening of vaginal atrophic changes. The effects of progestins on osteoporosis require further study.

Clinical Uses During the Reproductive Years

ENDOMETRIAL HYPERPLASIA.   Similar to cervical intraepithelial neoplasia, endometrial hyperplasia has been suggested as a precursor of endometrial carcinoma. With increasing degrees of atypia, better correlations exist between hyperplasia and carcinoma. Progestational agents have been shown to be effective in treating endometrial hyperplasia and are therefore believed to be effective in reducing the likelihood of progression to endometrial carcinoma. Oral regimens have varied from continuous administration of C-21 progestational compounds (i.e., megesterol 20 to 40 mg twice a day)[42] to a 10 to 14 day/month treatment protocol with medroxyprogesterone acetate 10 mg/day or norethindrone acetate 5 mg/day[40] for 3 to 6 months. Parenteral administration may also be used on a continuous basis for a 3- to 6-month period (medroxyprogesterone acetate suspension 400 mg IM every 2 weeks).[42] Continuous therapy is based on a rationale similar to that for endometrial carcinoma. Treatment may be complicated by bleeding from the atrophic endometrium. This may mandate further endometrial sampling to exclude the possibility of a focus of endometrial carcinoma not found during the first endometrial sampling. Once the appropriate diagnostic steps have been taken, discontinuation of the medication for 2 weeks or the addition of a 1-week course of estrogen are sufficient to stop the bleeding and allow for completion of the planned treatment regimen. The intermittent therapy relies on induction of progesterone receptors during the nontreatment portion of the cycle to promote a greater response. In addition, the superficial and intermediate layers of the endometrium are sloughed. Use of C-19 progestational compounds should cause endometrial atrophy by their androgenic characteristics as well as their progestational activity.

All patients being treated for endometrial hyperplasia should undergo a thorough endometrial biopsy the month after discontinuing progestational treatment. If intermittent therapy is to be utilized for a prolonged period, a biopsy should be repeated at 3 months after the initial diagnosis while off progestin therapy. Routine endometrial sampling should be performed as part of follow-up at 6-month to 1-year intervals in subjects at risk.

ANOVULATORY BLEEDING. The administration of progestins is effective in the control of bleeding resulting from unopposed estrogen. Progestins stabilize the endometrium and, on withdrawal, cause a synchronous shedding of the endometrium. Various 5 to 7 day treatment regimens have been used; medroxyprogesterone acetate 10 mg/day, norethindrone acetate 5 mg/day, and progestin-dominant oral contraceptives 4 tablets/day. Progesterone in oil (50 to 100 mg IM) has also been utilized. During the course of therapy bleeding should stop and should be followed by withdrawal bleeding 2 to 7 days after discontinuing therapy. The patient must be made aware that the ensuing bleeding is to be expected.

In patients with prolonged bleeding where the endometrium may be exhausted, estrogen therapy followed by a progestin is often more effective. With either treatment, after the expected withdrawal bleeding an investigation should be made to determine the cause of anovulation. Plans should be established to prevent recurrences either by correcting the cause of anovulation or establishing a monthly (or alternate month) course of exogenous progestins for a duration of 7 to 10 days. Clinical parameters (i.e., cervical mucus) should be used to evaluate the presence of unopposed estrogen and reduce the possibilities of an undiagnosed pregnancy prior to administration of prophylactic progestins. The alternate monthly use of progestins is advantageous in observing for spontaneous ovulation and reducing the number of physician visits. If spontaneous ovulation and menses occur, treatment need not be considered unless the patient fails to bleed within another 60 days. Premenstrual symptoms and temperature charts are useful in differentiating ovulatory from anovulatory bleeding.

If contraception is required, oral contraceptives may be used rather than progestins alone to prevent anovulatory, irregular bleeding. The patient should be informed that anovulation is likely to persist after discontinuation of the oral contraceptives.

In patients over the age of 35 or with a long history of anovulation, an office curettage should be performed prior to initiating therapy.

ENDOMETRIOSIS, CONTRACEPTION. For a discussion of this topic, see Chapters 16 and 22.

DYSMENORRHEA. Progestins have been used during the luteal phase to prevent dysmenorrhea. More effective agents are now available (Chap. 21).

DIAGNOSTIC AGENT IN AMENORRHEA. The most common cause of amenorrhea during the reproductive years is pregnancy. Progestin should not be used as a pregnancy test. If pregnancy is ruled out by a human chorionic gonadotropin determination or physical examination, progesterone or a progestin may be used. Withdrawal bleeding documents the presence of an intact, responsive, estrogen-primed endometrium. Progesterone in oil, 50 to 100 mg in a single injection, may be used or an oral progestin for 5 to 7 days (i.e., medroxyprogesterone acetate 10 mg/day).

INADEQUATE LUTEAL PHASE. Natural progesterone is effective in the treatment of an inadequate luteal phase resulting in infertility or habitual abortion.[43] Documentation relies on either endometrial histologic studies showing a lag of 2 or more days in secretory changes of the endometrium or serum progesterone concentrations 2 SD below those expected during any 3 days of the luteal phase. The etiology is believed to be inadequate follicle-stimulating hormone production during the follicular phase, hyperprolactinemia, an inadequate luteinizing hormone surge at midcycle, decreased progesterone receptors, or an unknown luteolytic factor. Gonadotropin therapy is an alternative treatment regimen to progestins. The inadequate luteal phase is more commonly seen with clomiphene citrate use.

Progesterone therapy is best accomplished by using vaginal suppositories containing 25 mg of progesterone twice a day.[43] Therapy is begun 2 days following a thermogenic rise in basal body temperature and continued for 6 weeks or until menstrual bleeding occurs. Progesterone in oil 12.5 mg/day IM may be substituted for the vaginal preparation. The serum progesterone concentrations obtained following either route of administration approximate those found during the normal luteal phase.[36] Use of synthetic progestins is strongly discouraged.

Progesterone as a fertility agent is not approved by the Food and Drug Administration. The patient must be familiar with the possible teratogenic risks involved with such treatment and the indications for its use. Treatment beyond 6 weeks after conception should not be necessary as the placenta becomes the major source of progesterone synthesis.

PREMENSTRUAL SPOTTING. Progestins have been recommended for the treatment of recurrent premenstrual spotting. A progestin is administered orally for the last 7 days of the luteal phase. It was initially conceived as treatment for a recurrent inadequate luteal phase. Treatment is occasionally effective, although the mechanism is not clear. Precautions should be taken to prevent the occurrence of conception during treatment.

THREATENED ABORTION. Genetic abnormalities account for 60 percent of all abortions. Recognizing the high percentage of threatened abortions that proceed normally to term, the empiric use of progestins in this situation is strongly discouraged. Use of progestins with threatened abortion results in an increased incidence of missed abortions. 17-α Hydroxyprogesterone caproate, the most commonly used agent in threatened abortions, is devoid of gestagen activity in the oophorectomized rat model, the classic bioassay of gestational activity.

PREVENTION OF PREMATURE LABOR. Progesterone has been shown to decrease uterine activity. A randomized study by Johnston[44] reported that 17-α hydroxyprogesterone caproate 250 mg/week administered after the first trimester resulted in prolongation of the gestational period in patients with a history of premature labor. The study population was small, although statistical significance was obtained. Many other agents are available for the acute treatment of premature labor. If 17-α hydroxyprogesterone caproate is to be used, treatment should not be initiated until 16 weeks, following major embryologic development.

Treatment Prior to Reproductive Age. Medroxyprogesterone acetate has been used in the treatment of precocious puberty. It appears to have little beneficial effect upon the rate of growth and ultimate height. Its use has been recommended to reduce breast development and produce an amenorrheic state. Except in extreme situations, counseling appears a safer and more logical treatment. An amenorrheic state may be obtained using doses of medroxyprogesterone acetate 150 mg IM every 3 to 6 months if the patient is felt to be incapable of managing menstrual bleeding in the opinion of the physician and her guardians. A thorough evaluation of the cause of precocious puberty is necessary prior to any treatment. Table 17-6 lists progestin products available for clinical use.

Complications Associated with Progestin Use

BLEEDING. During prolonged use of progestins uterine bleeding may occur. In using medroxyprogesterone acetate suspension

TABLE 17-6 PROGESTIN PRODUCTS AVAILABLE

Product	Trade Name	Route	Strength Supplied
Progesterone Inj USP	Femotrone, Progelan, and others	IM	In oil and aqueous* 25, 50, and 100 mg/ml
17-Hydroxyprogesterone caproate in oil	Delalutin, Gesterol LA, Hylutin, and others	IM	125 and 250 mg/ml
Medroxyprogesterone acetate	Depo Provera	IM	100 and 400 mg/ml†
	Amen, Curretab, Provera	PO	2.5 and 10 mg
Norethindrone	Norlutin	PO	5 mg
Norethindrone acetate	Norlutate	PO	5 mg
Dydrogesterone	Duphaston, Gynorest	PO	5 and 10 mg

* Progesterone suppositories are not commercially available but may be prepared from the progesterone suspension. See Ref. 43.
† Indicated only for advanced metastatic endometrial carcinoma.

as a contraceptive approximately 10 percent of subjects will discontinue the medication due to persistent abnormal uterine bleeding; however, estrogen is effective in correcting this complication.

HYPERTENSION. Most studies have failed to show a change in blood pressure with prolonged use of oral progestins.[45] Medroxyprogesterone acetate in high dosages, for the treatment of precocious puberty, has been reported to cause hypertension and other symptoms similar to Cushing's syndrome.[46]

DEPRESSION. The use of progestins for contraception or treatment of endometriosis and postmenopausal vasomotor symptoms is associated with mild depression. The mechanism for this phenomenon has not been determined nor is its frequency established.

WEIGHT GAIN. An increase in weight has been found following progestin therapy. The increase in weight is secondary both to water retention and residual anabolic activity in some of the synthetic progestins.

WATER RETENTION. Progesterone is a diuretic due to its inhibition of aldosterone. The body, however, readily compensates for this diuretic activity by increased production of aldosterone. Water retention during progestin therapy possibly results from fluctuating progestin concentrations with excessive compensatory increases in aldosterone production. The use of megesterol has been reported to produce a carpal tunnel-like syndrome.[47] This complication is believed to result from increased water retention in the collagen matrix of the aponeurosis, as may occur during pregnancy.

PROLONGED AMENORRHEA. The use of medroxyprogesterone acetate suspension may result in prolonged amenorrhea. The absorption and duration of action of this compound is exceedingly variable.

TERATOGENICITY. While speculation exists, there are few reports to support teratogenic effects resulting from the clinical use of natural progesterone. Controversy exists on the teratogenic actions of synthetic progestins. Administration of progestins during early pregnancy is reported to increase, by over eightfold, the incidence of the VACTERL syndrome.[44] VACTERL is an acronym for a complex of anomalies involving the vertebral, anal, cardiac, tracheal, esophageal, renal, or limb structures. Cardiac anomalies are the most commonly found abnormalities of the syndrome. In the Collaborative Perinatal Project[48] a relative increased risk of 1.8 was found for cardiac anomalies when progestins were used during early gestation. No other statistically significant increase in anomalies was found with the use of progestins. Therefore, their use during pregnancy should be restricted unless a specific indication necessitates their use.

REFERENCES

1. Bolt HM: Metabolism of estrogens—natural and synthetic. *Pharmacol Ther* 4:155, 1979
2. *Physicians' Desk Reference.* Available from Parke-Davis, Division of Warner-Lambert Co., Morris Plains, NJ 07950.
3. Clark JH, Peck EJ: Nuclear binding and biological response. In *Female Sex Steroid.* New York, Springer-Verlag, 1979, pp 70–97
4. Clark JH, Paszko Z, Peck EJ Jr: Nuclear binding and retention of the estrogen receptor complex: Relation to the agonist and antagonist properties of estriol. *Endocrinology* 100:91, 1977
5. Martucci C, Fishman J: Direction of estradiol metabolism as a control of its hormonal action—uterotrophic activity of estradiol metabolites. *Endocrinology* 101:1709, 1977
6. Hansten PD: Hormone interactions. In Hansten PD (ed): *Drug Interactions* Philadelphia, Lee and Febiger, 1975, p 165
7. Dickey RP: The pill: Physiology, pharmacology, and clinical use. In Typer LB, Isenman AW (eds): *American College of Obstetrics and Gynecology Seminar in Family Planning.* Chicago, Knox, 1974
8. Bullock JL, Massey FM, Gambrell RD: Use of progesterone medroxy acetate to prevent menopausal symptoms. *Obstet Gynecol* 46:165, 1975
9. Clayden JR, Bell JW, Pollard P: Menopausal flushing: Double blind trial of a nonhormonal medication. *Br J Med* 4:409, 1974
10. Rigg LA, Hermann H, Yen SSC: Absorption of estrogens from vaginal creams. *N Engl J Med* 298:195, 1978
11. Recker RR, Saville PD, Heaney RP: Effects of oestrogens and calcium carbonate on bone loss in postmenopausal women. *Ann Intern Med* 87:649, 1977
12. Nordin BE, Peacock M, Aaron J, Crilly RG, et al: Osteoporosis and osteomalacia. *Clin Endocrinol Metab* 9:177, 1980
13. Weiss NS, Ure CL, Ballard JH, et al: Decreased risk of fractures of the hip and lower forearm with postmenopausal use of estrogens. *N Engl J Med* 303:1195, 1980
14. Weinstein MC: Estrogen use in postmenopausal women—costs, risks, and benefits. *N Engl J Med* 303:308, 1980
15. Aitken JM: Osteoporosis and its relation to estrogen deficiency. In Campbell S (ed): *The Management of the Menopause and Post-Menopausal Years.* MTP Press, Lancaster, England, 1976, p 225
16. Nordin BE, Horsman A, Crilly RG, Marshall DH, Simpson M: Treatment of spinal osteoporosis in postmenopausal women. *Br Med J* 280:451, 1980
17. Heany RP, Recker RR, Saville PD: Menopausal changes in calcium balance. *J Lab Clin Med* 92:953, 1978
18. Scheider MA, Brotherton PL, Hailes J: The effect of exogenous estrogens on depression in menopausal women. *Med J Aust* 2:162, 1977
19. Schiff I, Ryan KJ: Benefits of estrogen replacement. *Obstet Gynecol Surv* 35:400, 1980
20. Speroff L: Dysfunctional uterine bleeding. In Speroff L, Glass RH, Kase NG (eds): *Clinical Gynecologic Endocrinology and Infertility.* Baltimore, Williams & Wilkins, 1978, p 151
21. Rezai P, Dmowski WP, Auletta F, Scommegna A: Effect of oral estriol on cervical secretions and on ovulatory response in infertile women. *Fertil Steril* 31:627, 1979
22. Morris JM, Van Wagenen G: Interception: The use of postovulatory estrogens to prevent implantation. *Am J Obstet Gynecol* 115:101, 1973
23. Kuhn N, Blunek W, Stahnke N, et al.: Estrogen treatment in tall girls. *Acta Paediatr Scand* 66:161, 1977
24. Horowitz RI, Feinstein AR: Alternative analytic methods for case control studies of estrogens and endometrial carcinoma. *N Engl J Med* 299:1089, 1978
25. Antunes CM, Stolley PD, Rosenhein NB, Davies JL, et al: Endometrial cancer and estrogen use. *N Engl J Med* 300:9, 1979
26. Patterson ME, Wade-Evans T, Sturdee DW, Thom M, Studd JW: Endometrial disease after treatment with oestrogens and progestogens in the climacteric. *Br Med J* 279:822, 1980
27. Gambrell RD, Massey FM, Castaneda TA, Ugenas A, et al: Use of the progestogen challenge test to reduce the risk of endometrial carcinoma. *Obstet Gynecol* 55:732, 1980
28. Ross RK, Pagonini Hill A, Gerkins VR, et al: A case control study of menopausal estrogen therapy and breast cancer. *JAMA* 243:1635, 1980
29. Gambrell RD, Massey FM, Castaneda TA, et al: Estrogen therapy and breast cancer in postmenopausal women. *Obstet Gynecol* 23:265, 1974

30. Hoover R, Gray LA, Cole P, et al: Menopausal estrogens and breast cancer. *N Engl J Med* 295:401, 1976

31. Surgically confirmed gallbladder disease, venous thromboembolism, and breast tumors in relation to postmenopausal estrogen therapy: A report from The Boston Collaborative Drug Surveillance Program, Boston University Medical Center. *N Engl J Med* 290:15–19, 1974

32. Rosenberg L, Armstrong B, Jick H: Myocardial infarction and estrogen therapy in postmenopausal women. *N Engl J Med* 299:1256, 1976

33. Hammond CB, Jelovsek FR, Lee K, et al: Effects of long term estrogen therapy. *Am J Obstet Gynecol* 133:525, 1979

34. Burch JC, Byrd BF, Vaughn WK: The effect of long term estrogen on hysterectomized women. *Am J Obstet Gynecol* 118:778, 1974

35. Aufrere MB, Benson H: Progesterone: An overview and recent advances. *J Pharm Sci* 65:783, 1976

36. Johansson ED: Plasma levels of progesterone achieved by different routes of administration. *Acta Obstet Gynecol Scand* 19 (suppl):17, 1972

37. Tachi C, Tachi S, Lindner HR: Modification by progesterone of estradiol-induced cell proliferation, RNA synthesis and estradiol distribution in the rat uterus. *J Reprod Fertil* 31:59, 1972

38. Tchernitchin A: Effects of progesterone on the in vivo binding of estrogens by uterine cells. *Experientia* 32:1069, 1976

39. Jick H, Watkins RN, Hunter JR, et al: Replacement estrogens and endometrial cancer. *N Engl J Med* 299:1089, 1978

40. Gambrell RD, Massey FM, Castaneda TA, et al: Reduced incidence of endometrial cancer amongst women treated with progestogens. *J Am Geriatr Soc* 27:389, 1979

41. Hammond CB, Jelovsek FR, Lee K, et al: Effects of long-term estrogen replacement: Neoplasia. *Am J Obstet Gynecol* 133:537, 1979

42. Disaia PJ: Cancer of the corpus. In Disaia PJ, Morrow CP, Townsend DE (eds): *Gynecologic Oncology*. New York, Wiley, 1975, p 111

43. Jones GS: The luteal phase defect. *Fertil Steril* 27:351, 1976

44. Chez RA: Proceedings of the symposium: Progesterone, progestins, and fetal development. *Fertil Steril* 30:16, 1978

45. Hall WD, Douglas MB, Blumenstein BA, Hatcher RA: Blood pressure and oral progestational agents. *Am J Obstet Gynecol* 136:34, 1980

46. Richman RA, Underwood LE, French FS, Van Wyk JJ: Adverse effects of large doses of medroxyprogesterone in idiopathic isosexual precocity. *J Pediatr* 79:963, 1971

47. Disaia PJ, Morrow CP: Unusual side effect of megesterol acetate. *Am J Obstet Gynecol* 129:460, 1977

48. Heinonen OP, Slone D, Monson RR, et al: Cardiovascular birth defects and antenatal exposure to female sex hormones. *N Engl J Med* 296:67, 1977

18. Induction of Ovulation

CHAD I. FRIEDMAN   MOON H. KIM

Treatment of oligo-ovulation and anovulation is one of the most rewarding endeavors in the treatment of infertility. The number of agents available in clinical practice is limited, each with its specific indications and mechanism of action. While relatively safe and effective, such medications require close medical follow-up. This chapter reviews the more commonly used agents for induction of ovulation.

Before proceeding with induction of ovulation it is necessary to acknowledge anovulation as a presenting symptom of several major disease entities. A working diagnosis of the cause of anovulation should be established before treatment is commenced. Emphasis is placed on the patient's medical history and physical examination, while the use of generalized baseline endocrine studies is discouraged. Several texts are available for consultation on the evaluation of anovulation.[1,2]

CLOMIPHENE CITRATE

Chemistry

Clomid (Merrell National Laboratory) is a mixture (1:1 ratio) of *cis*- and trans-isomers of (aminoethoxy) phenyl-1,2-diphenyl-2-chloroethylene (see Fig. 18-1). Being structurally related to diethylstilbestrol and chlorotrianisene (TACE), it was initially thought to possess estrogenic activity. However, greater attention was placed on its antiestrogenic effects. Early studies evaluated its potential in the treatment of endometrial hyperplasia. In the early 1960s Greenblatt et al.[3] reported the efficacy of MRL 41 (clomiphene citrate) to induce ovulation in patients with secondary amenorrhea.

Mechanism of Action

Clomiphene citrate binds readily to the cytoplasmic estrogen receptor, undergoes nuclear transport, and is retained within the nucleus. In contrast to natural estrogens, it fails to induce cytosol receptor replenishment.[4] Clomiphene citrate is capable of demonstrating short-term estrogen actions, but functions as an antiestrogen if endogenous estrogens are available. The mechanism of action is similar to tamoxifen, which has also been utilized in Europe for induction of ovulation. In the United States, tamoxifen has been used as an estrogen antagonist in the treatment of estrogen-dependent tumors (i.e., endometrial carcinoma and breast carcinoma).

Clomiphene citrate is most effective in inducing ovulation in individuals with endogenous estrogen production. Functioning as an antiestrogen, the hypothalamus is believed to sense a hypoestrogenic environment and to respond with increased secretion of gonadotropins (luteinizing hormone, LH; follicle stimulating hormone, FSH). The gonadotropin surge recruits several ovarian follicular units from quiescence or early maturation into maturing follicles. Once properly primed, the follicles continue to mature, recruiting the pituitary hypothalamic axis for further stimula-

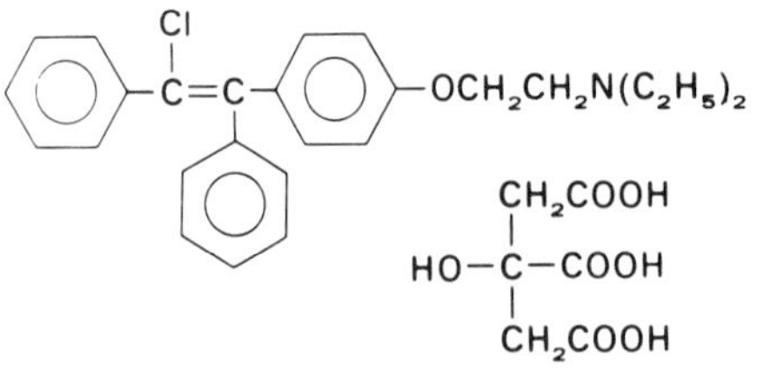

Figure 18-1. Chemical structure of clomiphene citrate. (From Csáky, TZ: *Cutting's Handbook of Pharmacology: The Actions and Uses of Drugs,* ed. 6, New York, Appleton-Century-Crofts, 1979, p 387)

tion of the follicle and a subsequent mid-cycle gonadotropin surge. It is apparent that in cases of severe pituitary or hypothalamic dysfunction clomiphene citrate is ineffective. In hypoestrogenic subjects its antiestrogenic activity is of little benefit in producing increased gonadotropin secretion. Figure 18-2 is an example of the expected changes in gonadotropins and steroids seen in a patient with polycystic ovarian disease (PCO) treated with clomiphene citrate.

Absorption and Metabolism

Clomiphene citrate is readily absorbed after oral administration. Up to 50 percent of the compound will be excreted within 5 days. Despite its relatively long half-life, less than 5 percent of the administered dose appears to be stored in fat.[5] It is excreted predominantly in feces, and traces may be found in feces 6 weeks after administration. The breakdown products of clomiphene citrate have not been well studied.

Pharmacologic Actions

Clinical Use. The use of clomiphene citrate in females should be restricted to individuals desiring a pregnancy. Clomiphene citrate has been used in adolescents with recurrent anovulatory bleeding, in the attempt to establish regular ovulatory cycles; however, there are few published reports to support long-term beneficial effects from clomiphene citrate.

The antiestrogenic action of clomiphene citrate makes it most useful as an ovulatory agent in patients with normal or increased endogenous estrogen production. Demonstration of withdrawal bleeding in response to an exogenous progestin helps to assess the likelihood of an ovulatory response to clomiphene citrate. Failure to bleed after progestin administration reduces the likelihood of an ovulatory response to therapy.

Dependent on the cause of anovulation, the administration of clomiphene citrate may be successful in inducing ovulation in greater than 80 percent of patients.[6] Pregnancy rates during six treatment cycles vary between 50 and 80 percent of the individuals ovulating successfully.[6,7] As the goal of treatment is pregnancy, a semen analysis and Huhner's test are performed before treatment is initiated. While it has been our practice to obtain a hysterosalpingogram before or within the first treatment cycle, others have advised deferring this diagnostic test until three ovulatory cycles have failed to result in pregnancy.[8] Laparoscopy is not performed until pregnancy has failed to occur despite six or more ovulatory cycles, unless the history or abnormal physical findings warrant intraperitoneal evaluation. Within three ovulatory cycles, the majority of clomid-related pregnancies will occur.[9] Beyond six ovulatory cycles, only a small percentage of pregnancies may be expected unless other causes of infertility are found and corrected. Pregnancies have been reported as late as the 29th ovulatory cycle[10] but the patient and physician must be cognizant of the diminishing benefit of continued treatment beyond six cycles.

Clomiphene citrate treatment is started at a dose of 50 mg/day for 5 days. Menstrual bleeding is usually induced, and clomiphene citrate begun on the fifth day of bleeding. Progestin administration before treatment has not been shown to alter the ovulation or pregnancy rate. The benefit of this regimen is a reduction in the likelihood of anovulatory bleeding during the course of treatment and the establishment of a uniform cyclic pattern of treatment.

Ovulation is expected to occur 5 to 11 days following discontinuation of clomiphene citrate. The daily dose of clomiphene citrate

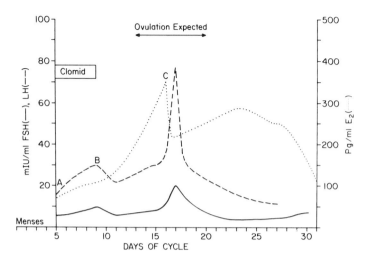

Figure 18-2. This is an idealized response of gonadotropins and estradiol to clomiphene citrate. A and B are labeled to draw attention to the persistent abnormal LH:FSH ratio in patients with PCO despite an ovulatory response. C represents the approximate time when human chorionic gonadotropins (HCG) may be administered in a clomiphene citrate-HCG regimen. A determination of serum estradiol would be helpful in determining follicular maturation in response to clomid at this point.

may be raised by 50-mg increments during each treatment cycle until ovulation is achieved. A positive correlation exists between the weight of the patient and the dose of clomiphene citrate required to achieve ovulation.[11] Clomiphene citrate in doses higher than required to achieve ovulation and a normal luteal phase will not increase the conception rate. Ovulation with the occurrence of ovarian hyperstimulation requires individualization of the therapeutic regimen. Decrements between standardized dose regimens may be achieved by prolonging treatment from 5 to 7 days at the preceding dose that failed to achieve ovulation. An alternative adjustment is to utilize the preceding dose for 2 days and the higher dose that resulted in hyperstimulation for the remaining 3 days of treatment. The use of dosages higher than required to achieve ovulation and treatment regimens in excess of 5 days are more likely to result in hyperstimulation.[12]

In addition to the use of clomiphene citrate in anovulatory patients, it has also been used in cases of oligo-ovulation. The average treatment cycle with clomiphene citrate is 34 days. The clinical definition of oligo-ovulation must be restricted to menstrual cycles in excess of 35 days to justify the risks and side effects associated with clomiphene citrate. Due to a relatively uniform response in repetitive cycles, clomiphene citrate may also be utilized

for regulation of ovulation when artificial insemination is required.[13]

Monitoring During Treatment. As documentation of ovulation is essential, one must by some means assess the presence of a functioning corpus luteum following treatment with clomiphene citrate. The basal body temperature recording has traditionally been used to document progesterone production from the corpus luteum. While assuring neither ovulation nor the adequacy of progesterone production, the basal body temperature graph is an inexpensive means of monitoring the response to treatment. In up to 20 percent of patients the temperature charts may be uninterpretable, and another means to assess ovulatory function is necessary. The occurrence of menstruation following clomiphene citrate treatment is supportive of ovulation but insufficient for documentation.

Since up to 80 percent of all conceptions during treatment with clomiphene citrate occur within the first three ovulatory cycles,[9] an assessment for the etiology of a failure to conceive should be performed during the fourth cycle. The postcoital sperm survival test should be repeated within a day or two prior to the presumed day of ovulation. An endometrial biopsy may also be performed during the luteal phase. As explained in the complication section, clomiphene citrate may preferentially exert a prolonged antiestrogen effect on the cervical mucus, and its use is occasionally associated with an inadequate luteal phase.

The incidence of ovarian enlargement during treatment with clomiphene citrate should be below 10 percent and without significant complications exceeding mild discomfort. To achieve this, ovarian size is determined before initiating a subsequent treatment cycle. If ovarian enlargement is noted, treatment should be withheld until resolution of the mass is noted. An intermediate dose between the preceding dose and that resulting in hyperstimulation should then be used.

Adverse Reactions

HYPERSTIMULATION. MacGregor[6] has reported a 13.6 percent incidence of ovarian enlargement following treatment with clomiphene citrate. While moderate and severe ovarian hyperstimulation has been reported with this agent, it is extremely rare. Monthly monitoring of ovarian size should be sufficient to prevent an advanced form of hyperstimulation. Future courses of induction of ovulation may proceed after regression of the cyst, with slightly reduced dosages.

MULTIPLE GESTATION. The occurrence of multiple gestations following clomid induction of ovulation is reported between 4 and 9 percent.[6-9] Patients with polycystic ovarian disease appear to be at increased risk. Ninety percent of the clomid-induced multiple gestations are dizygotic twins. Multiple gestations account for only a small percentage of the increased abortion rate associated with the use of clomiphene citrate. The incidence of multiple gestations in excess of two concepti is less than 1 percent of all pregnancies occurring after clomiphene citrate.[6]

INADEQUATE LUTEAL PHASE. This potential cause of ovulatory infertility or reproductive wastage is found with increased frequency when clomiphene citrate is required for induction of ovulation.[14] Whether this complication results from a hyperandrogenic environment within the ovary (i.e., PCO) or

from nonphysiologic gonadotropin priming of the follicle is not known. Increased doses of clomiphene citrate,[15] human chorionic gonadotropin,[14] and progesterone supplementation[14] have been used to correct this abnormality.

ABORTION. Clinically diagnosed abortion rates are higher in patients treated for infertility. This general statement is especially true for patients receiving clomiphene citrate. A 20 percent incidence of clinically diagnosed abortions may be found with this treatment.[6] The causes of the increased abortion rate appear to be heterogenous.

DYSMUCORRHEA. The use of clomiphene citrate may, in certain individuals, result in failure to produce periovulatory type cervical mucus despite appropriate endogenous estrogen concentrations.[14] It has been suggested that this adverse reaction may be dependent upon an increased sensitivity by the endocervix to the antiestrogen activity of clomiphene citrate.

TERATOLOGY. The incidence of congenital anomalies in pregnancies following the use of clomiphene citrate appears to be no different from the findings in an infertility population being treated by other modalities or for other causes.[16] In the case of inadvertent administration of clomiphene citrate following conception, a 5.1 percent incidence of major congenital anomalies has been reported.[17] No specific anomalies related to clomiphene citrate are known.

OTHER REACTIONS. Vasomotor symptoms (10 percent), bloating (approximately 5 percent), nausea and vomiting (approximately 2 percent), are the most common symptomatic complaints associated with clomiphene citrate.[6]

Adjuvants to Clomiphene Citrate Therapy.
Treatment with gonadotropins is an appropriate alternative in subjects failing to ovulate in response to clomiphene citrate. Because of the expense, the limitation of facilities for appropriate treatment with gonadotropins, and the greater inconvenience involved, combination therapies of clomiphene citrate and other

agents are often tried before proceeding to treatment with gonadotropins. Patients ovulating with clomiphene citrate but failing to become pregnant have in the past been treated with gonadotropins. While in many cases this would appear to be irrational, some of the causes of infertility found with the use of clomiphene citrate may have been avoided by the use of gonadotropins. Consideration of combined regimens in many of these cases may have diminished the need to use gonadotropins.[14] Table 18-1 is a summary of some combination regimens.

HUMAN MENOPAUSAL GONADOTROPIN (HMG) AND HUMAN CHORIONIC GONADOTROPIN (HCG)

Pergonal (Serono Laboratories, Inc., Braintree, Mass.) is the only commercial preparation of luteinizing hormone and follicle-stimulating hormone available for induction of ovulation in the United States. Early studies involving LH and FSH preparations were derived from human pituitaries. This made availability an extremely limiting factor. In 1962, Lunenfeld and co-workers reported a successful induction of ovulation with a gonadotropin preparation derived from human menopausal urine.[24] Pergonal is a preparation of LH and FSH extracted from human menopausal urine. It is available only as a 1:1 ratio (75 IU:75 IU) of LH and FSH.

The availability of human chorionic gonadotropin (HCG) predates that of human menopausal gonadotropin (HMG). HCG is known to possess potent LH-like activity. The combination of HMG for follicular maturation and HCG as the ovulatory stimulus results in a reliable means of inducing ovulation in subjects devoid of pituitary function. While it is conceptually a relatively simple and effective means of treating anovulation, its expense, significant side effects, and demand for careful monitoring have limited its use and appropriately delegated it as a secondary form of treatment.

Chemistry and Metabolism

LH, FSH, and HCG are all glycoproteins and consist of two subunits. The α-subunit is identical for all three hormones. The β-subunits have minor amino acid alterations capable of imparting very different biologic effects between LH, HCG, and FSH. Also differing among these three glycoproteins is the carbohydrate content. The β-subunit of LH consists of only one oligosaccharide, FSH-2, and HCG-5 oligosaccharide chains. Increasing oligosaccharide content not only alters the configuration of the molecule but positively correlates with the half-life of the hormone. The average half-life of endogenous LH in plasma is about 30 minutes, while for HCG it is about 6 hours. The longer functional activity and greater availability of HCG makes it the agent of choice to recreate the physiologic LH surge.

Little is known about the metabolism of gonadotropins. Of administered gonadotropins, 10 to 20 percent may be recovered in the urine. Gonadotropin preparations are effective only with parenteral administration because of their size and potential for degradation in the gastrointestinal tract.

Mechanism of Action

The biologic activity of gonadotropins is mediated through membrane receptors and cyclic adenosine 5'-monophosphate (AMP). FSH stimulation of the follicular unit results in steroid production and follicular maturation. Within the follicular unit, FSH and estrogen are necessary to induce LH receptors. LH actions are synergistic with FSH, causing increased production of estrogen precursors. An LH or LH-like surge is necessary for reinitiation of meiotic division within the ovum and for the release of the ovum from the ovary.

It is important to recognize that the follicular units exert considerable local control on their own development. Studies in rhesus monkeys have shown that high doses of gonadotropins early in follicular maturation may cause multiple follicles to reach a stage capable of ovulation. However, later in follicular maturation increased dosages of gonadotropins appear unable to rescue follicles destined for

TABLE 18-1 DRUGS UTILIZED CONCURRENTLY WITH CLOMIPHENE CITRATE

Adjuvant Agent	Indication	Regimen	Source(s)
Estrogen	Dysmucorrhea	Conjugated estrogens 0.3–0.625 mg or ethinyl estradiol 0.1 mg for 6–10 days prior to ovulation.	1
Glucocorticoids	Hyperandrogenism preventing adequate follicular maturation	Dexamethasone 0.5 mg q.h.s	18
Human chorionic gonadotropin (HCG)	Anovulation in estrogen-primed individual despite high doses of clomid; Hyperprolactinemic subjects; Inadequate luteal phase	10,000 IU IM on day 6 following discontinuance of clomiphene citrate.	12
		5000 IU IM on days 3 and 6 following ovulation.	19
Luteinizing hormone-releasing factor	Anovulation in estrogen primed individual despite high doses of clomid	Preparations presently not commercially available.	20, 21
Progesterone suppositories	Inadequate luteal phase	25 mg two times a day vaginally starting on second day of basal body temperature rise.	22
Human menopausal gonadotropin (+HCG)	Anovulation in estrogen-primed subject resistant to maximum doses of clomiphene citrate; hyperprolactinemic patients	HMG is begun after discontinuing clomiphene citrate. Monitoring is necessary.	23

atresia or to recruit new follicles into the process of maturation.[25] The mechanism by which the ovaries limit the follicular units eventually reaching maturation is unknown. This concept of production of a dominant follicle is important in the understanding of several empiric regimens for administeri g gonadotropins. Many of the concepts of induction of ovulation with gonadotropins were derived from experiments in animals that are naturally multiovulators.

Pharmacologic Actions

Clinical Use. With the exception of hypogonadotropic patients, gonadotropin therapy should be reserved for patients failing to ovulate in response to other appropriate treatment regimens (i.e., clomiphene citrate, bromocriptine, glucocorticoids). Gonadotropins have been used in patients ovulating in response to clomiphene citrate but failing to become pregnant after 6 to 12 months of continuous treatment. Pregnancy rates exceeding 50 percent have been reported in this group.[26] Neither clomiphene citrate nor gonadotropin therapy may be proposed as being more physiologic. Longer treatment regimens, higher dosages, and closer attention to cervical mucus, coital timing, and corpus luteum function during treatment with clomiphene citrate may have resulted in similar success rates.

Patients requiring gonadotropin treatment may be divided into two categories: Group 1 has primary or secondary amenorrhea with serum gonadotropins below the normal range and clinically demonstrable signs of estrogen deficiency. Group 2 patients have normal levels of gonadotropins and evidence of endogenous estrogen production.[27]

Clinically, these two groups of patients can be differentiated by response to a progesterone challenge. Serum concentrations of

FSH in patients failing to have withdrawal bleeding to progesterone are essential to confirm the presence of intact follicular units in the ovary. Markedly elevated levels of FSH imply primary ovarian failure or gonadotropin-resistant ovaries (Savage syndrome). Little benefit would be anticipated from gonadotropin therapy in these cases, although some exceptions exist.[28,29]

Most patients in group 1 with low gonadotropins are totally dependent on exogenous gonadotropins for follicular maturation and ovulation. While longer treatment cycles and larger amounts of gonadotropins are required, fewer complications are seen in these patients. In group 2 patients, treatment is begun at various stages of follicular maturation, and unplanned ovulations may occur.[26] The combination of endogenous ovarian stimulation and exogenous gonadotropin therapy may result in higher complication rates.[27]

Treatment Regimens. The ideal treatment regimen has (1) a high rate of ovulation and pregnancy, (2) a low incidence of hyperstimulation and multiple gestations, (3) a low incidence of abortion, and (4) relative economy. Numerous treatment regimens have been designed for induction of ovulation with gonadotropins. A daily individualized dosage regimen incorporating frequent monitoring techniques has been most widely accepted. The term "individualized" is perhaps deceiving, since proponents of different individualized treatment protocols advise strict adherence to specific predetermined dose schedules. Variation in ovarian responses to a set dose of gonadotropins during consecutive treatment cycles readily clarifies this apparent dilemma. Two treatment regimens and means of monitoring are presented. Other regimens and references are shown in Table 18-2.

March has reported his results in 108 treatment cycles with HMG.[30] A basal body temperature chart, daily palpation of the ovaries, and daily inspection of cervical mucus were used concurrently with daily determinations of total serum estrogen. Two ampules of HMG were administered daily for 3 or 4 days. If serum estrogens were noted to gradually increase, this daily dose was continued. The dose of gonadotropins was increased by 50 percent if serum estrogen concentrations did not increase. After 3 days more of therapy, consideration for a higher dosage was again made. Once a serum concentration of total estrogens of 200 pg/ml was obtained, the patient was seen twice daily. The patient was examined each morning, and the serum level of estrogen was measured. Based on the findings from the morning specimen, treatment was administered or withheld that afternoon. When serum estrogens were between 500 and 1000 pg/ml, with normal-sized, nontender ovaries, administration of HCG was planned. Twenty-four to 36 hours after the last HMG injection, 10,000 IU of HCG was administered. If the ovaries were not enlarged, a booster injection of HCG was given 4 and 8 days following the initial HCG injection to support the corpus luteum. In repeated cycles, treatment was initiated with the lowest dose of HMG that was capable of initiating adequate follicular steroidogenesis. In patients with endogenous ovarian estrogen production, a similar regimen was recommended but immediately preceded by a 5-day course of 200 mg/day of clomiphene citrate.

If ovarian enlargement or serum concentrations of estrogen beyond 1000 pg/ml were encountered, HCG was withheld. In this series no cases of severe hyperstimulation were reported, the ovulation rate exceeded 98 percent, the multiple pregnancy rate was 5 percent, and the overall pregnancy rate was 51 percent. A conceptualized treatment scheme is shown in Figure 18-3.

Oesler et al.[27] reported on over 1800 treatment cycles using a regimen similar to March's protocol for patients failing to have withdrawal bleeding to progesterone. However, reliance was placed on a cervical mucus scoring system rather than estrogen assays until good-quality mucus was obtained. Urinary estrogen concentrations were then used to assess the adequacy of the follicular maturation for an ovulatory response. They began with a lower initial dose (1 ampule of HMG/day)

**TABLE 18-2   COMBINED HMG AND HCG TREATMENT REGIMENS AND MEANS
OF MONITORING**

Administration HMG	Administration HCG	Overall Pregnancy Rate (%)	Incidence of Hyperstimulation	Monitoring	Source
Individualized dosing regimen with or without clomiphene citrate pretreatment	10,000 IU 24–36 hr following optimal E$_2$ concentration, then 3000 IU on days 4 and 8 after first dose	51	7% mild hyperstimulation, 0% severe hyperstimulation	Serum estrogens daily: opt. 500–1000 pg/ml, max. 1000 pg/ml	30
HMG 3–8 ampules on days 1, 3, 5 (group II patients only)	10,000 IU on day 8 with optional boost 5000 IU on day 15	32	None; withheld HCG in 8% of treatment cycles	Serum estrogens: opt. range day 8 300–1500 pg/ml, max. 2000 pg/ml	31
Individualized dosing regimen with stepdown	8000 IU administered 2–3 days after 3+ ferning is noted	57	14% moderate hyperstimulation, 5% severe hyperstimulation	No chemical monitoring	32
Individualized dosing regimen with possible stepdown	8000 IU following optimal 24-hr urinary estrogen concentration	58	8% moderate hyperstimulation, 0% severe hyperstimulation	Urinary estrogens: 100–200 mcg/24 hr, max. 200 mcg/24 hr	32
Individualized dosing regimen	10,000 IU HCG at time of optimal serum estrogen	55	4.1% moderate hyperstimulation, 0% severe hyperstimulation; withheld dose in 12% of cycles	Serum estradiol: opt. 1000–2000 pg/ml, max. 2000 pg/ml; sample obtained 12–15 hr after last injection	33

with changes in dosages being made on a weekly basis. In patients with endogenous estrogen production, early frequent determinations of urinary estrogens were advised. Follicular rupture was induced with 5000 IU of HCG followed by similar daily injections for 3 to 4 days, provided that the ovaries were not enlarged and urinary estrogen concentrations did not exceed 150 mcg/24 hours. In this series the incidence of severe hyperstimulation was 0.36 percent, the multiple pregnancy rate was 32.5 percent (78 percent being twins), and an overall pregnancy rate of 54.5

percent was achieved. The report stretches over 15 years with several refinements during recent years.

Monitoring of Treatment Effects.   The capacity for daily monitoring of serum or urinary estrogens is essential for treatment with gonadotropins. The point in therapy where daily measurements are initiated is, however, controversial. Generally, group 2 patients require hormonal monitoring immediately after initiating treatment. In group 1 patients, cervical mucus is frequently used during the early part

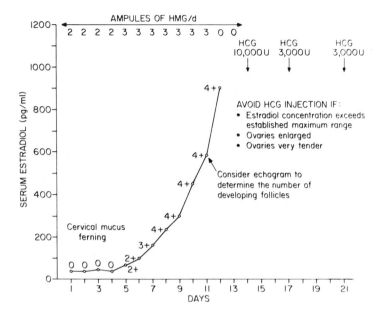

Figure 18-3. This diagram represents an ideal response to an individualized dosage regimen. Note that cervical mucus becomes an invalid monitor when estradiol serum concentrations exceed 200 pg/ml.

of therapy until good-quality mucus is obtained. This usually correlates with levels of serum estrogens between 200 and 300 pg/ml. Daily hormonal monitoring is then begun. With appropriate clinical experience, this form of monitoring is associated with few complications, although HCG treatment may be withheld in more treatment cycles using this monitoring regimen.

The ideal response to gonadotropin therapy is a cycle with gradually increasing estrogen production. Incremental rises of serum estrogens or estradiol should approximate a 100 percent rise over the value of the previous day during active follicular maturation. Too rapid a rise may be associated with the stimulation of multiple follicles or be an indicator of subsequent hyperstimulation.[14] If too rapid a rise is noted, a reduction in dose of HMG may be contemplated with consideration for withholding HCG if the preovulatory range of estrogens is exceeded.

The optimal range for administration of HCG varies in different laboratories. The serum concentration or urinary concentration of estrogens chosen as an endpoint is considerably in excess of the values found during the normal preovulatory period. These values are chosen to maximize the ovulation rate while maintaining an acceptable rate of multiple gestation and complications. The reader may refer to Table 18-2 to review these values in different treatment regimens.

Luteal function is confirmed by a serum concentration of progesterone approximately 7 to 10 days following the initial HCG injection. Pregnancy may be implied from a persistent thermogenic rise on the basal body temperature chart exceeding 14 days. A serum HCG (β-subunit) level may be used to confirm a pregnancy at that time.

Ultrasound has also been suggested as a means for monitoring follicular maturation.[34,35] While it would appear unlikely to replace hormonal monitoring, consideration should be given for its use as a means of determining whether multiple follicles have reached the preovulatory stage. Withholding HCG in these situations would reduce the incidence of multiple gestations. Further study is needed to assess the utility of this complementary monitoring modality.

Complications of Gonadotropin Treatment

OVARIAN HYPERSTIMULATION SYNDROME (OHSS). The use of estrogen monitoring and nonoverlapping administration of HCG have helped to reduce the occurrence of the hyperstimulation syndrome. The syndrome is characterized by ovarian enlargement, excessive ovarian hormone production, abdominal discomfort, and, in severe cases, by dehydration, increased capillary permeability, ascites, and hypercoagulability.

The initial signs of hyperstimulation generally manifest 3 to 6 days following the administration of HCG. Hyperstimulation in the absence of HCG administration generally results from spontaneous ovulation and is a rare phenomenon. Worsening of this complication may result if pregnancy was achieved during the cycle. Management of mild or moderate OHSS consists of observation and rest. Severe cases of OHSS mandate hospitalization, hydration, and careful monitoring of fluids, electrolytes, and coagulation factors. Benefit has been reported with the use of an antiprostaglandin agent (i.e., indomethecin),[36] antihistamines,[37] and plasma expanders like low-molecular-weight dextran.[36] Surgical intervention should be avoided, although it is occasionally required for ovarian torsion, ovarian hemorrhage, or the occurrence of a simultaneous ectopic pregnancy.

MULTIPLE GESTATIONS. An incidence of multiple gestations approaching 25 percent is to be expected with the use of gonadotropins, despite careful monitoring during treatment. Multiple gestations exceeding twins can be limited by careful estrogen monitoring. Determining the number of preovulatory follicles by ultrasound before administering HCG may further reduce the incidence of multiple gestations.

ABORTION. Abortion rates of 20 to 25 percent are found in subjects who conceived during gonadotropin treatment. While it is significantly greater than the incidence reported in a normal population, intermediate values are frequently reported in an infertility population. Multiple gestations account for a significant proportion of the reported abortions.

ECTOPIC PREGNANCY. The occurrence of ectopic pregnancies has been reported in association with the hyperstimulation syndrome.[38] While uncommon, it must be considered in the differential diagnosis of abdominal pain and hypotension following treatment with gonadotropins.

RAPID GROWTH OF PITUITARY ADENOMAS. Neurologic complications from rapidly enlarging pituitary tumors have been reported.[39] While not resulting from HMG therapy but rather from the ensuing pregnancy, the differential diagnosis preceding therapy must consider the possibility of a space-occupying lesion as the cause of severe pituitary dysfunction.

HYPERSENSITIVITY. Early use of gonadotropin preparations were associated with occasionally severe allergic reactions. Febrile reactions to HMG therapy have also been reported.[40]

Combination Treatments

CLOMIPHENE CITRATE PLUS HMG. In subjects capable of demonstrating withdrawal bleeding, March has reported that the use of clomiphene citrate immediately prior to HMG therapy reduces the amount of HMG required by 50 percent.[30] HCG is administered based on hormone monitoring. Although large series are not available to compare the incidence of multiple gestation or hyperstimulation, this reduction in time commitment and cost appears to be beneficial. Daily hormonal monitoring is required once gonadotropins are begun in these patients.

HMG–HCG AND BROMOCRIPTINE. In infertile patients with hyperprolactinemia failing to ovulate on bromocriptine alone or in combination with clomiphene citrate, HMG-HCG may be utilized.[41] The amount of gonadotropins required may be reduced if bromocriptine is utilized concurrently with HMG administration. Prior to such treatment, a thorough diagnostic evaluation should have been performed, with consideration for surgical treatment if a prolactin-producing tumor of the pituitary is present.

Bromocriptine has been suggested to reduce the requirement for HMG in euprolactinemic subjects.[41] Considering the present indications for the use of bromocriptine, this tenuous finding appears to be of little value in clinical practice.

BROMOCRIPTINE

Bromocriptine, a 2-bromo-ergocriptine mesylate (Parlodel, Sandoz Pharmaceutical, East Hanover, N.J.) is presently not approved as an agent for the treatment of infertility in the United States (Fig. 18-4). However, considerable data have been obtained on its use. Bromocriptine is extremely effective as an ovulatory agent in most patients with hyperprolactinemia.[42] It is effective in patients with hyperprolactinemia from a nontumorous source or from a neoplastic source.[43] The potential for rapid enlargement of pituitary tumors during pregnancy makes an evaluation of the cause of hyperprolactinemia mandatory before utilizing bromocriptine in patients desiring pregnancy.

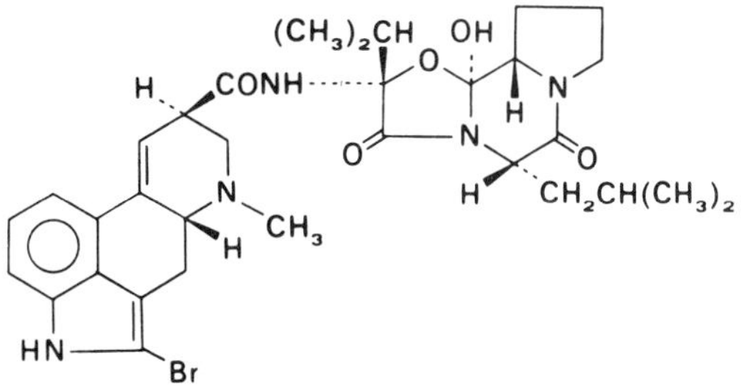

Chemistry and Metabolism

Bromocriptine is a semisynthetic ergot alkaloid that is rapidly and extensively absorbed from the gastrointestinal tract. Its peak plasma concentration occurs 2 to 3 hours following ingestion.[44] A single dose of bromocriptine will suppress prolactin for 8 to 12 hours.[43] Excretion is primarily accomplished through the biliary system and traces of the drug may be found up to 5 days after a single dose. Metabolism is extensive and varied, primarily involving the lysergic acid portion of the molecule.

Mechanism of Action

Dopamine is an endogenous catecholamine believed to be the major inhibiting factor for the release and synthesis of prolactin. Bromo-

Figure 18-4. Chemical structure of bromocriptine. (From Csáky, TZ: *Cutting's Handbook of Pharmacology: The Actions and Uses of Drugs*, ed. 6, New York, Appleton-Century-Crofts, 1979, p. 256, with permission)

criptine is a dopamine agonist, believed to interact at the dopamine receptors in prolactin-secreting cells. While extremely potent in its ability to suppress prolactin, bromocriptine exerts little influence on motor functions dependent on dopamine. Available evidence suggests the existence of multiple receptors for dopamine. Bromocriptine exerts its actions preferentially at the dopamine D_2 receptor, as defined by Kebabian and Calne.[45]

By suppressing central and peripheral concentrations of prolactin, bromocriptine allows for restitution of ovulatory function; however, it remains controversial how hyperprolactinemia results in anovulation.

Clinical Use for Induction of Ovulation

With the availability of radioimmunoassays for prolactin, a large proportion of anovulation (3 to 20 percent) has been found in association with hyperprolactinemia.[46] Anovulation may result from inhibition of hypothalamic tonic and cyclic secretion of gonadotropin-releasing factor, direct pituitary suppression, ovarian follicular disruption, or disturbances in catecholamine regulation. If iatrogenic causes of hyperprolactinemia are eliminated, microadenomas (less than 10 mm) or macroadenomas (greater than 10 mm) may be found in up to 45 percent of hyperprolactinemic amenorrheic subjects.[46] Bromocriptine is capable of suppressing pituitary prolactin secretion from almost all causes. With a return of prolactin levels to normal, an ovulatory rate of 80 percent may be achieved in previously anovulatory subjects.[42]

The dose of bromocriptine required for treatment of hyperprolactinemia is generally determined by the clinical response. There are several benefits to be achieved by using the lowest effective dose. High dosages reduce the specificity of bromocriptine for the D_2 receptor and may result in hypotensive episodes, excessive nausea, and motor dysfunction. Hypotension may be minimized by administering the drug at bedtime, the time of greatest prolactin secretion in idiopathic hyperprolactinemia. Nausea is reduced by using gradually increasing doses. Motor dysfunction is associated almost exclusively with very high doses of bromocriptine. In addition to these side effects, excessive suppression of prolactin by bromocriptine may result in decreased progesterone synthesis from the corpus luteum.[47]

To determine the lowest effective dose, treatment is begun with 1 tablet (2.5 mg) at bedtime. Maximum suppression of prolactin at a specific dose is achieved by 4 weeks.[39] The administered dose may be raised by 2.5-mg increments every 4 weeks, until ovulation occurs or a prolactin level within the normal range is obtained. The basal body temperature chart is used to monitor an ovulatory response. If a thermogenic rise consistent with ovulation is noted for 2 days, the medication is withheld until menstruation occurs. The average interval from achieving a euprolactinemic state to ovulation is 3 to 4 weeks.[39]

Once the dose required to achieve ovulation has been determined, treatment is begun with each ensuing menstruation at that dose. Because of nausea, some patients will require starting at the 2.5 mg/day dose, increasing daily until the dosage required for ovulation is achieved. Treatment is withheld once corpus luteum function has been demonstrated to avoid prolonged exposure of the possible embryo to bromocriptine. Resumption of hyperprolactinemia occurs during the luteal phase but does not appear to be detrimental.[48] Most patients will respond to a dose of 5 to 7.5

mg/day. This treatment scheme is shown in Figure 18-5.

Treatment with bromocriptine is effective in inducing ovulation only during the cycles in which it is used. Induction of ovulation with bromocriptine is therefore of limited value unless attempts at pregnancy are contemplated. While there have been reports of continued euprolactinemia following prolonged continuous treatment with bromocriptine, most patients return to their pretreatment level of hyperprolactinemia following discontinuation of the medication.[48]

Bromocriptine is presently approved for the treatment of anovulation in the United States. Other treatments that have been used for hyperprolactinemic amenorrhea include clomiphene citrate, HMG–HCG, transphenoidal excision of microadenomas, and radiation therapy. In amenorrhea-galactorrhea, clomiphene citrate has been reported to successfully induce ovulation in up to 42 percent of patients with a pregnancy rate of only 16 percent.[4] Successful induction of ovulation in hypoestrogenic hyperprolactinemia subjects is rare. Gonadotropin therapy in patients with amenorrhea and galactorrhea desiring pregnancy is relatively effective. Pregnancy rates greater than 75 percent are reported.[27] The high cost and potential complications associated with gonadotropin therapy make this form of treatment less than ideal. Pregnancies following transphenoidal surgery alone in most series occur in less than 40 percent of patients.[49] Radiation therapy involves a long lag phase before normal prolactin levels are achieved and often results in subsequent hypogonadotropism. To achieve pregnancy, exogenous gonadotropins are frequently required following radiation therapy.

Bromocriptine, when used in the treatment of infertility from anovulation and hyperprolactinemia, has resulted in a pregnancy rate of greater than 60 percent.[50,51] The abortion rate is less than that found with gonadotropin therapy and similar to the normal population.[50,52] Its ease of administration and relatively minor side effects makes it currently the best agent available for the medical man-

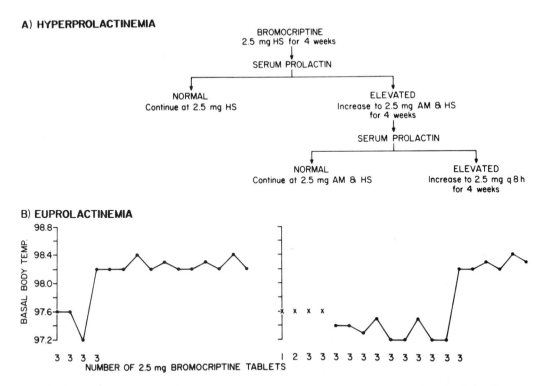

Figure 18-5. Induction of ovulation using bromocriptine. A is the scheme used to determine the dose of bromocriptine required to obtain a euprolactinemic state. B represents the treatment regimen to be used in a patient requiring 7.5 mg/day of bromocriptine to resume ovulation and obtain a euprolactinemic state.

agement of infertility resulting from hyperprolactinemia. Medical management for induction of ovulation is the appropriate treatment for nontumorous causes of hyperprolactinemia. Whether the criteria for differentiating microadenomas from hyperplastic causes of hyperprolactinemia is valid is presently being challenged. Medical treatment of hyperprolactinemic anovulation might also be advised for patients with microadenomas. Few neurologic complications are found in pregnancies occurring in patients with pituitary microadenomas.[52] The ability to manage neurologic complications during pregnancy with bromocriptine or with surgery without significant permanent sequelae is further support for the use of bromocriptine, even in cases of microadenomas.[52] The major question concerning the use of bromocriptine as an ovulatory agent

for patients with microadenomas concerns the long-term prognosis for growth of the microadenoma. Whether medical management during the reproductive years is only a temporary maneuver in a disease that will eventually require surgical treatment has not been answered. The ability to safely and successfully remove small pituitary tumors is well recognized, while the morbidity associated with the neglect of a rapidly growing pituitary tumor is also familiar.

Patients with macroadenomas appear to be at significantly greater risk if pregnancy is allowed to occur before surgical treatment is instituted.[52] Surgical removal of prolactinomas in excess of 10 mm or with suprasellar extension remains the treatment of choice in patients contemplating pregnancy. Radiologic studies of the sella turcica are therefore mandatory before attempts at induction of ovulation are considered.

The finding of hyperprolactinemia and polycystic ovarian disease has been reported in several series.[53] Treatment for anovulation in these cases should initially utilize the approved agent, clomiphene citrate. Failure to induce withdrawal bleeding with progesterone implies the need for bromocriptine. If ovulation fails to occur in response to bromocriptine and euprolactinemia, the addition of clomiphene citrate may be of value if progesterone-induced withdrawal bleeding can now be demonstrated. Bromocriptine has also been suggested as an effective agent in the treatment of euprolactinemic amenorrhea;[54] however, controlled studies have failed to substantiate this claim.[55]

Adverse Reactions

During initial therapy, a high incidence of nausea (52 percent), headaches (18 percent), orthostatic hypotension (6 percent), dizziness (16 percent), and vomiting (5 percent) may be encountered.[42] Stepwise increases in dosages and nocturnal administration appear to reduce these occurrences.

Alterations in awareness and behavior have been reported in 1 percent of patients.[43] Hallucinations have also been reported but are rare with the dosages utilized for hormonal control. Bromocriptine should not be used in patients with mental disturbances, coronary vascular disease, or peripheral vascular disease.

An abortion rate similar to the normal population is found when bromocriptine is used continuously[56] or in a cyclic fashion, as described previously. Malformations were noted in 2.9 percent of 375 offspring of mothers ingesting bromocriptine during the first month of pregnancy. Only two major malformations were seen in this population.[56]

OTHER AGENTS FOR INDUCTION OF OVULATION

Glucocorticoids

Glucocorticoids (i.e., dexamethasone, prednisone) have been used with success in hyperan-drogenic anovulatory patients. Resumption of regular ovulatory cycles are reported to occur in up to 60 percent of such patients.[57] By reducing the adrenal contribution to the excessive androgen pool, ovulation may resume. Doses utilized have varied with the patient's weight. Using 0.5 mg of dexamethasone at bedtime in patients weighing less than 150 lb and 0.75 mg in patients over 150 lb, serum levels of dehydroepiandrosterone sulfate are effectively suppressed.

With the exception of hyperandrogenism and anovulation resulting from adrenal hyperactivity (i.e., congenital adrenal hyperplasia), glucocorticoids should not be used as a primary agent for induction of ovulation. They are less reliable than clomiphene citrate, require daily administration, and have the potential for significant complications when used for long periods of time and during periods of stress.

Estrogens

Parenteral injection of estradiol has been used alone[58] or in combination with clomiphene citrate[59] for induction of ovulation. The treatment assumes that a mature follicle will respond to a LH surge induced by a bolus injection of estradiol. This is not a reliable means of inducing ovulation.

Epimestrol

Epimestrol, a methylated form of the natural estrogen 17 β-epiestriol, has been tested as an agent for induction of ovulation. It is presently not available in the United States for clinical use, and little data exist on its efficacy. Its actions are probably similar to clomiphene citrate, but antiestrogen effects on the cervical mucus are reported to be less frequent.[60]

Luteinizing Hormone-Releasing Hormone (LRH) and Analogues

Natural LRH, a simple polypeptide of 10 amino acids, can be used for inducing ovulation in a hypogonadotropic hypogonadal patient with an intact pituitary.[61,62] Its theoretical benefit over gonadotropin therapy is a lower cost and a lower incidence of multiple gestations and hyperstimulation. Treatment of hypogonadotropic hypogonadal patients is complicated by the need for a long priming period and frequent daily administration. Long-acting analogues, which may be administered intranasally and subcutaneously, have been synthesized. The greatest interest in these agents involves contraception rather than induction of ovulation.[63,64] The long-acting analogues or continuous administration of LRH can produce ovarian insensitivity to LH. Development of LRH analogues as inducers of ovulation in hypogonadotropic hypogonadal subjects requires more investigation.

Clinical experience with LRH and its analogues in conjunction with clomiphene citrate has been reported.[20,21] LRH has also been used for timing of ovulation. Whether LRH or its analogues are superior to HCG in these situations requires further investigation. Presently neither LRH nor its analogues is commercially available.

REFERENCES

1. Speroff L, Glass RH, Kase NG (eds): Anovulation, in *Clinical Gynecologic Endocrinology and Infertility*. Baltimore, Williams & Wilkins, 1978, p 123
2. Yen SSC: Chronic anovulation, in Yen SCC, Jaffe RB (eds): *Reproductive Endocrinology*, Philadelphia, Saunders, 1978, p 297
3. Greenblatt RB, Varfield WE, Junget EC, Roy AW: Induction of ovulation with MRL-41. *JAMA* 178:101, 1961
4. Clark JH, Peck EJ, Anderson JN: Oestrogen receptors and antagonisms of steroid hormone action. *Nature* 251:446, 1974
5. Schreiber EC: Clomiphene (abstract). Lawrence, Kan, American Society for Pharmacology and Experimental Therapeutics, Aug 1964
6. MacGregor AH, Johnson JE, Bunde CE: Further clinical experience with clomiphene citrate. *Fertil Steril* 19:616, 1968
7. Mishell DR, March GM: Induction of ovulation, in Mishell D, Davajan V (eds): *Reproductive Endocrinology Infertility and Contraception*. Philadelphia, Davis, 1979, pp 317–337
8. Drake TS, Tredway DR, Buchanan GC: Continued clinical experience with an increasing dosage regimen of clomiphene citrate administration. *Fertil Steril* 30:274, 1978
9. Ruse LA, Israel R, Mishell DR: An individualized graduated therapeutic regimen for clomiphene citrate. *Am J Obstet Gynecol* 120:785, 1974
10. March CM, Israel R, Mishell DR: Pregnancy following 29 cycles of clomiphene citrate therapy: A case report. *Am J Obstet Gynecol* 124:209, 1976
11. Shepard M., Balmaceda JP, Leija CG: Relationship of weight to successful induction of ovulation with clomiphene citrate. *Fertil Steril* 32:641, 1979
12. Huppert LC: Induction of ovulation with clomiphene citrate. *Fertil Steril* 31:1, 1979
13. Beck WW Jr, Barrett ATM: Adjunctive therapy to the women in couples undergoing artificial insemination (abstract). *Fertil Steril* 29:254, 1978
14. Wu CH: Monitoring of ovulation induction. *Fertil Steril* 30:617, 1978
15. Quagliarello J, Weiss G: Clomiphene citrate in the management of infertility associated with shortened luteal phase. *Fertil Steril* 31:373 1979
16. Adashi EY, Rock JA, Sapp KC, et al: Gestational outcome of clomiphene-related conceptions. *Fertil Steril* 31:620, 1979
17. Merrell-National Laboratories: *Product Information 1972*. Division of Richardson Merrell Inc., Cincinnati, Ohio 43215
18. Chang RJ, Abraham GE: Effect of dexamethasone and clomiphene citrate on peripheral steroid levels in a hirsute amenorrheic patient. Fertil Steril 27:640, 1976
19. Radwanska E, McGarrigle HH, Little V, et al: Induction of ovulation in women with hyperprolactinemic amenorrhea using clomiphene and human chorionic gonadotropins or bromocryptine. *Fertil Steril* 32:187, 1979
20. Phansey SA, Barnes MA, Williamson HO, Sagel J, et al: Combined use of clomiphene and intranasal luteinizing hormone-releasing hormone for induction of ovulation in chronically anovulatory women. *Fertil Steril* 34:448, 1980.
21. Huang KE: The induction of ovulation in amenorrheic patients with synthetic luteinizing hormone-releasing hormone: The significance of pituitary responsiveness. *Fertil Steril* 27:65, 1976
22. Jones GS: The luteal phase defect. *Fertil Steril* 27:351, 1976
23. March CM, Tredway DR, Mishell DR: Effect of clomiphene citrate on amount and duration of human menopausal gonadotropin therapy. *Am J Obstet Gynecol* 125:699, 1976
24. Lunenfeld B, Sulimovici S, Rabau E, Eshkol A: L' induction de l'ovulation dans les amenorrhea hypophysaires par un traitement com-

baine de gonadotropines urinaires menopausique et de gonadotropines chorioniques. *CR Soc Fr Gynecol* 35:346, 1962

25. Dizerega GS, Hodgen GD: The primate ovarian cycle: Suppression of human menopausal gonadotropin-induced follicular growth in the presence of the dominant follicle. *J Clin Endocrinol Metab* 50:819, 1980

26. Wang CF, Gemzell C: Use of human gonadotropin for the induction of ovulation in women with polycystic ovarian disease. *Fertil Steril* 33:479, 1980

27. Oesler G, Serr DM, Mashiach S, et al: The study of induction of ovulation with menotropins, analysis of results of 1897 treatment cycles. *Fertil Steril* 30:538, 1978

28. Johnson TR, Peterson EP: Gonadotropin-induced pregnancy following "premature ovarian failure." *Fertil Steril* 31:351, 1979

29. Zourlas P, Mantzaevinos T: Primary amenorrhea with normally developed secondary sex characteristics. *Fertil Steril* 34:112, 1980

30. March CM: Therapeutic regimens and monitoring techniques for human menopausal gonadotropin administration. *J Reprod Med* 21:198, 1978

31. Radwanska E, Hammond J, Hammond M, Smith P: Current experience with a standardized method of human menopausal gonadotropins/human chorionic gonadotropin administration. *Fertil Steril* 33:510, 1980.

32. Taymor ML: Induction of ovulation with gonadotropins. *Clin Obstet Gynecol* 16:201, 1973

33. Haning R, Levin R, Behrman HR, et al: Plasma estradiol window and urinary estriol glucuronide determinations for monitoring menotropin induction of ovulation. *Obstet Gynecol* 54:442, 1979

34. Smith DH, Picker RH, Sinosich M, Saunders DM: Assessment of ovulation by ultrasound and estradiol levels during spontaneous and induced cycles. *Fertil Steril* 33:387, 1980

35. Queenan JT, O'Brien G, Bains L, et al: Ultrasound scanning of ovaries to detect ovulation in women. *Fertil Steril* 34:99, 1980

36. Schenker J, Weinstein D: Ovarian hyperstimulation syndrome: A current survey. *Fertil Steril* 30:255, 1978

37. Gergeley RZ, Paldi E, Erlik Y, Makler A: Treatment of ovarian hyperstimulation syndrome by antihistamine. *Obstet Gynecol* 47:883, 1976

38. Evans JH, McBain JC, Pepperell RJ, et al: An increased ectopic pregnancy rate on gonadotropin therapy (abstract #444). Melbourne,

Australia, Sixth International Congress of Endocrinology, 1980

39. Gemzell C: Induction of ovulation in infertile women with pituitary adenomas. *Am J Obstet Gynecol* 121:311, 1975

40. *Physicians Reference.* Braintree, Mass., Serono Laboratories, Inc., 1975

41. Larsen S, Honore E: Estrogenic response in women with amenorrhea during treatment with human menopausal gonadotropin with and without the simultaneous administration of bromocriptine. *Fertil Steril* 33:378, 1980

42. Cuellar FG: Bromocriptine mesylate (Parlodel) in the management of amenorrhea/galactorrhea associated with hyperprolactinemia. *Obstet Gynecol* 55:278, 1980

43. Parkes D: Bromocriptine. *N Engl J Med* 301:873, 1979

44. Mehta AE, Tolis G: Pharmacology of bromocriptine in health and disease. *Drugs* 17:313, 1979

45. Kebabian JW, Calne DB: Multiple receptors for dopamine. *Nature* 277:93, 1979

46. Greer ME, Moraczewski T, Rakoff J: Prevalence of hyperprolactinemia in anovulatory women. *Obstet Gynecol* 56:65, 1980

47. Schulz KD, Geiger W, del Pozo E, et al: Pattern of sexual steroids, prolactin, and gonadotrophic hormones during prolactin inhibition in normally cycling women. *Am J Obstet Gynecol* 132:561, 1978

48. Herjan JT, Bennink C: Intermittent bromocriptine treatment for induction of ovulation in hyperprolactinemic patients. *Fertil Steril* 31:267, 1979

49. Gomez F, Reyes FI, Faiman C: Nonpuerperal galactorrhea and hyperprolactinemia: Clinical findings, endocrine features and therapeutic response in 56 cases. *Am J Med* 62:648, 1977

50. Zarate A, Canales E, Forsbach G, Fernandez-Lazala R: Bromocriptine: Clinical experience in the initiation of pregnancy in amenorrhea galactorrhea syndrome. *Obstet Gynecol* 52:442, 1978

51. Friesen HG, Tolis G: The use of bromocriptine in the galactorrhea amenorrhea syndrome: The Canadian cooperative study. *Clin Endocrinol* 6 (suppl): 91s, 1977

52. Gemzell C, Wang CF: Outcome of pregnancy in women with pituitary adenomas. *Fertil Steril* 31:363, 1979

53. Futterweit W, Kreiger DT: Pituitary tumors associated with hyperprolactinemia and polycystic ovarian disease. *Fertil Steril* 31:608, 1979

54. Corenblum B, Taylor P: A rationale for the use of bromocriptine in patients with amenorrhea and normoprolactinemia. *Fertil Steril* 34:239, 1980

55. Crosignani PG, Reschini E, Lombroso GC, Arosio M, Peracch M: Comparison of placebo and bromocriptine in the treatment of patients with normoprolactinemic amenorrhea. *Br J Obstet Gynecol* 85:773, 1978

56. Griffith RW, Turkalj I, Braun P: Outcome of pregnancy in mothers given bromocriptine. *Br J Clin Pharmacol* 5:227, 1978

57. Abraham GE, Maroulis GB, Boyers SP, et al: Dexamethasone suppression test in the management of hyperandrogenic patients. *Obstet Gynecol* 57:158, 1981

58. Weiss G, Nachtigall L, Ganguly M: Induction of an LH surge with estradiol benzoate. *Obstet Gynecol* 47:415, 1976

59. Canales ES, Cabezas A, Vasquez-Matute L, Zarate A: Induction of ovulation with clomiphene and estradiol benzoate in anovulatory women refractory to clomiphene citrate. *Fertil Steril* 29:496, 1978

60. Schmidt-Elmendorf H, Kammerling R: Vergleichende klinishe untersuchungen von clomiphen, cyclofenil und epimestrol. *Geburtshilfe Frauenhelikd* 37:531, 1977

61. Willus SJ, Fries H, Wide L: Successful induction of ovulation by prolonged treatment with LH releasing hormone in women with anorexia nervosa. *Am J Obstet Gynecol* 122:921, 1975

62. Leyendecker G, Wildt L, Hansmann M: Pregnancies following chronic intermittent (pulsatile) administration of GnRH by means of a portable pump ("Zyklomat")—a new approach to the treatment of infertility in hypothalamic amenorrhea. *J Clin Endocrinol Metab* 51:1214, 1980

63. Koyamo T, Ohkura T, Kumasaka T, Saito M: Effect of postovulatory treatment with a luteinizing hormone releasing hormone analogue on the plasma level of progesterone in women. *Fertil Steril* 30:549, 1978

64. Lemay A, Labrie F, Ferland L, Raynaud JP: Possible luteolytic of luteinizing hormone releasing hormone in normal women. *Fertil Steril* 31:29, 1978

19. Over-the-Counter Drugs for Gynecologic Use

Paul E. Hafner   William F. Rayburn

Over-the-counter (OTC) drugs can provide safe, convenient, and effective treatment for a variety of gynecologic disorders. Because OTC drugs may be purchased in various retail settings, including grocery stores, the patient may not come in contact with a health professional to provide guidance in product selection and use. Furthermore, much of the information the patient receives about OTCs comes from often misleading commercial advertisements or family members and friends. Present laws do not require manufacturers of OTC products to list the concentration or quantity of each ingredient. Therefore, this information is often unavailable and can only be guessed at. This chapter attempts to fill this information gap by discussing current knowledge about vaginal contraceptives, vaginal cleansing and deodorant products, menstrual preparations, and topical antipruritics or anesthetics.

VAGINAL CONTRACEPTIVES

Vaginal contraceptives, alone or in combination with a condom or diaphragm, are attractive alternatives for patients not desiring sterilization or adverse effects from either oral contraceptives or intrauterine devices. All nonprescription vaginal contraceptives work primarily as spermicides and as mechanical barriers to prevent sperm from entering the cervix and uterine cavity. The spermicide in most products is nonoxynol-9, a surfactant or

detergent, which solubilizes cell membranes and thus immobilizes the spermatozoa.[1] The extent of spermicidal activity in these alkylphenol compounds is influenced by the number of polyoxyethylene groups (5 to 15) in the side chain (Fig. 19-1). Nonoxynol-9 has nine groups in its side chain (n-9) and has been shown to be the most effective of the nonionic surfactants used in spermicidal contraceptives.[2]

Certain vaginal contraceptives contain acidic agents (boric acid, phenylmercuric acid), which lower the vaginal pH. A pH of less than 3.5 is considered to be spermicidal, and greater effectiveness is theoretically obtained as the pH is lowered. Phenylmercuric compounds are effective but may be absorbed systemically. Because of the possible adverse effects from mercury and the availability of other effective and less potentially harmful spermicides, mercury-containing vaginal contraceptives are not recommended.

Preparations

The major difference in vaginal spermicides is how the dose is delivered. Most preparations deliver 50 to 100 mg of nonoxynol-9 per dose, since human testing indicates a minimum of 50 mg of free nonoxynol-9 must be present in the vaginal vault to inhibit all spermatozoa.[3] No advantage has been shown among products with different nonoxynol-9 concentrations,[4] although spermicides designed to be used with a diaphragm are less concentrated and are in a base which has different diffusion

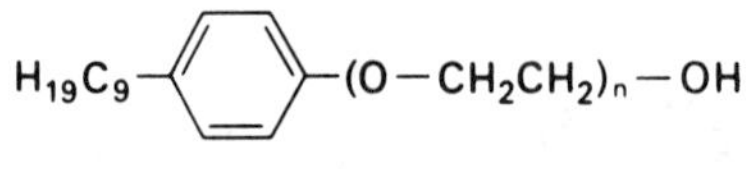

$$H_{19}C_9 - \langle \rangle - (O-CH_2CH_2)_n - OH$$

Figure 19-1. Chemical structure of nonoxynol-9. (From Csáky TZ: *Cutting's Handbook of Pharmacology: The Actions and Uses of Drugs*, ed. 6, New York, Appleton-Century-Crofts, 1979, p 137, with permission.)

or mechanical barrier characteristics. Vaginal spermicides come in cream, jelly, foam, and suppository or tablet form (Table 19-1). Jellies and creams are the least expensive, while convenience packages of prefilled applicators (foam or cream) and tablets or suppositories are the most expensive per dose.

Creams and jellies are applied near the cervix using an applicator at least 10 minutes but no longer than 1 hour before intercourse. Creams are more lubricating, but jellies are water soluble which enhances vaginal distribution and easy removal.

Foams are creams packaged in an aerosol form. Foams are also applied using an applicator which is filled from a dispenser. They should be applied no longer than 1 hour before intercourse and should remain in the vagina for at least 9 hours. For convenience, certain newer products allow one to prefill the applicator up to 7 days before use. Foams do not provide the lubrication of creams and jellies but tend to be less noticeable to the partners. They adhere well to vaginal surfaces and only a small amount of leakage usually occurs during and after intercourse.

Vaginal tablets and suppositories are easily inserted and deliver a consistent dose of spermicide in a base that melts, dissolves, or effervesces. Noneffervescent preparations should be inserted at least 20 minutes before intercourse to allow complete liquefaction and distribution. The manufacturers of effervescent forms recommend a wait of only 10 minutes before intercourse, but one recent study found the Encare suppository was still almost intact 15 minutes after insertion in 9 of 20 patients.[5] Effervescence and dispersion are influenced by the amount of vaginal fluid and the freshness of the tablet. Tablet freshness can be tested by moistening it with a drop of water prior to insertion. If bubbling begins, the tablet may be inserted. Effervescent tablets should be stored in a cool dry location and used within 6 months after purchase. Tablets and suppositories provide no lubrication. A warm or sometimes burning sensation for both partners is occasionally produced with effervescent preparations and can be relieved with discontinuation.

Effectiveness

If used properly, all vaginal spermicides are equally effective. Patient preference affects compliance and ultimately product effectiveness. When vaginal spermicides are used with barrier methods, such as condoms or diaphragms, the combined effectiveness is greater than either method alone (Table 19-2). One large-scale study indicates a first-year failure rate of 15 percent* for foams, creams and jellies, compared with 2 percent for oral contraceptives, 4 percent for intrauterine devices, 10 percent for condoms, 13 percent for diaphragms, and 19 percent for the rhythm method.[6] One application provides protection for one act of intercourse and repeated intercourse requires repeated applications.

Precautions

Spermicidal agents are considered nontoxic and usually cause no allergic reactions. Inflammatory changes in the vaginal epithelium of rabbits and rats from nonoxynol-9 exposure have been demonstrated and are related to the concentration and duration of use.[7] Ingredients such as fragrance additives may cause local burning or irritation, allergic reactions, or vaginal discharge. A change in or discontinuation of products should solve this problem.

Postcoital douching is inadequate for vaginal contraception. Active spermatozoa have been isolated in the endocervix within 1.5 to 3 minutes after coitus and have been recovered from the fallopian tubes within 5 minutes

---

* Failure rate relates to the number of pregnancies per 100 woman years of use.

TABLE 19-1 VAGINAL CONTRACEPTIVES

Product and Manufacturer	Active Ingredients	Other Ingredients
Creams		
Conceptrol (Ortho)	Nonoxynol-9, 5%	Oil-in-water emulsion
Delfen (Ortho)	Nonoxynol-9, 5%	Oil-in-water emulsion
Gels/Creams		
(to be used with a diaphragm)		
Koromex II (Cream) (Holland-Rantos)	Octoxynol, 3%	Cream base
Koromex II (Gel) (Holland-Rantos)	Octoxynol, 1%	Propylene glycol, cellulose gum, boric acid, sorbitol, starch, simethicone, fragrance
Ortho-Creme (Ortho)	Nonoxynol-9, 2%	Oil-in-water emulsion
Ortho-Gynol (Ortho)	p-Diisobutylphenoxy-polyethoxyethanol, 1%	Aqueous gel
Gels		
Koromex II-A (Holland-Rantos)	Nonoxynol-9, 2%	Propylene glycol, cellulose gum, boric acid, sorbitol, starch, simethicone, fragrance
Ramses 10-Hour (Schmid)	Dodecaethyleneglycol monolaurate, 5%	Boric acid, 1%; ethyl alcohol, 5%; water-miscible base
Foams		
Because Birth Control Foam (Schering)	Nonoxynol-9, 8%	Benzethonium chloride, 0.2%; oil-in-water emulsion
Dalkon (Robins)	Nonoxynol-9, 8%	Benzethonium chloride, 0.2%; oil-in-water emulsion
Delfen (Ortho)	Nonoxynol-9, 12.5%	Oil-in-water emulsion
Emko, Emko Pre-fil (Schering)	Nonoxynol-9, 8%	Benzethonium chloride, 0.2%; oil-in-water emulsion; stearic acid; triethanolamine; glyceryl monostearate; poloxamer 188; polyethylene glycol 600; substituted adamantane; dichlorodifluoro methane; dichlorotetrafluoroethane
Koromex (Holland-Rantos)	Nonoxynol-9, 12.5%	Propylene glycol, isopropyl alcohol, laureth 4, cetyl alcohol, polyethylene glycol stearate, fragrance, dichlorodifluro-methane, dichlorotetrafluoroethane
Suppositories		
Encare oval (Eaton)	Nonoxynol-9, 2.27%	Effervescent water-soluble base
Intercept (Ortho)	Nonoxynol-9 (100 mg), 5.56%	
Semicid (Whitehall)	Nonoxynol-9, 100 mg	Polyethylene glycol base
S'Positive (Jordan-Simner)	Nonoxynol-9, 5.56%	Vegetable oil base, benzethonium chloride

TABLE 19-2 COMPARATIVE EFFECTIVENESS OF CONTRACEPTIVE METHODS*

Method	% Effective Theoretical Use (100% compliance)	% Effective Actual Use (U.S. women not wanting more children)
Abortion	100	100
Tubal ligation	99.96	99.96
Vasectomy	99–85	99–85
Combined oral contraceptive	99.66	90–96
Condom plus spermicide	99	95
IUD	97–99	95
Condom	97	90
Diaphragm plus spermicide	97	83
Spermicidal	97	78
Coitus interruptus	91	75–80
Rhythm (calendar)	87	79
Lactation for 12 months	75	60
Chance (sexually active)	10	10

*From Hatcher RA, Stewart GK, Stewart F, et al: *Contraceptive Technology, 1978–79*, ed 9. New York: Irving, 1978, p 20, with permission.

after insemination, which is well before douching could be completed. Furthermore, douching should be avoided for at least 9 hours after intercourse when a vaginal spermicide is used, since douching will dilute the spermicide to ineffective levels and remove the mechanical barrier provided by the product base. Any increased risk of abortion or specific anomalies associated with vaginal contraceptive use is tentative in humans and not apparent in rat models.[9,10]

VAGINAL CLEANSING AND DEODORANT PRODUCTS

Vaginal Cleansers

The routine use of vaginal douches and deodorants by healthy women is controversial. The products listed in Table 19-3 are promoted as general vaginal and perineal cleansers that produce a refreshed feeling, relieve itching and burning, remove vaginal discharges, and deodorize. The benefits of their use appear to be minimal and offer no great advantage over perineal cleansing with mild soap and water or infrequent douching with 1 teaspoonful of white vinegar in 1 qt of warm water. If commercial products are used, the concentrates and stock bottle sizes of powder or solution are the most economical, while disposable and premeasured packages are least economical per dose. When used as directed, vaginal cleansers are not likely to be hazardous. Mixing with hot water, instillation with excessive pressure, and overuse are examples of improper self-administration. In addition, many ingredients in douche preparations may produce direct mucosal or dermal irritation or an allergic reaction.

Few OTC douches are medicinal and the user may delay seeking proper treatment. Povidone-iodine products (Betadine, Pharmadine) serve as adjunctive antimicrobial therapy

TABLE 19-3 DOUCHE PRODUCTS

Product and Manufacturer	Ingredients
Betadine (Perdue Frederick)	Solution: povidone-iodine, fragrance
Bo-Car-Al (Beecham Products)	Powder: boric acid, potassium aluminum sulfate, phenol, eucalyptus oil, methyl salicylate, thymol, menthol
Dismiss Disposable (Schering)	Solution: sodium chloride, sodium citrate, citric acid, cetearyl octoate, ceteareth-27
Gental Spring Disposable (Block Drug)	Powder: sodium edetate, sodium lauryl sulfate, sodium phosphate
Hygefem (Bluline)	Liquid: benzalkonium chloride, lactic acid, sodium lactate, potassium alum
Hygefem (Bluline)	Powder: benzalkonium chloride, citric acid, sodium phosphate, potassium alum
Hygette (Western Pharm)	Powder: boric acid, 75%; potassium alum, 16%; zinc sulfate, 8%
Inner Rinse (Block)	Solution: water, SD alcohol, sodium lauryl sulfate, sodium borate, disodium EDTA, citric acid, triethanolamine, methylparaben, propylparaben, fragrance
Jeneen (Norwich-Eaton)	Liquid: propylene glycol, octoxynol-9, lactic acid, sodium lactate
Massengill Disposable (Beecham Products)	Solution: alcohol, lactic acid, sodium lactate, octoxynol-9, cetylpyridinium chloride
Massengill (Beecham Products)	Liquid concentrate: lactic acid; sodium lactate; octoxynol-9; alcohol, 25%
Massengill Disposable (Beecham Products)	Liquid: vinegar, water
Massengill (Beecham Products)	Powder: boric acid, ammonium alum
New Freshness (Fleet)	Concentrate: vinegar, water Disposable: vinegar, water
Nylmerate II (Holland-Rantos)	Solution concentrate: boric acid; acetic acid; polysorbate 20; nonoxynol-9; sodium acetate; SD alcohol, 50%
Phemithyn (Scrip)	Solution: benzethonium chloride monohydrate, 3.17%
Stomaseptine (Berlex)	Powder: sodium perborate, sodium bicarbonate, sodium chloride, sodium borate

(Table 19-3 continues on page 268.)

TABLE 19-3 DOUCHE PRODUCTS—cont.

Product and Manufacturer	Ingredients
Summer's Eve Disposable (Fleet)	Solution, regular: sodium citrate, citric acid, propylene glycol, potassium alum, EDTA, quaternium-15 Solution, herbal scented: sodium citrate, citric acid, EDTA, quaternium-15, zinc sulfate, tartrazine Disposable: vinegar, water
Trichotine (Reed & Carnrick)	Liquid: sodium lauryl sulfate; sodium borate, EDTA; SD alcohol, 8% Powder: sodium lauryl sulfate, sodium perborate, sodium chloride
Trichotine-D Disposable (Reed & Carnrick)	Powder: sodium chloride, tetrasodium EDTA, sodium lauryl sulfate
Triva (Boyle)	Powder: oxyquinoline sulfate, 2%; aklyl aryl sulfonate, 35%; EDTA, 0.33%; sodium sulfate, 53%; lactose, 9.67%
Vagisec (Schmid)	Liquid: polyoxyethylene nonyl phenol, sodium edetate, docusate sodium

in selected cases of vaginitis by cleansing the vaginal vault or altering the vaginal pH (see Chap. 20).

Their multiple uses reflect the array of ingredients found in these products. With the exception of povidone-iodine and boric acid, the antimicrobials (benzalkonium chloride, cetylpyridinium chloride, benzethonium chloride) are merely preservatives. Acids (lactic, citric), bases (sodium bicarbonate, perborate, citrate, lactate) alone or in combination with buffers (sodium phosphate, EDTA) are added to alter or maintain a stable pH. Because of the short exposure time in the vaginal vault, the douche solution causes no sustained pH changes.

Phenol, menthol, and eucalyptol are included for their unproven antipruritic effect. Phenol has some local anesthetic effects but can cause irritation. Menthol produces a cooling effect that may temporarily relieve itching. Eucalyptol also provides a fragrance.

Astringents (ammonium alum, potassium alum, and zinc sulfate) may reduce inflammation, local edema, and exudation. Menthol,

methyl salicylate, and thymol have some counterirritant effect. Various surfactants are sometimes included to help spread the douche into the mucosal folds and rugae to aid in cleansing.

Feminine Deodorant Sprays

These products are deodorants and have no medicinal or therapeutic properties. The Food and Drug Administration has classified such sprays as cosmetic rather than "hygiene" products. Ingredients include perfumes to mask odor, antimicrobials to preserve the product, emollients to soothe the skin, and propellants to deliver the ingredients. Irritation is the most common adverse effect and is caused by overuse, application to previously inflamed surfaces, and holding the spray too close upon application.

MENSTRUAL DISCOMFORT PRODUCTS

OTC menstrual products are promoted to relieve premenstrual tension and edema along

TABLE 19-4 MENSTRUAL DISCOMFORT PRODUCTS

Product and Manufacturer	Ingredients
Aqua-Ban (Thompson Medical)	Ammonium chloride, 325 mg; caffeine, 100 mg
Cardui (Chattem)	Acetaminophen, 325 mg; pamabrom, 25 mg; pyrilamine maleate, 12.5 mg
Femcaps (Buffington)	Aspirin, 162 mg; phenacetin, 65 mg; caffeine, 32 mg; ephedrine sulfate, 8 mg; atropine sulfate, 0.0325 mg
Midol (Glenbrook)	Aspirin, 454 mg; caffeine, 32.4 mg; cinnamedrine, 14.9 mg
Odrinil "Water Pills" (Fox)	Powder extract of buchu, 34.4 mg; uva ursi, 34.4 mg, corn silk, 34.4 mg; juniper 16.2 mg; caffeine extract 16.2 mg
Pamprin (Chattem)	Acetaminophen, 325 mg; pamabron, 25 mg; pyrilamine maleate, 12.5 mg
Permathene H$_2$Off (Alleghany)	Ammonium chloride, 600 mg; caffeine, 200 mg
Sunril Premenstrual Capsules (Schering)	Acetaminophen, 300 mg; pamabron, 50 mg; pyrilamine maleate, 25 mg
Trendar Premenstrual Tablets (Whitehall)	Acetaminophen, 325 mg; pamabrom, 25 mg
Tri-Aqua Pfeiffer)	Extracts of buchu; uva ursi; triticum; zea; caffeine, 100 mg

with menstrual pain and discomfort. Ingredients include analgesics, diuretics, antihistamines, stimulants, and antispasmodics (Table 19-4). With the exception of the analgesics, these ingredients are of questionable value. The cost of multiple ingredient products is two to three times greater than brand name ones and as much as 10 times greater than generic aspirin or acetaminophen tablets.

Acetaminophen, followed by aspirin, is the analgesic most often included in these preparations. Both are effective in relieving mild to moderate pain. Aspirin has additional anti-inflammatory action. Acetaminophen is generally thought to be "safer than aspirin" by the public, since it does not cause gastrointestinal irritation. However, acetaminophen has been reported to cause hepatotoxicity in excessive doses,[8] and patients should be ad-

vised not to exceed recommended maximum daily doses.

The value of diuretics is questionable because of subtherapeutic doses or unsubstantiated effectiveness. Ingredients in these products that are thought to add diuretic effects include pamabrom, ammonium chloride, caffeine, and vegetable extracts.

Antihistamines may provide sedative effects to relieve tension, irritability, and nervousness; however, the doses used are less than recommended to produce sedation but may produce drowsiness. A drowsy patient is not necessarily less tense, irritable, or nervous. Pyrilamine maleate is the most common antihistamine in these compounds.

The stimulant caffeine is traditionally combined with OTC analgesics, but its relation to pain relief is unknown. One product

TABLE 19-5 TOPICAL ANTIPRURITICS AND ANESTHETICS

Product and Manufacturer	Ingredients
Antihistamines	
PBZ (Geigy)	Tripelennamine HCL, 2% Cream: water-washable base Ointment: petrolatum base
Benadryl (Parke-Davis)	Diphenhydramine HCl, 2%; water-miscible base
Anesthetics	
Americaine (Arnar-Stone)	Benzocaine, 20% Aerosol: water-dispersable base Ointment: water-soluble polyethylene glycol base; benzethonium chloride, 0.1%
Benzocaine (Various)	Benzocaine, 5%; cream, ointment base
Butesin Picrate (Abbott)	Butamben picrate, 1%; ointment base
Dibucaine (Various)	Dibucaine, 1%; ointment base
Nupercainal (CIBA)	Dibucaine, 0.5%; water-washable base
Pontocaine (Breon)	Tetracaine HCl, 1%; water-miscible base
Quotane (Menly & James)	Dimethisoquin HCl, 0.5%; thimerosal 1:50,000; water-miscible base
Surfacaine (Lilly)	Cream: cyclomethycaine, 0.5%; vanishing cream base Ointment: cyclomethycaine sulfate, 1%
Tronothane (Abbott)	Pramoxine HCl, 1% Cream: water-miscible base Jelly: water-soluble base
Xylocaine (Astra)	Lidocaine, 2.5%; water-miscible base
Corticosteroids	
Clear-Aid (Squibb)	Hydrocortisone, 0.5%
Cortaid (Upjohn)	Hydrocortisone acetate equivalent to hydrocortisone, 0.5%; ointment, cream, or spray
Dermolate Anti-itch (Schering)	Hydrocortisone, 0.5%; cream, spray
Combination Products	
Aerotherm (Aeroceuticals)	Spray: benzocaine, 13.6%; benzyl alcohol, 22.7%
Bicozene Creme (Ex-Lax Dist.)	Benzocaine, 5%; resorcinol, 1.67%
Derma Medicone (Medicone)	Benzocaine, 2%; oxyquinolone sulfate, 1.05%; menthol, 0.28%; ichthammol, 1%; zinc oxide, 13.7%; petrolatum, lanolin, perfume

(Table 19-5 continues on page 271.)

TABLE 19-5 TOPICAL ANTIPRURITICS AND ANESTHETICS—(cont.)

Product and Manufacturer	Ingredients
Dermoplast (Ayerst)	Spray: benzocaine, 20%; menthol, 0.5%; water-miscible base
Diothane (Merrell-National)	Diperodon, 1%; petrolatum; propylene glycol; sorbitan sesquioleate; oxyquinoline benzoate, 0.1%
Foille (Blistex)	Spray: benzocaine, 2%; benzyl alcohol, 4%; oxyquinoline, vegetable oil base
Pontocaine (Breon)	Tetracaine, 0.5%; menthol, 0.5%; white petrolatum, white wax
Tucks (Parke-Davis)	Cream, ointment: witch hazel, 50% Premoistened pads: witch hazel, 50%; glycerin, 10%; water; methyl paraben, 0.1%; benzethonium chloride, 0.003%
Vaginex (Schmid)	Benzocaine, resorcinol
Vagisil Feminine Itching Medication (Combe)	Benzocaine, 5%; resorcinol, 2%

contains ephedrine sulfate, which is a stimulant and a β-adrenergic receptor agonist on uterine smooth muscle. The effectiveness of ephedrine, cinnamedrine, and atropine in relieving muscle cramps is not well documented.

OTHER GYNECOLOGIC PRODUCTS

Topical Antipruritics and Anesthetics

A variety of products are available which contain local anesthetics, antihistamines, astringents, antimicrobials, and hydrocortisone. Their usefulness in relieving vulvar pruritis is limited and treatment for a serious underlying disorder may be delayed. The preparations are safe, but allergic reactions may occur and require discontinuation. Table 19-5 lists some topical antipruritic and anesthetic products currently available.

Lubricants

Lubricants are useful when treating dyspareunia from excessive dryness. A lack of estrogen

support of vaginal mucosa must be considered when prolonged dryness is evident. A water-soluble lubricant can be safely applied to the introitus or penis prior to intercourse. The least expensive but effective products are H-R Lubricating Jelly or K-Y Jelly. Transi-Lube, a more exotic product, is promoted as a sexual-foaming lubricant, because it is packaged as an aerosol foam and has a mild strawberry flavor and aroma.

REFERENCES

1. Helenius A, Simons K: Solubilization of membranes by detergents. *Biochem Biophys Acta* 415:29, 1975
2. Chvapil M, Droegemueller W, Owen J, et al: Studies on nonoxynol-9 III: Effect on fibroblast and spermatozoa. *Fertil Steril* 33(5) 521–525, May 1980
3. Chantler E, Duncan GW, Gallegos AJ, et al: Vaginal rings capable of constant release rate of spermicides. In Sciarra JJ, Zatuchni GI, Speidel JJ (eds): *Risks, Benefits and Controversies in Fertility Control*. New York: Harper & Row, 1977, p. 2
4. Topical spermacides for contraception. *Med Lett* 22(21):91–92, 1977

5. Stone SC, Cardinale F: Evaluation of a new vaginal contraceptive. *Am J Obstet Gynecol* 133:635, 1979

6. Vaughan B, et al: *Fam Plan Perspect* 9:251, 1977

7. Chvapil M, Droegemueller W, Owen J, et al: Studies on nonoxynol-9: I. The effect on the vaginas of rabbits and rats. *Fertil Steril* 33(4), 445–450, Apr 1980

8. Peterson RG, et al: Toxicity of acetaminophen overdose. *J Am Coll Emerg Phys* 7:202, 1978

9. Jick, H, Walker, A, Rothman, K, et al: Vaginal spermacides and congenital disorders. *JAMA* 245:1329, 1981

10. Abrutyn, D, McKenzie, B, Nadaskay, N: Teratology study of intravaginally administered nonoxynol-9-containing contraceptive cream in rats. *Fertil Steril* 37:113, 1982

20. Drugs to Treat Vulvovaginal Infections

JAMES K. CRANE

Vulvovaginal infections are the most common problems seen by the clinician who cares for women. The treatment of the various fungal, bacterial, viral, and other vulvovaginal disorders is a major part of gynecologic practice. Effective treatment of these sometimes debilitating problems is founded on a firm knowledge of the normal flora inhabiting the vulvovaginal area and the pathophysiology of each individual disease process. Advances in understanding the vaginal flora have given new insight into this ecologic niche and have made treatment regimens for such infections more rational. In this chapter, the common vulvovaginal infections are reviewed and the pharmacologic agents currently used for their treatment are discussed.

VULVOVAGINAL CANDIDIASIS

Candida albicans is a fungus found on many areas of the body. Differentiating the colonization of *Candida* from true infection becomes difficult, since the organism has been recovered in 25 to 50 percent of women who were considered free of vaginal disease.[1,2]

The diagnosis is based on a thorough medical history and physical examination with confirming laboratory studies. The patient may complain of dyspareunia, dysuria, or a mild to moderate curdy-white to yellow discharge. The onset is usually abrupt and often occurs in the luteal phase of the menstrual cycle just prior to menstruation. Pruritus is usually the most common presenting complaint with erythema, excoriations, and occasional white patches adherent to the vagina often being found on examination.

Examination of the vaginal discharge is imperative for proper diagnosis, with the wet mount having a sensitivity of 40 to 80 percent in detecting *Candida*.[3,4] This sensitivity is improved by adding a drop of 10 percent potassium hydroxide to the wet mount, but the opportunity to see trichomonads is lost. The organism may also be seen on Gram stain as gram-positive ovoid bodies with pseudohyphae with a sensitivity reported to be from 70 to nearly 100 percent.[3] The papanicolau smear has only a 20 to 46 percent positive rate in culture-positive patients.[3,4]

Testing of the vaginal pH may be useful. The normal pH of the vagina in the reproductive years is 3.5 to 4.5. During *C. albicans* infections the pH is usually 4 to 5, unless the infection is mixed. Culture may be done on Nickerson or Sabourand medium, but a positive growth is not an indication of disease, and culture is seldom necessary for diagnosis.

Predisposing factors in *Candida* vulvovaginitis include diabetes, pregnancy, broad-spectrum antibiotics, and oral antitrichomonal agents. Although there is a twofold increase in the incidence of positive *Candida* culture in women on steroidal antifertility drugs, there is no increase in the symptoms and signs of infection.[2]

Recurrent vaginal infections are a clinical dilemma. Miles et al.[5] report a virtual 100 per-

273

cent correlation between the anorectal candidiasis and vulvovaginal candidiasis. Patients without vulvovaginal involvement had negative anorectal cultures. This would seem to indicate that a "cure" in a certain number of patients is impossible due to persistent rectal colonization. A recent report by Syverson et al.[6] suggests "a poorly understood" lack of cellular immune response to *Candida* antigens in women with chronic *Candida* vaginitis.

Treatment of vulvovaginal candidiasis before the introduction of nystatin and the imidazole group of antifungal agents consisted of treatment with a 1 percent solution of gentian violet. Friedrick describes a 95-percent cure rate using this agent if it is carefully applied to the cervix, entire vagina, introitus, and inner vulva.[7] A second application is usually made 72 hours after the first. Charles reports the use of gentian violet three times for 1 or 2 weeks.[8] The application of gentian violet has not been popular, however, because of staining problems and the local reactions after treatment. The patient should also be given a fungicidal cream to be inserted morning and night for 2 weeks regardless of symptom relief or menses.

Nystatin

Nystatin (Nilstat) has replaced gentian violet because of its ease of use. Nystatin is produced by a strain of *Streptomyces noursei* and acts by binding to the sterol moiety present in the cellular membrane of the fungus. The cell permeability is thus altered, and intracellular potassium and other constituents of the cell are lost.

Nystatin comes as a vaginal suppository or cream. The suppository contains 100,000 units and is inserted in the deep vaginal vault twice daily for 14 days. Treatment must be continuous, regardless of menstruation. Nystatin cream should be used on the vulva and the skin of the male partner if he shows any signs of the disease. The combination of oral and topical therapy may be considered for recurrent vulvovaginal candidiasis. The oral dose (500,000 units four times daily for 1 week) will effectively treat the endogenous source.

Imidazole Drugs

The imidazole group includes miconazole (Monistat), clotrimazole (Gyne-Lotromin), and econazole. Their mode of action on the cell wall is similar to nystatin, and ribonucleic acid and protein synthesis is consequently disrupted.

Miconazole cream has been compared to nystatin.[9,10] Miconazole was used once daily for 2 weeks, while nystatin was used twice daily for 2 weeks. Miconazole had a slightly greater cure rate in both studies, but the patient population was small. Sargent then showed 2 percent miconazole nitrate in a 7-day course to be as effective as a 10- to 14-day course.[11] A recent report by VanLeusden and Nuijten showed a mycologic cure rate of 93 percent in patients on a 6-day course of 200-mg miconazole tablets compared to an 80-percent cure rate if a 3-day course of 400-mg miconazole nitrate was prescribed.[12] These were not significantly different, however, and it is implied that treatment with increased dosage and decreased duration remains effective. It should be noted that these findings are preliminary and require further verification.

The dosage schedule for clotrimazole (Gyne-Lotrimin) has also been investigated. The initial therapeutic treatment consisted of the insertion of a 100-mg vaginal tablet daily for 6 to 14 days, and occasionally, clotrimazole cream 1.0 percent to the vulva. Oates and Davidson compared 6-day and 12-day courses of clotrimazole, combined with the use of clotrimazole cream to the vulva twice daily.[13] The cure rate was similar. In addition, 50 percent of the women in each group were culture-positive at 10 weeks after therapy. Masterton, Napier, and Henderson[14] found that a 3-day course using two clotrimazole tablets high in the vagina each night resulted in a 24.3 percent failure rate 4 weeks after therapy in patients with a history of genital candidiasis, but only a 4.3 percent failure rate in women with a primary infection.

Econazole is available in Europe in a 150-mg vaginal suppository and a 1 percent vaginal cream. Balmer found a cure rate of 84.2 percent using a vaginal suppository for 3 consecu-

TABLE 20-1 DRUGS USED IN THE TREATMENT OF VULVOVAGINAL CANDIDIASIS

Generic Name	Dose	Adverse Effects
Gentian violet, 1%	Apply to vulvovaginal area—repeat in 72 hr	Local irritative effects, staining of skin and clothing
Nystatin (korostatin, mycostatin, nilstat)	One to two 100,000-unit vag tablet each day for 2 weeks	Mild local effects
Miconazole nitrate, 2% (Monistat-7 Cream) (Monistat-7 Vag. Suppos.)	1 applicatorful or suppos. intravaginally at bedtime for 7 days	Local irritative reactions, burning, itching, cramps
Clotrimazole (Gyne-Lotrimin 1% Cream and Tablets, Mycelex-	1 applicatorful or 1 tablet intravaginally at bedtime for 7–14 days	Local irritative symptoms, burning, erythema

tive days;[15] however, the agent is unavailable in the United States.

Table 20-1 summarizes current treatment schedules. There are minimal side effects with any of these drugs. The possible venereal nature of the disease and its predisposing conditions should be recalled in evaluating treatment failures. Individualization is important, and the adjustment of the duration of therapy depends on each case. The selection and duration of a specific agent is controversial. Masterton and co-workers[14] have found that half of patients suffering from sexually transmitted diseases fail to adhere to any course of treatment for more than 7 days.[16] Other studies have shown that patients who experience rapid symptomatic relief readily terminate their therapy.[14,17] The treatment of vulvovaginal candidiasis in pregnancy is identical to the nonpregnant state.

TRICHOMONAS VAGINALIS

Trichomoniasis is one of the most frequently occurring sexually acquired diseases. Of those patients with symptomatic vaginitis, 15 to 20 percent harbor this anaerobic, flagellated protozoan. The organism is capable of infecting the vagina, bladder, urethra, rectum, vas deferens, seminal vesicles, prostate, and prepuce. Catteral and Nicol reported that all female partners of 56 men with trichomonal urethritis harbored the organism, thus substantiating the venereal nature of the disease.[18] Only 12 percent of male consorts with *Trichomonas* will have symptoms.[18]

The peak incidence of trichomoniasis occurs between the ages of 16 and 35, which coincides with peak sexual activity. There is a high incidence of other venereal diseases, and about half of the women in a British study presenting with gonorrhea were found to have trichomoniasis as well.[19]

Patients may be asymptomatic or have an intense vulvovaginitis with pruritis, frothy discharge, foul odor, excoriations, dyspareunia, and dysuria. Symptoms usually occur after menstruation, which may explain the elevated pH (5.0 to 6.5) of the vagina seen in these infections.

Physical examination may reveal an erythematous, edematous vulvovaginal area with occasional excoriations. The vaginal discharge may be copious, foul smelling, and frothy. The vagina and cervix may display areas of punctuated hemorrhages, giving them a strawberry appearance.

Diagnosis may be made by saline wet mount visualization and further enhanced by culture techniques on hydrolysate serum media. The pap smear alone has false-positive and false-negative findings in 48.4 percent of partners.[20] In addition, *Trichomonas* can cause an atypical Pap smear, which is actually the indication of inflammatory changes and unrelated to the malignant change.

Metronidazole

The current treatment of trichomoniasis is metronidazole, an imidazole derivative. Metronidazole is directly trichomonacidal, although the mechanism is unknown. The drug is well absorbed after oral administration. Durel and associates found that oral doses of the drug imparted trichomonacidal activity to semen and urine, and showed that high cure rates could be obtained in both male and female patients.[21] Both unchanged metronidazole and several metabolites are excreted in various proportions in urine after oral administration, and may lead to a brownish discoloration of the urine. Low concentrations of metronidazole also appear in the saliva and in the breast milk during treatment. There are drugs similar to metronidazole used in Europe, including tinidazole which is undergoing testing in the United States.

The recommended dose of metronidazole has changed. The prior recommendation was one 250-mg tablet three times a day for 7 days. Morton (1972), Dykers (1975), and Fleury and associates (1977) found a single 2-gm dose of metronidazole to be as effective in treating vaginal trichomoniasis.[22-24]

The vast majority of treatment failures are probably due to reinfection, but continued reports of resistance are emerging.[25,26] Poor gastrointestinal absorption or too rapid metabolic transformation may also explain treatment failure.[27,28]

Side effects from metronidazole include gastrointestinal disturbances such as nausea, anorexia, diarrhea, epigastric distress, abdominal cramping, and vomiting. A metallic taste and a furry tongue are not uncommon. In some individuals the consumption of alcohol with metronidazole may produce nausea and vomiting. A sudden overgrowth of *Candida* may occur in the vagina. Neutropenia has been reported, and low neutrophil counts returned to normal in all cases after the course of medication was completed. The manufacturer recommends a total and differential leukocyte count before and after treatment, but most clinicians reserve this for retreatment. Dizziness, vertigo, incoordination, ataxia, and convulsive seizures have also been reported. Confusion, irritability, depression, weakness, insomnia, mild erythematous eruptions, and peripheral neuropathy characterized mainly by numbness or parasthesia of an extremity have been described. Metronidazole is contraindicated in patients with evidence or history of a blood dyscrasia, active organic disease of the central nervous system, first trimester of pregnancy, and prior sensitization to metronidazole.

Metronidazole has not been shown to be teratogenic in either animal or human studies, but has been reported to be mutagenic in bacteria.[29-31] The drug has been shown to be tumorogenic in rodents, and the manufacturer suggests that treatment in the second and third trimesters be limited to those in whom local palliative treatment has been inadequate in controlling symptoms.[32] There is, however, no consistently effective local treatment.

CORYNEBACTERIUM VAGINALE AND NONSPECIFIC VAGINITIS

The treatment of *Corynebacterium vaginale* (hemophilis vaginalis) has been under close scrutiny in recent years. Gardner and Dukes (1955) described the organism as being involved in most cases of nonspecific vaginitis.[33] *C. vaginale* has also been identified in 9.5 to 13 percent of women without any overt sign of infection.[34-36] This finding, however, should not be taken to dispute the role of *C. vaginale* in vaginal infection but to emphasize the nature of commensals becoming pathogens. In cases of overt vaginitis, the organism has been recovered in 31 to 57 percent of patients.[34-37]

Pruritis, a common complaint of candidiasis and trichomoniasis, is uncommon in *C. vaginale* infection unless a mixed infection is present. *C. vaginale* infection has a malodorous discharge with a vaginal pH in the 5.0 to 6.0 range. The discharge is moderately profuse and usually unrelated to the menstrual cycle. On wet smear, leukocytes and lactobacilli counts are reduced, and the "clue cell," as reported by Gardner and Dukes, is seen.[33]

Evidence to substantiate the venereal nature of *C. vaginale* vaginitis comes from work by Gardner and Kaufman, who studied the sexual partners of 101 women infected with the organism.[38] Positive urethral colonization was present in 91 (90 percent) of the males, who were also asymptomatic. Other research has shown the organism to be a primary commensal found in women and children without prior sexual contact.[39,40]

The use of a sulfonamide cream was initially considered to be a rational treatment, but Pheifer and associates have shown it to be ineffective in nonspecific vaginitis.[41] In addition, they found doxycycline and ampicillin to yield only a small percentage of cures when the *C. vaginale* culture was positive. Metronidazole cured vaginitis in 80 of 81 patients in this study, suggesting that anaerobic organisms are involved in a synergistic fashion in these infections.

Lee and Schmale reported successful treatment using ampicillin 500 mg every 6 hours for 5 days.[42] The use of this treatment regimen produced both clinical and culture cure in all 21 patients. However, when Pheifer et al. used the same protocol, clinical cure and eradication of *C. vaginale* occurred in only 9 of 27 patients.[41] These poor results of ampicillin therapy were unexplainable, since *C. vaginale* showed good in vitro sensitivity to ampicillin. Tetracycline and erythromycin have also been shown to be ineffective in treating these infections.[41,43,44] Table 20-2 summarizes current treatment plans. This is a venereal disease and failure to treat the sexual partner increases the likelihood of treatment failure.

The agent of choice at the time of this writing is uncertain, although the evidence

TABLE 20-2 TREATMENT FOR NONSPECIFIC VAGINITIS (CORYNEBACTERIUM VAGINALE)

Therapy	Treatment Regimen
Systemic	
Tetracycline	500 mg PO every 6 hr for 7 days
Ampicillin	500 mg PO every 6 hr for 5–7 days
Metronidazole (Flagyl)	500 mg PO every 6 hr for 7 days
Local	
Sulfonamide cream (Sultrin)	Apply intravaginally two times a day for 10 days

would indicate that metronidazole remains the most effective one.

GONORRHEA

Gonorrhea continues to be an epidemic disease of worldwide proportions. Penicillin has long been the treatment for gonorrhea and is discussed in detail in Chapter 24. The discovery of β-lactamase-producing strains of *Neisseria gonorrhea* by Ashford, Golash, and Hemming (1976) and Phillips (1976) has explained treatment failures.[45,46]

The symptomatic patient usually shows a vaginal discharge or dysuria. Barlow and associates showed that microscopic examination of cultures from infected sites produces the diagnosis in only 60 percent of females compared to 95 percent of males.[47] Cultures should be taken from the urethral orifice, vagina, endocervical, and anal canals. Omission of the anal culture will cause a missed diagnosis in almost 5 percent of infected patients. Repeated cultures may support initial negative results. Chipperfield and Catterall, using urethral and endocervical cultures, showed in 209 female patients that 91 percent were positive on first culture.[48] They were able to substantiate the diagnosis in another 7.1 percent by repeating the culture. Barlow and Phillips also showed that despite 85.6 percent positive cultures, only 60 percent of the women were symptomatic.[49]

Treatment for uncomplicated genitourinary gonorrhea has been outlined by the Center for Disease Control, and appears in Table 20-3.[50] All patients should be tested for syphilis and follow-up cultures obtained in 3 to 7 days after treatment. Spectinomycin should only be used in cases of β-lactamase-resistent N. gonorrhea or in those who fail to respond to other antimicrobial treatment.[51] Tetracycline is contraindicated during pregnancy (Chap. 2).

Treatment of N. gonorrhea infections is mandatory if the complications of infertility, pelvic inflammatory disease, and possible disseminated infection are to be prevented. The sexual partner(s) should also be treated.

ATROPHIC VAGINITIS

Atrophic vaginitis is most often found in postmenopausal women and in those who have been rendered menopausal through removal of their ovaries. The vaginal mucosa and vulva are usually thin and quite pale, and rugal folds are usually missing. The discharge is not usually diagnostic, but examination under the microscope is necessary to rule out candidiasis, trichomoniasis, or other forms of vaginitis.

Treatment consists of hormonal replacement by the judicious use of estrogen creams or tablets (see Chap. 17). Since estrogens are absorbed from the vaginal mucosa, they should be avoided in estrogen-sensitive tumors of the breast or uterus.[52] In addition, they are ineffective in vulvar dystrophies where 2 percent testosterone propionate in petrolatum is the drug of choice.

Gordon et al. found 17β-estradiol (Estrace vaginal cream) to also be effective in the treatment of postmenopausal vaginitis.[53] The patients were successfully treated for 1 or 2 months with 0.2 mg of micronized estradiol

TABLE 20-3   TREATMENT OF UNCOMPLICATED GENITOURINARY NEISSERIA GONORRHEA INFECTIONS

Treatment of Choice
Aqueous procaine penicillin G 4.8 million units IM with 1.0 gm probenecid by mouth.
Tetracycline hydrochloride 500 mg by mouth four times a day for 5 days

Slightly Less Effective
Ampicillin 3.5 gm with 1 gm probenecid by mouth
Amoxicillin 3.5 gm with 1 gm probenecid by mouth

For Penicillin Treatment Failures or Penicillin Allergies
Spectinomycin 2.0 gm IM (one dose)

intravaginally at bedtime. Dosage in each patient must be individualized regardless of the form of estrogen used. The minimal dose that achieves the desired therapeutic effect is the correct dosage.

HERPES VULVOVAGINITIS

The herpes simplex virus is a DNA-containing virus specific to humans with two antigenic groups (type I and type II). Type I herpes virus, initially found only in the oral cavity, has been seen in as many as 30 percent of genital herpes infections.

Primary infection with herpes virus (usually type II) may present without clinical manifestations or with both localized and systemic reactions. The patient may experience fever, malaise, inguinal adenopathy, erosions, labial edema and painful ulcerations. Small vesicles usually present on the labia minora, inner labia majora, or cervix. The vesicles often enlarge, rupture, and ulcerate before spontaneous healing. The ulcers last from 1 to 3 weeks in primary infection and last for a shorter period without systemic manifestations in recurrent infection. The virus then goes into a latent phase within the nerve ganglia and may recur with any form of stress. Recurrent lesions tend

TABLE 20-4 TOPICAL THERAPY OF HERPETIC VULVOVAGINITIS

Agent	Comments	Source
2 Deoxy-D-glucose	Inhibits synthesis or elongation of macromolecules required for envelope biogenesis and recognition phenomenon Effective in this study	54
3% Adenine arabinoside	Inhibits DNA synthesis Ineffective	55
5% Idoxuridine	Inhibits DNA synthesis Not effective in herpetic vulvovaginitis	56 57
Neutral-red photo- dynamic inactivation	Oncogenic potential Not effective	58
Proflavine photodynamic inactivation	Oncogenic potential Not effective	59
Burrow's solution	Soothing for local relief only	
Ether	Painful Ineffective	60
Nonoxynol-9	Nonionic surfactant Not effective	61
Povidone iodine douche (Betadine)	Antiseptic Antiviral 2 tsp betadine per quart warm water	62
Povidone iodine sitz bath	4 oz betadine solution to warm tub two to three times daily	

to be more localized and less painful. The diagnosis may be accomplished by observing intranuclear inclusion bodies on Pap smear or a positive culture.

Treatment successes have been limited. Table 20-4 lists agents that are currently in use or have been tried. Local treatment is ineffective due to the latent phase of the virus. In addition, the spontaneous healing of the ulcers makes it difficult to assess treatment regimens. Standard treatment includes the local use of sitz baths, topical povidone-iodine gels, and analgesics as necessary. Treatment during pregnancy consists of the use of sitz baths and topical povidone-iodine gels.

CHLAMYDIAL INFECTIONS

Chlamydia trachomatis has come under tremendous scrutiny in recent investigations. In the female genital tract, *C. trachomatis* most commonly infects the cervix to cause cervicitis. The organism appears to be specific for squamocolumnar cells and thus does not cause a vaginitis. Since most clinicians do not have culture facilities for *Chlamydia,* one should consider treatment for this organism if all other pathogens have been excluded. Recommended oral regimens of tetracycline include 2 gm/day for 7 days or 1 gm/day for 14 days. Erythromycin is an alternative drug for those

TABLE 20-5   RECOMMENDED TREATMENT FOR UNCOMMON VULVOVAGINAL INFECTIONS

Disease	Drug	Dose	Source(s)
Syphilis			
Primary, secondary, and early latent (less than 1 year's duration)	Benzathine penicillin Penicillin allergy: tetracycline or erythromycin	2.4 million units in divided doses each buttock

500 mg orally four times a day for 15 days | 63 |
During pregnancy	Benzathine penicillin	2.4 million units in divided doses each buttock (Charles prefers 2.4 million units in divided doses each buttock each week for 3 consecutive weeks)	63
	Penicillin allergy: erythromycin	500 mg orally four times a day for 15 days (Charles prefers 750 mg orally four times a day for 20 days)	63
Late latent (more than 1 year's duration)	Benzathine penicillin	2.4 million units in divided doses each buttock every week for 3 consecutive weeks	63
	Penicillin allergy: tetracycline or erythromycin	500 mg orally four times a day for 30 days	63
Granuloma inguinale (agent: Calymmato-bacterium granulomates)	Tetracycline or erythromycin	500 mg four times a day for 14 days	64
Chancroid (agent: Hemophilus ducreyi)	Sulfonamides (sulfisoxazole)	1 gm four times a day for 2 weeks	65
Condylomata acuminata	25% podophyllin in tincture of benzoin	1. Wash lesions with soap and water within 4 hr of application.
2. Do not apply to vagina or cervix.
3. Systemic toxic effects have been reported.
4. Contraindicated in the gravid patient. | 66

66
67,68

69,70 |
| Lymphogranuloma venereum (agent: Chlamydia trachomatis, subgroup A) | Sulfonamides (sulfisoxazole, sulfadiazine) Tetracycline | 1 gm four times a day for 3 weeks

500 mg four times a day for 1 week, followed by 250 mg four times a day for 2 weeks | 71

71 |
| | Doxycycline hyclate | 100 mg two times a day for 2 weeks | 71 |

unable to tolerate tetracyclines, or for use in pregnant women.

OTHER VULVOVAGINAL INFECTIONS

It is beyond the scope of this text to include each drug for every vulvovaginal infection; however, Table 20-5 lists and comments upon current drugs recommended for healing these less frequent infections.

REFERENCES

1. Drake TE, Mallbach HE: Candida and candidiasis, parts 1, 2. *Postgrad Med* 53:83, 120, 1973
2. Oriel JD, Partridge BM, Denny MJ, et al: Genital yeast infections. *Br Med J* 4:761, 1971
3. Eddie DAS: The laboratory diagnosis of vaginal infection caused by trichomonas and candida (monilial) species. *J Med Micro biol* 1:153, 1968
4. McHennon MT, Smith TM, McLennon CE: Diagnosis of vaginal mycosis and trichomoniasis: Reliability of cytologic smear, wet smear and culture. *Obstet Gynecol* 40:231, 1972
5. Miles MR, Olsen L, Rogers A: Recurrent vaginal candidiasis: Importance of an intestinal reservoir. *JAMA* 230:1836, 1977
6. Syverson RE, Buckley H, Gibian J, et al: Cellular and humoral immune status in women with chronic vaginitis. *Am J Obstet Gynecol* 134:624, 1979
7. Friedrick EG: *Vulvar Disease*. Philadelphia, Saunders, 1976, p 14
8. Charles D: *Infections in Obstetrics and Gynecology*. Philadelphia, Saunders, 1980 p 64
9. Culbertson C: Monistat: A new fungicide for treatment of vulvovaginal candidiasis. *Am J Obstet Gynecol* 120:973, 1974
10. Davis JE, Frudenfeld JH, Goddard JL: Comparative evaluation of "monistat" and "mycostatin" in the treatment of vulvovaginal candidiasis. *Obstet Gynecol* 44:403, 1974
11. Sargent EC Jr, Pasquale SA: Evaluation of monistat cream (miconazole nitrate 2%) in reduced regimen for treatment of vulvovaginal candidiasis. *J Reprod Med* 19:67, 1977
12. VanLeusden, HAIM, Nuijten STM: Miconazole in the treatment of vulvovaginal candidiasis: Comparison of a 6-day therapy and a 3-day treatment course. *Eur J Obstet Gynecol Reprod Biol* 10(3):203, 1980
13. Oates JK, Davidson F: Treatment of vaginal candidiasis with clotrimazole. *Postgrad Med J* 50(suppl):99, 1974
14. Masterton G, Napier I, Henderson J: Three-day clotrimazole treatment in candidal vaginitis, *Br J Vener Dis* 53:126, 1977
15. Balmer JA: Three-day therapy of vulvovaginal candidiasis with econazole: A multicentric study comprising 966 cases. *Am J Obstet Gynecol* 126:436, 1976
16. Masterton G, Henderson J, Napier I, et al: Vaginal candidiasis. *Br Med J* 1:712, 1976
17. Robertson WH: Vulvovaginal candidiasis treatment with clotrimazole cream in seven days compared with fourteen-day treatment with miconazole cream. *Am J Obstet Gynecol* 132:321, 1978
18. Catteral RD, Nicol CS: Is trichomonal infestation a venereal disease? *Br Med J* 1:1177, 1960
19. Rein JF, Chapel TA: Trichomoniasis, candidiasis and the minor venereal diseases. *Clin Obstet Gynecol* 18:73, 1975
20. Perl G: Errors in diagnosis of trichomonas vaginales infection: As observed among 1199 patients. *Obstet Gynecol* 39:70, 1972
21. Durel P, Roiron V, Seboulet A, Borel LJ: Systemic treatment of human trichomoniasis with a derivative of nitroimidazole, 8823 R.R. *Br J Vener Dis* 36:21, 1960
22. Morton RS: Metronidazole in the single dose treatment of trichomonal vaginitis in men and women. *Br J Vener Dis* 48:525, 1972
23. Dykers JR: Single-dose metronidazole for trichomonal vaginitis: Patient and consort. *N Engl J Med* 293:23, 1975
24. Fleury FJ, VanBergen WS, Prentice RL, et al: Single dose of two grams of metronidazole for trichomonas vaginalis infection. *Am J Obstet Gynecol* 128:320, 1977
25. Thurner J, Meingassner JG: Isolation of trichomonas vaginalis resistant to metronidazole (letter). *Lancet* 2(8092 pt 1):738, 1978
26. Meingassner JG: Strain of trichomonas vaginales resistant to metronidazole and other 5-nitroimidazoles. *Antimicrob Agents Chemother* 15(2):254, 1979
27. Kane PO, McFadzeam JA, Squires S: Absorption and excretion of metronidazole. *Br J Vener Dis* 37:276, 1961
28. Stambaugh JE, Feo LG, Manther RW: The isolation and identification of the urinary oxida-

tive metabolites of metronidazole in man. *J Pharmacol Exp Ther* 161:373, 1968

29. Voogd CE, van der Stel JJ, Jacobs JA: The mutagenic action of nitroimidazoles: I. Metronidazole, nimorazole, dimetridazole and ronidazole. *Mutat Res* 26:483–490, 1974

30. Legator MS, Connor TH, Stocker M: Detection of mutagenic activity of metronidazole and niridazole in body fluids of humans and mice. *Science* 188:1118–1119, 1975

31. Rosenkranz HS, Speck WT: Mutogenicity of metronidazole activation by mammalian liver microsomes. *Biochem Biophys Res Commun* 66:520–525, 1975

32. Rustia M, Shubik P: Induction of lung tumours and malignant lymphomas in mice by metronidazole. *J Natl. Cancer Inst* 48:721–729, 1972

33. Gardner H, Dukes CD: Haemophelus vaginales vaginitis: A newly defined specific infection previously classified "nonspecific" vaginitis. *Am J Obstet Gynecol* 69:962, 1955

34. Lewis JF, O'Brien SM, Ural UM, et al: Corynebacterium vaginale vaginitis. *Am J Obstet Gynecol* 112:87, 1972

35. Dunkelberg WE Jr, Hefner JD, Patow WE, et al: Hemophelies vaginalis among asymptomatic women. *Obstet Gynecol* 20:629, 1962

36. Josey WE, McKenzie WJ, Lambe DW: Corynebacterium vaginale (haemophelus vaginalis) in women with leukorrhea. *Am J Obstet Gynecol* 126:574, 1976

37. Alzerlund M, Mardh PA: Isolation and identification of corynebacterium vaginale (haemophelus vaginales) in women with infections of the lower genital tract. *Acta Obstet Gynecol Scand* 53:85, 1974

38. Gardner HL, Kaufman RH: *Benign Diseases of the Vulva.* St. Louis, Mosby 1969, pp 191–207

39. McCormack WH, Hayes CH, Rosner B, et al: Vaginal colonization with corynebacterium vaginale (haemophelus vaginalis). *J Infect Dis* 136:740, 1977

40. Hammerschlag MR, Alpert S, Rosner I, et al: Microbiology of the vagina in children: Normal and potentially pathogenic organisms. *Pediatrics* 62:57, 1978

41. Pheifer TA, Forsyth PS, Durfee MA, et al: Nonspecific vaginitis: Role of haemophelus vaginales and treatment with metronidazole. *N Engl J Med* 298:1429, 1978

42. Lee L, Schmale JD: Ampicillin therapy for corynebacterium vaginale (haemophelus vaginales) vaginitis. *Am J Obstet Gynecol* 115:786, 1973

43. Balsdon MJ, Pead L, Taylor GE, et al: Corynebacterium vaginale and vaginitis: A controlled trial of treatment. *Lancet* 8167(1):501, 1980

44. Durfee MA, Forsyth PS, Hale JA, et al: Ineffectiveness of erythromycin for treatment of haemophelus vaginales-associated vaginitis: Possible relationship to acidity of vaginal sections. *Antimicrob Agents Chemother* 16:635, 1979

45. Ashford WA, Golash RG, Hemming VG: Pencillinase-producing neisseria gonorrhoea. *Lancet* 2:657, 1976

46. Phillips I: Beta-lactamase producing penicillin-resistant gonococcus. *Lancet* 2:656, 1976

47. Barlow D, Nayyar K, Phillips I, et al: Diagnosis of gonorrhoea in women. *Br J Vener Dis* 52:326, 1976

48. Chipperfield EJ, Catterall RD: Reappraisal of gram-staining and culture techniques for diagnosis of gonorrhea in women. *Br J Vener Dis* 52:36, 1976

49. Barlow D, Phillips I: Gonorrhoea in women: Diagnostic, clinical, and laboratory aspects. *Lancet* 1:761, 1978

50. Center for Disease Control: Gonorrhea: Center for disease control recommended treatment schedules, 1979. *Ann Intern Med* 90:809, 1979

51. Thornsberry C, Jaffer H, Brown ST, et al: Spectinomycin resistant neisseria gonorrhoea. *JAMA* 237:2405, 1977

52. Rigg LA, Herman HW, Yen SCC: Absorption of estrogen from vaginal cream. *N Engl J Med* 298:195, 1978

53. Gordon WE, Herman HW, Hunter BS: Safety and efficacy of micronized estradiol vaginal cream. *South Med J* 72:1252, 1979

54. Blough HA, Giuntoli RL: Successful treatment of human genital herpes infection with 2-deoxy-D-glucose. *JAMA* 241:2798, 1979

55. Adams HG, Benson EA, Alexander ER, et al: Genital herpetic infection in men and women: Clinical course and effect of topical application of adenine arabenoside *J Infect Dis* 133 (suppl):A151, 1976

56. Taylor PK, Doherty NR: Comparison of the treatment of herpes genitales in men with proflavine photoinactivation, idoxuridine ointment and normal saline. *BR J Vener Dis* 51:125, 1975

57. Kibrick S, Katz AS: Topical idoxuridine in recurrent herpes simplex. *Ann NY Acad Sci* 173:83, 1970

58. Myers MG, Oxman MN, Clark JE, et al: Failure of neutral-red photodynamic inactivation in re-

current herpes simplex virus infection. *N Engl J Med* 293:945, 1975

59. Kaufman RH, Adam E, Mirkovic RR: Treatment of genital herpes simplex virus infection with photodynamic inactivation. *Am J Obstet Gynecol* 132:861, 1968

60. Corey L, Reeves WC, Chiang WT, et al: Ineffectiveness of topical ether for the treatment of genital herpes simplex virus infection. *N Engl J Med* 299:237, 1978

61. Vontver LA, Reeves WC, Rattray M: Clinical course and diagnosis of genital herpes simplex virus infection and evaluation of topical surfactant therapy. *AM J Obstet Gynecol* 133:548, 1979

62. Wilbanks GD, Chez RA: How to diagnose and treat genital herpes. *Contemp Obstet Gynecol* 16:81, 1980

63. Center for Disease Control: Syphilis: CDC recommended treatment schedules. *J Infect Dis* 134:97–99, 1976

64. Charles D: *Infections in Obstetrics and Gynecology.* Philadelphia, Saunders, 1980, p 38

65. Charles, D: *Infections in Obstetrics and Gynecology.* Philadelphia, Saunders, 1980, p 39

66. Charles D: *Infections in Obstetrics and Gynecology.* Philadelphia, Saunders, 1980, p 49

67. Montalde DH, Grombrone JP, Courney NG, et al: Podophyllin poisoning associated with the treatment of condyloma accumulation. *Am J Obstet Gynecol* 119:1130–1131, 1974

68. Slater GE, Rumack BH, Peterson RG: Podophyllin poisoning. Systemic toxicity following cutaneous application. *Obstet Gynecol* 52:94–96, 1978

69. Graber EA, Barber HRK, O'Rourke JJ: Simple surgical treatment for condyloma accumulation of the vulva. *Obstet Gynecol* 29:247–250, 1967

70. Chamberlain MJ, Reynolds AL, Yeoman WB: Toxic effects of podophyllin application in pregnancy. *Br Med J* 3:391–392, 1972

71. Fiumara NJ: *The Sexually Transmissible Diseases,* vol 25, no 3. Chicago, Yearbook Medical Publishers, 1978

72. Topical acyclovir for herpes simplex. *The Medical Letter* 24:55, 1982

21. Drugs and Urologic Disorders

James K. Crane

The past two decades have seen tremendous advancements in our knowledge of the dynamics of lower urinary tract function. Enhanced techniques in urodynamics have increased accuracy in diagnosing urologic disorders. The purpose of this chapter is to discuss drugs used in the treatment of certain urologic disorders in women. Their use should be based upon a thorough history, physical examination, and urodynamic evaluation. Only through proper evaluation and knowledge of lower urinary tract function can the proper pharmacologic agent be chosen.

NEUROPHYSIOLOGY OF THE LOWER URINARY TRACT

The lower urinary tract consists of the bladder, urethra, and their supporting structures. The bladder functions to store and evacuate urine and is innervated by the autonomic nervous system. During bladder filling, there is an increased sympathetic activity via the hypogastric nerves through β-adrenergic receptors in the detrusor muscle. At the same time, α-adrenergic receptors cause contraction of the outlet. The parasympathetic nerves are inhibited during this filling phase (Fig. 21-1).

Evacuation of urine involves a different process. The parasympathetic nerves mediate impulses for urine expulsion, while sympathetic impulses to contract the outlet are inhibited (Fig. 21-2).

By understanding these neurophysiologic principles, drugs may be more properly chosen in aiding either the evacuation or storage of urine. Agents that stimulate the parasympathetic nervous system or inhibit sympathetic effects assist in treating those conditions in which urine evacuation is desired, while agents that inhibit the parasympathetic nervous system aid in the storage of urine.

EVALUATION OF LOWER URINARY TRACT DYSFUNCTION

When evaluating urologic dysfunction, questionnaires have been found to be useful because they allow a more uniform and complete approach to the patient. There are several questionnaires that are available for this purpose.[1-3] In addition to a careful history, a thorough physical exam with a neurologic assessment is mandatory. Urodynamic assessment usually consists of measuring residual urines, cystometry, stress testing, and endoscopy. Depending on the facilities available, these may be combined with simultaneous cystometry and urethral pressure profiles, urine flow studies, and cystometry with urethral pressure profiles combined with electromyographic studies.

After an assessment of this sort, proper choice of drug therapy becomes more rational and has a greater chance of success. We are now able to evaluate lower urinary tract dys-

FILLING PHASE

Sympathetics

a = alpha (contract)

B = beta (relax)

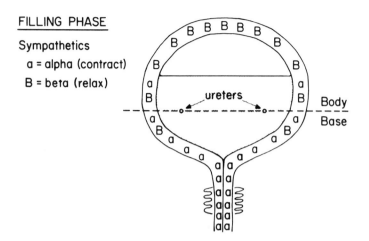

Figure 21-1. Filling phase. The filling phase is mostly a sympathetic process with α-contraction of the bladder base and urethra, β-relaxation of the dome, and α-inhibition of the increasing stimulus of the parasympathetics to discharge as the bladder fills.

function based on whether there is a problem in storage or evacuation of urine. Drugs that aid in the evacuation or storage of urine are listed in Tables 21-1 and 21-2 and are described there in greater detail.

DRUGS THAT PROMOTE URINE EVACUATION

Bethanechol (Duvoid, Myotonachol, Urecholine, Vesicholine)

Bethanechol is a synthetic choline ester (cholinergic) which is primarily muscarinic in activity; that is, it has effects similar to those of the alkaloid muscarine on smooth muscle, cardiac muscle, and exocrine glands.

Despite its widespread use, the literature is not firm on the effect of bethanecol on the bladder. Wein and associates found that in the normal male doses as high as 100 mg orally did not significantly affect the carbon dioxide cystometrogram.[4]

In voiding, there is a synchronous contraction of the detrusor with opening of the bladder neck and urethra. Bethanechol-induced contractions are not always synchronous, and the outlet may not relax because of the weak nicotinic properties of bethanechol that stimulate the sympathetic ganglia, increasing outlet resistance.[5]

Bethanechol may only be given orally or subcutaneously. The subcutaneous dose is usually 2.5 to 5.0 mg every 3 hours, and the

EXPULSION PHASE

Parasympathetics —— contraction ——>

Inhibition of Sympathetics

Relaxation of external striated sphincter

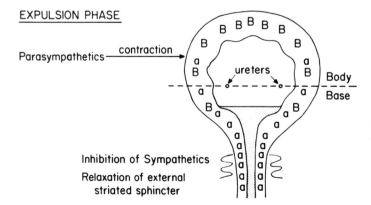

Figure 21-2. Expulsion phase. Expulsion of urine occurs when there is parasympathetic stimulation of the body with inhibition of the sympathetic system of the base. The external sphincter responds to β-autonomic and β-somatic control.

TABLE 21-1 DRUGS THAT AID IN THE EVACUATION OF URINE

Agent	Mode of Action	Dose	Adverse Reactions
Bethanechol: duvoid; myotonachol, urecholine, vesicholine	Stimulates parasympathetic nervous system	10–50 mg orally three to four times a day 2.5–5.0 mg sc three to four times a day	Lacrimation, flushing, sweating, GI disturbances, headaches, visual disturbance
Phenoxybenzamine: dibenzyline	α-Adrenergic blocker	10 mg PO one to three times a day	Postural hypotension, miosis, nasal stuffiness, sweating, dryness of mouth, tachycardia

oral dose is 50 to 100 mg four times a day. By the subcutaneous route, a significant rise in intravesical pressure is noted within 10 minutes, and most activity disappears in 2 hours.[6] When taken orally, the onset of action is slower (30 to 60 minutes) but is maintained for 2 to 6 hours.[6]

Side effects of bethanechol therapy include lacrimation, flushing, sweating, gastrointestinal disturbances such as abdominal cramps, difficulty with visual accommodation, and headaches.

The most common gynecologic use for bethanechol is in the atonic, postoperative bladder. Lapides suggests the following guidelines for the use of bethanechol in patients with atonic bladder:[7] If the patient is using a urethral catheter, this should be removed, or if a suprapubic catheter is in place, it should be clamped. Bethanechol is then given as a dose of 10 mg subcutaneous every 4 hours; this dose may be decreased to 7.5 mg if the patient is debilitated. The patient's urinary function is evaluated by noting the volume voided at each micturition and the time of micturition as related to time of drug administra-

TABLE 21-2 DRUGS THAT AID IN THE STORAGE OF URINE

Generic Name	Mode of Action	Dose	Adverse Reactions
Propantheline (Probanthine)	Inhibits parasympathetic nervous system	15–30 mg PO three to four times a day	Dryness of mouth, blurred vision, constipation, tachycardia, mydriasis
Methantheline (Banthine)	Inhibits parasympathetic nervous system	50–100 mg PO three to four times a day	Anticholinergic effects as above
Dicyclomine (Bentyl)	Inhibits parasympathetic nervous system	10–20 mg PO three to four times a day	Anticholinergic effects as above but less frequently
Imipramine (Tofranil)	Antimuscorinic, antispasmodic, inhibits parasympathetic nervous system, α-adrenergic stimulator	25 mg–50 mg PO three to four times a day	Sweating, weakness, fatigue, headache, and anticholinergic effects as above (but all are rare)
Oxybutynin (Ditropan)	Inhibit parasympathetic nervous system, local anesthetic, antispasmodic	5 mg PO two to four times a day	Anticholinergic effects as above are rare
Flavoxate HCl (Urispas)	Weak inhibitor of parasympathetic nervous system, local anesthetic, antispasmodic	100–200 mg PO three to four times a day	Anticholinergic effects as above are rare

tion. The patient is catheterized approximately 24 hours after initiation of drug therapy, and this is timed to follow the last voiding induced by the injection of bethanechol. When the residual is less than 30 ml, the subcutaneous dose is decreased to 2.5 mg. If the patient continues to respond, the regimen is converted to 50 to 100 mg orally four times a day. This is then progressively tapered.

One needs to be aware of the anatomic and functional status of the bladder outlet before initiating therapy. Bethanecol is contraindicated in bladder outlet obstruction and also in patients with asthma, peptic ulcer disease, enteritis, bowel obstruction, hyperthyroidism and cardiac disease (Table 1).

Phenoxybenzamine (Dibenzyline)

Phenoxybenzamine hydrochloride is a long-acting α-adrenergic receptor blocking agent. Since α-receptors are important in maintaining urethral resistance, effective α-blockade will lower urethral resistance. There is no firm evidence at this time that the drug has a significant effect on the bladder body or the striated external urethral sphincter.

Phenoxybenzamine has its present clinical use in patients with neurogenic bladder of a short-term nature and is useful in rehabilitating decompensated or atonic bladders when used in combination with bethanechol.[8-12] Since bethanechol has a weak nicotinic effect leading to increased resistance in the urethra, the combination of bethanechol and phenoxybenzamine will increase bladder contractibility and decrease urethral resistance.

Kleeman states that the therapeutic dose of phenoxybenzamine should rarely exceed 10 mg/day, since 30 mg/day commonly produces adverse effects such as sweating, dryness of the mouth, and tachycardia.[13] In addition, the drug may cause postural hypotension, miosis, and nasal stuffiness; however, side effects are rare using 10 mg/day (Table 21-1).

Diazepam (Valium) and Dantrolene (Dantrium)

The external sphincter is under somatic, parasympathetic, and sympathetic control. Drug therapy at the level of the external striated sphincter has been directed toward the use of skeletal muscle relaxants. These have mainly been used in urology for the treatment of both neurogenic and nonneurogenic lower tract dysfunctions.

Oral diazepam is effective in reducing anxiety through its depressant action on the brain stem reticular system. In addition, it also has some relaxant effect on striated muscle. Stanton, Cardozo, and Kerr-Wilson, in their work with women who had undergone colposuspension surgery, found that 10 mg given as a nightly dose was more effective than phenoxybenzamine, bethanechol chloride, and intravesical prostaglandin E_2 in shortening the time to spontaneous voiding postoperatively.[14] The patient population, however, was quite small.

Other investigators have reported some success with dantrolene (Dantrium) and baclofen (Lioresal) in urologic patients with neurogenic and nonneurogenic bladders.[15-17] Baclofen inhibits both monosynaptic and polysynaptic reflexes in the central nervous system and does not have the sedating effects of diazepam. Kiesswelter and Schober showed baclofen to be effective in treating patients with inhibited neurogenic bladders in multiple sclerosis and in those patients with detrusor-sphincter dyssynergia.[16] The drug was ineffective in bladder spasms due to cerebral lesions.

Dantrolene is a potent muscle relaxant. It does not appear to have any effect on peripheral nerves or neuromuscular junctions. Murdock, Sax, and Krane had success using this drug in treating external sphincter spasm.[17] They chose patients who otherwise might have undergone surgery consisting of pudendal neurectomy or external sphincterotomy and obtained favorable results.

The dosages and side effects of these drugs may be found in the literature. With the exception of diazepam, these drugs are usually used only in the individual with a neurologic lesion who is often cared for by the neurologist, urologist, or physical medicine specialist. Their use in gynecology for nonneurogenic bladder dysfunctions has not yet been established.

DRUGS THAT AID IN THE STORAGE OF URINE

Propantheline (Pro-Banthine) and Methaneline (Banthine)

Uncontrolled parasympathetic activity may be depressed by using anticholinergic agents. Agents having predominant anticholinergic activity include atropine, belladonna tincture, propantheline (Pro-Banthine), methantheline (Banthine), and dicyclomine. Atropine has less specific effects on the bladder than propantheline, and methantheline has less antimuscarinic effect. The most commonly used agent is propantheline.

Propantheline (Probanthine)

The predominant action of propantheline is interference with transmission at parasympathetic endings by competition with acetylcholine or similar agents. When used in clinically effective doses, propantheline has no effect on the tone of the empty bladder, urethral outlet pressures, or sensation. It will, however, abolish uncontrolled bladder contractions without significantly increasing residual urine, unless very high doses are used. When given orally, its onset of action occurs at 30 minutes and its duration of action is approximately 4 hours.[18] Finkbeiner and Bissada recommend the following adult dosage regimen:[19] The initial oral dose is 15 mg four times daily. This dose will usually decrease or abolish the amplitude and frequency of uncontrolled contractions and increase bladder capacity without a significant increase in residual urine. If the desired effect is not achieved, the dosage may be increased until either the desired effect is achieved, undesired side effects occur, or significant residual urine volumes ensue. An oral dose of 30 mg four times a day is the maximum a patient can usually tolerate.

Side effects of propantheline include dryness of mouth, blurred vision, constipation, tachycardia, and mydriasis. These drugs should therefore be used with caution in patients with heart disease and avoided in those with glaucoma, myasthenia gravis, and bowel or urinary obstruction.

In gynecology, the principal use of propantheline is for the uninhibited bladder. Here, the uninhibited bladder is defined as one which on filling shows uninhibited contractions above 15 cm H_2O without a detectable neurologic lesion. Propantheline in these cases is an effective drug with a relatively low cost.

Dicyclomine (Bentyl, Pasmin)

Dicyclomine has been used widely in a number of gastrointestinal disorders for some time. It has a direct smooth muscle relaxant effect along with antimuscarinic activity. Awad and associates evaluated this drug in patients with uninhibited bladder contractions and found that the symptoms of urge and urge incontinence were cured in all of the female patients using 20 mg three times a day for 4 to 8 weeks.[20] Side effects included difficulty in visual accommodation and mild dryness of the mouth. None of the patients in their study had a detectable neurologic disorder, so treatment was purely symptomatic. A noticeable improvement in symptoms was not usually observed for 7 to 10 days after beginning therapy, so an 8-week course was necessary to achieve a maximum effect in most cases. Dicyclomine may prove to be especially useful for the female patient with uninhibited bladder contractions because of its small number of side effects (Table 21-2).

Imipramine (Tofranil)

Imipramine is a dibenzapine derivative chemically similar in structure to the phenothiazines, whose urologic mechanism of action is still unclear. Maclean first reported the benefits from imipramine use in children with enuresis in 1960 using an effective dose of 25 mg at bedtime.[21] Labay and Boyarsky, using an in vitro canine model, found imipramine capable of relaxing the bladder musculature and blocking the cholinergic effect of acetycholine.[22] Mahoney, Laferte, and Mahoney, in examining the sphincter-augmenting effect of imipramine in children, felt that the drug exerted its beneficial effect by augmenting the tone of the involuntary urethral sphincter. Apparently both the α- and β-adrenergic receptors of the internal sphincter and the β-receptor become sensitized to sympathetic motor innervation.[23] Work by Benson and associates indicated that imipramine significantly decreased both bethanechol (cholinergic blockade) and barium-induced (antispasmodic or musculotropic) contractions.[24]

Imipramine seems to stimulate the central nervous system and have antimuscarinic, antispasmodic, and adrenergic activity. It also increases bladder outlet resistance.

The dose of imipramine in adults is 25 mg four times daily. Children require a lower dosage of 5 to 20 mg four times daily. Before therapy is begun, organic disease should be ruled out before a functional basis is assumed. Side effects include sweating, weakness, fatigue, headache, anticholinergic effects, and obstructive urinary symptoms. Some children have undergone personality changes. The drug should be used with caution in those patients with hypertension and cardiovascular disease. Imipramine is contraindicated in patients using monoamine oxidase inhibitors because of the possible potentiation of sympathomimetic substances by monoamine oxidase inhibitors, resulting in hypertensive crisis. Common monoamine oxidase inhibitors are toanylcypromine (Parnalt), phenizine (Nardil) and parqylene (Eutonye) (see Chap. 26).

Oxybutynin Chloride (Ditropan)

Oxybutymin chloride is a tertiary amine that is a cholinergic blocker, a potent local anesthetic, and a spasmolytic of induced contractions of smooth muscle from a variety of organs.[25] Using a 5-mg oral dose, the onset of action was present in 1 hour, and the height of effectiveness occurred within 3 to 6 hours. In patients with uncontrolled detrusor contractions, cystometrograms demonstrated a decrease in amplitude and/or a decrease in frequency of uncontrolled contractions. Some patients showed an increase in bladder volume. In eight adult patients with neurogenic bladders demonstrating uninhibited detrusor contractions, an oral dose of 5 mg two to three times a day resulted in a decrease in urinary frequency, urgency, and episodes of inconti-

nence. Oxybutynin has also been shown to be useful in those patients with urethralgia and vesicalgia due to infection, postoperation inflammation, irradiation, or following removal of catheters.

Fredericks found oxybutynin exposure in rabbits to be a potent inhibitor of barium chloride-induced contractions.[26] The drug was noted to possess an antispasmodic activity, which was weaker than propantheline or atropine.

Thompson and Lavretz, in a study of patients with neurovesical reflex activity (uninhibited bladders, eneuresis, and primary muscle spasm), found oxybutynin to have antispasmodic and anticholinergic effects.[27] Side effects have been rare, and minimal anticholinergic-type effects may be present. It appears, therefore, to be an excellent drug for use in those patients with uninhibited contractions secondary to infection, operation, or radiation. The usual dose is 5 mg two to four times daily.

Flavoxate Hydrochloride (Urispas)

Bladder irritation produces muscle spasms or reflex contractions that may be accompanied by urgency, frequency, dysuria, or suprapubic pain. Because of the side effects of anticholinergics, smooth muscle relaxants, which have their major action on the bladder, are desirable agents. Flavoxate hydrochloride is a flavone derivative known to have considerable smooth muscle relaxant effect.[28] In a double-blind crossover study with propantheline 50 mg, Kohler and Morales found flavoxate 200 mg to have an equal relaxant effect, without dehydration of the oropharynx or changes in intraocular pressure.[29] When compared to phenzopyridine HCl (Pyridium), flavoxate HCl was found to be superior to phenzopyridium in relieving symptoms of acute cystitis, urethritis, and trigonitis.[30] It was also better for relieving symptoms of prostatitis. Finkbeiner and Bissada have been unable to demonstrate any depressant action of flavoxate on the detrusor in vitro, and they were not impressed with the clinical effectiveness of flavoxate in patients with spastic bladders.[19]

Flavoxate appears to be an effective drug for relief of the symptoms of dysuria, urgency, nocturia, suprapubic pain, frequency, and incontinence that may occur in cystitis, prostatitis, urethritis, urethrocystitis, and urethrotrigonitis. In cases of urinary tract infection, it can be used in conjunction with the appropriate antibiotic.

Side effects have been very infrequent at a dose of one to two 100-mg tablets three to four times a day. The drug is contraindicated in obstructive conditions, achalasia, or gastrointestinal hemorrhage, and should be used with caution in patients with glaucoma.

DRUGS FOR URINARY STRESS INCONTINENCE

The treatment of urinary stress incontinence by pharmacologic means is an effective but often untried method. Some patients may refuse surgery, be poor operative candidates, or have only mild to moderate stress incontinence from sphincteric insufficiency. These individuals are candidates for medical therapy.

The sympathetic nervous system is involved in maintaining outlet resistance, and an increased pressure may be achieved by either β-blocker or α-stimulator drugs. The three commonly used agents are ephedrine sulfate, phenylpropanolamine, and propranolol. Ephedrine sulfate stimulates both the α- and β-adrenergic receptors to release norepinephrine, which then acts directly on the effector cells.[31] Phenylpropanolamine seems to have the same properties as ephedrine with less central nervous stimulation. Ornade is a combination drug containing 50 mg phenylpropanolamine, 8 mg chlorpheniramine maleate (antihistamine), and 2.5 mg isopropamide iodide (a drying agent). Since Ornade contains an antihistamine, drowsiness may occur as an unwanted side effect.

Diokno and Taub used ephedrine sulfate in doses of 44 to 200 mg daily in four divided doses to improve urinary incontinence of mild

to moderate nature.[32] It was of little benefit in cases with an uninhibited neurogenic bladder or with severe stress incontinence. In addition, tachyphylaxis has occasionally been seen with ephedrine use but not with phenylpropanolamine.[19]

Awad, Downie, and Kiruluta found phenylpropanolamine to be effective in 11 of 13 female patients with sphincteric insufficiency.[33] Side effects were uncommon, and any beneficial response depended on the therapy being continuous.

The side effects of sympathomimetic agents include palpitations, arrhythmias, insomnia, epigastric distress, anxiety, hyperexcitability, and nervousness. They should be used with caution in patients with glaucoma, hypertension, hyperthyroidism, and cardiovascular disease.

Propranolol, through its β-blocking effect, may potentiate α-receptors and increase outlet resistance. Gleason and associates found propranolol to be useful in treating stress incontinence in five women scheduled for incontinence surgery when a 10-mg dose was given four times a day.[34] Propranolol holds promise for patients with cardiovascular or hypertensive disease in whom α-stimulators are contraindicated (Table 21-3).[9]

ESTROGEN AND PROGESTERONE EFFECTS ON THE URINARY TRACT

Reports on the beneficial effects of estrogen used in stress incontinence in postmenopausal women have been published by Raz, Zeigler, and Caine, who reported that improvement occurred in 65 percent of postmenopausal women with urinary stress incontinence who received estrogen, whereas 60 percent of those treated with medroxyprogesterone acetate became worse.[35] These findings were reversed when treatment was stopped. These experiments were done using urethral pressure profiles, which showed an increase in profile closure pressure with estrogen and a corresponding decrease with progesterone. Al-

TABLE 21-3   DRUGS THAT HAVE EFFECTS ON THE URINARY SPHINCTER AND URINARY STRESS INCONTINENCE

Generic Name	Mode of Action	Dose	Adverse Reactions
Ephedrine (Ephedrine)	Adrenergic stimulation	15–50 mg PO three to four times a day	CNS stimulation with palpitations, GI disturbance, hyperexcitability, nervousness, etc.
Phenylpropanolamine Propadrine	α-Adrenergic stimulator	25–50 mg PO three to four times a day	As above and: cardiac palpitations, cardiac arrhythmia, insomnia, epigastric distress, anxiety, nervousness, hyperexcitability
Ornade	α-Adrenergic stimulator, antihistamine	1 cap two times a day	
Propranolol (Inderal)	β-adrenergic blocker	10–40 mg PO three to four times a day	Bradycardia, hypotension, depression, GI disturbances, bronchospasm
Imipramine (Tofranil)	See Table 2	See Table 2	See Table 2

though estrogen is known to enhance incontinence by its effects on both the urethral mucosa and urethral vasculature, these actions do not account for the deleterious effect of progesterone on the urethral pressure profile.[36,37] The appropriate dose of estrogen for treatment of urinary incontinence is the lowest amount that will achieve the desired goal, either by the intravaginal or oral route.

PROSTAGLANDINS AND DETRUSOR DYNAMICS

Prostaglandins E_2 and F_2 are released during the nervous stimulation of the bladder, and studies have shown this to cause an increased detrusor muscle activity.[38,39] It has been hypothesized that a reduction in circulating prostaglandin levels may help to reduce detrusor hypercontractility. Indomethacin is a prostaglandin synthetase inhibitor which has been shown by Ghoneim and associates to reduce urethral resistance observed during vesical distention.[40]

Cardozo and Stanton undertook a study to compare bromocriptine and indomethacin in the treatment of detrusor instability.[41] Primary detrusor instability was diagnosed in 66 percent, multiple sclerosis in 19 percent, cerebrovascular accident in 9 percent, and other upper motor neuron lesions in 6 percent. Indomethacin was found to be useful in treating the symptom of frequency with detrusor instability, but bromocriptine was not helpful.

Neither drug was effective against urgency or urge incontinence and side effects with indomethacin and bromocriptine were numerous (nausea, vomiting, dizziness). Nevertheless, investigations of the use of prostaglandin inhibitors for the unstable bladder deserve further attention.

REFERENCES

1. Hodgkinson CP: Stress urinary incontinence—1970. *Am J Obstet Gynecol* 108:1149, 1970
2. Corlett RC Jr: Gynecologic urology, part 1. *Curr Probl Obstet Gynecol* 12(1):32–34, 1978
3. Robertson JR: *Genitourinary Problems in Women.* Springfield, Ill, Thomas, 1978, p 32
4. Wein AJ, Hanno PM, Dixon DO, et al: The effect of oral bethanechol chloride on the cystometrogram of the normal male adult. *J Urol* 120:330, 1978

5. Yalla SV, Rossier AB, Fam B: Synchronous cystosphincterometry in patients with spinal cord injury. *Urology* 6:777, 1975

6. Diokno AC, Lapides J: Action of oral and parenteral bethanecol on decompressed bladder. *Urology* 10:23, 1977

7. Lapides J: Urecholine regimen for rehabilitating the atonic bladder. *J Urol* 91:658, 1964

8. Krane RJ, Olsson CA: Phenoxybenzaminde in neurogenic bladder dysfunction: II. Clinical considerations. *J Urol* 110:653, 1973

9. Khanna OP: Disorders of micturition: Neuropharmacologic basis and results of drug therapy. *Urology* 8:316, 1976

10. Stockamp K: Treatment with phenoxybenzamine of upper urinary tract complications caused by intravesical obstruction. *J Urol* 113:128, 1975

11. Krane RJ, Olsson CA: Phenoxybenzamine in neurogenic bladder dysfunction—clinical considerations. *J. Urol* 110:653, 1973

12. Khanna OP: Disorders of micturition: Neuropharmacologic basis and results of drug therapy. *Urology* 8:316, 1976

13. Kleeman FJ: Phenoxybenzamine: Letter to the editor. *J Urol* 117:814, 1977

14. Stanton SL, Cardozo LD, Kerr-Wilson R: Treatment of delayed onset of spontaneous voiding after surgery for incontinence. *Urology* 13:494, 1979

15. From A, Heltberg A: A double-blind trial of baclofen (Lioresal) and diazepam in spasticity due to multiple sclerosis. *Acta Neurol Scand* 51:158, 1975

16. Kiesswelter H, Schober W: Lioresal in the treatment of neurogenic bladder dysfunction. *Urol Int* 30:63, 1975

17. Murdock M, Sax D, Krane RJ: Use of dantrolene sodium in external sphincter spasm. *Urology* 8:133, 1976

18. Kiesswelter H, Popper L: A cystometrographic study to assess the influence of atropine, propantheline and mebeverine on the smooth muscle of the bladder. *Br J Urol* 44:31, 1972

19. Finkbeiner AE, Bissada NK: Drug therapy for lower urinary tract dysfunction. *Urol Clin North Am* 7:3, 1980

20. Awad SA, Bryreak S, Downie JW, et al: The treatment of the uninhibited bladder with dicyclomine. *J Urol* 117:161, 1977

21. Maclean REG: Imipramine hydrochloride (Tofranil) and enuresis. *Am J Psychiatry* 117:551, 1960

22. Labay P, Boyarsky S: The action of imipramine on the bladder musculature. *J Urol* 109:385, 1973

23. Mahoney DT, Laferte RO, Mahoney JE: Observations on sphincteric augmenting effect of imipramine in children with urinary incontinence. *Urology* 1:317, 1973

24. Benson GS, Sarshek SA, Raezer D, et al: Bladder muscle contractility: Comparative effects and mechanisms of action of atropine, propantheline, flavoxate and imipramine. *Urology* 9:31, 1977

25. Diokno AC, Lapides J: Oxybutynin: A new drug with analgesic and anticholinergic properties. *J Urol* 108:307, 1972

26. Fredericks CM, Anderson GF, Kreulen DC: A study on the anticholinergic and antispasmodic activity of oxybutynin (Ditropan) on rabbit detrusor. *Invest Urol* 12:317, 1975

27. Thompson IM, Lavretz R: Oxybutynin in bladder spasm, neurogenic bladder and enuresis. *Urology* 8:452, 1976

28. Setrikar I, Ravaer MT, Dare P: Pharmacological properties of peperideno ethyl-3-methylflavone 8-carboxylate hydrochloride, a smooth-muscle relaxant. *J Pharmacol Exp Ther* 130:356, 1960

29. Kohler RP, Morales PA: Cystometric evaluation of flavoxate hydrochloride in normal and neurogenic bladder. *J Urol* 100:729, 1968

30. Gould S: Urinary tract disorders: Clinical comparison of flavoxate and phenzopyridium. *Urology* 5:612, 1975

31. Irnes IR, Nickerson M: Drugs acting on postganglionic adrenergic nerve endings and structures innervated by them, in Goodman LS, Gilman A (eds): *The Pharmacologic Basis of Therapeutics*, ed. 3 New York, Macmillan, 1965, p 505–526

32. Diokno AC, Taub M: Ephedrine in treatment of urinary incontinence *Urology* 5:624, 1975

33. Awad SA, Downie JW, Kiruluta HG: Alpha-adrenergic agents in urinary disorders of the proximal urethra: Part 1. Sphincter incontinence. *Br J Urol* 50:332, 1978

34. Gleason DM, Reilly RJ, Bottacini MR, et al: The urethral continence zone and its relation to stress incontinence. *J Urol* 112:81, 1974

35. Raz S, Ziegler M, Caine M: The role of female hormones in stress incontinence. Paper read before the Congress of the International Society of Urology, Amsterdam, 1973

36. Smith P: Age changes with the female urethra. *Br J Urol* 44:667, 1972

37. Berkow SG: Corpus spongeosum of urethra: Its possible role in urinary control and stress incontinence in women *Am J Obstet Gynecol* 65:346, 1953

38. Abrams PH, Feneley RCL: The actions of prostaglandins on the smooth muscle of the human urinary tract in vitro. *Br J Urol* 47:909, 1976

39. Bultitude MI, Huls NH, Shuttleworth KED: Clinical experimental studies on the action of prostaglandins and their synthesis inhibitors on detrusor muscle in vitro and in vivo. *Br J Urol* 48:631, 1976

40. Ghoneim MA, Fretin JA, Gagnon, DJ, et al: The influence of vesical distention on the urethral resistance to flow: A possible role for prostaglandins? *J Urol* 116:739, 1976

41. Cardozo LD, Stanton SL: A comparison between bromocriptine and indomethacin in the treatment of detrusor instability. *J Urol* 123:399, 1980

22. Drugs for Treating Endometriosis, Dysmenorrhea, and Pelvic Pain

JEFFREY M. DICKE   GERALD L. CABLE

The treatment of endometriosis, dysmenor-rhea, and chronic pelvic pain often represents a therapeutic challenge to the family physician and gynecologist. These are common conditions with significant implications regarding the patient's physical and emotional well-being. Medical management has formerly been limited to the use of agents that were relatively ineffective or undesirable because of potential side effects. Recent advances in the pathophysiology of these disorders have resulted in the development of many new agents which are more specific and effective in their ability to provide relief from these conditions, while causing fewer adverse effects. The following is a brief discussion of these disease entities including their etiology, pathophysiology, and therapy.

ENDOMETRIOSIS

Endometriosis is a pathologic entity resulting from the presence of viable endometrial glands and stroma in various extrauterine locations. Sites of occurrence commonly include the ovaries, uterosacral, round and broad ligaments, rectovaginal septum, and pelvic peritoneum covering the uterus, fallopian tubes, rectum, sigmoid, and bladder. Less frequently it involves the cervix, vagina, vulva, appendix,

small bowel, and laparotomy scars, with occasional occurrence in extraabdominal locations such as the pleura, lung, skeletal muscle, and bone.

The etiology of endometriosis is uncertain, but the following theories are considered to be the most credible:

1. The tubal reflux theory, advanced by Sampson, in which transtubal regurgitation of menstrual blood and endometrial fragments occur with subsequent implantation on peritoneal surfaces of viable, aberrant tissue.

2. The coelomic-epithelium metaplasia theory, in which ectopic-functioning endometrium develops as a result of atypical development of germinal epithelium and various parts of pelvic peritoneum which are embryologically derived from totipotential coelomic epithelial cell elements.

3. The theory of lymphatic dissemination, which suggests that aberrant tissue is a result of metastases of normal endometrium via uterine lymphatic vessels.

4. The vascular theory, which supposes hematogenous spread of endometrium as an explanation for endometriosis in distant sites.

295

5. The theory of Mullerian cell differentiation, which allows that cell rests of embryonic Mullerian epithelium develop into functioning ectopic endometrial implants as a result of cyclic ovarian stimulation.

Although published reports indicate that endometriosis may be found at any age after the menarche, the diagnosis is usually made in the third and fourth decades.[1] At the present time, data from women undergoing pelvic laparotomy for whatever reason indicate an incidence of 10 to 25 percent.[1] Such women often present as nulliparas in their late 20s or early 30s with a history of delayed childbearing or involuntary infertility. The progress of the disease is related to the number of uninterrupted progestational cycles, and improvement is noted during periods of anovulation and amenorrhea. Thus, it is not a disease of premenarchal, pregnant, or postmenopausal females.

Endometriosis may have either an acute or chronic presentation, and the site of involvement determines the symptomatology. The four most common manifestations of the disease include infertility, dysmenorrhea and pelvic pain, dyspareunia, and menstrual irregularities. Symptomatology is not proportional to the extent of disease. Patients with extensive palpable disease may be relatively asymptomatic, while those with relatively small peritoneal implants may experience significant pain resulting from fibrosis and stretching of the involved peritoneum.

The diagnosis of endometriosis is often suggested by these characteristic signs and symptoms. An almost diagnostic finding on pelvic examination is the hard, immobile, fibrotic nodule presenting as irregular thickening in the cul-de-sac, uterosacral ligaments, and rectovaginal septum. A definitive diagnosis of endometriosis requires at least visual confirmation via laparoscopy or laparotomy. Endometriotic implants appear as brown or black nodules frequently surrounded by hemorrhagic areas, fibrosis, and adhesions. Larger lesions, known as endometriomas, often involve ovaries and intestines. Thus, as Kistner

notes, the diagnosis is "suggested by history, corroborated by the pelvic exam, and verified by endoscopy and/or biopsy."[2]

Therapy for endometriosis is surgical and/or hormonal. Surgical treatment is considered to be either conservative or radical, depending upon intent. Conservative surgery is that done to preserve and improve reproductive potential, while radical surgery attempts to alleviate the disease completely. Ectopic endometrial implants typically soften and regress with cessation of cyclic ovarian function. Thus, hormonal therapy is aimed at inhibiting both the proliferation and subsequent bleeding of aberrant endometrium by pharmacologically providing a pseudopregnancy or pseudomenopause. The following is a discussion of agents used for such purposes.

Danazol (Danocrine)

First available for clinical and animal studies in 1967, danazol is a synthetic (2,3-isoxyl) derivative of 17 α-ethinyl testosterone. An orally active pituitary gonadotropin inhibitory agent, danazol has no estrogenic or progestational activity and only mild androgenic activity. Gonadotropin secretion or release is inhibited even though overt sex hormone activity is not manifested. Danazol acts by suppressing the cyclical release of luteinizing hormone (LH) and follicle-stimulating hormone (FSH) with inhibition of ovarian steroidogenesis. Evidence also suggests that danazol has direct actions at the gonadal and endometrial levels with probable competitive blocking of estrogen and progesterone receptors. Over several weeks, plasma levels of estradiol and estrone are markedly suppressed, resulting in peripheral changes similar to castration or menopause. Atrophy of the vaginal mucosa, uterine endometrium, and the aberrant endometrium of endometriosis may occur. Studies evaluating the effect of danazol therapy on pituitary, thyroid, and adrenal function in relatively small numbers of women reveal a decrease in thyroid-binding globulin, thyroid-stimulating hormone (TSH), T_3, and T_4 with slight increases in free T_4 and free T_3 index.[3] Metyrapone challenge tests to evaluate pituitary-adrenal response reveal a normal ability of the pituitary to secrete adrenocorticotropic hormone (ACTH) and of the adrenal gland to respond.[4] Glucose tolerance and serum concentrations of prolactin, cortisol, and testosterone are unaffected by danazol therapy.[4] Likewise, no changes in fibrinolysis, coagulation, or platelet function have been demonstrated.[5]

Clinical Uses. Several large studies utilizing danazol 200 mg four times daily for periods of 3 to 18 months have demonstrated good clinical success.[6-8] The average course of therapy was 6 months, with the goal of treatment being to achieve suppression and atrophy of endometrial deposits. Effective treatment therefore was usually accompanied by complete amenorrhea. (Amenorrhea, vaginal cytology, and endometrial biopsies provide evidence of the pseudomenopausal state and are measures of the effectiveness of danazol therapy.) Subjective symptomatology showed improvement after only a few weeks of therapy, with eventual amelioration of dysmenorrhea and pelvic pain in 90 to 100 percent of all patients.[5,9] Clinical findings on pelvic exam revealed a slower response and provided a measure of the adequacy of therapy duration. Gradual improvement in pelvic induration and tenderness occurred in 80 to 90 percent of patients after 3 to 7 months of treatment.[4,5]

The manufacturers' current recommended dosage is 200 mg four times daily. Ongoing studies with lower dose treatments of 600, 400, and 200 mg/day suggest that relief of symptoms may be possible with a lower incidence of side effects.[10,11] Regular ovulatory menses usually return within 1 to 3 months following discontinuation of therapy, thus relieving the pseudomenopausal state and its beneficial effect on endometriosis. The interval between cessation of therapy, rate of recurrence, and subsequent progression of the disease is variable. Approximately one-third of study populations experienced exacerbation of symptoms within the first year.[7,9]

The efficacy of danazol in treating infertility resulting from endometriosis has been evaluated by posttreatment follow-up. Pregnancy rates have been reported to be 43 percent in 4 months, 50 percent in 6 months, and 56 percent in 1 year.[4] Up to 52 months of follow-up care in one large study yielded a corrected pregnancy rate of 72 percent, with many patients conceiving more than once and most remaining symptom-free.[7]

Danazol has also been approved for the treatment of severe fibrocystic disease of the breast, a disorder characterized by pain, tenderness, and nodularity exacerbated premenstrually. In clinical studies using 50 to 800 mg (usually 100 to 400 mg) of danazol daily for 3 to 6 months, relief of pain and nodularity was achieved in 54 to almost 90 percent of patients. These signs and symptoms recurred in approximately one-third of patients 11 to 32 months following cessation of therapy. The manufacturer claims the disease may recur in one-half of patients within 1 year after discontinuation of the drug. The long-term safety and cost-effectiveness are not well established for such use.[10]

Side Effects and Precautions. The side effects of danazol are generally the result of its primary pharmacologic actions. Those attributable to inhibition of the pituitary-gonadal axis include symptoms referable to depressed ovarian function, such as vasomotor instability, breast changes, and vaginitis, and have been reported to occur in 1.5 to 4.5 percent of 704 treated women.[2] Side effects attributable to danazol's androgenic activity and their incidence include acne (13.4 percent), hirsutism (5.8 percent), edema (5.8 percent), weight gain (2.8 percent), voice change (2.8 percent), and oiliness of skin (1.8 percent).[3] General side effects reported in a small percentage of patients include emotional (depression, anxiety, fatigue), gastrointestinal (nausea, vomiting, diarrhea, constipation), and musculoskeletal complaints. These effects were those recorded by patients treated with 800 mg/day. Studies in progress indicate that the incidence of side effects is decreased in women maintained on lesser dosages.[11,13]

A disadvantage of danazol therapy and a

potentially limiting factor in its use is cost. Current retail cost often exceeds $1/200-mg capsule. This may render danazol unavailable to patients with limited budgets and should be considered when evaluating the advantages and disadvantages of therapy.

Other Steroids. Since signs and symptoms of endometriosis regress during pregnancy and for a varying length of time thereafter, gestation has long been suggested as a prophylactic and therapeutic modality. Such regression is thought to be the result of anovulation and amenorrhea induced by pituitary-gonadal suppression. If pregnancy is not a desirable or obtainable means of therapy, anovulation may be achieved using estrogens, progestins, androgens, or a combination thereof.

Estrogens

Based on the observation that endometriosis is associated with ovulatory cycles, constant estrogen administration has been used to inhibit ovulation and suppress further growth of the aberrant endometrium. The daily administration of large doses of estrogen results in symptomatic improvement but little change in the size and location of ectopic endometrial implants.[14] Despite subjective improvement, prolonged estrogen administration is associated with a variety of serious side effects including cystic and adenomatous hyperplasia of the endometrium, thrombophlebitis, breakthrough bleeding, peripheral edema, nausea, and vomiting (see Chap. 17). Furthermore, estrogen-stimulated proliferative growth of endometrium will not cause regression of the disease. Because of potential side effects and alternate methods of therapy, the routine use of estrogens is currently considered unacceptable in treating endometriosis.

Progestins

The use of progestational agents to inhibit ovulation has been advocated. Progestational agents are generally better tolerated with fewer complications than estrogen administration (see Chap. 17). With progestational therapy, gonadotropin release is inhibited and

ovarian steroid production is reduced. Progesterone also exerts a direct effect on the endometrium, resulting in endometrial atrophy. With excessive suppression of estrogen, breakthrough bleeding may occur and necessitate low-dose estrogen to stabilize the endometrium. Other side effects are minor and include weight gain, depression, breast tenderness, and vaginitis. Depomedroxyprogesterone acetate 100 mg every 2 weeks for 2 months, followed by 200 mg each month for 4 to 6 months has been used to achieve subjective remission. A disadvantage of progestin therapy in the patient desiring pregnancy is delayed ovulation for possibly 6 to 12 months following the cessation of treatment.

Androgens

Androgens are thought to be effective in treating endometriosis by acting directly on areas of endometriosis. Androgen therapy is unique among hormonal treatments for endometriosis, because neither gonadotropin release, ovarian steroid production, nor ovulation is inhibited. The use of androgens has centered around their effectiveness in relieving both dysmenorrhea and dyspareunia. Methyltestosterone 5 to 10 mg daily for 6 to 12 weeks has been shown to provide symptomatic improvement in approximately 80 percent of patients, although most patients experienced a recurrence of symptoms within several months after discontinuation.[2] Pregnancy rates following therapy have been reported to be 10 to 60 percent.[15] A comparison with untreated patients is difficult because of the lack of standardization. Androgens may cause virilization of female fetuses, so early pregnancy must be excluded if menses are delayed (see Chap. 2). Side effects of androgen treatment include acne, menstrual irregularities, hirsutism, clitoromegaly, hoarseness, and hepatocellular jaundice.

Estrogen/Progestin Combination Therapy

The observation that pregnancy induces both subjective and objective improvement in patients with endometriosis is the basis for administration of estrogen and progestin in a manner simulating the hormonal profile in pregnancy. Similar to true pregnancy, the pseudopregnant state results in the decidualization, necrosis, and resorption of aberrant endometrium. A common regimen involves the continuous use of oral contraceptives with an initial dose of 1 tablet daily. After several weeks, this is increased to 2 or 3 tablets daily, with additional increases as necessary to prevent breakthrough bleeding. An exacerbation of symptoms may occur during the initial 2 to 3 months of therapy, which resolves following decidual necrosis and absorption. Subjective improvement has been reported in various studies in approximately 85 to 90 percent of patients.[16,17] Objective improvement as manifested by the regression of endometrial nodules has also been noted to occur within 4 months of treatment.[17] Recurrence of symptoms has been shown to occur in approximately one-third of patients, commonly within 1 year.[16] Treatment is usually continued for 6 to 9 months, with spontaneous ovulation often occurring within 6 to 8 weeks following therapy. Corrected pregnancy rates after pseudopregnancy treatment vary from 26 to 72 percent. Interpretation is difficult because of the variety of drugs used, patient preselection, and lack of standards for therapy and effectiveness. Spontaneous rupture of endometriomas has been reported in patients with severe disease treated with induction of pseudopregnancy.[15] Other complications of oral contraceptive therapy include reproductive system and systemic side effects (see Chap. 16).

DYSMENORRHEA AND CHRONIC PELVIC PAIN

Historical Perspective

As stated by Karl Abraham, "Many women suffer temporarily or permanently, in childhood or in adult age, from the fact they have been born females."[18] Dysmenorrhea has presented a therapeutic challenge to physicians throughout the ages with popular remedies of the past rooted in traditions having little scientific basis. Ancient Greek medicine described the analgesic effect of sweet wine, fennel root, and rose oil when applied to the external genitalia of menstruating women. Chinese women were treated with moxibustion, wherein a cone of wormwood on a slice of ginger was placed on a specific point on the abdomen, ignited, and allowed to burn down to the skin. In the mid-1800s bilateral oophorectomy became popular for the treatment of dysmenorrhea and other functional disorders. At the turn of the century, a number of plant extracts and synthetic chemicals were used, with opium being the most popular. Nitroglycerine was recommended for symptoms of vasomotor lability and pallor. The association between dysmenorrhea and ovulation was first noted in the 1930s, with Sturgis and Albright, in 1940, the first investigators to demonstrate that estrogens suppress ovulation by inhibiting pituitary gonadotropins. Pending the development of oral contraceptives, estrogens remained the treatment of choice for dysmenorrhea. Following their introduction, oral contraceptives became the preferred hormonal therapy for dysmenorrhea, although with further elucidation of side effects the risks of such treatment became arguably greater than the benefits. In 1965, Dickles postulated the role prostaglandins play in the etiology of dysmenorrhea, and in 1971 Vane speculated that aspirin-like compounds act by inhibiting prostaglandin synthesis. Dickles subsequently suggested that anti-inflammatory agents might be used to treat dysmenorrhea, and since then the efficacy of prostaglandin synthesis inhibitors has been demonstrated in multiple clinical studies.[19] Future development of drugs that act more specifically on uterine prostaglandins may allow the physician an even more effective means of treating the symptoms of dysmenorrhea and chronic pelvic pain.

Primary dysmenorrhea, or menstrual discomfort in the absence of pelvic pathology, generally begins with the initiation of ovulatory cycles and thus first occurs 6 to 12 months following menarche and becomes progressively worse with time. The characteristic history is that of colicky lower quadrant pain radiating to the thighs and lower back. Additional symptoms include nausea, vomiting, diarrhea, dizziness, and emotional lability. The pain usually occurs immediately prior to menstruation, and symptoms may continue for several hours up to 2 days. The diagnosis of primary dysmenorrhea is confirmed by history and the absence of pelvic pathology.

Menstrual pain initially occurring later in reproductive life is known as secondary dysmenorrhea and is related to pelvic pathology or anatomic abnormalities. These may include endometriosis, myomas, pelvic inflammatory disease, polyps, or Mullerian anomalies resulting in outflow obstruction. The pain of secondary dysmenorrhea contrasts with primary dysmenorrhea in that it often begins several days before menstruation and may occur at various times during the menstrual cycle. Furthermore, treatment of secondary dysmenorrhea is less amenable to drug manipulation and more curable by operative intervention.

Etiology

The pathophysiology of primary dysmenorrhea is thought to involve a variety of factors including uterine blood flow, myometrial activity, ovarian-pituitary hormones, cervical factors, and, most recently, prostaglandins.

Uterine blood flow has been advanced as a possible factor in the etiology of dysmenorrhea based on studies recording local endometrial blood flow in dysmenorrheic women during pain.[20] Decreases in local endometrial blood flow were noted during uterine contractions and correlated with maximal colicky pain. The relation between blood flow and pain demonstrated by these recordings has led to the hypothesis that primary dysmenorrhea may result from uterine ischemia occurring secondary to uterine hyperactivity or to other factors acting on the uterine vasculature.

Using microtransducer catheters, myometrial hyperactivity during painful menstruation was demonstrated in almost all dysmenorrheic women.[20] Although previous investigators sought to ascribe the pain of dysmenorrhea to specific contractile patterns, such as regular

or dysrhythmic activity, no single activity pattern has been shown to be responsible.[20]

Estrogen and progesterone may have a role in the pathology of dysmenorrhea since anovulatory women seldom experience such discomfort, and therapy with oral contraceptives is effective in relieving dysmenorrhea. The mechanism wherein ovarian steroids are involved in the pathophysiology of dysmenorrhea is unknown, although it has been suggested that these steroids may affect uterine production of and response to prostaglandins.

Vasopressin stimulates myometrial activity and exerts a direct effect on the vasculature to decrease uterine blood flow.[21] To date, its precise role in dysmenorrhea is unclear and further studies are pending.

Cervical obstruction and subsequent retention of menstrual secretion as a cause of painful menstruation is a theory of dysmenorrhea ascribed to Hippocrates.[20] Early reports indicating improvement of dysmenorrhea following cervical dilatation gave credence to this concept. More recent evaluation of such therapy has demonstrated an occasionally favorable but usually temporary response. Further observations arguing against this theory include the lack of dysmenorrhea in cases of known cervical stenosis, its occurrence in patients with unobstructed and profuse menstrual flow, and the pain secondary to mechanical obstruction (as in hematometra) being dissimilar in character to typical dysmenorrhea. Although cervical obstruction alone may not be a direct cause of dysmenorrhea, it may delay the discharge of menstrual fluid. Uterine distension may result, and myometrial hyperactivity can occur from the increased absorption of prostaglandins from the menstrual fluid.

Role of Prostaglandins

Prostaglandins are oxygenated metabolites of certain 20-carbon polyunsaturated, essential fatty acids and are composed of a central five-membered ring with two side chains. Precursor fatty acids are membrane bound in cells and require release by phospholipase enzymes before prostaglandin synthesis can be initiated. A variety of stimuli are known to activate phospholipase for prostaglandin biosynthesis. These include chemical, neural, mechanical, and hormonal stimuli including estrogen and progesterone. Prostaglandin synthesis occurs throughout the body with all cell types demonstrating the capacity for converting fatty acids into prostaglandins. The ratio of different prostaglandins varies in different tissues and within the same tissue depending on the circumstances.

Uterine prostaglandin synthesis is apparently initiated by lysosomal enzymes released late in the menstrual cycle. The action of these enzymes, induced by the alteration in the hormonal environment, may be responsible for the release of phospholipids from the cell membrane. These phospholipids provide the common denominator, arachidonic acid, along with other fatty acids necessary for prostaglandin synthesis. The initial step in the conversion of arachidonic acid to prostaglandins is the formation of prostaglandin G_2, a cyclic endoperoxide. This reaction is inhibited by nonsteroidal anti-inflammatory agents.[22] Prostaglandins E_2 and F_2 are subsequently formed from prostaglandin G_2. Progesterone induces prostaglandin production. Since primary dysmenorrhea is observed only during ovulatory cycles, progesterone may function to regulate endometrial prostaglandin production.

A role for prostaglandins in primary dysmenorrhea is suggested by the observation that the concentrations of prostaglandins E_2 and F_2, present in the endometrium throughout the cycle, are maximal at the time of menstruation.[23] In addition, increased prostaglandin levels have been demonstrated in endometrial jet-wash specimens, menstrual blood, and endometrial tissue from patients with primary dysmenorrhea.[23]

A recent theory advanced by Henzel and Izu to explain the mechanism of action of prostaglandins in producing dysmenorrhea is as follows: Lysosomal enzymes released as a result of the changing balance of ovarian hormones at menstruation activate phospholipases. These stimulate the release of phospholipids, which are rearranged into arachidonic acid and other prostaglandin precursors, which are then converted to prostaglandins by the enzyme complex prostaglandin synthetase.[24] Prostaglandins so formed subsequently cause myometrial hyperactivity, vascular constriction, decreased uterine blood flow, and tissue ischemia, resulting in the typical symptoms of dysmenorrhea.

The direct relation between prostaglandin synthesis and painful menstruation is supported by the observation that decreased uterine prostaglandin synthesis is accompanied by relief of symptoms.[23] In addition, systemic symptoms often associated with dysmenorrhea such as nausea, vomiting, diarrhea, and headache can be induced with IV injection of prostaglandins, lending further credence to their role in the pathogenesis of dysmenorrhea.

Although effective in the treatment of primary dysmenorrhea, prostaglandin synthesis inhibitors are not always of benefit, with success rates reported to be 70 to 80 percent.[23]

Nonsteroidal anti-inflammatory medications such as aspirin and the newer aspirin-like compounds (Table 22-1) inhibit the production of prostaglandins (Fig. 22-1). Because of this characteristic, they are often called prostaglandin synthetase inhibitors (PGSI). This inhibition may only partly explain the anti-inflammatory effect of PGSIs, but it offers a rationale for their use in treating primary dysmenorrhea. Their ability to reduce prostaglandin F_2 (PGF$_2$) and prostaglandin E_2 (PGE$_2$) levels in dysmenorrhic patients has coincided with excellent pain relief.[25-27] Double-blind clinical trials versus placebo have also confirmed the benefit of using indoleacetic acids, propionic acid derivatives, and fenemates to relieve pain and cramping in primary dysmenorrhea. Preliminary reports also suggest these agents may reduce excess menstrual bleeding, particularly during IUD use.

Aspirin. Aspirin is still the most commonly used PGSI. Low cost and wide availability make it well suited for treatment of mild dysmenorrhea. Unfortunately, 1 table (0.5 gm) given four times daily for 3 days is not significantly more effective than placebo or acet-

TABLE 22-1   DRUGS TO TREAT DYSMENORRHEA AND CHRONIC PELVIC PAIN

Drug	Doses for Treatment of Dysmenorrhea	Relative Cost*	5-Day Course ($)
Indolacetic acids			
Indomethacin	25-mg capsules three times a day	1.0/capsule	2.24
(Indocin)	50-mg capsules three times a day	1.6/capsule	3.72
Indeneacotic acid			
Sulindac	N/A	1.8/150-mg tablet	N/A
(Clinoril)		2.4/200-mg tablet	N/A
Propionic acids			
Naproxen	250 mg × 2 stat, then	1.7/tablet	5.70
(Naprosyn)	250 mg every 4–6 hr		
Naproxen sodium	275 mg × 2 stat, then	N/A	
(Anaprox)	275 mg every 6–8 hr		
Ibuprofen	400 mg three times a day	1.0/tablet	2.31
(Motrin)			
Fenoprofen			
(Nalfon)	200 mg every 4–6 hr		
Fenemate			
Mefenamic acid	250 mg × 2 stat, then	1.4/capsule	4.47
(Ponstel)	250 mg every 6 hr		

* From *American Druggist Blue Book,* New York, American Druggist, *July 1980–June 1981,* with permission. Relative cost comparisons are based on wholesale costs for 60–100 doses.

aminophen (0.5 gm four times daily for 3 days).[8] The recommended dose of aspirin for analgesia is 0.3 to 1.0 gm every 3 to 4 hours.[9] Higher doses of either aspirin or acetaminophen may prove to be more effective. One trial has demonstrated this potential, as 62 percent of patients on 1.0-gm doses of acetaminophen achieved relief.[30]

Indolacetic Acid Derivatives. In 1953, before prostaglandins were recognized as a factor in dysmenorrhea, women taking phenylbutazone for treatment of rheumatic disease experienced a decrease in menstrual pain.[31] Despite this finding, phenylbutazone has not been widely used to treat dysmenorrhea, because it is poorly tolerated by many patients. Nausea, vomiting, epigastric discomfort, and skin rashes are the most frequently reported side effects, while more serious effects include edema, peptic ulcer, and hematologic toxicity (aplastic anemia, leukopenia, agranulocytosis, and thrombocytopenia). Another member of this pharmacologic class, indomethacin (Indocin), has been used more often in doses of 25 to 50 mg three times daily. Pain relief is

reported in 71 to 100 percent of patients receiving indomethacin whether the medication is begun 3 days before the onset of menses or when symptoms occur. Central nervous system side effects, such as dizziness, headache, and fatigue have limited its effectiveness.[32] Headache has been reported to occur in 50 percent of patients receiving total daily doses

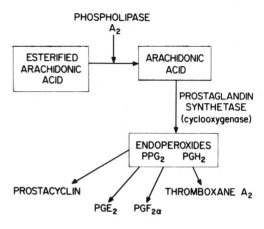

Figure 22-1: PGSI inhibition of prostaglandin biosynthesis.

exceeding 100 mg.[33] Indomethacin also causes gastrointestinal discomfort, including peptic ulcer, and although it has not been associated with edema, is occasionally a factor in aplastic anemia. The use of sulindac (Clinoril), a compound with a similar therapeutic spectrum, has not yet been studied in dysmenorrhea, and this agent may have less central nervous system side effects than indomethacin.[34]

Propionic Acid Derivatives. Propionic acid derivatives provide good pain relief in dysmenorrhea without the bothersome central nervous system effects of indomethacin. Drugs included in this classification are ibuprofen (Motrin), fenoprofen (Nalfon), naproxen (Naprosyn), and naproxen sodium (Anaprox).

Naproxen and naproxen sodium have been studied extensively. The sodium content of each 275-mg tablet of naproxen sodium is 25 mg (1mEq). The significant pain relief using either agent compared to placebo is closely associated with a significant decrease in uterine tonicity.[34,35] Of patients who were previously incapacitated by dysmenorrhea, 77.3 percent were able to function normally during treatment.[36] Most data support a dose of 550 mg (2 tablets of naproxen sodium) started with the onset of symptoms, then 275 mg every 4 to 6 hours until symptoms disappear. Side effects have been minimal and are often indistinguishable from the nausea or diarrhea that often accompany dysmenorrhea.

The use of ibuprofen in treating dysmenorrhea has also been studied. Measurable decreases in menstrual fluid PG levels, uterine pressures, and good to excellent pain relief have been reported in patients receiving this agent. Side effects have not been reported at doses of 400 mg given three times daily or every 4 hours. Ibuprofen has been reported to be more efficacious than indomethacin.[37] Evidence suggests that treatment should begin with the onset of symptoms.[38]

Fenemates. The only fenemates available for use in the United States are mefenamic acid (Ponstel) and meclofenamate sodium (Meclomen). Of these two, mefenamic acid has been used in dysmenorrhea. It is considered equivalent to aspirin as an analgesic. The use of mefenamic acid to treat moderate pain should not exceed 1 week since serious gastrointestinal effects or nephrotoxicity have been associated with prolonged use. Mefenamic acid may have two advantages over the other PGSIs. First, it not only inhibits prostaglandin synthesis, but also reduces the activity of already synthesized prostaglandins.[33] Second, in patients with menorrhagia, a significant reduction in menstrual blood loss has been described.[39] Treatment is begun with the onset of symptoms, using 250 to 500 mg initially followed by 250 mg every 6 hours. Side effects are reported to be minimal, but if diarrhea occurs, mefenamic acid should be discontinued because of its association with ulceration or inflammation of either the upper or lower gastrointestinal tract.

Other Drugs. Many other medications have been utilized in the management of primary dysmenorrhea. Anticholinergic agents, such as methoscopolamine bromide (Pamine) and methantheline bromide (Banthine), are atropine-like medications. Their inhibition of the parasympathetic nervous system produces some degree of uterine relaxation, but may be accompanied by unwanted effects such as tachycardia, dry mouth, blurred vision, and urinary retention. β-adrenergic receptor stimulants, such as isoxsuprine (Vasodilan) and terbutaline (Bricanyl, Brethine), have the potential to produce relaxation in the nonpregnant uterus.[40] The response to these agents is variable, and side effects such as tachycardia and nervousness may limit their use. Isoxsuprine is significantly less effective than placebo in relieving pain of dysmenorrhea and may even increase uterine vascular congestion.[41] Terbutaline is significantly more effective than placebo in relieving symptoms of dysmenorrhea, but has not been used extensively to treat this disorder.[42]

Estrogens have been used since the early 1940s to treat dysmenorrhea. Ovulation is inhibited, followed by a painless episode of bleeding.[43] Along with inhibition of ovulation, endometrial growth is suppressed, resulting in reduced endometrial prostaglandin production. This may account for the relief of dysmenorrhea symptoms.[25] Estrogens, combined with progesterone in oral contraceptive medications, have been administered on a cyclic basis to treat dysmenorrhea. Because dysmenorrhea is of short duration, the rationale for using this treatment is questionable, unless the patient also desires contraception, or the PGSI medications prove ineffective.

Guidelines for Managing Chronic Pelvic Pain

Careful evaluation of the patient's history and a thorough physical examination is important for the diagnosis and proper treatment of dysmenorrhea and chronic pelvic pain. The absence of obvious pelvic pathology permits the patient to be a suitable candidate for medical management.

Of the currently available classes of drugs, the prostaglandin synthetase inhibitors have been shown to be highly effective with minimal side effects. The fenemates, such as Ponstel, have some advantage over the priopionic derivatives, such as Naprosyn and Motrin, since they inhibit the activity of prostaglandins already formed. Indoleacetic acid derivatives have proven efficacy but with a high incidence of side effects. Despite its relative low cost, aspirin may be significantly less effective in the recommended doses in comparison to other medications. Anticholinergic agents and β-adrenergic receptor stimulants may have some future use in the treatment of dysmenorrhea and pelvic pain, but are currently not popular because of their variable response and side effects.

Exploratory surgery, usually by laporoscopy, is indicated in the presence of pelvic pathology or if medical management fails after at least a 3-month trial.

REFERENCES

1. Current concepts in endometriosis. *J Reprod Med* 19(suppl 5):299, 1977

2. Kistner RW: Management of endometriosis in the infertile patient. *Fertil Steril* 26:1151, 1975

3. Thorell JI, Rannevik G, Dymling JF: Effect of danazol on thyroid function in women. *Postgrad Med J* 55(suppl 5):33, 1979

4. Young MD, Blackmore WP: The use of danazol in the management of endometriosis. *J Int Med Res* 5(suppl 3):86, 1977

5. Fraser IS: Danazol—a steroid with a unique combination of actions. *Scot Med J* 24:147, 1979

6. Mettler L, Semm K: Clinical and biochemical experiences with danazol in the treatment of endometriosis in cases with female infertility. *Postgrad Med J* 55(suppl 5):27, 1979

7. Dmowski WT, Cohen MR: Antigonadotropin (danazol) in the treatment of endometriosis. *Am J Obstet Gynecol* 130:41, 1978

8. Audebert AJM, Emperaire JC, Larrve CS: Endometriosis and infertility: A review of sixty-two patients treated with danazol. *Postgrad Med J* 55(supl 5):10, 1979

9. Greenblatt RB, Tzigounis V: Danazol treatment of endometriosis: Long-term follow up. *Fertil Steril* 32:518, 1979

10. Danazol for fibrocystic disease of the breast. *Med Lett* 23:5, 1981

11. Chalmers JA, Shervington PC: Follow-up of patients with endometriosis treated with danazol. *Postgrad Med J* 55(suppl 5):44, 1979

12. Spooner JB: Classification of side-effects to danazol therapy. *J Int Med Res* 5(suppl 3):15, 1977

13. Ward GD: Dosage aspects of danazol therapy in endometriosis. *J Int Med Res* 5(suppl 3):75, 1977

14. Hoskins AL, Woolf RB: Stilbestrol-induced hyperhormonal amenorrhea for the treatment of pelvic endometriosis. *Obstet Gynecol* 5:113, 1955

15. Hammond CB, Haney AF: Conservative treatment of endometriosis. *Fertil Steril* 30:497, 1978

16. Kistner RW: The treatment of endometriosis by inducing psuedopregnancy with ovarian hormones. *Fertil Steril* 10:539, 1959

17. Hammond CB, Rock JA, Parker RT: Conservative treatment of endometriosis: The effects of limited surgery and hormonal pseudopregnancy. *Fertil Steril* 7:756, 1976

18. Abraham K: Manifestation of the female castration complex, in *Selected Papers of Karl Abraham, M.D.* Honolulu, Hogarth Press, 1927, p 338

19. Henzel MR, Massey S, Hanson FW, Buttram VC, Rosenwaks Z, Pauls FD: Primary dysmenorrhea: The therapeutic challenge. *J Reprod Med* 25(suppl 4): 226, 1980

20. Akerlund M: Pathophysiology of dysmenorrhea. *Acta Obstet Gynecol* 87(suppl):27, 1979

21. Akerlund M, Anderson KE: Vasopressin response and terbutaline inhibition of the uterus. *Obstet Gynecol* 48:528, 1976

22. Samuelsson B, Granstrom E, Green K, Hamberg M, Hammarstrom S, Malmsten C: Prostaglandin and thromboxanes. *Ann Rev Biochem* 47:997, 1978

23. Rosenwaks Z Seegar-Jones G: Menstrual pain: Its origin and pathogenesis. *J Reprod Med* 25(suppl 4):207, 1980

24. Henzel MR, Izu A: Naproxen and naproxen sodium in dysmenorrhea: Development from in vitro inhibition of prostaglandin synthesis to suppression of uterine contractions in women and demonstration of clinical efficacy. *Acta Obstet Gynecol Scand* 87(suppl):105, 1979

25. Chan WY, Hill JC: Determination of menstrual prostaglandin levels in non-dysmenorrheic and dysmenorrheic subjects. *Prostaglandins* 15(2):365–375, 1978

26. Chan WY, et al: Relief of dysmenorrhea with the prostaglandin synthetase inhibitor ibuprofen: Effect on prostaglandin levels in menstrual fluid. *Am J Obstet Gynecol* 135:102, 1979

27. Halbert DR, Demers LM: A clinical trial of indomethacin and ibuprofen in dysmenorrhea. *J Reprod Med* 21(4):219–222, 1978

28. Janbu T, et al: Effect of acetylsalicylic acid, paracetamol and placebo on pain and blood loss in dysmenorrheic women. *Acta Obstet Gynecol Scand* 87(suppl):81–85, 1979

29. Flower RJ, Moncada S, Vane JR: Analgesic-antipyretics and anti-inflammatory agents, in Gilman AG, Goodman LS, Gilman A (eds): *The Pharmacological Basis of Therapeutics,* ed. 6. New York, Macmillan, 1980, pp 682–728

30. Layes Molla A, Donald JF: A comparative study of ibuprofen and paracetamol in primary dysmenorrhea. *J Int Med Res* 2:395, 1974

31. Fox WW: Butazolidine: Letter to the editor. *Lancet* 1:195, 1953

32. Kajanoja P, Vesanto T: Naproxen and indomethacin in the treatment of primary dysmenorrhea. *Acta Obstet Gynecol Scand* 87(suppl):87–89, 1979

33. Simon LS, Mills JA: Nonsteroidal anti-inflammatory drugs. *N Engl J Med* 302(22):1238, 1980

34. Joelsson I, Lalos O: The effect of inhibitors of prostaglandin synthesis in primary dysmenorrhea studied with hysterametry. *Acta Obstet Gynecol Scand* 87:(suppl):45–50, 1979

35. Henzel MR, et al: Anaprox in dysmenorrhea: Reduction of pain and intrauterine pressure. *Am J Obstet Gynecol,* 135:455, 1979

36. Jacobson J, et al: Prostaglandin synthetase inhibitors and dysmenorrhea—a survey and personal clinical experience. *Acta Obstet Gynecol Scand* 87(suppl):73–79, 1979

37. Halbert DR, Demers LM: A clinical trial of indomethacin and ibuprofen in dysmenorrhea. *J Reprod Med* 21(4):219–222, 1978

38. Larkin RM, et al: Dysmenorrhea: Treatment with an antiprostaglandin. *Obstet Gynecol* 54(4):456–459, 1979

39. Anderson AB, et al: Reduction of menstrual blood loss by prostaglandin synthetase inhibitors. *Lancet* 1:774, 1976

40. Koelle, GB: Neurohumoral transmission and the autonomic nervous system, in Goodman LS, Gilman A (eds): *The Pharmacological Basis of Therapeutics,* ed. 5. New York, Macmillan, 1975, pp 404–444

41. Rubin A: Isoxsuprine for the treatment of dysmenorrhea: A double-blind study of 143 subjects. *Obstet Gynecol* 19:9, 1962

42. Akerlund M, Andersson KE, Ingemarsson I: Effect of terbutaline on myometrial activity, uterine blood flow, and lower abdominal pain in women. *Br J Obstet Gynecol* 83(9):673–678, 1976

43. Sturgis SH, Albright F: The mechanism of estrin therapy in the relief of dysmenorrhea. *Endocrinology* 26:68–72, 1940

23. Chemotherapy in Gynecologic Oncology

JOHN G. BOUTSELIS
GEORGE A. JOHNSTON   WILLIAM F. RAYBURN

A remarkable advancement in the management of cancer during the past two decades has been the demonstration that certain disseminated malignancies may be controlled or cured using chemotherapy.[1] Although surgery and radiation remain the primary modes for treating gynecologic malignancies, adjuvant chemotherapy provides the only means of systemic therapy for disseminated disease.[1] Promising results have been shown using adjuvant drugs in treating trophoblastic, ovarian, and endometrial neoplasms. Investigations are also continuing in determining the efficacy of adjuvant chemotherapy in widespread squamous cell carcinoma of the vulva or cervix.

This chapter reviews general principles of cancer chemotherapy, particularly as they relate to cellular biology and kinetics. The proposed mechanisms of action, usual dose ranges, and adverse effects are described for each of the commonly used agents, classified in Table 23-1. The role of these drugs in the management of gynecologic malignancies is then briefly discussed; however, the treatment of each specific malignancy is beyond the scope of this chapter.

PRINCIPLES OF CANCER CHEMOTHERAPY

Principles of chemotherapy are derived from their original successful application to the treatment of choriocarcinoma, Burkitt's lymphoma, acute lymphocytic leukemia, Hodg-

kin's disease, Wilms tumor, Ewing's sarcoma, and testicular carcinoma.[2] The one common denominator in these tumors is a rapid proliferation of cells. Conversely, tumors with a slower growth rate are usually less responsive to antineoplastic agents. Utilizing the L-1210 mouse leukemia model, it has been established that a given dose of an effective chemotherapeutic drug kills a constant fraction of cells regardless of the number of cells present in a tumor (fractional kill hypothesis).[3] A single course of drug therapy will result in a 90 percent decrease of a 10^{10} (10 billion) cell population/cm^3 of tumor. With each succeeding dose, the number of surviving cells is proportionately decreased. Li, Hentz, and Spencer have demonstrated this hypothesis of fractional kill through the use of the human-chorionic gonadotropin (HCG) tumor marker in choriocarcinoma.[4]

Variables to be considered in administering chemotherapy include the immunocompetence of the host, the volume of the tumor, the growth rate, the number and sensitivity of cells entering the resting phase of the cell cycle (G-0), the specific agents, and the dose schedules utilized. If the tumor volume is small and the fractional kill large, then resistant clones are less apt to develop during therapy.

Cell Growth Kinetics
To understand growth kinetics of cancer cells with uncontrolled proliferative characteristics, one must understand the kinetics of *normal* cell growth. Cell growth kinetics may be divided

TABLE 23-1. CLASSIFICATION OF CURRENTLY USED CHEMOTHERAPEUTIC AGENTS

I   Alkylating Agents
    Cyclophosphamide (Cytoxan)
    Melphelan (Alkeran)
    Chlorambucil (Leukeran)
    Triethylenethiophosphoramide (Thiotepa)
    Mechlorethamine (Mustargen)

II Antimetabolites
    Methotrexate (Amethopterin)
    5-Fluorouracil (5-FU, Fluorouracil)
    6-Mercaptopurine (6MP) (Purinethol)

III Antibiotics
    Dactinomycin (Cosmegen)
    Doxorubicin (Adriamycin)
    Bleomycin (Blenoxane)
    Mitomycin-C (Mutamycin)
    Mithramycin (Mithracin)

IV Plant Alkaloids—Vinca Alkaloids (Periwinkle Drugs)
    Vinblastine (Velban)
    Vincristine (Oncovin)

V   Hormones (Progestins)
    Medroxyprogesterone Acetate (Depo-Provera)
    Hydroxyprogesterone Caproate (Delalutin)
    Megestrol Acetate (Megace)

VI Other Drugs (Miscellaneous)
    Hydroxyurea (Hydrea)
    Cis-Diamininodichloroplatinum II (Platinol)
    Tamoxifen (Nolvadex)
    Hexamethylmelamine
    Dacarbazine (DTIC)
    Nitrosourea (Carmustine)

into three tissue groups (expanding, static, and renewing) that relate to parenchymal cell production and loss. The *expanding* tissues (kidney, liver, endocrine glands) are composed of differentiated cells that do not require replacement and will survive the lifetime of the organism. They maintain their ability to replicate and replace accidental cell loss. *Static* tissues (nerve and striated muscle) are highly differentiated, and these cells have lost their capacity to divide. *Renewing* tissues (bone marrow, gastrointestinal mucosa, epidermis, and hair follicles) are composed of differenti-

ated cells with a short life span; these are constantly renewed from a stem cell or clonogenic subpopulation. Cancer cells possess the attribute of uncontrolled cell growth and most closely resemble the renewing cell tissues, since they depend on the stem cell or a subpopulation of cells.[3]

The Cell Cycle

Cell growth kinetics are best illustrated in Figure 23-1, which depicts the cell cycle. The S, G-1, and M phases are relatively constant for any cell type. As the G-1 phase becomes more prolonged, the cell enters a resting or nondividing phase (G-0). After an undetermined length of time, the resting cell can either enter into the dividing cell cycle or remain as a permanently nondividing cell and eventually die. Hence, the G-0 phase can act as a reservoir from which cell proliferation can occur.[5]

The metabolic characteristics of the various phases of the cell cycle are important to the clinician, since various chemotherapeutic agents have damaging effects at one or more phases of the life cycle of the cell (Table 23-2). In general, some agents are characterized as being cell cycle-specific or phase-specific, while other agents are cell cycle-nonspecific or phase nonspecific. The distinction between specific and nonspecific agents is relative rather than absolute.

High doses of phase-specific agents have been used intermittently when a tumor has a rapid growth potential. The continuous exposure of a tumor to cycle- and phase-specific drugs should destroy any resistant, resting tumor cells which eventually enter the more drug-sensitive proliferating cycle.[5]

MECHANISMS OF ACTION

The mechanisms of action of chemotherapeutic agents relate to the different stage of the cancer cell cycle and whether or not the agents are cycle-nonspecific or cycle-specific.[6] Although antineoplastic agents vary in their mechanisms of action, they all destroy rapidly proliferating cells by interfering with one or

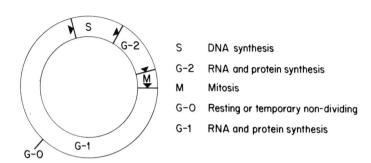

S   DNA synthesis

G-2   RNA and protein synthesis

M   Mitosis

G-0   Resting or temporary non-dividing

G-1   RNA and protein synthesis

Figure 23-1. The cell life cycle.

more of the sequences in cell replication, and toxic effects extend to the life cycles of normal cells.

Alkylating Agents

This is the single most commonly used group of antineoplastic agents. Despite much investigation, the mechanism of cytotoxicity remains poorly understood. These agents form cross-linkages between two DNA molecules to prevent replication and alter the biologic proper-

TABLE 23-2. RELATION BETWEEN THE CELL CYCLE AND DAMAGING EFFECTS FROM CHEMOTHERAPEUTIC AGENTS

Cycle-nonspecific Agents
    Alkylating agents

Cycle-specific Agents
    Antimetabolites
    Antibiotics
    Plant alkaloids
    Miscellaneous group

Phases of the Cell Cycle and Effective Agents
    S   (DNA synthesis) = Alk. agents, MTX, 5-FU, H. urea, 6-MP, ARA-C, Actinomycin D, adriamycin
    G-2   (RNA + Protein Synthesis) = Alk. agents, 5-FU, actinomycin D
    M   (Mitosis) = Alk. agents, vincristine, vinblastine, bleomycin, nitrogen mustard
    G-0   (Resting) = Alk. agents, adriamycin, actinomycin D, mitomycin D, bleomycin
    G-1   (RNA + Protein synthesis) = Alk. agents, MTX, 5-FU, actinomycin D

ties of the chromosomes. The alkylating agents act during the G-0 to M cell phases of the cell cycle. These drugs are cycle-nonspecific agents, since they do not depend on DNA synthesis for their effect and are best suited for slow-growing bulky tumors. The cells, which remain unaltered after alkylating therapy, tend to divide very rapidly and are more susceptible to attack by cycle-specific agents.

Antimetabolites

Antimetabolites are a large heterogenous group of cycle-specific or phase-specific agents which act by inhibiting essential metabolic processes that are necessary for DNA or RNA synthesis. The most common folic acid antagonist, methotrexate, acts to prevent the reduction of folic acid to folinic acid. It combines with the enzyme, dihydrofolinic acid reductase, to interfere with the formation of tetrahydrofolinic acid, a coenzyme necessary for DNA synthesis. Hence, it behaves as an enzyme-blocking agent, inhibiting DNA and RNA synthesis.

5-Fluorouracil (5-FU) is the most effective and widely prescribed pyrimidine analogue. It binds with thymidylate synthetase after being incorporated into the nucleic acid complex. Thymidine deficiency results from this enzyme inhibition, and cell replication is prevented.

Antibiotics

Antibiotics are phase- or cycle-specific agents which form a complex with DNA. This is caused by a selective binding at the guanine-cytosine segment to block the enzyme, DNA-dependent RNA synthetase, and inhibit the formation of messenger RNA and subsequent cell protein synthesis.

Plant Alkaloids

Plant alkaloids from the periwinkle plant, *Vinca rosea,* are cycle-specific agents which arrest mitosis during metaphase by binding to the protein necessary for mitotic spindle formation.

Hormones

Although the mechanism of action is poorly understood, the progestins are thought to cause immunosuppression, changes in endogenous sex steroid support, and directly affect cellular action.

Other Drugs

cis-*Platinum.* The biochemical properties of *cis*-platinum are similar to that of the alkylating agents which cause interstrand and intrastrand cross-links in DNA. Its action is cell cycle-nonspecific by inhibiting translation of DNA precursors for DNA and protein synthesis.

Hexamethylamine. Hexamethylamine acts in an unknown manner. It was originally thought to be a member of the alkylating agent group but its action is more similar to the antimetabolites.

Hydroxyurea. Hydroxyurea enhances radiosensitivity, perhaps by freezing cells into the relatively radiosensitive, late phase of G-1 rather than permitting them to proceed to the radioresistant S-phase of the cycle.

Tamoxifen. Tamoxifen is an antiestrogen-like compound, similar to clomiphene in chemical structure, which competes with circulating estrogen at intracellular receptor sites in the cytoplasm and nucleus complex.

DOSES AND ROUTES OF ADMINISTRATION

The doses and routes of administration of the various agents are listed in Tables 23-3 and

23-4. The goal of adjunctive chemotherapy is maximal tumor cell kill with minimal toxic effects. The highest tolerable dose of each agent is to be used until either (1) tumor cells are successfully eradicated, or (2) tolerable signs of reversible toxicity are maximized. For chemotherapy to be most effective, the tumor must be decreased to a subclinical or occult size following surgery or radiation. Otherwise, presumed tumoricidal doses during continuous or intermittent therapy may achieve inadequate concentrations in these less accessible tissues. The tumor size is also important to follow during therapy, since tumor growth would indicate a drug failure and the development of a resistant clone of cells. A drug regimen is considered ineffective only after a trial of two or more courses of chemotherapy.

Cancer drugs are usually administered initially by the IV route. Premedication with antiemetics or sedatives is often necessary. Oral administration is begun after parenteral therapy, and may also require premedication with an antiemetic or ingestion during a meal or at bedtime. The physician must read the package insert, since the efficacy of many agents is influenced by light exposure or temperature changes.

SINGLE VERSUS COMBINATION THERAPY

Although single-agent chemotherapy may be used in certain circumstances, most disseminated gynecologic malignancies are more effectively treated with multiple agents. This varies with the type of malignancy and stages of disease.

Single-agent chemotherapy is more commonly used for slow-growing solid tumors, while rapidly proliferating solid tumors may be more amenable to combination chemotherapy. Combination chemotherapy ideally acts synergistically by increasing the fractional kill of tumor through their different mechanisms of action. Table 3 describes the various single agents presently used in treating a number of highly malignant neoplasms, while Table

TABLE 23-3   DOSAGE REGIMENS AND SIDE EFFECTS OF THE VARIOUS CHEMOTHERAPY AGENTS

Drug	Dose and Route of Administration	Acute Side Effects	Toxicity
I Alkylating Agents			
Cyclophosphamide (Cytoxan)	750–1000 mg/M² IV as single dose every 3 weeks	Nausea and vomiting	Bone marrow depression (thrombocytopenia), hemorrhagic cystitis, alopecia
Melphalan (Alkeran)	0.2 mg/kg/day PO × 5 days, 4–6 weeks	Nausea and vomiting	BM depression (thrombocytopenia)
Chlorambucil (Leukeran)	0.1–0.2 mg/kg/day PO Decrease dose with BM depression	Nausea and vomiting with high dose	BM depression
Thiotepa (triethylenothiophosphoramide)	0.2 mg/kg/day IV × 5 days	Nausea and vomiting	BM depression
DTIC (Carbazine)	150–250 mg/M²/day × 5	Nausea and vomiting	BM depression and hepatotoxicity
II Antimetabolites			
Methotrexate (Amethopterin)	15–25 mg OD/IV or IM × 5 days for choriocarcinoma. Dose variable with type malignancy.	Usually none; stomatitis	BM toxicity, liver or renal failure; GIT disturbance as acute stomatitis, nausea, vomiting and diarrhea; alopecia; pulmonary toxicity
5-Fluorouracil (5-FU, Fluorouracil)	12–15 mg/kg IV weekly 12–15 mg/kg IV/OD × 5 days per month 5 mg/kg OD/IV × 5 days as part of act fu cy	Nausea and vomiting	Liver fibrosis rare. BM depression, stomatitis, ileitis, alopecia, diarrhea, cerebellar ataxia
6-Mercaptopurine (GMP, Purinethol)	2.5–5.0 mg/kg PO daily	Nausea and vomiting	BM depression, hepatotoxicity, dermatitis, mucosal ulceration
III Antibiotics			
Dactinomycin (Actinomycin D, Cosmegen)	12–15 mg/kg IV daily × 5 days (0.5 mg/day × 5 days)	Pain with extravasation and local skin necrosis; nausea, vomiting, diarrhea, cramps	BM depression, GIT symptoms, skin rash; pigmentation and desquamation if had previous irradiation
Doxorubicin (Adriamycin)	40–100 mg/M² IV every 3 weeks (maximum dose 550 mg/M²)	Nausea and vomiting; local phlebitis, fever, extravasation necrosis, red urine	BM depression, stomatitis; cardiotoxicity related to cumulative dose
Bleomycin (Blenoxane)	10–20 mg/M² IV or IM one to two times per week (maximum dose total of 400 mg)	Nausea, vomiting, fever, chills, localized pain, stomatitis, skin blisters	Pulmonary fibrosis, BM depression, GIT symptoms, skin changes, alopecia, kidney toxicity
Mitomycin C (Mutamycin)	0.05 mg/kg OD/IV × 6 days, then alternate days until total dose of 50 mg	Nausea and vomiting, extravasation necrosis	BM depression, nausea, vomiting, oral ulceration, diarrhea, irreversible thrombocytopenia

(Table 23-3 continues on page 312.)

TABLE 23-3   (Continued)

Drug	Dose and Route of Administration	Acute Side Effects	Toxicity
Mithramycin (Mithracin)	.02–.05 mg/kg	Nausea and vomiting, hypocalcemia	BM depression, hepatotoxicity
IV Plant Alkaloids (Periwinkle Drugs)			
Vinblastine (Velban)	0.1–0.2 mg/kg IV per week	Localized severe and prolonged extravasation, skin reaction, headache, nausea and vomiting, parasthesia, stomatitis	BM suppression (especially neutropenia), alopecia, muscle weakness, peripheral neuropathy, depression
Vincristine (Oncovin)	1.5 mg/M² IV per week in VAC; 0.4–1.4 mg/M² IV weekly in adults, 2 mg/M² weekly in children	Extravasation, local inflammation	Neuropathy, constipation, paralytic ileus, weakness and loss of reflexes, foot cramp, hoarseness, depression, BM toxicity (mild), alopecia
V Antineoplastic Hormones			
Medroxyprogesterone acetate (Depo-Provera)	400–800 mg IM or PO per week	None	Occasional liver function abnormality, alopecia and hypersensitivity with any of the progestational agents
Hydroxyprogesterone caproate (Delalutin)	1000 mg IM two times per week	None	Same as above
Megestral acetate (Megace)	120–320 mg daily	None	Same as above with caution in cardiac patients
VI Miscellaneous Drugs			
Hydroxyurea (Hydrea)	80 mg/kg PO every 3 days during radiation therapy or 20–30 mg/kg PO daily	Anorexia and nausea	BM depression, alopecia, stomatitis, diarrhea, megaloblastic anemia
Cis-Diammine di-chloroplatinum (Cis-Platinum)	50–100 mg/M² IV every 3 weeks	Severe nausea and vomiting	Renal toxicity, neurotoxicity, ototoxicity, moderate BM depression
Hexamethylmelamine	4–8 mg/kg PO daily 2 weeks per month, or 3 weeks every 6 weeks	Nausea and vomiting	BM depression, CNS depression, peripheral neuropathy
Tamoxifen citrate (Nolvadex)	10–20 mg PO daily	Nausea	Minimal, if any

TABLE 23-4 MULTIPLE AGENT CHEMOTHERAPY REGIMENS

Drug	Dose and Route of Administration	Acute Side Effects	Toxicity
MAC			
Methotrexate	0.3 mg/kg IM or IV, five times daily	Refer to individual	Potential severe
Actinomycin D	0.01 mg/kg IV, every	drug for acute	BM depression,
Chlorambucil	0.2 mg/kg PO, 2–3 weeks	side effects	gut toxicity, alopecia,
	Cytoxan 3–5 mg/kg/day		dermatitis, nausea,
	IV in place of chlorambucil		stomatitis
VAC			
Vincristine	1.5 mg/M² weekly	Refer to individual	BM toxicity;
	× 4–6 weeks, then every	drug for acute	neurologic toxicity;
	2 weeks	side effects	alopecia, constipation, stomatitis, dermatitis, ileus
Actinomycin D	0.5 mg, five times daily every 4–6		
Cyclophosphamide	8 mg/kg, weeks		
	When used with XRT, give vincristine only until XRT completed.		
PAC			
Cis-Platinum	50 mg/M², IV every 3	Refer to individual	Potential severe BM
Adriamycin	50 mg/M², weeks	drug for acute	toxicity; stomatitis;
Cyclophosphamide	500 mg	side effects	renal toxicity; cardiotoxicity

23-4 describes some of the most common agents used in combination chemotherapy.[5]

ADVERSE EFFECTS

The physician must be familiar with any potential immediate or delayed toxic effects before any agent is administered (Table 23-3). Immunosuppression is the most common side effect, especially with continuous drug therapy. No myelosuppressing agent should be given without initial and periodic blood counts. Recommended dosages and regimens are very schedule-dependent, but should be decreased in the presence of myelosuppression or if drug elimination processes are impaired. The best indicators of hematopoetic reserve are the neutrophil and platelet counts. Therapy should be delayed if the white blood count is less than 3000, neutrophil count is less than 1500, or platelet count is less than 100,000. Furthermore, any drug should be discontinued if signs of severe toxicity develop. This usually occurs in 1 to 3 weeks after beginning the administration of most agents.

Mild signs of toxicity are frequent and include nausea, vomiting, diarrhea, hair loss, and slight temperature elevations. The patient should be aware of these effects and report them to the physician when treated on an outpatient basis.

Supportive care of adverse effects is necessary. Treatment frequently consists of pain relief or management of infectious or myelosuppression complications. Pain is dependent on tumor aggressiveness, tumor location, and patient sensitivity. Drugs used to relieve pain include narcotics, mild analgesics, and Brompton's cocktail (morphine 5 mg, cocaine 10 mg,

**TABLE 23-5   ROLE OF CHEMOTHERAPY IN THE MANAGEMENT OF VARIOUS GYNECO-
LOGIC NEOPLASMS***

Neoplasm	Role of Surgery and XRT	Role of Chemotherapy
Squamous cancer of cervix Stage IB, IIA	1. Radical hysterectomy with pelvic lymphadenectomy *or* T & C plus ext. radiation.	Chemotherapy is less promising for squamous carcinoma than other gynecologic malignancies. Drug regimens have included: 1. Bleomycin + Mitomycin + Vincristine
Stage II-B, III, IV	2. Complete radiation therapy.	2. As above + *C. platinum* 3. Bleomycin + methotrexate
Radiation failures	3. Total pelvic exenteration when lesion resectable and deemed operable.	4. Adriamycin + methotrexate 5. Hydroxyurea + radiation 6. *C. platinum* + methotrexate 7. Adriamycin + 5-fluorouracil 8. Cytoxan, adriamycin, bleomycin, vincristine, actinomycin D (Barker)
Squamous cancer of vagina	1. Complete radiation is procedure of choice. 2. Radical pelvic surgery for recurrent cancer.	5-Flurouracil cream if intraepithelial neoplasia
Squamous cancer of vulva	1. Radical vulvectomy, groin lymphadenectomy. Pelvic node dissection when indicated. 2. Radical vulvectomy and pelvic radiation in selected cases.	
Adenocarcinoma cervix	T & C plus TAHBSO.	Adriamycin, 5-Flourounacil, cytoxan
Special gonadal-stromal ovarian tumors Granulosa cell tumor	1. TAHBSO 2. Debulk if needed 3. Irradiation	VAC or Act Fu Cy
Thecoma	TAHBSO	Unnecessary
Sertoli-Leydig tumors	USO or TAHBSO	VAC or Act Fu Cy
Gynandroblastoma	TAHBSO	VAC or Act Fu Cy
Lipid cell tumor	USO or TAHBSO + irradiation	Act Fu Cy in advanced stages.
Secondary (metastatic) ovarian tumors Metastatic from breast, GI tract, and lymphatic system to ovary	1. Locate primary tumor. 2. Treatment of metastatic tumor is secondary to that of the primary tumor site therapy.	Varies with primary tumor.
Endometrial carcinoma Stage I, G-1	1. TAHBSO.	No chemotherapy indicated in Stage IA, G-1.

* Abbreviations: T & C—tandem and culpostat internal radiation (radium and cesium); TAH, BSO—total abdominal hysterectomy, bilateral salpingo-oophorectomy; USO—unilateral salpingo-oophorectomy

(Table 23-5 continues on pages 315 and 316.)

TABLE 23-5 (Continued)

Neoplasm	Role of Surgery and XRT	Role of Chemotherapy
All other stage I	2. T & C + TAHBSO; Ext. rad. with myometrial invasion; T & C + ext. rad. plus TAHBSO	Extrapelvic metastases requires chemotherapy: 1. Estrogen and progesterone receptors may be guide. Provera 500 mg three times per week × five doses. Then Megace: Megace 240 mg/PO daily × 1 year.
Stage II	3. T & C + radical hysterectomy and pelvic lymphadenectomy; T & C + ext. rad. with TAHBSO	2. ADR and cytoxan nine times per 3 weeks × 12 courses. 3. Platinum may be added to CTX and ADR.
Stage II and IV	4. TAHBSO	
Endometrial sarcoma	1. Ext. rad. and TAHBSO in 6 weeks. 2. Radical surgery may be used in ca/sa or sarcoma botryoides.	Progestational chemotherapy in stromal sarcoma. All endometrial sarcomas should receive VAC chemotherapy × 12 courses.
Leiomyosarcoma	TAHBSO	Low mitotic count—no chemotherapy High mitotic count—VAC or ADR + DTIC
Fallopian tube carcinoma	1. TAHBSO 2. Radiation therapy is controversial	ADR + CTX ± *C. platinum* Melphelan may be used with minimal disease.

Epithelial cancer of ovary (mesotheliomas)
  Serous carcinoma
  Mucinous carcinoma
  Endometrial carcinoma
  Clear cell carcinoma
	TAHBSO + omentectomy (maximum primary surgical effort to reduce tumor to less than 2 cm in diameter); diaphragm and periaortic biopsies, appendectomy, peritoneal washings	*Single drug therapy (stage IA)*
		1. Melphalan 0.2 mg/kg/day IV 5 days/month
		2. Cytoxan 1000 mg/M² IV every 3 weeks
		3. Thiotepa 0.2 mg/kg/day IV for 5 days/month
		4. Leukoran 0.1–0.2 mg/kg/day PO
		5. *C. platinum* 50 mg/M² IV every 3 weeks
		6. Adriamycin 60–90 mg/M² IV every 3 weeks
		Multiple drugs (advanced disease)
		1. Adriamycin 60 mg/M² IV every 3 weeks; cytoxan 100 mg IV every 3 weeks
		2. ADR + CTX as above, plus *C. platinum* 50 mg/M² IV every 3 weeks

Germ-cell ovarian tumors Pure dysgerminomas	USO or TAHBSO + total abdominal radiation therapy	Chemotherapy optional (VAC) for pure dysgerminomas. Otherwise, VAC, MAC or Act Fu Cy for all other germ-cell tumors
Endodermal sinus	USO or TAHBSO	*VAC:*
Embryonal carcinoma	USO or TAHBSO	Vinc. 1.5/M² IV weekly × 12 weeks
Choriocarcinoma	USO OR TAHBSO	ADR 60 mg/M² IV every 3 weeks
Malignant immature teratoma	USO or TAHBSO	CTX 1000 mg/ IV every 3 weeks
Mixed germ-cell tumors	TAHBSO	*MAC:*
Polyembryoma	TAHBSO	MTX 0.3 mg/kg IM or IV ⎱ daily × 5 days Act. D 0.01 mg/kg IV ⎰ every 4 weeks CTX 4 mg/kg IV ——— (trophoblast element)
		Act Fu Cy: Act. D. 0.01 mg/kg IV ⎱ daily × 5 days 5-Fu 5 mg/kg IV ⎰ every 4 weeks CTY 5 mg/kg IV ———

TABLE 23-5   (Continued)

Neoplasm	Role of Surgery and XRT	Role of Chemotherapy
Hydatidiform mole	1. Suction and sharp curettage uterus 2. Hysterectomy for sterilization	If persistent β-subunit HCG after 2 months or plateau or rising titer, treat with methotrexate (20 mg/day IM $\times$ 5 days every 10–14 days until weekly negative HCG $\times$ 3 weeks) or actinomycin D (0.5 mg IV $\times$ 5 days, every 10–14 days). Then interval HCG for 1 year.
Invasive mole	Need examination of removed uterus for positive diagnosis	If diagnosis can be made, treat as above with 25 mg methotrexate (or actinomycin D) daily $\times$ 5 days.
Choriocarcinoma (low risk)	1. Hysterectomy with localized uterine lesions, while on methotrexate only if sterilization desired 2. Chemotherapy otherwise	Methotrexate 25 mg IM or IV or actinomycin D 0.5 mg IV daily $\times$ 5 days every 10–14 days until negative β-subunit HCG for 3 weeks.
Choriocarcinoma (High risk): (100,000 IU/24-hr urine or 40,000 mIU/ml serum) Initial high HCG Delayed therapy (4 + months) Brain or liver metastasis Resistant to single agent Following term pregnancy	1. Surgery may be used to remove localized lesion resistant to chemotherapy (uterus, liver, lung, etc.) 2. External radiation— 2000–3000 rads for brain or liver metastasis 3. Radiation until patient is stablilized for use of chemotherapy	1. MTX 15 mg IM, actinomycin D 0.5 mg IV and chlorambucil 10 mg PO = all given daily $\times$ 5 days every 12–14 days until negative β-subunit HCG weekly for 3 weeks, as with mole. 2. Modified Bagshawe Regimen*

Day	Hour	Treatment
1	0600	Hydroxyurea 500 mg PO
	1200	Hydroxyurea 500 mg PO
	1800	Hydroxyurea 500 mg PO
	1900	Actinomycin D 200 μg IV
	2400	Hydroxyurea 500 mg PO
2	0700	Vincristine 1 mg/M² IV
	1900	MTX 100 mg/M² IV
		MTX 200 mg/M² IV infusion in 12 hr
		Actinomycin D 200 μg IV
3	1900	Actinomycin D 200 μg IV
		Cytoxan 500 mg/M² IV
		Folic Acid 14 mg IM
4	0100	Folic Acid 14 mg IM
	0700	Folic Acid 14 mg IM
	1300	Folic Acid 14 mg IM
	1900	Actinomycin 500 mcg IV
5	0100	Folic Acid 14 mg IM
	1900	Actinomycin 500 mcg IV
6	No Rx	
7	No Rx	
8	1900	Cytoxan 500 mg/M² IV
		Adriamycin 30 mg/M² IV

*Currently used at Southeast Regional Center for T. Disease

and 95 percent ethanol/20 ml).[7] Brompton's cocktail may be given with a phenothiazine every 4 hours to prevent rather than to treat the pain. Transfusion is recommended to replace specific blood cell lines. A blood transfusion is usually necessary if the patient is remarkably symptomatic or if the hematocrit is 24 percent or less. Platelet transfusion is necessary if the count is less than 20,000/mm³ or if spontaneous bleeding occurs. Multiple vitamins are routinely prescribed to anyone taking a chemotherapy agent. Infectious morbidity and mortality are increased with myelosuppression and impaired host defenses. Fever evaluations with surveillance cultures, removal of indwelling catheters, and isolation precautions are indicated.

GUIDELINES FOR THE USE OF CHEMOTHERAPY IN TREATING GYNECOLOGIC MALIGNANCIES

Chemotherapy is used in gynecology to eliminate microscopic metastatic tumors or for palliation of advanced, disseminated, or recurrent disease. Table 23-5 illustrates the relation between chemotherapy and other therapeutic modalities in the management of specific neoplasms. Surgery for treating choriocarcinoma has been replaced by methotrexate or actinomycin D therapy. Similarly, in germ-cell tumors of the ovary, multiagent chemotherapy has resulted in cure rates otherwise unattainable by surgery alone. For ovarian epithelial tumors, a combination of therapeutic modalities includes an initial maximal surgical debulking effort, followed by the utilization of appropriate chemotherapeutic agents. In advanced endometrial carcinoma, antineoplastic agents play a key role in the induction of prolonged or complete remission. There is still a need for continued research in the manage-

ment of metastatic squamous cell carcinomas of the cervix using surgery and/or radiation along with adjunctive chemotherapy.

Although chemotherapeutic agents are considered valuable adjuncts to standard therapeutic modalities, their effectiveness is often difficult to assess and requires continued clinical trials. The effectiveness of chemotherapy has been enhanced by new protocols and revisions in drug scheduling. The additional use of immunotherapy may also be promising, but it too requires years of refinement to assess its clinical value.[8] Undoubtedly, newer drugs and new forms of drug delivery will be developed through research efforts and will place chemotherapy at greater heights of successful treatment of gynecologic malignancies.

REFERENCES

1. Smith JP, Rutledge F: Advances in chemotherapy for gynecologic cancer. *Cancer* 36:669, 1975
2. Barber H: Chemotherapy, in Barber H (ed): *Manual of Gynecologic Oncology.* Philadelphia, Lippincott 1980, p 111–125
3. Disaia P, Morrow P, and Towns D (eds): Chemotherapy, in *Synopsis of Gynecologic Oncology.* New York, Wiley, 1975, p 265–281
4. Li MD, Hertz R, Spencer DB: Effects of methotrexate upon choriocarcinoma and chorioadenoma. *Proc Exp Biol Med* 93:361, 1956
5. Disaia P, Creasman W: *Clinical Gynecologic Oncology,* Chap 11. St. Louis, Mosby, 1981, p 285–298
6. McGowan D: *Gynecologic Oncology,* Chap 5, New York, Appleton, 1978, pp 92–145
7. Mount BM, Ayemian I, Scott JF: The use of brompton mixture in treating chronic pain of malignant disease. *CMA Journal* 115:122, 1976
8. Barber H: Immunotherapy and immunopotentiation, in Barber H (ed): *Manual of Gynecologic Oncology.* Philadelphia, Lippincott, 1980, p 130
9. Bagshowe KD: Treatment of trophoblastic tumors. *Ann Acad Med* 5:273, 1976

PART THREE: DRUGS FOR GENERAL USE

24. Antibiotic Therapy

JAMES A. VISCONTI   JAY D. IAMS
WILLIAM E. COPELAND, JR.

It is useful to regard bacterial infections of the female genital tract as alterations in the relationship between the host and her normal bacterial flora. When normal vaginal flora gain access to the upper tracts and multiply, pelvic infection may result. Surgical or obstetrical procedures, foreign bodies, and exogenous pathogenic bacteria may produce a change in the location and number of endogenous organisms sufficient for infection to be manifested (Fig. 24-1). Principal among aerobic organisms are the gram-positive aerobic streptococci and the gram-negative rods, including *Escherichia coli* and *Bacteroides fragilis*, peptostreptococci, streptococci, and *Clostridia* organisms. Other than *Neisseria gonorrhoeae*, *Listeria monocytogenes*, and aerobic β-hemolytic streptococci (groups A and B), exogenous pathogens are rarely implicated in pelvic infections.

When clinical symptoms suggest an infection of the lower genital tract, cultures may be useful to identify the presence of exogenous bacteria that might be responsible for clinical infection. Cultures obtained transvaginally or transcervically are unlikely to be clinically useful unless one of these organisms is isolated. Recently, a technique that allows for uncontaminated transcervical cultures of the endometrial cavity has been reported.[1] Should further evaluation confirm the accuracy of culture data obtained with this technique, this device may allow recognition of patients in whom host flora have colonized the endometrium in clinically significant numbers. The specific diagnosis of salpingitis and pelvic inflammatory disease is more difficult because of the inaccessibility of the upper genital tracts. Clinical diagnosis is accurate in only 65 percent of patients with visually documented pelvic inflammatory disease.[2] Culture data are helpful but not possible to obtain without the use of invasive techniques (culdocentesis or laparoscopy), which increase patient discomfort and risk. Any cultures taken directly from infected tissues at surgery are accurate if processed correctly and are helpful in choosing an appropriate treatment plan.

Monif has described the "progressive anaerobic syndrome," a useful concept to explain many of the clinical features of pelvic infection.[3] The initial insult occurs as a disruption of the integrity of the upper genital tract through surgery, delivery, or presence of a foreign body (e.g., an intrauterine device, IUD). Aerobic bacteria produce the initial infection and, as these organisms multiply and destroy tissue, available oxygen is consumed and a progressively anaerobic and acidotic environment is produced. This is followed by the secondary invasion of facultative aerobes and subsequently the obligate anaerobes. This progression can often be arrested in the early stages by antimicrobials without anaerobic activity, if the diagnosis is made early. Infections of longer duration or greater severity, includ-

319

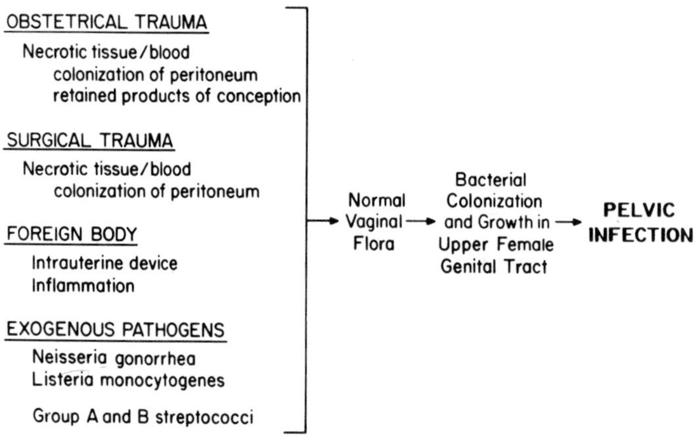

OBSTETRICAL TRAUMA
  Necrotic tissue/blood
    colonization of peritoneum
    retained products of conception

SURGICAL TRAUMA
  Necrotic tissue/blood
    colonization of peritoneum

FOREIGN BODY
  Intrauterine device
  Inflammation

EXOGENOUS PATHOGENS
  Neisseria gonorrhea
  Listeria monocytogenes

  Group A and B streptococci

Normal   Bacterial
Vaginal → Colonization   PELVIC
Flora   and Growth in → INFECTION
              Upper Female
              Genital Tract

Figure 24-1. Surgical or obstetrical procedures, foreign bodies, and exogenous pathogenic bacteria may produce a change in the location and number of endogenous organisms sufficient for infection to manifest.

ing tubovarian abscesses, require the addition of antibiotics with an anaerobic spectrum. Whether the early utilization of antimicrobials effective against anaerobes will improve long-term results is still unknown. However, this concept accounts for the reported excess of antimicrobial agents of limited spectrum as prophylactic drugs in gynecologic surgery.

The rationale for clinical use of antibiotics in pelvic infections is based on numerous factors. The single most important concept is that of the polymicrobial nature of these mixed aerobic-anaerobic infections. Penicillin remains an excellent choice for the majority of anaerobic organisms, with the significant exception of B. fragilis. Most gram-positive cocci, specifically aerobic streptococci, are also sensitive to penicillin therapy. Antibiotics effective against B. fragilis include clindamycin, chloramphenicol, β-lactamase-resistant cephalosporins, and metronidazole. The aerobic gram-negative rods significant in pelvic infections are usually sensitive to the various aminoglycosides.

Multiple regimens of various antibiotics have been investigated in pelvic infections without one specific combination demonstrating a definite superiority based on acute response or long-term sequelae. This has been documented in both acute salpingitis[4] and postpartum endometritis.[5-7] In recent studies, the most significant feature in altering both short- and long-term outcome was early diagnosis and treatment.[8]

Chlamydia trachomatis has emerged as a pathogen in acute pelvic inflammatory disease.[9-11] This protozoan is responsible for a variety of infections, including lymphogranuloma venereum, neonatal conjunctivitis, and nonspecific urethritis in the male. C. trachomatis is now implicated as an etiologic agent in acute salpingitis as well as being identified in an asymptomatic carrier state in approximately 5 percent of the population. The treatment of choice for C. trachomatis is a natural or synthetic tetracycline. Erythromycin is an effective substitute in patients allergic to the tetracyclines.

On occasion, antibiotic therapy, regardless of bacterial spectrum, is ineffective. These conditions should strongly suggest abscess formation, retained products of conception, or presence of a foreign body such as an IUD. These conditions should be corrected to maximize the effect of the administered medication.

Antimicrobial drugs can prevent infection in some surgical patients, but are not without risk. Potential adverse effects include toxic or allergic drug reactions and superinfection. It should be noted that an effective prophylactic antibiotic regimen need not be active against all potential pathogens.

The effective use of prophylactic antibiotics depends on the timing of administration. Antimicrobials should first be given 1 hour before surgery, sufficient to achieve therapeutic tissue levels during the procedure. Prophylactic drugs should be stopped within 24 hours following surgery since continuing prophylaxis beyond 24 hours increases the risk of drug toxicity and bacterial superinfection, and does not increase prophylactic efficiency. In several studies antimicrobial prophylaxis has been reported to decrease morbidity after vaginal hysterectomy. A 2-year prospective double-blind study of prophylactic antibiotics in 317 patients who had elective vaginal hysterectomies found that patients given either penicillin G or cefazolin intravenously 30 minutes before surgery and at 6-hour intervals thereafter for 48 hours had significantly fewer postoperative infections than those given a placebo.[12] Prophylactic antibiotics did not lower the incidence of infection associated with abdominal hysterectomy. The recommended dose (in patients with normal renal function) for cephalosporins is 1 gm parenterally every 4 to 8 hours.

Physicians have a bewildering array of antimicrobial agents at their disposal. The number of agents and their doses, side effects, and actions make it nearly impossible to think of them in an organized manner. Accordingly, they are discussed in the following sections as chemically related groups of drugs. The material on each group of drugs is subdivided into similar areas (mechanism, pharmacology, indications, dosing, adverse effects) for ease of retrieval.

PENICILLINS

Pharmacology and Preparations

The penicillins remain among the most effective and least toxic of available antimicrobials. The various preparations (see Table 24-1) of the penicillins are obtained by chemical or biologic modifications of the 6-aminopenicillanic acid nucleus of this compound. Penicillins act by inhibiting bacterial cell wall synthesis, but many different mechanisms are involved in this process.

The potassium salt of penicillin V is better absorbed than the sodium salt. Penicillin G, methicillin, carbenicillin, and nafcillin are all highly acid labile, which accounts for their poor bioavailability. Patients should be advised to ingest penicillins 1 hour before meals, because the presence of food delays and impairs their absorption.

Once in the blood stream penicillins bind to serum proteins to varying degrees. Despite many studies, the precise influence of protein-binding on therapy is a clouded issue. Only unbound drug exerts antibacterial activity, and bound drug cannot enter a microorganism or diffuse into tissue. Penicillins are distributed to the lungs, liver, kidney, muscle, and bone in sufficient quantities to treat infections. However, levels of penicillins in the eye, brain, cerebrospinal fluid (CSF), and prostate are inadequate to treat the usual pathogens.

All penicillins are highly excreted by the kidney and produce high urine concentrations. A portion of all of these agents is metabolized, but much is eliminated without degradation. Most penicillins are actively secreted into the bile, producing concentrations that exceed

TABLE 24-1 PENICILLINS COMMERCIALLY AVAILABLE IN THE UNITED STATES

Natural penicillins
  Benzylpenicillin G
  Phenoxymethylpenicillin (V)

Penicillinase-resistant penicillins
  Methicillin
  Nafcillin
  Isoxazolyl penicillins
    Cloxacillin
    Dicloxacillin
    Oxacillin

Aminopenicillins
  Ampicillin
  Amoxicillin
  Cyclacillin

Antipseudomonas penicillins
  Carbenicillin
  Indanyl carbenicillin
  Ticarcillin
  Mezlocillin
  Piperacillin*
  Azlocillin*

* Investigational status at this time, but soon to be released to U.S. market.

TABLE 24-2 RECOMMENDED PENICILLIN MAINTENANCE DOSES FOR ADULT PATIENTS WITH NORMAL AND REDUCED RENAL FUNCTION*

Drug	PO Dose	Normal Renal Function IM Dose	IV Dose
Penicillin G (1.7 mEq K+/ mil.units)	1.0 gm every 6 hr before meals	600,000– 1.2 million units	10–12 mu up to 40 mil. u/day
Procaine		300,000 units	1.2 mil. u every 24–72 hr
Benzathine		600,000 units	1.2 mil. u every 15–30 days
Penicillin V	0.250–0.5 gm every 6 hr before meals		
Methicillin		1–2 gm every 4– 6 hr	8–12 gm/day (2 gm every 4 hr)
Nafcillin	0.250 gm every 6 hr ac	0.5–1.0 gm every 4–6 hr	8–12 gm/day (2 gm every 4 hr)
Oxacillin	0.5–1.0 gm every 6 hr		8–12 gm/day (2 gm every 4 hr)
Cloxacillin	0.25–0.5 gm every 6 hr before meals		
Dicloxacillin	0.25–0.5 gm every 6 hr ac	0.25–0.5 gm every 6 hr	
Ampicillin	0.250–0.5 gm every 6 hr ac	0.25–0.5 gm every 6 hr	8–12 gm/day (2 gm every 4 hr)
Amoxicillin	0.25 gm every 8 hr		
Carbenicillin disodium (4.7 mEq Na+/gm)			24–36 gm/day (2–3 gm every 2 hr)
Indanyl carbenicillin	0.382–0.764 gm every 6 hr		
Ticarcillin (5.2–6.5 mEq Na+/gm)		1 gm every 6 hr	16–20 gm/day (3 gm every 4 hr)
Piperacillin (~2 mEq Na+/gm)			12–18 gm/day (4 gm every 6 hr)
Mezlocillin (~2 mEq Na+/gm)			12–18 gm/day (4 gm every 6 hr)

* From Ref. 13.

TABLE 24-2 (Continued)

Mild RF (> 50 ml/min)	Moderate RF (50 ml/min to 10 ml/min)	Severe RF (< 10 ml/min)
		1 mil. u every 6 hr
1–2 gm every 4 hr	1–2 gm every 4 hr	1–2 gm every 8–12 hr
2 gm every 4 hr	2 gm every 4 hr	2 gm every 4 hr
0.25–0.5 gm every 6 hr	0.25–0.5 gm every 6 hr	0.25–0.5 gm every 6 hr
0.25–0.5 gm every 6 hr	0.25–0.5 gm every 6 hr	0.25–0.5 gm every 6 hr
0.25–0.5 gm every 6 hr	0.25–0.5 gm every 6–12 hr	0.25 gm every 12–16 hr
0.25–0.5 gm every 8 hr	0.250 gm every 6–12 hr	0.250 gm every 12–16 hr
2–3 gm every 8–12 hr	2–3 gm every 12–24 hr	2–3 gm every 24–48 hr
3 gm every 8–12 hr	3 gm every 12–24 hr	3 gm every 24–48hr
16 gm/day (4 gm every 6 hr)	12 gm/day (4 gm every 8 hr)	8 gm/day (2.5 gm every 8 hr)
12–18 gm/day (4 gm every 6 hr)	9 gm/day (3 gm every 8 hr)	6 gm/day (2 gm every 8 hr)

those in serum. Penetration, however, is poor in the presence of common duct obstruction. Because most penicillins are rapidly secreted into the urine, their half-lives in serum are short. Therefore, renal failure is important when considering their elimination, since it prolongs the half-life of several agents. Even in the presence of marked renal impairment (creatinine clearance < 20 ml/minute), urinary levels of ampicillin, carbenicillin, and ticarcillin are adequate for effective therapy. Urinary levels of indanyl carbenicillin may not be adequate when renal function is significantly reduced.

Recommended penicillin dosages for adults with renal insufficiency are also given in Table 24-2. The renal excretion of all penicillins can be impaired by probenecid, increasing serum levels and prolonging drug half-life. The major use of probenecid is to increase serum levels of penicillin G, ampicillin, and amoxicillin in the treatment of gonorrhea by single-dose administration.

Penicillin G is available as two repository salts for IM use only, procaine penicillin G and benzathine penicillin G. Procaine penicillin G produces detectable blood levels for 12 hours. Doubling the dose does not double the blood level, unless the drug is administered in different body sites. This is the primary rationale for splitting the 4.8 million units of procaine penicillin G into two sites to treat gonorrhea. Benzathine penicillin G provides detectable blood levels for 4 weeks. Mixtures of procaine penicillin and benzathine penicillin are available, but their use is irrational since this preparation actually dilutes the level of benzathine penicillin.

Antibacterial Activity

Streptococci. Streptococci of the *Streptococcus pyogenes* (group A), *St. agalactiae* (Group B), *St. viridans*, *St. pneumoniae* (pneumococcus), peptostreptococci, and the anaerobes have remained extremely sensitive to penicillin G.[14-16] Group D streptococci include *St. bovis*, which is penicillin-sensitive, and the true enterococci (*St. fäecalis*, *St. fecium*, *St. durans*, and

St. liquifaciens), which have always been relatively resistant to penicillin. The levels of penicillin V and the aminopenicillins needed to inhibit these organisms are about the same. Amoxicillin, however, may be more active against enterococci. The semisynthetic antistaphylococcal penicillins have the advantage over methicillin in their effectiveness against not only penicillinase-resistant staphylococci but against other gram-positive organisms as well.

The population at risk of developing bacterial endocarditis has expanded and now includes patients with rheumatic heart disease, congenital heart disease, mitral valve prolapse, idiopathic hypertrophic subaortic stenosis (IHSS), and prosthetic valves. The most recent recommendations[17] from the American Heart Association for the prevention of bacterial endocarditis are given in Table 24-3.

Staphylococci. Both *Staphylococcus aureus* and *S. epidermis* have become increasingly resistant to penicillin G. Greater than 80 percent of hospital-acquired staphylococci are resistant to penicillin G because of β-lactamase production. Staphylococci resistant to penicillin G are also resistant to the aminopenicillins, ampicillin, amoxicillin, cyclacillin, carbenicillin, and ticarcillin. *S. aureus* or *S. epidermis* resistant to methicillin are also resistant to oxacillin, nafcillin, and cloxacillin.

Neisseria. *Neisseria* are more sensitive to penicillin G than to penicillin V. They are almost as sensitive to ampicillin as to penicillin G but carbenicillin is much less active. For practical purposes, the antistaphylococcal agents have only minimal activity against *N. meningitidis* or *N. gonorrhoeae*. Antibiotics and the doses used to treat gonorrhea are shown in Table 24-4.

Clostridium. Penicillin G is effective against most of the gram-positive bacilli that are clinically important including *Cl. tetani*, *Cl. perfringens*, *Corynebacterium diphtheriae*, *Bacillus anthracis*, and *Listeria monocytogenes*. While the antistaphylococcus agents are less active than penicillin G, they do adequately inhibit all

TABLE 24-3   BACTERIAL ENDOCARDITIS PROPHYLAXIS

I.   For dental procedures and surgery of the upper respiratory tract:
  A. Aqueous penicillin G 1 million units IM mixed with 600,000 units of procaine penicillin G administered 30–60 min prior to the procedure followed with penicillin V, 500 mg by mouth every 6 hr for eight doses.
  B. For patients with prosthetic heart valves who are at high risk; an aminoglycoside such as streptomycin 1 gm IM is recommended *in addition* to the aqueous procaine penicillin G and the penicillin V.
  C. Oral prophylactic therapy includes penicillin V, 2 gm by mouth administered 30–60 min before the procedure followed by 500 mg by mouth every 6 hr for eight doses.
  D. Penicillin-allergic patients may be given:
    1. Erythromycin, 1 gm by mouth 1.5 hr prior to the procedure, followed by 500 mg by mouth every 6 hr for eight doses.
    2. Vancomycin, 1 gm IV over 30–60 min. The infusion should be started 1 hr prior to the procedure. This is followed by erythromycin, 500 mg by mouth every 6 hr for eight doses.

II. Urethral, gynecologic and abdominal procedures. The American Heart Association recommends that antibiotics be administered before urethral catheterization in patients with valvular heart disease, but they are not required in most patients with heart disease for upper GI endoscopy (without biopsy), percutaneous liver biopsy, sigmoidoscopy, barium enema, pelvic examination, dilation and curettage of the uterus, uncomplicated vaginal delivery, and insertion or removal of intrauterine devices.
  A. Aqueous penicillin 2 million units or ampicillin 1 gm, both IV or IM plus gentamicin 1.5 mg/kg IM or IV (or streptomycin 1 gm IM) 0.5–1 hr prior to the procedure. If gentamicin is used, repeat the dose of penicillin or ampicillin and gentamicin every 8 hr for two additional doses. If streptomycin is used, give penicillin or ampicillin with streptomycin every 12 hr for two additional doses after the procedure.
  B. If the patient is allergic to penicillin, vancomycin 1 gm, IV infused over 30 min about 1 hr prior to the procedure plus streptomycin 1 gm IM can be used. A single dose of these antibiotics is probably sufficient. The same dose of these agents may be repeated in 12 hr.

these organisms except Listeria. Other species of *Clostridium* may resist penicillin, ampicillin, and cephalosporins while showing suceptibility to chloramphenicol and metronidazole.[18]

Bacteroides.   There are a number of gram-negative rods of clinical importance that are sensitive to penicillin G. *Fusobacterium nudeatum, B. melanenogenicus,* and *B. oralis* are inhibited by penicillin G and, to a lesser extent, to penicillin

V. Intravenous administration provides adequate levels. The antistaphylococcal agents do not show good activity against these organisms.

There is still considerable disagreement about the agents of choice in the treatment of intra-abdominal anaerobic infections, in which *B. fragilis* is an important pathogen. At present, clindamycin and chloramphenicol seem to be agents of first choice followed by

TABLE 24-4   ANTIBIOTICS AND TREATMENT SCHEDULES FOR VENEREAL DISEASES

Disease	Treatment	
	FIRST CHOICE	ALTERNATE
Uncomplicated gonorrhea	Procaine penicillin G 4.8 mil. u, IM (in two injections) plus probenecid 1 gm by mouth 30 min prior to injection	Tetracycline* 0.5 gm PO four times a day for 5 days or ampicillin 3.5 gm PO or amoxicillin 3.0 gm PO plus 1 gm probenecid PO given simultaneously
Pregnant patients	Same as above	Spectinomycin 2 gm IM (not established as safe for fetus) or erythromycin 1.5 gm PO then 0.5 gm four times a day for 4 days (high failure rate)
Penicillinase-producing *N. gonorrhoeae*	Spectinomycin 2 gm IM	Cefoxitin 2 gm IM plus 1 gm probenecid PO
Acute salpingitis (PID), outpatients	Procaine penicillin G 4.8 mil. u or ampicillin 3.5 gm PO or amoxicillin 3.0 gm each with 1 gm probenecid followed by ampicillin or amoxicillin 0.5 gm four times a day for 10 days *or* tetracycline 0.5 gm PO four times a day for 10 days	
Acute salpingitis, hospitalized	Aqueous penicillin G 20 mil. u/day IV until improvement then ampicillin 0.5 gm PO four times a day to complete 10 days of therapy	Tetracycline 0.25 gm IV every 6 hours until improvement, then 0.5 gm PO four times a day to complete 10 days of therapy
Disseminated gonococcal infection	Ampicillin 3.5 gm PO or amoxicillin 3.0 gm PO each with probenecid 1 gm PO followed by ampicillin or amoxicillin 0.5 gm PO four times a day for 7 days	Spectinomycin 2 gm IM four times a day for 3 days or erythromycin 0.5 gm PO four times a day for 7 days Tetracycline 0.5 gm PO four times a day for 7 days

(continued)

TABLE 24-4 (Continued)

Disease	Treatment	
	FIRST CHOICE	ALTERNATE
	Aqueous penicillin G 10 mil. u IV/day until improvement then ampicillin 0.5 gm PO four times a day to complete 7 days of therapy	
Nongonococcal or post gonococcal urethritis	Tetracycline 500 mg PO four times a day for 7–14 days	Erythromycin 500 mg PO four times a day for 7–14 days
Primary syphilis	Benzathine penicillin G 2.4 mil. u IM or aqueous procaine penicillin G 600,000 units IM daily for 8 days	Tetracycline or erythromycin 0.5 gm PO four times a day for 15 days
Latent or late secondary syphilis	Benzathine penicillin G 2.4 mil. u, IM every week for 3 weeks	Erythromycin or tetracycline 0.5 gm PO four times a day for 30 days
Neurosyphilis	Aqueous procaine penicillin G 600,000 units, IM for 15 days or aqueous penicillin G 2–4 mil. u, IV every 4 hours for 10 days	Benzathine penicillin G 2.4 mil. u, IM every week for 3 weeks or erythromycin or tetracycline 0.5 gm PO four times a day for 30 days

* Avoid tetracycline in pregnant patients.

secondary agents including penicillin G, ampicillin, and carbenicillin. In spite of this, penicillin G succeeds in eradicating most pelvic infections. Carbenicillin may be effective, but a substantial percentage of *B. fragilis* strains are resistant. Ticarcillin is active against most anaerobes, including *B. fragilis,* but the role of this agent in pelvic infections needs further investigation.

Other Gram-Negative Organisms. The activity of penicillins against gram-negative enteric bacilli depend on the susceptibility patterns of the local organisms. In general, penicillin G will inhibit many *E. coli* and *Proteus mirabilis* found in urinary tract infections, but penicillin G shows a more limited antibacterial spectrum than ampicillin. Penicillin V has poor activity against gram-negative bacilli and the antistaphylococcal agents possess no activity against these organisms.

The aminopenicillins inhibit about 85 percent of *E. coli* and *P. mirabilis* isolated in the community.[19] Most *Klebsiella, Enterobacter, Serratia,* indole-positive *Proteus* (*P. morganii* and *P. vulgaris*), and *Providencia* are resistant. Although most *Salmonella typhii* are sensitive, some isolates from Central America are resistant. Many *Sa. typhimurium* are resistant and at present most *Shigella sonnei* are resistant, except for *Sh. flexneri*, which is inhibited by ampicillin.

Carbenicillin and ticarcillin are active against *E. coli* and *P. mirabilis*. In addition to their activity against *Pseudomonas aeruginosa*, they are active against many *Enterobacter*, most indole-positive *Proteus*, some *Serratia*, most *Providencia*, and *Acinetobacter* organisms.[20] Table 24-4 summarizes the antibiotics and their doses used in the treatment of syphilis.

The most recent semisynthetic penicillins (piperacillin, mezlocillin, and azlocillin) offer a broader spectrum that includes increased activity against *P. aeruginosa*. Piperacillin has greatest activity against *Pseudomonas*. All three are readily hydrolyzed by beta-lactamase; therefore, resistant strains may be encountered. Piperacillin is also very active against *H. influenzae* and *N. gonorrhoeae*. All three penicillins are active against *E. coli*, *Proteus sp.*, and *S. marcescens*. Piperacillin and mezlocillin are active against *B. fragilis*. The place for these new agents in the therapy of gynecologic and obstetric infections has not been established.

Adverse Effects

All of the penicillins can produce untoward reactions. Hypersensitivity reactions are the major adverse effect. Allergic reactions to penicillin are estimated to occur in 2 to 5 percent of the general population; approximately 10 percent of patients who have previously been exposed to penicillin will experience an allergic reaction.[21] Penicillin preparations administered by the parenteral route are associated with a higher incidence of sensitivity reactions (procaine penicillin IM ~ 5 percent; penicillin G IV ~ 2.5 percent; penicillin G, PO ~ 0.3 percent) than are oral products.[22] Ampicillin produces about twice as many rashes (7 percent) as do other penicillins and is particularly likely to develop in patients with infectious mononucleosis, cytomegalovirus infection, or leukemics receiving allopurinol. Other reactions that

have been noted with the various penicillins include:

1. Coombs'positivity, hemolytic anemia being rare

2. Nephritis, interstitial with fever and eosinophilia, appears to be most common with methicillin

3. Hepatitis and elevations of SGOT

4. Bleeding tendency because of platelet dysfunction seen with carbenicillin and ticarcillin

5. Diarrhea, commonly with ampicillin- and pencillinase-resistant products

6. Pain and tenderness at injection site, especially with benzathine products

7. Stomatitis, glossitis

8. Convulsions, usually associated with high-dose parenteral therapy in patients with renal insufficiency

9. Central nervous system reactions (not seizures) in some patients receiving procaine penicillin G, probably due to the procaine

10. Hyperkalemia with potassium penicillin G (contains 1.7 mEq potassium ion/1 million units)

11. Hypernatremia and excess sodium load with carbenicillin (contains 4.7 mEq sodium ion/gm)

CEPHALOSPORINS

Pharmacology

Cephalosporins are compounds containing 7-amino cephalosporanic acid and are derived by a number of modifications of cephalosporin C. These agents are similar to penicillin in respect to structure, mechanism of action, and general antimicrobial activity. Like penicillins, cephalosporins inhibit peptoglycan transpeptidase and D-alanine carboxypeptidase in bacterial cells; thus, they prevent cross-linking of muramic acid-containing peptidoglycan strands. This results in a defective bacterial cell wall which is osmotically unstable.[23] The β-lactam moiety, unlike that in the 5-member penicillin ring, is attached to a 6-member ring in the cephalosporins. It is this structural characteristic which makes cephalosporins more resistant to penicillinase.

The pharmacokinetic characteristics of the cephalosporins have been studied extensively. The primary route of excretion of the cephalosporins is renal, mainly by glomerular filtration and tubular secretion. Cephalothin and cephapirin are also metabolized (20 to 30 percent) to the less active desacetyl metabolite. From 60 to 80 percent of both cephalothin and cephapirin are eliminated in the unchanged form by renal tubular secretion. Cefazolin is primarily cleared by glomerular filtration. Table 24-5 summarizes the pharmacokinetic properties of the cephalosporins.

Cefoxitin is not strictly considered a cephalosporin, because it is derived from cephamycin C and contains a 7-α methoxy moiety which is responsible for resistance to β-lactamase.[24]

Antibacterial Activity

The cephalosporins are drugs of choice only for infections caused by *Klebsiella*. Urinary tract infection with *Klebsiella* is not uncommon in reproductive-age women, and may be particularly difficult to eradicate during pregnancy. Combination therapy with two agents showing bactericidal urinary concentrations in vitro is often required.

Because the cephalosporins are not often agents of first choice, they are especially suitable for antimicrobial prophylaxis. Many agents have been shown to diminish postoperative febrile morbidity in premenopausal women following vaginal hysterectomy, but use of a first-line or potentially toxic antibiotic for this indication is not recommended. A

course of cefazolin, 1 gm IM or IV 1 to 2 hours before surgery, and then 6 and 12 hours postoperatively is effective and safe. Cefoxitin and cefamandole are agents with a broader spectrum of activity, active against some anaerobes and resistant gram-negative organisms. Therefore, these drugs are less suited for prophylactic use.

The cephalosporins continue to be used frequently, although less costly and equally effective drugs are available.

Gram-Positive Organisms. The cephalosporins are active against most gram-positive organisms including penicillinase-producing staphylococci.

Gram-Negative Organisms. Cephalothin, cefazolin, cephapirin and cephradine are considered effective against three common gram-negative bacilli, that is, *E. coli, P. mirabilis,* and *Klebsiella.*[25-27] Though these agents have some activity against *Haemophilus influenzae,* ampicillin and chloramphenicol are considered the agents of choice.[28] With the exception of cefamandole and cefoxitin, the cephalosporins have marginal effects on the enterobacteriaceae (*Serratia; Enterobacter; Enterococci; Salmonella; Shigella;* and indole-positive *Proteus* including *P. morganii, P. vulgaris, P. rettgeri; Citrobacter;* and *Providencia*), *Pseudomonas,* and *Bacteroides* organisms.

Cefamandole and cefoxitin have a broader spectrum of activity. Cefamandole has been shown to be effective against *H. influenzae, En. cloacae, Acinetobacter,* and indole-positive *Proteus* besides the common gram-positive organisms.[26,29,30-32] Cefoxitin also has an extended spectrum of activity over the older cephalosporins and has more in vitro activity against β-lactamase-producing bacteria. It is effective against indole-positive *Proteus* (*P. morgani, P. rettgeri,* and *P. vulgaris*), *Serratia, Providencia,* and *Bacteroides fragilis.*[32-34] Cefoxitin is, however, not as active as penicillin against other anaerobes: peptostreptococci, *Fusobacteria,* and *Clostridia.*[33] It is also less effective than penicillin or ampicillin against *St. pneumoniae,*

TABLE 24-5   RECOMMENDED CEPHALOSPORIN DOSES FOR ADULT PATIENTS WITH NORMAL REDUCED RENAL FUNCTION[36-39]

Drug	Normal Renal Function	Moderate Renal Function	Severe Renal Failure
Cephalothin	1–2 gm every 4 hr IV	1–2 gm every 4–6 hr	1 gm every 8 hr
Cefazolin	250–500 mg IV every 6–8 hr IM	250 mg every 6 hr	250 mg every 24 hr
Cephapirin	1–2 gm every 4 hr IV	1–2 gm every 4–6 hr	1 gm every 8 hr
Cefamandole	1–2 gm every 4–6 hr	1.5–2.0 gm every 8 hr	1 gm every 12 hr
Cefoxitin	1–2 gm every 4–6 hr	1–2 gm every 12–24 hr	0.5–1.0 gm every 12–24 hr
Cephalexin	250–500 mg every 6 hr PO	250 mg every 6 hr	250 mg every 24 hr
Cephradine	500 mg to 2 gm every 6 hr PO	500 mg every 24–40 hr	500 mg every 40–70 hr
Cefadroxil	250–500 mg every 8–12 hr	500 mg every 12–24 hr	500 mg every 36 hr
Cefaclor	250–500 mg every 8 hr	Dose usually unchanged	
Cefotaxime	2 gm every 4 hr	2 gm every 4 hr	1 gm every 4 hr
Moxalactam	4 gm every 8 hr	2 gm every 8 hr or 3 gm every 12 hr	Further adjustment only necessary for patient with hepatic and renal insufficiency

St. pyogenes, H. influenzae, and has poor activity against *Enterobacter, Citrobacter, Acinetobacter,* and *Pseudomonas.*[33] Though gentamicin remains the drug of choice in *Serratia* infections, resistant strains may respond to cefoxitin.[35] For treating anerobes, the increased activity of cefoxitin against bacteroides may prove useful, particularly when treating mixed infections caused by both aerobic and anaerobic pathogens where *B. fragilis* is suspected to be the primary pathogen.

Preparations and Doses

Cephalothin, cefazolin, and cephapirin have very similar therapeutic effectiveness and antimicrobiologic activity.[25,26,31,36,39] Cefazolin may have some advantages since it causes the least pain on IM injection, can be administered either intramuscularly or intravenously and attains higher serum and tissue levels. It therefore can be administered less frequently, and in smaller doses. Recommended doses of cephalothin and cephapirin and their microbi-

ologic spectra are similar. The authors are unaware of reports in the literature indicating cephapirin to be any more or less effective than cephalothin, and therefore these two drugs should be considered interchangeable. However, since cephalothin has been shown to be the most stable cephalosporin against inactivation by the cephalosporinases produced by some strains of *S. aureus,* it should be considered the cephalosporin of choice for treating difficult staphylococcal infections. Cephradine and cephalexin are also similar and can be considered therapeutically equivalent[27] when oral therapy is necessary. At equivalent doses, cefazolin achieves serum levels that are between two and four times those of cephalothin.[36,37]

Cefamandole and cefoxitin should be held in reserve for more resistant organisms that do not normally respond to other cephalosporins. Indications for cefamandole might include (1) infections where organisms may include cefamandole-sensitive *Citrobacter, Entero-*

bacter, and indole-positive *Proteus* (*P. morganii, P. vulgaris,* and *P. rettgeri*); (2) *H. influenzae* infections in patients with documented penicillin allergy (not previous anaphylactic reaction) or the organism is ampicillin-resistant; and (3) serious life-threatening infections where the etiology cannot be immediately established.

Cefoxitin should be considered in (1) infections where organisms include cefoxitin-sensitive indole-positive *Proteus, Serratia* (resistant to gentamicin), and *B. fragilis* (resistant to clindamycin); and (2) abdominal infections or sepsis where there is a high probability of mixed aerobic and anaerobic organisms and where there is concern of clindamycin toxicity (pseudomembranous colitis) or chloramphenical toxicity. Where *Pseudomonas* may be present, an aminoglycoside as well as cefoxitin may have to be used.

Cefadroxil is a cephalosporin that has a longer half-life and slower urinary excretion rate than either cephalexin or cephradine, and as a result may be administered less frequently (twice daily) than other oral cephalosporins in the therapy of infections of the urinary tract.

Cefaclor is highly active against *E. coli, K. pneumoniae, P. mirabilis,* and *H. influenzae.* Following oral administration of a 500-mg dose, peak serum concentrations of 12 to 14 μg/ml (total antibiotic) are achieved in 1 hour. The mean urinary concentration is greater than 1500 μg/ml in 4 to 6 hours following ingestion of a dose.

With all oral cephalosporins, oral absorption is probably best and most complete when these are taken on an empty stomach.

The third generation cephalosporins and cephalosporin-like drugs are cefotaxime, cefoperazone and moxalactam. They are useful for beta-lactamase-producing organisms because of their resistance to these enzymes. All three are highly active against the *Enterobacteriacae,* and show moderate activity against *Pseudomonas* and *B. fragilis.* Moxalactam activity is similar to that of Cefoxitin for *B. fragilis.* The third generation cephalosporins are less active than the earlier cephalosporins against *S. aureus* and *S. epidermidis.* These new cephalosporins should be reserved for serious gram-negative

infections and not for less serious infections easily handled by the penicillins and earlier cephalosporins. Because of moxalactam's *B. fragilis* activity, it may become established in the therapy of intra-abdominal infections. However, comparative in vivo studies of this new agent versus combination therapy (clindamycin, metronidazole or cefoxitin with an aminoglycoside) in intra-abdominal infections are not yet available. The use of these drugs as single therapy in neutropenic or immunosuppressed patients is not recommended. The usual doses of these drugs are shown in Table 24-5.

Cost-Effectiveness

The purchase of cephalosporins often represents the largest single drug expenditure in most United States hospitals. Where the cephalosporins are comparative and are marketed by more than one company, significant cost savings can be achieved by competitive bidding. A comparative cost analysis of the cephalosporins based on daily cost to patients shows cefamandole and cefoxitin to be more expensive than cefazolin, cephalothin, and cephapirin. With the exception of cefamandole and cefoxitin, all the cephalosporins are comparable. Cefazolin, however, seems to have some distinct advantages in that lower and fewer doses are necessary for most infections, therefore greater savings can be realized.

Adverse Effects

The cephalosporins may be associated with the production of serious untoward effects including hypersensitivity reactions, hematologic reactions, nephrotoxicity, and local reactions such as thrombophlebitis. Allergic reactions may occur. The precise incidence of cross-reactivity between penicillins and cephalosporins is not well defined. Cephalosporins probably should not be administered to individuals who have immediate-type reactions such as urticaria or anaphylaxis to the administration of penicillins. Cephalosporins may elicit allergic reactions in patients who are not allergic to penicillin. Such reactions include anaphylaxis, serum sickness, eosinophilia, fever, and skin eruptions. Therapy with cephalothin and cephaloridine have been associated with a positive Coombs' test, but hemolytic anemia is uncommon. Prolongation of the prothrombin time (PT) has been reported after 5 to 7 days of therapy, especially in malnourished patients and vitamin K may be administered if necessary to improve clotting function. Colonization and superinfection have been reported in 2 to 5 percent of patients receiving cephalosporins. Leukopenia has been rarely reported with high doses (> 12 gm/day) and is reversible in 2 to 7 days after therapy is discontinued.

Central nervous system toxicity with mental confusion has been reported after high doses in patients with renal failure. Reversible renal tubular necrosis may result from cephaloridine administration. Pain and sterile abscesses at injection sites and phlebitis have been reported. Cefamandole has been associated with a disulfiram-like reaction with nausea and vomiting, flushing, and hypotension happening about 30 minutes after administration. The oral cephalosporins have been associated with abdominal distress, diarrhea, hypersensitivity reactions, and rarely, antibiotic-induced pseudomembranous colitis.

TETRACYCLINES

Tetracyclines have a broad spectrum of antimicrobial activity, are relatively well absorbed after oral administration, and are generally well tolerated with few serious adverse effects. Tetracyclines, however, are regarded as the drugs of choice for relatively few microbial pathogens because of their often unpredictable and incomplete coverage of most pathogenic species.

Pharmacology
Tetracyclines block the binding of transfer RNA-amino acid complexes to the ribosome, thus making amino acids unavailable to messenger RNA for protein synthesis.

The major differences in the various tetracycline products relate to their pharmacokinetic characteristics (see Table 24-6). The

completeness of oral absorption when taken on an empty stomach ranges from 60 to nearly 100 percent with various preparations. Food interferes with absorption. Divalent ions, calcium, aluminum, magnesium, as well as iron preparations, and sodium bicarbonate impair absorption significantly.

Peak serum levels with a 250-mg oral dose of tetracycline are 1 to 3 μg/ml at 1 to 2 hours and up to 5 μg/ml with a 500-mg dose.[40] Intravenous therapy with tetracycline, doxycycline or minocycline gives levels of 15 to 30 μg/ml depending on the rate of infusion and dose.[39] Intramuscular administration is not recommended due to severe pain and poor absorption. Tetracyclines penetrate tissue and body fluids well. Liver and bile levels are 5 to 10 times higher than simultaneous serum levels. Protein-binding ranges from 55 to 80 percent for all tetracyclines except oxytetracycline, which is 30 percent bound. Elimination of tetracyclines is primarily by the gastrointestinal tract and urinary tract. Tetracycline and oxytetracycline give the highest urinary levels and are sometimes preferred for urinary tract infections. In patients with impaired renal function, doxycycline may be administered without reduction in dosage and is the drug of choice for extrarenal infections. In these patients, the half-life of tetracycline and oxytetracycline increases to about 100 hours. The half-lives of chlortetracycline, doxycycline, and minocycline are about doubled by impaired renal function. Tetracyclines cross the placental barrier and relatively high concentrations are found in human milk and therefore should not be prescribed to nursing mothers. Tetracyclines should not be used for the treatment of urinary tract infections in pregnant women (see Chap. 2). Doxycycline and minocycline are more convenient for patients due to twice-daily dosing and are least affected by concomitant food.

Clinical Uses—Spectrum of Activity
The tetracyclines are active against many gram-positive and gram-negative bacteria as well as rickettsia, mycoplasma, and chlamydia. The antibacterial spectrum, although broad, is often unpredictable. Most gonococci, *H. in-*

TABLE 24-6 PHARMACOKINETICS OF TETRACYCLINES[41, 42]

Product	Adult Dose		%Oral Absorption	Half-Life (hr)	Peak Serum Concentration (µg/ml)	Excretion
	ORAL	IV				
Chlortetracycline (Aureomycin)	250–500 mg four times a day	250–500 mg every 12 hr	30	7	2–7	20% renal + biliary
Demeclocycline (Declomycin)	250–300 mg four times a day		70	15	2–4	40% renal
Doxycycline (Vibramycin)	100 mg every 12 hr first day, then 100–200 mg/day in one or two doses	200 mg initially, then 100 mg every 12 hr	90	15 (15–36) ESRD*	2–6 PO 15–30 IV	10% renal
Methacycline (Rondomycin)	150 mg every 6 hr	150 mg every 6 hr				
Minocycline (Minocin, Vectrin)	200 mg initially, then 100 mg every 12 hr	200 mg initially, then 100 mg every 12 hr	100	17 (17–30) ESRD	2–4 PO 15–30 IV	Metabolized
Tetracycline	250–500 mg four times a day	250–500 mg every 12 hr should not exceed 2 gm/day	80	10	2–4 PO 15–30 IV	60% renal

* ESRD = End-stage renal disease

fluenza, and *St. pneumoniae* are sensitive, but there is increasing resistance among each of the species. Resistance among gram-positive bacteria include about 50 percent of *S. aureus*, 30 percent of β-hemolytic streptococci, and virtually all enterococci. Susceptibility of *E. coli*, *P. mirabilis*, *Klebsiella*, *Shigella*, and *Salmonella* organisms is quite variable. Most strains of indole-positive *Proteus*, *Serratia*, *Ps. aeruginosa*, *Providencia*, and *Enterobacter* are resistant. Activity against anaerobes is erratic—as many as 40 percent of peptostreptococci, 40 percent of *B. melanerogenicus* and 30 to 60 percent of *B. fragilis* are resistant.

The analogues of tetracyclines show similar spectra of activity. An exception would be minocycline, which is more active against *S. aureus* and *Nocardia asteroides*. In all instances, other antimicrobials are considered the agents of choice for infection involving these pathogens. Minocycline and doxycycline are somewhat more active against anaerobes and facultative gram-negative bacilli. While doxycycline is the best tetracycline against anaerobes, one-third of *B. fragilis* strains remains resistant at readily achievable blood concentrations.

Adverse Effects

Common Effects. Gastrointestinal side effects are common and include nausea, vomiting, anorexia, unpleasant taste, pruritis, and diarrhea. Superinfections are common and include oral candidiasis and vulvovaginitis. Hypersensitivity reactions are also common and include rashes, fever, and eosinophilia. Photosensitivity may occur with any tetracycline, especially with demeclocycline. Photosensitivity may be treated with a sunscreen preparation. Vestibular toxicity is unique to minocycline and has been reported in up to 90 percent of patients receiving this drug. This effect is dose-related and reversible.

Tetracyclines are deposited in developing teeth during early stages of calcification and may cause a dose-related yellow-brown mottling effect. There may also be disturbances in fetal bone growth. These potential complications contraindicate the use of tetracycline

in children under 8 years old and in any pregnant woman.

Intravenous administration frequently causes thrombophlebitis. Increases in BUN may occur because of the inhibition of hepatic protein synthesis while catabolism continues. In the presence of impaired renal function there may be increasing acidosis, hyperphosphatemia, anorexia, nausea, vomiting, weight loss, and severe electrolyte disturbances. These effects may be noted with any tetracycline other than doxycycline.

Uncommon Effects. Hepatotoxicity ranges from mildly abnormal liver function tests to severe hepatic failure with jaundice followed by azotemia, acidosis, shock, and death. Hepatotoxicity is usually related to excessive dose (> 2 gm/day), pregnancy, renal disease, or previous hepatic disease. Pregnant women also appear to have a greater than normal chance of developing pancreatitis following tetracycline administration. Because many alternative drugs are available, tetracyclines should be avoided entirely in the pregnant patient.

Rare Effects. The ingestion of outdated tetracycline has been associated with the Fanconi syndrome. Pseudomembranous enterocolitis has also been rarely reported. A number of recent cases of injury to the esophagus have been reported with tetracyclines, especially doxycycline capsules. The pH of a solution of doxycycline in water is about 1.0 and when passage of such capsules down the esophagus is delayed, injury is likely to result. Patients should be counseled to swallow tetracycline products with a glass of water with the patient in an upright position. These drugs should not be taken immediately before bedtime or when lying down.

CHLORAMPHENICOL

Pharmacology
Chloramphenicol has bacteriostatic activity through an inhibition of microbial protein pro-

duction by suppressing peptidyl transferase activity on the 50 S-subunit of the ribosome.

It is well absorbed after oral administration with peak blood levels of 3 to 6 μg/ml following a 500-mg dose and 8 to 15 μg/ml following a 1-gm dose. Absorption from IM injection is poor. Peak serum concentrations with intravenous administration in the usual doses are 10 to 20 μg/ml, depending on the infusion rate. Chloramphenicol penetrates well into tissues and body fluids because of its high lipid solubility. Most of the drug is inactivated by conjugation with glucuronide in the liver. The half-life of 2 to 3 hours in patients with normal liver function increases in the presence of severe hepatic disease with jaundice. Chloramphenicol may inhibit the metabolism of tolbutamide, phenytoin, and warfarin, and increases in half-lives of these drugs have been reported.[43] Most of the drug is excreted in the urine with about 5 percent excreted unchanged. Renal failure results in the accumulation of nontoxic metabolites with minimal influence on the half-life of the active form. Severe liver disease increases the potential for high levels of free chloramphenicol due to decreased glucuronide conjugation. Serum concentrations greater than 25 μg/ml should be avoided due to potential for hematologic toxicity.[41]

Chloramphenicol is available for oral and intravenous use. The usual dose is 50 to 100 mg/kg/day in four divided doses. Maximum doses for adults with severe renal disease are 2 to 3 gm/day. Ascites or jaundice due to liver disease is a relative contraindication to chloramphenicol.

Antibacterial Activity

Chloramphenicol is highly active in vitro against all anaerobic microorganisms. Chloramphenicol has failed in a small number of *B. fragilis* sepsis patients even though the organism was sensitive in vitro. Chloramphenicol is the drug of choice for treatment of typhoid fever and other systemic *Salmonella* infections. Chloramphenicol should *not* be used to treat infections caused by staphylococci, *St. pneumoniae* or β-hemolytic strepto-cocci. These microorganisms are susceptible in vitro to chloramphenicol, but safer, more effective therapy is available. Penicillin G is the drug of choice for all anaerobic infections except those caused by *B. fragilis*. Activity against aerobic gram-negative bacilli is erratic, but *E. coli*, *Shigella* and *P. mirabilis* are generally sensitive. About 30 to 60 percent of *Klebsiella*, *Citrobacter*, indole-positive *Proteus*, *Providencia*, and *Serratia* are susceptible, but *Ps. aeruginosa* is almost always resistant.

Adverse Effects

The most important toxic effect of chloramphenicol is bone marrow suppression, which occurs in a dose-related form and as an idiosyncratic reaction. Dose-related bone marrow suppression occurs particularly when plasma concentrations exceed 25 μg/ml with daily doses of 4 gm or more and with prolonged therapy. The clinical picture is characterized by anemia, pancytopenia, and increased serum iron concentration. Serious granulocytopenia is rare if treatment with chloramphenicol is discontinued when white blood cell counts decrease to less than 4000/mm³ and the neutrophil percentage decreases to less than 40 percent.[41] Recovery from dose-related bone marrow suppression usually occurs within 3 weeks after use of the drug has been stopped.

Idiosyncratic aplastic anemia is rare. It has only been documented in cases where the drug is administered orally, usually in persons who have received prolonged therapy and especially in those who have received the drug on multiple occasions.[44] Idiosyncratic aplastic anemia is unrelated to dose. Other side effects include nausea, vomiting, glossitis, stomatitis, diarrhea, and pseudomembranous colitis.

ERYTHROMYCIN

Erythromycin is a macrolide antimicrobial with activity against most gram-positive bacteria, many anaerobes, *Mycoplasma pneumonia* and Legionella pneumonophilia (Legionnaire's disease).

Pharmacology

Erythromycin inhibits protein synthesis by binding with the 50 S-ribosomal subunit, thereby interfering with the site where amino acids are transferred to protein. The drug is bacteriostatic but may be bactericidal at high concentrations. It is available as estolate, ethylsuccinate, gluceptate, lactobionate, and stearate salts.

Absorption of all erythromycin preparations is mainly in the duodenum. The bioavailability of oral preparations depends on formulation, the gastric acidity and emptying time, and the effect of multiple dosing.[45] Erythromycin base is acid labile and therefore commercially available as an enteric-coated tablet (resistant to gastric acid). The stearate is less water soluble and therefore protected to some extent against gastric acid. The ethylsuccinate is partially dissociated in the intestine, and once absorbed, it is hydrolyzed to free erythromycin. Erythromycin estolate is acid stable and dissociates in the intestine and becomes hydrolyzed in the blood to the free base.

Peak blood levels of active drug after a 500-mg oral dose usually range from 3 to 10 μg/ml. Serum levels obtained with a 500-mg IV infusion of the lactobionate are 8 to 12 μg/ml. Peak blood levels are seen 30 to 90 minutes after oral administration, and the half-life is 1.5 to 2.5 hours.

Erythromycin is excreted primarily in the bile while only 2 to 5 percent is excreted in the urine. Erythromycin is present in maternal milk and crosses the placental barrier (although fetal levels are < 25 percent of maternal blood levels).[46]

Antibacterial Activity

Erythromycin is active against most gram-positive bacteria, including streptococci such as *St. pneumoniae*, group A and B β-hemolytic streptococci and most enterococci. Most strains are sensitive to concentrations of 0.5 μg/ml or less at neutral pH. The activity of erythromycin increases at a pH of 8. Susceptibility of *S. aureus* is variable: Most community-acquired strains are susceptible, but up to 50 percent of hospital-acquired strains are resistant in institutions where the drug is extensively used.

H. influenzae, Neisseria, C. diphtheriae, Pasteurella mutlocida, Listeria, brucella, rickettsia, mycoplasma, chlamydia, and treponemes strains are usually sensitive. Activity versus anaerobic bacteria is erratic.[47] Less than half of *F. nucleatum* and *B. fragilis* are susceptible to 4 μg/ml. Most anaerobic gram-positive cocci are susceptible. Aerobic and facultative gram-negative bacteria are resistant but may be susceptible to urinary levels in alkaline media.

Indications

The parenteral use of erythromycin is limited because of the frequency of thrombophlebitis. In most instances the drug is given orally where the primary uses are for respiratory tract infections. Penicillins are preferred for most of these infections but erythromycin is a suitable alternative for patients who are penicillin-sensitive. Erythromycin is the agent of choice for *M. pneumoniae* and Legionnaires' disease.[41] The American Heart Association recommends erythromycin as an alternative to penicillin for both treatment and prevention of pharyngeal infections caused by group A β-hemolytic streptococci. For venereal disease, erythromycin is an alternative agent for penicillin-allergic patients with syphilis or pregnant patients with uncomplicated gonorrhea. (Table 24-4). It may also be used as an alternative to tetracyclines for genital infections due to *C. trachomatis*. Cystitis and pyelonephritis caused by gram-negative bacilli may be treated with erythromycin and urine alkalinization with 12 to 15 gm of sodium bicarbonate daily.

Dosage

Adult oral doses range from 250 to 1000 mg (30 to 60 mg/kg/day) every 6 hours. The usual dose is 500 mg every 6 hours. No dosage adjustment is necessary in renal failure.

Intravenous preparations are usually administered in 1 to 4 gm/day in two to four divided doses.

Adverse Reactions

The major adverse reactions with oral preparations are epigastric distress, nausea, and diarrhea. These are dose-related and rarely necessitate discontinuing the drug.

The most serious toxicity is cholestatic hepatitis, which occurs only with the estolate. Symptoms include fever, abdominal pain, nausea, vomiting, jaundice, and dark urine. The onset usually occurs 10 to 20 days after initial exposure or immediately after reexposure. Laboratory abnormalities include leukocytosis, eosinophilia with increased bilirubin, alkaline phosphatase, and serum glutamic pyruvic transaminase (SGPT). Most patients improve promptly when the drug is discontinued. Hypersensitivity reactions such as rash and drug fever are rare. Intramuscular administration is extremely painful and is therefore not recommended. Intravenous administration may cause pain during infusion with a high incidence of phlebitis.[41]

CLINDAMYCIN

Clindamycin inhibits the initiation of peptide chain synthesis, and is similar to chloramphenicol and erythromycin. Clindamycin is bactericidal against some, but not all, susceptible bacteria.

Pharmacokinetics

Oral preparations are nearly completely absorbed. Peak serum levels of 3 to 5 μg/ml are achieved at 30 to 45 minutes after oral administration of 300 mg of clindamycin hydrochloride or palmitate. Concurrent food administration has little effect on serum levels. There is only a modest increase in peak levels with repeated dosing at 6- to 8-hour intervals. Intramuscular injections of 300 mg produce levels of 3 to 5 μg/ml, while 600-mg doses give peak levels of about 8 μg/ml. Intravenous administration of 600 mg yields peak levels of 10 to 45 μg/ml.[41] Clindamycin is extensively distributed throughout body tissues with the exception of the eye and central nervous system. The half-life is 2 to 3 hours and only slightly increased in renal failure. Half-life increases dramatically ($\sim$ five times) in hepatic failure. Clindamycin readily (10 to 20 percent) crosses the placental barrier.[46]

Spectrum of Activity

Clindamycin is active against most gram-positive bacteria, streptococci (not enterococci), and *S. aureus*. Most anaerobic bacteria are susceptible to clindamycin at 0.5 μg/ml or less. This includes *B. fragilis,* which accounts for 75 percent of anaerobic bacteremias and is a major isolate in female genital tract infections.

Indications

One indication for clindamycin is serious infection in which *B. fragilis* is an established or suspected pathogen. This includes intra-abdominal sepsis, infections of the female upper genital tract, and selected soft tissue infections. In most instances the drug is combined with another agent that is active against aerobic gram-negative bacilli, since these conditions are usually mixed aerobic-anaerobic infections.

Dosage

Clindamycin preparations are the hydrochloride, the 2-palmitic acid ester and the 2-phosphoric acid ester. The two esters are not biologically active and must be hydrolyzed in the blood. Clindamycin hydrochloride is recommended for oral use with adult doses of 150 to 450 mg every 6 to 8 hours, usually 300 mg every 6 hours. Concurrent food administration has little effect on serum levels. IM or IV doses are usually 300 to 600 mg every 6 to 8 hours. No dose modification is necessary in renal failure. The usual parenteral dose in patients with severe liver disease is 300 mg every 8 hours.

Adverse Reactions

Major adverse reactions are gastrointestinal complications ranging from common, uncomplicated diarrhea to serious pseudomembranous colitis. This colitis is believed to be caused by an enterotoxin produced by *Cl. difficile*, and probably occurs in about 0.01 percent of cases. While both the oral and parenteral forms of clindamycin may cause pseudomembranous colitis, there appears to be a modest increase in the incidence of this complication with oral administration.[48] Treatment consists of discontinuing clindamycin, avoiding antiperistaltic medications such as diphenoxylate, and the use of vancomycin (500 mg orally four times daily for at least 1 week).[49]

Other side effects include a morbilliform rash in 3 to 5 percent of patients. Transient abnormalities of liver function are relatively common. These are not dose-related and they return to baseline values when the drug is discontinued or treatment continued.

AMINOGLYCOSIDES

Pharmacology

Aminoglycoside antibiotics in clinical use include streptomycin, kanamycin, gentamicin, tobramycin, and amikacin. They bind irreversibly to bacterial ribosomes, blocking the recognition step in protein synthesis and causing misreading of the genetic code.

The aminoglycosides are (1) bactericidal for a wide range of gram-positive and gram-negative species and mycobacteria, (2) minimally absorbed from the gut, (3) their dosage is more accurately calculated on the basis of lean rather than total body weight, and (4) elimination occurs almost entirely by the kidney.

These antibiotics are well absorbed by IM injection producing peak serum levels after about 1 hour. Less than 1 percent of an oral dose is absorbed and the resultant serum levels are usually insignificant in patients with normal renal function. Repeated oral dosing may result in accumulation in patients with impaired renal function. These drugs have similar volumes of distribution and are minimally protein bound. Aminoglycosides are distributed in extracellular fluid volume which constitutes about 30 percent of lean body weight (about 20 liters in the average adult).

Intrathecal administration is necessary to ensure adequate concentration in the CSF. Placental tissue levels are approximately 25 to 50 percent of those in the serum. These drugs have a marked affinity for renal cortical tissue, accumulating in concentrations that are 10 to 50 times those in serum. Aminoglycosides are eliminated from the body by renal glomerular filtration. The half-life of 2 to 3 hours in patients with normal renal function is markedly increased in the renally impaired patient.

Antimicrobial Activity

All aminoglycosides are negligibly bound to plasma proteins and excreted primarily unchanged by the kidneys. Although the average half-life in patients with normal renal function is 2 to 3 hours, it may range from 0.5 to 10 hours. Patients with impaired renal function excrete the drug more slowly and the half-life in an anuric patient may range from 50 to 80 hours.

Indications for monitoring serum levels of aminoglycosides include: (1) assuring that peak concentrations are in the therapeutic range, (2) patients not responding to therapy, (3) patients with conditions associated with lower peak levels (e.g., obesity and expanded extracellular fluid volume), (4) patients who develop signs or symptoms of ototoxicity or nephrotoxicity, (5) patients undergoing dialysis, and (6) patients who have received more than 5 days of therapy—even those without obvious impaired renal function.

Streptomycin. The introduction of newer agents with a broader spectrum of activity has limited the indications for streptomycin. Penicillin G or ampicillin in combination with streptomycin is the treatment of choice for enterococcal endocarditis. Streptomycin in combination with penicillin is recommended for prophylaxis of bacterial endocarditis in patients with cardiac valvular defects at times of gastrointestinal or genitourinary manipulation or surgery (see Table 24-3 for doses).

Kanamycin. Serious infection due to members of the Enterobacteriaceae family is the main indication for this agent. It is effective against a wide range of gram-negative organisms; however, it exhibits very little activity against *Ps. aeruginosa.*

Gentamicin, Tobramycin, and Amikacin. All these agents are indicated for serious aerobic gram-negative infections including those in which *Ps. aeruginosa* is suspected of being an etiologic agent. Where possible, culture and sensitivity results as well as resistance patterns should guide the physician in the selection of one of these agents.

Tobramycin is similar to gentamicin, and bacteria highly resistant to gentamicin are usually also resistant to tobramycin. While most strains of *Pseudomonas* are sensitive to tobramycin and gentamicin, tobramycin is inhibitory at one-third the concentration of gentamicin. *Serratia* may be less sensitive to tobramycin than to gentamicin. Amikacin is similar to gentamicin but active against many isolates of *Proteus* and *Serratia* that are resistant to gentamicin and tobramycin.

Seriously ill patients should receive a loading dose in order to initially achieve therapeutic plasma concentrations (see Table 24-7). For tobramycin or gentamicin this should be 2 mg/kg, and for amikacin this should be 7.5 mg/kg. Although these drugs do not completely distribute to adipose tissue, it is recommended to administer the loading dose based upon total body weight in a critically ill patient to avoid subtherapeutic levels. Amikacin should be considered only where organisms are resistant to gentamicin and tobramycin. The initial maintenance dose should be based on the nomogram in Table 24-8.[52] This nomogram is based upon average data and should be employed for initial therapy only. The recommended dosing interval for gentamicin and tobramycin for patients with creatinine clearance < 50 ml/minute is 12 hours, and 24 hours for those with a creatinine clearance < 10 ml/minute. An IV dose should be administered over 30 minutes. In patients with relatively stable renal function, peak plasma concentration can be obtained by sampling 15 minutes after the loading dose infusion is com-

pleted and again immediately before the maintenance dose. These values represent peak and trough levels. In patients with unstable renal function or those who did not have drug levels drawn after the loading dose, serum levels may be drawn 15 minutes after the infusion is complete and immediately before the next dose. Where gentamicin, tobramycin, or amikacin are administered intramuscularly, peak serum levels should be drawn at 1 hour for gentamicin and amikacin and 1½ hours for tobramycin and again immediately before the next dose. Peak and trough levels should be checked every 2 to 3 days to avoid toxicity and assure therapeutic levels.

Peritonitis and suppurative pelvic disease (including pelvic inflammatory disease, chorioamnionitis, postpartum endomyometritis, and postsurgical infections) are generally caused by a mixture of anaerobic and facultatively aerobic organisms. These infections usually respond well to a combination of antibiotics designed to cover this spectrum. If there is any likelihood of the presence of the gonococcus, penicillin G or ampicillin should be added. Although aminoglycosides are not drugs of choice, they cover unsuspected *S. aureus* and *S. epidermidis, Salmonella,* and *H. influenzae* until more effective and safer therapy can be selected.

The aminoglycosides are not effective against anaerobic bacteria, anaerobic cocci, most strains of streptococci (including β-hemolytic streptococci and *St. viridans*), enterococci, and pneumococci. Staphylococci are readily inhibited by aminoglycosides, but penicillins and cephalosporins provide much safer therapy for infections due to these organisms.

Adverse Effects
Allergic reactions such as eosinophilia and rash occur in approximately 1 percent of patients receiving aminoglycosides. The most important adverse effects of this group of drugs are toxic rather than allergic in nature, affecting the auditory-vestibular apparatus and the kidneys. These reactions can be roughly correlated to the length of treatment, preexisting renal impairment, and other factors. It is

TABLE 24-7 AMINOGLYCOSIDE DOSES IN ADULTS WITH NORMAL AND IMPAIRED RENAL FUNCTION*

Antibiotic	Desirable Serum Level (mg/ml)		Toxic Range (mg/ml)	Loading Dosage, Normal Renal Function IM or IV (mg/kg/bw)†	Impaired Renal Functions	
	PEAK	TROUGH			INITIAL LOADING DOSE (mg/kg/bw)	MAINTENANCE DOSE
Gentamicin	5–8	< 2	> 10–12	IM/IV 1.5–2.0 every 8 hours	1.5–2.0	Adjusted based on creatinine clearance
Tobramycin	5–8	< 2	> 10–12	IM/IV 1.5–2.0 every 8 hr	1.5–2.0	Same as above
Kanamycin	20–25	5–10	> 30–35	IM 5.0–7.5 every 8 hr	5.0–7.5	Same as above
Amikacin	15–25	< 8–10	> 30–35	IM/IV 5.0–7.5 every 8 hr	5.0–7.5	Same as above
Streptomycin	5–20	< 5	> 40–50	IM 7.5 every 12 hr (~ 500 mg)	15 (~ 1 gm)	Same as above

* From Refs. 50 and 51, with permission.
† In obese patients, doses should be calculated based on "ideal" or "lean" body weight:
Male = 160 lb + 5 lb/in over 5 ft, female = 100 lb + 5 lb/in over 5 ft.

TABLE 24-8 MAINTENANCE DOSE SELECTION (AS PERCENTAGE OF CHOSEN LOADING DOSE) TO CONTINUE PEAK SERUM LEVELS INDICATED*

Percentage of Loading Dose Required for Dosage Interval Selected

CREAT. CLEAR. (ML/MIN)	HALF-LIFE (HR)	8 HR	12 HR	24 HR
90	3.1	84	—	—
80	3.4	80	91	—
70	3.9	76	88	—
60	4.5	71	84	—
50	5.3	65	79	—
40	6.5	57	72	92
30	8.4	48	63	86
25	9.9	43	57	81
20	11.9	37	50	73
17	13.6	33	46	70
15	15.1	31	42	67
12	17.9	27	37	61
10	20.4	24	34	56
7	25.9	19	28	47
5	31.5	16	23	41
2	46.8	11	16	30
0	69.3	8	11	21

* According to desired dosing interval and the patient's correct creatinine clearance. From Ref. 52, with permission.

not clear whether the toxicity is primarily related to an excessively high peak serum concentration or to an excessively high trough concentration.

Two types of ototoxity have been observed. Cochlear damage manifested by varying degrees of high-tone hearing loss (kanamycin, amikacin) and vestibular impairment with nystagmus, nausea, and vertigo (gentamicin, tobramycin, and streptomycin). There is considerable disagreement as to the evidence of ototoxicity (and its reversibility) caused by aminoglycosides. The ototoxic effects of aminoglycosides are potentiated by coadministration of ethacrynic acid, furosemide, and mannitol.

Aminoglycosides may damage the proximal tubular cells of the kidney. The resultant clinical picture is that of acute tubular necrosis of greater or lesser degree. The mechanism of this phenomenon is not established; however, it is known that these antibiotics accumulate in renal cortical tissue in concentrations

that greatly exceed those in serum and persist there for days following a single dose of drug. The incidence of clinically significant renal damage varies widely among the congeners. Recent data suggest that in controlled comparisons in humans the rate of nephrotoxicity of tobramycin (12 percent) is less than that of gentamicin (26 percent).[53] Renal damage is usually reversible if the aminoglycoside is discontinued at the first signs of renal dysfunction such as a rising BUN, serum creatinine, or the presence of protein and tubular cells in the urine.

Other potentially important adverse reactions include neuromuscular blockage. This effect is similar to that produced by d-tubocurarine. Patients with myasthenia gravis or severe hypoglycemia as well as patients who have recently received other neuromuscular-blocking drugs appear to be particularly sensitive to this effect. The propensity of the various congeners to block neuromuscular transmission is neomycin > streptomycin > kanamycin and amikacin > gentamicin and tobramycin. Blockage can be partially or completely reversed by the intravenous administration of calcium salts.

REFERENCES

1. Knrypel RA, Scerbo JC, Dzink J, et al: Quantitative transcervical uterine cultures with a new device. *Obstet Gynecol* 57:243, 1981
2. Jacobson L, Westrom L: Objectivized diagnosis of acute pelvic inflammatory disease. *Am J Obstet Gynecol* 105:1088, 1969
3. Monif GRG, Welkos SL: Infectious morbidity due to *Bacteroides fragilis* in obstetric patients. *Clin Obstet Gynecol* 19:131, 1976
4. Ledger WJ: Laparoscopy in the diagnosis and management of patients with suspected salpingo-oophoritis. *Am J Obstet Gynecol* 138:1012, 1980
5. di Zerega G, Yonekura L, Roy S, et al: A comparison of clindamycin-gentamicin and penicillin-gentamicin in the treatment of post-cesarean section endomyometritis. *Am J Obstet Gynecol* 134:238, 1979
6. Sweet RL, Ledger WJ: Cefoxitin: Single-agent treatment of mixed aerobic-anaerobic pelvic infections. *Obstet Gynecol* 54:193, 1979
7. Platt LD, Yonekura ML, Ledger WJ: The role of anaerobic bacteria in postpartum endomyometritis. *Am J Obstet Gynecol* 135:814, 1979
8. Westrom L: Effect of acute pelvic inflammatory disease on fertility. *Am J Obstet Gynecol* 121:707, 1975
9. Mardh PA, Ripa T, Svensson L, et al: *Chlamydia trachomatis* infection in patients with acute salpingitis. *N Engl J Med* 296:1377, 1977
10. Paavonen J: *Chalmydia trachomatis* in acute salpingitis. *Am J Obstet Gynecol* 138:957, 1980
11. Ripa KT, Svensson L, Treharne JD, et al: *Chlamydia trachomatis* infection in patients with laparoscopically verified acute salpingitis. *Am J Obstet Gynecol* 138:960, 1980
12. Grossman JH, Greco TP, Minkin MJ, et al: Prophylactic antibiotics in gynecologic surgery. *Obstet Gynecol* 53:539, 1979
13. Bennett WM, et al: Drug therapy in renal failure: Dosing guidelines for adults. *Ann Int Med* 93:62, 1980
14. Findland M, et al: Susceptibility of pneumococci and *Haemophilus influenzae* to antibacterial agents. *Antimicrob Agents Chemother* 9:274, 1976
15. Findland M, et al: Susceptibility of beta-hemolytic streptococci to 65 antibacterial agents. *Antimicrob Agents Chemother* 9:11–19, 1976
16. Sutter VL: Susceptibility of anaerobic bacteria to 23 antimicrobial agents. *Antimicrob Agents Chemother* 10:736–752, 1976
17. American Heart Association: Recommendations on bacterial endocarditis. *Circulation* 56:139A, 1977
18. Finefold SM: Anaerobic infections. *Arch Int Med* 139:144, 1979
19. Neu HC: Antimicrobial activity and human pharmacology of amoxicillin. *J Infect Dis* 129:123, 1974
20. Neu HC, Garvey GJ: Comparative *in vitro* activity and clinical pharmacology of ticarcillin and carbenicillin. *Antimicrob Agents Chemother* 8:462, 1972
21. Pitts JC: Allergic penicillin reactions. *J Kansas Med Soc* 72:322, 1971
22. Maheras MG: Penicillin hypersensitivity. *Minn Med* 52:1811, 1969
23. Sanders WF Jr, Sanders CC: Toxicity of antibacterial agents: Mechanism of action on mammalian cells. *Ann Rev Pharmacol Toxicol* 19:53, 1979
24. Miller AK, et al: Cephamycins: A new family of β-lactam. *Antibiot Antimicrob Agents Chemother* 5:25, 1974
25. Thrupp LD: Newer cephalosporins and "extended spectrum" penicillins. *Ann Rev Pharmacol* 14:435, 1974
26. Washington JA: The *in vitro* spectrum of cephalosporins. *Mayo Clin Proc* 51:237, 1976
27. Klastersky J, et al: Cephradine: Antibacterial activity and clinical effectiveness. *Chemotherapy* 18:191, 1973
28. Handbook of antimicrobial therapy. *Med Lett*, Revised Edition. New Rochelle, New York, The Medical Letter, Inc., 1980
29. Neu HC: Comparison of the pharmacokinetics of cefamandole and other cephalosporin compounds. *J Infect Dis* 137(suppl):S80, 1978
30. Neu HC: Cefamandole, a cephalosporin with unusually wide spectrum of activity. *Antimicrob Agents Chemother* 16:177, 1974
31. Kirby ER, et al: Clinical pharmacology of cefamadole compared with cephalothin. *Antimicrob Agents Chemother* 9:653, 1976
32. Tally FP, et al: Cefoxitin therapy of anaerobic and aerobic infections. *J Antimicrob Chemother* 5:101, 1979

33. Neu HC: A new β-lactam antibiotic: Is it a major advance? *Drugs* 17:153, 1979

34. Wise R: Use of antibiotics: Cephalosporins. *Br Med J* 2:40, 1978

35. Yu, VL: *Serratia marcescens:* Historical perspective and clinical review. *N Engl J Med* 300:887, 1979

36. Nightingale CH, et al: Pharmacokinetics and clinical use of cephalosporins. *J Pharm Sci* 64:1899, 1975

37. Barza M, Miao VW: Antimicrobial spectrum pharmacology and therapeutic use of antibiotics: Part 3. Cephalosporins. *Am J Hosp Pharm* 34:521, 1977

38. Czerwinski AW, Pederson JA: Pharmacokinetics of cefamandole in patients with renal impairment. *Antimicrob Agents Chemother* 15:161, 1979

39. Quintiliani R, Nightingale C: Drugs five years later: Cefazolin. *Ann Intern Med* 89:650, 1978

40. Barr WH, et al: Assessment of the biologic availability of tetracycline products in man. *Clin Pharm Ther* 13:97–108, 1972

41. Wilson WR: Tetracyclines, chloramphenicol, erythromycin and clindamycin. *Mayo Clin Proc* 52:635–640, 1977

42. Barza M, Scheife RT: Tetracyclines. *J Maine Med Assoc* 67:368–376, 1976

43. Christensen LK, Skousted L: Inhibition of drug metabolism by chloramphenicol. *Lancet* 2:1397–1399, 1969

44. Holt R: Bacterial degradation of chloramphenical. *Lancet* 1:1259–1260, 1967

45. Nicholas P: Erythromycin: Clinical review. *NY State J Med* 77:2088–2094, 1977

46. Philipson A, et al: Transplacental passage of erythromycin and clindamycin. *N Engl J Med* 288:1219, 1973

47. Sutter LV, Finegold SM: Susceptibility of anaerobic bacteria to 23 antimicrobial agents. *Antimicrob Agents Chemother* 10:736–752, 1976

48. Bartlett JG: Antibiotic-associated diarrhea, in Remington JS, Swartz MN (eds): *Current Clinical Topics in Infectious Diseases.* New York, McGraw-Hill, 1980, pp 240–264

49. Keighley MRB, et al: Randomized controlled trial of vancomycin for pseudomembranous colitis and postoperative diarrhea. *Br Med J* 2:1667, 1978

50. Giusti DL: The clinical use of antimicrobial agents in patients with renal and hepatic insufficiency: The aminoglycosides. *Drug Intell Clin Pharm* 7:540–556, 1973

51. Jackson EA, McLeod DC: Pharmacokinetics and dosing of antimicrobial agents in renal impairment. *Am J Hosp Pharm* 31:36–52, 1974

52. Sarubbi FA, Hull HJ: Amikacin serum concentrations: Predictions of levels and dosage guidelines. *Ann Intern Med* 89:612–618, 1978

53. Smith CR, et al: Double-blind comparison of the nephrotoxicity of gentamicin and tobramycin. *N Engl J Med* 302:1106–1109, 1980

25. Anticoagulants and Antiplatelet Agents

CARL P. WEINER

Coagulative complications are a major source of morbidity and mortality in gynecology and obstetrics. Thromboembolic phenomena (TEP), which include deep vein thrombosis or thrombophlebitis (DVT), pelvic vein thrombosis or thrombophlebitis, and pulmonary embolus formation, account for half of obstetrical morbidity and mortality.[1] In one study, pulmonary embolus formation was second only to abortion as the most common cause of maternal death.[1]

The gynecologic patient following surgery is also prone to thromboembolic phenomena, despite care to prevent TEP by eliminating leg compression and stressing early ambulation (Table 25-1). The incidence of TEP in one obstetric and gynecologic service exceeded the surgical services' by 2.5 times. While 20 percent of those with clinically detectable deep venous thrombosis develop a pulmonary embolus,[2] 50 percent who have a fatal pulmonary embolus lack premonitory signs.[3] Clinical findings are absent in half of those patients who have demonstrable DVT using [125I]fibrinogen scanning.[4] Long-term sequelae from thromboembolism is often unpredictable and may lead to future lost work time or an extension or recurrence of the underlying disease process. The likelihood of symptoms later recurring has been reported as high as 74 percent.

Virchow proposed in 1847 that venous stasis, blood hypercoagulability, and vascular injury were the major factors that predisposed to thromboembolic disease.[5] These conditions are present during pregnancy, and Table 25-2 lists these changes in coagulation. Furthermore, a progressive increase in the levels of fibrin split products is found during the third trimester.[6] It is therefore not surprising that in the presence of venous stasis and hypercoagulability to find the incidence of thrombophlebitis to increase during the antepartum period (Table 25-3). In the postpartum period, thromboembolic phenomena have been reported to increase four to five times over the antepartum period, and the incidence of postpartum deep venous thrombosis using [125I]fibrinogen scanning is estimated to be 30 in 1000.[7] In addition, pulmonary embolism increases in patients with a history of prior DVT, prolonged antenatal bedrest, in the older or obese patient, after cesarean section, and where estrogens are used to suppress lactation.[8]

Surgical procedures also result in a relative hypercoagulable state. Platelet hypercoagulability from thromboplastin mediated aggregation, antithrombin III consumption, release of tissue thromboplastin, venous stasis from immobilization and general anesthesia, and dehydration contribute to this hypercoagulability. Restraining straps, poorly fitting vascular stockings, and inadequate postoperative ambulation contribute to stasis.

Thromboembolic phenomena may be arterial or venous. Because the basic pathologic mechanism of arterial and venous disease differs, adequate treatment necessitates identification of the thrombus site. Arterial thrombi

345

TABLE 25-1 INCIDENCE OF THROMBOEMBOLIC PHENOMENA AFTER COMMON GYNECOLOGIC PROCEDURES USING [125I]SCANNING*

	%TEP
Vaginal hysterectomy	7
Abdominal hysterectomy (benign pathology)	13
Radical hysterectomy for cervical carcinoma	25
Pelvic surgery for carcinoma other than cervix	45
Overall incidence of clinically detectable pulmonary emboli	2.9
Fatality rate of thromboembolism	0.7

* From Walsh JJ, Bonnar J, Wright FW: A study of pulmonary embolism and deep leg vein thrombosis after major gynecological surgery using labelled fibrinogen—phlebography and lung scanning. *Br J Obstet Gynaecol* 81:311, 1974, with permission.

result from vascular injury; platelets interact with the damaged vascular intima, while coagulation factors have a limited role. Venous thrombosis is propagated by thrombin generation with or without intimal damage.

Drugs used to medically manage disorders interrupting the coagulation process include anticoagulants (heparin, warfarin) and antiplatelets (aspirin, sulfinpyrazone, dipyridamole). An understanding of the agents available for the treatment and/or prevention of these pathologic alterations is essential. The indications, therapeutic doses, complications, and mechanisms of these agents are reviewed in this chapter.

HEPARIN

Chemical Composition and Preparations

Heparin is a heterogenous, mucopolysaccaride organic acid, composed of sulfated D-glucosamine and D-glucuronic acid with a molecular weight of 6000 to 20,000 daltons. It is prepared from two principal sources: the porcine intestine and the bovine lung. These preparations differ significantly in chemical makeup, and possibly, physiologic action. Porcine gut heparin results in a more variable anticoagulation effect than the bovine lung.

The effect of porcine and bovine heparin on platelet aggregation varies. Porcine heparin decreases the time for adenosine diphosphate (ADP) induced platelet aggregation, snow storm phenomena, and platelet plug formation. Bovine heparin has an opposite and more desirable effect.[9] In normal volunteers, lung heparin had significantly less effect on mean prothrombin time compared to porcine heparin when measured 30 minutes after IV injec-

TABLE 25-2 CHANGES IN COAGULATION FACTORS DURING PREGNANCY

Increased	Unchanged	Decreased
Fibrinogen (II)	Antithrombin III	
VII		XI
X		XIII
VIII		
VIIIR-AG		
Platelets		
Fibrinolytic activity		

TABLE 25-3 INCIDENCE OF THROMBOEMBOLIC DISEASE IN OBSTETRICS

Type of Thromboembolic Disease	% Incidence
Superficial Thrombophlebitis (lower extremity only)	
Antepartum	0.016–0.15
Postpartum	0.08–1.35
Deep Vein Thrombophlebitis	
Antepartum	0.11–0.36
Postpartum	0.15–0.27–3.0
Pulmonary Embolus	
Postpartum	0.04–0.05

tion. In addition, it is more difficult to reverse the effects of gut heparin with protamine sulfate than it is bovine lung heparin.[10]

The variability between in vitro and in vivo assays of heparin potency is striking. The Bureau of Standards, the National Institute of Health, and the departments of public health in most states confirm this in that there has been and presently is no standard for heparin in this country.[11] In clinical practice, both bovine and porcine calcium and sodium salts are used interchangeably, although the potential toxic side effects differ between the types of preparations.

Mechanism of Action

Heparin inhibits blood clotting in a dose-dependent manner. In large doses, heparin reversibly neutralizes activated thrombin (Fig. 25-1). Both high and low doses of heparin potentiate the action of antithrombin III (AT-III), a serine protease inhibitor which irreversibly inhibits the activated factor X to prevent thrombin formation. The activity of AT-III is profoundly increased by small amounts of heparin. The amount of heparin required to neutralize formed thrombin is 30 to 40 times the amount required to block its generation.[12]

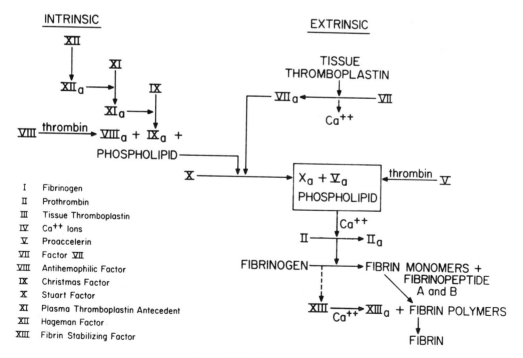

Figure 25-1. Coagulation cascade.

Heparin also inhibits the thrombin-induced aggregation of platelets at all dose levels. In a prospective double-blind study, patients therapeutically anticoagulated with bovine lung heparin were noted to have a threefold increase in the incidence of thrombocytopenia compared to those anticoagulated with porcine gut.[13] The thrombocytopenia resolved within 8 days in all groups and no relationship between route of administration or dose and the development of thrombocytopenia was detected. The thrombocytopenia may be associated with complement-mediated platelet injury.[14] Ultra-low doses of heparin (1 unit/kg/hour) appear to decrease platelet adhesiveness by increasing platelet lipoprotein lipase activity,[15] while having little effect on the activity of the intrinsic and extrinsic pathways of coagulation (Fig. 25-1). It may also cause release of vessel endothelial cell heparin.[17]

Routes of Administration, Metabolism

Heparin must be administered parenterally, either by SC or IV routes. IM injection should be avoided because of hematoma formation.

Heparin is cleared at a dose-related exponential rate by both the liver and kidney. Half of heparin administered intravenously is rapidly excreted in the urine. It does not cross the placenta nor is it transferred into the breast milk, which makes it attractive for obstetrical use.[16]

Antidote

Therapeutic heparin levels are cleared within 4 hours after cessation of therapy, but protamine sulfate may be used for a more rapid reversal. The dosage of protamine varies with the quantity of circulating heparin. It is administered in a 2 mg/ml concentration at a rate not to exceed 50 mg over a 10-minute period or 200 mg within 2 hours. Rarely is more than 100 mg of protamine required. This neutralizing effect should be monitored by activated partial thromboplastin time (aPTT) determination.

Side Effects and Precautions

Complications from heparin use include leucopenia, thrombocytopenia, osteoporosis, fat necrosis, and hemorrhage. Only hemorrhage appears to be closely dose-related. Heparin-associated thrombocytopenia occurs in 0.8 to 26 percent of cases and may be rarely associated with arterial thrombosis. Thrombosis has not been described with doses of 10,000 units or less per day[18] and is not dependent on the route of administration. Osteoporosis has been reported in patients on long-term heparin therapy (6 months or more) in doses greater than 15,000 units/day.[18,19] Heparin-associated osteoporosis has been reported during pregnancy.[19] Three cases of heparin-related fat necrosis have been reported, and in each case 15,000 units/day were used. The etiology was uncertain, but the lesions were similar microscopically to previously reported coumadin-associated cutaneous necrosis.[20]

The anticoagulation effect of heparin is altered by aspirin-like drugs in an unknown fashion. Presumably, there is an additive effect on platelet aggregation inhibition.

ORAL ANTICOAGULANTS

All commercially available oral anticoagulants are water-soluble derivatives of coumaric acid or a synthetic relative (Table 25-4). They act by inhibiting the generation of vitamin K-dependent coagulation factors—II, VII, IX, and X. Oral anticoagulants have no in vitro activity, while the in vivo actions of coumarin and indandione derivatives are essentially the same.

Acenocoumarol, a synthetic warfarin-like drug which differs from warfarin (coumadin) by a shorter duration of action (36 to 48 hours), may be of value in the obstetric patient in whom a relatively rapid reversal may be desirable. Because oral anticoagulants have no antiplatelet activity, they are of minimal use in arterial disease. Phenprocoumon should not be used since its plasma half-life ranges up to 160 hours.

TABLE 25-4 PHARMACOKINETICS OF COUMARINS IN HUMANS

Coumarin	GI Absorption	Percentage Bound to Plasma Protein	Plasma Half-Life (hr)
Acenocoumarol	Rapid, complete	?	20.0
Bishydroxycoumarin	Slow, incomplete, variable	99	24.0*
Ethylbiscoumacetate	Rapid, complete	90	2.5*
Phenprocoumon	Complete	99	160.0
Warfarin sodium	Rapid, complete	97	42.0

* Plasma half-life increases with plasma concentration.

Mechanism of Action

Vitamin K promotes the γ-carboxylation of specific glutamic acid residues necessary for calcium- and phospholipid-binding by the cascade factors. The action of vitamin K can be readily blocked by coumarin drugs to decrease the production of factors II, VII, IX, and X within 2 to 24 hours (Fig. 25-1). This inhibitory effect by coumarin can be eliminated only by large vitamin K doses. The prothrombin time (PT) determination is the most sensitive laboratory test for factors VII and X measurement and may be used as a gauge of coumarin effects.

Side Effects

Side effects of oral anticoagulants are limited to allergy and hemorrhage. All oral anticoagulants cross the placenta, and all are excreted into breast milk to produce fetal and neonatal hypoprothrombinemia. A coumarin-induced allergic hepatitis has been reported.[21] Coumarin cutaneous necrosis is a rare complication with an unknown etiology. Possible etiologies that have been advanced include allergic vasculitis, a localized Schwartzman reaction, and an abnormality of the clotting mechanisms.[22]

Antidote

Reversal of coumarin anticoagulation may be hastened by parenteral administration of phytonadione (vitamin K). Fifty milligrams administered parenterally will correct the PT within 12 hours. When given intravenously, phytonadione should be given at a rate less than 5 mg/minute to avoid hypotension.

Drug Interactions

Drugs that potentiate or inhibit coumarin action are numerous. A suitable reference should be consulted prior to prescribing a new drug to a patient on coumarin. Coumarin is highly protein bound, and altered coumarin-albumin binding induced by other drug-protein binding is the dominant mode of action. Commonly used drugs which alter the anticoagulant activity of coumarin include aspirin, acetomenophen, mefenamic acid, sulfa compounds, oral contraceptives, and any acidic compound.

ANTIPLATELET DRUGS

Antiplatelet drugs retard the formation and growth of arterial thrombi by interfering with platelet aggregation at the site of vascular injury. These agents also minimize the risk of hemorrhage by interfering with platelets after their adherence to collagen.[23] Because they act predominantly upon arterial lesions, antiplatelet drugs have limited applicability in gynecology and obstetrics. The three most commonly used agents are aspirin, sulfinpyrazone, and dipyridamole.

Aspirin

Mechanism of Action. Aspirin profoundly affects platelet function in a number of ways. It irreversibly inhibits cyclooxygenase,[24] the enzyme central to the formation of the most potent platelet aggregating agent known— thromboxane A_2.[25] Aspirin inhibits the release of platelet ADP to permanently impair ADP-mediated aggregation in these platelets.[26] The acetylation of platelets by aspirin prevents collagen-induced aggregation which can result in increased bleeding times.[27]

Metabolism. Aspirin is readily absorbed following oral or rectal administration. While the plasma half-life is approximately 20 minutes, the acetylation effect of aspirin on platelets lasts the 10-day life span of the exposed platelets. This effect is not reflected in either the PT or PTT clotting tests. Aspirin is rapidly distributed throughout the body, predominantly by a pH-dependent passive transport system, and placental transfer occurs readily. The effect on hemostasis is apparent within 60 minutes after ingestion of 2 tablets (650 mg). Aspirin metabolism occurs primarily within hepatic microsomes and mitochondria, and the three chief metabolites are salicyluric acid, phenolic glucuronide, and acyl glucuronide. These metabolites and nonmetabolized aspirin are excreted primarily by the kidneys.

Side Effects. Complications of aspirin ingestion are many. Problems at low doses include gastric irritation, production of or exacerbation of hepatitis, asthma, and bleeding associated with gastric ulceration or concomitant anticoagulant administration. Patients with underlying platelet abnormalities (e.g., Von Willebrands) are especially prone to hemorrhagic complications. The combined use of aspirin with heparin is contraindicated.

Efficacy. Controlled studies relating to aspirin and thromboembolic prophylaxis are few. Most surgical studies have involved orthopedic patients, and the ability of aspirin to reduce this risk was demonstrated clearly only in males undergoing hip replacement. Long-term aspirin trials for the prevention of cerebrovascular accidents have revealed a reduction in thromboembolism only among males.[28] Aspirin is effective in the treatment of recurrent transient ischemic attacks.

Coagulation-related indications for aspirin in gynecologic and obstetric patients are limited to the treatment of patients with known arterial thromboembolic disease with symptoms of dysmenorrhea or pelvic pain (see Chap. 21) and possibly to prevent premature labor (see Chap. 9).

Sulfinpyrazone, Dipyridamole

Sulfinpyrazone, a uricosuric agent, and dipyridamole (Persantine) a coronary vasodilating agent, have both demonstrated the in vitro inhibition of platelet aggregation. Both have been advocated as prophylactic agents for arterial thrombi.

CLINICAL USES OF ANTICOAGULANT AND ANTIPLATELET DRUGS

Short-Term, Low-Dose Therapy

Thromboembolism Prophylaxis. Since the incidence of thromboembolic phenomena in gynecology and obstetrics is remarkably high, prevention must be the goal. Risk versus benefit analysis indicates that gynecologic patients undergoing major operative procedures should receive some form of TEP prophylaxis. Nonambulatory patients or patients with malignant disease also benefit from prophylaxis during their hospitalization.

The decision to use an anticoagulant or antiplatelet agent during pregnancy requires individualization. High-risk categories are listed in Table 25-5. Those patients undergoing operative delivery (mid-forceps or cesarean) are at particular risk. There are two pharmacologic techniques for short-term prophylaxis which involve the administration of heparin in a minidose or ultra-low dose manner.

TABLE 25-5 OBSTETRICAL CRITERIA FOR TEP PROPHYLAXIS

1. Prior history of TEP during or prior to conception
2. Anemia (< 9.9 gMs)
3. Operative delivery
4. Concurrent malignant disease
5. Possibly Preeclampsia-eclampsia (Demonstrates decreased AT III levels)

Minidose heparin (low dose) is defined as the administration of 5000 units SC every 12 hours. The efficacy of prophylactic minidose heparin is well established in patient populations undergoing nonorthopedic surgery. Data from studies involving abdominal surgery using minidose heparin have indicated a 72 percent reduction in DVT and an 86 percent reduction in pulmonary embolus (PE) (Table 25-6). No added protection resulted from higher prophylactic heparin doses (15,000 units/day or greater), and bleeding complications were increased.[29] Minidose levels peak 2 to 4 hours after injection at 0.05 to 0.5 units/ml.[25]

Minidose heparin may be used in pregnancy for TEP prophylaxis without significant complication. An increase in plasma volume, renal clearance, and the activity of placental heparinase necessitates a dosage in excess of 5000 units every 12 hours to obtain prophylactic levels. Early in pregnancy, 7500 units every 12 hours is required to reliably obtain presumed adequate plasma heparin levels. The dose is further increased in the third trimester to 10,000 units every 12 hours. After delivery, the dose is halved to the nonpregnant range.[30]

Minidose heparin has been used in pregnancies complicated by a chronic consumptive coagulopathy, with variable results. These conditions would include intrauterine fetal demise after 12 to 15 weeks' gestation, chronic abruption, placenta previa, sepsis, and toxemia.[31] Since antithrombin III levels are decreased in toxemia and placental abruption,[32] heparin therapy has not been conclusively ef-

fective. Heparinization during sickle-cell crisis has been suggested but has not yet been found to be effective. Consumption coagulopathy conditions associated with obstetric complications include amniotic fluid embolus, hydatidiform mole, septic abortion, and hypertonic saline abortion. None of these entities is an indication for heparin therapy.[33]

It has been conservatively estimated that when used on a large scale, minidose heparin could save 4000 to 8000 lives each year in the United States alone.[34] Side effects from minidose heparin prophylaxis are minimal, and the common coagulation tests are not altered in patients with normal platelet and renal function. Aspirin ingestion or traumatic surgery in conjunction with minidose heparin may lead to a prolongation of the aPTT.[35] This finding has not been substantiated in larger studies, but stresses the need to avoid concomitant aspirin. Transfusion requirements are not increased with minidose heparin. The incidence of wound hematoma is slightly increased, but hospitalization is not prolonged.

Prophylactic minidose heparin is administered 5000 units SC 2 hours preoperatively, and thereafter every 12 hours. Therapy is continued until the patient is ambulating well. An alternative regimen is to initiate minidose heparin preoperatively and then switch to ultralow dose heparin postoperatively.

A double-blind, randomized, prospective study involving surgical patients demonstrated that an infusion of ultra-low dose heparin (1 unit/kg/hour) significantly reduced the incidence of TEP in a high-risk population. The incidence of DVT detected by [^{125}I]fibrinogen scan was reduced from 22 to 4 percent, and the incidence of documented pulmonary emboli was reduced from 2 percent to zero.[36] At this infusion rate, the calculated plasma level is only 0.007 units/ml, below the 0.01 units/ml thought necessary for effective TEP prophylaxis. There is no alteration of the aPTT.

This ultra-low dose regimen may be ideal for the laboring and parturient patient and requires further investigation. The piggyback infusion technique would eliminate the risk of injection site hematoma formation from sub-

TABLE 25-6   SUMMARY OF SURGICAL LITERATURE REVIEW COMPARING MINIDOSE HEPARIN TREATMENT WITH NO PROPHYLACTIC ANTICOAGULATION (CONTROL)

Author	Pt. No.	Study Pop.	Thrombophlebitis		Pulmonary Embolus		Findings and Complications with Minidose Heparin
			CONTROL (%)	HEPARIN (%)	CONTROL (%)	HEPARIN (%)	
Kakkar[61] et al.	53	Gen. Surg.	26	4	0	0	No complications.
Kakkar[62] et al.	261	Gen. Gyn.	42	8/9	0	0	No complications. Lower response in orthopedic cases.
Gordon-Smith[60] et al.	161	Gen. Surg.	41	13.5/8.3	0	0.2	No complications. Two different treatment durations.
Nicolaides[48] et al.	251	Gen. Gyn.	24	.8	0	0	No complications. Documented elimination of propagating thrombi.
Gallus[56] et al.	226	Gen. Surg.	16.1	1.9	0	0	Three times daily dose. Increased transfusion requirements. Results comparable to twice daily dosing.
Macintyre[57]	256	Gen. Gyn.	37	12	3.1	0.79	No difference in measured blood loss. One fatal control group—pulmonary embolus.
Ribaudo[58] et al.	150	Gen. Surg.	4/53	4/32	2.7/5.3	0	2.6% suffered postoperative bleeds of some type—equal in both groups.
Lahnborg[59]	112	Gen. Surg.	11	3.4	0	0	
Kakkar[63] et al.	4121	Gen. Gyn.	24.6	7.7	2.2	.6	Decreased number of heparin-treated deep venous thrombosis required further treatment; wound hematoma—5.6% control, 7.7% heparin patients; fatal PE—0.58% control, .09% heparin.

cutaneous administration, require less nursing time, and reduce the incidence of infusion phlebitis.[37]

Short-Term, Full-Dose Therapy

The term "full dose" heparin refers to a dosage sufficient to alter coagulation time as measured by the aPTT. Therapeutic doses of heparin may be administered subcutaneously or by intermittent or continuous IV infusion. Continuous infusion is preferred, since a steady-state level of heparin is obtained and the probability of a bleeding episode is decreased. A loading dose of 75 to 85 units/kg is given and then followed by constant infusion of approximately 1000 units/hour in a 1-liter solution containing 20,000 units of heparin (Table 25-7).

Heparin anticoagulation is monitored by the aPTT, a reflection of the intrinsic cascade (Fig. 25-1). The goal of therapeutic heparinization, regardless of the indication, is an aPTT value of 1.5 to 2 times the patient's control time. The aPTT is monitored every few hours after the infusion has begun and fine adjustments in heparin rate are made as necessary. Once the desired aPTT is reached, serial aPTTs *are not* required for the first 36 to 48 hours.

The amount of heparin required for anticoagulation is a reflection of the severity of the disease.[38] The resolution of active thrombotic disease is associated with a sudden and significant reduction in the quantity of heparin required for anticoagulation. In addition, *Bacteroides fragilis*, an organism frequently associated with pelvic thrombophlebitis, has demonstrated an ability to produce heparinase in vitro.[39] Whether secondary to successful antibiosis or the cessation of active thrombotic disease, this sudden reduction in heparin need must be identified, and the heparin rate decreased appropriately.

Pelvic Vein Thrombophlebitis. The incidence of febrile morbidity following delivery or other operative procedures varies greatly. Of obstetric cases with fever, 90 to 95 percent respond to a regimen of one, two, or three antibiotics.

TABLE 25-7 THERAPEUTIC HEPARINIZATION

Day 1
  Loading dose
    75–85 units/kg IV push
  Maintenance
    20,000 units/liter IV piggyback
    by timed pump arrangement at
    1000 units/hr continuous infusion
    aPTT every 3–4 hr after loading
    dose—then every 3–4 hr until stable at 1½ to
    2 times control value

Day 2–3
  Observe for decreased heparin requirements.
  Adjust as necessary.

Day 10–12
  Begin oral anticoagulants if desired.

Of the 5 to 10 percent with persistent fevers, approximately half will have an abscess, while the remainder will have pelvic thrombophlebitis.[40] The incidence of pelvic thrombophlebitis in gynecologic patients is less clear but remains a concern.

Therapeutic (full-dose) heparinization is indicated in a patient who remains febrile in the absence of a detectable abscess, ureteral damage, or drug fever following an adequate trial of antibiotics whose spectrum covers enterococcus and anaerobes. After an adequate trial of antibiosis and heparinization, deffervescence should occur 12 to 48 hours after heparinization.[41] Heparin therapy is continued 10 to 15 days after deffervescence. Failure to respond to therapy strongly suggests the presence of an abscess, and operative intervention should be contemplated.[42]

Ovarian Vein Thrombosis. The syndrome of acute ovarian vein thrombosis has been reported to occur postpartum in 1 of 4000 pregnancies.[43] It commonly presents with severe pain localized to the involved adnexa (usually the right) at 2 to 3 days postpartum. Fever is consistently present, and pain in the flank and abdomen may present initially.[43,44] A trial of therapeutic heparinization is indicated after ureteral obstruction has been excluded by an IV pyelogram. In practice, the diagnosis of ovarian vein thrombosis is often made at laparotomy. Ligation of the involved ovarian vessel should be performed if extension of clot to the vena cava is evident. Heparin therapy should be continued 10 to 15 days, but the value of subsequent oral anticoagulation in the absence of embolus is unclear.

Deep Vein Thrombosis and Thrombophlebitis. Therapeutic heparinization is the treatment of choice for deep vein thrombosis or thrombophlebitis. Heparinization prevents extension of venous thrombi to decrease the risk of subsequent embolus formation. Furthermore, the frequency of the postphlebitic syndrome is reduced, and the intrapulmonary extension of thrombi that have already embolized to the lung is limited. Full heparinization is necessary for 10 to 15 days, and the subsequent use of coumarin or low-dose heparin has been advocated for an additional 3 months.

Disseminated Intravascular Coagulopathy. Disseminated intravascular coagulation (DIC) is not uncommon in a busy gynecologic and obstetric service, and the sequence of events in altered coagulation is shown in Figure 25-2. Results from treatment with heparin have been mixed, and frequently, success is inversely related to the degree of fulminance. Fulminant DIC, regardless of the initiating mechanism, quickly depletes AT-III levels. Therapeutic heparinization would result in reversible inhibition of thrombin, but with the continued consumption of prothrombin components, bleeding may increase. Since most hospitals cannot provide a rapid accurate plasma assay of AT-III activity, therapeutic heparinization should be avoided in patients with clinically evident DIC. AT-III concentrates alone have been used successfully to manage DIC.[45] Treatment of DIC should instead be directed toward the elimination of the initiating event and the replacement of

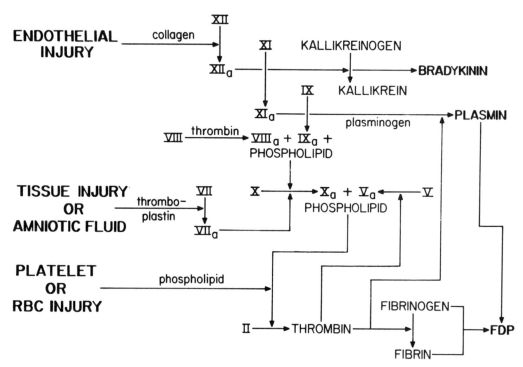

Figure 25-2. Sequence of events in disseminated intravascular coagulation (DIC).

prothrombin factors with a combination of fresh frozen plasma, cryoprecipitate, or fresh, whole blood.

Long-Term Anticoagulation

Anticoagulation for more than 15 days is indicated in patients who have recently experienced a thrombo-embolic event or who have a past history of TEP and are again subjected to increased risk (e.g., pregnancy).[46,47] There are major problems associated with the use of long-term oral anticoagulation. Major hemorrhagic morbidity with oral anticoagulation can occur in 4 to 17 percent of cases and 38 percent when major and minor bleeds are combined.[56]

Coumarinization is begun at 10 to 15 mg/day for 3 to 5 days prior to discontinuing heparin. The PT measurement is the most sensitive monitoring technique. Once a therapeutic time of 18 to 24 seconds is reached, heparin is discontinued and the dosage of coumarin is adjusted downward to a daily maintenance dose of 2 to 10 mg/day. Weekly PTs are indicated initially with a reduction to every other week eventually being feasible. These guidelines apply to all oral anticoagulants, but an appropriate drug reference is necessary before determining the proper dose for each.

All oral anticoagulants readily cross the placenta. In the past, when long-term therapy was required, coumarin was the drug of choice. However, evidence suggests that minidose heparin is preferable to oral anticoagulation, since minidose heparin has a lower complication rate with equal or greater efficacy than oral anticoagulation in patients whose disease is limited to deep venous thrombosis of the calves. Minidose heparin stabilizes and prevents the extension of preexisting thrombi, while allowing time for the endogenous fibrinolysins to function.[48] It is unclear whether patients with proximal venous disease are better treated with low-dose heparin or oral anticoagulants, but proximal venous disease does not require a longer treatment period than does calf disease.

Minidose heparin administered at home has been accepted by patients who are prop-erly educated.[49] A randomized, long-term study comparing minidose heparin with oral anticoagulation for the prevention of recurrent TEP in a high-risk population revealed a significant reduction in bleeding complications among the minidose heparin group with a thrombo-embolic recurrence rate equal to or lower than that with oral anticoagulation.[47]

Heparin does not cross the placenta and has been used successfully in pregnancy to avoid coumarin teratogenicity. Osteopenia and thrombocytopenia associated with long-term heparin administration in doses greater than 20,000 units/day are very rare side effects during pregnancy. Platelet counts are required each week in patients receiving long-term, low-dose heparin. Until further experience is acquired, spinal and epidural anesthesia should be contraindicated in obstetric patients because of possible epidural bleeding and subsequent spinal cord compression.

The use of minidose heparin in the obstetric patient has not been examined in large trials,[50] and most reports have used doses greater than those recommended here. In a review of the obstetric literature, fetal morbidity and mortality was equal in both the oral anticoagulant and heparin group. Both resulted in a normal outcome in 65 percent of pregnancies;[51] however, the causes of morbidity and mortality differed markedly. Complications in the coumarin group were directly related to the effects of coumarin (hemorrhage, placental abruption, fetal anomalies), while in the heparin group complications were not directly related to heparin, even at the higher doses. The patient population possibly differed in that only the most ill patients were maintained on heparin. If clinical management dictates its use, coumarin should be discontinued at 37 weeks' gestation, and subcutaneous heparin administered instead.

WARFARIN EMBRYOPATHY

Oral anticoagulants pose a significant risk of malformation and/or hemorrhage to the fetus. Exposure during organogenesis (the first 8 weeks) may result in the abnormal development of facial structures, hypoplastic digits, stippled epiphyses and mental retardation (Table 25-8). Second-trimester exposure may result in optic nerve atrophy, faulty brain growth, and developmental retardation. Third-trimester exposure may produce fetal anticoagulation.

The etiology of warfarin embryopathy is unclear. While microhemorrhages have been implicated, the reproducibility of the syndrome suggests a relation with vitamin K deficiency.[52,53] This is supported indirectly by autopsy data. The risk of malformations from first-trimester warfarin exposure is estimated to be 15 to 25 percent, while many studies suggest that a risk of perinatal hemorrhage from second- and third-trimester exposure to warfarin (coumarin) is between 5 and 10 percent.[54]

TABLE 25-8 FEATURES NOTED IN 15 INFANTS EXPOSED TO ORAL ANTICOAGULANTS DURING FIRST TRIMESTER OF GESTATION*,†

Early delivery	10/15††
Polyhydramnios	3/5
Prenatal growth retardation	4/14
Respiratory distress	10/11
Hypotonia	3/3
Postnatal growth retardation	1/3
Blindness	1/5
Delayed development	2/7
Mental retardation	2/6
Seizures	1/2
Death in infancy	4/15
Midface hypoplasia	9/9
Nasal hypoplasia	15/15
Optic atrophy	3/10
Low-set or malformed pinnae	1/1
Cardiac defect	1/3
Short extremities	5/7
Epiphyseal stippling	10/12
Calcification of thyroid tracheal or laryngeal cartilages	4/14

* In individual cases, hydrocephaly, encephalocele, cataracts, microphthalmos, single umbilical artery, limb asymmetry, joint contractures, dislocation of hips, simian lines, scoliosis, and hemangiomala have been noted.
† From Stevenson RE, Burton OM, Ferlanto GL, Taylor HA: Hazards of oral anticoagulants during pregnancy. *JAMA* 253:1549, 1980, with permission (Ref. 54).
†† Denominator indicates the number of reports in which specific mention of the feature is made.

REFERENCES

1. Arthure M: Maternal mortality. *J Obstet Gynaecol Br Commonw* 75:1309, 1968
2. Coon WW, Coller FD: Clinic pathologic correlation in thromboembolism. *Surg Gynecol Obstet* 109:254, 1959
3. Sevitt S, Gallagher NG: Pulmonary embolus. *Lancet* 2:981, 1954
4. Tlanc D, Kakkar VV, Clarke MB: Detection of venous thrombosis of the legs using ^{125}I labelled fibrinogen. *Br J Surg* 55:742, 1968
5. Virchow R: *Gesammelte Abhandlungen Zurwissensch Aftlichen Medizin.* Frankfurt, Von Meidinger, 1856, p 219
6. Bonnar J, Davidson JF, Pidgeon CF, McNicol GP, Douglas AS: Fibrin degradation products in normal and abnormal pregnancy. *Br Med J* 3:1137, 1969
7. Friend JR, Kakkar VV: The diagnosis of deep vein thrombosis in the puerperium. *J Obstet Gynaecol Br Commonw* 77:820, 1970
8. Howie PW: Thromboembolism. *Clin Obstet Gynecol* 4:397, 1977
9. Boldberg E, O'Reilly J, Chaithiraphan S: Prevention of postbrachial arteriotomy thrombosis. *Lancet* 1:789, 1972
10. Novak E, Sekhar NC, Dunham NW, Coleman LL: A comparative study of the effect of lung and gut heparins on platelet aggregation and protamine neutralization in man. *Clin Med* 79:22, 1972
11. Broders CA, Wilson JW: Heparin: Help or hindrance? *J Reprod Med* 10:269, 1973
12. Wessler S, Yen ET: Theory and practice of minidose heparin in surgical patients. *Circulation* 47(4):671, 1973
13. Bell WR, Royall RM: Heparin associated with thrombocytopenia: A comparison of three heparin preparations. *N Engl J Med* 303(16):902, 1980

14. Cincs DB, Kaywin P, Birva M, Tomaski A, Schreiber AD: Heparin associated thrombocytopenia. *N Engl J Med* 303(14):780, 1980

15. Negus D, Pinto DJ, Slack WW: Effect of small doses of heparin on platelet adhesiveness and lipoprotein-lipase activity before and after surgery. *Lancet* 2:1202, 1971

16. Heaf DJ, Kaijser L, Eklund B: Differences in heparin-released lipolytic activity on the superficial and deep veins of the human. *Eur J Clin Invest* 7:195, 1977

17. Kraemer PM: Heparin releases heparin sulfate from the cell surface. *Thromb Haemostasis* 42:418, 1979

18. Griffith GC, Nichols G, Asher JD, et al: Heparin osteoporosis. *JAMA* 193:85, 1965

19. Wise PH, Hall AJ: Heparin-induced osteopenia in pregnancy. *Br Med J* July 12, 1980, p 110

20. Hall JC, McConahay D, Gibson D, et al: Heparin necrosis—an anticoagulation syndrome. *JAMA* 244(16):1831, 1980

21. Slagboon G, Loeliger EA: Coumarin associated hepatitis—report of two cases. *Arch Int Med* 140:1028, 1980

22. Nalbandian RM, Mader IJ, Barrett JL, et al: Petechiae, ecchymoses, and necrosis of skin induced by coumarin congeners. *JAMA* 192:603, 1965

23. Deykin D: Antithrombotic therapy—rationale and application. *Postgrad Med* 65:135, 1979

24. Roth GJ, Majerus PW: The mechanism of the effect of aspirin on human platelets: I. Acetylation of a particulate fraction protein. *J Clin Invest* 56:624, 1975

25. Kelton JG, Hirsh J: Bleeding associated with antithrombotic therapy. *Semin Hematol* 17:259, 1980

26. Zucker MB, Peterson J: Inhibition of adenosine diphosphate-induced secondary aggregation and other platelet functions by acetyl salicyclic acid. *Proc Soc Exp Biol Med* 127:547, 1967

27. Rosenberg FJ, Gimber-Phillips PE, Grublewski GE, et al: Acetylsalicyclic acid: Inhibition of platelet aggregation in the rabbit. *J Pharmacol Exp Ther* 179:410, 1971

28. Canadian Cooperative Study Group: A randomized trial of aspirin and sulfinpyrazone in threatened stroke. *N Engl J Med* 299:53, 1978

29. Verstraete M: The prevention of postoperative deep vein thrombosis and pulmonary embolism with low dose subcutaneous heparin and dextran. *Surg Gynecol Obstet* 143:981, 1976

30. Kruse-Blinkenberg HO, Bech-Jansen P, Jensen P, et al: Low dose heparin in major surgery:

31. Pritchard JA, MacDonald PC (eds): *Williams Obstetrics*, ed 15. New York, Appleton, 1976

32. Weiner CP, Brandt J: Plasma antithrombin III activity in normal pregnancy. *Obstet Gynecol* 56:601, 1980

33. Redman CWG: Coagulation problems in human pregnancy. *Postgrad Med J* 55:367, 1979

34. Sherry S: Low-dose heparin in prophylaxis for postoperative venous thromboembolism. *N Engl J Med* 293:300, 1975

35. Gurewich V, Nunn T, Kuriakose TT, et al: Hemostatic effects of uniform, low-dose subcutaneous heparin in surgical patients. *Arch Int Med* 138:41, 1978

36. Negus D, Friedgood A, Cox SJ, et al: Ultralow dose intravenous heparin in the prevention of postoperative deep-vein thrombosis. *Lancet* 1:891, 1980

37. Stradling JR: Heparin and infusion phlebitis. *Lancet* 2:1195, 1978

38. White TM, Berene JL, Marino AM: Continuous heparin infusion requirements—diagnostic and therapeutic implications. *JAMA* 241:2717, 1979

39. Gesner BM, Jenkin CR: Production of heparinase by bacteroides. *J Bacteriol* 81:595, 1961

40. Ledger WJ: *Infection in the Female*. Philadelphia, Lea and Febiger, 1977

41. Ledger WJ: Infections in obstetrics and gynecology: New developments in treatment. *Surg Clin North Am* 52:1447, 1972

42. Gibbs RS: Treatment of refractory postpartum fever. *Clin Obstet Gynecol* 219:83, 1976

43. Rosenblum R, Derrick FC, Willis A: Postpartum ovarian vein thrombosis. *Obstet Gynecol* 28:121, 1966

44. O'Lane JM, Lebherz TB: Puerperal ovarian vein thrombosis. *Obstet Gynecol* 26:676, 1965

45. Buller HR, Weenink AH, Treffers PE, et al: Severe antithrombin: III. Deficiency in a patient with pre-eclampsia. *Scand J Haematol* 25:81, 1980

46. Coon WW, Willis PW, Symons MJ: Assessment of anticoagulant treatment of venous thromboembolism. *Ann Surg* 70:559, 1969

47. Moser KM: Pulmonary embolism. *Am Rev Resp Dis* 115:829, 1977

48. Nicolaides AN, Dupont PA, Desai S, et al: Small doses of subcutaneous heparin in preventing deep venous thrombosis after major surgery. *Lancet* 2:890, 1972

49. Bynum LJ, Wilson JE: Low-dose heparin ther-

apy in the long-term management of venous embolism. *Am J Med* 67:553, 1979

50. Baskin HF, Murray JM, Harris RE: Low-dose heparin for prevention of thromboembolic disease in pregnancy. *Am J Obstet Gynecol* 129:590, 1977

51. Hall JG, Pauli RM, Wilson KM: Maternal and fetal sequelae of anticoagulation during pregnancy. *Am J Med* 68:122, 1980

52. Becker MH, Genieser NB, Finegold M, et al: Chondro-dysplasia punctata. Is maternal warfarin a factor? *Am J Dis Child* 129:356, 1975

53. Beyer WA, Hakami N, Shepard TH: The development of hemostasis in the human fetus and newborn infant. *J Pediatr* 79:838, 1971

54. Stevenson RE, Burton OM, Ferlauto GL, Taylor HA: Hazards of oral anticoagulants during pregnancy. *JAMA* 243:1549, 1980.

55. Davis FE, Estruch MT, Samson-Corvera EB, et al: Management of anticoagulation in outpatients. *Arch Int Med* 137:197, 1977

56. Gallus AS, Hirsh J, Tuttle RJ, et al: Small subcutaneous doses of heparin in prevention of venous thrombosis. *N Engl J Med* 288:545–551, 1973

57. MacIntyre IMC: Heparin versus Dextran in the prevention of deep vein thrombosis. *Lancet* 1:118–120, 1974

58. Ribaudo JM, Hoellrich RG, McKinnon WM, et al: Evaluation of minidose heparin administration as a prophylaxis against postoperative pulmonary embolus—a prospective double blind study. *Am Surg* 289–295, 1975

59. Lahnborg G, Bergstrom J: Clinical and hemostatic parameters related to thromboembolism and low dose heparin in major surgery. *Acta Chir Scand* 141:590, 1975

60. Gordon-Smith IC, Grundy DJ, LeQuesne LP, et al: *Lancet* 2:1133, 1972

61. Kakkar UV, Corrigan T, Spindler J, et al: Efficacy of low doses of heparin in prevention of deep vein thrombosis after major surgery—a double blind randomized study. *Lancet* 2:101, 1972

62. Kakkar UV, Spindler J, Flute PJ, et al: Efficacy of low doses of heparin in prevention of deep vein thrombosis after major surgery. *Lancet* 2:101, 1976

63. Kakkar UV, Corrigan TP, Fossard DP: Prevention of fatal postoperative pulmonary embolism by low doses of heparin—an international multicentre trial. *Lancet* 1:45–51, 1975

26. Psychoactive Drugs

NICHOLAS A. VOTOLATO   STEPHEN F. PARISER

More than 20 million people in this nation have symptoms of psychiatric origin that warrant treatment. Physicians need to understand the pharmacotherapeutics of psychoactive drugs to facilitate the treatment of psychiatric symptoms and syndromes. This chapter focuses on major considerations of the diagnosis and drug treatment for the affective or "mood" disorders, anxiety states, insomnia, and schizophrenia. To understand and identify these disorders, reference is made to the *Diagnostic and Statistical Manual (DSM-III) 1980,* of the American Psychiatric Association. The *DSM-III* offers specific contemporary criteria for psychiatric diagnosis. Psychotropic drugs for use in treatment are discussed after each syndrome is identified.

AFFECTIVE DISORDERS

The pharmacologic treatment of patients with affective disorders can be accomplished through an understanding of the two major mood disorders, *major depressive disorder* and *bipolar affective disorder.* Affective disorders are of particular interest for those caring for women because of the sex preference ratio (2:1) of this condition: Depression is twice as common in women as men.

A major depressive disorder is a clinical syndrome that represents more than simply an unhappy mood resulting from such things as marital conflict, personality conflicts, or so-cial pressures. The essential and classic feature of depression is a persistent dysphoric mood. Variable signs of depression are listed in Table 26-1. It can disrupt normal functioning and has significant morbidity and mortality. This syndrome includes features such as a significant loss of interest in usual activities, an inability to derive pleasure from various aspects of the individual's life, fatigue, and either hypersomnia or insomnia.

Other psychiatric conditions that need to be excluded in order to justify this diagnosis include schizophrenia, adjustment reactions, hysteria, organic brain syndromes, drug-induced disorders, and drug use disorders. The latter condition can range from the abuse of alcohol and "street drugs" to the abuse of prescribed medications such as central nervous system (CNS) depressants, antihypertensive medications, and oral contraceptives. Although drug-related depressive symptoms may coexist with major depression, evaluation and elimination of any potential causative agents are important.

The duration of an untreated major depression is frequently 6 to 12 months, although episodes vary considerably. Of all depressed patients 50 to 85 percent completely recover; however, some patients have chronic mood disorders requiring lifetime drug treatment.[1] The disruption of normal function and potential for morbidity and mortality make it necessary to intervene pharmacologically in many patients. Major depression might be recurrent and may lead to personal or fam-

TABLE 26-1   CRITERIA FOR DIAGNOSING AFFECTIVE DISORDERS

Major Depression

A. General loss of interest or pleasure in areas of usual activities and/ or dysphoric mood.

B. At least four of the following symptoms have been persistent at least 2 weeks:
  1. Appetite or weight change
  2. Sleep change (insomnia or hypersomnia)
  3. Psychomotor change (agitated/retarded)
  4. Loss of energy, fatiguability
  5. Loss of interest in usual activities
  6. Feelings of worthlessness, guilt, or self-reproach
  7. Decreased ability to concentrate
  8. Recurrent thoughts of death or suicide

C. Not superimposed on schizophrenic symptoms.

Bipolar Illness, Manic

A. One or more distinct periods with a predominantly elevated, expansive, or irritable mood. The elevated or irritable mood must be a prominent part of the illness and relatively persistent, although it may alternate or intermingle with depressive mood.

B. Duration of at least 1 week (or any duration if hospitalization is necessary) during which, for most of the time, at least three of the following symptoms have persisted (four if the mood is only irritable) and have been present to a significant degree:
  1. Increase in activity (either socially, at work, or sexually) or physical restlessness
  2. More talkative than usual or pressure to keep talking
  3. Flight of ideas or subjective experience that thoughts are racing
  4. Inflated self-esteem (grandiosity, which may be delusional)
  5. Decreased need for sleep
  6. Distractibility (i.e., attention too easily drawn to unimportant or irrelevant external stimuli)
  7. Excessive involvement in activities that have a high potential for painful consequences which are not recognized (i.e., buying sprees, sexual indiscretion, foolish business investments, reckless driving)

---

ily chaos, hostility, and suicide. The patient's discomforting experience can be minimized by relieving the vegetative signs through the use of antidepressants. Even in the small percentage of cases of depression where symptoms remit quickly, the skillful use of antidepressant agents can shorten the episode considerably.

The other major category of affective disorder, bipolar affective disorders, refers to patients who have had at least one episode of mania and may also at other times experience a major depressive illness. The manic phases

seen in this illness commonly consist of one or more manic episodes, which are described in Table 26-1. Bipolar affective disorders are recurrent and tend to be familial. An untreated manic state may continue for several months before remitting. Manic episodes are characterized by a predominately elevated, expansive, or irritable mood, not due to substance intoxication, although certain agents such as L-dopa, antidepressants, and stimulants can precipitate an attack.[2] The hypomanic episode is a disturbance similar to, but not as severe as a manic episode, and may or may not be treated.

Drug treatment of mood disorders involves the use of tricyclic antidepressants, monoamine oxidase (MAO) inhibitors, and lithium carbonate. The duration of drug treatment may vary from 6 months to a lifetime. In patients with recurrent episodes of major depression, maintenance antidepressant or even lithium carbonate treatment may be of prophylactic value.[3,4]

Tricyclic Antidepressants

Patients who meet the diagnostic criteria for major depression are candidates for therapy with tricyclic antidepressants. These drugs are safer and simpler to prescribe than MAO inhibitors. Since Kuhn's discovery of the antidepressant prototype imipramine in 1957, these drugs have been, and are, the primary medical treatment of major depression.[5]

Research has focused on the "catecholamine hypothesis" of depression, which proposes that depression is related to the reduced levels or diminished turnover of serotonin and/or norepinephrine.[6] This theory initially seemed to account for the efficacy of the tricyclics, such as imipramine, which block the reuptake of these neurotransmitters. The tertiary amine tricyclics, such as amitriptyline, seem to be more serotonergic, while the secondary amines such as desipramine appear to be more noradrenergic. Current research suggests a far more complex neurotransmitter-neuroendocrine relationship than that expressed by the catecholamine hypothesis.

A patient's previous drug response is usually a good guideline in the selection of the specific drug and dosage, and provides information as to potential side effects. Responses to these drugs are frequently similar among blood relatives, and a positive familial experience with a particular drug is a good guide to choosing a therapeutic drug for the depressed patient.[7]

There are seven tricyclic antidepressants currently available in the United States (Table 26-2). All are similar in their efficacy, although individual responses may vary. Differences in

response to the various agents may be related to the basic subtypes of affective disorders, pharmacokinetics, side effects, or combinations of these factors. Although side effects are generally similar (Table 26-3), differences in the drugs lie in the degree of these side effects. The most common side effects of these agents are anticholinergic. These are more common on initiation of therapy and are frequently transient. Patients frequently complain of dry mouth, blurred vision, and constipation. Other symptoms, such as urinary retention and toxic psychosis, are more common in the elderly. A common cardiovascular side effect is orthostatic hypotension, which is more dangerous in the elderly or cardiovascularly vulnerable patient. Other cardiac effects include conduction defects. Imipramine and similar agents have a quinidine-like effect, lengthening the QRS interval.[8] Because of potential cardiotoxicity, patients with arrhythmias or organic heart disease may benefit from careful cardiac monitoring (including Holter monitoring), electrocardiograms, and observation for postural hypotension. Neurologic side effects are rare and seem to be dose-related. Nightmares, tremor, and mild or severe confusion are also secondary to the atropine-like effects.

At this time there are no clear, documented guidelines for determining which particular agent should be used to initiate treatment. While investigations suggest the usefulness of measuring urinary or spinal fluid levels of neurotransmitter metabolites in determining which particular agent may be beneficial, their validity is not commonly accepted.[9] Knowledge of the differences in side effects is important for drug selection. For example, doxepin (Sinequan) and amitriptyline (Elavil) are the most sedating antidepressants and may be of greater benefit in patients where insomnia, anxiety, and agitation are a major part of their syndrome. Protriptyline (Vivactil) and desipramine (Norpramin) are the least sedating, possibly activating, and may be of greater benefit in patients with hypersomnia and/or anergia. In patients who are sensitive to the anticholinergic effects of drugs, particularly

TABLE 26-2 ANTIDEPRESSANT AGENTS

Generic Name (Brand)	Oral Preparations (mg)	Average Daily Dose (mg)	Adverse Effects	
			ANTI-CHOLINERGIC EFFECTS	SEDA-TION
Tricyclics				
Amitriptyline (Elavil, Endep, others)	10, 25, 50, 75, 100, 150	150–300	High	High
Desipramine (Norpramin, Pertofran)	25, 50	150–250	Low	Low
Doxepin (Adapin, Sinequan)	10, 25, 50, 75, 100, 150	150–300	Moderate	High
Imipramine (Presamine, Tofranil)	10, 25, 50, 75—PM, 100—PM, 150—PM	150–300	Moderate	Moderate
Nortriptyline (Aventyl, Pamelor)	10, 25	50–150	Moderate	Moderate
Protriptyline (Vivactil)	5, 10	10–60	High	Low
Trimipramine (Surmontil)	25, 50	150–250	Moderate	Moderate
Monoamine Oxidase (MAO) Inhibitors				
Hydrazines				
Isocarboxazine (Marplan)	10	10–50		
Phenelzine (Nardil)	15	15–75		
Nonhydrazine				
Tranylcypromine (Parnate)	10	20–40		
Combination Agents				
Amitriptyline/perphenazine (Etrafon, Triavil)	2–10, 4–10, 2–25, 4–25, 4–50			
Amitriptyline/chlordiazepoxide (Limbitrol)	5/12.5, 10/25			

the elderly, desipramine (Norpramin) is the logical choice because of its relatively low anticholinergic activity.[10]

A protocol for managing depression medically is shown in Figure 26-1. The patient is likely to benefit by initially using smaller dosages of the tricyclic of choice which may be increased every 24 to 48 hours according to target symptom (such as sleep) improvement (or lack of improvement) and any observed side effects.[1] If after a 10- to 14-day period the patient does not improve, referral to a psychiatrist may be considered. If the patient improves, therapy should be maintained for 3 to 6 months, then slowly tapered if symptoms permit.

Because of their long duration of action, tricyclic antidepressants may be given in a sin-

gle daily dose to physically healthy patients. This schedule reduces certain side effects, avoids the need for bedtime sedatives, improves compliance, and is less expensive. Divided doses may be of greater benefit in patients where side effects such as sedation or postural hypotension become troublesome.

The lag period for visible improvement is 7 to 21 days, and supportive therapy may be necessary. This lack of immediate improvement or the presence of side effects may decrease compliance. Constipation may be relieved with stool softeners such as dioctyl sodium sulfosuccinate (Colace®). Urinary retention may improve with bethanechol (Urecholine) 25 mg two to three times a day.[11] Dry mouth may be made more tolerable by employing sugarless candy or gum, or com-

TABLE 26-3 POTENTIAL SIDE EFFECTS OF COMMONLY USED ANTIDEPRESSANTS

Tricyclic Antidepressants
  Anticholinergic effects
    Dry mouth
    Visual accommodation difficulties
    Aggravation of narrow-angle glaucoma
    Urinary retention, hesitancy
    Constipation
    Tachycardia
    Toxic psychosis (central anticholinergic)
    Impotence
  Cardiovascular effects
    Orthostatic hypotension
    Conduction defects (quinidine-like effects)
    ECG abnormalities (lengthened QRS)
    Negative ionotropic effect
    Congestive heart failure
    (direct cardiac depressant effect)
  Neurologic effects
    Nightmares
    Confusional states (elderly)
    Insomnia, hypersomnia
    Fine tremor of the extremities
  Psychiatric effects
    Activation of psychotic symptoms in schizophrenics
    Activation of mania in bipolar patients
    Weight gain

Monoamine Oxidase Inhibitors
  Hypertension following tyramine-containing foods or sympathomimetic amines
  Hypotension
  Activation of psychosis in schizophrenics
  Activation of mania in bipolar patients
  Impaired hepatic function (rare)
  Restlessness
  Hyperreflexia

viduals. Plasma-level assays are increasingly available and aid in identifying compliant but nonresponding patients. For most of the tricyclics there appears to be a linear relationship between plasma levels and response, with a minimum level necessary for clinical improvement. One exception is nortriptyline (Pamelor®) where a "therapeutic window" seems to exist in which plasma levels between 50 and 150 ng/ml are necessary for clinical improvement.[12] Another reason for nonresponse may be the specific agent chosen, since affective disorders vary in neurochemical-neuroendocrine pathology. Some nonresponding patients often improve after the initiation of a different antidepressant agent.

The role of tricyclics in the treatment of bipolar patients remains unresolved. Many clinicians hesitate to use tricyclic antidepressants alone in the treatment of depressed bipolar patients for fear of inducing a manic episode. The combination of lithium and tricyclics is now widely used clinically in patients with bipolar mood disorders who fail to respond with lithium alone.[13]

One of the fears clinicians have is the use of these drugs in the pregnant female. These drugs pose no known increased hazard to the fetus and the newborn in therapeutic dosages, but should be used with caution, as should most drugs in the pregnant female.

Suicide by overdose of tricyclics is a concern. Although the tricyclics are of tremendous benefit, they are lethal when ingested in toxic quantities. Toxicity of acute overdose is characterized by hyperpyrexia, hypertension, seizures, and coma. Cardiac complications include conduction aberrations involving multiple focal ectopic beats, which can be life-threatening.[14] Gastric lavage and ingestion of activated charcoal should be used to prevent any further absorption. Plasma levels of the drug may be beneficial in evaluating the patient's progress.

Monoamine Oxidase Inhibitors

Monoamine oxidase inhibitor drugs are usually prescribed in patients unresponsive to tricyclics. Recent evidence suggests that MAO inhibitors are more effective in young patients

mercially available artificial saliva preparations such as Xerolube®.

Some patients with well-documented depression fail to improve with drug treatment. Efforts should then be made to determine the etiology of this lack of improvement. A common reason is patient noncompliance. Another reason may be subtherapeutic plasma levels. Tricyclic antidepressants are enterohepatically cycled, which may result in up to a 40-fold difference in plasma levels among indi-

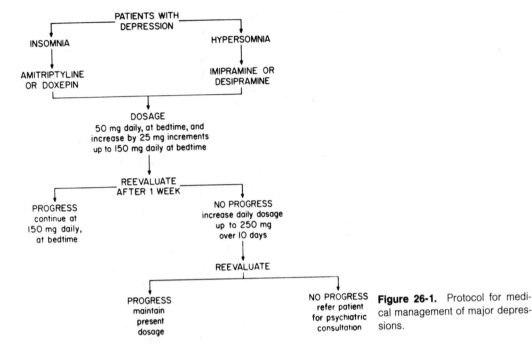

Figure 26-1. Protocol for medical management of major depressions.

with atypical depressions characterized by marked somatic anxiety, hypochondriasis, irritability, agoraphobia, social phobias, and who complain of anergia.[15,16]

The two most studied drugs in this class are the hydrazine phenelzine (Nardil®) and the nonhydrazine tranylcypromine (Parnate). Tranylcypromine is structurally similar to the amphetamines and has stimulant effects in some patients. It should be given early in the day so as not to interfere with sleep. In atypical depressions with coexisting somatic anxiety, phenelzine (Nardil) is preferred.

These drugs were thought to act by blocking MAO, which is the main metabolizing enzyme of the catecholamines. Recent studies suggest a more complex mechanism. Like the tricyclic antidepressants, the MAO inhibitors may require 1 to 6 weeks of continuous therapy until a clinical response is evident. If a therapeutic response occurs, the dosage should be maintained at the lowest level providing adequate clinical response. Maintenance therapy can be continued for about 6 to 12 months, with the drug dosage tapered

down as the patient response permits. MAO levels return to normal in 1 to 2 weeks.

The potential side effects of these drugs make it necessary for only those physicians with experience in the use of these agents to use them (Table 26-3). A major side effect especially common with tranylcypromine is central stimulation, which may cause insomnia, irritability, motor restlessness, and agitation. The appearance of symptoms of hypomania or the precipitation of psychosis in patients with a history of schizophrenia have also been reported. Orthostatic hypotension and hyperreflexia are also seen with some degree of frequency. Hepatic dysfunction reported in early trials with these drugs is rare. The most serious side effect is hypertensive crisis when the drugs have been combined with food of high tyramine content or sympathomimetics.[17] Great care should be taken to inform the patient of this potential interaction. Meperidine (Demerol), other narcotics, and CNS depressants are to be avoided or used cautiously in small dosages. Alcohol-containing drinks should be avoided mainly because of their tyramine content. Distilled drinks such as vodka contain little or no tyramine and can be used in small quantities without difficulty. Other adverse effects from the MAO inhibitor-tyramine interactions such as mild headache need only to be followed, with no treatment. If hypertension becomes severe, the α-adrenergic blocking agent phentolamine (Regitine) in 5-mg doses given slowly intravenously is indicated.

Several early reports of serious and often fatal adverse interactions with concomitant use of MAO inhibitors and tricyclic antidepressants have caused physicians to avoid this combination. Newer evidence by many authors has shown this combination to be safe and effective in certain refractory patients; however, it should be restricted only to inpatients and prescribed by physicians with experience in the use of both drugs.[18]

Lithium Carbonate

Lithium carbonate is the salt of an alkali metal and is the most important agent available for the treatment of mania. Lithium also acts to reduce the frequency and severity of recurrences in patients with bipolar mood disorders. Lithium carbonate was discovered in 1949 by Cade in Australia when he serendipitously observed that lithium carbonate promoted lethargy and had a calming effect on manic patients. It is also documented to be of benefit in recurrent unipolar depressions. Lithium is distributed throughout the body, being almost totally excreted through the kidneys. It is thought that the mechanism of action lies in its ability to alter membrane excitability, presumably by decreasing the amount of catecholamines at the receptor by enhancing the reuptake of norepinephrine from the synaptic cleft. It also causes a decrease in norepinephrine release and increases intracellular turnover.[19-21]

Common side effects include gastrointestinal disturbances such as nausea, vomiting, diarrhea, and abdominal pain. These effects may be diminished if the drug is taken with meals. Muscle weakness, fine tremors, stiffness, dizziness, blurred vision, polydipsia, and polyuria are other common symptoms. Effects

not related to dosage include diffuse thyroid enlargement, nontoxic goiter, nephrogenic diabetes insipidus, and leukocytosis. The early symptoms of lithium toxicity frequently include drowsiness, muscle twitching, coarse tremors, and increased muscle tone, and can lead to convulsions and even death.[22,23]

Before initiating treatment, a careful medical history and examination are essential. Relative contraindications for lithium include kidney or cardiovascular disease and severe debilitation. Patients on low-sodium diets or who are taking diuretics may be more at risk for lithium toxicity, since the kidney may reabsorb more lithium with sodium depletion. Laboratory tests of value in monitoring lithium therapy include periodic renal function tests, a CBC, and thyroid function tests. An electrocardiogram and serum electrolytes may be needed in certain patients.

In acute mania, a dosage of 600 to 1800 mg in divided doses should be initiated, depending on serum lithium level monitoring. The small therapeutic index for this drug makes it necessary to monitor serum levels closely, since there is a strong correlation between the serum levels of lithium and therapeutic and toxic results. Serum levels should be evaluated two to three times a week during the acute phase, then every other month for maintenance. Measurement of lithium levels should be done at 10 to 12 hours following the last dose. A desired therapeutic serum level is 0.5 to 1.2 mEq/liter. Levels greater than 1.6 mEq/liter are frequently toxic.

Because symptoms of mania require 5 to 10 days to improve with lithium treatment, it may be appropriate to administer an antipsychotic agent along with lithium during the acute phase. Early reports, particularly with haloperidol (Haldol) suggested this combination to be potentially toxic, but more conclusive evidence indicates this combination to be both safe and effective.[24]

There is some concern about the use of lithium during pregnancy. Lithium freely crosses the placental barrier (see Chap. 2). Although danger to the fetus is not definite, cardiac anomalies (Ebstein's anomaly) have been

TABLE 26-4 COMMON SUBJECTIVE DESCRIPTIONS OF ANXIETY EXPERIENCES

Behavioral Symptoms:
  Keyed up
  Panicky
  Phobic
  Frightened for no reason
  Threatened

Emotional Symptoms:
  Anxious
  Apprehensive
  Fearful
  Feeling of dread
  Nervous
  Overconcerned
  Worried

Physical Symptoms:
  Breathless
  Choking sensations
  Dizzy
  Flushed
  Giddy
  Head pounding
  Heart pounding
  Muscles tense
  Restless
  Shaky
  Sweating
  Tense
  Tightness in chest
  Tire easily
  Trembling
  Urge to urinate

practical perspective, anxiety symptoms commonly represent awareness of autonomic nervous system activity regardless of the etiology (Table 26-4).[25] This subjective state is clinically defined as being similar to fear, yet it is different in that the source of the danger that produced the fear is unknown.

In evaluating the patient with anxiety symptoms, it must be determined if the symptoms represent psychologic conflicts or are secondary to some medical illness (Table 26-5). In certain patients anxiety symptoms occur in the form of panic attacks where there are sudden feelings of impending doom usually accompanied by severe autonomic symptoms. There is some evidence that these panic attacks occur frequently in conjunction with mi-

TABLE 26-5 CONDITIONS THAT MAY PRESENT WITH ANXIETY SYMPTOMS

Angina

ASA intolerance

Drug intoxication

Drug withdrawal

Caffeinism

Organic brain syndromes

Seizure disorders

Hypoglycemia

Chronic obstructive pulmonary disease

Hyperdynamic β-adrenergic circulatory state

Ménière's disease

Pain

Paroxysmal atrial tachycardia (and other arrhythmias)

Pheochromocytoma

Premenstrual tension/dysphoria

Pulmonary embolism

Myocardial infarction

Thyrotoxicosis

Mitral valve prolapse

Akathisia

Affective disorders (mania/depression)

Schizophrenia

reported. Because of this evidence, the potential damage must be weighed against the benefits. Lithium also crosses into the breast milk, and patients must be advised not to breastfeed if lithium therapy is to be continued (see Chap. 15).

ANTIANXIETY AGENTS

Anxiety has traditionally been defined as apprehension, tension, or uneasiness produced in a person by a generalized expectation of danger from an unknown source. From a more tral valve prolapse and/or major depression.[26] These attacks become so terrifying to the patient that they become phobic trying to avoid all the things that seem to precipitate them. Some of these patients become agoraphobic or "housebound" in the process.

Probably the most commonly encountered types of anxiety symptoms are secondary to some life stress. These symptoms can become severe enough to cause dysfunction of normal activity. At the same time, support, empathy, and ventilation are frequently useful in the treatment of these anxiety symptoms associated with daily living.

The categories of drugs that have been used in the treatment of these symptoms are the benzodiazepines, barbiturates, propanediols, β-blocking agents, certain antihista-

mines, and tricyclic antidepressants, particularly the more sedating ones (see Table 26-6). The benzodiazepines are the safest and the most effective of all the anxiolytic agents. Unless combined with other drugs, overdosage with the benzodiazepines is virtually never lethal. This is important in reducing the risk of overdose whether or not it is intentional. The benzodiazepines lack the ability to stimulate microsomal enzymes and are also effective at relieving anxiety while producing minimum reduction in alertness.

Benzodiazepines

The benzodiazepines are the drug treatment of choice for the symptoms of uncomplicated tension or anxiety when pharmacologic treatment is selected. Although there are no

TABLE 26-6 ANTIANXIETY AGENTS

Generic Name (Brand)	Oral Preparations (mg)	Average Daily Dose (mg)
Benzodiazepines		
Chlordiazepoxide (Librium)	5, 10, 25	15–100
Chorazepate dipotassium (Tranxene)	3.75, 7.5, 15	15–60
Clorazepate monopotassium (Azene)	3.25, 6.5, 13	13–52
Diazepam (Valium)	2, 5, 10	5–60
Lorazepam (Ativan)	1, 2	2–10
Oxazepam (Serax)	10, 15, 30	30–120
Prazepam (Centrax)	5, 10	20–60
Nonbenzodiazepine Alternatives		
Propanediols		
Meprobamate (Equanil, Miltown)	200, 400	600–2000
Tybamate (Solacen, Tybatran)	250, 350	750–2500
Antihistamines		
Diphenhydramine (Benadryl)	25, 50	75–300
Hydroxyzine (Atarax, Vistaril)	10, 25, 50, 100	75–400
Tricyclic Antidepressants		
Doxepin (Adapin, Sinequan)	10, 25, 50, 75, 100, 150	50–150

marked differences in the pharmacologic properties of these drugs, there are differences in their pharmacokinetics. Benzodiazepines may be separated into those that have a longer duration of action because of active metabolites, and those with no active metabolites and a shorter duration of action (Table 26-6). The newer agents have gained popularity, particularly in the elderly, but whether they are therapeutically better than other agents at lower dosages is yet to be resolved.[27-29]

Pharmacologic intervention with benzodiazepines is usually indicated when anxiety interferes with the patient's daily functioning and is not caused by affective illness, medical illness (such as hyperthyroidism), caffeine, or other drug toxicity. They are particularly valuable in acute stress situations or as a pretreatment for medical or surgical procedures. It is less clearly indicated for the treatment of chronic anxiety or for diminishing the tension caused by everyday life.

The benzodiazepines should be prescribed over a short term, in the lowest possible dose, and limited to times of extreme stress. These limitations must be discussed openly with the patient, and each patient must be closely monitored to avoid overuse of these drugs.

The benzodiazepines are remarkably free of serious side effects when used alone, but they can cause drowsiness and ataxia in higher dosages. Their additive effects with other CNS depressants, particularly alcohol, can cause serious problems. Paradoxical rage, although more likely with barbiturates, occurs occasionally. Although these agents are less likely to cause severe dependence and addiction, dependence and addiction are possible and can be a problem. The long half-life of the benzodiazepines and phenobarbital have a lesser potential for severe withdrawal since they have a built-in tapering factor, at least in moderate doses. Not only are the type of the drug and the dose important, but so is the duration of the intake in determining the character of withdrawal.

Drowsiness, ataxia, nystagmus, dysarthria, dizziness, and vertigo are sometimes severe adverse effects, and generally occur in the elderly. Their use in the elderly can also cause some impairment of intellectual performance and even prolonged confusional states.[30] These and all CNS depressants should be avoided in seriously depressed patients because they may aggravate their depression.

Teratogenic effects have not been definitely established, although there is evidence indicating that when used in the first 6 weeks of gestation, anomalies are greater than drug-free controls (see Chap. 2).

Propanediols

The propanediols, with meprobamate being the most commonly prescribed, are less effective as anxiolytics than the benzodiazepines and are associated with the same potential hazards as the barbiturates. The propanediols have great potential for tolerance and dependence, and withdrawal reactions may be very severe, at least in the case of meprobamate.

β-Adrenergic Blocking Agents

Although they have no well-defined indications for specific treatment of anxiety at this time, the β-blocking agents have been used in blocking the autonomic responses of panic attacks associated with certain cardiac arrhythmias. The relief of panic attacks has also been accomplished with MAO inhibitors and tricyclic antidepressants.[31,25]

Antihistamines

Antihistamines are the active agent in over-the-counter "antianxiety" preparations and seem to be of limited benefit. In particular, two antihistamines, hydroxyzine (Atarax) and diphenhydramine (Benadryl), are occasionally used and are somewhat more successful. Although they are less efficacious than the benzodiazepines, they have the advantage of having little potential for habituation or physical dependence. These agents may be useful in patients having a history of medication abuse.

Tricyclic Antidepressants

Tricyclic antidepressants, particularly doxepin (Sinequan), have been promoted as having anxiolytic properties, in part because of their antihistaminic effects. They are effective when anxiety coexists with depression, but should not be used in simple anxiety.

HYPNOTIC AGENTS

Complaints of insomnia, specifically the inability to fall asleep, to remain asleep, and the subjective feeling that the quality of sleep is poor despite a normal duration, are common. Patients with these complaints may request "sleeping pills"; however, further understanding of the nature of their insomnia is necessary before prescribing any of the available hypnotic agents. Interviews with insomniac patients often uncover a history of alcohol or hypnotic abuse, with tolerance to the already ingested drugs. Before initiating treatment with these agents, the physician must recognize that once started, it is difficult to persuade patients to discontinue their use. As previously noted, sleep disruption is a major symptom of depression, and patients with insomnia must be screened to rule this out. This type of insomnia may be relieved quite effectively by the antidepressant drugs. Hypnotics should be avoided in the affective disturbances, since depression may be aggravated. Insomnia may also be associated with physical conditions requiring medical or surgical care.

The major appropriate indication for the prescribing of hypnotic drugs is the short-term symptomatic treatment of insomnia from stressful adjustment situations. Used in this way, these agents are safe and effective. Hypnotic agents are quite similar or identical to the anxiolytic agents, with similar benefits and risks.

In patients for whom insomnia requires drug treatment, the benzodiazepines are the best choice when compared to the barbiturates and other nonbarbiturate hypnotic agents. Benzodiazepines are less likely to affect REM sleep, do not induce liver enzymes, and have less potential for dependency. In proper dosages these agents effectively induce sleep, with little effect on the quality. On the contrary,

the barbiturates and nonbarbiturates can affect the quality of sleep after 2 to 3 days of usage and have a greater potential for abuse and lethality.

Flurazepam (Dalmane), despite its longer duration of action, has been approved by the Food and Drug Administration as a hypnotic. Diazepam (Valium), frequently used for symptomatic anxiety, may be effectively used as a hypnotic. The newer and shorter-acting benzodiazepines oxazepam (Serax) and lorazepam (Ativan) have become popular for sleep induction. These two agents do not have psychoactive metabolites. Their onset of action is not as rapid as other benzodiazepines. Temazepam (Restoril) has both a shorter duration of action and more rapid onset, and may be a more rational choice.

Other alternatives such as chloral hydrate (Noctec), meprobamate (Equanil), glutethimide (Doriden), methaqualone (Quaalude), or the antihistamines used in the over-the-counter sleep remedies, may be effective for occasional, brief use, but tend to lose their efficacy with prolonged use. With the exception of the antihistamines, patients on all of these agents develop tolerance quickly and have a greater potential for abuse and toxicity with overdose.

ANTIPSYCHOTIC AGENTS (NEUROLEPTICS)

The agents in this group are best used in the treatment of schizophrenia. Symptoms characteristic of schizophrenia frequently include thought disorders (unusual content and conceptual disorganization, delusions, and hallucinations) and severe agitation. These symptoms often respond well to antipsychotic treatment.

The neuroleptics listed in Table 26-7 are all similar. They are equally effective in the relief of symptoms if equivalent dosages are given. Major differences involve the types of side effects (sedative, extrapyramidal, and anticholinergic) produced by each of the chemi-

TABLE 26-7   ANTIPSYCHOTIC AGENTS

Generic Name (Brand)	Oral Preparations (mg)	Daily Dose (mg)	Adverse Effects		
			ANTICHO-LINERGIC EFFECTS	SEDATION	EXTRAPYRA-MIDAL REACTIONS
Phenothiazines					
Aliphatic					
Chlorpromazine (Thorazine)	10, 25, 50, 100, 200, 30-SP, 75-SP, 150-SP, 200-SP	50–400	High	High	Moderate
Piperidine					
Mesoridazine (Serentil)	10, 25, 50, 100	25–200	High	High	Low
Piperacetazine (Quide)	10, 25	10–40	High	Moderate	Moderate
Thioridazine (Mellaril)	10, 15, 25, 50, 100, 150, 200	50–400	High	High	Low
Piperazine					
Fluphenazine (Prolixin)	1, 2.5, 5, 10	2–15	Low	Low	High
Perphanazine (Trilafon)	2, 4, 8, 16	8–32	Moderate	Moderate	Moderate
Trifluoperazine (Stelazine)	1, 2, 5, 10	5–30	Moderate	Moderate	Moderate
Nonphenothiazines					
Thioxanthines					
Thiothixene (Navane)	1, 2, 5, 10, 20	5–30	Low	Low	High
Butyrophenones					
Haloperidol (Haldol)	0.5, 1, 2, 5, 10	2–15	Low	Low	High
Dibenzoxazepines					
Loxapine (Daxolin, Loxitane)	5, 10, 25, 50	25–75	Low	Moderate	Moderate
Dihydroindolones					
Molindone (Lidone, Moban)	5, 10, 25, 50	25–75	Low	Low	Moderate

cal groups. Dosages must be increased gradually on an outpatient basis until a therapeutic dose is achieved or a serious side effect occurs. Gradual increases are necessary because individual patient tolerance to these drugs is highly variable. The young and the elderly, for example, not only need smaller dosages, but have a greater potential for sedative or extrapyramidal side effects. The "correct" dosage is not absolute and therefore requires the clinical judgment of the physician.[32-34]

The half-life of these medications is very long. In most cases, the drugs can be given as a single daily dose at bedtime or twice daily (one-third in the morning and two-thirds at bedtime). There is a lower incidence of side effects when these drugs are administered as a single dose at bedtime rather than in divided doses, and compliance is improved. More frequent dosing may be necessary in more agitated patients, where sedative and motor-inhibiting effects are necessary, and in patients where side effects such as postural hypotension or hangover become clinical problems.[37] As with other drugs that undergo enterohepatic cycling, the IM injection gives plasma levels two to three times higher than the oral route. This is an important consideration

TABLE 26-8   ADVERSE EFFECTS OF PSYCHOTROPIC DRUGS ON ORGAN SYSTEMS

System	Effects	Drugs
Autonomic	Anticholinergic: dry mouth and skin, urinary retention, poor visual accommodation	Tricyclics, antipsychotics
Cardiac	ECG abnormalities and arrhythmias	Tricyclics, phenothiazines, lithium
Cardiovascular	Hypotension	Tricyclics, MAO inhibitors, antipsychotics (esp. thioridazine)
	Hypertension	MAO inhibitors + adrenergic stimulants (tyramine, amphetamine, L-dopa, etc.)
Dermatologic	Skin rash	All drugs
	Photosensitivity	Antipsychotics (esp. chlorpromazine)
	Pigmentation	Antipsychotics (esp. chlorpromazine)
Endocrinologic	Amenorrhea	Antipsychotics
	Galactorrhea and gynecomastia	Antipsychotics
	Nontoxic goiter	Lithium
Gastrointestinal	Nausea and vomiting	Antipsychotics, lithium (with or without toxicity)
	Constipation	Antipsychotics, tricyclics
	Paralytic ileus	Phenothiazines, tricyclics, antiparkinsonian agents
	Increased body weight	Tricyclics, antipsychotics (except Molindone)
Hematologic	Leukopenia and agranulocytosis	Antipsychotic (rare)
	Leukocytosis	Lithium
Hepatic	Induction of metabolic enzymes	Barbiturates
	Toxic reactions	Antipsychotics (esp. chlorpromazine)
	Cholestasis	Tricyclics (both rare)
	Hepatotoxicity	MAO inhibitors (rare)
Neurologic	Extrapyramidal reactions Pseudo-parkinsonian Acute dystonias Akathisia	Antipsychotics
	Tardive dyskinesia	Antipsychotics
	Fine tremor	Lithium
Opthalmologic	Lens pigmentation	Antipsychotics (esp. chlorpromazine)
	Pigmentary retinopathy	Thioridazine (dosage limit: 800 mg)
Renal	Polyuria	Lithium

when approaching the acutely agitated patient who is unable to take medication orally.

The elimination of symptoms may take 6 weeks or longer. The lack of understanding of this lag period may expose the patient to much higher levels of medication than is necessary. Once the patient is stabilized, a reduc-

tion to a maintenance dose is desired. A relapse of symptoms is possible during the first 4 months after treatment, and maintenance therapy should continue for at least 2 to 4 months.

Although the different classes of antipsychotic drugs are equally efficacious, their side effects are quite different and may actually be utilized to the clinician's advantage (Table 26-8). The aliphatic and piperidine derivatives produce more sedation and hypotension, while having less potential for extrapyramidal side effects (EPS). Thioridazine (Mellaril) is a piperidine derivative that has a particularly low potential for EPS.[33] Although they have less sedation and hypotension, the piperazines and butyrophenones have a greater potential for EPS. EPS not only causes discomfort, but partially explains why some patients stop taking their medication. Extrapyramidal signs can be controlled by reducing the dosage, changing the patient to a less EPS-producing antipsychotic, or adding an antiparkinsonian agent to the regimen (Table 26-9). Although most antipsychotic drugs do not have an absolute maximum dosage, thioridazine (Mellaril) should not be given in dosages exceeding 800 mg/day as pigmentary retinopathy has been reported at higher dosages. Thioridazine may also cause inhibition of ejaculation or retrograde ejaculation, which may be distressing to both sexual partners. Weight gain may be a problem with many patients on antipsychotic therapy. The exception to this side effect is molidone (Moban), which causes no weight gain and at times may initiate weight loss.

Perhaps because of dopamine blockade, elevated prolatin levels seen with antipsychotic agent use may explain any amenorrhea, galactorrhea, and gynecomastia that occurs. A reduction in dosage may relieve the symptoms, although some authors suggest that a change to another agent (molindone) can accomplish this without a reduction in effective dosage. This advantage of molidone (Moban) needs further investigation.[36]

With the exception of thioridazine, all the antipsychotics are good antiemetics at very low dosages, and for this reason they are used frequently for the nausea and vomiting associated with cancer chemotherapy, particularly haloperidol (Haldol).

Antipsychotics do not appear to cause congenital abnormalities and thus are not absolutely contraindicated in pregnancy. A psychiatry consultation is useful before changing any drugs during pregnancy, so that the risks and benefits can be weighed. These drugs can cause extrapyramidal and anticholinergic symptoms to the newborn. Drug effects on the nursing infant are significant, particularly if the aliphatics or piperidines are used, and breastfeeding is therefore discouraged.

Tardive dyskinesia is a major concern for patients and is usually seen after long-term antipsychotic therapy.[37] These involuntary movements of a choreathetoid type may involve the mouth, lips, tongue, trunk, and extremities. Antiparkinsonian agents do not help with this type of EPS and may even worsen the condition. Although initially thought to be irreversible, these movements may disappear in approximately one-third of the patients after discontinuing the antipsychotic. Recently, large dosages of lecithin have been used with some success to control these movements.[35]

TABLE 26-9 ANTIPARKINSONIAN DRUGS

Generic	Brand	Dose (mg)	Frequency of Doses/Day
Benztropine mesylate	Cogentin	1–2	1–4
Biperidine HCl	Akineton	2–4	1–4
Procyclidine HCl	Kemadrin	5–10	1–4
Trihexyphenidyl HCl	Artane	2–5	1–4
Diphenhydramine HCl	Benadryl	25–50	1–3
Amantadine	Symmetrel	100	1–3

Although many side effects are associated with the use of antipsychotic agents, most are mild and controlled easily. The more dangerous side effects are rare, and the benefits afforded previously institutionalized schizophrenic patients would appear to make neuroleptic medication well worth the inherent risks.

In summary, psychotropic drug treatment mandates a reasonable understanding of psychiatric syndromes and patient personal style. Because of the common nature of psychiatric syndromes such as depression and adjustment reactions, the obstetrician-gynecologist would benefit by devoting time toward developing a better understanding of patients and the management of their psychiatric complaints.

REFERENCES

1. Pariser SF, Young EA, Jones BA, et al: Depression: A new approach to an old syndrome. *Am Fam Physician* 18(4):130, 1978
2. Bunney WE, Murphy DL, Goodwin FK: The switch process in manic-depressive illness. *Arch Gen Psychiatry* 27:295, 312, 1972
3. Mendels J, Ramsey A, Dyson W, et al: Lithium as an antidepressant. *Arch Gen Psychiatry* 36(8):845, 1979
4. Schou M: Lithium as a prophylactic agent in unipolar affective illness. *Arch Gen Psychiatry* 36(8):849, 1979
5. Kuhn R: Treatment of depressive states with G 22355 (imipramine hydrochloride). *Am J Psychiatry* 115:459, 1958
6. Maas JW: Biogenic amines and depression. *Arch Gen Psychiatry* 32:1357, 1975
7. Hollister LE: Tricyclic antidepressants. *N Engl J Med* 299:1106, 1168, 1978
8. Bigger JT Jr, Giardina EGV, Perel JM, et al: Cardiac antiarrhythmic effect of imipramine hydrochloride. *N Engl J Med* 296:206, 1977
9. Goodwin FK, Cowdy RW, Webster MH: Predictors of drug response in the affective disorders: Toward an integrated approach, in Lipton MA, DiMascio A, Killam KF (eds): *Psychopharmacology: A Generation of Progress.* New York, Raven, 1978, pp 1277–1288
10. Snyder SH, Yamamura HI: Antidepressant and the muscarinic acetylcholine receptor. *Arch Gen Psychiatry* 34(2):236, 1977
11. Everett HC: The use of bethanechol chloride with tricyclic antidepressants. *Am J Psychiatry* 132:1202, 1975
12. Risch SC, Huey LY, Janowsky DS: Plasma levels of tricyclic antidepressants and clinical efficacy: Review of the literature. *J Clin Psychiatry* 40(1):4 and 40(2):58, 1979
13. Wehr TA, Goodwin FK: Rapid cycling in manic-depressives induced by tricyclic antidepressant. *Arch Gen Psychiatry* 36(5):555, 1979
14. Munoz RA: Treatment of tricyclic intoxication. *Am J Psychiatry* 133:1085, 1976
15. Tyrer P: Towards rational therapy with monoamine oxidase inhibitors. *Br J Psychiatry* 128:354, 1976
16. Robinson DS, Nies A, Ravaris CL, et al: Clinical pharmacology of phenelzine. *Arch Gen Psychiatry* 35(5):629, 1978
17. Ayd FJ Jr, Blackwell B (eds): *Discoveries in Biological Psychiatry.* Philadelphia, Lippincott, 1970
18. Goldberg RS, Thorton WE: Combined tricyclic—MAOI therapy for refractory depression: A review with guidelines for appropriate usage. *J Clin Pharmacol* 18(2–3):143, 1978
19. Lipton MA: Lithium: Developments in basic and clinical research. *Am J Psychiatry* 135:1059, 1978
20. Goodwin FK, Zis AP: Lithium in the treatment of mania. *Arch Gen Psychiatry* 36(8):840, 1979
21. Grof P: Some practical aspects of lithium treatment. *Arch Gen Psychiatry* 36(8):891, 1979
22. Reisberg B, Gershon S: Side effects associated with lithium therapy. *Arch Gen Psychiatry* 36(8):879, 1979
23. Jenner FA: Lithium and the question of kidney damage. *Arch Gen Psychiatry* 36(8):888, 1979
24. Cohen WJ, Cohen NH: Lithium carbonate, haloperidol, and irreversible brain death. *JAMA* 230(9):12, 1974
25. Pariser SF, Jones BA, Young EA: Diagnosis and management of anxiety symptoms and syndromes. *N Engl J Med* 296:16; 909, 1977
26. Pariser SF, Pinta E, Jones B: Mitral valve prolapse syndrome and anxiety neurosis/panic disorder. *Am J Psychiatry* 135:246, 1978
27. Greenblatt DJ, Allen MD, Locniskar A, et al: Lorazepam kinetics in the elderly. *Clin Pharmacol Ther* 26(1):103, 1979
28. Hoyumpa AM: Disposition and elimination of minor tranquilizers in the aged and in patients with liver disease. *South Med J* 71(suppl 2), Aug 1978
29. Shader RI, Greenblatt DJ: Clinical implications

of benzodiazepam pharmacokinetics. *Am J Psychiatry* 134:6, 1977

30. Greenblatt DJ. Allen MD, Shader RI: Toxicity of high-dose flurazepam in the elderly. *Clin Pharmacol Ther* 21 (3), March 1977

31. Jefferson W: Beta-adrenergic receptor blocking drugs in psychiatry. *Arch Gen Psychiatry* 31(5):681, 1974

32. Branchey MH, Lee JH, Amin R, et al: High and low potency neuroleptics in the elderly patients. *JAMA* 239:1860, 1978

33. DiMascio A, Sovner RD: Neuroleptic-induced extrapyramidal side effects. *Drug Ther* 6:99, 1976

34. Werry JS: The use of psychotropic drugs in children. *J. Child Psychiatry* 16:446, 1977

35. Jackson IV, Nuttall EA, Perez-Cruet J: Treatment of tardive dyskinesia with lecithin. *Am J Psychiatry* 136:11, 1979

36. Krumholz WV, Sheppard C, Merlis S: Menstruation changes as an unusual side effect in a molindone trial. *Curr Ther Res* 12(2):94, 1970

37. Klawans HL: The pharmacology of tardive dyskinesia. *Am J Psychiatry* 130:1, Jan 1973

APPENDIX

I. Chemical Properties of Drugs for Obstetrics and Gynecology

BRIAN D. ANDRESEN

Name	Structure (page number)*	Molecular Weight	pKa	T$_{1/2}$ (hr)	% Protein Binding
Anesthetics, local					
Bupivacaine	534	288	8.1	2.7	96
Lidocaine	534	234	7.9	1.6	64
Mepivacaine	534	246	7.6	1.9	77
Analgesics, nonnarcotic					
Aspirin	540	180	3.5	2–5 (<3 gm) 16–19 (>3 gm)	50–90
Acetaminophen	541	151	9.5	2–2.4	25
Ibuprofen	548	206	4.4	2	99
Indomethacin	547	357	5.5	4–12	92–99
Phenylbutazone	543	308	4.5	29–175	98
Naproxen	548	230	5	10–17	98–99
Analgesics, narcotic					
Meperidine	563	247	8.7	2.4–4	65–75
Morphine	553	285	8	1.9–3.1	35
Pentazocine	556	285	9	2	60–70
Methadone	560	309	8.6	18–97	71–87
Naloxone	559	327	8	1–1.7	—
Codeine	556	299	8.2	3–4	7
Antianxiety Agents					
Chlordiazepoxide	611	299	4.8	5–30	94–97
Diazepam	611	284	3.3	24–48	94–98
Oxazepam	613	286	1.7, 11.6	6–25	90
Lorazepam	612	321	1.3, 11.5	9–16	90
Antiarrhythmics					
Procainamide	178	235	9.2	2.2–4	15
Propranolol	179	259	9.4	2–6	90–96

* The structure of each drug may be found on the page number shown in Csáky TZ: Cutting's Handbook of Pharmacology: The Actions and Uses of Drugs, ed. 6, New York, Appleton-Century-Crofts, 1979

Name	Structure (page number)*	Molecular Weight	pKa	$T_{1/2}$ (hr)	% Protein Binding
Antimicrobial Agents					
Gentamicin	33	477	8.2	2–3	< 10
Kanamycin	34	484	7.2	2.5	0–3
Cefoxitin	19	427	—	1	65–80
Cephalothin	18	396	5.5	0.5–1	70
Cefazolin	17	454	2.3	2	84
Chloramphenicol	31	323	5.5	1.6–3.3	60–80
Clindamycin	24	424	7.5	2–4	94
Erythromycin	23	733	8.8	1.4	73
Metronidazole	72	171	2.5	6–12	< 20
Nitrofurantoin	50	238	7.2	0.3–0.6	25–60
Ampicillin	15	349	2.5, 7.2	1–1.5	15–29
Benzyl penicillin	13	334	2.8	0.5	65
Sulfamethoxazole	7	253	5.7	7–12	62
Sulfisoxazole	7	267	4.9	3–7	84
Doxycycline	28	444	3.4, 7.7	15–24	25–31
Tetracycline	29	444	3.3, 7.7	1.3–1.6	20–40
Anticoagulants					
Heparin	273	6,000–20,000	—	1.5–2	95
Warfarin	100	308	4.8	35–45	> 99
Anticonvulsants					
Carbamazepine	592	236	—	18–65	70–80
Phenobarbital	587	232	7.2	48–144	50–60
Phenytoin	589	252	8.3	8–60	87–93
Primidone	587	218	—	3.3–12.5	0
Trimethadione	590	143	—	12–24	0
Valproic acid	593	144	4.8	13–21	80–90
Antidepressants					
Amitryptyline	631	277	9.4	32–40	82–96
Imipramine	631	280	—	3.5	85–92
Antihistamines					
Chlorpheneramine	329	275	9.2	30	172
Diphenhydramine	327	255	8.3	4–10	⁺ 98
Pseudoephedrine	443	165	9.9, 5.8	9–16	—
Antihypertensives					
Diazoxide	238	230	8.7	21–36	90–93
Hydralazine	226	160	7.1	2–4	88–90
Methyldopa	236	211	2.2, 9.2, 10.6, 12	8	< 20

* The structure of each drug may be found on the page number shown in Csáky TZ: Cutting's Handbook of Pharmacology: The Actions and Uses of Drugs, ed. 6, New York, Appleton-Century-Crofts, 1979

Name	Structure (page number)*	Molecular Weight	pKa	$T_{1/2}$ (hr)	% Protein Binding
Antipsychotic Drugs					
Chlorpromazine	596	318	9.3	16–30	98–99
Lithium	615	6.9	6.8	8–35	0
Prochlorperazine	597	373	8.1	23	—
Thioridazine	598	370	9.5	26–36	96–99
Antituberculosis Drugs					
Ethambutol	42	204	6.9, 9.5	6–8	8–40
Isoniazid	40	137	2.0, 3.9	0.7–4	low
PAS (para-amino salicylic acid)	38	153	1.7, 3.2	0.5–1.5	50–70
Rifampin	42	822	1.7, 7.9	1.5–5	70–90
Streptomycin	35	581	—	2–3	20–30
Antiulcer Drugs					
Cimetidine	333	252	7	2	18–26
Bronchodilators					
Terbutaline	453	225	8.8, 10.1, 11.2	3.4	25
Theophylline	186	180	0.7, 8.8	3–13	53–65
Cardiac Gycosides					
Digoxin	173	780	—	30–40	20–40
Corticosteroids					
Betamethasone	356	393	—	≥ 5	—
Cortisone	353	360	—	0.5–2	90
Dexamethasone	357	392	—	3–4.5	77
Hydrocortisone	353	362	—	1.5–2	90–95
Prednisone	360	358	—	3.4–3.8	70
Diuretics					
Chlorothiazide	191	295	6.7, 9.5	13	20–80
Furosemide	194	330	3.8	0.3–1.6	91–99
Hydrochlorothiazide	192	297	7.9, 9.2	2–15	—
Hypoglycemic Agents					
Insulin (regular)	400	6,000	—	1.5–2	1–10
Tolazamide	403	311	3.5, 5.7	7	—
Tolbutamide	404	270	5.3	3–27	95–97

* The structure of each drug may be found on the page number shown in Csáky TZ: Cutting's Handbook of Pharmacology: The Actions and Uses of Drugs, ed. 6, New York, Appleton-Century-Crofts, 1979

Name	Structure (page number)*	Molecular Weight	pKa	$T_{1/2}$ (hr)	% Protein Binding
Sedatives					
Flurazepam	612	387	1.9, 8	47–100	—
Secobarbital	581	238	7.4	20–28	46–70
Thyroid/Antithyroid Drugs					
Methimazole	368	114	—	6–7	—
Propylthiouracil	368	170	7.8	1.2–1.5	75
Thyroxine	366	776	2.2, 6.7, 10.1	144–168	>99
Triiodothyroxine	366	690	—	35–60	>99
Tocolytic Agents					
Ritodrine	454	287	—	2–10	—
Terbutaline	453	225	8.8, 10.1, 11.2	3.4	25
Isoxsuprine	453	301	8.0, 9.8	1.25	—
Uterine Stimulants					
Oxytocin	258	1,007	—	0.08–0.1	30
Methylergonovine	257	339	—	—	—
Miscellaneous					
Caffeine	624	194	3.5	3.5	1–5
Ethanol	642	46	14	4.33	1–5
Tetrahydrocannabinol	645	314	—	—	>99
Amphetamine	645	135	9.9	10–30	—
Lysergic acid (LSD-25)	647	323	—	1.7–3.0	—
Cocaine	529	303	8.4	1	—
Methaqualone	584	250	2.5	16–42	80

* The structure of each drug may be found on the page number shown in Csáky TZ: Cutting's Handbook of Pharmacology: The Actions and Uses of Drugs, ed. 6, New York, Appleton-Century-Crofts, 1979

II. Cost Comparisons Between Commonly Prescribed Drugs

PAUL E. HAFNER

Prices listed in this appendix are wholesale prices based on 100 doses, unless otherwise noted. The data were gathered from the *1980–1981 American Druggist Blue Book* or *February 1981 Medi-Span Pricing Guide*. These prices are for relative cost comparison only; the actual cost to the patient will vary from one pharmacy to another. This table does not consider the frequency of administration or the duration of therapy.

Product	Pharmaceutical Company	Wholesale Cost Per 100 ($)
Decongestants/Antihistamines		
Sudafed 60 mg tab	Burroughs-Wellcome	4.50
Pseudoephedrine HCl 60 mg tab	Various	1.75–2.95
Actifed tab	Burroughs-Wellcome	5.50
Dimetapp tab	A. H. Robins	10.89
Ornade cap	SKF	14.80
Drixoral tab	Schering	13.84
Antibiotics		
Polycillin 500 mg cap	Bristol	37.70
Ampicillin 500 mg cap	Various	9.75–21.95
Keflex 500 mg cap	UpJohn	65.96
Cephalexin 500 mg cap	Various	39.95–61.40
Vibramycin 100 mg cap	Pfizer	84.12
Doxycyline Hyclate 100 mg cap	Various	49.80–80.84
Achromycin-V 500 mg cap	Lederle	9.27
Tetracycline HCl 500 mg cap	Various	3.50–9.90
Erythrocin 250 mg tab	Abbott	15.45
Erythromycin Stearate 250 mg tab	Various	5.75–12.47
Septra tabs	Burroughs-Wellcome	21.00
Septra DS tabs	Burroughs-Wellcome	32.67
Bactrim tabs	Roche	20.10
Macrodantin 50 mg cap	Eaton	16.10
Nitrofurantoin 50 mg cap	Various	7.60
Gantrisin 500 mg tab	Roche	5.16
Sulfisoxazole 50 mg tab	Various	2.10–3.59

Product	Pharmaceutical Company	Wholesale Cost Per 100 ($)
Antidepressants		
Elavil 50 mg tab	MSD	16.35
Amitriptyline 50 mg tab	Various	3.00–12.65
Tofranil 50 mg tab	Geigy	22.35
Imipramine HCl 50 mg tab	Various	3.00–12.50
Vivactyl 10 mg tabs	MSD	15.71
Sinequan 50 mg cap	Pfizer	21.42
Antianxiety Drugs		
Valium 5 mg tab	Roche	10.32
Librium 25 mg cap	Roche	14.65
Chlordiazepoxide HCl 25 mg cap	Various	1.25–6.75
Tranxene 7.5 mg cap	Abbott	13.26
Ativan 2 mg tab	Wyeth	19.23
Serax 15 mg cap	Wyeth	12.05
Miltown 400 mg tab	Wallace	7.45
Meprobamate 400 mg tab	Various	0.60–2.95
Vistaril 25 mg cap	Pfizer	16.49
Atarax 25 mg tab	Roerig	15.76
Hydroxyzine HCl 25 mg tab	Various	6.75–10.35
Antihypertensives		
Aldomet 250 mg tab	MSD	10.66
Apresoline 25 mg tab	CIBA	5.36
Hydralazine 25 mg tab	Various	1.25–5.00
Inderal 40 mg tab	Ayerst	8.46
HydroDiuril 50 mg tab	MSD	6.43
Hydrochlorothiazide 50 mg tab	Various	0.50–5.83
Diuril 500 mg tab	MSD	6.43
Chlorothiazide 500 mg tab	Various	3.48–7.65
Lasix 40 mg tab	Hoechst-Roussel	10.30
Dyazide cap	SKF	10.30
Insulins		
Regular U-100	Squibb	4.61/vial
Regular U-100	Lilly	5.03
NPH U-100	Squibb	5.26
NPH U-100	Lilly	5.38
Lente U-100	Squibb	5.26
Lente U-100	Lilly	5.38
Semilente U-100	Squibb	5.26
Semilente U-100	Lilly	5.38
Anticonvulsants		
Dilantin 100 mg cap	Parke-Davis	5.57
Sodium Phenytoin 100 mg cap	Various	0.90–2.29
Phenobarbital Sodium 32 mg tab	Various	0.23–1.50
Mysoline 250 mg tab	Ayerst	6.70
Primidone 250 mg tab	Various	3.80–4.75
Tegretol 200 mg tab	Geigy	13.91

Product	Pharmaceutical Company	Wholesale Cost Per 100 ($)
Tridione 300 mg cap	Abbott	7.22
Zarontin 250 mg cap	Parke-Davis	15.04
Depakene 250 mg cap	Abbott	17.36
β-Adrenergic Tocolytic Agents		
Vasodilan 10 mg tab	Mead-Johnson	13.55
Isoxsuprine HCl 10 mg tab	Various	3.09–9.25
Brethine 2.5 mg tab	Geigy	9.22
Bricanyl 2.5 mg tab	Astra	8.34
Yutopar 10 mg tab	Merrell-National	55.00
Antiemetics		
Bendectin tab	Merrell-National	13.55
Phenergan 25 mg supp	Wyeth	5.19/12
Compazine 25 mg supp	SKF	5.00/12
Oral Contraceptives		
Ortho Novum 1/50 21 or 28	Ortho	5.90/cycle
Norinyl 1/50 21 or 28	Syntex	5.80/cycle
Ovral 21 or 28	Wyeth	7.63/cycle
Ovcon-50 21	Mead-Johnson	5.82/cycle
Norlestrin 1/20 21 or 28	Parke-Davis	6.89/cycle
Demulen 21 or 28	Searle	7.99/cycle
Ortho Novum 1/35 21 or 28	Ortho	5.98/cycle
Norinyl 1/35 21 or 28	Syntex	5.80/cycle
LoOvral 1/35 21 or 28	Wyeth	7.63/cycle
Brevicon 21 or 28	Syntex	5.76/cycle
Modicon 21	Ortho	5.96/cycle
Ovcon 35 21	Mead-Johnson	5.99/cycle
Loestrin 1/20 21	Parke-Davis	6.84/cycle
Loestrin 1.5/30	Parke-Davis	6.84/cycle
Drugs for Pelvic Pain		
Danocrine 200 mg cap	Winthrop	96.00
Indocin 25 mg cap	MSD	14.90
Clinoril 150 mg tab	MSD	28.36
Naprosyn 250 mg tab	Syntex	25.90
Anaprox 275 mg tab	Syntex	28.85
Motrin 400 mg tab	UpJohn	15.42
Ponstel 250 mg cap	Parke-Davis	20.30
Bayer 325 mg tab	Glenbrook	1.72
Aspirin 325 mg tab	Various	.27–.99
Tylenol 325 mg tab	McNeil	2.24
Acetaminophen 325 mg tab	Various	.90–1.75
Urologic Disorders		
Urecholine 10 mg tab	MSD	17.72
Bethanechol HCl 10 mg tab	Various	1.65–12.38
Dibenzyline 10 mg cap	SKF	4.85
Anticholinergics/Anti-spasmodics		
Urispas 100 mg tab	SKF	9.25

Product	Pharmaceutical Company	Wholesale Cost Per 100 ($)
Enuretrol tab	Berlex	6.60
Ditropan 5 mg tab	Marion	11.57
Bentyl 10 mg cap	Merrell-National	6.25
Dicyclomine HCl 10 mg cap	Various	1.30–4.70
Probanthine 15 mg tab	Searle	11.68
Propantheline HBr 15 mg tab	Various	1.25–7.25
Vulvovaginal Candidiasis Preparations		
Mycostatin Vag tabs 100,000 U	Squibb	3.75/15
Nilstat Vag tabs 100,000 U	Lederle	3.81/15
Nystatin Vag tabs 100,000 U	Various	1.45–2.30/15
Monistat-7 Vag cream	Ortho	6.00/47 gm
Gyne-Lotrim 100 mg tabs	Schering	6.00/7
Gyne-Lotrim Vag Cr 7 day	Schering	6.00/45 gm
Mycelex-G 100 mg tabs	Dome	5.15/7
Mycelex Vag Cr 7 day	Dome	4.86/45 gm
Nonspecific Vaginitis Preparations		
Tetracycline cap—see Antibiotics		
Ampicillin cap—see Antibiotics		
Flagyl 250 mg tab	Searle	44.46
Metronidazole 250 mg tab	Generix	34.45
Sultrin Vag Cr	Ortho	6.00/78 gm
Triple Sulfa Vag Cr	Various	2.50–4.10/78 gm
Estrogens		
Estrace 1 mg tab	Mead-Johnson	6.38
Diethylstilbestrol 0.5 mg tab	Various	0.65–1.65
Premarin 0.625 mg tab	Ayerst	6.00
Conjugated Estrogens 0.625 mg tab	Various	1.87–6.82
Estrovis 100 mcg tab	Parke-Davis	30.92
Menest 0.625 mg tab	Beecham	5.04
Amnestrogen 0.625 mg tab	Squibb	7.20
Evex 0.625 mg tab	Syntex	5.79
Ogen 0.75 mg tab	Abbott	5.86
Estinyl 0.05 mg tab	Schering	8.14
Feminone 0.05 mg tab	UpJohn	2.51

III. Adverse Interactions Between Commonly Used Drugs

R. Michael Gendreau

Drugs	Interaction	Proposed Mechanism
Aminoglycosides		
Cephaloridine	Increased nephrotoxicity	Not established
Cephalothin	Increased nephrotoxicity	Not established
Curaiform drugs	Neuromuscular blockade	Additive
Digoxin	Possible decreased digoxin effect	Inhibition of gastro-intestinal absorption
Ethacrynic acid	Increased ototoxicity	Additive
Polymyxins	Increased nephrotoxicity	Additive
Ampicillin		
Contraceptives, oral	Decreased contraceptive effect	Not established
Anesthetics, general		
Antihypertensive drug	Hypotension	Usually additive
Antacids		
Digoxin	Decreased drug levels	Decreased digoxin absorption
Indomethacin	Decreased drug levels	Decreased indomethacin absorption
Isoniazid	Decreased isoniazid effect with aluminum antacids	Decreased absorption of isoniazid
Salicylates	Decreased salicylate levels	Increased renal clearance
Tetracyclines, oral	Decreased tetracycline levels	Decreased tetracycline absorption
Anticoagulants, oral		
Anabolic and androgenic steroids	Increased anticoagulant effect	Not established
Barbiturates	Decreased anticoagulant effect	Induction of microsomal enzymes
Carbamazepine	Decreased anticoagulant effect	Induction of microsomal enzymes
Cimetidine	Increased anticoagulant effect	Inhibition of microsomal enzymes
Contraceptives, oral	Decreased anticoagulant effect	Increased factor VII and X (prothrombin may decrease)
Dextrothyroxine	Increased anticoagulant effect	Not established
Hypoglycemics	Increased sulfonylurea hypoglycemia	Inhibition of microsomal enzymes
Indomethacin	Increased bleeding risk	Inhibition of platelet function
Metronidazole	Increased anticoagulant effect	Inhibition of microsomal enzymes
Miconazole	Increased anticoagulant effect	Not established

Drugs	Interaction	Proposed Mechanism
Phenylbutazone or oxyphen-butazone	Increased anticoagulant effect	Displacement from binding sites; inhibition of microsomal enzymes
Phenytoin	Increased phenytoin toxicity with dicumarol	Inhibition of microsomal enzymes
Rifampin	Decreased anticoagulant effect	Induction of microsomal enzymes
Salicylates	Increased bleeding time	Inhibition of platelet function
more than 2 gm/day	Increased hypoprothrombinemic effect	Reduction in plasma prothrombin
Sulfinpyrazone	Increased anticoagulant effect	Not established
Sulfonamides	Increased anticoagulant effect	Inhibition of microsomal enzymes; displacement from binding sites
Thyroid hormones	Increased anticoagulant effect	Increased clotting factor catabolism
Barbiturates		
β-Adrenergic blockers	Decreased β-blocker effect	Induction of microsomal enzymes
Anticoagulants, oral	Decreased anticoagulant effect	Induction of microsomal enzymes
Antidepressants, tricyclic	Decreased antidepressant effect	Induction of microsomal enzymes
Chloramphenicol	Increased barbiturate effect	Inhibition of microsomal enzymes
Contraceptives, oral	Decreased contraceptive effect	Induction of microsomal enzymes
Corticosteroids	Decreased steroid effect	Induction of microsomal enzymes
Digitoxin	Decreased digitoxin effect	Induction of microsomal enzymes
Doxycycline	Decreased doxycycline effect	Induction of microsomal enzymes
Meperidine	Increased CNS depression	Increased meperidine metabolites
Phenothiazines	Decreased phenothiazine effect	Induction of microsomal enzymes
Rifampin	Decreased barbiturate effect	Induction of microsomal enzymes
Valproic acid	Increased phenobarbital effect	Decreased phenobarbital metabolism
Benzodiazepines		
Cimetidine	Increased effect of chlordiazepoxide and diazepam	Inhibition of microsomal enzymes
β-adrenergic (see sympathomimetic amines)		
Cephaloridine		
Aminoglycoside antibiotics	Increased nephrotoxicity	Not established
Ethacrynic acid	Increased nephrotoxicity	Additive
Furosemide	Increased nephrotoxicity	Additive
Cephalothin		
Aminoglycoside antibiotics	Increased nephrotoxicity	Not established
Chloramphenicol		
Barbiturates	Increased barbiturate effect	Inhibition of microsomal enzymes
Phenytoin	Increased phenytoin toxicity	Inhibition of microsomal enzymes
Cimetidine		
Anticoagulants, oral	Increased anticoagulant effect	Inhibition of microsomal enzymes
Benzodiazepines	Increased effect of chlordiazepoxide	Inhibition of microsomal enzymes
Theophylline	Increased theophylline toxicity	Inhibition of microsomal enzymes
Contraceptives, oral		
Ampicillin	Decreased contraceptive effect	Induction of microsomal enzymes
Anticoagulants, oral	Decreased anticoagulant effect	Increased factor VII and X (prothrombin may decrease)

Drugs	Interaction	Proposed Mechanism
Barbiturates	Decreased contraceptive effect	Induction of microsomal enzymes
Carbamazepine	Decreased contraceptive effect	Induction of microsomal enzymes
Guanethidine	Decreased guanethidine effect	Not established
Hypoglycemics, oral	Increased glucose levels	Increase glucose tolerance
Phenytoin	Decreased contraceptive effect	Induction of microsomal enzymes
Primidone	Decreased contraceptive effect	Induction of microsomal enzymes
Tetracyclines	Decreased contraceptive effect	Not established
Diazepam	Slower diazepam elimination	Impaired metabolism
Corticosteroids		
Barbiturates	Decreased corticosteroid effect	Induction of microsomal enzymes
Diuretics (except spironolactone and triamterene)	Increased potassium loss	Additive
Ephedrine	Decreased dexamethasone effect	Not established
Estrogens	Usually increased corticosteroid effect	Increased protein-binding
Phenytoin	Decreased corticosteroid effect	Induction of microsomal enzymes
Rifampin	Decreased corticosteroid effect	Induction of microsomal enzymes
Danazol		
Estrogens	Decreased estrogen effects	Inhibition of gonadotropins
Diazoxide		
Anesthetics, general	Hypotension	Usually additive
Phenytoin	Decreased anticonvulsant effect	Not established
Sympathomimetic amines	Decreased antihypertensive effect	Pharmacologic antagonism
Digoxin		
Antacids, oral	Decreased digoxin effect	Decreased digoxin absorption
Diuretics (except K+ sparing)	Increased digoxin toxicity	Hypokalemia
Sympathomimetic amines	Increased tendency to cardiac arrythmias	Additive
Ergot Alkaloids (ergotamine, ergotrate, cafergot and similar agents)		
Ephedrine	Postpartum hypertension	Additive
Methoxamine	Postpartum hypertension, headaches	Additive
Propranolol	Headaches, vasoconstriction	Additive
Sympathomimetics	Hypertension, headaches	Additive
Estrogens		
Anticoagulants	Usually decreased anticoagulant effect	Increased coagulation factors
Corticosteroids	Potentiation of corticosteroid (esp. anti-inflammatory) effects, esp. with hydrocortisone	Possibly due to increased steroid being protein bound
Hypoglycemics	Increased blood glucose levels	Decreased glucose tolerance
Oxytocin	Increased uterine contractility	Not established
Phenobarbital	Decreased drug levels	Induction of microsomal enzymes
Vitamins	Decreased folate levels	Not established
Furosemide		
Cephaloridine	Increased nephrotoxicity	Additive
Corticosteroids	Increased potassium loss	Additive
Digitalis drugs	Increased digitalis toxicity	Hypokalemia
Indomethacin	Decreased antihypertensive and natriuretic effect	Prostaglandin inhibition

Drugs	Interaction	Proposed Mechanism
Lithium	Increased lithium toxicity	Decreased renal lithium clearance
Phenytoin	Reduced diuresis	Not established
Propranolol	Increased β-blockade	Not established
Heparin		
Aspirin	Increased bleeding risk	Inhibition of platelet function
Hydralazine		
Anesthetics, general	Hypotension	Usually additive
Sympathomimetic amines	Decreased antihypertensive effect	Pharmacologic antagonism
Hypoglycemics, oral		
Contraceptives, oral	Increased blood glucose levels	Decreased glucose tolerance
Dicumarol	Increased hypoglycemia	Inhibition of microsomal enzymes
Propranolol	Prolonged hypoglycemia	Reduced glycogenolysis
	Masks tachycardia and tremor	β-receptor blockade
	Hypertension during hypoglycemia	Blocked β effects of epinephrine
Rifampin	Decreased hypoglycemic effect	Induction of microsomal enzymes
Salicylates	Increased hypoglycemia, especially with chlorpropamide	Displacement from binding sites; additive
Indomethacin		
Antacids, oral	Decreased indomethacin effect	Decreased indomethacin absorption
Anticoagulants, oral	Increased bleeding risk	Inhibition of platelet function
β-adrenergic blockers	Decreased antihypertensive effect	Possibly by prostaglandin inhibition
Diuretics	Decreased antihypertensive and natriuretic effect of thiazides and furosemide	Possibly by prostaglandin inhibition
Lithium	Increased lithium toxicity	Decreased renal lithium clearance
Sympathomimetic amines	Severe hypertension	Not established
Influenza Vaccine		
Theophylline	Increased theophylline effect	Decreased theophylline metabolism
Insulin		
Anticoagulants, oral	Decreased glucose levels	Decreased protein-binding
Corticosteroids	Increased glucose levels	Antagonism
Diuretics (Thiazide)	Increased glucose levels	Antagonism
Oral Contraceptives	Increased glucose levels	Decreased glucose tolerance
Phentolamine	Increased insulin secretion	Blockade of adrenergic suppression of insulin secretion
Propranolol	Increased insulin activity, hypoglycemia	Pharmacologic action
Salicylates	Decreased glucose levels	Decreased protein-binding
Sulfonamides	Decreased glucose levels	Decreased protein-binding
Iron, oral		
Tetracyclines	Decreased tetracycline effect	Decreased tetracycline absorption
Isoniazid		
Aluminum antacids	Decreased isoniazid effect	Inhibition of isoniazid absorption
Phenytoin	Increased phenytoin toxicity	Inhibition of microsomal enzymes
Lithium		
Diuretics (except spironolactone and triamterene)	Increased lithium toxicity	Decreased renal lithium clearance

Drugs	Interaction	Proposed Mechanism
Indomethacin	Increased lithium toxicity	Decreased renal lithium clearance
Methyldopa	Increased lithium toxicity	Not established
Phenothiazines	Decreased phenothiazine levels	Not established
Meperidine		
Barbiturates	Increased CNS depression	Increased meperidine metabolites
MAO Inhibitors	Hypertension; hypotension and coma	Not established
Methadone		
Curariform drugs	Increased respiratory depression	Additive
Rifampin	Methadone withdrawal symptoms	Induction of microsomal enzymes
Methyldopa		
Anesthetics, general	Hypotension	Usually additive
Lithium	Increased lithium toxicity	Not established
Sympathomimetic amines	Decreased antihypertensive effect	Pharmacologic antagonism
Tolbutamide	Increased hypoglycemia	Inhibition of microsomal enzymes
Metronidazole		
Alcohol	Increased alcohol toxicity	Inhibition of aldehyde dehydrogenase
Anticoagulants, oral	Increased anticoagulant effect	Inhibition of microsomal enzymes
Miconazole		
Amphotericin B	Decreased anticandidal effect	Not established
Anticoagulants, oral	Increased anticoagulant effect	Not established
Oxytocics		
Ephedrine	Severe hypertension	Additive
Estrogens	Increased uterine contractility	Not established
Sympathomimetic amines	Severe hypertension, vasoconstriction, migraine headache	Additive
Phenothiazines		
Barbiturates	Decreased phenothiazine effect	Induction of microsomal enzymes
Propranolol	Increased effects of chlorpromazine and propranolol	Inhibition of metabolism of both drugs
Phenytoin		
Antidepressants, tricyclic	Increased phenytoin toxicity with imipramine	Not established
Contraceptives, oral	Decreased contraceptive effect	Induction of microsomal enzymes
Corticosteroids	Decreased corticosteroid effect	Induction of microsomal enzymes
Doxycycline	Decreased doxycycline effect	Induction of microsomal enzymes
Furosemide	Decreased diuresis	Decreased furosemide absorption
Isoniazid	Increased phenytoin toxicity	Inhibition of microsomal enzymes
Phenylbutazone	Increased phenytoin toxicity	Inhibition of microsomal enzymes
Primidone		
Contraceptives, oral	Decreased contraceptive effect	Induction of microsomal enzymes
Progesterone and Similar Agents		
Antihistamines	Progesterone inhibition	Direct
Phenobarbital	Decreased drug effect	Induction of microsomal enzymes
Phenothiazines	Increased phenothiazine effect	Inhibition of microsomal enzymes
Phenylbutazone	Decreased progestin effects	Induction of microsomal enzymes

Drugs	Interaction	Proposed Mechanism
Propranolol		
Anesthetics, general	Hypotension	Usually additive
Barbiturates	Decreased β-blocker effect	Induction of microsomal enzymes
Chlorpromazine	Increased effects of both drugs	Inhibition of metabolism of both drugs
Ergots	Headaches, vasoconstriction	Additive
Hypoglycemics, oral	Prolonged hypoglycemia	Decreased glycogenolysis
	Masks tachycardia and tremor	β-receptor blockade
	Hypertension during hypoglycemia	Blocked β effects of epinephrine
Indomethacin	Decreased antihypertensive effect	Possibly by prostaglandin inhibition
Lidocaine	Increased lidocaine effect	Decreased lidocaine clearance
Sympathomimetic amines	Decreased antihypertensive effect	Pharmacologic antagonism
	Hypertension with epinephrine, possibly others	Unopposed α-adrenergic stimulation
Theophylline	Increased theophylline effect with propranolol	Decreased theophylline clearance
Prostaglandins		
Antagonists, including:	Assorted, including:	Inhibition of enzymes in pathway leading to production
Aspirin	Asthma	
Caffeine	Fever	
Indomethacin	Inflammation	
Procaine	Coagulation and platelet function	
Theophylline	Inhibition of uterine stimulation	
Ritodrine		
Anesthetics (general)	Hypotension	Vasodilitation
Corticosteroids	Pulmonary edema	Increased diastolic pressure
Digitalis	Cardiac arrhythmias	Increased conduction velocities
Hypoglycemics	Increased glucose levels	Pharmacologic effect
Propranolol	Antagonism	Pharmacologic antagonism
Salicylates		
Antacids	Decreased salicylate levels	Increased renal clearance
Anticoagulants, oral	Possible increased bleeding risk with aspirin	Inhibition of platelet function
	Increased hypoprothrombinemic effect (more than 2 gm/day of salicylates)	Reduction of plasma prothrombin
Heparin	Increased bleeding risk	Inhibition of platelet function
Hypoglycemics	Increased hypoglycemia	Displacement from binding sites; additive
Sulfamethoxazole-Trimethoprim	Same as Sulfonamides	
Sulfonamides		
Anticoagulants, oral	Increased anticoagulant effect	Displacement from binding sites
Hypoglycemics	Increased sulfonylurea hypoglycemia	Not established
Sympathomimetic Amines		
Antihypertensive drugs	Decreased antihypertensive effect	Inhibition of norepinephrine uptake by neuron
β-adrenergic blockers (nonselective)	Hypertension with epinephrine, possibly with others	Unopposed α-adrenergic stimulation

Drugs	Interaction	Proposed Mechanism
Digitalis drugs	Increased tendency to cardiac arrhythmias	Additive
Tetracyclines		
Antacids, oral	Decreased tetracycline effects	Decreased tetracycline absorption
Barbiturates	Decreased doxycycline effect	Induction of microsomal enzymes
Carbamazepine	Decreased doxycycline effect	Induction of microsomal enzymes
Contraceptives, oral	Decreased contraceptive effect	Not established
Iron, oral	Decreased tetracycline effect	Decreased tetracycline absorption
Phenytoin	Decreased doxycycline effect	Induction of microsomal enzymes
Theophylline		
Cimetidine	Increased theophylline toxicity	Inhibition of microsomal enzymes
Erythromycin	Increased theophylline effect	Inhibition of theophylline metabolism
Influenza vaccine	Increased theophylline effect	Inhibition of theophylline metabolism
Propranolol	Increased theophylline effect	Decreased theophylline clearance
Smoking (tobacco and marijuana)	Decreased theophylline effect	Increased metabolism
Thiazide Diuretics		
Corticosteroids	Increased potassium loss	Additive
Digitalis drugs	Increased digitalis toxicity	Hypokalemia
Indomethacin	Decreased antihypertensive and natriuretic	Possibly by prostaglandin inhibition
Salicylates	Increased CNS toxicity with acetazolamide	Increased plasma nonionized salicylate with increased CNS levels
Thyroid hormones		
Anticoagulants	Increased anticoagulant effect	Increased clotting factor catabolism
Tobramycin	See Aminoglycosides	
Vitamin K		
Antibiotics	Decreased clotting factor synthesis	Inhibition of bacterial production of vitamin K due to antibiotic usage
Mineral oil	Decreased clotting factor synthesis	Decreased adsorption of vitamin K

Index